contents

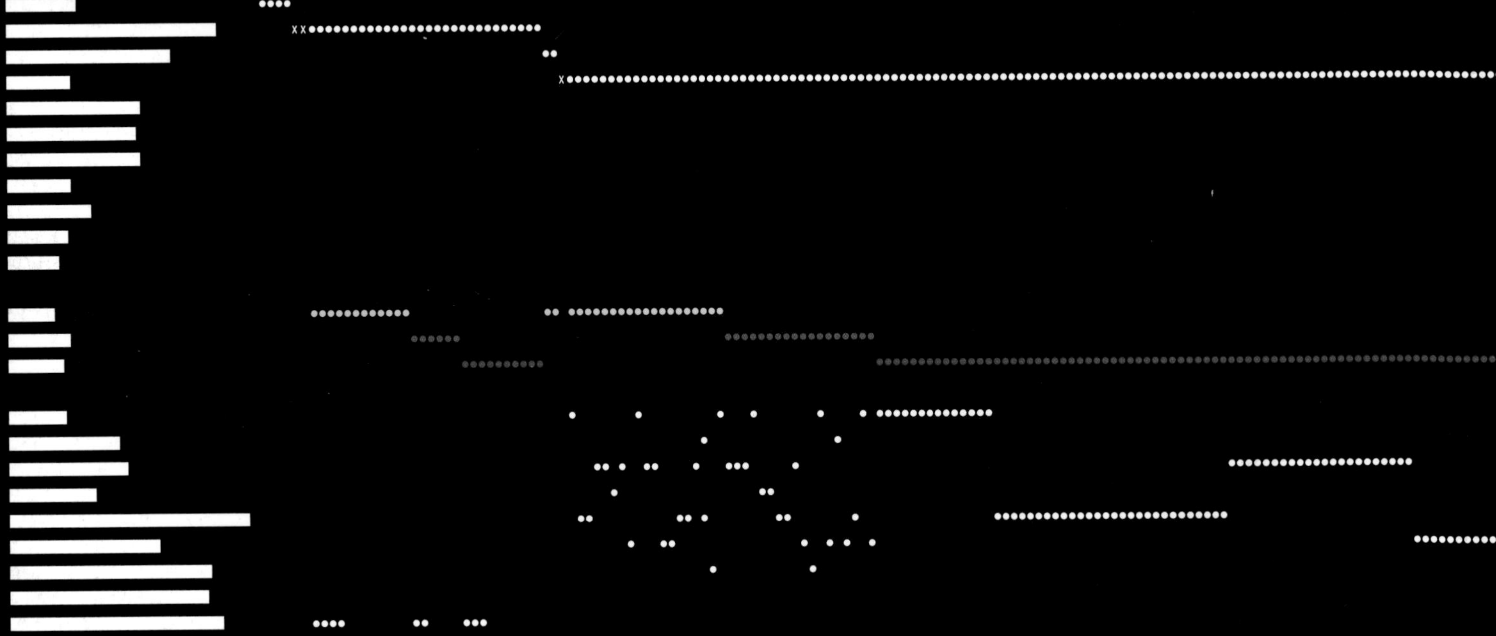

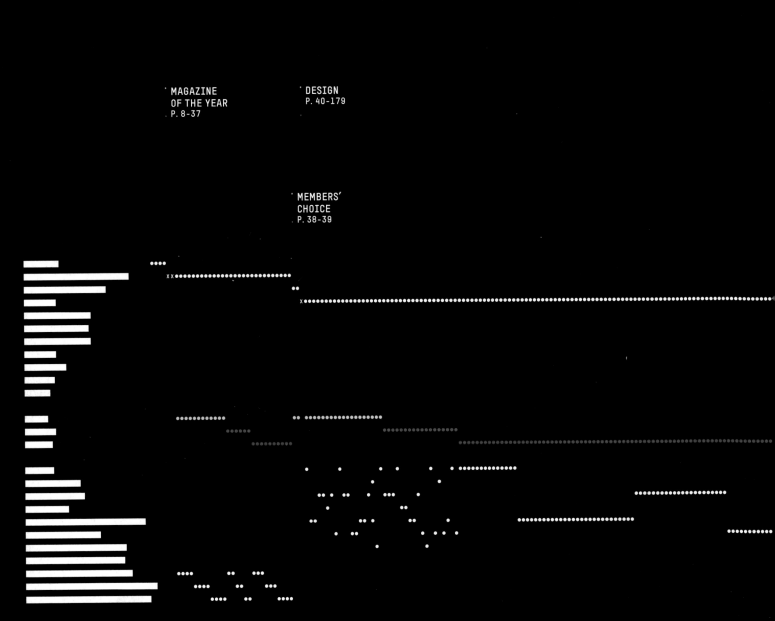

COVER AND ANNUAL DESIGN
Todd Albertson & Tom Brown, WEAPON OF CHOICE

CONTRIBUTING DESIGN
Jennifer Roberts & Dian Holton

judges

CO-CHAIRS

Dirk Barnett
Creative Director,
Blender

Scott Dadich
Creative Director,
WIRED

13

14

15

16

17

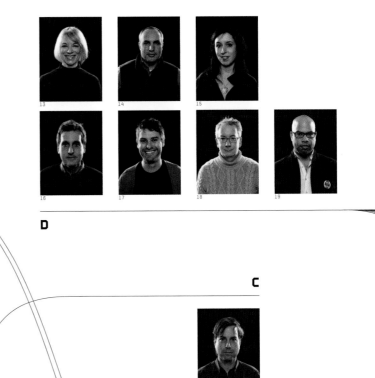

18

19

D

C

12

B

4

5

6

7

8

9

10

11

F

20

21

22

A

1

2

3

A: (1) **Todd Albertson** Creative Director, Todd Albertson Design (2) **Alice Alves** Deputy Art Director, Fortune (3) **Gail Anderson** Creative Director/Design, SpotCo. **B:** (4) **Florian Bachleda** Creative Director, FB Design (5) **Oksana Badrak** Illustrator (6) **Lisa Berman** Director of Photography, Entertainment Weekly (7) **Phil Bicker** Creative Director, The Fader (8) **Deb Bishop** Creative Director, More (9) **Tom Brown** Principal, TBA+D
(10) **Peter Buchanan-Smith** Principal, Buchanan-Smith, LLC (11) **Stella Bugbee** Design Director, Domino
C: (12) **David Carthas** Director of Photography, Blender **D:** (13) **Lynda Decker** President, Decker Design (14) **Ken DeLago** Design Director, Golf Digest (15) **Kristina DiMatteo** Art Director, Print (16) **Chris Dixon** Design Director, New York Magazine (17) **Jeff Docherty** Art Director, SEED (18) **Stephen Doyle** Principal, Doyle Partners (19) **Arem Duplessis** Art Director, The New York Times Magazine **F:** (20) **Andrea Fella** Art Director (21) **Carla Frank** Creative Director, Carla Frank Creative (22) **Tobias Frere-Jones** Principal, Director of Typography, Hoefler & Frere-Jones **G:** (23) **Jeff Glendenning** Art Director (24) **Carin Goldberg** Principal, Carin Goldberg Design (25) **Kim Gougenheim** Director of Photography, Every Day with Rachael Ray
(26) **Michael Grossman** Editorial & Design Consultant (27) **Eddie Guy** Illustrator **H:** (absent) **David Harris** Design Director, Vanity Fair (28) **Rob Hewitt** Art Director, Key, The New York Times Real Estate Magazine + Play, The New York Times Sports Magazine (29) **Maili Holiman** Art Director, WIRED (30) **Amy Hoppy** Photo Editor (31) **Andrew Horton** Art Director, Business Week **I:** (32) **Nancy Jo Iacoi** Director of Photography, Orchard
J: (33) **Andre Jointe** Art Director, Details

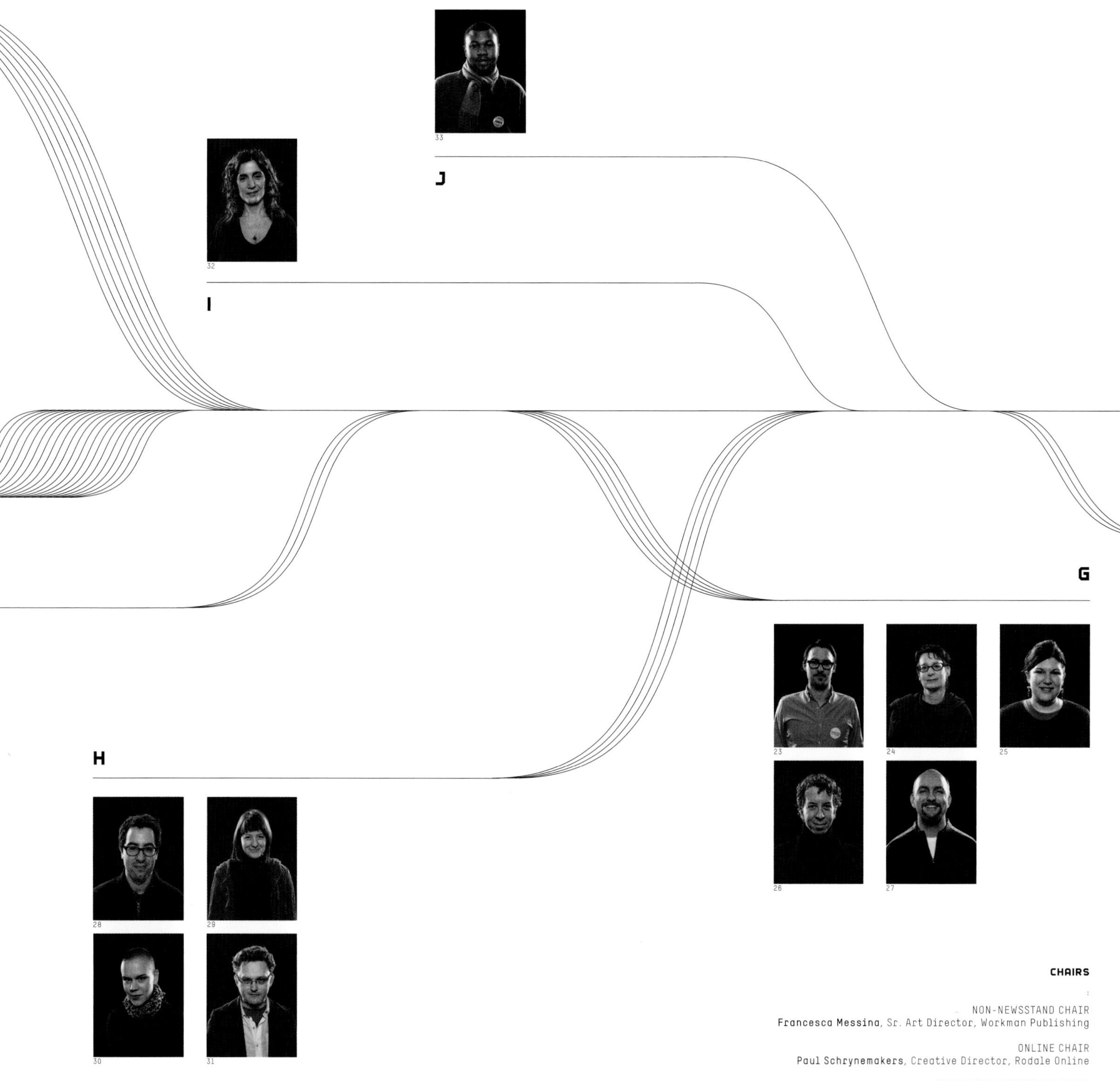

CHAIRS

NON-NEWSSTAND CHAIR
Francesca Messina, Sr. Art Director, Workman Publishing

ONLINE CHAIR
Paul Schrynemakers, Creative Director, Rodale Online

MAGAZINE OF THE YEAR CHAIR
Linda Root, Design Director, Studio Incubate

Photographs by **Brent Humphreys**

judges

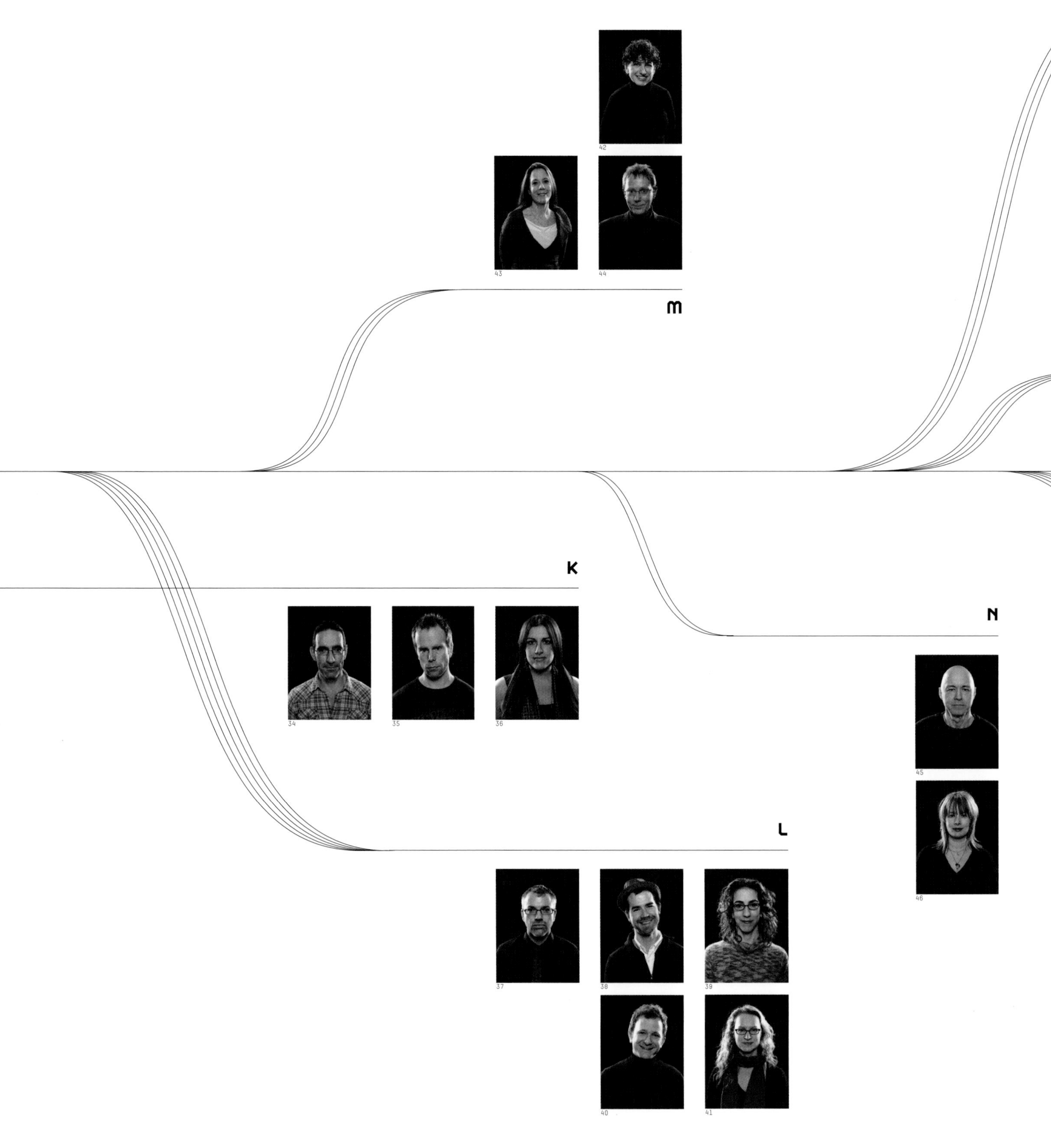

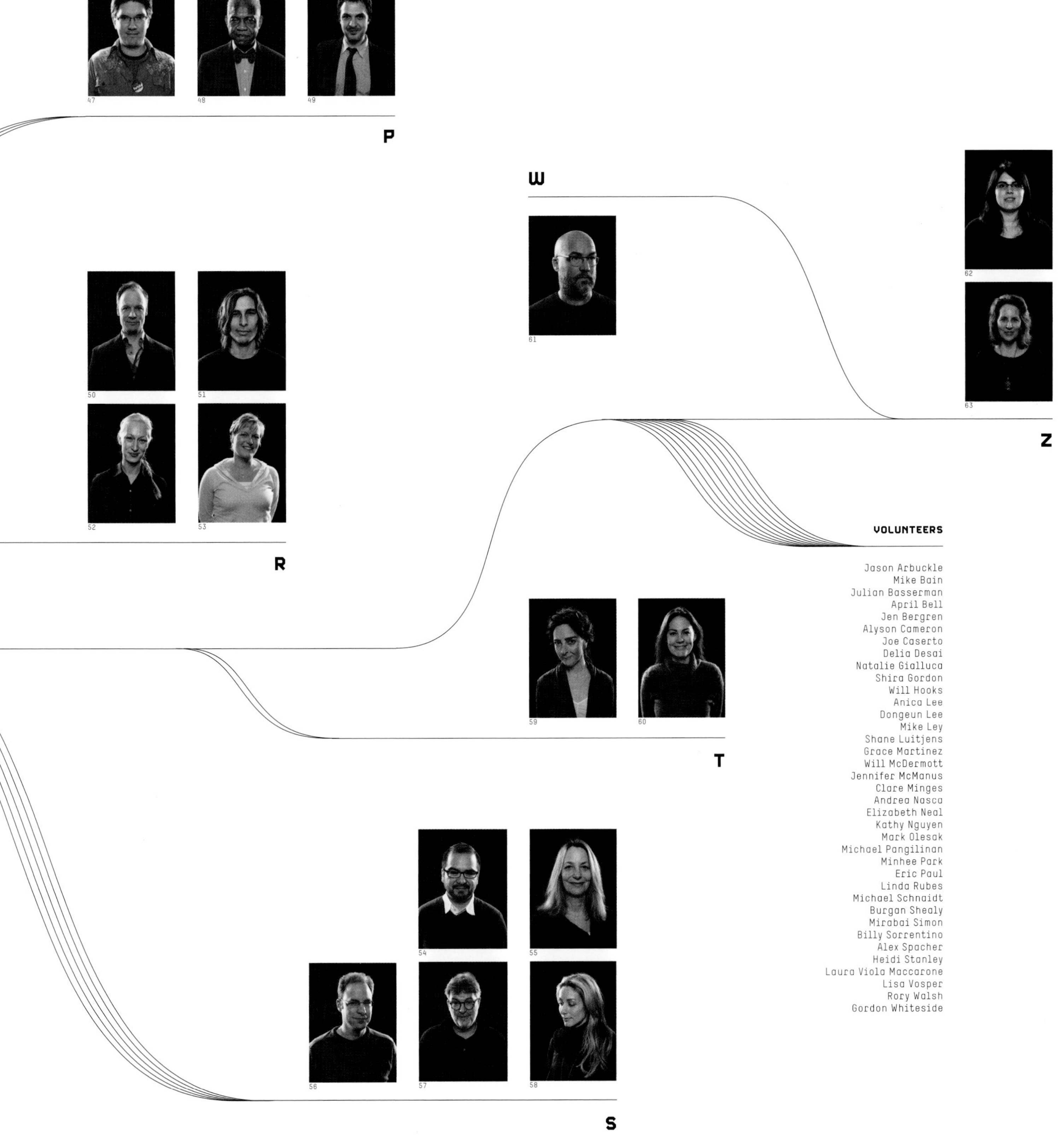

K: (34) **George Karabotsos** Design Director, Men's Health (35) **Brandon Kavulla** Art Director, Best Life (36) **Nathalie Kirsheh** Art Director, W **L:** (37) **Jeremy LaCroix** Creative Director, CHOW.com (38) **Matthew Lenning** Design Director, Bon Appétit (39) **Alissa Levin** Founder/Partner, Point Five Design (40) **Josh Liberson** Principal, Helicopter (41) **Deanna Lowe** Art Director, Fortune **M:** (42) **Melanie McLaughlin** Design Consultant (43) **Francesca Messina** Sr. Art Director, Workman Publishing (44) **Don Morris** Principal, Don Morris Design **N:** (45) **Robert Newman** Art Director (46) **Catriona Ni Aolain** Director of Photography, ESPN The Magazine **P:** (47) **Donald Partyka** Creative Director, America's Quarterly (absent) **Deborah Paul** Editorial Director, Emmis Publications (48) **George Pitts** Director of Photography, Latina (49) **Platon** Photographer **R:** (50) **Bruce Ramsay** Director of Covers, Newsweek (51) **Jose Reyes** Art Director, Paste (52) **Judith Puckett-Rinella** Photo Editor, T, The New York Times Magazine (53) **Linda Root** Design Director, Studio Incubate **S:** (54) **Hector Sanchez** Design Director, Atlanta Magazine (55) **Paula Scher** Partner, Pentagram (56) **Paul Schrynemakers** Creative Director, Rodale Online (57) **Mitch Shostak** Creative Director, Shostak Studios (58) **Gretchen Smelter** Creative Director, Brides **T:** (59) **Catherine Talese** Photo Consultant (60) **Casey Tierney** Photo Director, Real Simple **W:** (61) **Dan Winters** Photographer **Z:** (62) **Liana Zamora** Art Director (63) **Ellen Zaslow** Design Director, San Francisco Magazine

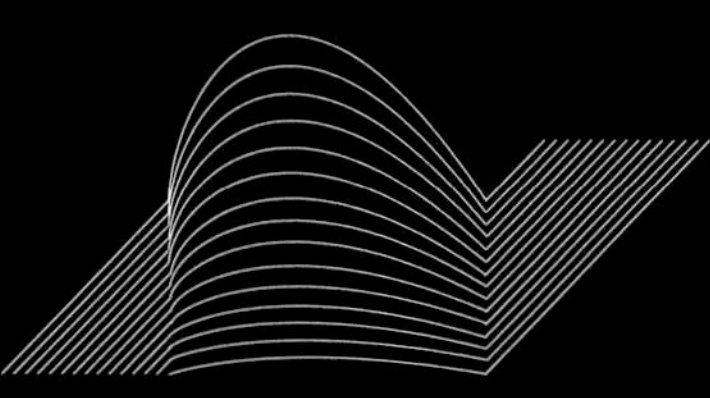

magazine of the year

ENTRIES: 49

GOLD: 3
SILVER: 3
MERIT: 9

INCLUDING:
MEMBERS' CHOICE
ENTRIES: 34
GOLD: 1

: SECTION
MAGAZINE OF THE YEAR

: AWARD
GOLD

: CATEGORY
CIRCULATION 1 MILLION+

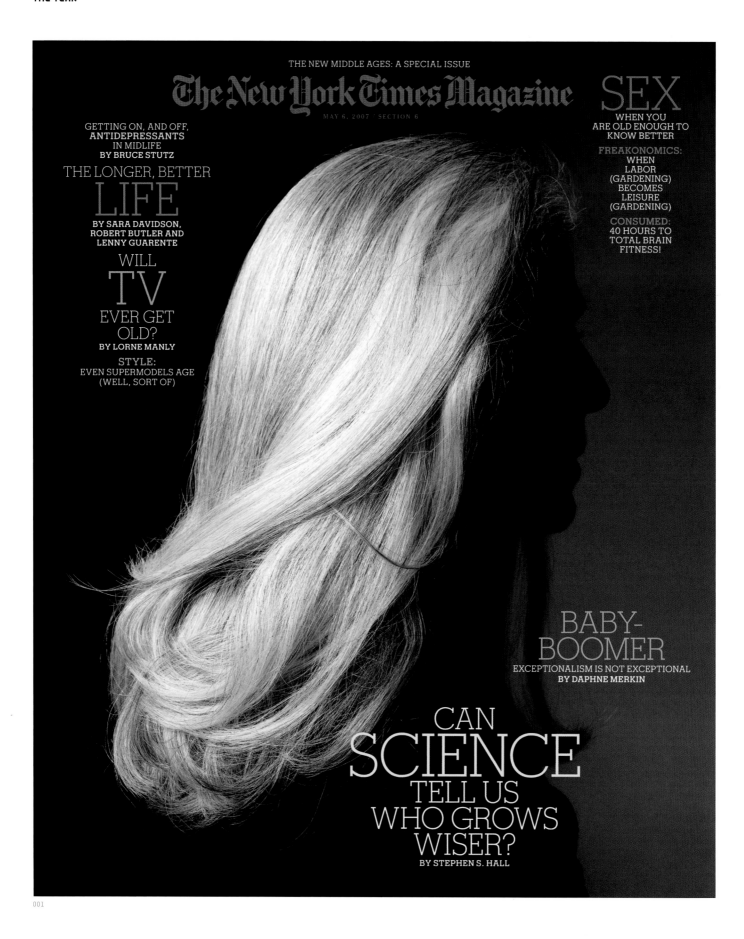

THE NEW MIDDLE AGES: A SPECIAL ISSUE

The New York Times Magazine

MAY 6, 2007 / SECTION 6

GETTING ON, AND OFF, **ANTIDEPRESSANTS** IN MIDLIFE
BY BRUCE STUTZ

THE LONGER, BETTER LIFE
BY SARA DAVIDSON, ROBERT BUTLER AND LENNY GUARENTE

WILL TV EVER GET OLD?
BY LORNE MANLY

STYLE: EVEN SUPERMODELS AGE (WELL, SORT OF)

SEX
WHEN YOU ARE OLD ENOUGH TO KNOW BETTER

FREAKONOMICS: WHEN LABOR (GARDENING) BECOMES LEISURE (GARDENING)

CONSUMED: 40 HOURS TO TOTAL BRAIN FITNESS!

BABY-BOOMER
EXCEPTIONALISM IS NOT EXCEPTIONAL
BY DAPHNE MERKIN

CAN SCIENCE TELL US WHO GROWS WISER?
BY STEPHEN S. HALL

001

001 THE NEW YORK TIMES MAGAZINE

Creative Director_**Janet Froelich** Art Director_**Arem Duplessis** Deputy Art Director_**Gail Bichler**
Designers _**Arem Duplessis, Jeff Glendenning, Leo Jung, Gail Bichler, Jeff Docherty, Nancy Harris Rouemy, Catherine Gilmore-Barnes, Holly Gressley, Julia Moburg, Hilary Greenbaum** Director of Photography_**Kathy Ryan** Photo Editors_**Kira Pollack, Luise Stauss, Joanna Milter, Clinton Cargill, Leonor Mamanna, Stacey Baker**
Editor-In-Chief_**Gerry Marzorati** Publisher_**The New York Times** Issues_**May 6, 2007, September 30, 2007, October 14, 2007** Category_**Design: Magazine of the Year**

LONGEVITY

A LONGER, BETTER LIFE

SARA DAVIDSON TALKS TO TWO MEDICAL SCIENTISTS ABOUT HOW THE BODY AGES AND THE RESEARCH ON TRYING TO EXTEND OUR HEALTHY LIFE SPAN.

Participants

LENNY GUARENTE, PH.D.: Novartis professor of biology at M.I.T. and author of "Ageless Quest: One Scientist's Search for Genes That Prolong Youth."
ROBERT N. BUTLER, M.D.: Founding director of the National Institute on Aging, a founder of the Alzheimer's Disease Association and winner of a Pulitzer Prize in 1976 for "Why Survive? Being Old in America." He heads the International Longevity Center.
SARA DAVIDSON: Author, most recently, of "Leap! What Will We Do With the Rest of Our Lives?"

PHOTOGRAPH BY HORACIO SALINAS

52

001

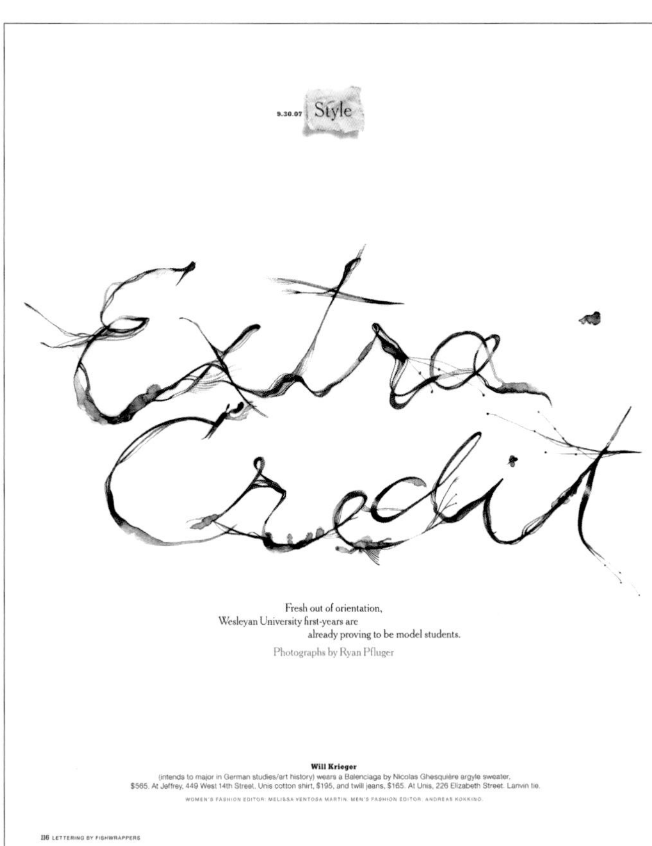

9.30.07 Style

Extra Credit

Fresh out of orientation, Wesleyan University first-years are already proving to be model students.

Photographs by Ryan Pfluger

Will Krieger
(intends to major in German studies/art history) wears a Balenciaga by Nicolas Ghesquière argyle sweater, $565. At Jeffrey, 449 West 14th Street. Unis cotton shirt, $195, and twill jeans, $165. At Unis, 226 Elizabeth Street. Lanvin tie.

WOMEN'S FASHION EDITOR: MELISSA VENTOSA MARTIN. MEN'S FASHION EDITOR: ANDREAS KOKKINO.

96 LETTERING BY FISHWRAPPERS

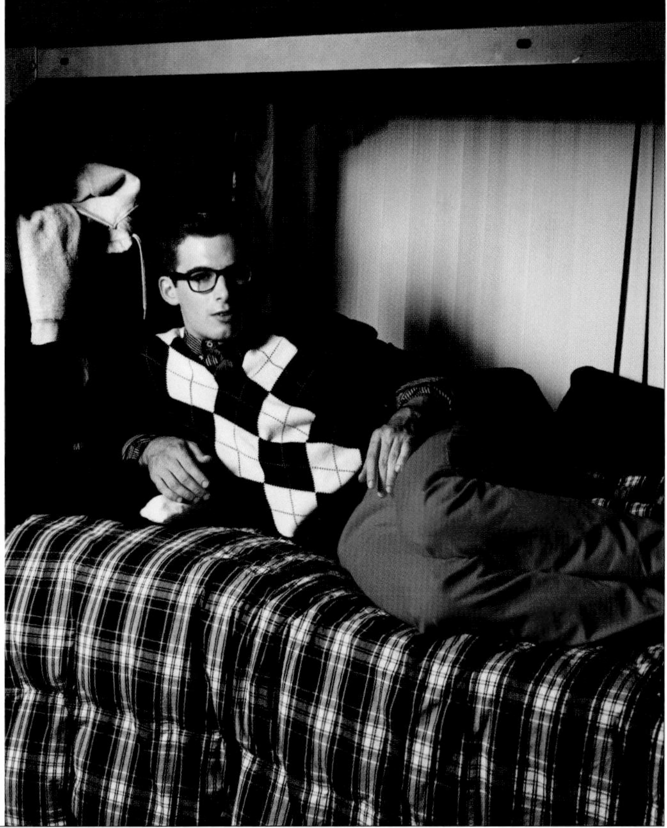

001

: SECTION
MAGAZINE OF THE YEAR

: AWARD
GOLD

: CATEGORY
CIRCULATION 1 MILLION+

10.14.07 **Style**

'Are You Talkin' to Me?'

The story of a man, a blabbermouth suit and the forces of evil.

By Shalom Auslander

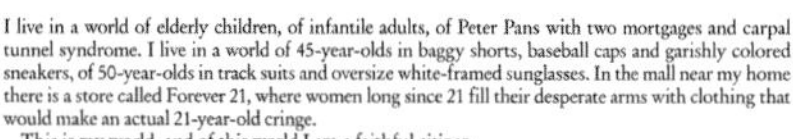

I live in a world of elderly children, of infantile adults, of Peter Pans with two mortgages and carpal tunnel syndrome. I live in a world of 45-year-olds in baggy shorts, baseball caps and garishly colored sneakers, of 50-year-olds in track suits and oversize white-framed sunglasses. In the mall near my home there is a store called Forever 21, where women long since 21 fill their desperate arms with clothing that would make an actual 21-year-old cringe.

This is my world, and of this world I am a faithful citizen.

I wear ripped jeans and T-shirts. I wear hoodies and Crocs. I wear Chuck Taylors.

"Look, Dad," says my 3-year-old son, pointing to a classmate as we walk across the schoolyard. "Zachary is wearing the same thing as you!"

I wonder what Suit Me is doing right now. Perhaps he is at the opera, understanding Italian and shouting *Bravo!* as the curtain falls. Perhaps he is at dinner with other Suit People, swirling red wine around a glass as he discusses the past week's lead article in The Economist. "They fundamentally misunderstand China's relationship to the something something something," he says. He mentions Turkey, and they all nod. Perhaps he is, if nothing else, feeling ever-so-slightly less lousy about him-

Photo Illustration by Jeff Riedel

92

Cantarelli suit, $2,295, Thom Browne.New York shirt, $230, Alexander Olch tie, $130. Bergdorf Goodman Collection belt, $250, vintage Rolex watch with 18-karat-gold face, $8,295, and Church's shoes, $680. All at Bergdorf Goodman the Men's Store.

001

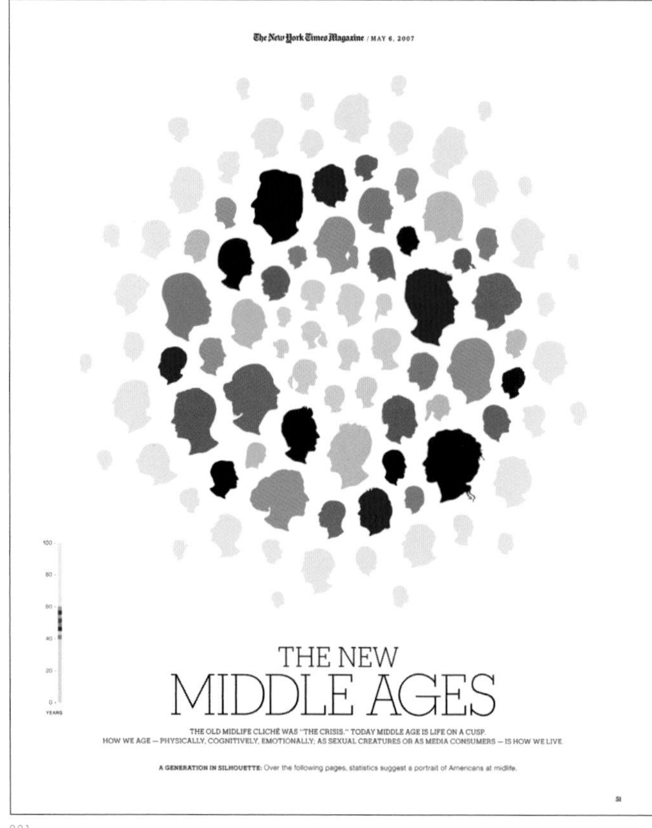

The New York Times Magazine / MAY 6, 2007

THE NEW
MIDDLE AGES

THE OLD MIDLIFE CLICHÉ WAS "THE CRISIS." TODAY MIDDLE AGE IS LIFE ON A CUSP.
HOW WE AGE — PHYSICALLY, COGNITIVELY, EMOTIONALLY; AS SEXUAL CREATURES OR AS MEDIA CONSUMERS — IS HOW WE LIVE.

A GENERATION IN SILHOUETTE: Over the following pages, statistics suggest a portrait of Americans at midlife.

51

001

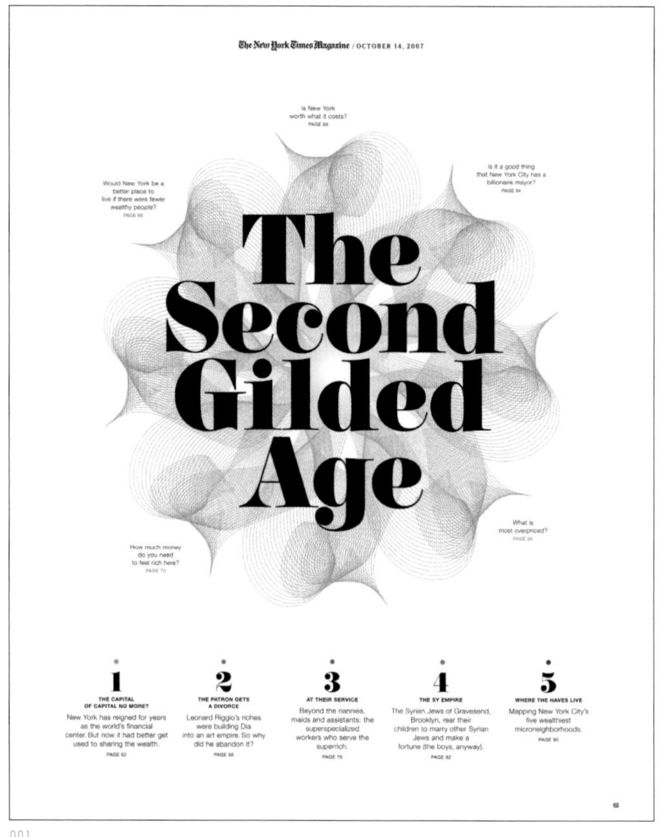

The New York Times Magazine / OCTOBER 14, 2007

Is New York worth what it costs? PAGE 88

Would New York be a better place to live if there were fewer wealthy people? PAGE 95

Is it a good thing that New York City has a billionaire mayor? PAGE 94

The Second Gilded Age

How much money do you need to feel rich here? PAGE 70

1 THE CAPITAL OF CAPITAL NO MORE? New York has reigned for years as the world's financial center. But now it had better get used to sharing the wealth. PAGE 62

2 THE PATRON GETS A DIVORCE Leonard Riggio's riches were building Dia into an art empire. So why did he abandon it? PAGE 66

3 AT THEIR SERVICE Beyond the nannies, maids and assistants: the superspecialized workers who serve the superrich. PAGE 76

4 THE SY EMPIRE The Syrian Jews of Gravesend, Brooklyn, rear their children to marry other Syrian Jews and make a fortune (the boys, anyway). PAGE 82

5 WHERE THE HAVES LIVE Mapping New York City's five wealthiest microneighborhoods. PAGE 90

61

001

001 THE NEW YORK TIMES MAGAZINE

Creative Director_**Janet Froelich** Art Director_**Arem Duplessis** Deputy Art Director_**Gail Bichler**
Designers_**Arem Duplessis, Jeff Glendenning, Leo Jung, Gail Bichler, Jeff Docherty, Nancy Harris Rouemy, Catherine Gilmore-Barnes, Holly Gressley, Julia Moburg, Hilary Greenbaum** Director of Photography_**Kathy Ryan** Photo Editors_**Kira Pollack, Luise Stauss, Joanna Milter, Clinton Cargill, Leonor Mamanna, Stacey Baker**
Editor-In-Chief_**Gerry Marzorati** Publisher_**The New York Times** Issues_**May 6, 2007, September 30, 2007, October 14, 2007** Category_**Design: Magazine of the Year**

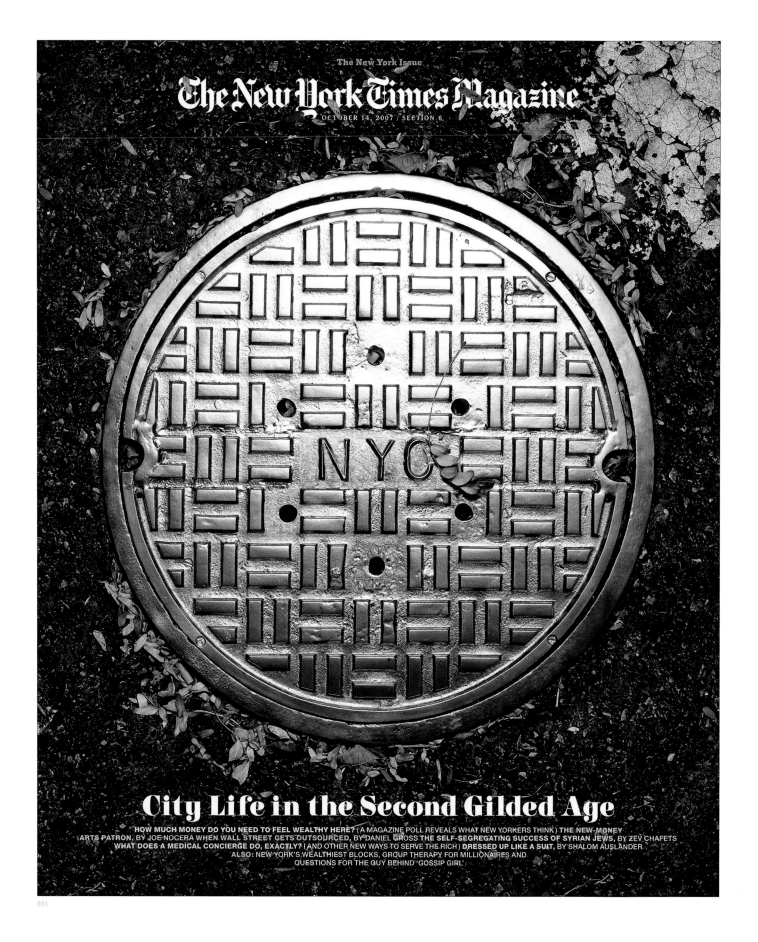

The New York Issue

The New York Times Magazine

OCTOBER 14, 2007 / SECTION 6

City Life in the Second Gilded Age

HOW MUCH MONEY DO YOU NEED TO FEEL WEALTHY HERE? (A MAGAZINE POLL REVEALS WHAT NEW YORKERS THINK) **THE NEW-MONEY ARTS PATRON,** BY JOE NOCERA **WHEN WALL STREET GETS OUTSOURCED,** BY DANIEL GROSS **THE SELF-SEGREGATING SUCCESS OF SYRIAN JEWS,** BY ZEV CHAFETS **WHAT DOES A MEDICAL CONCIERGE DO, EXACTLY?** (AND OTHER NEW WAYS TO SERVE THE RICH) **DRESSED UP LIKE A SUIT,** BY SHALOM AUSLANDER

ALSO: NEW YORK'S WEALTHIEST BLOCKS, GROUP THERAPY FOR MILLIONAIRES AND QUESTIONS FOR THE GUY BEHIND 'GOSSIP GIRL'

001

SECTION
MAGAZINE OF THE YEAR

AWARD
GOLD

CATEGORY
CIRCULATION 500,000–1 MILLION

WIRED

08.15-WIRED

Martha Geeks Out!

How To:

> Land a Fat Raise
> Rule the Blogosphere
> Take Killer Digipics
> Outsmart a Mechanic
> Snag a Cell Phone Deal
> Weasel Free Drinks
> Keep Batteries Charged
> Email Like a Pro
> Get Fired Properly
> Bake a Wii Cake

+

LOST AT SEA
The Epic Search for a Tech Hero

SMOG AND MIRRORS
China's Plan for a Green Olympics

TB, EBOLA, SARS
The New Science of Diagnosis

Wii

PIECE OF CAKE AUG.2007

002

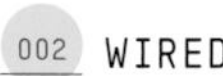 WIRED

Creative Director_Scott Dadich Design Director_Wyatt Mitchell Art Directors_Maili Holiman, Jeremy LaCroix, Carl DeTorres
Designers_Carl DeTorres, Chris Imlay, Margaret Swart, Christy Sheppard, Victor Krummenacher Illustrators_Eddie Guy, Bryan Christie, Seth Ferris, Christoph Niemann, Bruce Hutchison, Pietari Posti, Yochiro Ono, Atshuisa Okura, Nicholas Felton, Florian Bachleda, Riccardo Vecchio, Luke Hayman, John Knoll
Photo Editors_Anna Goldwater Alexander, Zana Woods, Carolyn Rauch Photographers_Jill Greenberg, Baerbel Schmidt, John Clard, Darren Braun, Todd Hido, Chris Buck, Alessandra Petlin, Gregg Segal, Ofer Wolberger, Donald Milne, Dan Winters, Peter Yang, Emily Shur, Robert Maxwell, Mauricio Alejo
Editor-In-Chief_Chris Anderson Publisher_Condé Nast Publications, Inc. Issues_August 2007, October 2007, November 2007 Category_Design: Magazine of the Year

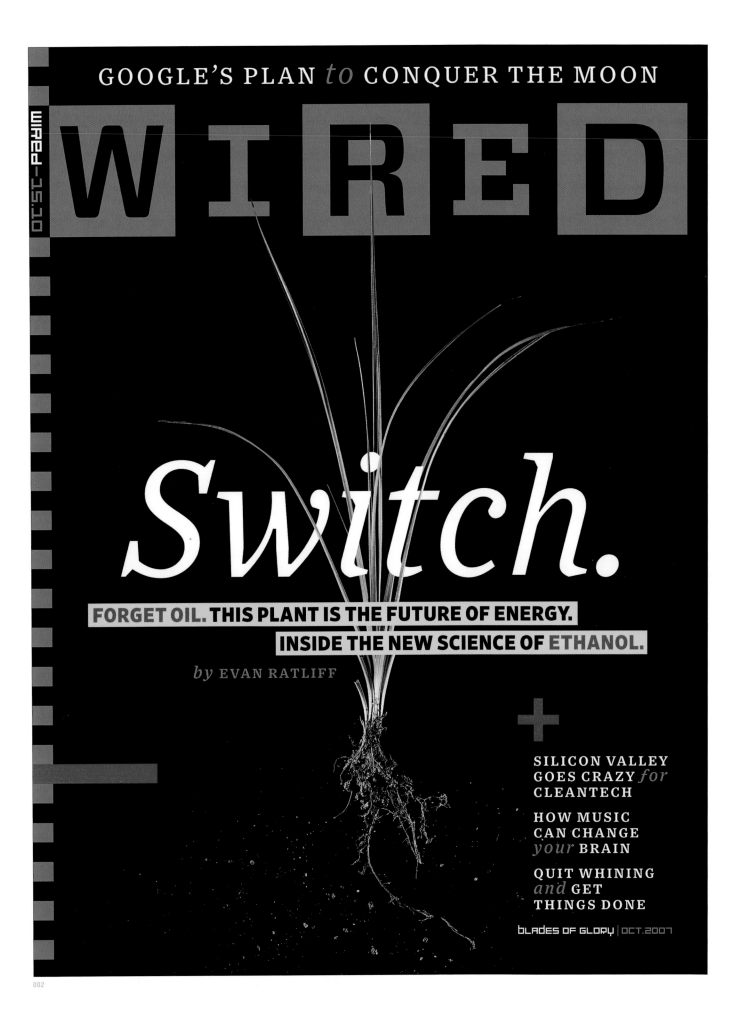

GOOGLE'S PLAN *to* CONQUER THE MOON

WIRED

WIRED–15.10 OCT

Switch.

FORGET OIL. THIS PLANT IS THE FUTURE OF ENERGY.
INSIDE THE NEW SCIENCE OF ETHANOL.

by EVAN RATLIFF

SILICON VALLEY GOES CRAZY *for* CLEANTECH

HOW MUSIC CAN CHANGE *your* BRAIN

QUIT WHINING *and* GET THINGS DONE

BLADES OF GLORY | OCT.2007

: SECTION
MAGAZINE OF THE YEAR

: AWARD
GOLD

: CATEGORY
CIRCULATION 500,000-1 MILLION

The *Other* Other White Meat

It looks the same, it cooks the same, it tastes the same. But this pig, a Hampshire from Indiana named Nelly, is a clone. And cloned bacon? It may already be at your supermarket.
by BEN PAYNTER

KARYN SCHAUF SETS A FROSTY GLASS OF MILK on the red-checkered tablecloth in front of me; a plate of Oreo knockoffs sits beside it. Two identical cows prance across the glass. In fact, nearly everything in the kitchenette—plates, cookie jars, wallpaper trim—is emblazoned with cows. And why not? We're next door to the Schaufs' 99-cow milking stables, Indianhead Holsteins, in Barron, Wisconsin. ¶ I swirl the glass: A thick lather coats the sides. I sniff: It has a rich, almost buttery aroma. I hate the idea of milk over ice, but the drink is on the rocks because it was squeezed in a steamy, unpasteurized froth just half an hour ago from Mandy2, a 5½-foot-tall behemoth with hindquarters as big as truck wheels and a posterior as flat and broad as the

PHOTOGRAPHS BY ALESSANDRA PETLIN

NOV 2007 NOV 2007

002

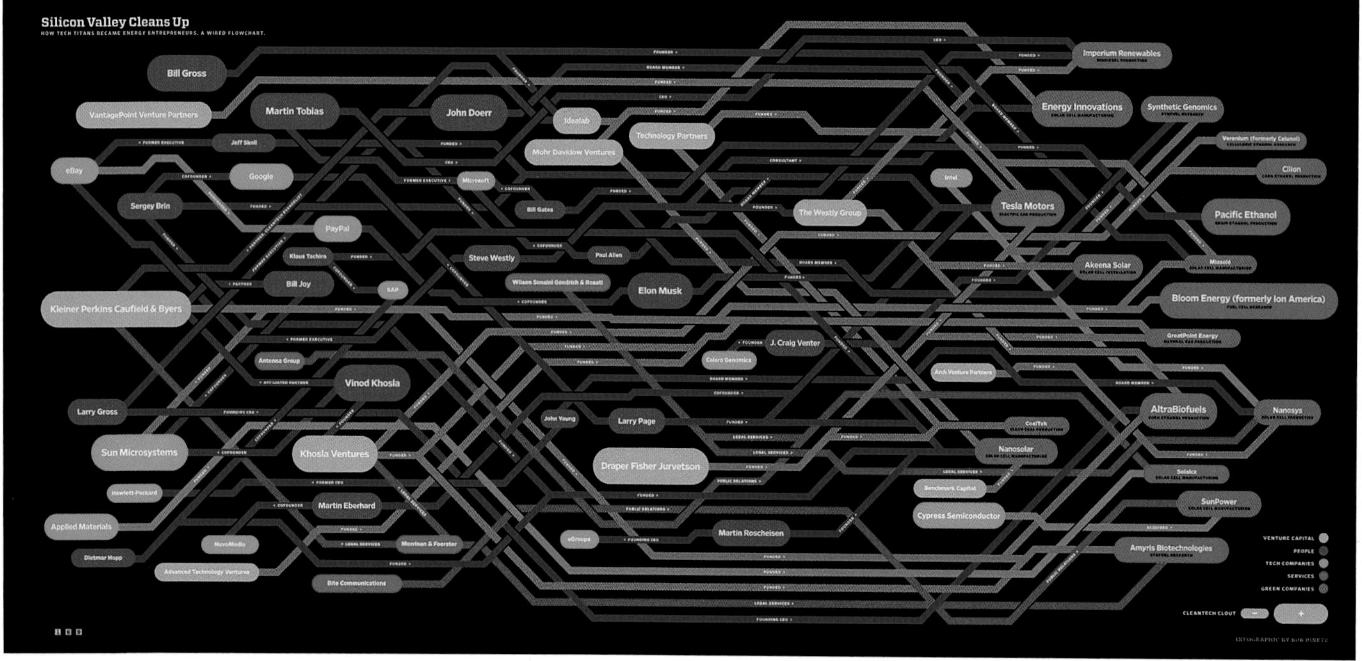

002

002 **WIRED**

Creative Director_**Scott Dadich** Design Director_**Wyatt Mitchell** Art Directors_**Maili Holiman, Jeremy LaCroix, Carl DeTorres**
Designers_**Carl DeTorres, Chris Imlay, Margaret Swart, Christy Sheppard, Victor Krummenacher** Illustrators_**Eddie Guy, Bryan Christie, Seth Ferris, Christoph Niemann, Bruce Hutchison, Pietari Posti, Yochiro Ono, Atshuisa Okura, Nicholas Felton, Florian Bachleda, Riccardo Vecchio, Luke Hayman, John Knoll**
Photo Editors_**Anna Goldwater Alexander, Zana Woods, Carolyn Rauch** Photographers_**Jill Greenberg, Baerbel Schmidt, John Clard, Darren Braun, Todd Hido, Chris Buck, Alessandra Petlin, Gregg Segal, Ofer Wolberger, Donald Milne, Dan Winters, Peter Yang, Emily Shur, Robert Maxwell, Mauricio Alejo**
Editor-In-Chief_**Chris Anderson** Publisher_**Condé Nast Publications, Inc.** Issues_**August 2007, October 2007, November 2007** Category_**Design: Magazine of the Year**

THE FRESH, FUN GUIDE TO PERSONAL STYLE | A MARTHA STEWART MAGAZINE
Blueprint
NOVEMBER | DECEMBER 2007
DESIGN YOUR LIFE
issue No 7
MODERN Holidays
175 BRIGHT Ideas for November to New Year's
Festive DECORATING Without the Fuss
Surprise! GIFTS TO WOW EVERYONE On Your List
Pretty PARTY DRESSING 15 Standout Looks
Plus: SETTING YOUR TABLE WITH STYLE A Clip-and-Save Guide

SECTION
MAGAZINE OF THE YEAR

AWARD
GOLD

CATEGORY
CIRCULATION UNDER 500,000

Blueprint

HOLIDAYS

GLAM I AM

CALL OFF THE DOGS.
WE'VE TRACKED DOWN DAZZLING DRESSES AND SMART SEPARATES FOR EVERY SOIRÉE FROM NOW UNTIL THE NEW YEAR.

TEXT BY *Alexa Yablonski*
PHOTOGRAPHS BY *Myers Robertson*

TYPE FLOURISH BY NATASHA TIBBOTT. HAIR BY ROBERT LYON AT JED ROOT FOR KERASTASE PARIS. MAKEUP BY WADA FOR JED ROOT.

100 Blueprintmag.com

003

003 BLUEPRINT

Creative Director_Eric A. Pike Design Director_Deb Bishop Art Directors_Cybele Grandjean, Lisa Thé, Jamie Prokell, Jennifer Merrill Illustrators_Natasha Tibbot, Tina Chang, Arthur Mount, Si Scott, Sara Singh, Kate Francis Director of Photography_Heloise Goodman Senior Photo Editor_Mary Cahill Assistant Photo Editor_Darlene Schrack Photographers_Sang An, Roland Bello, Craig Cutler, Timothy Kolk, Thomas Loof, Douglas Friedman, Charles Masters, John Kernick, Johnny Miller, Jens Mortensen, Eric Piasecki, Myers Robertson, Mikkel Vang Stylists_Page Marchese Norman, Shane Powers, Rebecca Robertson, Katie Hatch Editor-In-Chief_Sarah Humphreys Publisher_Martha Stewart Living Omnimedia Issues_March/April 2007, September/October 2007, November/December 2007 Category_Design: Magazine of the Year

Snow Angel

"Wearing winter white sets you apart in a sea of black," says fashion editor Katie Hatch. "And it's not exactly fuchsia, so it's easy to pull off." What makes this tank-and-pants outfit even more appealing: its loose silhouette, great for entertaining at home. Candela NYC "Harry" TOP, $250, Runway, 847-444-0064. Tory Burch "Laura" PANTS, $325, Nordstrom, 619-295-4441. Amrita Singh silver-plated BANGLES, $55 to $75 for three, *shop amritasingh.com*. Shelley Cooper for Sweet Romance "Diamond Ribbon" EARRINGS (worn as barrette), $60, *sweetromanceonline.com*. Cubic zirconia stud EARRINGS, $12, Nine West, 800-999-1877

DOUBLE ISSUE

DECEMBER 31, 2007 / JANUARY 7, 2008

Person of the Year [And the Runners-Up Al Gore, J.K. Rowling, Hu Jintao & General David Petraeus]

TIME

Vladimir Putin

Tsar of The New Russia

www.time.com

004

TIME

Art Director_**Arthur Hochstein** Director of Photography_**MaryAnne Golon** Picture Editor_**Alice Gabriner** Editor-In-Chief_**Richard Stengel** Publisher_**Time Inc.** Issues_**April 30, 2007, May 14, 2007, December 31, 2007** Category_**Design: Magazine of the Year**

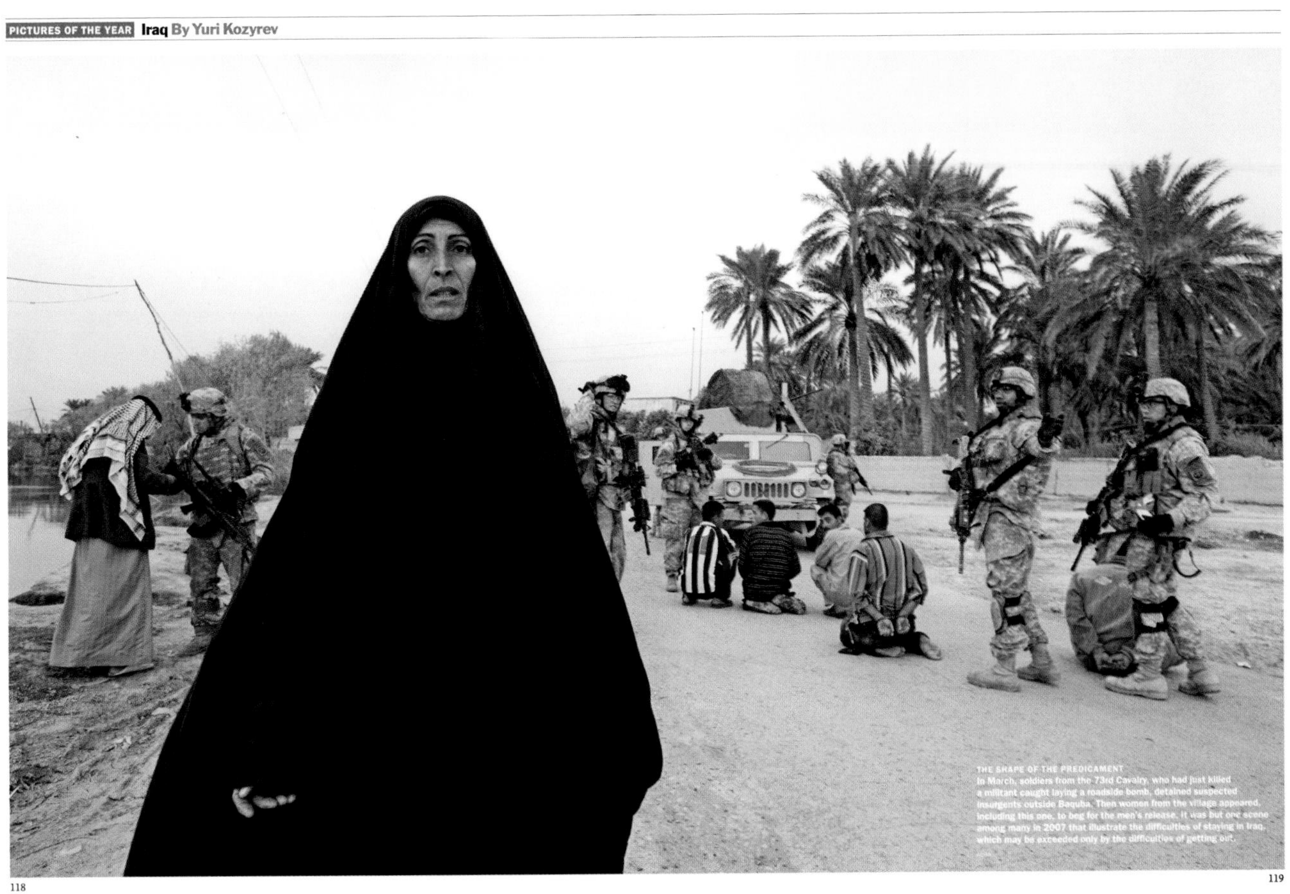

PICTURES OF THE YEAR **Iraq** By Yuri Kozyrev

THE SHAPE OF THE PREDICAMENT
In March, soldiers from the 73rd Cavalry, who had just killed a militant caught laying a roadside bomb, detained suspected insurgents outside Baquba. Then women from the village appeared, including this one, to beg for the men's release. It was but one scene among many in 2007 that illustrate the difficulties of staying in Iraq, which may be exceeded only by the difficulties of getting out.

118 119

004

TIME 100

Artists & Entertainers

Cate Blanchett. Never a starlet, she always gets to play the women worth dying for

BY RICHARD CORLISS

SO MANY ACTRESSES IN THEIR EARLY PRIME SEEM IN ARRESTED adolescence. Their coquetry and little-girl voices suggest they're campaigning for prom queen, not great film roles. Cate Blanchett is gloriously different. She's a grownup, radiating an aristocracy that has no fancy airs, just a warm, alert intelligence. Beauty helps, and height (she's 5 ft. 8½ in.), but what's crucial is that regal poise. Onscreen her magic can ennoble those in her orbit (when she's a virgin queen in *Elizabeth* or the Lady of Lórien in *The Lord of the Rings*). Sometimes it dashes them on the rocks of malice (as in *Veronica Guerin* and *Notes on a Scandal*). Either way, as an icon or a threat, the Blanchett woman is a prize worth fighting, scheming, dying for.

From the start, acclaim came to her as easily as tabloid headlines to other young stars. Within a year of her 1992 graduation from the Australian national drama school, she was the It girl of the Sydney stage, playing Shakespeare's Ophelia and Miranda, one of Caryl Churchill's *Top Girls* and the accusing student in David Mamet's *Oleanna*. Her first lead film role, in *Oscar and Lucinda*, glowed not with promise but with an early, ripe achievement. Her first movie outside Australia, *Elizabeth*, won her an Oscar nomination.

Blanchett, 38 this month, has graced heist movies *(Bandits)* and angsty art films *(Coffee and Cigarettes)*. But she's really an emissary from another, older world: the empyrean of classic movie glamour. Directors trying to capture the mature allure of old Hollywood think of her first: to play Katharine Hepburn in *The Aviator*, a Marlene Dietrich type in *The Good German*, the ideal match for a grizzled archaeologist in the next *Indiana Jones* epic.

The actress who can do anything is now, it seems, doing everything. In films she'll play Bob Dylan (kind of) in Todd Haynes' *I'm Not There*, Queen Elizabeth again (with Clive Owen as Sir Walter Raleigh) and the voice of Mrs. Fox in the cartoon *The Fabulous Mr. Fox*. She was a superb Hedda Gabler onstage and was named co-director of the Sydney Theatre Company with her husband Andrew Upton. Is there anything she can't do? Well, odds are that if some impossible acting challenge occurs to her, she'll try it.

Years from now, when cinephiles are asked to name the movies' golden age, they'll say it was when Cate Blanchett was in them.

128

RICHARD BAILEY—ICON

005

005

005 GQ

Design Director_Fred Woodward Art Director_Anton Ioukhnovets Deputy Art Director_Thomas Alberty Designers_Michael Pangilinan, Drue Wagner, Rob Hewitt, Delgis Canahuate, Eve Binder, Chelsea Cardinal Illustrators_Jean-Philippe Delhomme, John Ritter, Zohar Lazar, John Ueland Director of Photography_Dora Somosi Senior Photo Editor_Krista Prestek Photo Editors_Justin O'Neill, Jesse Lee, Halena Green, Roberto Deluna, Jolanta Bielat Photographers_Mark Seliger, Dan Forbes, David Bailey, Brian Finke, Richard Burbridge, Michael Thompson, Carter Smith, Tom Schierlitz, Peggy Sirota, Ellen Von Unwerth, Ben Watts, Tim Richardson, Brigitte LaCombe, Jeff Riedel, Nathaniel Goldberg, Terry Richardson, Francois Dischinger, Ilan Rubin, Zachary Scott, Vadukul, Platon, Danielle Levitt Creative Director_Jim Moore Editor-In-Chief_Jim Nelson Publisher_Condé Nast Publications Inc. Issues_January 2007, September 2007, October 2007 Category_Design: Magazine of the Year

LOOK SHARP//LIVE SMART

*Dress Like A Winner

50+ PAGES OF THE BEST FALL CLOTHES

AND A LIBERAL DOSE OF UNIMPEACHABLE FASHION ADVICE

Barack Obama Rules

>ON THE ROAD WITH THE GREAT CONTENDER

+THE 50 MOST POWERFUL PEOPLE IN D.C.

>Men & Money
He's Rich.
He's Your Friend.
So Why Do You
Want To Punch
His Face In?

>The Most Annoying Man On TV
PAGE 325

...And The Funniest
PAGE 358

NFL KICKOFF '07

>All Hail The Young QBs

The Future Of The Game Is Here

STARRING
Vince Young
Ben Roethlisberger
Matt Leinart
JaMarcus Russell
Brady Quinn
& Tony Romo

GQ ● COM → SEE EVAN RACHEL WOOD PHOTOS WE COULDN'T PRINT

SECTION
MAGAZINE OF THE YEAR

AWARD
SILVER

CATEGORY
CIRCULATION UNDER 500,000

print

DESIGN CULTURE
JULY/AUGUST 2007

Blogging Your Obsessions

Ersatz German Packaging

Overnight Stores Pop Up!

Virtuous Magazines

The Consumption Issue

How Design Drives Spending, Saving, and Desire

006

PRINT

Art Director_Kristina DiMatteo Associate Art Director_Lindsay Ballant Designers_Kristina DiMatteo, Lindsay Ballant, Holly Gressley
Illustrators_Chragokyberneticks, Joon Mo Kang, Siggi Eggertsson, Happy Pets, Kate Bingaman, Nicholas Felton, Ellie Harrison, John D. Freyer, Phil Lublin
Photographers_Beat Schweizer, Peter Tannenbaum, Erin Gleeson, Sven Knauth, Brad Dickson, Mark Weiss, Erin Gleeson, Brad Dickson, Jason Fulford, Jeon Mee Yoon, Sasha Nialla, Mark Mahaney Editor-In-Chief_Joyce Rutter Kaye Publisher_F & W Publications Issues_March/April 2007, May/June 2007, July/August 2007
Category_Design: Magazine of the Year

STATE OF PLAY

Governments are giving new funding and support to European video games. But what makes a game European?

By Sean Ashcroft

Illustrations by Siggi Eggertsson

77

006

new visual artists

2007

MONOGRAMS, once used to identify clothing at Roman baths, are now mainly machine-rendered tokens of convention. But Phil Lubiner's hand-drawn monogrammed initials (right), for each of our New Visual Artists, have their own distinct personalities. They're a perfect introduction to the overwhelming diversity and talent on the following pages.

Judge for yourself: Kingston, Jamaica–born Simon Benjamin makes motion graphics inspired by Michel Gondry, and Bob Chen uses the cultural past of his native China to create a rich body of work; Cybu Richli's cerebral infographics contrast with Japan native Masayoshi Nakamura's artfully imperfect animations. The existential, high-concept illustrations from Milan-based Shout offer an elegant counterpoint to John Pobojewski's irreverent mix of biblical and pop culture references and Erik Adams's devout sensibility. Our U.S. artists have roots in locales stretching from New York, Connecticut, and North Carolina to California, Washington, and Hawaii.

And they're as accomplished as they are diverse. Whether you're paging through magazines like *T: The New York Times Style Magazine*, admiring a tricked-out commercial featuring Pharrell, browsing the latest Barbara Kruger monograph, watching MTV, or downing a Coke Zero, these innovators are shedding their own bright lights on the stuff you see (and love) every day. Given Emily Lessard's political-campaign design ambitions, Joe Marianek's "design for good" philosophy, and Mark Mahaney's quiet conscience, their hearts are in the right place as well.

And yet—they're so young! It's hard to believe, but two of our winners were little children on the other side of the Iron Curtain in 1989. Thomas Porostocky left Czechoslovakia for Canada when he was 8; Helen Yentus was born in Moscow but landed in Brooklyn in time to start fourth grade. We're a little jealous, of course, but mostly, we're just proud, like a parent showing off a wallet full of pictures. We know we can't claim them forever, but we're keeping the bragging rights.

44

**Where do you see yourself in five years?*

PHOTOGRAPH BY MARK MAHANEY
ILLUSTRATION BY PHIL LUBINER

006

007

007

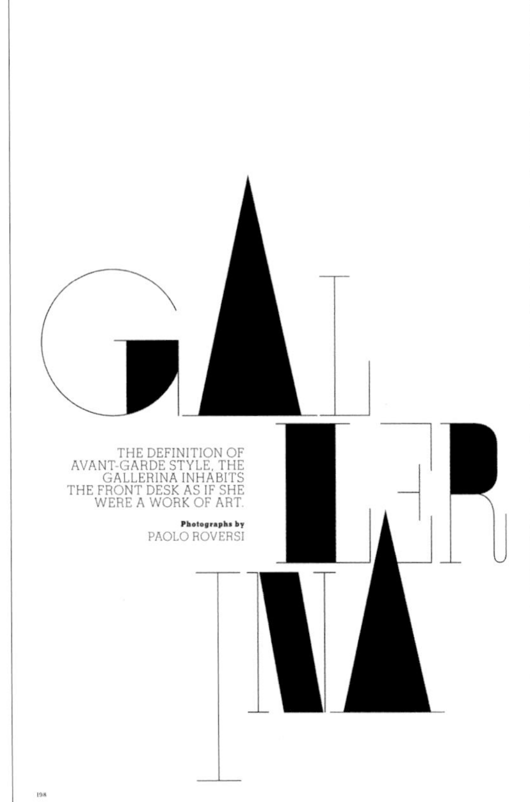

007

007 T, THE NEW YORK TIMES STYLE MAGAZINE

Creative Director_**Janet Froelich** Senior Art Director_**David Sebbah** Art Director_**Christopher Martinez**
Designer_**Elizabeth Spiridakis** Director of Photography_**Kathy Ryan** Photo Editors_**Judith Puckett-Rinella, Scott Hall, Jennifer Pastore**
Editor-In-Chief_**Stefano Tonchi** Publisher_**The New York Times** Issues_**September 16, 2007, October 21, 2007, December 2, 2007**
Category_**Design: Magazine of the Year**

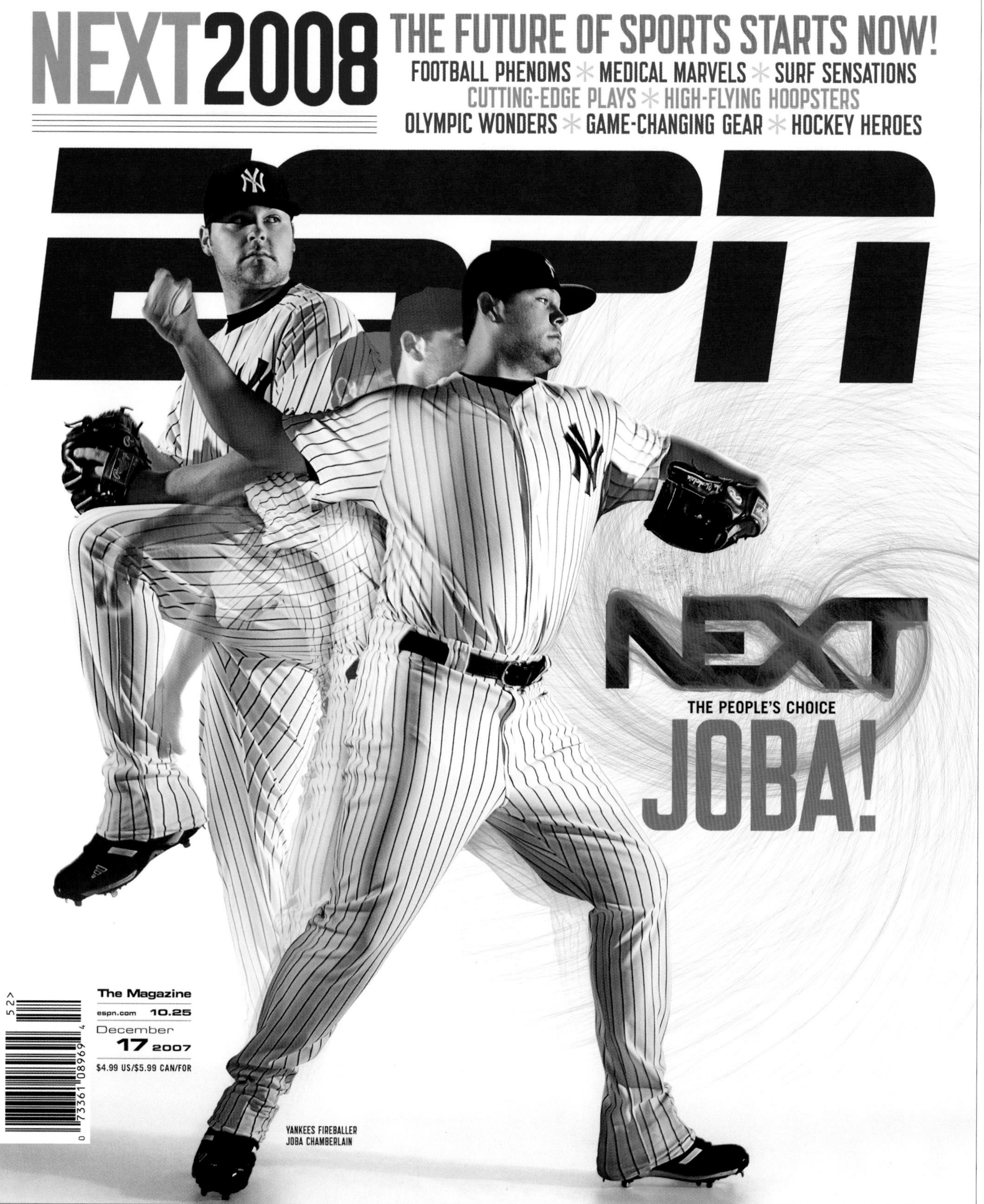

008

008 ESPN THE MAGAZINE

Creative Director_Siung Tjia Art Director_Robert Festino Designers_Jason Lancaster, Lou Vega, Hitomi Sato, Kathie Scrobanovich, Oliver Yoo Illustrators_Jason Lee, Quickhoney, Frank Stockton, Koren Shadmi, Tomby, Brian Stauffer, Mark Zingarelli, Martin French, Leonardo Solaas, Ulla Puggaard, Siggi Eggertsson Director of Photography_Catriona Ni Aolain Photo Editors_Nancy Weisman, Jennifer Aborn, Jim Surber, Amy McNulty, Daniela Corticchia, Tricia Reed, Julie Claire, Maisie Todd, Shawn Vale Photographers_Jeff Minton, Jamie Squire, Chris McPherson, Bryce Duffy, Patrik Giardino, Matthew Mahon, Justin Stephens, Jason Tanaka Blaney, Nathaniel Welch, Phil Mucci, Peter Yang, Michael Muller, Matthias Clamer, Jeff Riedel, Adam Weiss, Sye Williams, Lego, Alex Tehrani Publisher_ESPN, Inc. Issues_March 26, 2007, August 27, 2007, December 12, 2007 Category_Design: Magazine of the Year

: SECTION
MAGAZINE OF THE YEAR

: AWARD
MERIT

: CATEGORY
CIRCULATION 1 MILLION+
CIRCULATION 500,000-1 MILLION

The New York Times Sports Magazine NOVEMBER 2007
PLAY
MICHAEL LEWIS
THE TOUGHEST TWO SECONDS IN FOOTBALL
RICHARD FORD
THE PROBLEM WITH SPORTS
THE SUBVERSIVE
STEVE NASH, LOOKING FOR MEANING AT FAST-BREAK SPEED
BY CHIP BROWN
SUNS
THE DIVINE CALLING OF ALBERTO SALAZAR By John Brant
UP KILIMANJARO, BARELY By Tom Bissell
BASEBALL'S SILLY SEASON By Will Leitch & Will Carroll
COLLEGE FOOTBALL'S RUNAWAY MONEY TRAIN By Joe Nocera
PLUS: HOW TO CURE ATHLETE'S BACK / SNOWBOARDING THE REALLY BIG STUFF / SURFING'S IT GIRL
BILL COWHER ON THE SCIENCE OF PASS DEFENSE / THE GUILTY PLEASURES OF THE JOCK TELL-ALL / FIXING GAMES THE GOODFELLA WAY

009

009 PLAY, THE NEW YORK TIMES SPORTS MAGAZINE

Creative Director_Janet Froelich Art Directors_Dirk Barnett, Christopher Martinez Designers_Dirk Barnett, Christopher Martinez, Dragos Lemnei, Julia Moburg Director of Photography_Kathy Ryan Photo Editor_Kira Pollack Photographers_Vincent Laforet, Dan Winters, Tierney Gearon, Finlay MacKay, Olaf Blecker, Larry Sultan, Lynsey Addario, Brent Humphreys Publisher_The New York Times Issues_June 2007, September 2007, November 2007 Category_Design: Magazine of the Year

Hungry Heart David Chang always felt like a misfit cooking in fine dining establishments. How ironic, then, that his two New York City restaurants serve some of the finest food around
Photographs by Marcus Nilsson

010

Gourmet
THE MAGAZINE OF GOOD LIVING

010

Gourmet
THE MAGAZINE OF GOOD LIVING

010

010 GOURMET

Creative Director_**Richard Ferretti** Art Director_**Erika Oliveira**
Designers_**Erika Oliveira, Richard Ferretti, Kevin DeMaria, Flavia Schepmans** Photo Editors_**Megan M. Re, Amy Koblenzer** Editor-In-Chief_**Ruth Reichl**
Publisher_**Condé Nast Publications, Inc.** Issues_**September 2007, October 2007, December 2007** Category_**Design: Magazine of the Year**

011

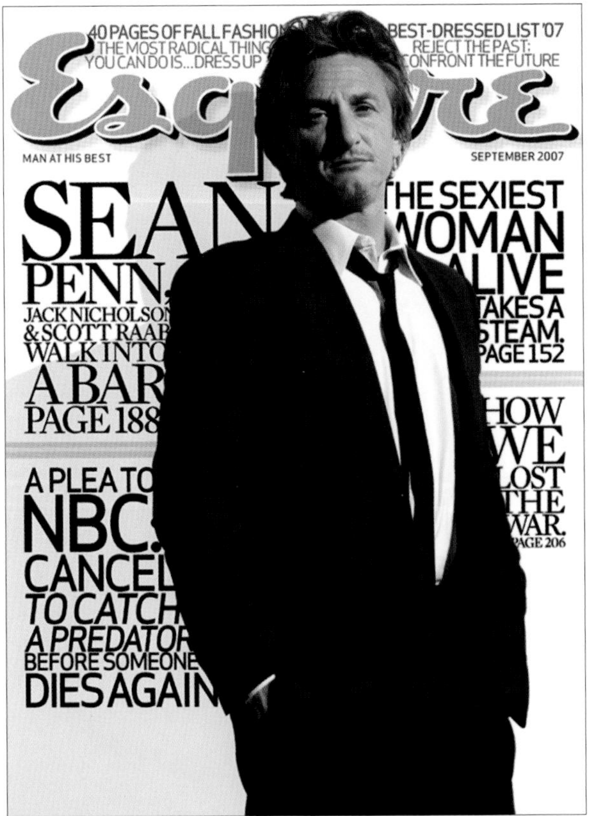

011

011

011 ESQUIRE

Design Director_David Curcurito Art Director_Darhil Crooks Designer_Colin Tunstall Photo Directors_Nancy Jo Iacoi, Michael Norseng Photo Editor_Michael Norseng Design Assistants_Soni Khatri, Derya Hanife Altan Editor-In-Chief_David Granger Publisher_The Hearst Corporation-Magazines Division Issues_March 2007, May 2007, September 2007 Category_Design: Magazine of the Year

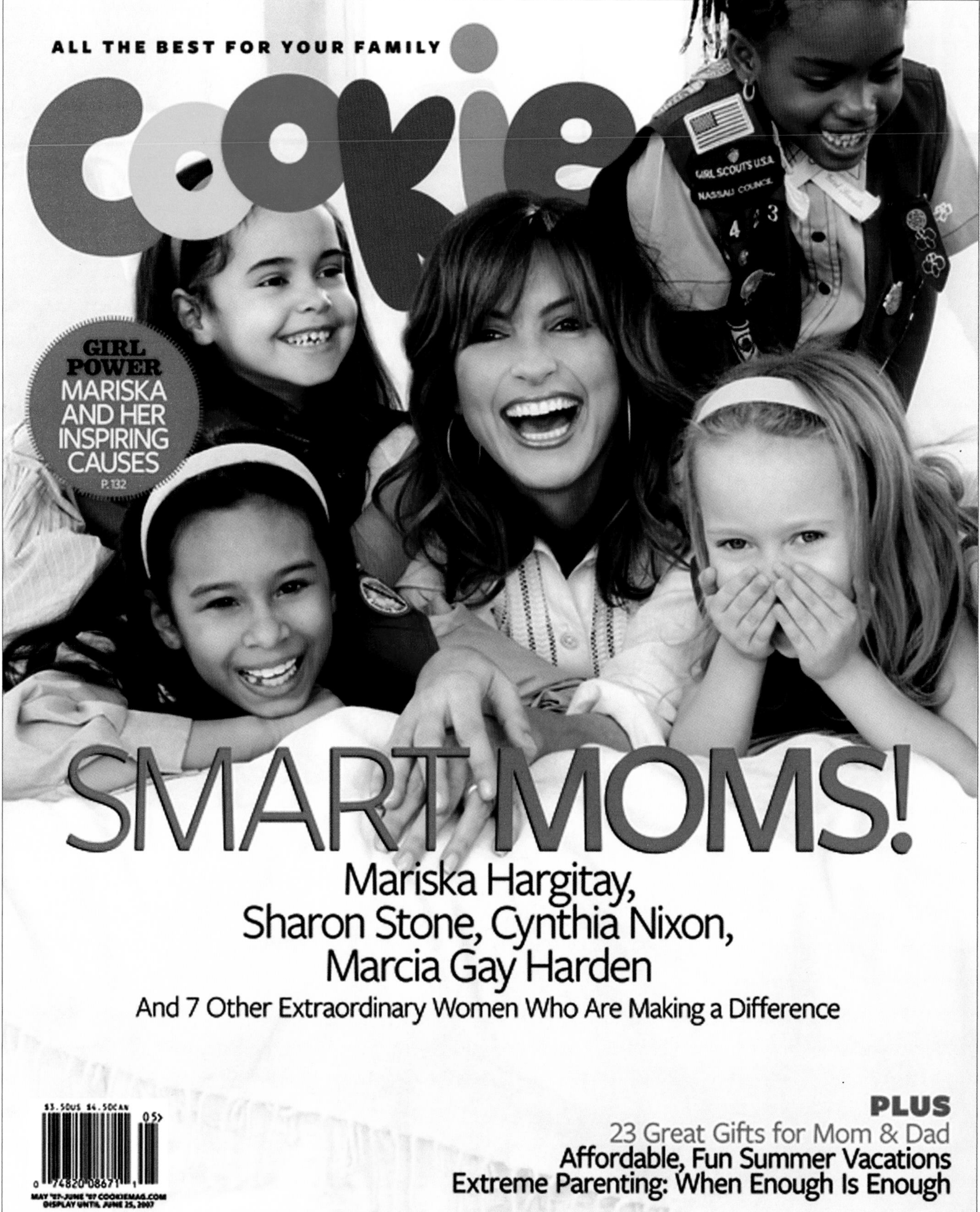
ALL THE BEST FOR YOUR FAMILY
cookie
GIRL POWER
MARISKA AND HER INSPIRING CAUSES
P. 132
SMART MOMS!
Mariska Hargitay,
Sharon Stone, Cynthia Nixon,
Marcia Gay Harden
And 7 Other Extraordinary Women Who Are Making a Difference
PLUS
23 Great Gifts for Mom & Dad
Affordable, Fun Summer Vacations
Extreme Parenting: When Enough Is Enough

012

012 COOKIE

Design Director_Kirby Rodriguez Art Director_Alex Grossman Designers_Shanna Greenberg, Nicolette Berthelot
Photo Editors_Darrick Harris, Rebecca Etter Editor-In-Chief_Pilar Guzmán Publisher_Condé Nast Publications Inc.
Issues_May/June 2007, September 2007, October/November 2007 Category_Design: Magazine of the Year

: SECTION
MAGAZINE OF THE YEAR

: AWARD
MERIT

: CATEGORY
CIRCULATION UNDER 500,000

GOP'S IRAQ ZOMBIES

REDGRAVE & DIDION

DISCO-ROCK

100-PERSON POLL ON THE FILTHIEST WORDS

THE SAD, MAD GENIUS OF GEORGE W.S. TROW

NEW YORK

MARCH 26, 2007

Plus Adam Platt eats his way through the U.K.

NEW YORK (YAY!)

In finance, restaurants, art, even sex, our pesky rival across the pond is getting cocky. Can they beat us with our own moves?

VS.

LONDON (HISS!)

A world-capital title fight, featuring Nick Hornby, Kate Winslet, the Klaxons, Christopher Hitchens, Bill Nighy, Helena Christensen, Michael Kinsley, and many others.

$2.99 (CANADA $3.99)

13

0 71486 01912 1

WWW.NYMAG.COM

PROFESSION
Graphic Designers
ESSENTIAL DESIGN
New York Subway Signs and Map
PEAK
1965 to 1985
2 Design Revolutionaries
THE VIGNELLIS
IN AN INSTANT, THEIR PARED-DOWN DESIGNS—FOR THE SUBWAY, BLOOMINGDALE'S, AMERICAN AIRLINES—CONJURE A PARTICULAR MOMENT IN THE CITY'S HISTORY.
Photograph by DEAN KAUFMAN
Massimo and Lella Vignelli, photographed in their Upper East Side apartment in September.

013

New York

ON A RAINY NIGHT IN 1971, THE NOTORIOUS SKYJACKER JUMPED OUT OF A 727 AND INTO AMERICAN LEGEND. BUT RECENTLY, A CHANCE LEAD TO A MANHATTAN P.I. MAY HAVE FINALLY CRACKED THE CASE.

UNMASKING D.B. COOPER

By GEOFFREY GRAY

(Opposite) An FBI sketch of "D.B. Cooper."

(This page) Kenneth Christiansen, Northwest purser and former paratrooper: the suspect.

43

013

013 NEW YORK

Design Director_Chris Dixon Art Directors_Randy Minor, Kate Elazegui Designers_Robert Vargas, Katie Van Syckle Illustrators_Fabien Baron, Joe Darrow, John Burgoyne, Sean McCabe, Wes Duvall Director of Photography_Jody Quon Photographers_Mackenzie Stroh, Dean Kaufman, Perry Moore, Mark Heithoff, Levi Brown, Christian Witkin, Mitchell Feinberg, Davies + Starr, Jake Chessum, Kang Kim, Rachel Papo, Michael Edwards, Andrew Eccles, Nigel Parry, Morini & Montanari, Todd Selby, Anne Hall, Brigitte Lacombe, James Day, Tim Richardson Editor-In-Chief_Adam Moss Publisher_New York Magazine Holdings, LLC Issues_March 26, 2007, October 29, 2007, December 7, 2007 Category_Design: Magazine of the Year

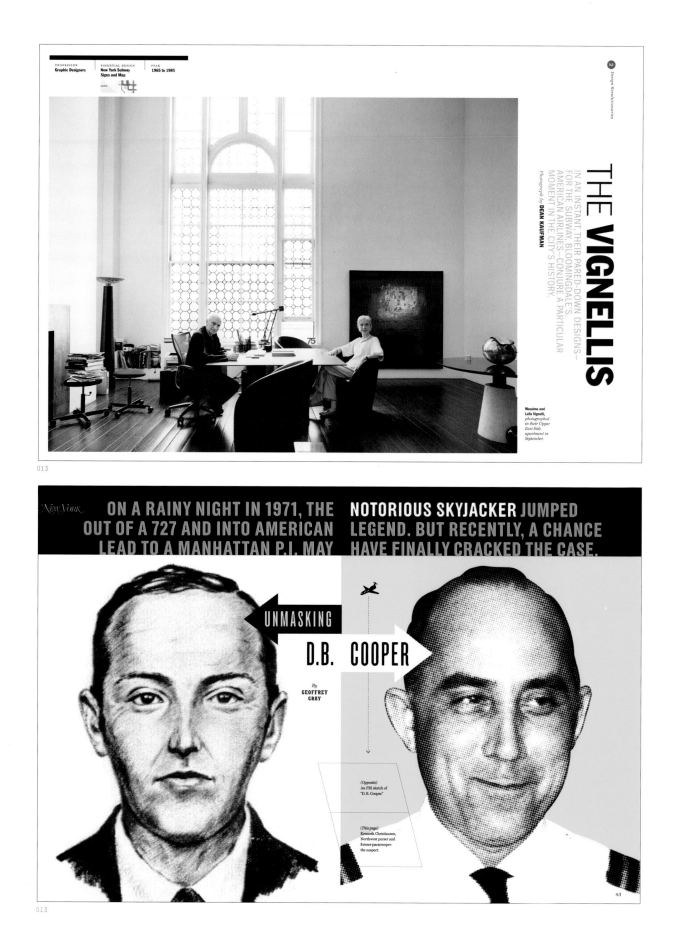

:SECTION
MAGAZINE OF THE YEAR

:AWARD
MERIT

:CATEGORY
CIRCULATION UNDER 500,000

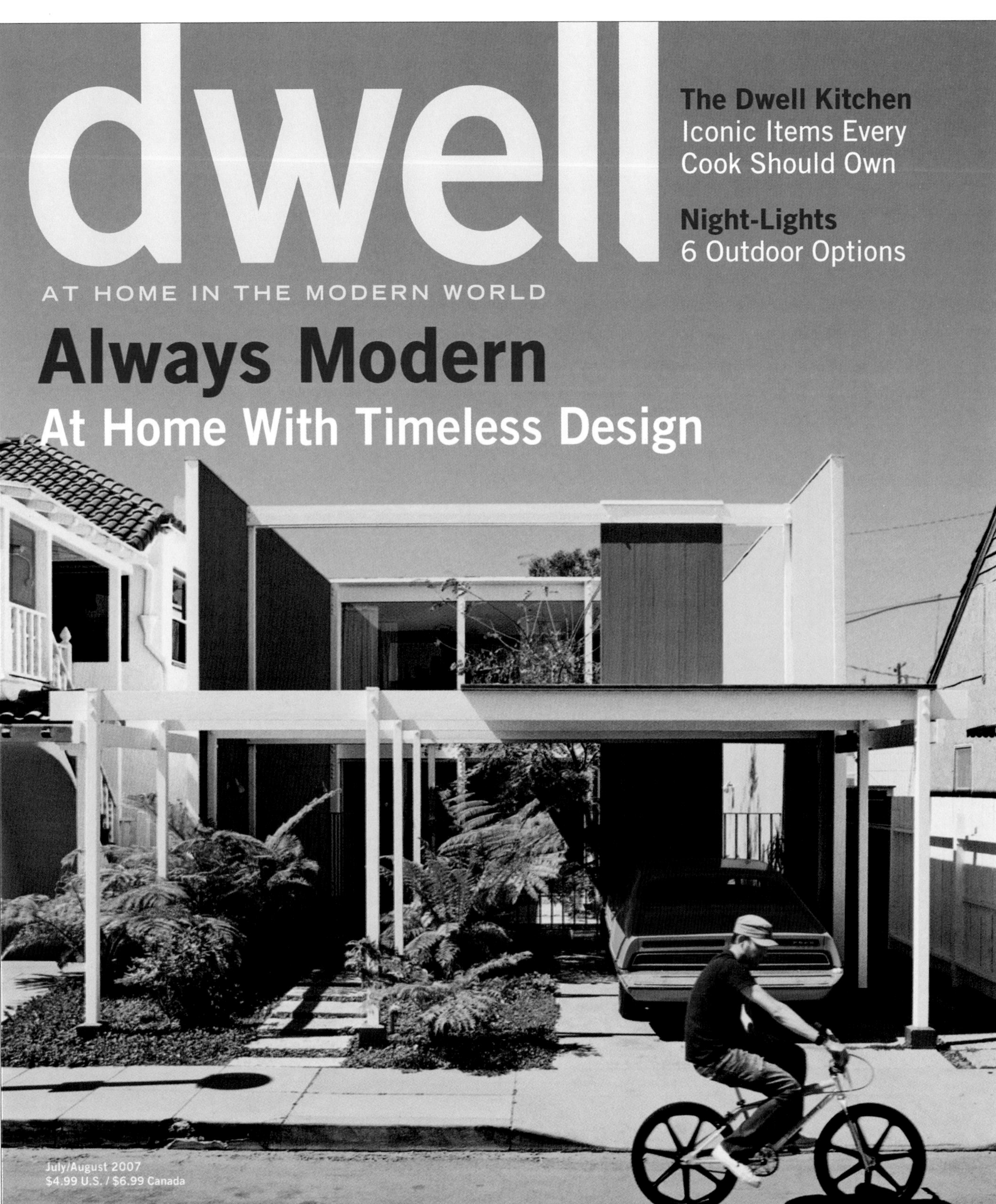

014

014 DWELL

Design Director_Kyle Blue Designers_Brendan Callahan, Suzanne La Gasa, Geoff Halber
Director of Photography_Kate Stone Foss Photo Editors_Andrea Lawson, Alexis Tjian Production_Kathryn Hansen
Editor-In-Chief_Sam Grawe Publisher_Dwell LLC Issues_May 2007, July/August 2007, October 2007
Category_Design: Magazine of the Year

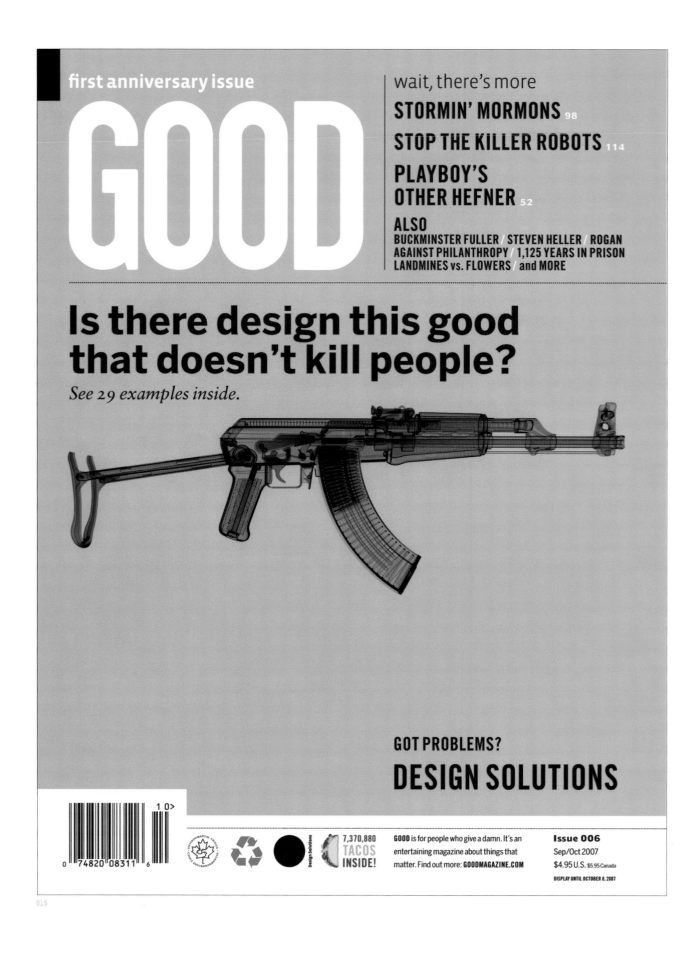

first anniversary issue

GOOD

wait, there's more

STORMIN' MORMONS 98

STOP THE KILLER ROBOTS 114

PLAYBOY'S OTHER HEFNER 52

ALSO
BUCKMINSTER FULLER / STEVEN HELLER / ROGAN
AGAINST PHILANTHROPY / 1,125 YEARS IN PRISON
LANDMINES vs. FLOWERS / and MORE

Is there design this good that doesn't kill people?

See 29 examples inside.

GOT PROBLEMS?

DESIGN SOLUTIONS

GOOD is for people who give a damn. It's an entertaining magazine about things that matter. Find out more: **GOODMAGAZINE.COM**

Issue 006
Sep/Oct 2007
$4.95 U.S. $5.95 Canada
DISPLAY UNTIL OCTOBER 8, 2007

015

015 GOOD

Creative Director_Casey Caplowe Design Director_Scott Stowell
Designers_Susan Barber, Rob Dileso, Gary Fogelson, Carol Hayes, Serifcan Özcan, Nick Rock, Scott Stowell, Ryan Thacker
Director of Photography_Joaquin Trujillo Studio_Open Publisher_Good Magazine, LLC
Client_Good Magazine, LLC Issues_March/April 2007, July/August 2007, September/October 2007 Category_Design: Magazine of the Year

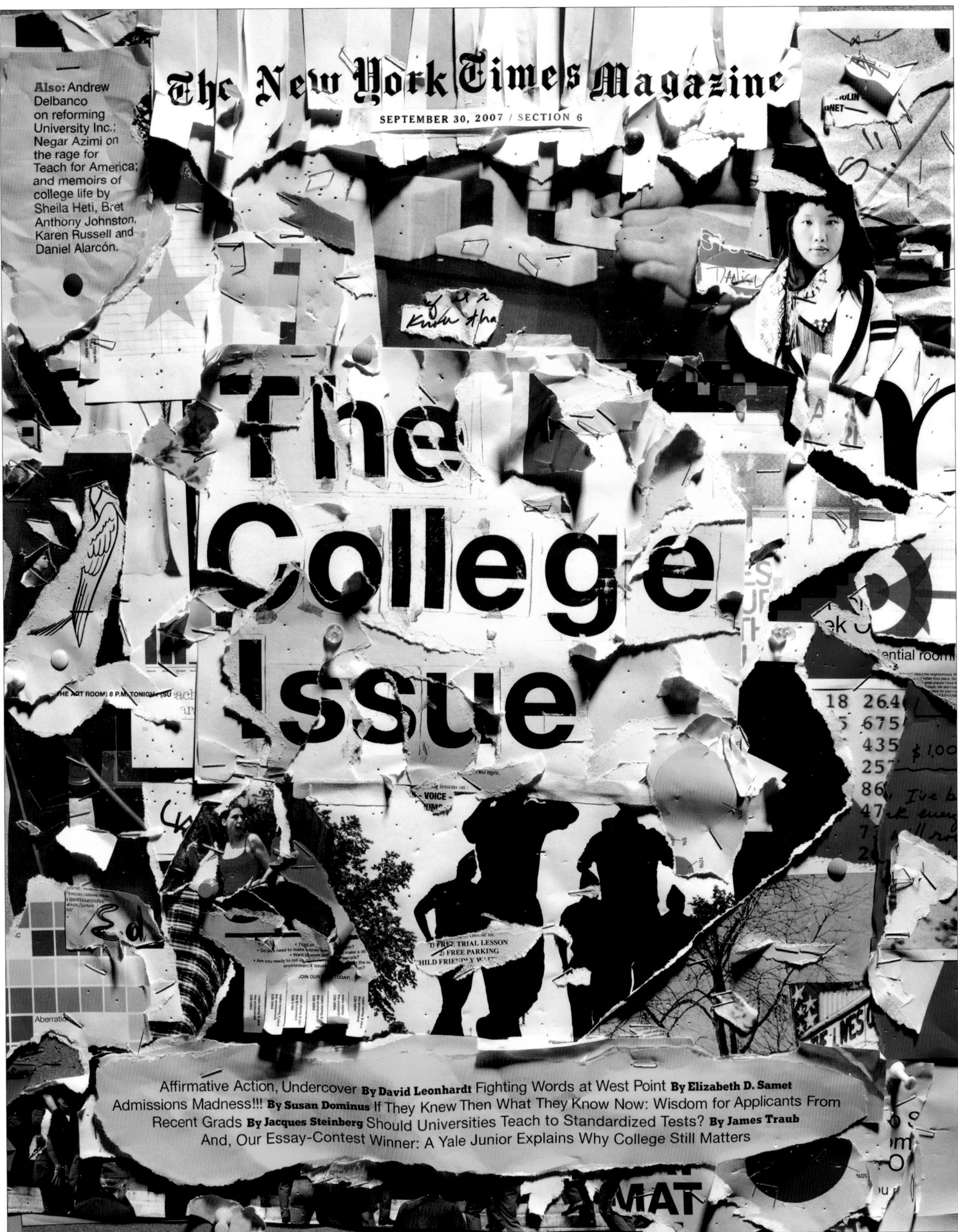

016

016 THE NEW YORK TIMES MAGAZINE

Creative Director_Janet Froelich Art Director_Arem Duplessis Designers_Arem Duplessis, Jeff Glendenning, Julia Moburg, Holly Gressley Director of Photography_Kathy Ryan Photo Editors _Stacey Baker, Clinton Cargill Editor-In-Chief_Gerry Marzorati Publisher_The New York Times Issue_September 30, 2007 Category_Design: Entire Issue

Fear and loathing pave the road to college.
But ask recent graduates to reflect on their experience,
and they advise kids to forget rankings, chill out and
get ready to savor the best years of their lives.

By Jacques Steinberg

LAURIE HOACHLANDER'S PARENTS may have spent tens of thousands of dollars on the psychology courses she took as an undergraduate at the University of Pennsylvania, but ask the 27-year-old, a member of the class of 2002, what was most valuable about her college years, and her thoughts drift far beyond the classroom window.

There was her year as a resident adviser to a cluster of freshmen in her dormitory at Penn, an experience colored by the attempted suicide of one of her charges, followed by his recovery and return to the hall. "That taught me a lot about crisis management," she says. Then there was her work as a campus tour guide, which taught her "how to be a better public speaker." That, she says, wound up serving her well in one of her first jobs, as a leader of seminars for real estate brokers: they would interrupt her presentations with offbeat questions,

How would you rate
your **overall experience** as an undergraduate student?

UNLESS OTHERWISE INDICATED
THESE GRAPHICS REFLECT THE RESULTS OF A NATIONAL POLL OF
RECENT COLLEGE GRADUATES BY THE NEW YORK TIMES AND MTVU

Infographics by Yokoland

72 LETTERING BY FISHWRAPPERS. PHOTOGRAPHS BY JORGEN GOMNAES.

73

016

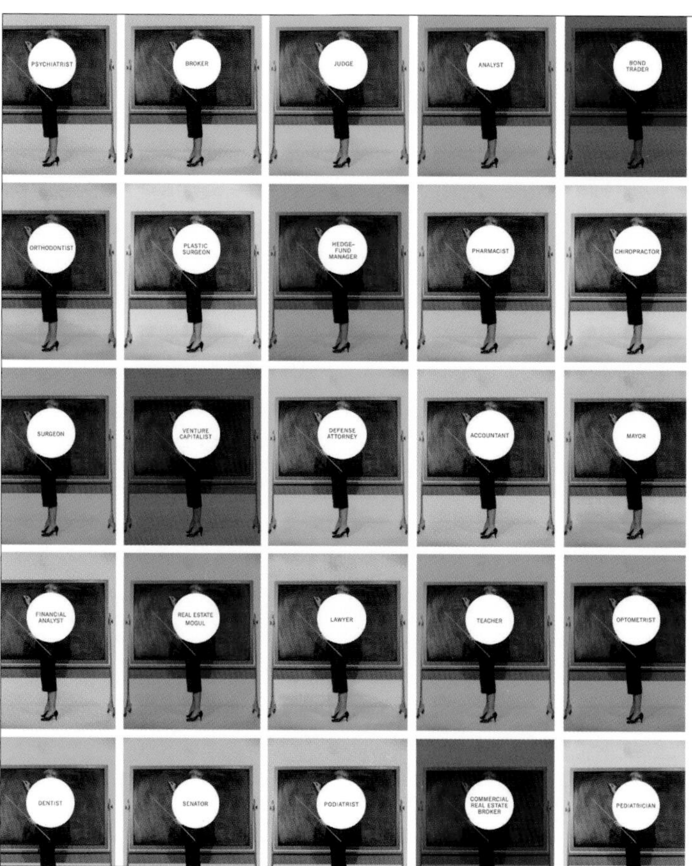

? why | teach | 4 for | America

A volunteer program
for ambitious college graduates is great for the résumé.
But is it good for the country?

By Negar Azimi

HOUSTON'S FIFTH WARD has an abundance of overgrown grass fields and dilapidated chicken restaurants: chicken and barbecue, chicken and waffles and just plain chicken. Along railroad tracks that run past a string of cavernous warehouses is John L. McReynolds Middle School, a brick building with Art Deco flourishes that suggest a glorious past. Until 2006, McReynolds had been ranked "academically unacceptable" for three years running by the Texas Education Agency. Three principals had come and gone over five years. I went to McReynolds in early July to observe Teach for America, a program that promises to place America's best and brightest college graduates into the nation's neediest public schools for two-year stints. For three years, Teach for America has been working with the McReynolds summer-school program.

Hada Flores, a 22-year-old Texan of El Salvadoran origin, had tied her jet-black hair into a tight ponytail and was facing down a room of emphatically bored young people. Some weeks before, she marched in her graduation ceremony at Stanford. Now, while most of her friends were either at the beach or backpacking around Europe,

Illustrations by Alan Dye

LETTERING BY FISHWRAPPERS. PHOTOGRAPH FROM EVERETT COLLECTION. 111

016

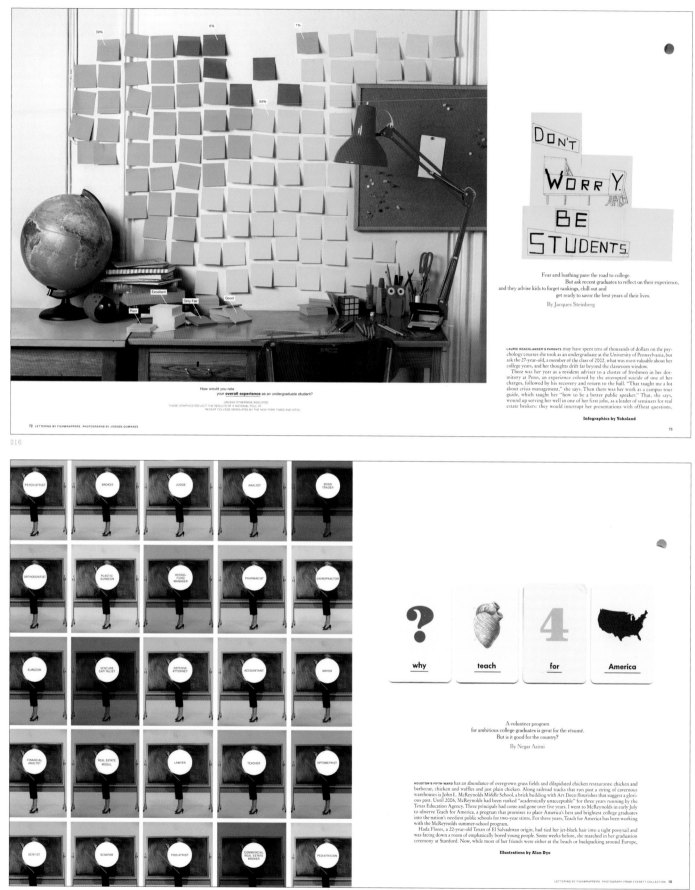

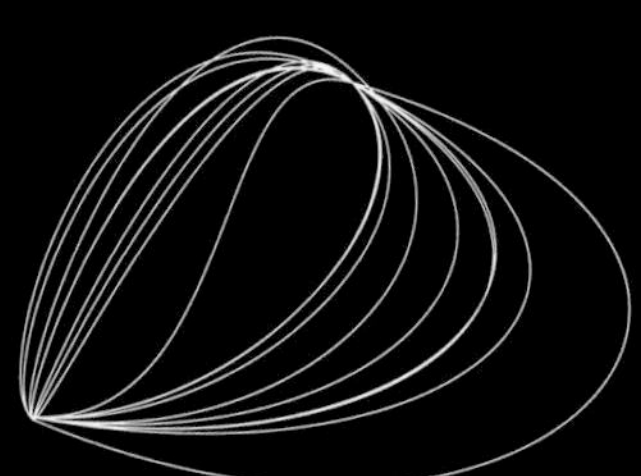

design

ENTRIES: 3,716
CATEGORIES: 7

GOLD: 13
SILVER: 13
MERIT: 243

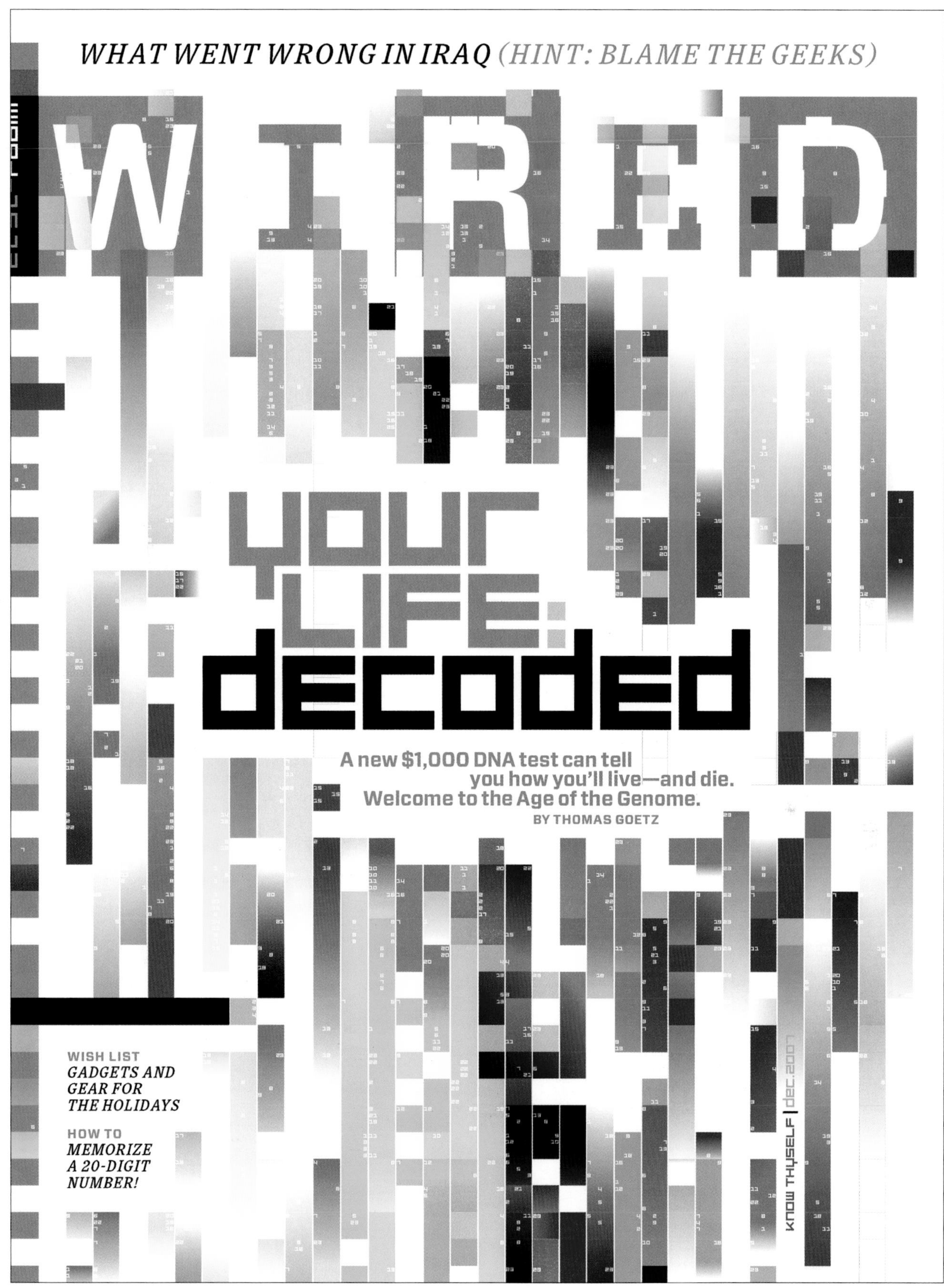

WHAT WENT WRONG IN IRAQ (HINT: BLAME THE GEEKS)
WIRED
your LIFE: decoded
A new $1,000 DNA test can tell you how you'll live—and die. Welcome to the Age of the Genome.
BY THOMAS GOETZ
WISH LIST
GADGETS AND GEAR FOR THE HOLIDAYS
HOW TO
MEMORIZE A 20-DIGIT NUMBER!
KNOW THYSELF | dec.2007

017

017 WIRED

Creative Director_**Scott Dadich** Design Director_**Wyatt Mitchell** Designer_**Mark Makers**
Publisher_**Condé Nast Publications, Inc.** Issue_**December 2007** Category_**Design: Cover**

HOT BETTY

018

W Profile
BY JENNY COMITA
As the endearingly dowdy star of *Ugly Betty*, actress America Ferrera
has achieved her Hollywood dreams at the tender age of 23.
Now comes the hard part: learning to enjoy it.
PHOTOGRAPHED BY MICHAEL THOMPSON
STYLED BY CAMILLA NICKERSON
MAY 2007 W | 165

Creative Director_Dennis Freedman Design Director_ Edward Leida Art Director_Nathalie Kirsheh Designer_Nathalie Kirsheh Photographer_Michael Thompson Publisher_Condé Nast Publications Inc. Issue_May 2007 Category_Design: Feature: Spread/Single Page

: SECTION
DESIGN

: AWARD
GOLD

: CATEGORY
ENTIRE ISSUE

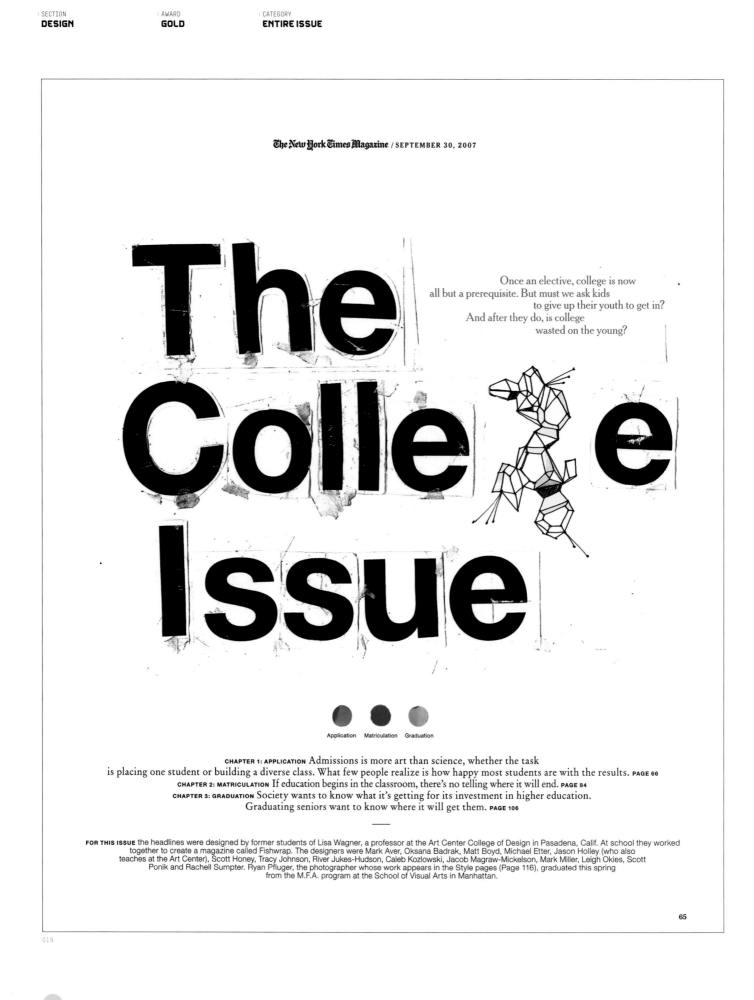

The New York Times Magazine / SEPTEMBER 30, 2007

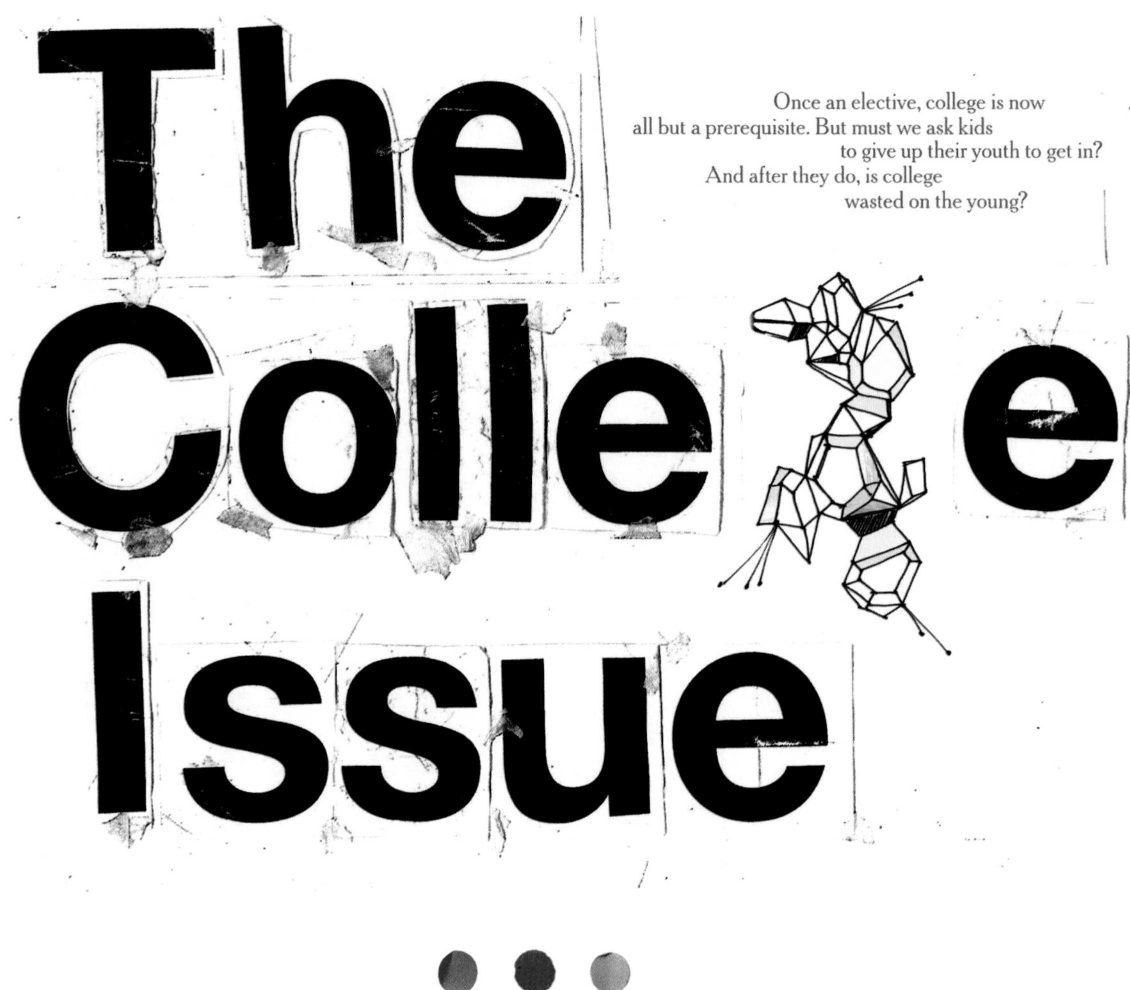

The College Issue
Once an elective, college is now all but a prerequisite. But must we ask kids to give up their youth to get in? And after they do, is college wasted on the young?

Application Matriculation Graduation

CHAPTER 1: APPLICATION Admissions is more art than science, whether the task is placing one student or building a diverse class. What few people realize is how happy most students are with the results. **PAGE 66**
CHAPTER 2: MATRICULATION If education begins in the classroom, there's no telling where it will end. **PAGE 84**
CHAPTER 3: GRADUATION Society wants to know what it's getting for its investment in higher education. Graduating seniors want to know where it will get them. **PAGE 106**

FOR THIS ISSUE the headlines were designed by former students of Lisa Wagner, a professor at the Art Center College of Design in Pasadena, Calif. At school they worked together to create a magazine called Fishwrap. The designers were Mark Aver, Oksana Badrak, Matt Boyd, Michael Etter, Jason Holley (who also teaches at the Art Center), Scott Honey, Tracy Johnson, River Jukes-Hudson, Caleb Kozlowski, Jacob Magraw-Mickelson, Mark Miller, Leigh Okies, Scott Ponik and Rachell Sumpter. Ryan Pfluger, the photographer whose work appears in the Style pages (Page 116), graduated this spring from the M.F.A. program at the School of Visual Arts in Manhattan.

65

019

019 THE NEW YORK TIMES MAGAZINE

Creative Director_**Janet Froelich** Art Director_**Arem Duplessis**
Designers_**Arem Duplessis, Jeff Glendenning, Julia Moburg, Holly Gressley** Director of Photography_**Kathy Ryan**
Photo Editors_**Stacey Baker, Clinton Cargill** Editor-In-Chief_**Gerry Marzorati**
Publisher_**The New York Times** Issue_**September 30, 2007** Category_**Design: Entire Issue**

The New York Times Magazine
SEPTEMBER 30, 2007 / SECTION 6
Andrew Delbanco on reforming University Inc.; Negar Azimi on the rage for Teach for America; and memoirs of college life by Sheila Heti, Bret Anthony Johnston, Karen Russell and Daniel Alarcón.
The College Issue
Affirmative Action, Undercover By David Leonhardt Fighting Words at West Point By Elizabeth D. Samet Admissions Madness!!! By Susan Dominus If They Knew Then What They Know Now: Wisdom for Applicants From Recent Grads By Jacques Steinberg Should Universities Teach to Standardized Tests? By James Traub And, Our Essay-Contest Winner: A Yale Junior Explains Why College Still Matters

019

9.30.07

THE INFORMATION

Degree Requirements In Fund-Raising

Higher ed seeks even higher levels of giving.

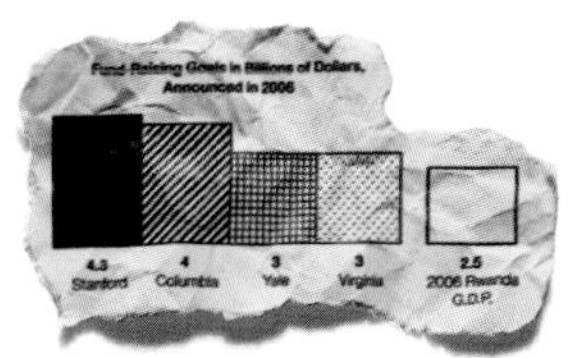

College presidents are likely to spend more time raising money than doing anything else, suggests a recent survey by The Chronicle of Higher Education. But because the transition from the life of the mind to the life of the wallet does not always come easily, several prominent university officials provide a few basic rules when it comes to high-stakes fund-raising.

1

SET AN OUTRAGEOUS GOAL

If you're at a major university, start at a billion dollars. Last year, the University of Virginia, Yale, Columbia and Stanford all announced comprehensive fund-raising campaigns of $3 billion or more. In 2008, New York University will conclude a seven-year, $2.5 billion campaign that has led to the school's raising money at a pace of $1 million a day, 7 days a week, 365 days a year.

1a

MAKE THAT OUTRAGEOUS GOAL NECESSARY — AND URGENT!

Leon Botstein, the longtime president of Bard College, says that the current multibillion-dollar fund-raising campaigns define fiscal solidity in this way: "If there is a nuclear attack, can we survive that attack and pay our faculty for another 100 years?" Even if the answer is yes, do not say so in your letters to would-be donors.

2

SPEND TIME WITH THE DONOR

When courting a top contributor, wait before suggesting an amount for a gift. There may be an urge to ask a wealthy donor in the first conversation to sponsor a chaired professorship for $2 million, Debra LaMorte, senior vice president of development at N.Y.U., says. "But if I spend a little more time with you, I may find out that your mother died of breast cancer, and you may be willing to spend $25 million to have your name on the new cancer center."

3

PUT THE DONOR IN THE MIDDLE OF THE STORY

Philanthropists give not simply out of loyalty but also because they want to shape the narrative of their own lives and legacies. "Part of leadership is creating a story about your university that is attractive to people and in which they want to participate," says John Sexton, president of N.Y.U. Appeals on behalf of student financial aid tend to have a very powerful psychological draw for alumni, according to Neil Rudenstine, who was Harvard's president from 1991 to 2001. They make alumni "feel like they're not just helping the institution, but they're really helping somebody else have that experience they had," Rudenstine says.

4

REMEMBER: YOU'RE NOT BEGGING; YOU'RE DISPENSING FAVORS

It helps considerably to think of yourself not as a beggar but rather as if you're "doing that person a favor," LaMorte says. "People joke with me, 'Oh no, here comes Debra, look out for your wallet.' But I have to feel as though I am helping people focus their philanthropy in a way that gives them meaning and that will enhance their lives."

5

REACH OUTSIDE THE ALUMNI COMMUNITY

"Alumni alone are a limited constituency," says Carol P. Herring, president of the Rutgers University Foundation. Botstein says that his fund-raising requires more than stroking graduates. "Our alumni are not investment bankers," he says. "They are not in general very rich. So I'm going after unaffiliated philanthropy. Fund-raising should be driven by ideas, like doing something about homelessness, AIDS, fostering the arts. Success in philanthropy is linking the person with the idea that appeals to that person."

6

DON'T FORGET THE LITTLE GUY

Roughly 5 percent of donors give 95 percent of the money in some large universitywide fund-raising campaigns. Why, then, do schools solicit gifts of $25 or $50? One significant reason is that the college rankings in U.S. News & World Report factor in the percentage of undergraduate alumni who give — whether the gift is $20 or $20 million.

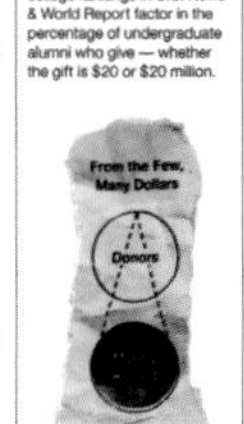

7

THINK ABOUT OTHER THINGS TOO

Maintaining a former interest in, say, medieval literature can be daunting for the academic-turned-administrator. President John T. Casteen III of the University of Virginia says that he used to read for eight or nine hours a day when he was primarily a scholar; now, he says, he's lucky if he reads for more than two.

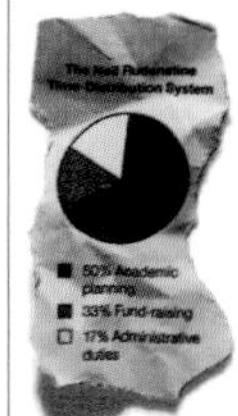

At Harvard, Neil Rudenstine created a private time-distribution formula to keep his priorities straight: he told himself he would devote no less than half his time to the intellectual life of the institution — academic planning, faculty searches, tenured appointments — and no more than a third to fund-raising. The rest of his time was for administrative duties. "If I went through a week where I hardly had a chance to think about academic planning, then I would make a very powerful correction the next couple of weeks," Rudenstine says.

7a

ACKNOWLEDGE THAT MONEY ISN'T EVERYTHING

"Excessive wealth engenders self-satisfied mediocrity," Leon Botstein says. "It's true in families, and it's true in universities."

CHARLES WILSON

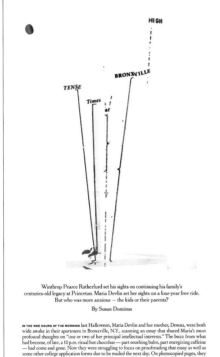

44

019

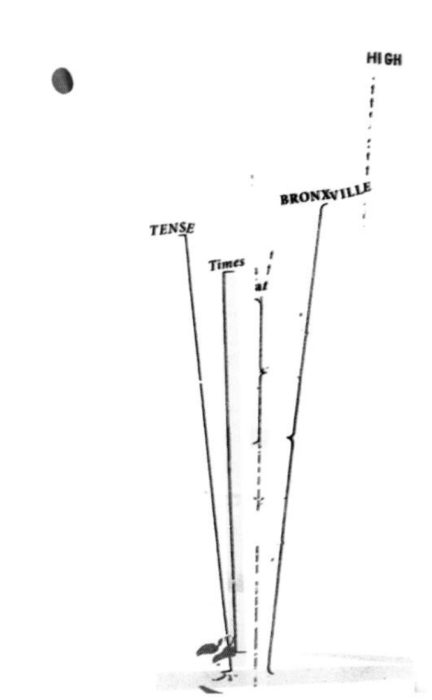

Winthrop Pearce Rutherfurd set his sights on continuing his family's centuries-old legacy at Princeton. Maria Devlin set her sights on a four-year free ride. But who was more anxious — the kids or their parents?

By Susan Dominus

IN THE WEE HOURS OF THE MORNING last Halloween, Maria Devlin and her mother, Donna, were both wide awake in their apartment in Bronxville, N.Y., scanning an essay that shared Maria's most profound thoughts on "one or two of her principal intellectual interests." The buzz from what had become, of late, a 10 p.m. ritual hot chocolate — part soothing balm, part energizing caffeine — had come and gone. Now they were struggling to focus on proofreading that essay as well as some other college application forms due to be mailed the next day. On photocopied pages, they practiced squeezing Maria's many accomplishments — National Merit finalist, area all-state flutist (honor ensemble), numerous playwriting awards — into the too-small lines scattered throughout the page. Once Maria's mother found a way to make it all fit, with abbreviations and tiny, neat letters, Maria would commit the list to the official page in clean, precise writing. Around 2 in the morning, a friend sent Maria an e-mail message: What are you doing? Maria told her and fired back the same question. A.P. American history, the friend wrote. Gotcha, wrote

66 LETTERING BY FISHWRAPPERS

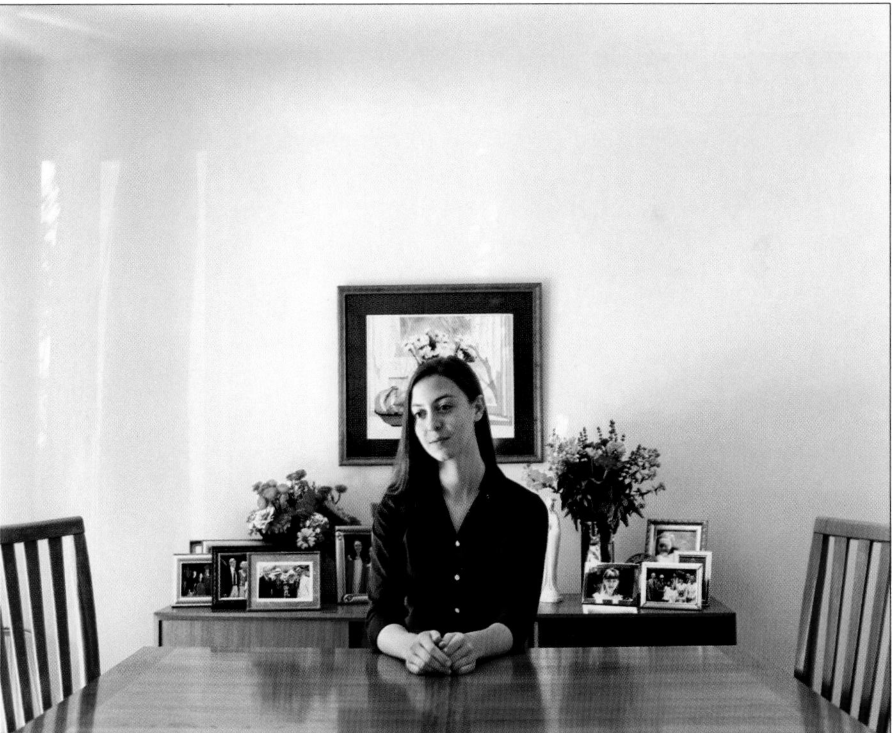

Photographs by Amy Elkins

Maria Devlin was striving to match the right school with the right scholarship.

67

019

SECTION
DESIGN

AWARD
GOLD

CATEGORY
REDESIGN ENTIRE ISSUE

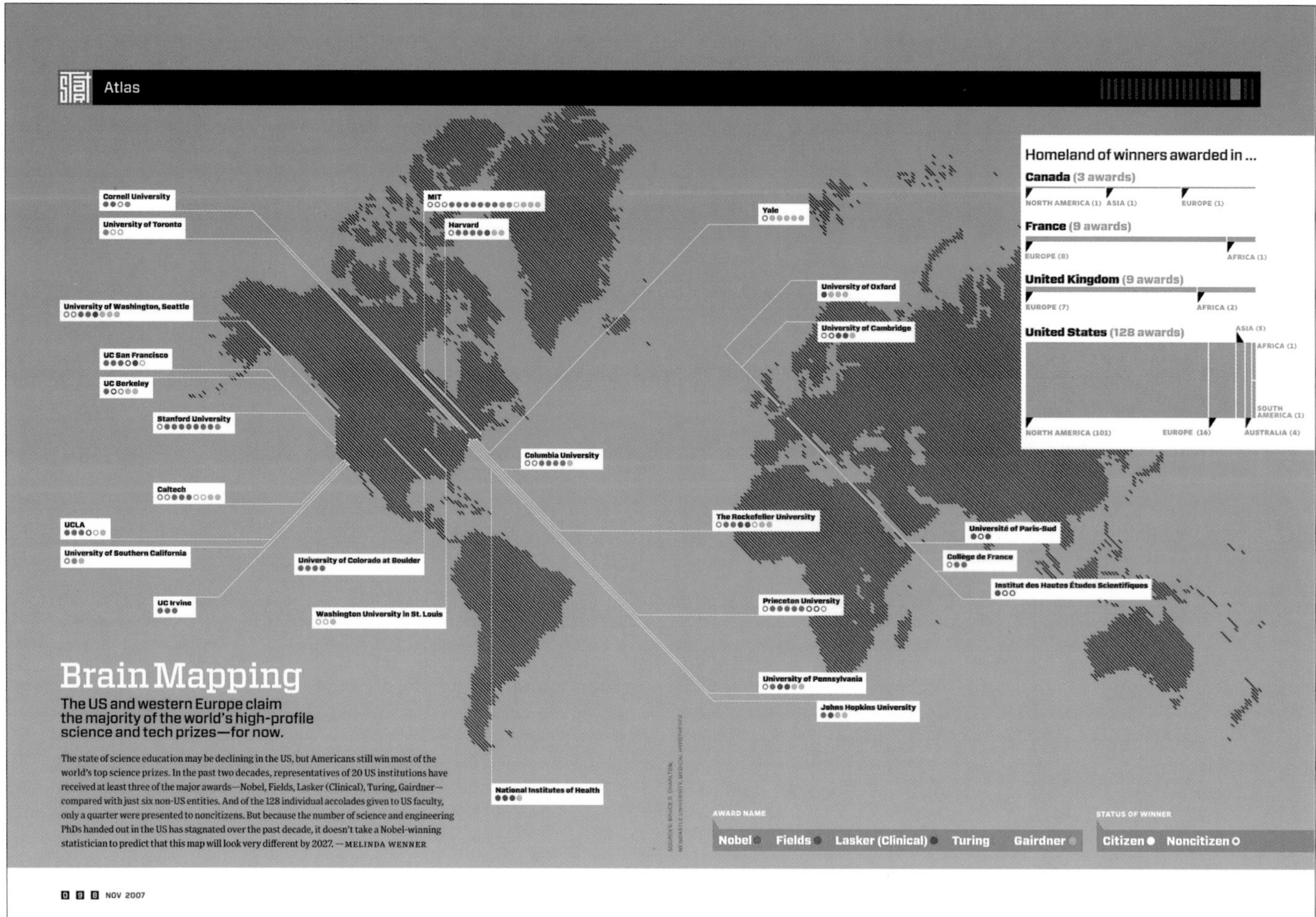

Brain Mapping

The US and western Europe claim the majority of the world's high-profile science and tech prizes—for now.

The state of science education may be declining in the US, but Americans still win most of the world's top science prizes. In the past two decades, representatives of 20 US institutions have received at least three of the major awards—Nobel, Fields, Lasker (Clinical), Turing, Gairdner—compared with just six non-US entities. And of the 128 individual accolades given to US faculty, only a quarter were presented to noncitizens. But because the number of science and engineering PhDs handed out in the US has stagnated over the past decade, it doesn't take a Nobel-winning statistician to predict that this map will look very different by 2027. —MELINDA WENNER

020

020

MEDIA CAN'T BE TOO FAST OR TOO RICH. Four years ago, James Murdoch, second son of you-know-who, took over as executive director of British Sky Broadcasting—better known as Sky in the UK, where nearly one in three households subscribes to its flagship satellite TV service. Over the past year, Murdoch, 34, has led the company in an $800 million bid to complement Sky's high-flying television circus with a screaming-fast DSL broadband network. The result: a unique engine for channeling both content and interactivity, whatever size the screen. WIRED dropped into Sky's studio-lot headquarters west of London to learn about a bitfest Americans can only dream of.

Sky began as a satellite TV provider, optimized for pumping out the opiate of the UK masses—English Premier League soccer. Now it's also a high-end ISP. What happened?

020

 WIRED

Creative Director_**Scott Dadich** Design Director_**Wyatt Mitchell** Art Directors_**Maili Holiman, Carl DeTorres**
Designers_**Chris Imlay, Christy Sheppard, Margaret Swart** Illustrators_**Yoichiro Ono, Atshuisa Okura, Nicholas Felton, Florian Bachleda**
Photo Editors_**Anna Goldwater Alexander, Zana Woods, Carolyn Rauch** Photographers_**Chris Buck, Alessandra Petlin, Gregg Segal, Ofer Wolberger, Donald Milne, Todd Hido** Publisher_**Condé Nast Publications, Inc.** Issue_**November 2007** Category_**Design: Redesign**

021

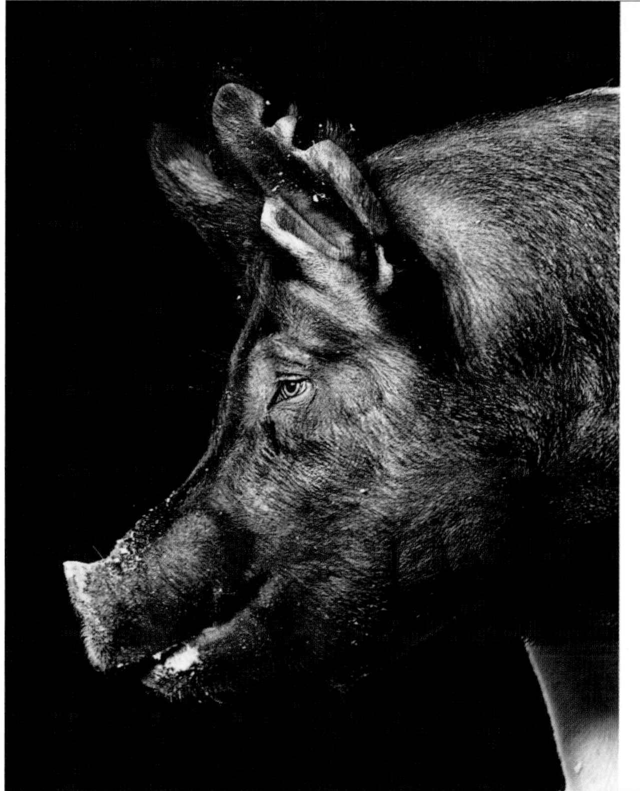

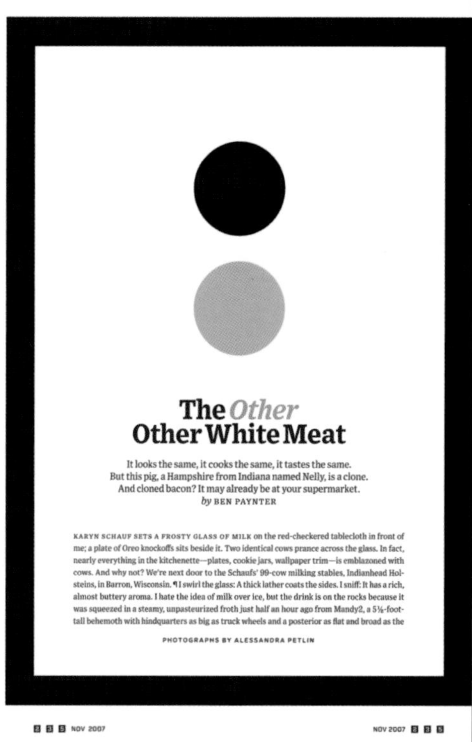

021

021 WIRED

Creative Director_Scott Dadich Design Director_Wyatt Mitchell Art Directors_Maili Holiman, Carl DeTorres Designers_Chris Imlay, Christy Sheppard, Margaret Swart Illustrators_Yoichiro Ono, Atshuisa Okura, Nicholas Felton, Florian Bachleda Photo Editors_Anna Goldwater Alexander, Zana Woods, Carolyn Rauch Photographers_Chris Buck, Alessandra Petlin, Gregg Segal, Ofer Wolberger, Donald Milne, Todd Hido Publisher_Condé Nast Publications, Inc. Issue_November 2007 Category_Design: Entire Issue

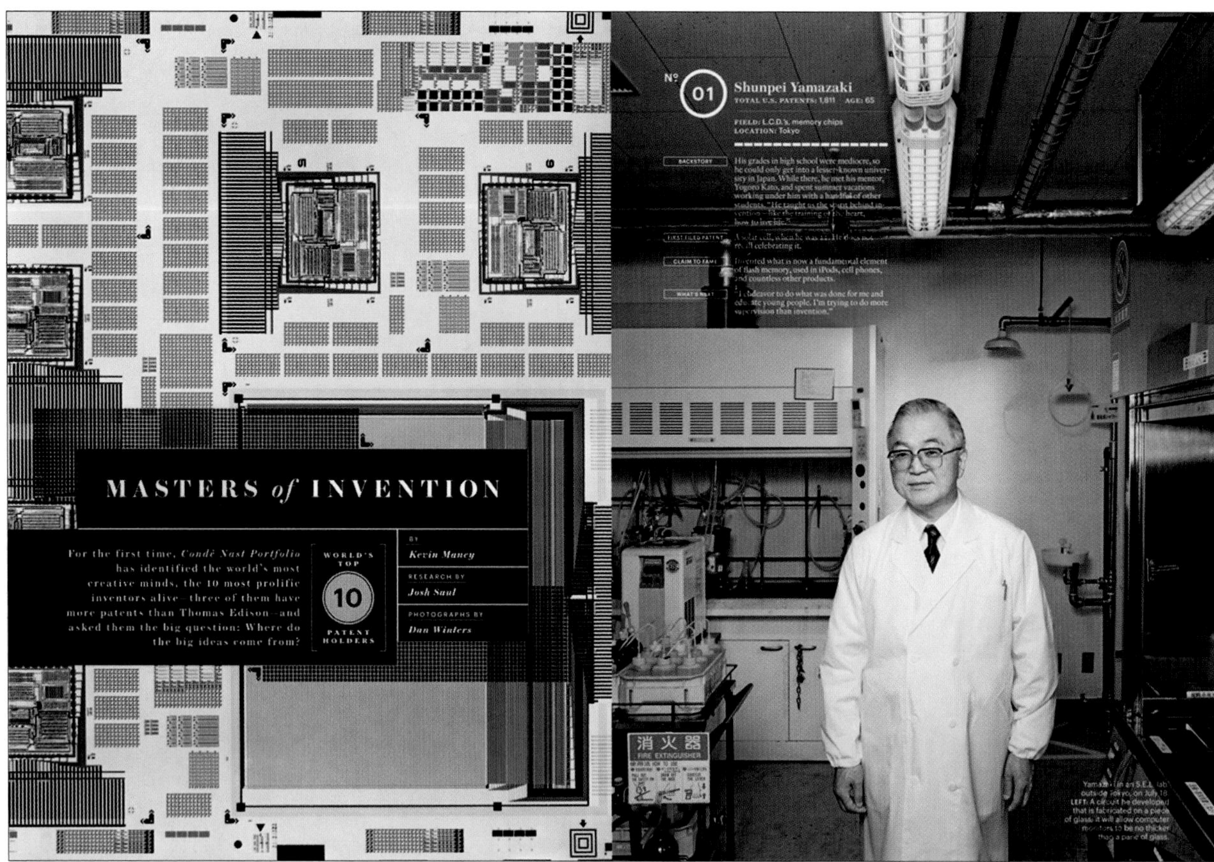

022

→ **SHUNPEI YAMAZAKI** is the most prolific inventor in history, but you've probably never heard of him. He is 65, runs a research and development company—Semiconductor Energy Laboratory, in Atsugi, Japan—and holds 1,811 U.S. patents, nearly 700 more than Thomas Edison. This neatly dressed, polite, trumpet-voiced man, who comes across as something of a mystical seeker, attributes his success to six years under a mentor who taught him the "emotional spirit" of inventing. For Yamazaki and his peers, inventing is much more than just making money from intellectual properties; it's anything from a compulsion to a calling. Invention is the engine of industry and the raison d'être of nearly every technology company. More than that, it advances civilization. Yet our greatest creators don't have rock-star status. Oh, there's Edison, the Elvis of inventors, and a thin sliver of society knows about contemporary pioneers like Dean Kamen, who created the Segway, and Tim Berners-Lee, who is credited with envisioning the World Wide Web. But the most successful living exemplars have a Q rating somewhere below that of an extra in *Gigli*.

Inventors are undervalued but not without controversy. Nearly 90,000 U.S. patents were granted in 2006, up 50 percent from a decade ago—an explosion that has created a mess for some companies. Rampant legal fights over who devised what have become yet another cost of doing business, especially in the technology sector. Overwhelmed examiners sometimes grant questionable patents, and the U.S. Patent and Trademark Office is so inundated that years can go by between submission and approval.

Despite the systemic muddle, anyone who ranks in Edison's class has lived a remarkable life. I wanted to interview the top 10 living patent holders worldwide—ranked here in order of their number of U.S. patents—in the hope of gaining some insight into the creative spark behind invention. But first I had to find out who they are. Astoundingly, the patent office does not keep such a list. No one does. At the request of *Condé Nast Portfolio*, the Patent Board, a Chicago patent research and advisory firm, ran the query and came back with the names. (Granted, a tally of the number of patents does not necessarily identify the "greatest" inventors, just as book sales rarely reveal the finest writers. But such a list is the only objective measure we have.) These men—the group is all male—have rarely, if ever, talked to the media. During *(continued on page 214)*

206 Condé Nast Portfolio.November.07

022

022 CONDÉ NAST PORTFOLIO

Design Director_**Robert Priest** Art Director_**Grace Lee** Designer_**Grace Lee** Director of Photography_**Lisa Berman**
Photo Editor_**Brian Marcus** Deputy Photo Editor_**Sarah Czeladnicki** Photographer_**Dan Winters** Editor-In-Chief_**Joanne Lipman**
Publisher_**Condé Nast Publications Inc.** Issue_**November 2007** Category_**Design: Feature: Story**

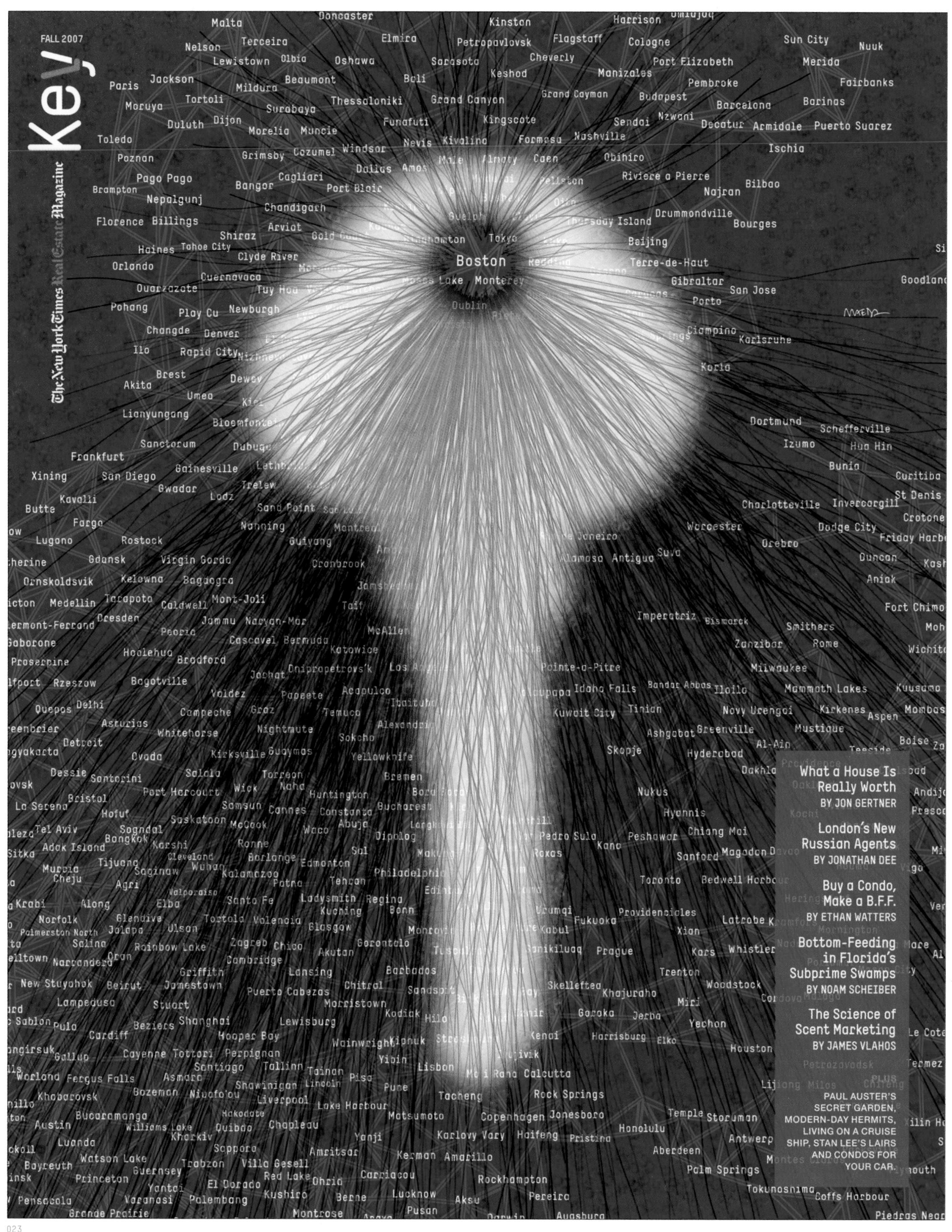

023

023 KEY, THE NEW YORK TIMES REAL ESTATE MAGAZINE

Creative Director_Janet Froelich Art Directors_Dirk Barnett, Arem Duplessis
Designer_Dirk Barnett Artist_John Maeda Editor-In-Chief_Gerry Marzorati Publisher_The New York Times
Issue_Fall 2007 Category_Design: Cover

:SECTION
DESIGN

:AWARD
GOLD

:CATEGORY
ENTIRE ISSUE

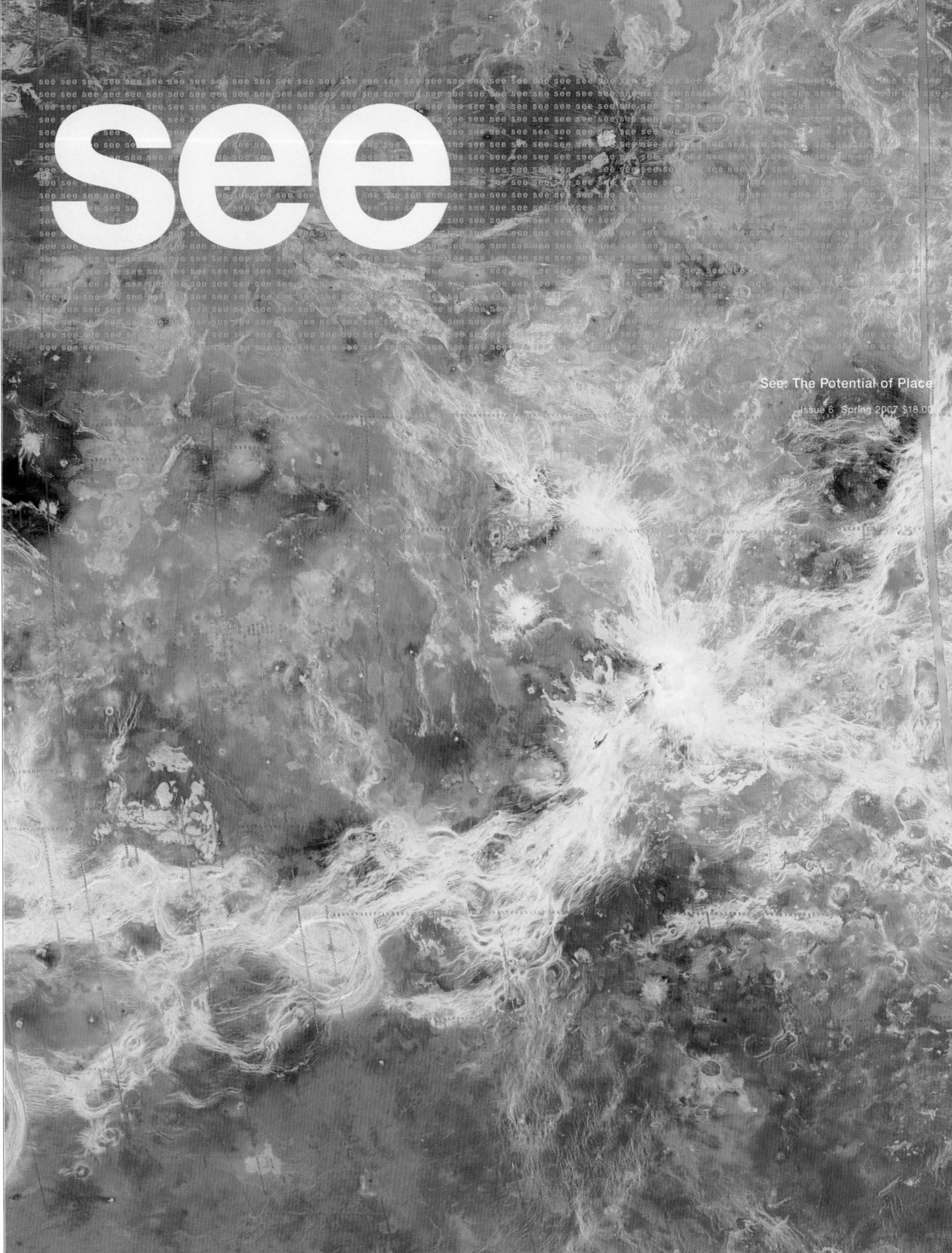

024

024 SEE: THE POTENTIAL OF PLACE

Creative Director_**Bill Cahan** Art Directors_**Bill Cahan, Steve Frykholm, Todd Richards**
Designers_**Todd Richards, Erik Adams** Illustrator_**Kevin Christy** Photographers_**Mark King, Julian Dufort, Kenji Toma, Catherine Ledner, Nicholas Nixon**
Production Artists_**Clare RhineLander, Marlene Capotosto** Studio_**Cahan & Associates**
Publisher_**Herman Miller, Inc.** Client_**Herman Miller** Issue_**May 2007** Category_**Design: Entire Issue**

024

024

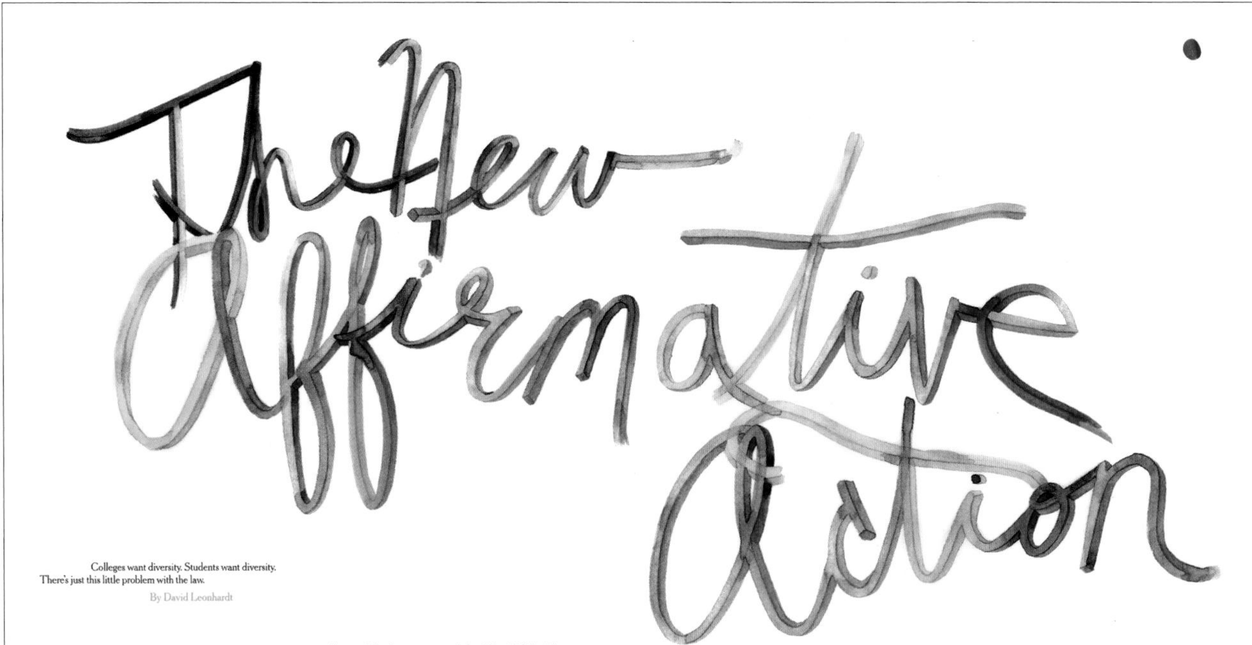

Colleges want diversity. Students want diversity.
There's just this little problem with the law.

By David Leonhardt

IN ANOTHER TIME, it wouldn't have been too hard to guess where Frances Harris would have ended up going to college. She has managed to do very well in very difficult circumstances, and she is African-American. Her high school, in the Oak Park neighborhood of Sacramento, was shut down as an irremediable failure the spring before her freshman year, then reopened months later as a charter school. Midway through high school, her father developed heart problems and became an irritable fixture around the home. She also discovered that he was not actually her biological father. That was a man named Leroy who, when her mother took Harris to see him, simply said his name was George and waited for her to leave. In Harris's senior year, her mother lost her job at a nursing home and the family filed for bankruptcy.

Harris somehow stayed focused on teenage life. She earned an A-minus average and she distinguished herself as a debater. Her basketball teammates sometimes teased her for using big words, but they also elected her co-captain. As she led me on a tour of her school and her neighborhood one day this summer, she introduced me around with an assured ease that most adults can't manage, even if her sentences are peppered with "like," "you know" and "Oh, my God." Her bedroom in the bungalow she shares with her parents is a masterpiece of teenage energy, the walls covered with her prom-queen tiara, her purple-and-white basketball jersey (No. 3) and photos of her friends. "The hardest part of high school," she says, "was to be smart and cool at the same time." She decided her dream college was the University of California, Los Angeles.

Ten or 20 years ago, Frances Harris almost certainly would have been admitted. Her excellent grades might not have even been necessary, because Berkeley and U.C.L.A. — the jewels in the U.C. system — accepted almost all of the African-Americans who met the basic application requirements. To an admissions officer, Harris would have seemed like gold: diversity and achievement, wrapped up in a single kid.

But in the early 1990s, the elite campuses began to pull back from their aggressive affirmative-action policies, and in 1996, California voters passed the California Civil Rights Initiative, also known as Proposition 209. After that, race could no longer be a factor in government hiring or public-university admissions. The number of black students at both Berkeley and U.C.L.A. plummeted, and at U.C.L.A. the declines continued through-

76 LETTERING BY FISHWRAPPERS

77

025

NO GR_DU_TE LEFT BEHIND

A college degree increases your value in the job market. But how much does it increase your knowledge? The Bush administration is backing a movement to put colleges to the test.

By James Traub

AT THE UNIVERSITY OF CHARLESTON, a not-exactly-selective institution on the banks of the Kanawha River in the capital city of West Virginia, incoming students take a standardized test designed to measure reasoning and writing skills and then take the test again after sophomore year and once again as seniors — to see if their education is doing them any good. Courses are constructed around a series of defined "liberal learning outcomes" like critical thinking and creativity, and if the students' work shows that many of them aren't hitting the outcomes, the teachers go back to the drawing board. Ditto with the standardized tests. "We take data seriously," says Alan Belcher, a member of the Faculty Center that rides herd on the whole process, "and we act on it." Apparently they act well: in its promotional materials, U.C. boasts that it posted "the largest learning gain from first to final year" of any of the 40 schools that participated in a trial of the Collegiate Learning Assessment, one test it uses.

This orientation toward measurable outcomes has already colonized many spheres of life — K-12 education, medicine, government services — but in the world of higher education, places like the University of Charleston are lonely outliers. They may soon become the vanguard. The Bush administration, having used the No Child Left Behind Act to impose accountability — and, critics would say, a sterile uniformity — on the reluctant world of public elementary and secondary schools, is now seeking to accomplish something similar in post-secondary education. A commission impaneled by Education Secretary Margaret Spellings

Illustrations by Patrick Thomas

106 LETTERING BY FISHWRAPPERS

025

025 THE NEW YORK TIMES MAGAZINE

Creative Director_**Janet Froelich** Art Director_**Arem Duplessis**
Designers_**Jeff Glendenning, Arem Duplessis**
Illustrator_**Alan Dye** Director of Photography_**Kathy Ryan**
Infographics_**Yokoland** Editor-In-Chief_**Gerry Marzorati**
Publisher_**The New York Times** Issue_**September 30, 2007**
Category_**Design: Feature: Story**

026 WIRED

Creative Director_**Scott Dadich** Design Director_**Wyatt Mitchell**
Art Director_**Carl DeTorres** Designers_**Wyatt Mitchell, Carl DeTorres**
Illustrator_**Atsuhisa Okura** Photo Editor_**Zana Woods**
Photographer_**Ofer Wolberger**
Publisher_**Condé Nast Publications, Inc.**
Issue_**November 2007** Category_**Design: Feature: Story**

ジャパンインク
Japan, Ink
In a nation obsessed with comics, the big publishers get rich. But now amateur rip-offs are taking over, making fan fiction the hottest thing on the street. Inside the manga industrial complex.
BY DANIEL H. PINK

026

VIZ STARTED PUBLISHING THE DRAGON BALL Z MANGA IN 1998. AT THE BEHEST OF CREATOR AKIRA TORIYAMA, THE MANGA WAS NOT FLOPPED. KIDS HAD TO READ IT IN ITS ORIGINAL RIGHT-TO-LEFT SEQUENCE IF THEY WANTED THEIR ACTION FIX.
228
IN 1996, AMERICAN TV WELCOMED ANOTHER SMASH HIT ANIME, CALLED DRAGON BALL Z—A SHONEN KUNG FU SLUGFEST BELOVED BY TWEEN BOYS. EVEN IF YOU WEREN'T A FAN OF THE SHOW, YOU'VE PROBABLY SEEN THE HALLOWEEN COSTUMES.
TORIYAMA, LIKE MANY MANGA ARTISTS, HATED FLOPPING. IT MADE ALL THE CHARACTERS LOOK LEFT-HANDED AND AS THOUGH THEY WERE WEARING THEIR KIMONOS BACKWARD! THINK OF A MOVIE DIRECTOR WHO DOESN'T WANT THEIR WIDESCREEN EPIC REFORMATTED FOR A SQUARE TV SCREEN. THE ORIGINAL PUBLISHER OF DRAGON BALL Z, SHUEISHA, FELT THE SAME WAY.
SHUEISHA PUBLISHES WEEKLY SHONEN JUMP, WHICH HAS A CIRCULATION OF 3 MILLION IN JAPAN.
"AK OF TROY" IS THE FOUNDER OF THE SCANLATION SITE CALLED TORIYAMA'S WORLD.
IN THE MID-'90S, MORE AND MORE MANGA FANS WERE DOING THEIR OWN TRANSLATIONS AND SCANS AND TRADING THEM OVER IRC, THEN LATER ON THE WEB. THEY DIDN'T FLOP THE PAGES BECAUSE IT WAS EASIER NOT TO (AND READING IT IN THE ORIGINAL FORMAT WAS A BADGE OF HONOR).
THE UNFLOPPED DRAGON BALL Z SOLD SURPRISINGLY WELL. AT THE TIME, IT WAS HARD TO FIND UNFLOPPED MANGA IN ENGLISH ... UNLESS YOU KNEW WHERE TO LOOK. MANY POPULAR TITLES WERE BEING TRANSLATED AND DISSEMINATED ILLEGALLY BY DIY "SCANLATION" GROUPS.
I HAD NO SKILLS WITH IMAGE EDITING OR WEB DESIGN ... I JUST USED MS PAINT AND A GEOCITIES SITE. I PUT UP ABOUT 10 CHAPTERS OF KINNIKUMAN (ULTIMATE MUSCLE) AND GOT A FEW HITS AND SOME NICE EMAILS. WHEN I STARTED DOING CURRENT SERIES LIKE NARUTO AND HIKARU NO GO, THE SITE EXPLODED!
IN FIVE YEARS, THE FRONT PAGE OF TORIYAMAWORLD.COM HAS RECEIVED 20 MILLION HITS!
Latest titles
SHOJO (GIRLS') MANGA FOCUSES ON ROMANCE AND RELATIONSHIPS. IT HAS NO EQUIVALENT IN AMERICAN COMICS. THE ART IS FULL OF ABSTRACT IMAGERY, FLOWER PATTERNS, AND FULL-PAGE CLOSE-UPS OF CHARACTERS WITH HUGE EYES THAT BRIM WITH EMOTION.
少女
HOWEVER, MANGA WASN'T JUST GRISLY ACTION AND EXPLICIT SEX. CASE IN POINT: TITLES AIMED AT GIRLS.
229
CONVERSELY, SHONEN (BOYS') MANGA INVOLVES NONSTOP ACTION, SHOUTING, AND GRATUITOUS PEEKS UP GIRLS' DRESSES. MOST OF WHAT CAME TO AMERICA WAS EITHER SHONEN OR THE DARKER, MORE EXPLICIT SEINEN (MEN'S) MANGA.
少年
SAILOR MOON, A POPULAR TITLE ABOUT A KICK-ASS BLOND SUPERHEROINE IN A SHORT SKIRT, WAS A MAJOR HIT IN JAPAN. THE ANIME CAME TO AMERICAN TV IN 1995, GIVING MANY U.S. GIRLS THEIR FIRST TASTE OF SHOJO.
SAILOR MOON PROVED THERE WAS A SOLID AMERICAN FEMALE AUDIENCE FOR MANGA. ONE SIGN WAS THE GROWTH OF COSPLAY—FANS DRESSING UP AS THEIR FAVORITE CHARACTERS AT INCREASINGLY COMMON ANIME CONVENTIONS.
EXPO 97
MIXX ZINE
MANY OF THE POPULAR IMPORTS IN THE '90S WERE ROMANCES AND TENDER SITCOMS, NOT JUST NINJAS BATTLING CYBORGS. THEY APPEALED TO BOTH GENDERS.
IN 1997, THE SAILOR MOON MANGA WAS TRANSLATED IN A U.S. PERIODICAL CALLED MIXXZINE, WHICH OFFERED SERIALIZED BLACK-AND-WHITE STORIES CLOSER IN FORMAT TO A JAPANESE MANGA THAN A U.S. COMIC. THE COMPANY, MIXX ENTERTAINMENT, DIDN'T MARKET ITS PRODUCTS AS COMICS: IT DUBBED THEM MOTIONLESS PICTURE ENTERTAINMENT.

026

PHOTOGRAPH BY TOM SCHIERLITZ

SHE'S NOT

XL

ROB SHEFFIELD was your
He never expected to be
never expected to be

027

 GQ

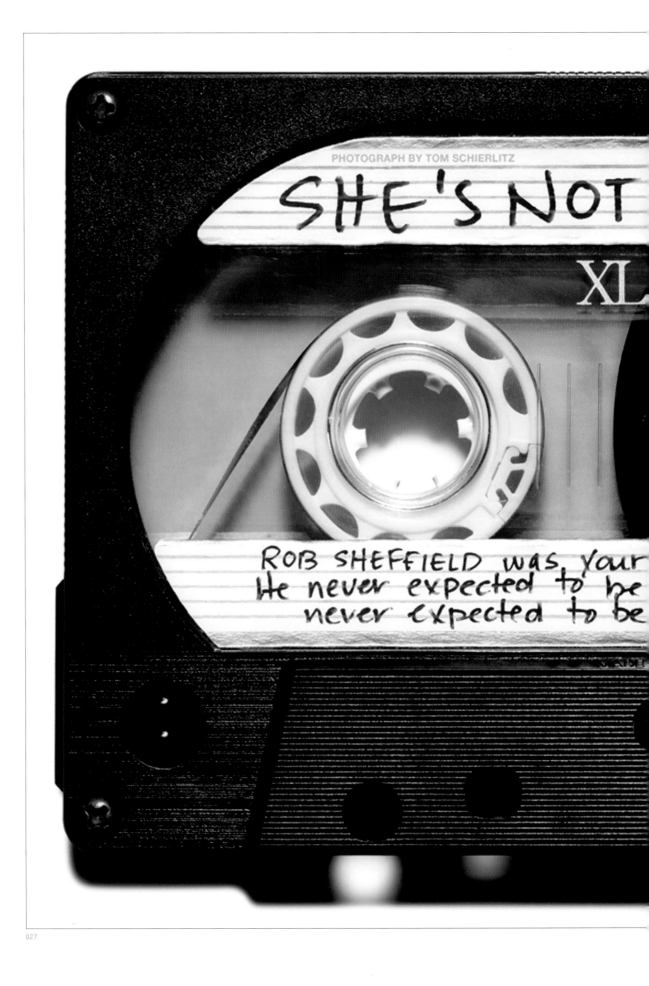

Design Director_Fred Woodward Designer_Drue Wagner Director of Photography_Dora Somosi Photo Editor_Justin O'Neill Photographer_Tom Schierlitz
Editor-In-Chief_Jim Nelson Publisher_Condé Nast Publications Inc. Issue_January 2007 Category_Design: Feature: Spread/Single Page

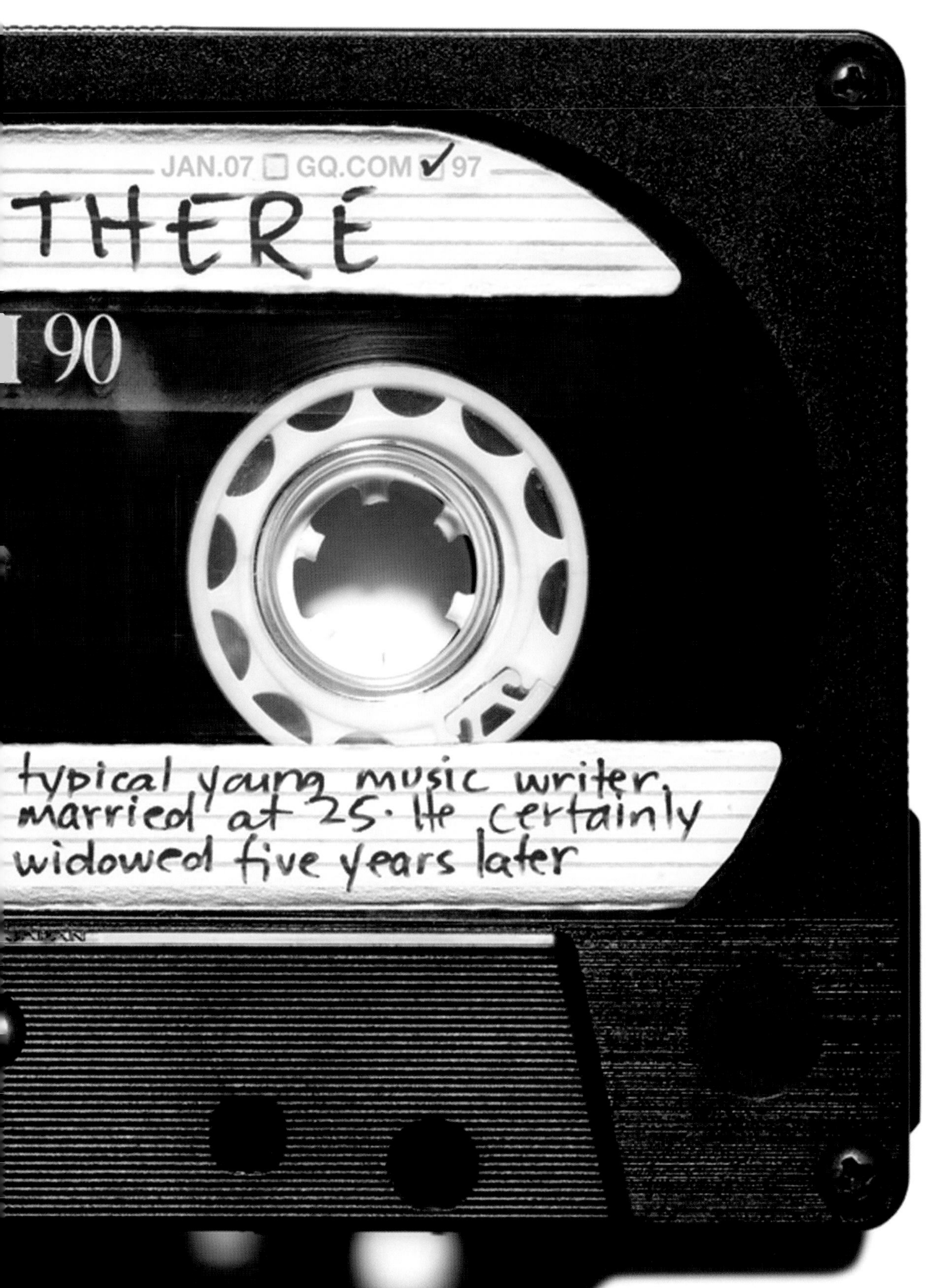
JAN.07 GQ.COM 97
THERE
90
typical young music writer,
married at 25. He certainly
widowed five years later

: SECTION
DESIGN

: AWARD
GOLD

: CATEGORY
ENTIRE ISSUE
FEATURE: SPREAD/SINGLE
FRONT PAGE

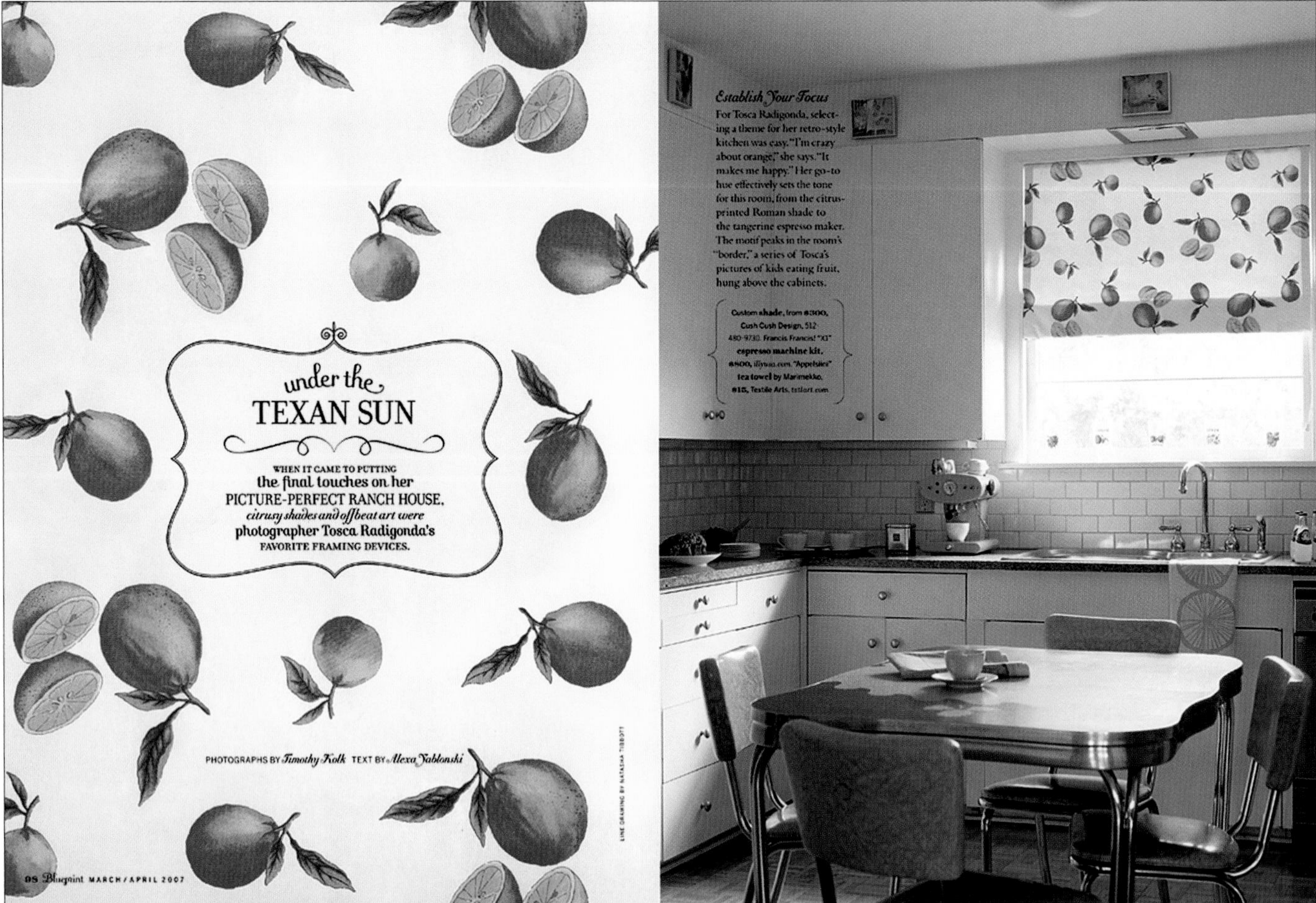
under the
TEXAN SUN

WHEN IT CAME TO PUTTING the final touches on her PICTURE-PERFECT RANCH HOUSE, citrusy shades and offbeat art were photographer Tosca Radigonda's FAVORITE FRAMING DEVICES.

PHOTOGRAPHS BY Timothy Kolk TEXT BY Alexa Yablonski

LINE DRAWING BY NATASHA TIBBOTT

Establish Your Focus

For Tosca Radigonda, selecting a theme for her retro-style kitchen was easy. "I'm crazy about orange," she says. "It makes me happy." Her go-to hue effectively sets the tone for this room, from the citrus-printed Roman shade to the tangerine espresso maker. The motif peaks in the room's "border," a series of Tosca's pictures of kids eating fruit, hung above the cabinets.

Custom shade, from $300, Cush Cush Design, 512-480-9730. Francis Francis! "X1" **espresso machine kit**, $800, illyusa.com. "Appelsiini" **tea towel** by Marimekko, $15, Textile Arts, txtlart.com

98 Blueprint MARCH/APRIL 2007

028

THE FRESH, FUN GUIDE TO PERSONAL STYLE | A MARTHA STEWART MAGAZINE
Blueprint
DESIGN YOUR LIFE
MARCH | APRIL 2007
issue No 3
An INCREDIBLE SMALL-SPACE MAKEOVER
15 Floor-to-Ceiling Solutions
The Truly DOABLE DINNER PARTY
FASHION'S NEW Necessities
REJIGGER YOUR HOME BAR
A Clip & Save Handbook

028

shoe RACK

PAGE No 74

CUTE, COMFORTABLE FLATS

CREATED BY JOHANNAH MASTERS

PHOTOGRAPHS BY JENS MORTENSEN

Sweet & Low

Kick-start your spring wardrobe without inflicting lasting injury on your budget—or your toes. We've rounded up the season's best flats, starting with nine cheeky-yet-comfy ways to perk up a dull day (or outfit).

1. Corso Como "Floral," **$130,** *nordstrom.com* for stores. **2. Poetic Licence** "Checkmate," **$69,** *nordstrom.com* for stores. **3. J.Lo by Jennifer Lopez** "Chao," **$100,** *macys.com* for stores. **4. French Connection** suede flat, **$98,** *frenchconnection.com* for stores. **5. Laundry by Shelli Segal** "Beckin," **$155,** *nordstrom.com* for stores. **6. BCBGgirls** "Limber," **$79,** select Macy's stores. **7. Steven by Steve Madden** striped trim flat, **$100,** *stevemadden.com* for stores. **8. Beverly Feldman** "For Real," **$140,** *beverlyfeldmanshoes.com*. **9. Beatrix Ong** "Capella," **$308,** *shopbop.com*

Blueprint MARCH/APRIL 2007

028

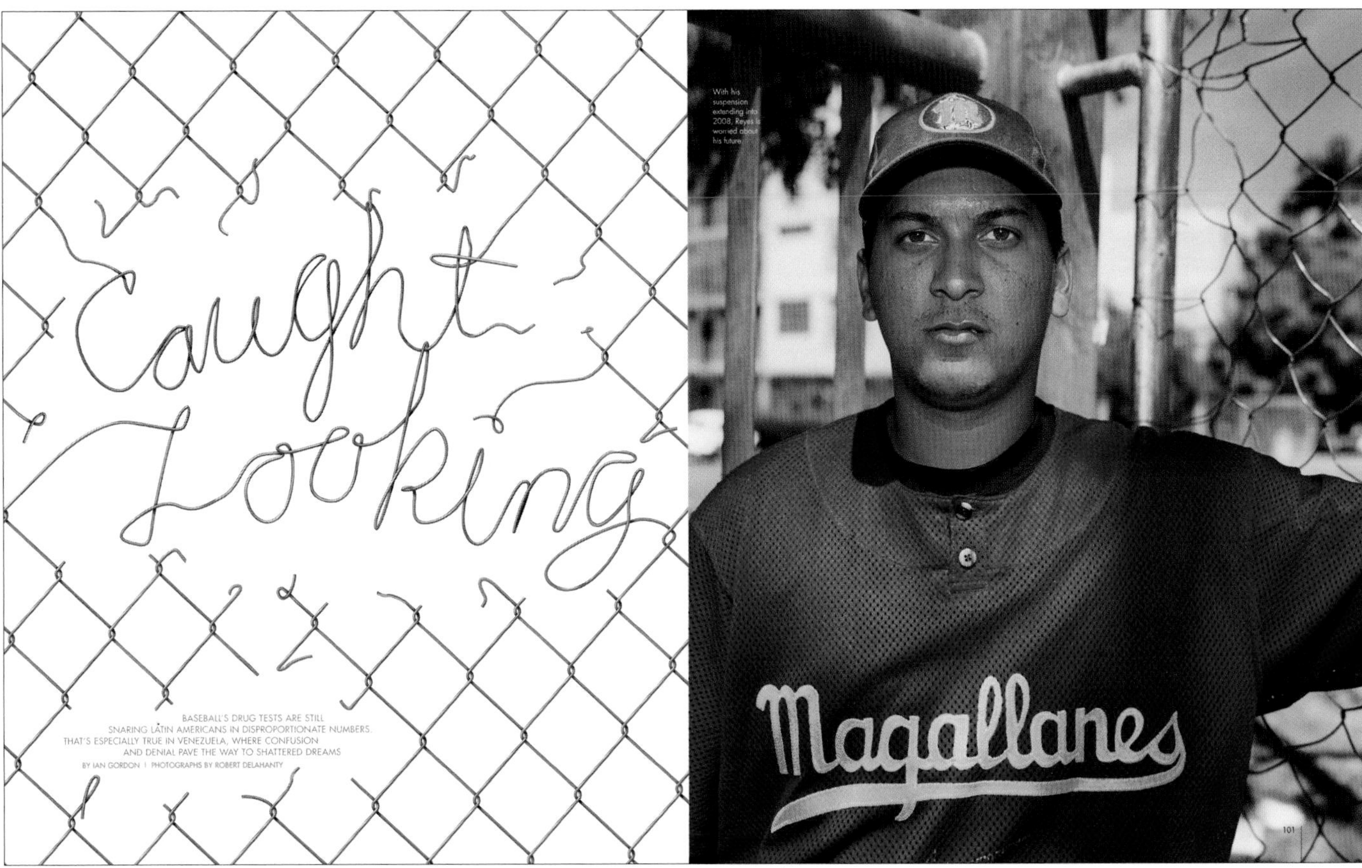

029

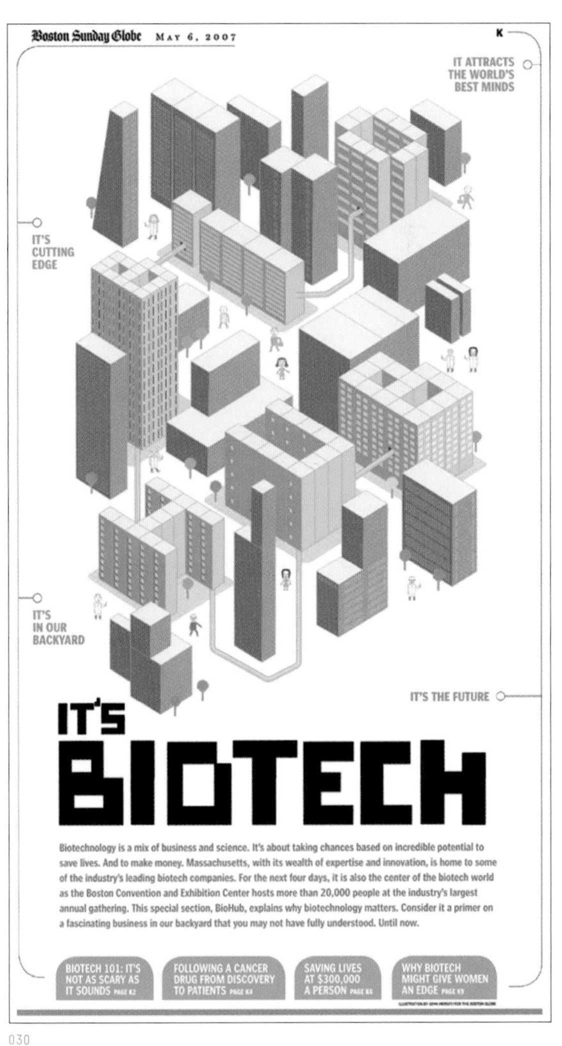

Boston Sunday Globe MAY 6, 2007

K

IT ATTRACTS THE WORLD'S BEST MINDS

IT'S CUTTING EDGE

IT'S IN OUR BACKYARD

IT'S THE FUTURE

IT'S BIOTECH

Biotechnology is a mix of business and science. It's about taking chances based on incredible potential to save lives. And to make money. Massachusetts, with its wealth of expertise and innovation, is home to some of the industry's leading biotech companies. For the next four days, it is also the center of the biotech world as the Boston Convention and Exhibition Center hosts more than 20,000 people at the industry's largest annual gathering. This special section, BioHub, explains why biotechnology matters. Consider it a primer on a fascinating business in our backyard that you may not have fully understood. Until now.

BIOTECH 101: IT'S NOT AS SCARY AS IT SOUNDS PAGE K2

FOLLOWING A CANCER DRUG FROM DISCOVERY TO PATIENTS PAGE K4

SAVING LIVES AT $300,000 A PERSON PAGE K6

WHY BIOTECH MIGHT GIVE WOMEN AN EDGE PAGE K9

030

028 BLUEPRINT

Creative Director_Eric A. Pike Design Director_Deb Bishop
Art Directors_Cybele Grandjean, Lisa Thé, Jamie Prokell, Jennifer Merrill Illustrators_Natasha Tibbot, Tina Chang, Arthur Mount, Si Scott Director of Photography_Heloise Goodman
Senior Photo Editor_Mary Cahill Assistant Photo Editor_Darlene Schrack
Photographers_Sang An, Roland Bello, Craig Cutler, Timothy Kolk, Thomas Loof Stylists_Page Marchese Norman, Shane Powers, Rebecca Robertson, Katie Hatch Editor-In-Chief_Sarah Humphreys
Publisher_Martha Stewart Living Omnimedia
Issue_March/April 2007 Category_Design: Entire Issue

029 ESPN THE MAGAZINE

Creative Director_Siung Tjia Designer_Jason Lancaster
Illustrator_Jason Lee Director of Photography_Catriona Ni Aolain
Photo Editor_Maisie Todd Photographer_Robert Delahanty
Publisher_ESPN, Inc. Issue_June 4, 2007
Category_Design: Feature: Spread/Single Page

030 THE BOSTON GLOBE

Design Director_Dan Zedek Art Director_Grant Staublin
Illustrator_John Hersey Publisher_The New York Times Co.
Issue_May 6, 2007 Category_Design: Front Page

: SECTION
DESIGN

: AWARD
GOLD

: CATEGORY
FRONT/BACK OF BOOK COVER

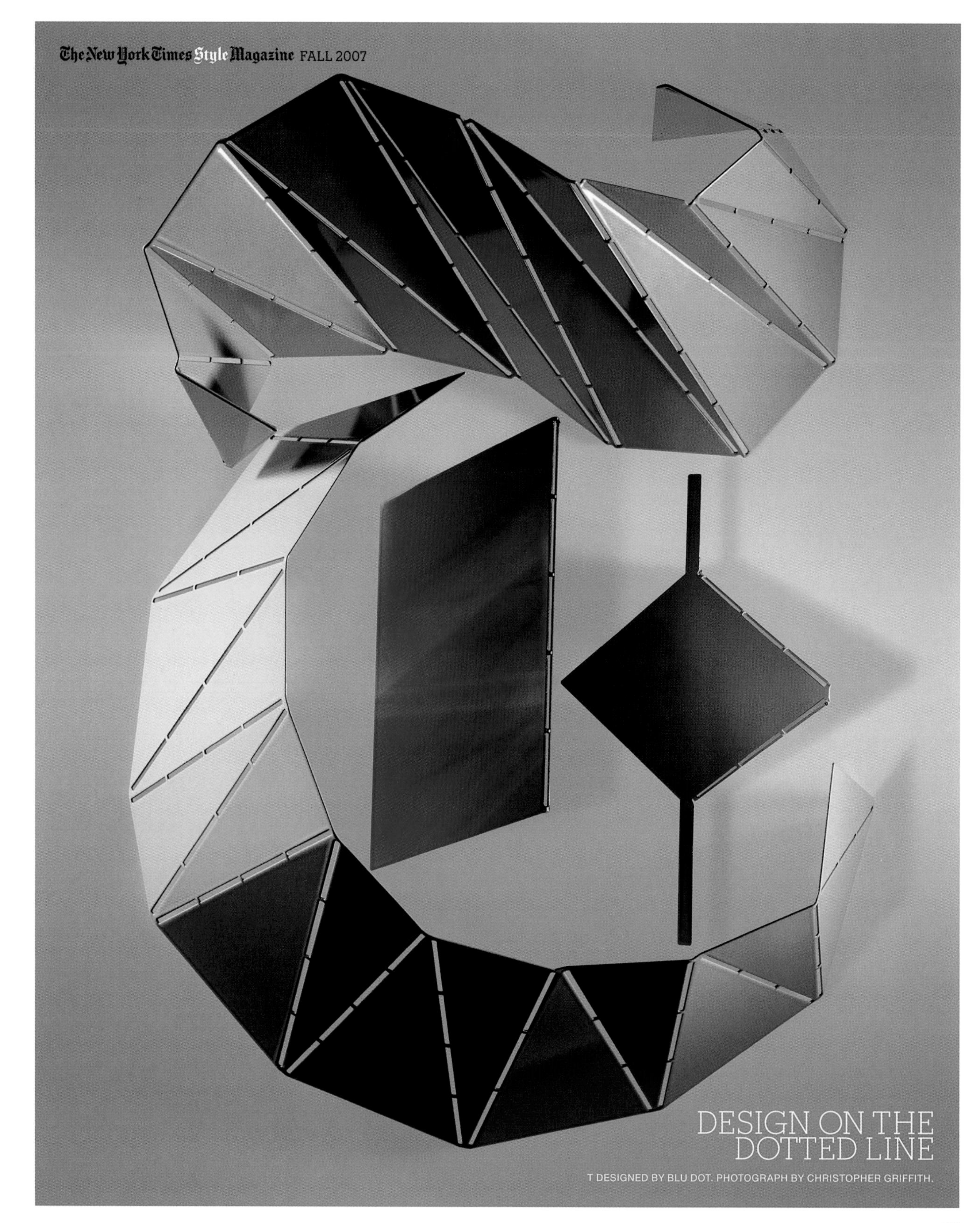

The New York Times Style Magazine FALL 2007
DESIGN ON THE DOTTED LINE
T DESIGNED BY BLU DOT. PHOTOGRAPH BY CHRISTOPHER GRIFFITH.
137

031

031 T, THE NEW YORK TIMES STYLE MAGAZINE

Creative Director_Janet Froelich Senior Art Director_David Sebbah
Art Director_Christopher Martinez Designer_David Sebbah
Photo Editor_Judith Puckett-Rinella Editor-In-Chief_Stefano Tonchi
Publisher_The New York Times Issue_April 2007, September 2007, October 2007, November 2007
Category_Front of Book/Back of Book

031

The New York Times Style Magazine
Playing the Field
HERE, THERE AND EVERYWHERE

031

031

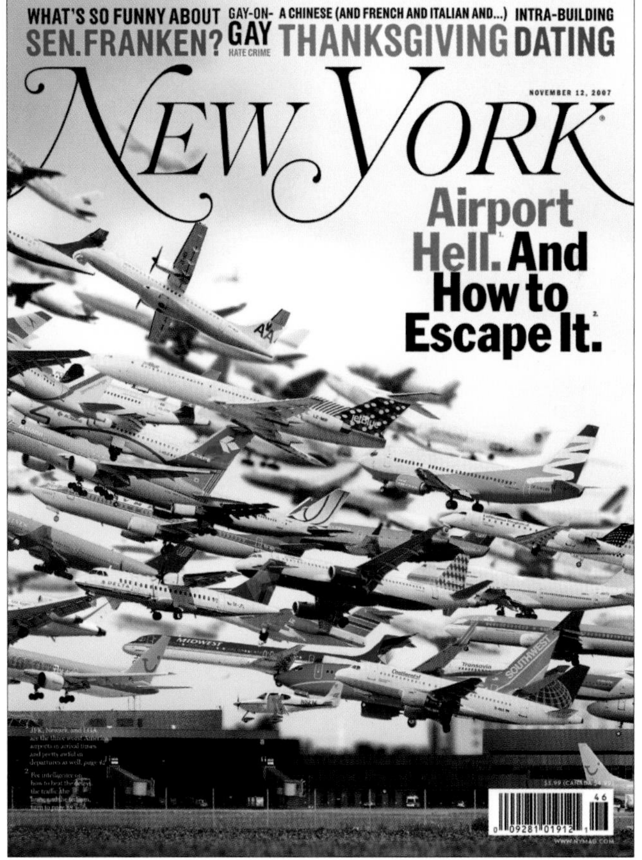

WHAT'S SO FUNNY ABOUT SEN. FRANKEN?
GAY-ON-GAY HATE CRIME
A CHINESE (AND FRENCH AND ITALIAN AND...) THANKSGIVING
INTRA-BUILDING DATING
NOVEMBER 12, 2007
NEW YORK
Airport Hell. And How to Escape It.

032

032 NEW YORK

Design Director_**Chris Dixon** Art Directors_**Randy Minor, Kate Elazegui**
Designer_**Chris Dixon** Director of Photography_**Jody Quon**
Photographer_**Ho-Yeol Ryu** Photo Illustrator_**Ho-Yeol Ryu**
Editor-In-Chief_**Adam Moss** Publisher_**New York Magazine Holdings, LLC**
Issue_**November 12, 2007** Category_**Design: Cover**

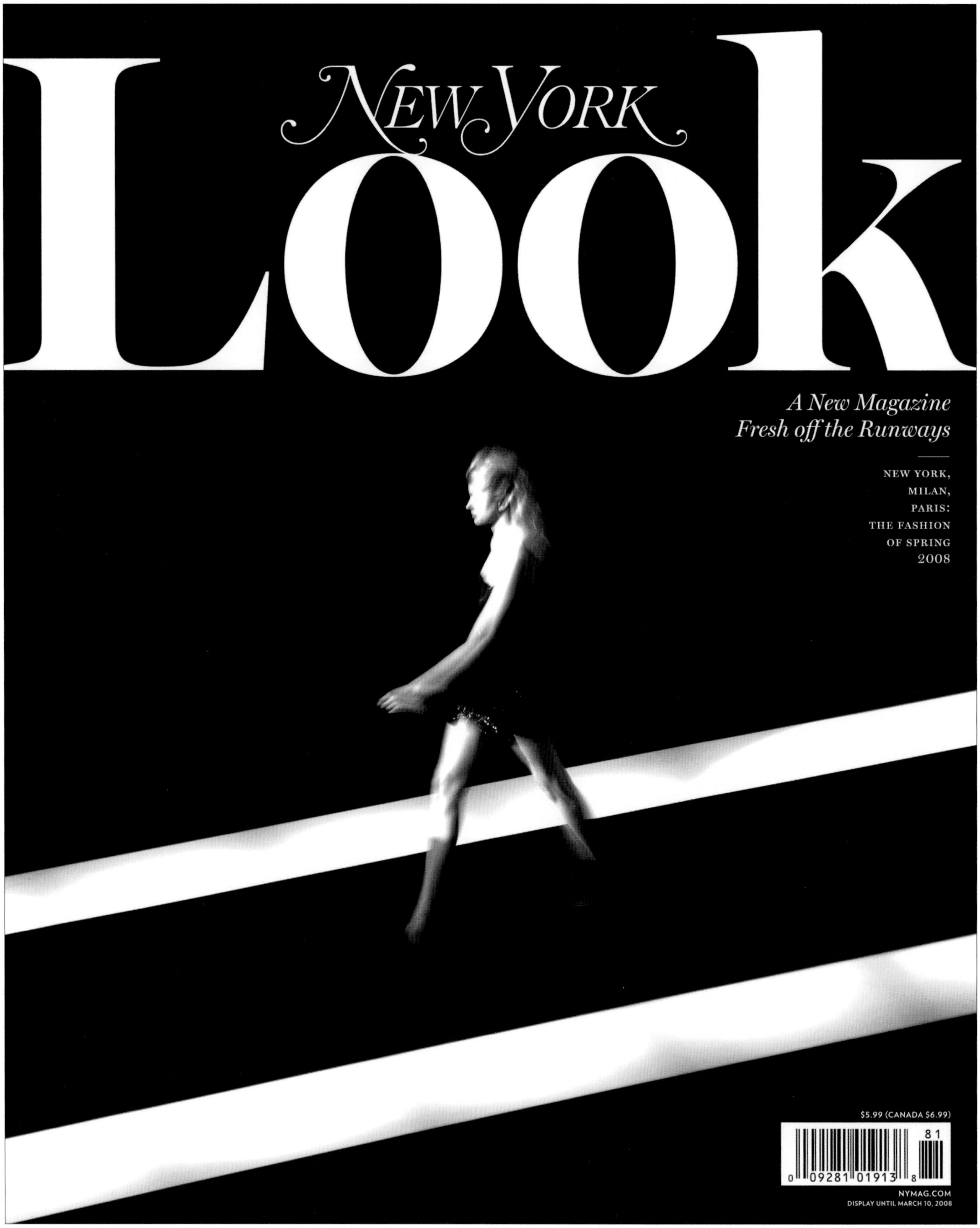

: SECTION
DESIGN

: AWARD
SILVER

: CATEGORY
ENTIRE ISSUE

NEW YORK

Look

A New Magazine
Fresh off the Runways

NEW YORK,
MILAN,
PARIS:
THE FASHION
OF SPRING
2008

$5.99 (CANADA $6.99)

0 09281 01913 8 81

NYMAG.COM
DISPLAY UNTIL MARCH 10, 2008

033

NEW YORK LOOK

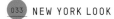

Design Director_**Chris Dixon** Art Director_**Randy Minor** Designer_**Caroline Jackson Crafton**
Director of Photography_**Jody Quon** Photographers_**Paolo Pellegrin, Davies + Starr, Levi Brown**
Editor-In-Chief_**Adam Moss** Publisher_**New York Magazine Holdings, LLC** Issue_**Fall 2007**
Category_**Design: Entire Issue**

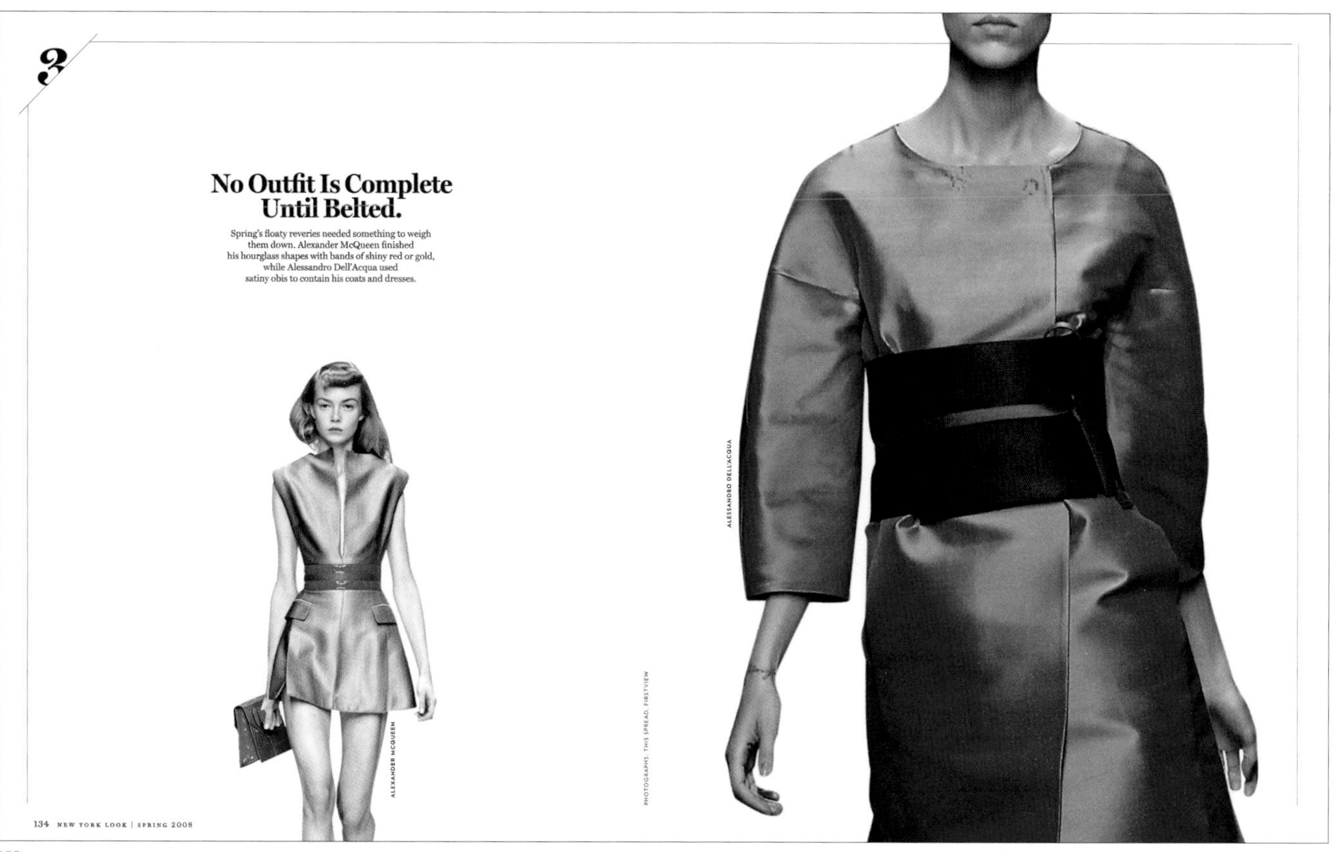

3

No Outfit Is Complete Until Belted.

Spring's floaty reveries needed something to weigh them down. Alexander McQueen finished his hourglass shapes with bands of shiny red or gold, while Alessandro Dell'Acqua used satiny obis to contain his coats and dresses.

ALEXANDER MCQUEEN

PHOTOGRAPHS: THIS SPREAD, FIRSTVIEW

ALESSANDRO DELL'ACQUA

134 NEW YORK LOOK | SPRING 2008

033

2

DOCUMENTARY

FROM EVERY ANGLE

Photographs by
PAOLO PELLEGRIN

Makeup-ready models, from left, Siri Tollerød, Tanya Dziahileva, Lyoka Tyagnereva, Ali Michael, Elsa Sylvan, Serafima Vakulenko, and Taryn Davidson, rehearse at Lanvin, Paris, October 7.

88 NEW YORK LOOK | SPRING 2008

033

SECTION
DESIGN

AWARD
SILVER

CATEGORY
ENTIRE ISSUE COVER

WHO WILL we remember fifty years from now? Who is creating a body of work—making the music, pioneering the thinking, building the highlight reels—that will endure? Here are fifteen men we believe will change our future
GREG VEIS
GQ@50
OCTOBER 2007
386
THE LEGACY PROJECT
a PORTFOLIO BY RICHARD BURBRIDGE
TOM BRADY

034

Off the Record with Don Rumsfeld
(former)
(But don't write that down!)
Photographs By
453

034

 GQ

Design Director_**Fred Woodward** Art Director_**Anton Ioukhnovets** Deputy Art Director_**Thomas Alberty**
Designers_**Michael Pangilinan, Drue Wagner, Chelsea Cardinal, Rob Hewitt, Eve Binder, Delgis Canahuate, Liana Zamora**
Illustrators_**Jean-Philippe Delhomme, John Ritter** Director of Photography_**Dora Somosi** Senior Photo Editor_**Krista Prestek**
Photo Editors_**Justin O'Neil, Jesse Lee, Melissa Goldstein, Jolanta Bielat, Roberto DeLuna, Halena Green**
Photographers_**Jeff Riedel, Richard Burbridge, Nathaniel Goldberg, Platon, Terry Richardson, Francois Dischinger, Ilan Rubin, Zachary Scott, Max Vadukul, Danielle Levitt** Creative Director_**Jim Moore** Editor-In-Chief_**Jim Nelson**
Publisher_**Condé Nast Publications Inc.** Issue_**October 2007** Category_**Design: Entire Issue**

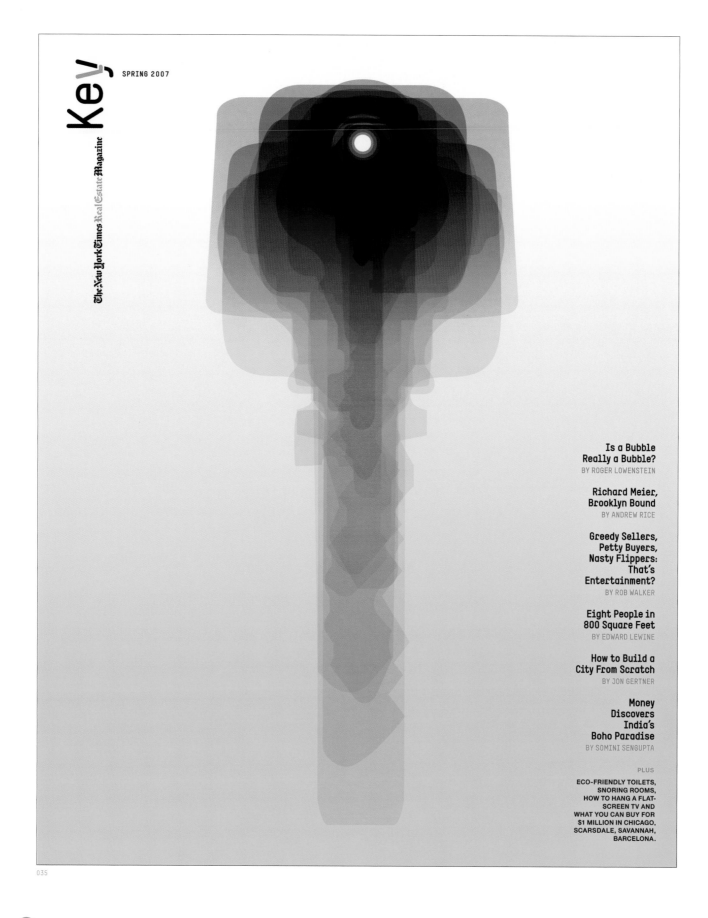

Key SPRING 2007

The New York Times Real Estate Magazine

Is a Bubble Really a Bubble?
BY ROGER LOWENSTEIN

Richard Meier, Brooklyn Bound
BY ANDREW RICE

Greedy Sellers, Petty Buyers, Nasty Flippers: That's Entertainment?
BY ROB WALKER

Eight People in 800 Square Feet
BY EDWARD LEWINE

How to Build a City From Scratch
BY JON GERTNER

Money Discovers India's Boho Paradise
BY SOMINI SENGUPTA

PLUS

ECO-FRIENDLY TOILETS, SNORING ROOMS, HOW TO HANG A FLAT-SCREEN TV AND WHAT YOU CAN BUY FOR $1 MILLION IN CHICAGO, SCARSDALE, SAVANNAH, BARCELONA.

035

035 KEY, THE NEW YORK TIMES REAL ESTATE MAGAZINE

Creative Director_Janet Froelich
Art Directors_Jeff Glendenning, Arem Duplessis
Designer_Jeff Glendenning
Illustrator_2x4, New York
Publisher_The New York Times Issue_Spring 2007
Category_Design: Cover

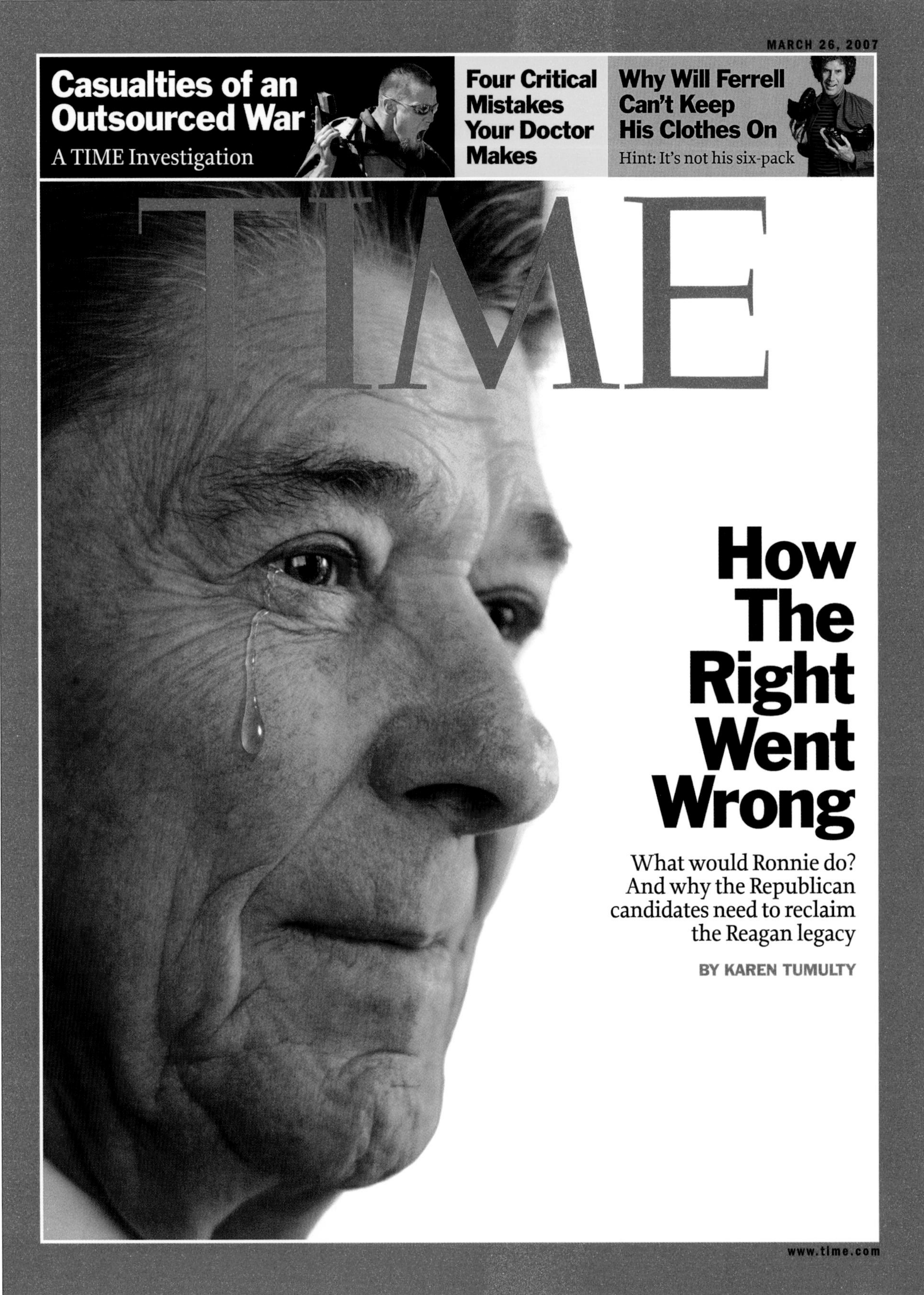

036

036 TIME

Art Director_Arthur Hochstein Designers_Luke Hayman, Cynthia Hoffman, D.W. Pine
Director of Photography_MaryAnne Golon Picture Editor_Alice Gabriner Publisher_Time Inc.
Issue_December 31, 2007 Category_Design: Redesign

NATION

How The Right Went Wrong

Conservatives are gloomy. The Republican candidates are struggling. Can the party reclaim Reagan's legacy?

BY KAREN TUMULTY

A GENERATION AGO, FRESH OFF the second biggest electoral landslide in American history, Ronald Reagan surveyed the wreckage that had been the opposition and declared victory. Standing before 1,700 true believers at the 1985 Conservative Political Action Conference (CPAC), he proclaimed, "The tide of history is moving irresistibly in our direction. Why? Because the other side is virtually bankrupt of ideas. It has nothing more to say, nothing to add to the debate. It has spent its intellectual capital." At this year's conference two weeks ago, Reagan's name was invoked more than anyone else's. But the mood at the most storied annual gathering of conservatives was anything but triumphal. John McCain, the Establishment favorite to win the 2008 Republican nomination, skipped CPAC entirely but did show up on *David Letterman* the night before, choosing the most aggressively glib venue to semiofficially announce his candidacy. Former Massachusetts Governor Mitt Romney was there to make his pitch for 2008 but had to compete with a man who was working the crowd in a dolphin costume and a T shirt identifying him as FLIP ROMNEY: JUST ANOTHER FLIP FLOPPER FROM MASSACHUSETTS. Ex–New York Mayor Rudy Giuliani barely mentioned the social issues on which he parts ways with conservatives, except to joke, "I don't agree with myself on everything." And the only memorable sound bite of the whole affair came from right-wing telepundit Ann Coulter, whose idea of an ideological rallying cry was to declare Democratic hopeful John Edwards a "faggot." The condemnation that followed, in which at least seven newspapers banished her column from their opinion pages, became a ragged coda for the state of a movement that had once been justly proud of its ability to win an argument.

These are gloomy and uncertain days for conservatives, who—except for the eight-year Clinton interregnum—have dominated political power and thought in this country since Reagan rode in from the West. Their tradition goes back even further, to Founding Fathers who believed that people should do things for themselves and who shook off a monarchy in their conviction that Big Government is more to be feared than encouraged. The Boston Tea Party, as Reagan used to point out, was an antitax initiative.

But everything that Reagan said in 1985 about "the other side" could easily apply to the conservatives of 2007. They are hand-

Can he win the right back? *Ronald Reagan introduced John McCain to conservative activists in 1974. Now they are worried he's unreliable*

Photograph for TIME by Joe Pugliese

036

Index TIME VOL. 169, NO. 13 | 2007

TIME March 26, 2007 5

036

Dashboard WASHINGTON MEMO ... NEWSREEL ... LOVE THE U.S., HATE THE U.S. ... A SAFER RIDE IN IRAQ ... MORTGAGE MELTDOWN ... LEXICON **Verbatim** "I SHOULD HAVE FOCUSED ... LESS ON MY PERSONAL MORAL VIEWS" **People** THE SCORE ... DIDDY AND SNOOP: HAS HIP-HOP HEALED? **Milestones** BYE-BYE, BETTY ... CAPTAIN AMERICA SALUTED ... LAST WORD: BRONX FIRE FUNERAL

Briefing

2007 | #13

THE MOMENT

The Confession Procession. These are days of absolution in the nation's capital

"MISTAKES WERE MADE," Attorney General Alberto Gonzales admitted when pressed about the purge of eight U.S. Attorneys viewed as unfriendly to the Administration. "Mistakes were made," President Bush agreed the next day. It's a bad sign when officials are left quoting Nixon spokesman Ron Ziegler, whose handling of Watergate set the standard for nonconfessions as well as nondenials. Flamboyant apology has never been in the Bush script. This is an Administration known for firing people for independence, not incompetence. But campaign season has arrived, subpoena power has changed hands, and suddenly everyone is in a purgative mood.

This was Gonzales' second round in as many weeks, having joined FBI chief Robert Mueller in admitting how far the FBI had stretched the Patriot Act in order to probe the phone and bank records of 52,000 people suspected of terrorism. Setting the pace in the accountability race was Defense Secretary Bob Gates, who fired the Army Secretary for not firing those responsible for the Walter Reed scandal.

In private life the conscience is our secret police, driving us to repent, but in public life contrition is often more about opportunity than obedience. With epic misconduct on every front page—the Vice President's man a convicted perjurer, the sacred trust of wounded soldiers betrayed—there was a window for anyone accused of more commonplace crimes to wipe the slate clean.

In public life, contrition is more about opportunity than obedience

Newt Gingrich confesses his serial marital sins to Focus on the Family founder James Dobson and wins absolution; Mitt Romney admits the error of his earlier tolerance of abortion rights. John Edwards seldom misses a chance to repent of his vote for the war, to highlight Hillary Clinton's refusal to do likewise. As for paying for past mistakes, Barack Obama took care of $400 worth of parking tickets left over from his law-school days—two weeks before he announced his candidacy.

Talk is cheap when confession plays as entertainment on daytime TV. In politics, as in church, there's no telling when penitence is sincere, for God alone knows the human heart. But it's a useful test in judging character to ask whether admitting failure comes at a cost—or a discount. —BY NANCY GIBBS

TIME March 26, 2007 15

036

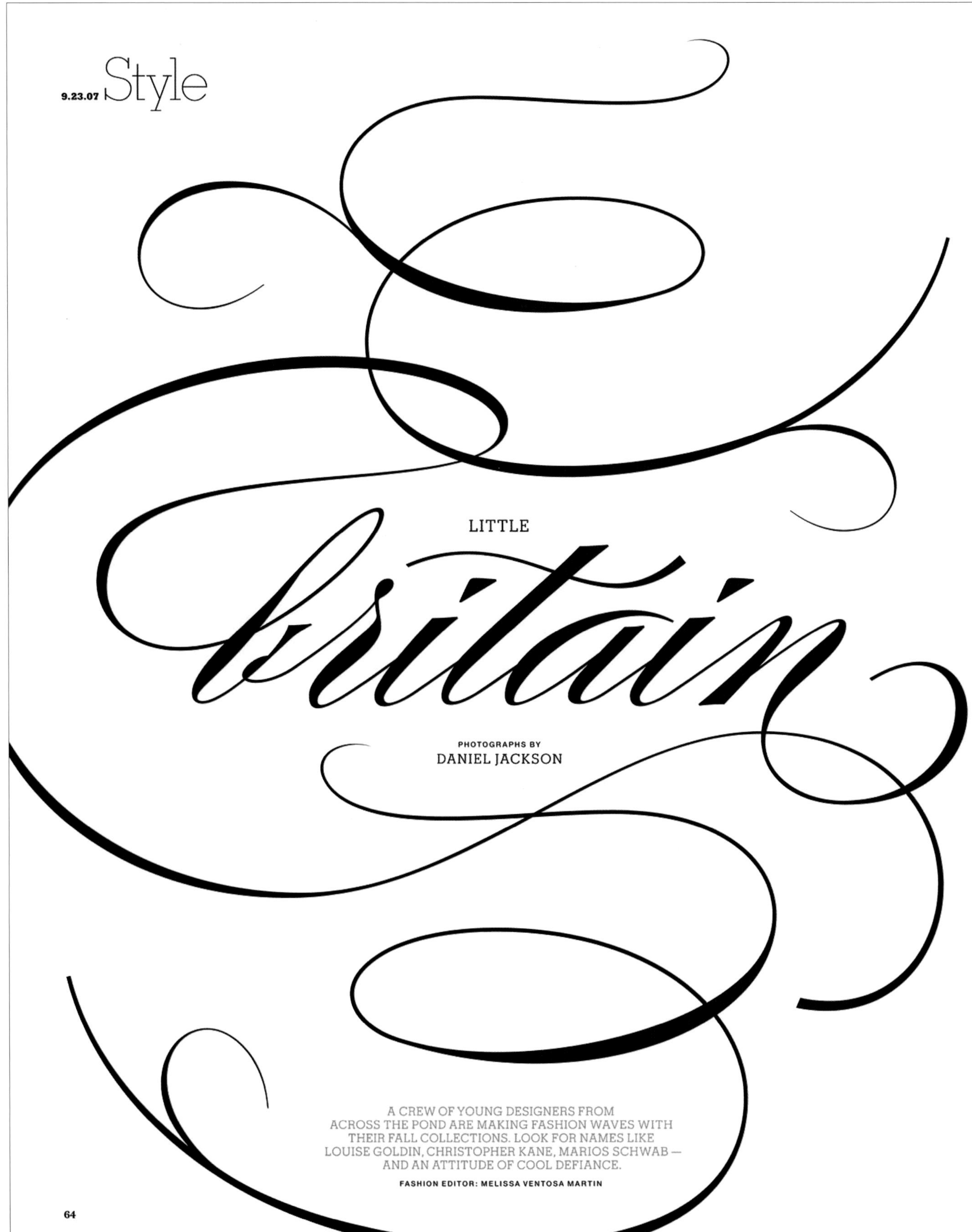

9.23.07 Style
LITTLE
Britain
PHOTOGRAPHS BY
DANIEL JACKSON
A CREW OF YOUNG DESIGNERS FROM ACROSS THE POND ARE MAKING FASHION WAVES WITH THEIR FALL COLLECTIONS. LOOK FOR NAMES LIKE LOUISE GOLDIN, CHRISTOPHER KANE, MARIOS SCHWAB — AND AN ATTITUDE OF COOL DEFIANCE.
FASHION EDITOR: MELISSA VENTOSA MARTIN
64

GILES BLACK DOUBLE-DUCHESS FEATHER DRESS, MADE TO ORDER. AT BARNEYS NEW YORK. FALKE HOSIERY. MANOLO BLAHNIK FOR CHRISTOPHER KANE SHOES.

037 THE NEW YORK TIMES MAGAZINE

Creative Director_**Janet Froelich** Art Director_**Arem Duplessis** Designer_**Nancy Harris Rouemy** Photographer_**Daniel Jackson** Fashion Editor_**Melissa Ventosa Martin** Editor-In-Chief_**Gerry Marzorati** Publisher_**The New York Times** Issue_**September 23, 2007** Category_**Design: Feature: Spread/Single Page**

:SECTION **DESIGN** | :AWARD **SILVER** | :CATEGORY **ENTIRE ISSUE** **FEATURE: STORY**

The New York Times Magazine
NYC
City Life in the Second Gilded Age

038

The New York Times Magazine

10.14.07

MONEY

62
The Capital of Capital No More?
New York has reigned for years as the world's financial center. But now it had better get used to sharing the wealth.
BY DANIEL GROSS

76
At Their Service
Beyond the nannies, maids and assistants: the superspecialized workers who serve the superrich.
PHOTOGRAPHS BY NADAV KANDER

90
Where the Haves Live
Mapping New York City's five wealthiest microneighborhoods.
TEXT BY EMILY BIUSO
ILLUSTRATION BY IAN DINGMAN

66
The Patron Gets a Divorce
Leonard Riggio's riches were building Dia into an art empire. So why did he abandon it?
BY JOE NOCERA

82
The SY Empire
The Syrian Jews of Gravesend, Brooklyn, rear their children to marry other Syrian Jews and make a fortune (the boys, anyway).
BY ZEV CHAFETS

On the cover: Photo illustration by Vik Muniz. Manhole cover: Suzanne Couture Modelmaking.

Continued on Page 14

THIS WEEK ON THE WEB

THE POWER OF THE PURSE The Questions For columnist Deborah Solomon takes to the streets — with a video camera — to ask New Yorkers about their designer handbags and the mainstreaming of luxury purchases.

URBANE LEGEND Martha Stewart, a puzzle devotee, writes the clues for a special online-only crossword with a New York theme.

BEHIND THE NUMBERS An in-depth breakdown of responses to our exclusive poll of more than 1,000 New York City residents, plus information on how the poll was conducted.

THE FUNNY PAGES Previous installments of Cathleen Schine's serial and Daniel Clowes's graphic novel.

FROM THE ARCHIVE Jonathan Mahler on Michael R. Bloomberg.

MAGAZINE ARTICLES ARE ONLINE all week at The New York Times on the Web, **nytimes.com/magazine**, or on America Online. Keyword: NYT magazine.

13

038

1
56TH TO 59TH STREETS, MADISON TO PARK AVENUES
Average household income: $577,170
Average household income in 1980: $85,178*
Median age: 57.2
Non-Hispanic white: 85%
Postgraduate degree: 38.2%
Rent: 21.8%
Own: 78.2%

2
91ST TO 94TH STREETS, FIFTH TO MADISON AVENUES
Average household income: $394,084
Average household income in 1980: $161,517
Median age: 44.6
Non-Hispanic white: 90.2%
Postgraduate degree: 48%
Rent: 39.9%
Own: 60.1%

3
77TH TO 79TH STREETS, FIFTH TO MADISON AVENUES
Average household income: $392,089
Average household income in 1980: $128,327
Median age: 50.2
Non-Hispanic white: 94.1%
Postgraduate degree: 48.3%
Rent: 41.6%
Own: 58.4%

4
79TH TO 82ND STREETS, FIFTH TO MADISON AVENUES
Average household income: $373,880
Average household income in 1980: $137,372
Median age: 47.5
Non-Hispanic white: 90.8%
Postgraduate degree: 48.7%
Rent: 48.4%
Own: 51.6%

5
49TH TO 54TH STREETS, AVENUE OF THE AMERICAS TO FIFTH AVENUE
Average household income: $370,900
Average household income in 1980: $33,693
Median age: 52.5
Non-Hispanic white: 76.4%
Postgraduate degree: 40.2%
Rent: 24.1%
Own: 75.9%

5 Where the Haves Live

Mapping New York City's five wealthiest microneighborhoods. Text by Emily Biuso

Other sections of the city might lay claim to more absurd real estate prices or more visible celebrities, but residents of the five areas shown above can say they live in the city's richest neighborhoods, at least by one measure. Earlier this year, the magazine asked the demographers Andrew Beveridge and Susan Weber-Stoger of Queens College to determine the wealthiest places in New York. Analyzing 2000 census data (the most recent data available), the team determined the average household income for each of the city's so-called block groups, the smallest geographic areas for which the census provides income information.

At first glance, the results confirm common knowledge. There's a high concentration of wealthy people living along Fifth, Park and Madison Avenues between 77th and 82nd Streets, for example. But two of the top-ranked block groups have changed considerably since the '80s. In the area from 56th to 59th between Madison and Park, average household income increased almost 700 percent between 1980 and 2000. A few blocks south, between 49th and 54th Streets and Fifth and Sixth Avenues, income rose more than 1,000 percent in that time. What caused such a surge in an area more associated with Rockefeller Center, Christie's and Fifth Avenue shopping than with residential buildings? One likely factor is Museum Tower, at 15 West 53rd Street, the superluxury building overlooking MoMA that opened its $85,000 bronze doors in 1985. Since then, the building has been home to the likes of the architect Philip Johnson, Sirio Maccioni, the proprietor of Le Cirque, and Sharon Percy Rockefeller. ■

● In 2000, New York ranked No. 5 among the 10 largest metropolitan areas in the United States in percentage of the population with at least a college degree.

Illustration by Ian Dingman

*DOLLARS ARE ADJUSTED TO 2000 CENSUS RATE. EDUCATION APPLIES ONLY TO ADULTS 25 AND OLDER. SOURCE: U.S. CENSUS BUREAU.

90 91

038

THE NEW YORK TIMES MAGAZINE

Creative Director_**Janet Froelich** Art Directors_**Arem Duplessis, Gail Bichler** Designer_**Leo Jung**
Director of Photography_**Kathy Ryan** Photo Editor_**Luise Stauss** Editor-In-Chief_**Gerry Marzorati** Publisher_**The New York Times**
Issue_**October 14, 2007** Category_**Design: Entire Issue**

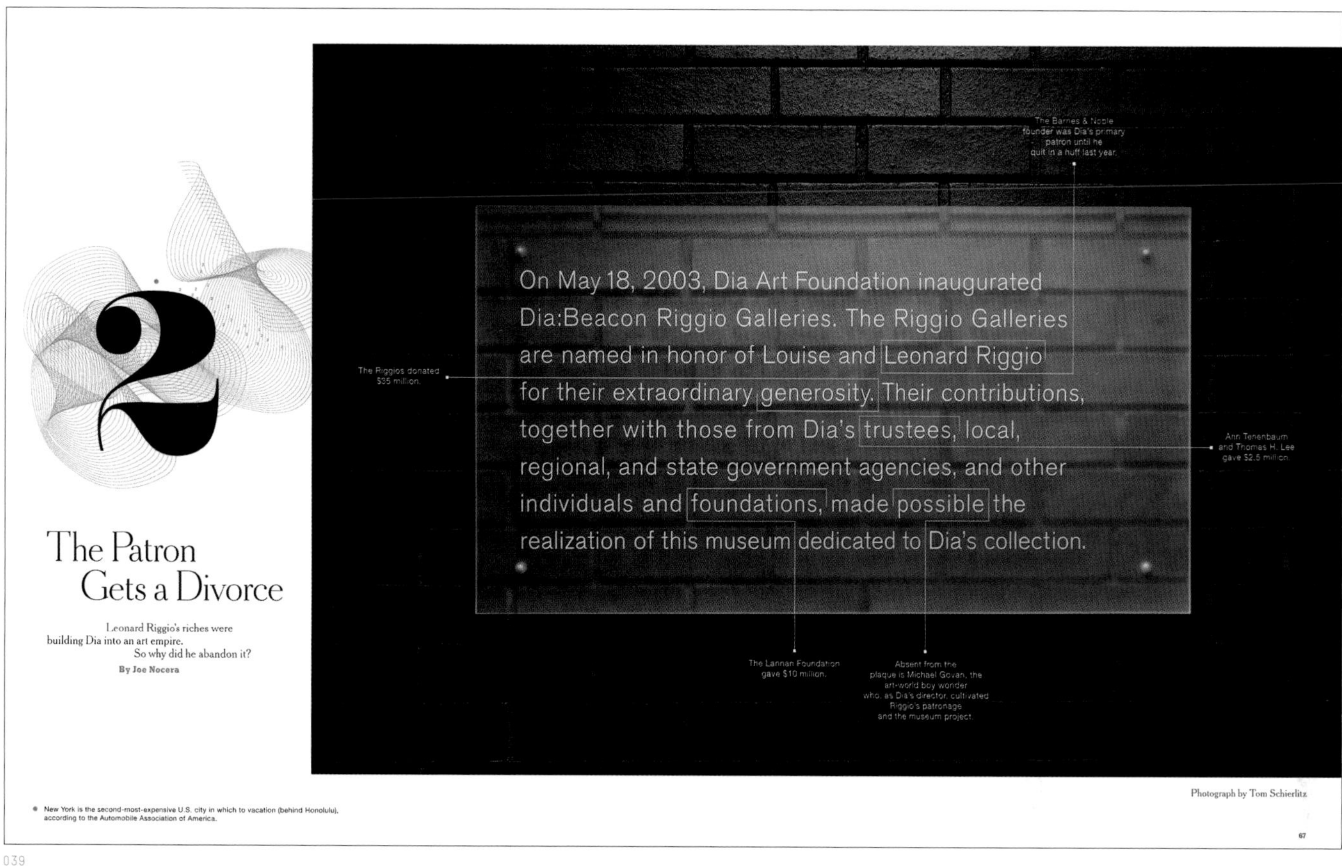

2
The Patron
Gets a Divorce
Leonard Riggio's riches were building Dia into an art empire. So why did he abandon it?
By Joe Nocera
On May 18, 2003, Dia Art Foundation inaugurated Dia:Beacon Riggio Galleries. The Riggio Galleries are named in honor of Louise and Leonard Riggio for their extraordinary generosity. Their contributions, together with those from Dia's trustees, local, regional, and state government agencies, and other individuals and foundations, made possible the realization of this museum dedicated to Dia's collection.
The Barnes & Noble founder was Dia's primary patron until he quit in a huff last year.
The Riggios donated $35 million.
Ann Tenenbaum and Thomas H. Lee gave $2.5 million.
The Lannan Foundation gave $10 million.
Absent from the plaque is Michael Govan, the art-world boy wonder who, as Dia's director, cultivated Riggio's patronage and the museum project.
New York is the second-most-expensive U.S. city in which to vacation (behind Honolulu), according to the Automobile Association of America.
Photograph by Tom Schierlitz
67

039

The SY Empire
The Syrian Jews of Gravesend, Brooklyn, rear their children to marry other Syrian Jews and make a fortune (the boys, anyway).
By Zev Chafets
4
Geographically speaking, the Syrian Jewish community of Brooklyn — 75,000 strong and growing fast — inhabits an enclave running from Avenue I in the north to Avenue V in the south and stretching eastward to Nostrand Avenue from West 6th Street. But the community's true boundaries are at once more expansive and more constricted.
The SY's, as the community members call themselves (pronounced "ess-why" — it's a shorthand for "Syrian"), live in a self-created entrepreneurial and mercantile empire whose current sources of wealth are found everywhere from Coney Island to Shanghai. They are rich beyond the dreams of their immigrant forebears. Many live in multimillion-dollar mansions in the Gravesend neighborhood of Brooklyn, summer in fabulous seafront homes
Photograph by Domingo Milella
New York County (Manhattan) ranks No. 4 in the nation among median home values. The median home value for the county is $788,000.
83

039

039 THE NEW YORK TIMES MAGAZINE

Creative Director_**Janet Froelich** Art Directors_**Arem Duplessis, Gail Bichler** Designer_**Leo Jung** Illustrator_**Ian Dingman**
Director of Photography_**Kathy Ryan** Photo Editors_**Clinton Cargill, Stacey Baker** Photographers_**Ralph Gibson, Tom Schierlitz, Nadav Kander, Domingo Milella**
Editor-In-Chief_**Gerry Marzorati** Publisher_**The New York Times** Issue_**October 14, 2007** Category_**Design: Feature: Story**

SECTION
DESIGN

AWARD
SILVER

CATEGORY
FRONT/BACK OF BOOK COVER

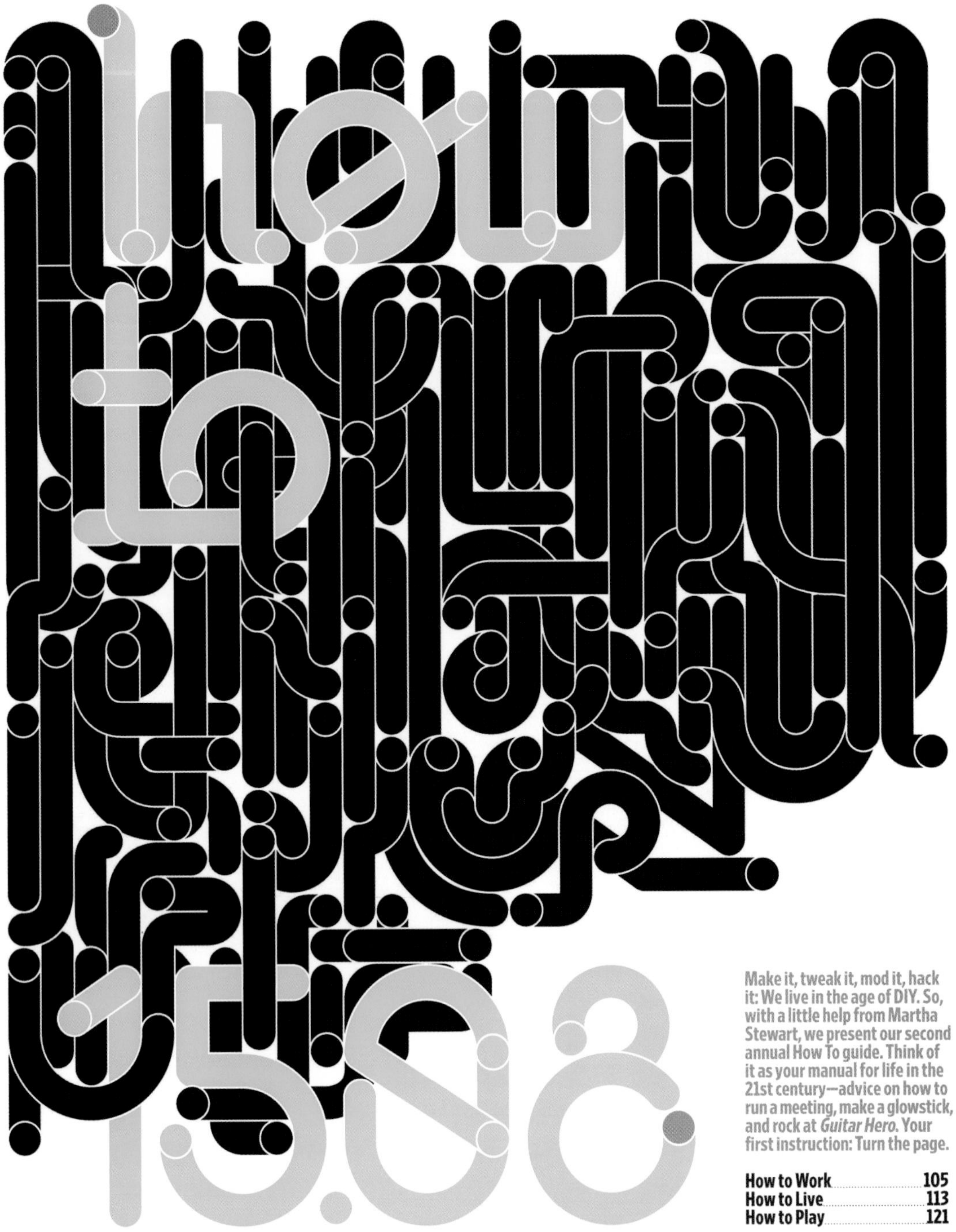

15.08

Make it, tweak it, mod it, hack it: We live in the age of DIY. So, with a little help from Martha Stewart, we present our second annual How To guide. Think of it as your manual for life in the 21st century—advice on how to run a meeting, make a glowstick, and rock at *Guitar Hero*. Your first instruction: Turn the page.

Features | 15.08 WIRED

TYPOGRAPHY BY Seth Ferris

AUGUST 2007 

040

 WIRED

Creative Director_Scott Dadich Designers_Maili Holiman, Scott Dadich
Illustrators_Seth Ferris, Mario Hugo, Marian Bantjes, Stephen Doyle Publisher_Condé Nast Publications, Inc.
Issues_February 2007, May 2007, December 2007 Category_Front of Book/Back of Book

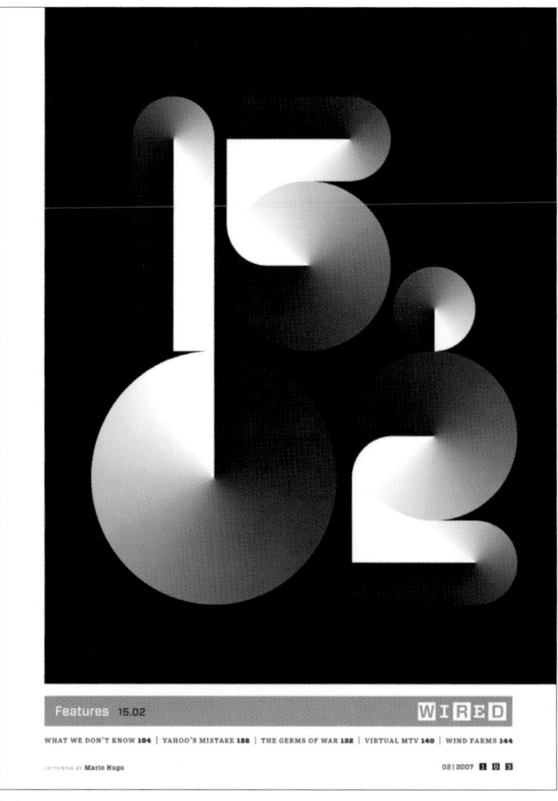

040

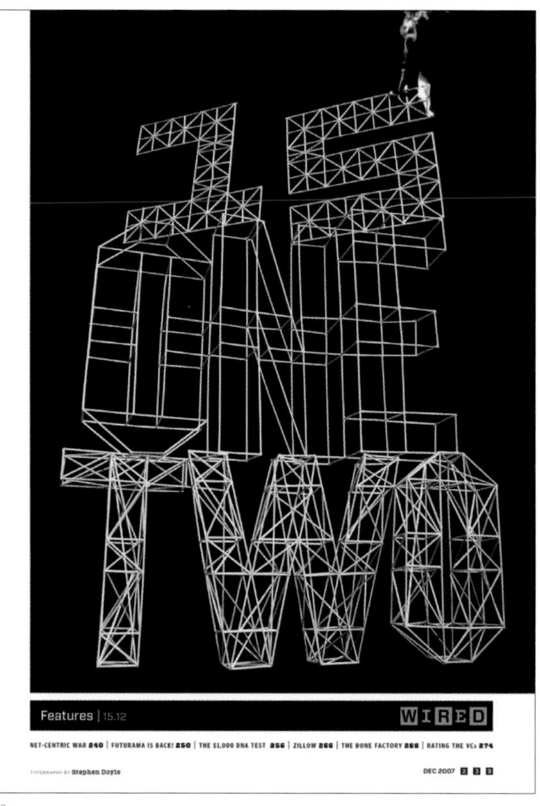

040

15.05

130 TIM KRING FOR HEROES | 134 HENRY LOUIS GATES JR. | 135 J. K. ROWLING | 136 THE ALLEN BRAIN ATLAS | 138 BRIAN K. VAUGHAN | 139 CLIFF BLESZINSKI & TIM SWEENEY | 140 ALFONSO CUARÓN | 142 ARIANNA HUFFINGTON | 143 GREGG GILLIS | 144 WALTER DE'SILVA | 146 JEN CHUNG | 147 WORLDVISTA | 148 MICHAEL WESCH | 149 MARK SHUTTLEWORTH | 150 ARNOLD SCHWARZENEGGER

WIRED

the 2007 RAVE AWARDS

To find the 22 innovators, instigators, and inventors to honor with a Rave Award this year, we started by looking for the most intriguing breakthroughs in the world today—then tracked down the individuals who made them happen. Each honoree told a unique story, but they tended to have one thing in common: Before changing the game in technology, business, or culture, they first changed themselves. There's the actor who became a politician (Arnold Schwarzenegger) and the politician who became an entrepreneur (Arianna Huffington), not to mention an entrepreneur turned philanthropist (Paul Allen) and a philanthropist turned open source warrior (Mark Shuttleworth). The lesson seems obvious: Reinvent yourself, reinvent the world.

LETTERING BY MARIAN BANTJES

1 3 1

040

041

041 WIRED

Creative Director_Scott Dadich Design Director_Wyatt Mitchell Art Director_Carl DeTorres
Designer_Carl DeTorres Illustrator_Yoichiro Ono Publisher_Condé Nast Publications, Inc.
Issue_November 2007 Category_Design: Cover

: SECTION
DESIGN

: AWARD
SILVER

: CATEGORY
FEATURE: STORY FRONT PAGE

042

042

GOLF DIGEST INDEX

Design Director_Ken DeLago Designer_Marne Mayer
Director of Photography_Ryan Cline Photographer_Roxanne Lowit
Issue_Fall 2007 Category Design: Feature: Story

May 6, 2007

The New York Times

Book Review

Section 7 Copyright © 2007 The New York Times

JONATHAN MILES ON SMOKING — ROBERT R. HARRIS ON DRINKING — DAVE BARRY ON E-MAIL — EMILY BAZELON ON DIETING — TONI BENTLEY ON DRUG ADDICTION — DANIELLE TRUSSONI ON BARFLIES — SUSAN CASEY ON GAMBLING — CAMILLE PAGLIA ON TEENAGERS

10 11 13 22 14 6 8 20

BAD FOR YOU BAD FOR YOU BAD FOR YOU

WARNING: Benjamin Kunkel on Nirvana · Joe Queenan on bad books
Diane Johnson on New Age spirituality · Tom Carson on Warren Zevon

Rodrigo Corral

043

THE NEW YORK TIMES BOOK REVIEW

Design Director_Tom Bodkin Art Director_Nicholas Blechman
Illustrator_Rodrigo Corral Publisher_The New York Times
Issue_May 6, 2007 Category_Design: Front Page

: SECTION
DESIGN

: AWARD
SILVER

: CATEGORY
FEATURE: STORY
FEATURE: SPREAD/SINGLE

044

F

OR TWO GLORIOUS YEARS, OPTIMUS PRIME was America's hero. He starred in *Transformers*, a thriftily animated series (cynics would call it a half-hour toy commercial) that pitted Prime and his army of Autobots against the vicious Megatron and his Decepticons. On the small screen, these robots in disguise were more than cartoons, they were towering titanium gods, massive in their machine carapaces: tractor trailers, cop cars, fighter jets. // In toy form, Transformers combined the tantalizing tactility of a Rubik's Cube with the vroom-vroom automotive voyeurism of Hot Wheels. Add a touch of Cold War moral clarity and we were hooked. Boys ages 5 to 11—and it *was* boys—faithfully tuned in week after week to watch the saga of these doughty bots, who struck out from their home planet, Cybertron, with vague and mixed motives—conquest, freedom, resources, defense—and brought their civil war to our planet. We welcomed them as liberators and adopted Prime as our mech-daddy. Some quite literally: In 2001, a 30-year-old National Guardsman from Cuyahoga Falls, Ohio, legally changed his name to Optimus Prime. "I really latched onto him when I was a kid," Prime said to TV reporters before shipping out to the Middle East in 2003. "My dad passed away and I didn't really have anybody around." // Then in 1986, the original Prime did something that distinguished him from most other cartoon heroes. He died. He died for freedom, for righteousness, and for shelf space. In the toy biz, there's no room for fatherly affection—only next year's line. *The Transformers: The Movie*, released in August of that year, was Prime's swan song. For nearly two decades, through various toy lines and dubious toon reboots (a gorilla named Optimus Primal? Please.), the sons of Prime waited for Papa Bot. // At last, in July 2004, it was decreed from the throne of Steven »

139

044

WIRED

Creative Director_Scott Dadich
Art Directors_Scott Dadich, Carl DeTorres
Designer_Carl DeTorres Illustrators_The Designers Republic, Industrial Light & Magic Photo Editor_Carolyn Rauch
Photographer_Thomas Hannich Publisher_Condé Nast Publications, Inc.
Issue_July 2007 Category_Design: Feature: Story

100 REASONS TO GET RID OF IT

BECAUSE YOU HAVE TOO MUCH STUFF

1 **1.4 million** Americans suffer from chronic hoarding & clutter.

2 PEOPLE BURN **55** MINUTES A DAY LOOKING FOR THINGS.

3 **80%** of what we own we never use.

4 **1800GOTJUNK.COM** PAY SOMEONE ELSE TO TAKE OUT THE (BIG, CUMBERSOME) TRASH.

5 **PUBLIC STORAGE.COM** Lock it up in more than 2,100 locations around the U.S.

6 redshield.org *Schedule a pickup with your local Salvation Army.*

7 EARTH911.ORG Find local recycling and reuse programs for all kinds of household items.

BECAUSE SOMEONE ELSE NEEDS IT

CELL PHONES

12 VERIZONWIRELESS.COM Put a refurbished phone (of any brand) into the hands of a domestic violence victim… 13 ECO-CELL.COM …Or let its sale benefit an environmental charity. 14 CARE.ORG Send a phone to the field staff of a poverty-fighting mission.

DIGITAL CAMERAS

15 OPERATIONHOMEFRONT.NET Help keep service members in touch with their families.

ALL TECHNOLOGY

16 RETHINK.EBAY.COM Work with charities to find homes for consumer electronics. 17 YOUTHFORTECHNOLOGY.ORG Put scanners, computers, and cameras in the hands of deserving, impoverished kids around the world.

Air Miles

18 REDCROSS.ORG For Red Cross staff and volunteers 19 HEROMILES.COM For deployed soldiers 20 MARROW.ORG For transplant patients 21 CHILDRENSCANCERASSOCIATION.ORG For terminally ill kids

FURNITURE & APPLIANCES

22 EXCESSACCESS.ORG *Match your household items with a local non-profit's wish list.* 23 HELPITUP.ORG *Furnish homes for disaster victims.* 24 DRESSFORSUCCESS.ORG *Give interview and work clothing to disadvantaged women.* 25 MAKINGMEMORIES.ORG *Donate a wedding gown to benefit breast-cancer patients.* 26 WWW.OPERATIONFAIRYDUST.ORG *Send formalwear to teenage girls who need help getting to the prom.* 27 ONEWARMCOAT.ORG *A free coat to anyone who needs one.* 28 BOULDERRUNNING.COM *Ship shoes and sportswear to struggling athletes around the world.*

Other

29 SUITCASESFORKIDS.ORG Supply children in foster care with luggage. 30 UNITEFORSIGHT.ORG & GIVETHEGIFTOFSIGHT.ORG Send eyewear to men and women in underdeveloped countries. 31 SAVETHECHILDREN.ORG Convert American Express credit card points to cash donations. 32 CARTALK.COM Donate a used vehicle to support your local public radio station. 33 BOOKSFORAFRICA.ORG Give everything from storybooks to encyclopedias. 34 CAP4PETS.ORG Send towels and newspapers to animal shelters. 35 GOODWILL.ORG Fund job training programs and social services. 36 FREECYCLE.ORG Post donations for charities (and regular folks) to claim. 37 HABITAT.ORG Donate leftover building supplies to Habitat for Humanity's ReStores.

COMPUTERS

38 CRISTINA.ORG Technology and training for the disabled and disadvantaged. 39 SHARETECHNOLOGY.ORG Connecting donations with charities across the U.S. 40 WORLDCOMPUTEREXCHANGE.ORG Send computers to more than 50 developing countries.

BECAUSE IT CAN BE TURNED INTO SOMETHING ELSE

41 NIKEREUSEASHOE.COM Recycled footwear materials become sports and playground surfaces. 42 PATAGONIA.COM Donated Capilene base layers become polyester fibers for new Capilene garments. 43 PANGEA ORGANICS' packaging becomes an herb garden when planted in soil. 44 CARGO COSMETICS' PlantLove lipstick tubes come in plantable boxes that sprout wildflowers. 45 PENCILTHINGS.COM Old newspapers become colored pencils. 46 VIVATERRA.COM Rubber tires become sleek purses… 47 PASSCHAL.COM …or rugged iPod covers. 48 GAIAM.COM Plastic soda bottles become durable hammocks. 49 RECYCLINE.COM Yogurt containers become colorful plates, flatware, toothbrushes, and razors.

BECAUSE IT'S FUN

8 127SALE.COM Set up shop at the WORLD'S LONGEST YARD SALE, August 2–5, along 450 miles of Highway 127 in the Southeastern U.S.… 9 Or peddle your wares in your own front yard on NATIONAL GARAGE SALE DAY, August 10. 10 SWAPORAMARAMA.ORG Attend nationwide clothing exchanges and do-it-yourself alteration workshops. 11 WILDZIPPER.COM Watch as a pile of your favorite old T-shirts is converted into a quilt.

BONUS REASON

Because if you recycle this magazine, you can still go to blueprintmag.com to view all of these links. (And don't worry, we won't hold it against you.)

138 Blueprint MARCH…

Blueprint

BECAUSE IT WILL MAKE YOUR LIFE BETTER

50 Getting rid of clutter will *reduce* HOUSEWORK BY **40%**

51 YOU CAN USUALLY **ERASE A $10K CREDIT CARD DEBT** (with an average interest rate) 65% faster—and pay 75% less total interest—when you pay double the typical minimum monthly payment.

52 DOWNLOAD SECURITY SOFTWARE LIKE STOPZILLA TO KEEP A LID ON COMPUTER POP-UPS.

53 AROUND **23%** OF PEOPLE PAY LATE FEES ON BILLS THEY CANNOT FIND.

BECAUSE YOU CAN GET SOMETHING BACK

54 Return six MAC Cosmetics containers to any MAC store and receive a free lipstick. 55 Trade in an old iPod and receive a 10% discount on a new one. 56 COINSTAR.COM Easily convert spare change into "real" money. 57 CRAIGSLIST.ORG Sell it to your neighbors. 58 EBAY.COM Sell it to anyone. 59 GIFTCARDBUYBACK.COM Get cash for gift cards you'll never use. 60 PAPERBACKSWAP.COM Trade the books you have for the ones you want. 61 PEERFLIX.COM Trade the DVDs you've seen for the ones you haven't. 62 SPUN.COM Clear off your CD shelves, and make money in the process. 63 TITLETRADER.COM The great entertainment exchange: books, music, movies, and games, all swapped in one place.

BECAUSE YOU DON'T WANT TO SUFFER FROM "Stuck Song Syndrome"

77 And these five tunes are among the most persistent: Chili's "BABY BACK RIBS" jingle, "WE WILL ROCK YOU," the "MISSION IMPOSSIBLE" theme, "YMCA," and "IT'S A SMALL WORLD AFTER ALL." (Tip: Try drowning them out with classical music, which is less likely to haunt you after it's turned off.)

BECAUSE THE LAST THING YOU NEED IS MORE PAPER LYING AROUND

78 FILE YOUR TAXES THROUGH AN AUTHORIZED IRS E-FILE PROVIDER. 79 ELIMINATE PAPER STATEMENTS BY BANKING AND PAYING BILLS ONLINE. 80 CALL 1-888-567-8688 TO STOP UNWANTED CREDIT CARD SOLICITATIONS. 81 OPT OUT OF MAILING AND TELEMARKETING LISTS BY LOGGING ON TO DMACONSUMERS.ORG.

BECAUSE THERE'S A BETTER OPTION

82 *Search for phone numbers online instead of storing bulky Yellow and White Pages volumes.* 83 *Lose the road maps and get a GPS system to download up-to-date travel guides.* 84 *Read* Dating Up: Dump the Schlump and Find a Quality Man, *by J. Courtney Sullivan (Warner Books, $14, 2007).*

BECAUSE YOU DON'T WANT TO END UP LIKE THEM

85 *Miss Havisham* in Great Expectations 86 *Big Edie* and *Little Edie Bouvier Beale* in Grey Gardens 87 *Oscar Madison* on The Odd Couple 88 The *family in the documentary* Packrat (packratthemovie.com) 89 The *Bronx, New York, man* who, in 2003, was trapped in his home under an avalanche of books and newspapers for two days before being rescued.

BECAUSE IT'S OLD/EXPIRED

64 ENERGYSTAR.GOV *Replacing old* APPLIANCES *with new, energy-efficient ones saves money and fuel.* 65 RUNNING SHOES *should be retired after 300 to 500 miles in order to prevent injuries.* 66 *Deep-six your* TOOTHBRUSH *every three to four months.* 67 *Swap your pitcher's* WATER FILTER *every two months (or as directed).* 68 *Change out disposable* AIR CONDITIONER FILTERS *once a month during cooling season.* 69 *Replace the batteries in your* SMOKE DETECTOR *at least once a year.* 70 FOODSAFETY.GOV *Find the* USDA'S *recommended storage limits for refrigerated and frozen* FOOD. 71 *Throw out* MASCARA AND MOISTURIZER *after three months.* 72 *Discard* FOUNDATION *and* SUNSCREEN *after six months to a year.* 73 *Keep* CONCEALER, LIPSTICK, EYE- AND LIP LINERS, FRAGRANCES, POWDERS, BLUSHES, AND SHADOWS *for only a year and a half to two years.* 74–76 *Say goodbye to the dried-out remnants of your favorite no-longer-available* LIPSTICK, *and check out* THREECUSTOM.COM, T.J.MAXX *stores, or* LANCÔME'S BEAUTY BYE-BYE *program for replacements or duplicates of discontinued cosmetics.*

BECAUSE IF THEY SAID IT, IT'S PROBABLY TRUE

90 "SIMPLICITY IS THE ULTIMATE SOPHISTICATION." –Leonardo da Vinci

91 "LESS IS MORE." –Ludwig Mies van der Rohe

92 "HAVE NOTHING IN YOUR HOUSES THAT YOU DO NOT KNOW TO BE USEFUL OR BELIEVE TO BE BEAUTIFUL." –William Morris

93 *"You've got to accentuate the positive, eliminate the negative."* –Johnny Mercer

94 "THE JOY OF GIVING IS INDEED A PLEASURE, ESPECIALLY WHEN YOU GET RID OF SOMETHING YOU DON'T WANT." –Frank Butler and Frank Cavett, Going My Way

OR JUST BECAUSE

95 IT HAS NO VALUE, SENTIMENTAL OR MONETARY. 96 IT HASN'T BEEN USED IN OVER A YEAR. 97 THERE IS NO LOGICAL PLACE TO KEEP IT. 98 IT DOESN'T WORK. 99 AN EX GAVE IT TO YOU.

100 *And what's the worst that can happen if you throw it out?*

PHOTOGRAPH BY KATE MATHIS

MARCH/APRIL 2007 Blueprint 139

045

TheFunded.com
"Trashing VCs Since 2007"

Ted
ANGRY ENTREPRENEUR

by Carlye Adler • Wired • December 2007 • photographs by Rainer Hosch

046

045 **BLUEPRINT**

Creative Director_**Eric A. Pike** Design Director_**Deb Bishop** Art Director_**Cybele Grandjean** Designer_**Cybele Grandjean** Director of Photography_**Heloise Goodman** Photographer_**Kate Mathis** Assistant Photo Editor_**Darlene Schrack** Editor-In-Chief_**Sarah Humphreys** Publisher_**Martha Stewart Living Omnimedia** Issue_**March/April 2007** Category_**Design: Feature: Spread/Single Page**

046 **WIRED**

Creative Director_**Scott Dadich** Design Director_**Wyatt Mitchell** Designers_**Scott Dadich, Carl DeTorres** Photo Editor_**Zana Woods** Photographer_**Ranier Hosch** Publisher_**Condé Nast Publications, Inc.** Issue_**December 2007** Category_**Design: Feature: Spread/Single Page**

: SECTION
DESIGN

: AWARD
SILVER

: CATEGORY
COVER
FEATURE: STORY

print
DESIGN CULTURE PLACE
MAY/JUNE 2007
EUROPEAN DESIGN 2007
ANIMATION PUNKS IN LITHUANIA
TIME LESS
BELGIUM'S FASHION VISIONARY
EMO TION AL
MYTH IC
TWIST ED
DO DESIGN WEEKS MATTER?
RADICAL

047

PRINT

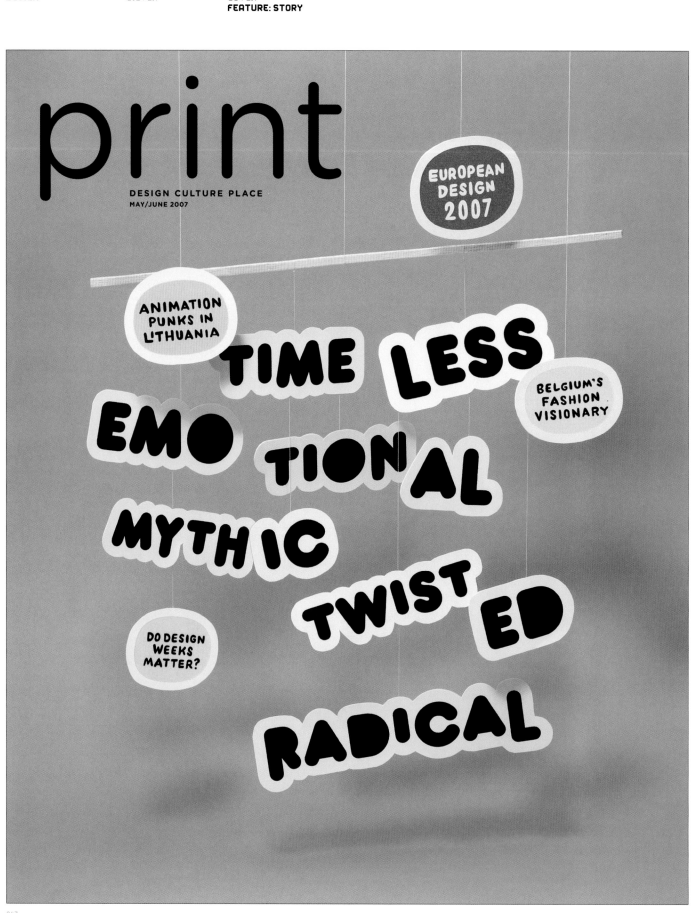

Art Director_**Kristina DiMatteo** Associate Art Director_**Lindsay Ballant**
Illustrator_**Chragokyberneticks** Photographer_**Beat Schweizer** Editor-In-Chief_**Joyce Rutter Kaye**
Publisher_**F & W Publications** Issue_**May/June 2007** Category_**Design: Cover**

The Obsessives

A week's worth of time, money, and resources—gone in a flash! Or is it? We asked four artists known for their clever online record-keeping to show us exactly how they spent those precious 604,800 seconds.

By Emily Gordon

NAME KATE BINGAMAN (29)
LIVES IN STARKVILLE, MISS.
OCCUPATION ASST. PROFESSOR OF GRAPHIC DESIGN
WEBSITE OBSESSIVECONSUMPTION.COM

NAME NICHOLAS FELTON (29)
LIVES IN NEW YORK CITY
OCCUPATION GRAPHIC DESIGNER, MEGAFONE
WEBSITE FELTRON.COM, MGFN.NET

NAME ELLIE HARRISON (28)
LIVES IN NOTTINGHAM, U.K.
OCCUPATION ARTIST, CURATOR, LECTURER
WEBSITE ELLIEHARRISON.COM

NAME JOHN D. FREYER (34)
LIVES IN IOWA CITY, IOWA
OCCUPATION LECTURER IN PHOTOGRAPHY, ARTIST, WRITER
WEBSITE TEMPORAMA.COM

The four artists whose intent expressions and busy workspaces are pictured at left are, in many ways, quite ordinary. They read, they eat toast, they buy fishing videos. Then they take it a big step further. Kate Bingaman created a dazzling online archive of years' worth of purchases—and bills—all illustrated in minute detail. Designer Nicholas Felton charms the blogosphere yearly with his Feltron Report, an elegant, meticulous annual report of himself. Ellie Harrison, a self-described "recovering data collector," has photographed many dimensions of her life and objects; she also keeps a blog of ideas hatched while drinking tea (she's a Brit). And John D. Freyer made a riveting narrative about selling his possessions on eBay in his book *All My Life for Sale*. We asked all four to document what they consumed for one week. They all produced a vivid record that says volumes about who they are.

Kate: "I think the minute and mundane information is the most interesting, so if the receipt had a bar code or a tear, I drew it. A 13-year-old girl who loves to shop can find something she's interested in with my work, and so can an anti-consumerist activist. I like that I can have a conversation with both."

Nicholas: "I'm a list-maker, and tend to keep records of things naturally. This is mirrored by an economy that is constantly tracking and accumulating statistics on us. Some of these records are open, and some are not—I'm interested in both, as well as things that are only interesting to me."

Ellie: "I became aware that I was consuming in small amounts nearly all the time. The most relaxing moments were the ones when I knew I was consuming nothing, lying in bed at night or walking down the street. These moments became really important to me, and I found myself treasuring and prolonging them."

John: "After reviewing the hundreds of photographs I took, I kept coming back to the bags. I liked the way they revealed their contents—they contained nearly all of what I consumed during the week, and really talked about the way I (and we) consume stuff, in such volume that we need giant plastic bags to carry it with us."

68 PRINTMAG.COM 69

048

048

PRINT

Art Director_Kristina DiMatteo Associate Art Director_Lindsay Ballant Designers_Kristina DiMatteo, Lindsay Ballant
Illustrators_Happy Pets, Kate Bingaman, Nicholas Felton, Ellie Harrison, John D. Freyer
Editor-In-Chief_Joyce Rutter Kaye Publisher_F & W Publications Issue_July/August 2007 Category_Design: Feature: Story

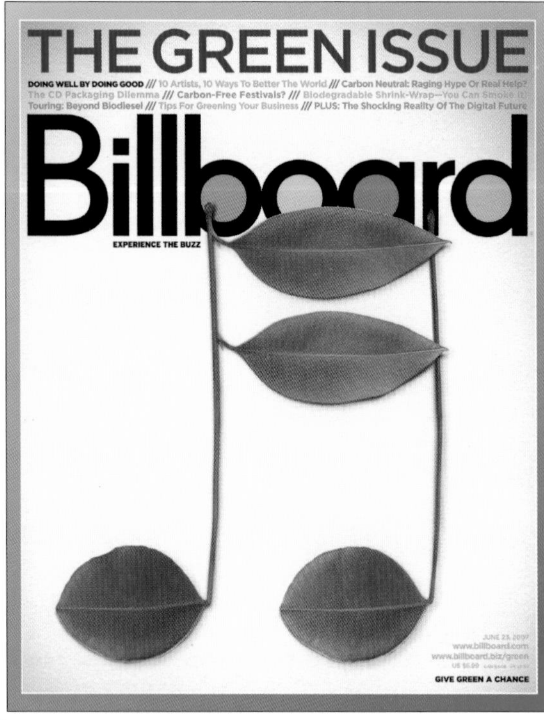

049

051

050

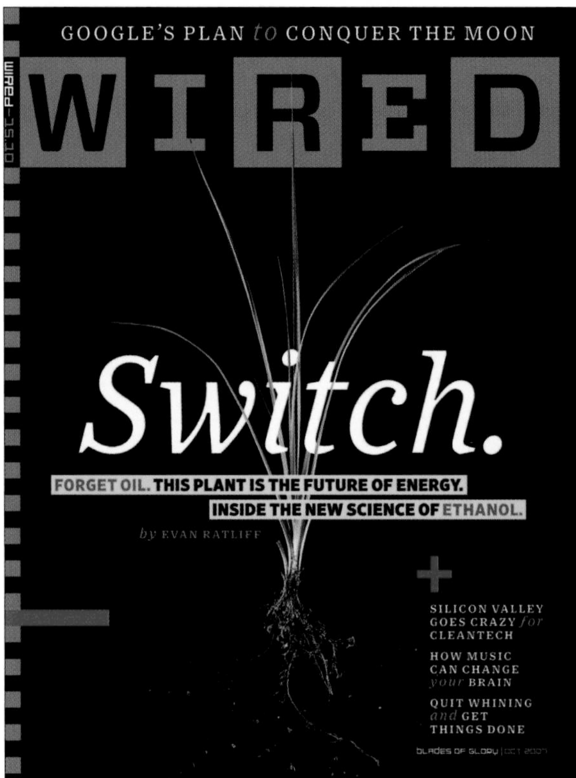

052

049 BILLBOARD

Creative Director_Josh Klenert Art Director_Christine Bower
Designer_Greg Grabowy Illustrator_National Forest
Photo Editor_Amelia Halverson Publisher_Nielsen Business Media
Issue_June 23, 2007 Category_Design: Cover

050 PURSUITS

Art Director_Mary Ann Salvato Designer_Mary Ann Salvato
Photo Editor_Michael Green Photographer_Johnathan Kantor
Issue_February 25, 2007 Category_Design: Cover

051 THE NEW YORK TIMES MAGAZINE

Creative Director_Janet Froelich Art Directors_Arem Duplessis, Gail Bichler Designer_Arem Duplessis
Director of Photography_Kathy Ryan Photo Editor_Kira Pollack
Photographer_Vik Muniz Editor-In-Chief_Gerry Marzorati
Publisher_The New York Times Issue_April 15, 2007
Category_Design: Cover

052 WIRED

Creative Director_Scott Dadich
Photo Editor_Anna Goldwater Alexander Photographer_Dan Winters
Publisher_Condé Nast Publications, Inc. Issue_October 2007
Category_Design: Cover

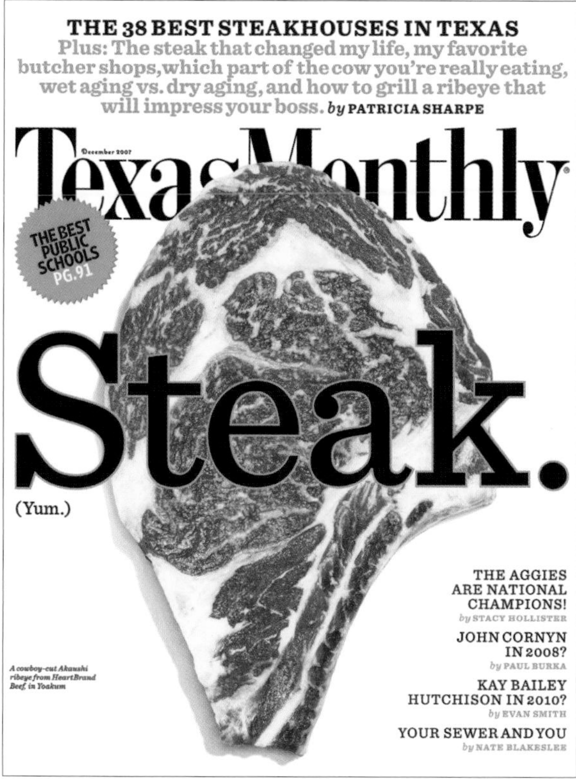

053

055

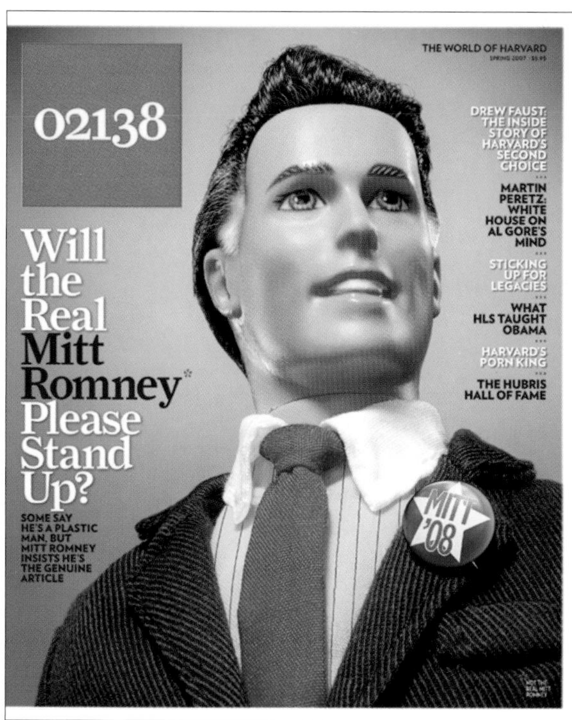

054

056

053 TEXAS MONTHLY

Art Director_T.J. Tucker Designer_Andi Beierman
Photo Editor_Leslie Baldwin Photographer_Dan Winters
Publisher_Emmis Communications Corp. Issue_December 2007
Category_Design: Cover

054 02138

Creative Director_Patrick Mitchell Art Director_Susannah Haesche
Designer_Ashley Bond Illustrator_Christopher Harting
Director of Photography_Katharine MacIntyre Studio_PlutoMedia
Publisher_Atlantic Media Issue_Spring 2007 Category_Design: Cover

055 NEW YORK

Design Director_Chris Dixon Art Directors_Randy Minor, Kate Elazegui
Designer_Chris Dixon Director of Photography_Jody Quon
Photographer_James Wojcik Editor-In-Chief_Adam Moss
Publisher_New York Magazine Holdings, LLC Issue_July 30-August 6, 2007 Category_Design: Cover

056 PLASTIQUE MAGAZINE

Design Director_Matt Willey Art Director_Matt Willey
Designers_Matt Willey, Matt Curtis Photo Editor_Brylie Fowler
Studio_Studio8 Design Issue_Summer/Autumn 2007
Category_Design: Cover

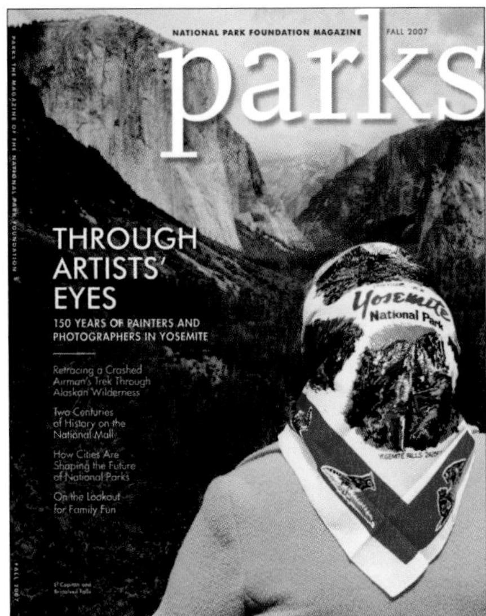

057

058

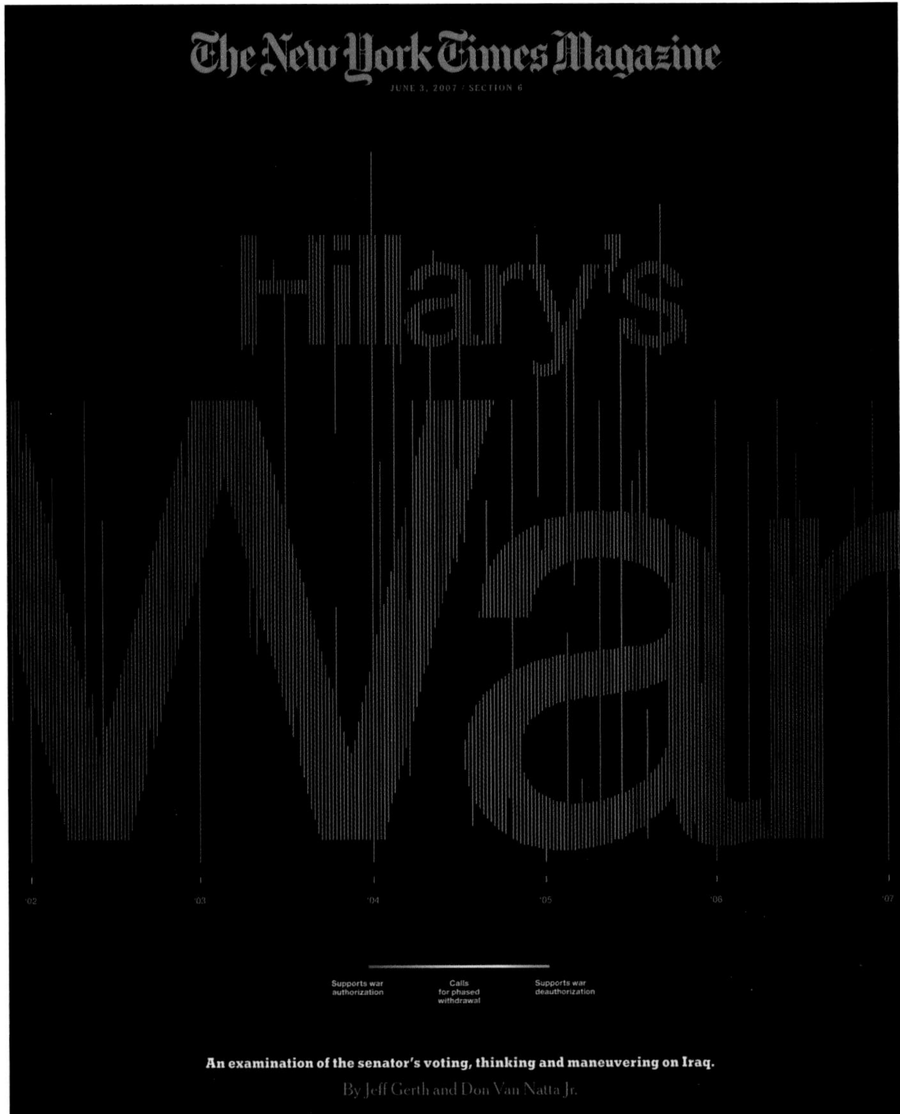

059

057 PARKS

Creative Director_Charlene Benson
Design Director_Syndi Becker
Designer_Syndi Becker
Director of Photography_Ann de Saussure
Photo Editor_Kate Giel
Photographer_Roger Minick
Issue_Fall 2007
Category_Design: Cover

058 02138

Creative Director_Patrick Mitchell Art Director_Susannah Haesche
Designer_Ashley Bond
Illustrator_Walter Smith Director of Photography_Katharine MacIntyre
Studio_PlutoMedia
Publisher_Atlantic Media
Issue_November/December 2007
Category_Design: Cover

059 THE NEW YORK TIMES MAGAZINE

Creative Director_Janet Froelich
Art Director_Arem Duplessis
Designer_Arem Duplessis
Lettering_Tom Brown Art+Design
Editor-In-Chief_Gerry Marzorati
Publisher_The New York Times
Issue_June 3, 2007
Category_Design: Cover

060

061

062

060 LING

Creative Director_Ricardo Feriche
Art Director_Joel Dalman
Illustrators_Óscar Aragón, Celine Robert, Vincens Castelltorr, Jari Mas
Photographer_Óscar Aragón
Issue_November 2007
Category_Design: Cover

061 COLUMBIA JOURNALISM REVIEW

Design Directors_Alissa Levin, Benjamin Levine
Designer_Benjamin Levine
Photographer_Cara Barer
Studio_Point Five Design
Editor-In-Chief_Mike Hoyt
Publisher_Columbia School of Journalism
Client_Columbia Journalism Review
Issue_September/October 2007
Category_Design: Cover

062 LING

Creative Director_Ricardo Feriche
Art Director_Joel Dalman
Illustrators_Óscar Aragón, Celine Robert, Vincens Castelltorr, Jari Mas
Photographer_Getty Images
Issue_June 2007
Category_Design: Cover

063

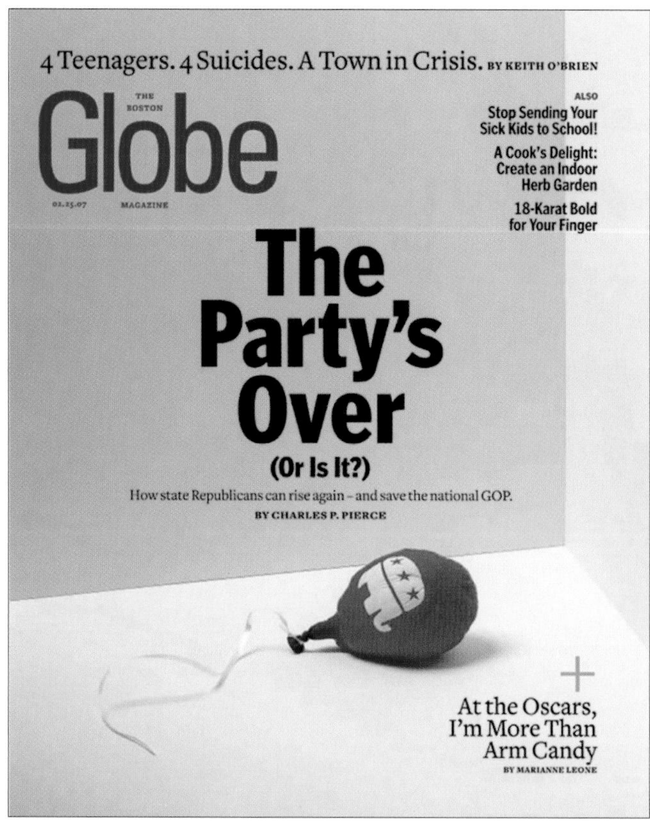

065

064

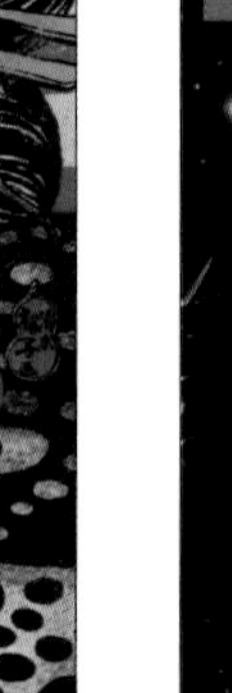

066

067

063 NEW YORK

Design Director_Chris Dixon
Art Directors_Randy Minor, Kate Elazegui
Designers_Chris Dixon, Paul Sahre
Illustrator_Sean McCabe
Director of Photography_ Jody Quon
Editor-In-Chief_Adam Moss
Publisher_New York Magazine Holdings, LLC
Issue_June 25, 2007
Category_Design: Cover

064 3X3

Design Director_Charles Hively
Art Director_Sarah Munt
Designer_Charles Hively
Illustrator_Yuko Shimizu
Publisher_3x3
Issue_March 2007
Category Design: Cover

065 THE BOSTON GLOBE MAGAZINE

Design Director_Dan Zedek
Art Director_Brendan Stephens
Designer_Josue Evilla
Photographer_Christopher Hartig
Assistant Managing Editor/Design_Dan Zedek
Publisher_The New York Times
Issue_February 25, 2007
Category_Design: Cover

066 02138

Creative Director_Patrick Mitchell
Art Director_Susannah Haesche
Illustrator_Joseph Darrow
Director of Photography_Katharine MacIntyre
Photographer_Catherine Ledner
Studio_PlutoMedia
Publisher_Atlantic Media
Issue_September/October 2007
Category_Design: Cover

067 AMERICAN WAY

Design Director_J.R. Arebalo, Jr.
Art Director_Samuel Solomon
Photographer_Gavin Bond
Publisher_American Airlines Publishing
Issue_May 15, 2007
Category_Design: Cover

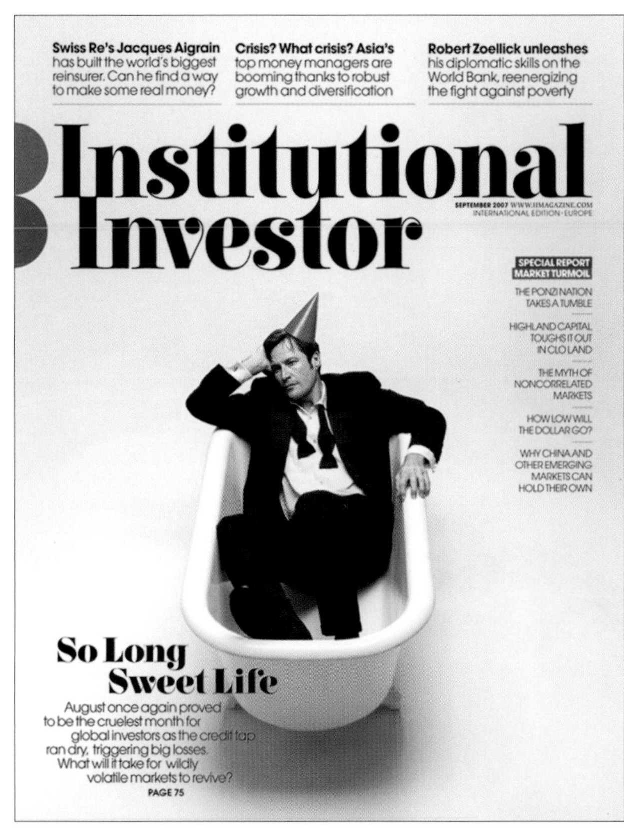

068

070

069

071

072

068 INSTITUTIONAL INVESTOR

Creative Director_Tom Brown
Art Director_Nathan Sinclair
Designer_Nathan Sinclair
Photo Editor_Daniella Nilva
Photographer_Fredrik Broden
Publisher_Institutional Investor Inc.
Issue_September 2007
Category_Design: Cover

069 UD&SE

Design Director_Torsten Hogh Rasmussen
Photographer_Per Morten Abrahamsen
Publisher_DSB
Issue_February 2007
Category_Design: Cover

070 WIRED

Creative Director_Scott Dadich
Designer_Scott Dadich
Illustrators_ILM, Ryan Jones, Alex Jaeger, Rick O'Connor, Ron Woodall
Photo Editor_Carolyn Rauch
Publisher_Condé Nast Publications, Inc.
Issue_July 2007
Category_Design: Cover

071 PLASTIQUE MAGAZINE

Design Director_Matt Willey
Art Director_Matt Willey
Designers_Matt Willey, Matt Curtis
Photo Editor_Brylie Fowler
Studio_Studio8 Design
Issue_Spring 2007
Category_Design: Cover

072 BLUEPRINT

Creative Director_Eric A. Pike
Design Director_Deb Bishop
Designer_Deb Bishop
Director of Photography_Heloise Goodman
Senior Photo Editor_Mary Cahill
Photographer_Hugh Stewart
Stylists_Page Marchese Norman, Katie Hatch
Editor-In-Chief_Sarah Humphreys
Publisher_Martha Stewart Living Omnimedia
Issue_March/April 2007
Category_Design: Cover

LA LUNA DE METROPOLI

DI CAPRIO, AL RESCATE DE ÁFRICA

LA PELÍCULA DE AVENTURAS "DIAMANTE DE SANGRE" DENUNCIA EL TRÁFICO ILEGAL DE DIAMANTES PARA FINANCIAR LA GUERRA CIVIL DE SIERRA LEONA

073

074

075

073 METROPOLI

Creative Director_**Rodrigo Sánchez**
Designer_**Rodrigo Sánchez**
Illustrator_**Raúl Arias**
Publisher_**Unidad Editorial S.A.**
Issue_**February 9, 2007**
Category_**Design: Cover**

074 UCLA MAGAZINE

Design Director_**Charles Hess**
Designers_**Alicia Patel, Janet Park**
Photo Editor_**Charles Hess**
Photographer_**Dave Lauridsen**
Studio_**Chess Design**
Editor-In-Chief_**Jack Feuer**
Publisher_**UCLA**
Client_**UCLA**
Issue_**October 2007**
Category_**Design: Cover**

075 UCLA MAGAZINE

Design Director_**Charles Hess**
Designer_**Nicholas Pavkovic**
Illustrator_**Charles Hess**
Studio_**Chess Design**
Editor-In-Chief_**Jack Feuer**
Publisher_**UCLA**
Client **UCLA**
Issue_**January 2007**
Category **Design: Cover**

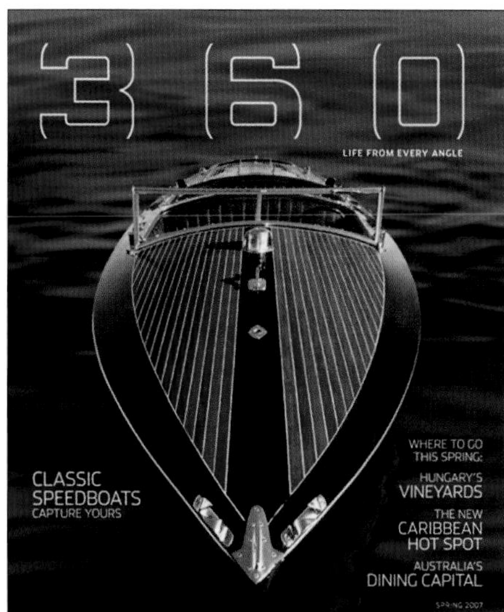

076

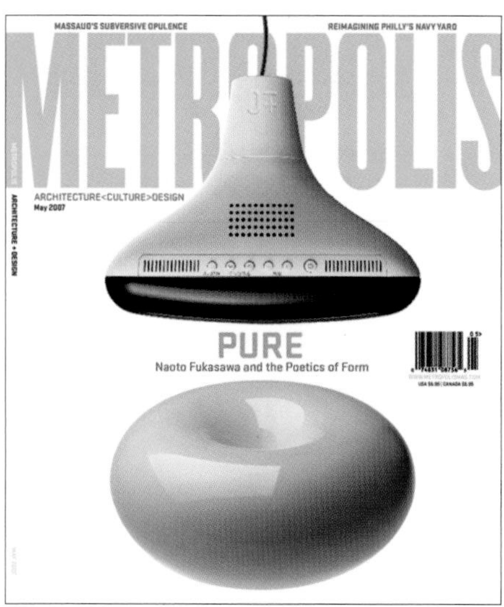

077

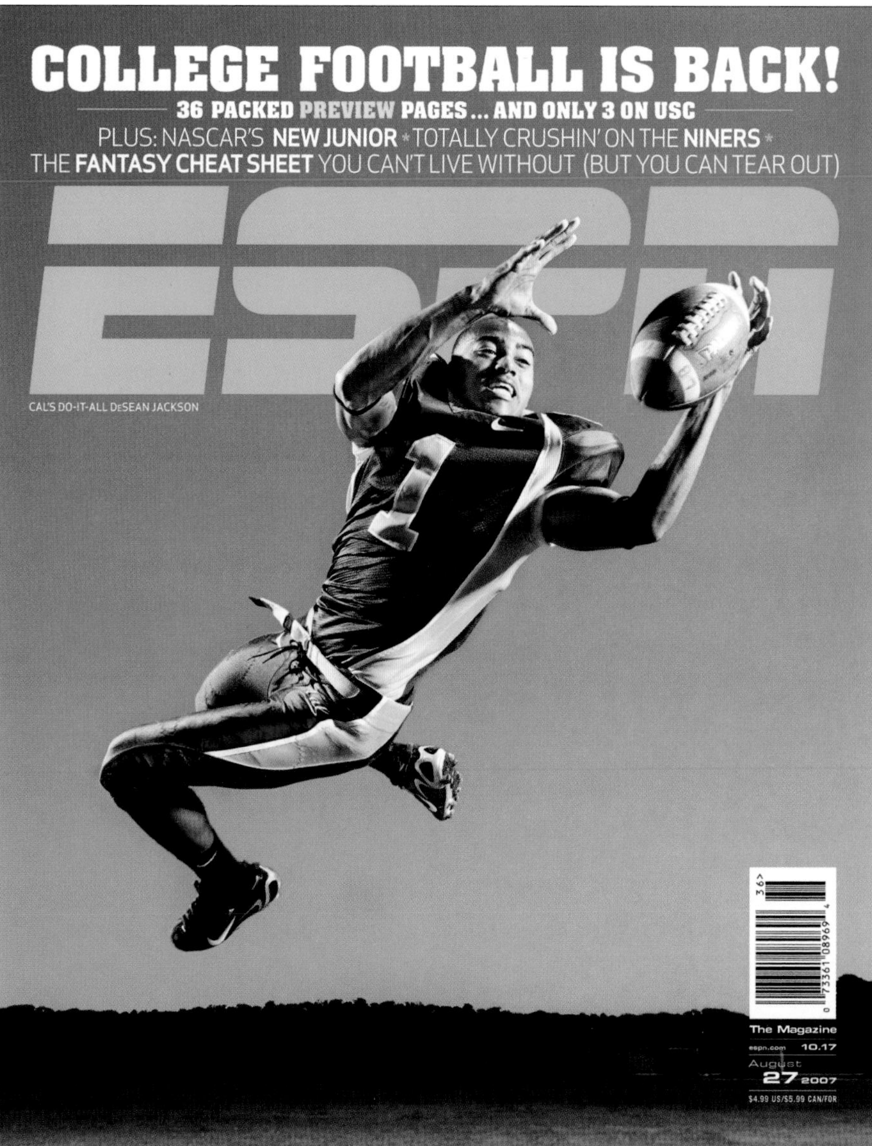

078

076 360

Design Director_Don Morris
Art Directors_André Mora, Leslie Steiger
Photo Editor_Meg Matyia
Photographer_Curtis Johnson
Assistant Photo Editor_Meg Ambrose
Studio_Don Morris Design
Editor-In-Chief_Liz Buffa
Publisher_American Express Publishing
Client_American Express Publishing
Issue_Spring 2007
Category_Design: Cover

077 METROPOLIS

Creative Director_Criswell Lappin
Designer_Erich Nagler
Photo Editor_Bilyana Dimitrova
Photographer_Hidetoyo Sasaki
Publisher_Bellerophon Publications
Issue_May 2007
Category_Design: Cover

078 ESPN THE MAGAZINE

Creative Director_Siung Tjia
Designer_Siung Tjia
Director of Photography_Catriona Ni Aolain
Photographer_Patrik Giardino
Publisher_ESPN, Inc.
Issue_August 27, 2007
Category_Design: Cover

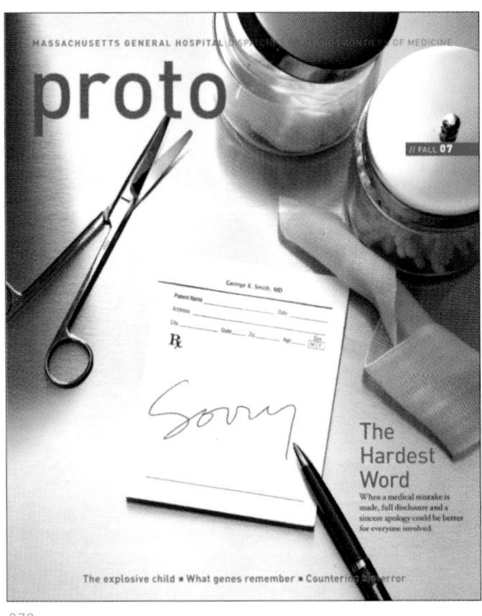

079

081

083

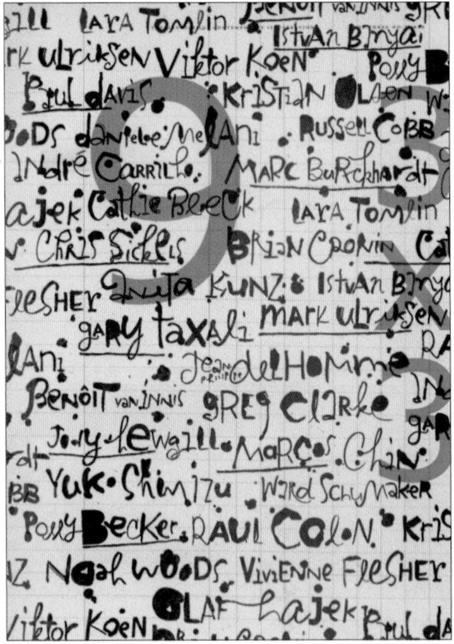
080

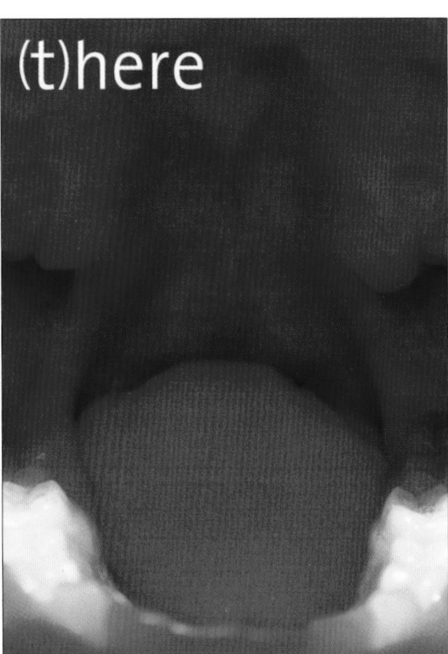

082

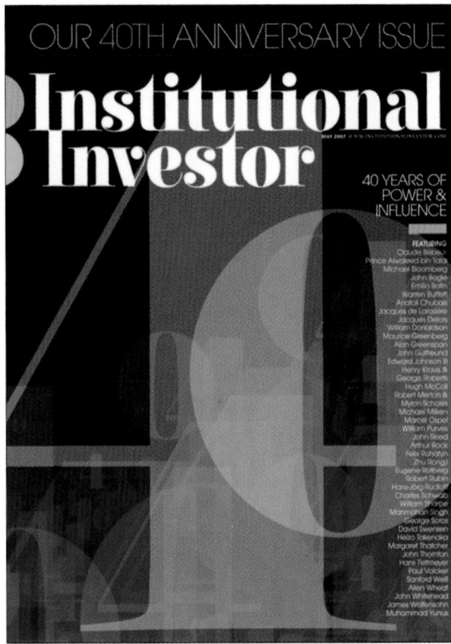

084

079 PROTO

Creative Director_**Charlene Benson**
Designer_**Lee Williams**
Director of Photography_**Denise Bosco**
Photographer_**Kenji Toma**
Studio_**Time Inc. Content Solutions**
Publisher_**Time Inc. Strategic Communications**
Client_**Massachusets General Hospital**
Issue_**Fall 2007**
Category_**Design: Cover**

080 3X3

Design Director_**Charles Hively**
Art Director_**Sarah Munt**
Designer_**Charles Hively**
Illustrator_**Ward Schumaker**
Publisher_**3x3**
Issue_**September 2007**
Category_**Design: Cover**

081 DEPARTURES

Creative Director_**Bernard Scharf**
Art Director_**Adam Bookbinder**
Associate Art Director_**Lou Corredor**
Director of Photography_**Jennifer Laski**
Photo Editors_**Jennifer Geaney, Brandon Perlman**
Photographer_**Doug Rosa**
Publisher_**American Express Publishing Co.**
Issue_**January/February 2007**
Category_**Design: Cover**

082 (T)HERE

Creative Director_**Christopher Wieliczko**
Design Director_**Jason Makowski**
Designer_**Meredith Resas**
Photographer_**David Incorvaia**
Editor-In-Chief_**Jason Makowski**
Publisher_**There Media, Inc.**
Issue_**Fall 2007**
Category_**Design: Cover**

083 BLACK INK

Creative Director_**Bernard Scharf**
Art Director_**Adam Bookbinder**
Illustrator_**Leanne Shapton**
Director of Photography_**Jennifer Laski**
Issue_**Winter 2007**
Category_**Design: Cover**

084 INSTITUTIONAL INVESTOR

Creative Director_**Tom Brown**
Art Director_**Nathan Sinclair**
Designer_**Nathan Sinclair**
Publisher_**Institutional Investor Inc.**
Issue_**May 2007**
Category_**Design: Cover**

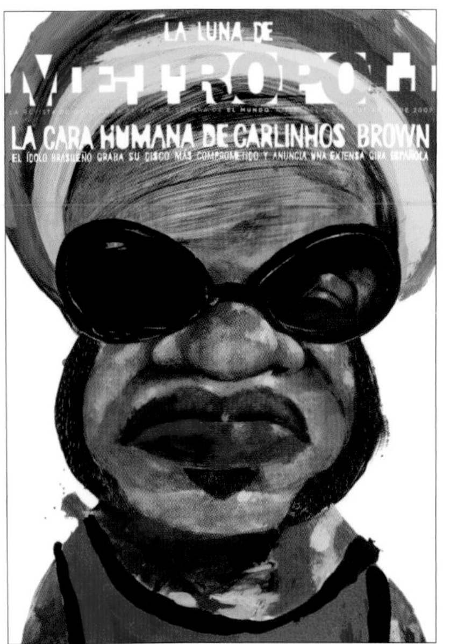

085

087

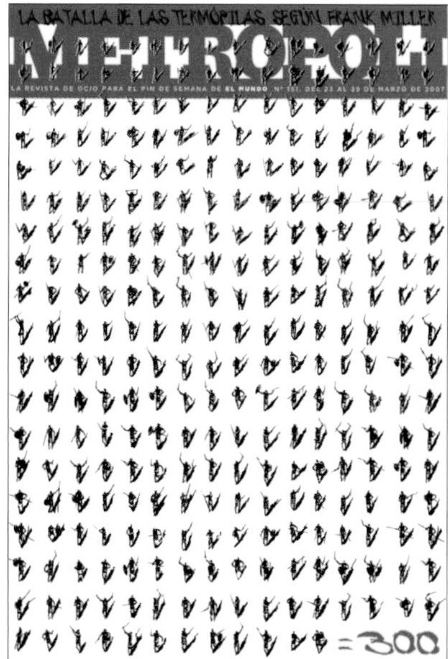

089

086

088

090

085 METROPOLI

Creative Director_Rodrigo Sánchez
Designer_Rodrigo Sánchez
Illustrator_Raúl Arias
Publisher_Unidad Editorial S.A.
Issue_April 6, 2007
Category_Design: Cover

086 CONDÉ NAST PORTFOLIO

Design Director_Robert Priest
Art Director_Grace Lee
Designers_Robert Priest, Grace Lee
Director of Photography_Lisa Berman
Photo Editor_Rossana Shokrian
Deputy Photo Editor_Sarah Czeladnicki
Photographer_Scott Peterman
Editor-In-Chief_Joanne Lipman
Publisher_Condé Nast Publications Inc.
Issue_May 2007
Category_Design: Cover

087 METROPOLI

Creative Director_Rodrigo Sánchez
Designer_Rodrigo Sánchez
Illustrator_Raúl Arias
Publisher_Unidad Editorial S.A.
Issue_March 27, 2007
Category_Design: Cover

088 COLUMBIA JOURNALISM REVIEW

Design Directors_Alissa Levin, Benjamin Levine
Designer_Benjamin Levine
Photographer_Airedale Brothers
Studio_Point Five Design
Editor-In-Chief_Mike Hoyt
Publisher_Columbia School of Journalism
Client_Columbia Journalism Review
Issue_November/December 2007
Category_Design: Cover

089 METROPOLI

Creative Director_Rodrigo Sánchez
Designer_Rodrigo Sánchez
Illustrator_Raúl Arias
Publisher_Unidad Editorial S.A.
Issue January 4, 2007
Category_Design: Cover

090 COLUMBIA JOURNALISM REVIEW

Design Directors_Alissa Levin, Benjamin Levine
Designers_Alissa Levin, Benjamin Levine
Photographer_Raymond Depardon
Studio_Point Five Design
Editor-In-Chief_Mike Hoyt
Publisher_Columbia School of Journalism
Client_Columbia Journalism Review
Issue_March/April 2007
Category_Design: Cover

097

099

101

098

100

097 02138

Creative Director_Patrick Mitchell Art Director_Susannah Haesche
Designer_Ashley Bond Director of Photography Katharine MacIntyre
Photographer_Robert Ascroft Studio_PlutoMedia
Publisher_Atlantic Media
Issue_May/June 2007 Category_Design: Cover

098 TIME

Art Director_Arthur Hochstein Designer_Arthur Hochstein
Director of Photography_MaryAnne Golon Picture Editor_Alice Gabriner
Publisher_Time Inc. Issue_July 30, 2007 Category_Design: Cover

099 METROPOLIS

Creative Director_Criswell Lappin Designer_Garrett Niksch
Photo Editor_Bilyana Dimitrova Publisher_Bellerophon Publications
Issue_March 2007 Category_Design: Cover

100 NEW YORK

Design Director_Chris Dixon Art Directors_Randy Minor, Kate Elazegui
Designer_Chris Dixon Director of Photography_Jody Quon
Photographer_Andrew Eccles Editor-In-Chief_Adam Moss
Publisher_New York Magazine Holdings, LLC Issue_October 1, 2007
Category_Design: Cover

101 BLACK INK

Creative Director_Bernard Scharf Art Director_Adam Bookbinder
Designer_Tivadar Bote Director of Photography_Jennifer Laski
Issue_Summer 2007 Category_Design: Cover

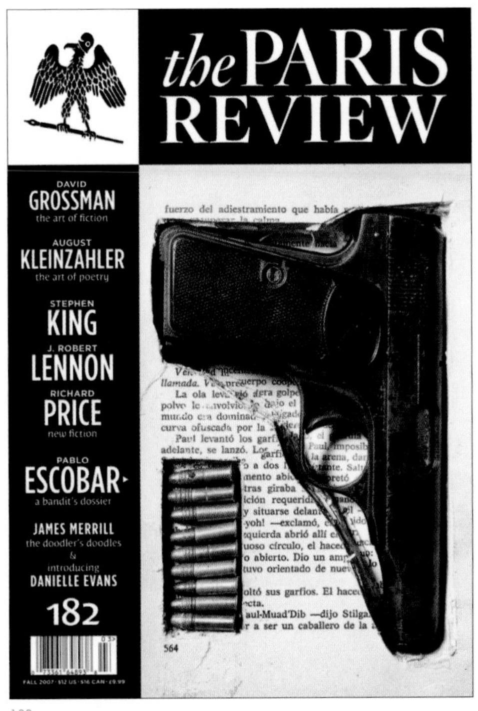

102

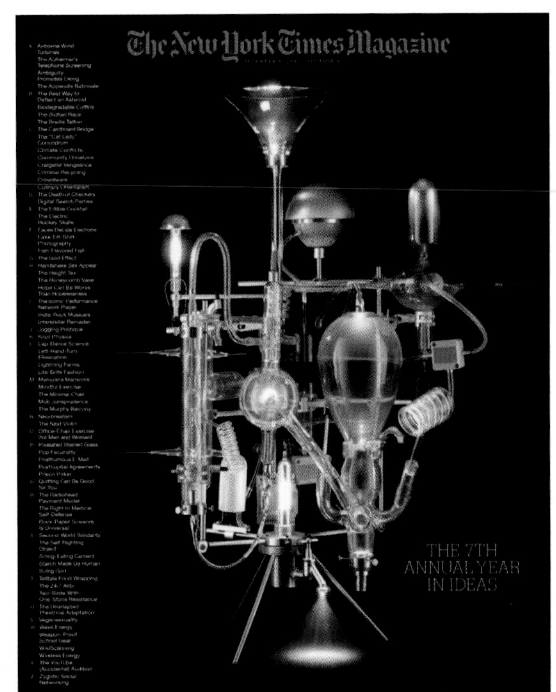

104

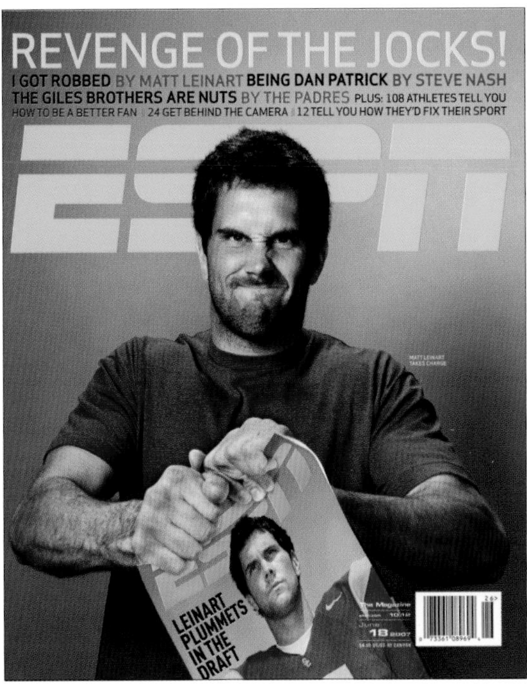

103

105

102 THE PARIS REVIEW

Design Directors_**Alissa Levin, Benjamin Levine** Designers_**Alissa Levin, Benjamin Levine** Photographer_**James Mallison** Studio_**Point Five Design** Editor-In-Chief_**Philip Gourevitch** Publisher_**The Paris Review Foundation** Client_**The Paris Review** Issue_**Fall 2007** Category_**Design: Cover**

103 ESPN THE MAGAZINE

Creative Director_**Siung Tjia** Designer_**Siung Tjia** Director of Photography_**Catriona Ni Aolain** Photographer_**Peter Yang** Publisher_**ESPN, Inc.** Issue_**June 18, 2007** Category_**Design: Cover**

104 THE NEW YORK TIMES MAGAZINE

Creative Director_**Janet Froelich** Art Director_**Arem Duplessis** Designer_**Gail Bichler** Director of Photography_**Kathy Ryan** Photographer_**Reinhard Hunger** Editor-In-Chief_**Gerry Marzorati** Publisher_**The New York Times** Issue_**December 9, 2007** Category_**Design: Cover**

105 RIGAMAROLE

Creative Director_**Thomas Hull** Art Director_**Thomas Hull** Designer_**Daniel Pagan** Director of Photography_**Thomas Hull** Photo Editor_**Daniel Pagan** Photographer_**Drew Donovan** Studio_**Rigsby Hull** Client_**Diamond Offshore Drilling, Inc.** Issue_**Fall 2007** Category_**Design: Cover**

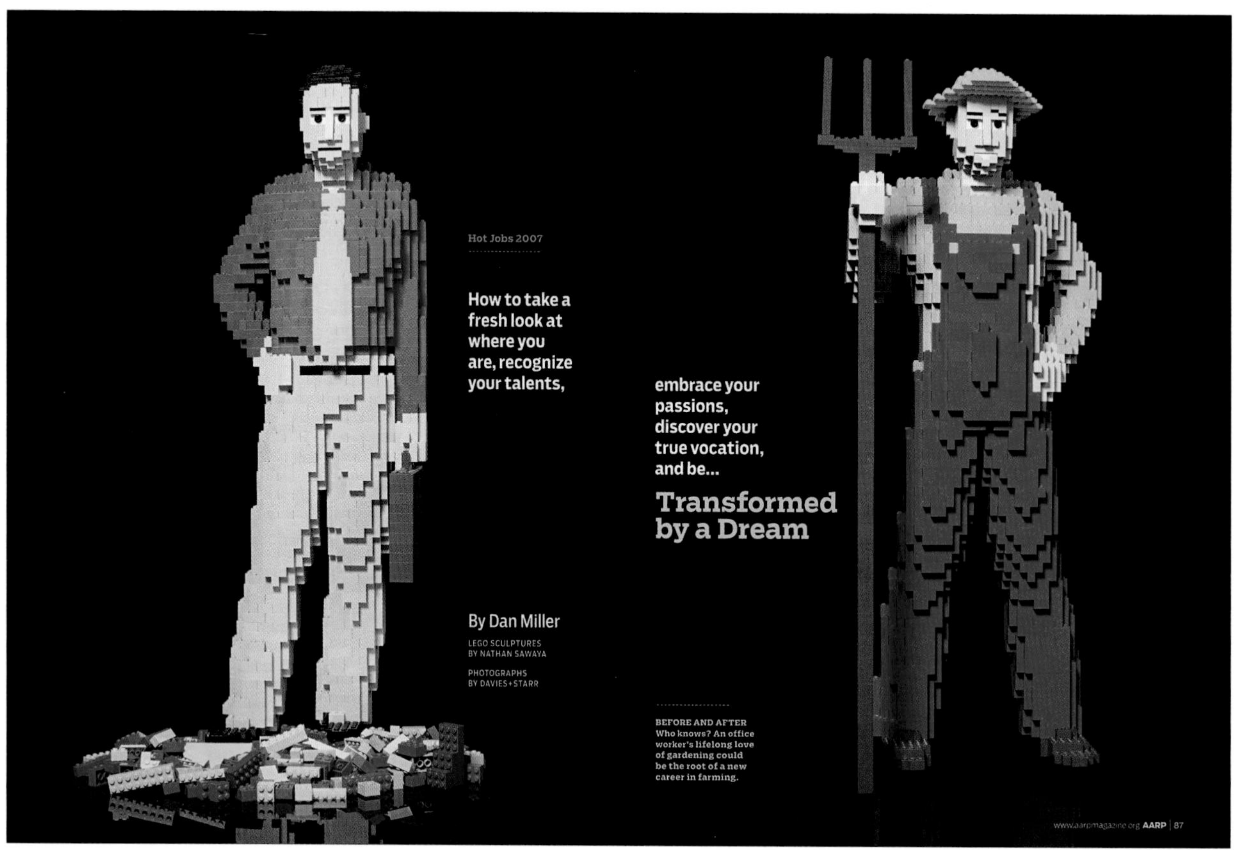

106

107

106 AARP THE MAGAZINE

Design Director_**Andrzej Janerka** Art Director_**Todd Albertson**
Designer_**Todd Albertson** Illustrator_**Nathan Sawaya**
Photographer_**Davies+Starr** Editor-In-Chief_**Steve Slon**
Publisher_**AARP Publications** Issue_**November/December 2007**
Category_**Design: Feature: Spread/Single Page**

107 DESTINASIAN

Creative Director_**Tom Brown** Art Director_**Ingrid Tedjakunmala**
Designer_**Tom Brown** Photographer_**Tony Law**
Studio_**Tom Brown Art+Design** Publisher_**DestinAsian Communications Ltd.**
Client_**DestinAsian** Issue_**December 2007/January 2008**
Category_**Design: Feature: Spread/Single Page**

108

109

108 PREMIERE

Art Director_**Rob Hewitt** Designer_**Rob Hewitt** Illustrator_**Jason Lee**
Director of Photography_**David Carthas** Photographer_**Platon**
Editor-In-Chief_**Peter Herbst** Publisher_**Hachette Filipacchi Media U.S.**
Issue_**March 2007** Category_**Design: Feature: Spread/Single Page**

109 PLAY, THE NEW YORK TIMES SPORTS MAGAZINE

Creative Director_**Janet Froelich** Art Director_**Dirk Barnett**
Designer_**Dirk Barnett** Photo Editor_**Kira Pollack**
Photographer_**Finlay MacKay** Publisher_**The New York Times**
Issue_**November 2007** Category_**Design: Feature: Spread/Single Page**

110

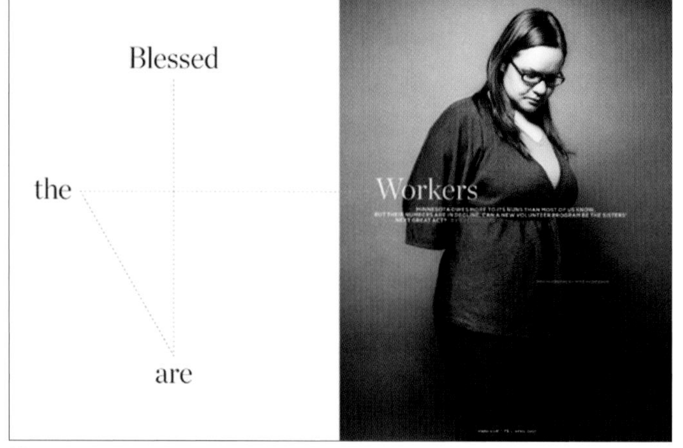

111

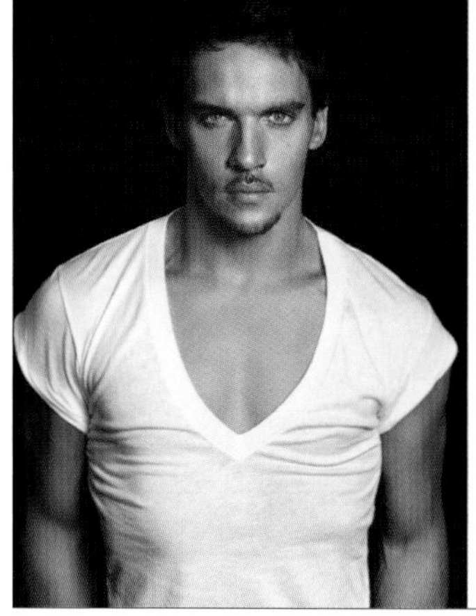

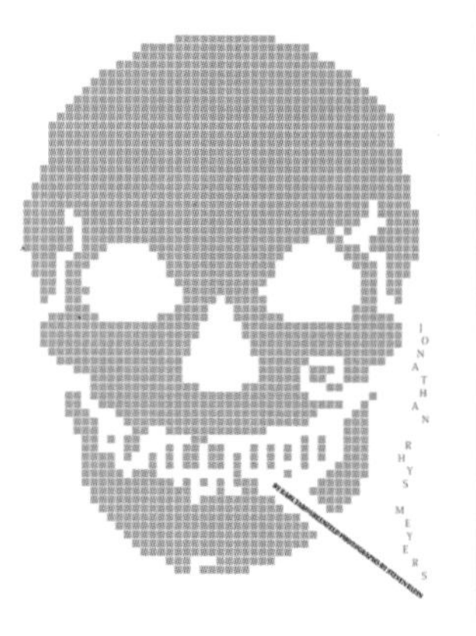

112

110 GQ

Design Director_Fred Woodward
Designer_Thomas Alberty
Director of Photography_Dora Somosi
Photo Editor_Krista Prestek
Photographer_Marc Joseph
Publisher_Condé Nast Publications Inc.
Issue_January 2007
Category_Design: Feature: Spread/Single Page

111 MINNESOTA MONTHLY

Art Director_Brian Johnson
Photographer_Mike McGregor
Publisher_Greenspring Media Group
Issue_April 2007
Category_Design: Feature: Spread/Single Page

112 DETAILS

Creative Director_Rockwell Harwood
Art Director_Andre Jointe
Designer_Rockwell Harwood
Photo Editors_Hali Tara Feldman, Alexandra Ghez, Chandra Glich Photographer_Steven Klein
Publisher_Condé Nast Publications
Issue_November 2007
Category_Design: Feature: Spread/Single Page

STICKER SHOCK

Sustainable

4.2¢ $2.64 1/2 GAL LFT MLK

6.0¢ $3.78 1/2 GAL LFT ORGNC MLK

113

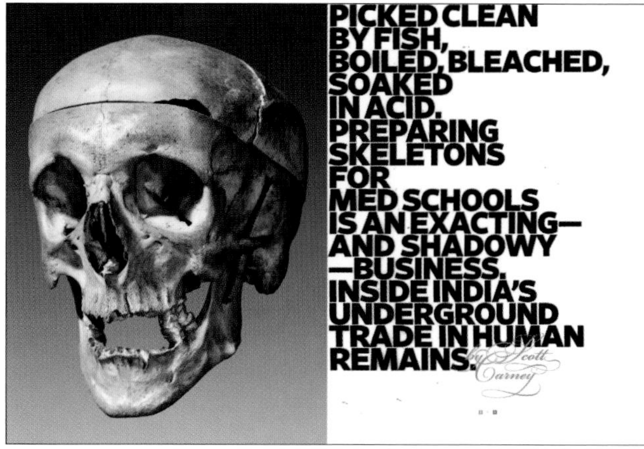

114

How do more and more professors write books at Harvard? With the help of a small army of student assistants who research, edit, and sometimes even write material for which they are never credited. Welcome to the world of celebrity academics—and the behind-the-scenes scribes who help make their fame and fortune possible.

A Million Little Writers

By Jacob Hale Russell

115

113 AMERICAN WAY

Design Director_J.R. Arebalo, Jr.
Designer_Caleb Bennett
Photographer_Pat Haverfield
Publisher_American Airlines Publishing
Issue_October 1, 2007
Category_Design: Feature: Spread/Single Page

114 WIRED

Creative Director_Scott Dadich
Design Director_Wyatt Mitchell
Designers_Scott Dadich, Victor Krummenacher
Photo Editor_Carolyn Rauch
Photographer_Rennio Maifredii
Publisher_Condé Nast Publications, Inc.
Issue_December 2007
Category_Design: Feature: Spread/Single Page

115 02138

Creative Director_Patrick Mitchell
Art Director_Susannah Haesche
Designer_Ashley Bond
Illustrator_Thomas Fuchs
Director of Photography_Katharine MacIntyre
Studio_PlutoMedia
Publisher_Atlantic Media
Issue_November/December 2007
Category_Design: Feature: Spread/Single Page

116

119

117

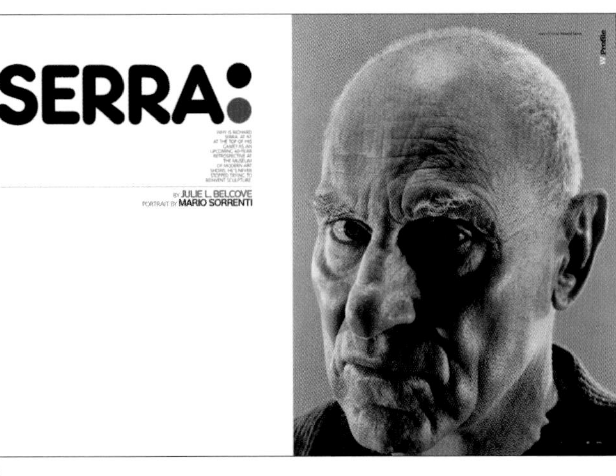

118

120

116 AMERICAN WAY

Design Director_J.R. Arebalo, Jr.
Designer_Caleb Bennett
Photographer_Daniele Dainelli
Publisher_American Airlines Publishing
Issue_April 15, 2007
Category_Design: Feature: Spread/Single Page

117 GOLF DIGEST INDEX

Design Director_Ken DeLago
Designer_Ken DeLago
Director of Photography_Matthew M. Ginella
Photo Editor_Kerry Brady
Photographer_Tom Fowlks
Issue_Spring 2007
Category_Design: Feature: Spread/Single Page

118 W

Creative Director_Dennis Freedman
Design Director_Edward Leida Art Director_Nathalie Kirsheh
Designer_Nathalie Kirsheh
Photo Editor_Nadia Vellam
Photographer_Mario Sorrenti
Publisher_Condé Nast Publications Inc.
Issue_May 2007
Category_Design: Feature: Spread/Single Page

119 OUTSIDE

Creative Director_Hannah McCaughey
Art Directors_Kate Iltis, John McCauley
Designer_Mace Fleeger
Director of Photography_Lesley Meyer
Photo Editors_Amy Feitelberg, Amber Terranova
Publisher_Mariah Media, Inc. Issue_July 2007
Category_Design: Feature: Spread/Single Page

120 BLUEPRINT

Creative Director_Eric A. Pike
Design Director_Deb Bishop
Art Director_Lisa Thé
Illustrator_Si Scott
Director of Photography_Heloise Goodman
Assistant Photo Editor_Darlene Schrack
Editor-In-Chief_Sarah Humphreys
Publisher_Martha Stewart Living Omnimedia
Issue_March/April 2007
Category_Design: Feature: Spread/Single Page

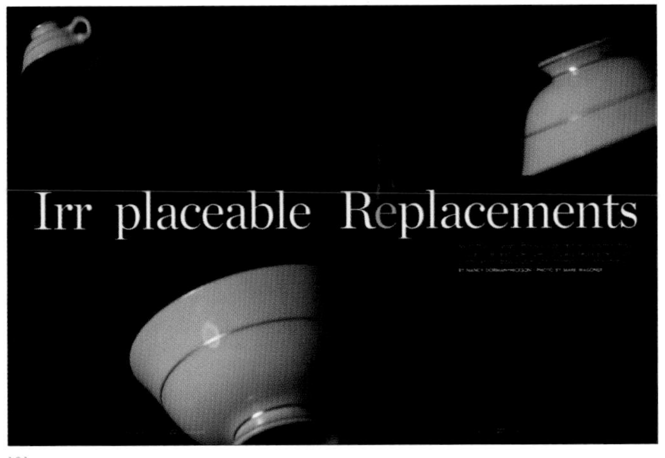

121

123

W EYE

Letter From London

The latest news from Britain's mad, mad art world.

Photograph by JENS MORTENSEN

He's like a greedy octopus, grabbing everything in his long tentacles," says a London curator about Sir Nicholas Serota, the director of the Tate and, according to *ArtReview,* the third most powerful person in the art world, after François Pinault and Larry Gagosian. Serota, who looks more like a neatly dressed asparagus than a cephalopod, was once seen as the savior of the British art scene; many now consider him a monopolist trying to make everything a subsidiary of Tate Inc. He has just announced a new venture, the Tate Channel, an online TV station serviced by the museum's own production company and sister to its publishing and education arms.

A defender retorts that Serota has no choice but to go corporate as art prices reach new heights of ridiculousness: "Nick is a strategist who realizes that public institutions can't compete with private individuals anymore." Still, artists themselves aren't always willing to be part of the big machine. At the recent opening of the Venice Biennale, Tracey Emin overlooked the fact that Culture Secretary Tessa Jowell

Asked why he collects art, one hedge fund manager said, "It impresses girls when they see big bucks on the wall."

AUGUST 2007 www.wmagazine.com

122

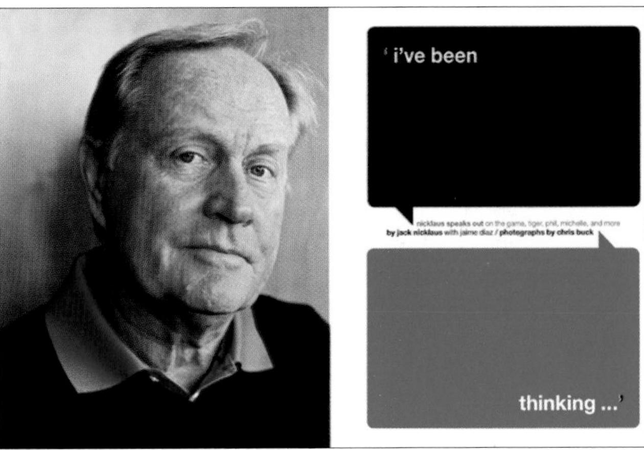

124

125

121 **GREENSBORO MONTHLY**

Art Director_Larry Williams
Photographer_Mark Wagoner
Editor-In-Chief_Lauren Rippey
Publisher_Media General
Issue_October 2007
Category_Design: Feature: Spread/Single Page

122 **W**

Design Director_Edward Leida
Art Director_Nathalie Kirsheh
Designer_Laura Konrad
Photo Editor_Nadia Vellam
Photographer_Jens Mortensen
Publisher_Condé Nast Publications Inc.
Issue_August 2007
Category_Design: Feature: Spread/Single Page

123 **W**

Creative Director_Dennis Freedman
Design Director_Edward Leida
Designer_Edward Leida
Photographer_Craig McDean
Publisher_Condé Nast Publications Inc.
Issue_December 2007
Category_Design: Feature: Spread/Single Page

124 **GOLF DIGEST**

Design Director_Ken DeLago
Designer_Ken DeLago
Director of Photography_Matthew M. Ginella
Photographer_Chris Buck
Publisher_Condé Nast Publications Inc.
Issue_March 2007
Category_Design: Feature: Spread/Single Page

125 **UD&SE**

Design Director_Torsten Hogh Rasmussen
Photographer_Asger Carlsen
Publisher_DSB
Issue_January 2007
Category_Design: Feature: Spread/Single Page

126

127

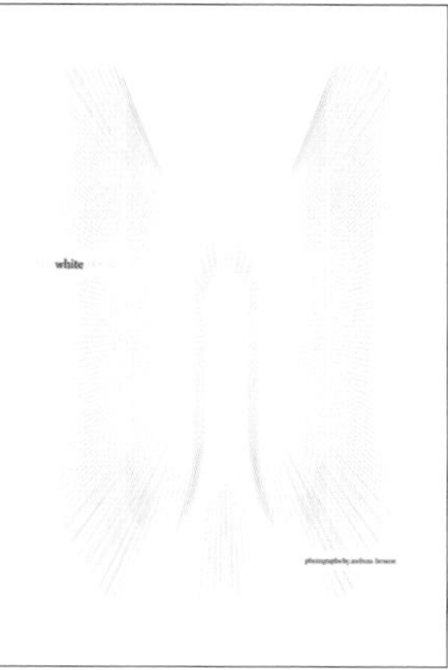

128

126 W

Creative Director_Dennis Freedman
Design Director_Edward Leida
Designer_Edward Leida
Artist_Doug Aitken
Publisher_Condé Nast Publications Inc.
Issue_January 2007
Category_Design: Feature: Spread/Single Page

127 02138

Creative Director_Patrick Mitchell
Art Director_Susannah Haesche
Designer_Ashley Bond
Director of Photography_Katharine MacIntyre
Photographer_Catherine Ledner
Studio_PlutoMedia
Publisher_Atlantic Media
Issue_November/December 2007
Category_Design: Feature: Spread/Single Page

128 DETAILS

Creative Director_Rockwell Harwood
Art Director_Andre Jointe
Designer_Robert Vargas
Photo Editors_Hali Tara Feldman, Alexandra Ghez, Chandra Glich
Photographer_Andreas Larsson
Publisher_Condé Nast Publications
Issue_June/July 2007
Category_Design: Feature: Spread/Single Page

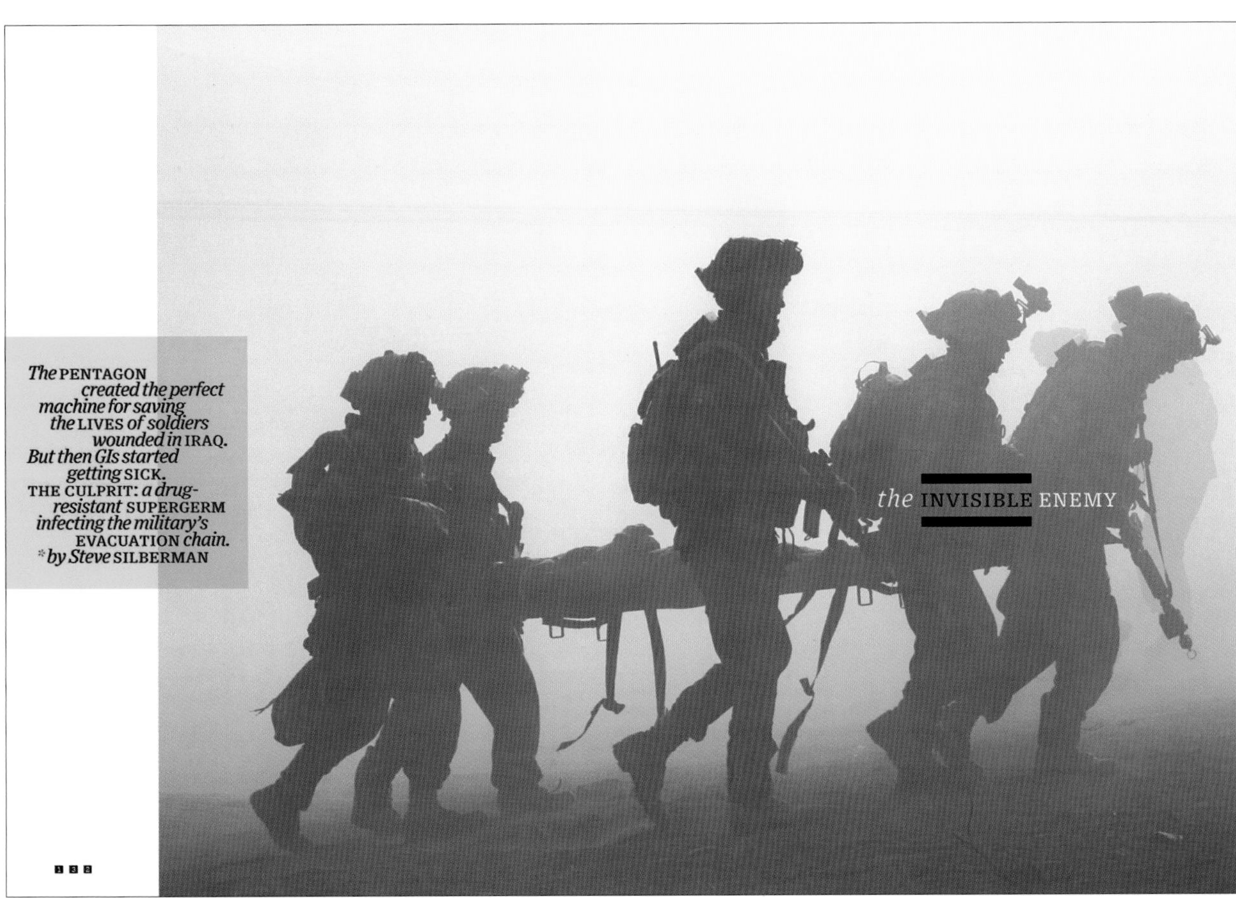

The PENTAGON created the perfect machine for saving the LIVES of soldiers wounded in IRAQ. But then GIs started getting SICK. THE CULPRIT: a drug-resistant SUPERGERM infecting the military's EVACUATION chain.
by Steve SILBERMAN
the INVISIBLE ENEMY

129

130

131

129 WIRED

Creative Director_Scott Dadich
Art Director_Jeremy LaCroix
Designers_Jeremy LaCroix, Scott Dadich
Illustrators_ILM, Ryan Jones, Alex Jaeger, Rick O'Connor, Ron Woodall
Photo Editor_Zana Woods
Publisher_Condé Nast Publications, Inc.
Issue_February 2007
Category_Design: Feature: Spread/Single Page

130 W

Creative Director_Dennis Freedman
Design Director_Edward Leida
Designer_Edward Leida
Photographer_Mario Sorrenti
Publisher_Condé Nast Publications Inc.
Issue_May 2007
Category_Design: Feature: Spread/Single Page

131 PREMIERE

Art Director_Rob Hewitt
Designer_Rob Hewitt
Director of Photography_David Carthas
Photographer_Martin Schoeller
Editor-In-Chief_Peter Herbst
Publisher_Hachette Filipacchi Media U.S.
Issue_April 2007
Category_Design: Feature: Spread/Single Page

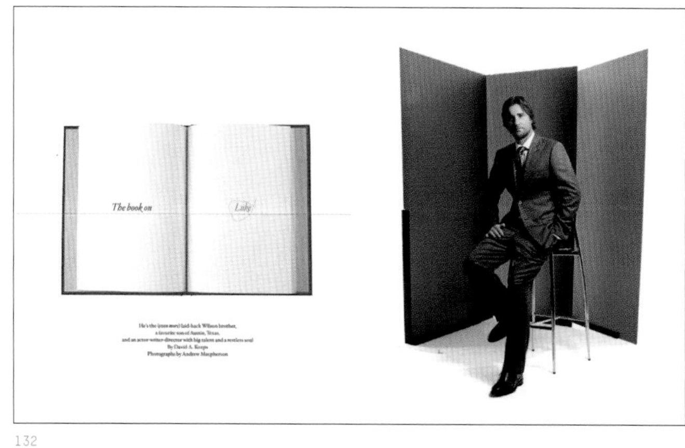

132

135

133

136

134

137

132 BEST LIFE

Art Director_Brandon Kavulla
Designer_Brandon Kavulla
Director of Photography_Ryan Cadiz
Photographer_Andrew Macpherson
Publisher_Rodale
Issue_May 2007
Category_Design: Feature: Spread/Single Page

133 GOLF DIGEST INDEX

Design Director_Ken DeLago
Designer_Ken DeLago
Director of Photography_Matthew M. Ginella
Photo Editor_Kerry Brady
Photographer_Dom Furore
Issue_Spring 2007
Category_Design: Feature: Spread/Single Page

134 W

Creative Director_Dennis Freedman
Design Director_Edward Leida
Art Director_Nathalie Kirsheh
Designer_Nathalie Kirsheh
Photo Editor_Nadia Vellam
Photographer_Hannah Starkey
Publisher_Condé Nast Publications Inc.
Issue_June 2007
Category_Design: Feature: Spread/Single Page

135 TEXAS MONTHLY

Art Director_T.J. Tucker
Designers_Andi Beierman, Rachel Wyatt
Photo Editor_Leslie Baldwin
Photographer_Dan Winters
Publisher_Emmis Communications Corp.
Issue_June 2007
Category_Design: Feature: Spread/Single Page

136 AMERICAN AIRLINES NEXOS

Design Director_Marco Rosales
Designer_Marco Rosales
Photographer_Patrick Price
Publisher_American Airlines Publishing
Issue_February 1, 2007
Category Design: Feature: Spread/Single Page

137 DESTINASIAN

Creative Director_Tom Brown
Art Director_Ingrid Tedjakunmala
Designer_Tom Brown
Photographer_Frédéric Lagrange
Studio_Tom Brown Art+Design
Publisher_DestinAsian Communications Ltd.
Client_DestinAsian
Issue_April/May 2007
Category_Design: Feature: Spread/Single Page

138

141

139

142

140

143

138 BYU MAGAZINE

Creative Director_David Eliason Art Director_Bruce Patrick Designer_John Petersen Illustrator_Edel Rodriguez Publisher_Brigham Young University Issue_January 2007 Category_Design: Feature: Spread/Single Page

139 AMERICAN WAY

Design Director_J.R. Arebalo, Jr.
Art Director_J.R. Arebalo, Jr.
Photographer_Sean McCormick
Publisher_American Airlines Publishing
Issue_November 15, 2007
Category_Design: Feature: Spread/Single Page

140 ESPN THE MAGAZINE

Creative Director_Siung Tjia
Designer_Jason Lancaster
Director of Photography_Catriona Ni Aolain
Photo Editor_Julie Claire
Publisher_ESPN, Inc.
Issue_August 27, 2007
Category_Design: Feature: Spread/Single Page

141 TEXAS MONTHLY

Art Director_T.J. Tucker
Designers_Andi Beierman, Rachel Wyatt
Illustrator_Robert Risko
Publisher_Emmis Communications Corp.
Issue_April 2007
Category_Design: Feature: Spread/Single Page

142 EARNSHAW'S MAGAZINE

Creative Director_Nancy Campbell
Art Director_Trevett McCandliss
Designer_Trevett McCandliss
Photographer_Colin Clark
Issue_September 2007
Category_Design: Feature: Spread/Single Page

143 AMERICAN WAY

Design Director_J.R. Arebalo, Jr.
Art Director_Samuel Solomon
Photographers_Sean McCormick, Pat Haverfield
Publisher_American Airlines Publishing
Issue_November 15, 2007
Category_Design: Feature: Spread/Single Page

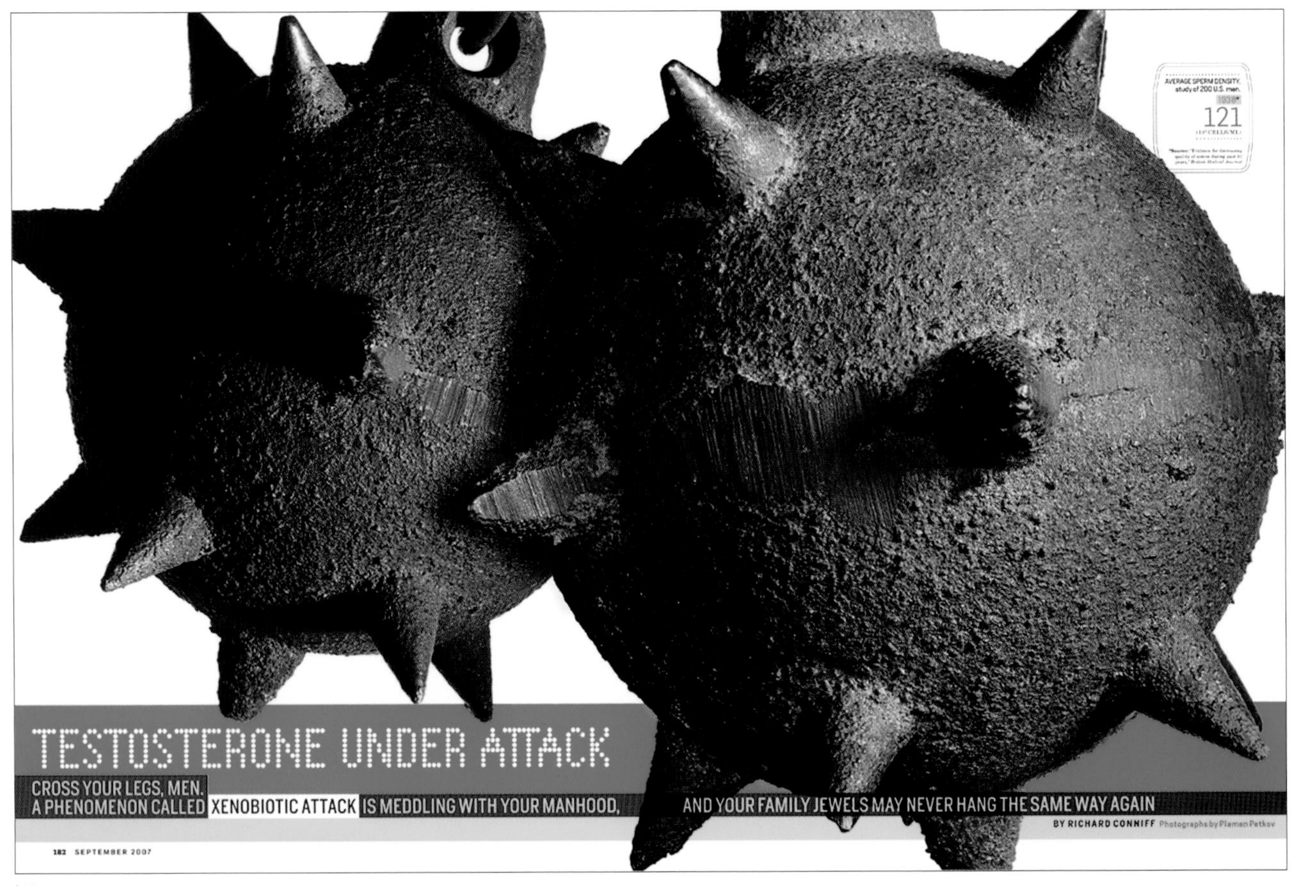

144

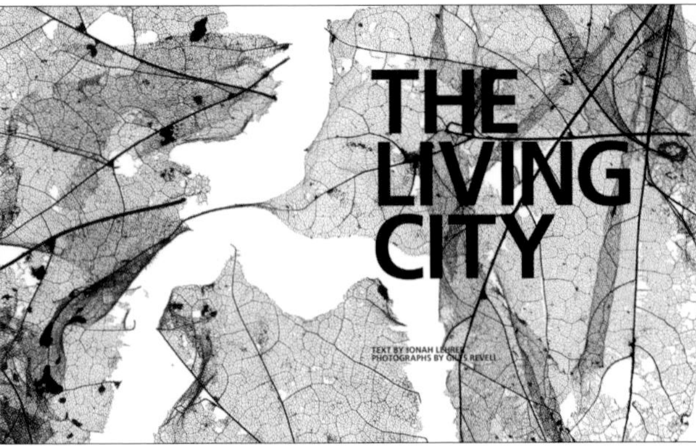

145

146

144 MEN'S HEALTH

Design Director_George Karabotsos Art Director_John Dixon
Designers_John Dixon, Elizabeth Neal Illustrator_ Lee Woodgate
Director of Photography_Laurie Kratochvil Photo Editor_Brenda Milis
Photographer_Plamen Petkov Publisher_Rodale Inc.
Issue_September 2007 Category_Design: Feature: Spread/Single Page

145 SEED

Art Director_Adam Billyeald Photographer_Giles Revell
Editor-In-Chief_Adam Bly Publisher_Seed Media Group
Issue August 2007 Category Design: Feature: Story

146 PLAY, THE NEW YORK TIMES SPORTS MAGAZINE

Creative Director_Janet Froelich Art Director_Dirk Barnett
Designer_Dirk Barnett Photo Editor_Kira Pollack
Photographer_Finlay MacKay Publisher_The New York Times
Issue_September 2007 Category_Design: Feature: Spread/Single Page

ENCHANTED
Creatures

With their spellbinding details, pins and other insect-motif jewelry are wearable collector's items.

If you have ever been captivated by a butterfly alighting on a thistle or a ladybug meandering along a garden wall, chances are you will adore insect jewelry. The playful pieces allow you to delight in nature's beauty—a dragonfly's diaphanous wings, a grasshopper's attenuate legs—without anything buzzing or crawling. Yet these bugs are imbued with vibrancy and personality, as if they were really alive.

These are several of the traits that prompted Nancy Heckler, a *Martha Stewart Living* contributing editor, to start amassing insect brooches thirty years ago. "I'm drawn to the whimsical quality of these pins," says Heckler, who displays the creatures on framed velvet panels in her bedroom and

PHOTOGRAPHS BY ANITA CALERO
TEXT BY JILL GERSTON

winged beauties
THIS PAGE: Graceful dragonfly pins come in myriad materials, including silver, horn, enamel, mother-of-pearl, brass, tigereye, clear and amber plastic, and green Bakelite. OPPOSITE: Grasshoppers are among the most sought-after insect art, whether they are made of smooth or etched silver or studded with rhinestones.

147

148

Child's Play

Traveling with the little tax deductions? Keeping them occupied is a breeze – we kid you not.

By Tracy Staton | Illustration by Headcase Design

149

147 MARTHA STEWART LIVING

Creative Director_**Eric A. Pike** Design Director_**James Dunlinson** Art Director_**Amber Blakesley** Designer_**Kevin Brainard** Director of Photography_**Heloise Goodman** Photographer_**Anita Calero** Stylist_**Fritz Karch** Editor-In-Chief_**Margaret Roach** Publisher_**Martha Stewart Living Omnimedia** Issue_**March 2007** Category_**Design: Feature: Spread/Single Page**

148 ATLANTA MAGAZINE

Design Director_**Hector Sanchez** Art Director_**Eric Capossela** Designer_**Eric Capossela** Photographer_**Peter Yang** Publisher_**Emmis** Issue_**April 2007** Category_**Design: Feature: Spread/Single Page**

149 AMERICAN WAY

Design Director_**J.R. Arebalo, Jr.** Art Director_**Samuel Solomon** Illustrator_**Headcase Design** Publisher_**American Airlines Publishing** Issue_**July 15, 2007** Category_**Design: Feature: Spread/Single Page**

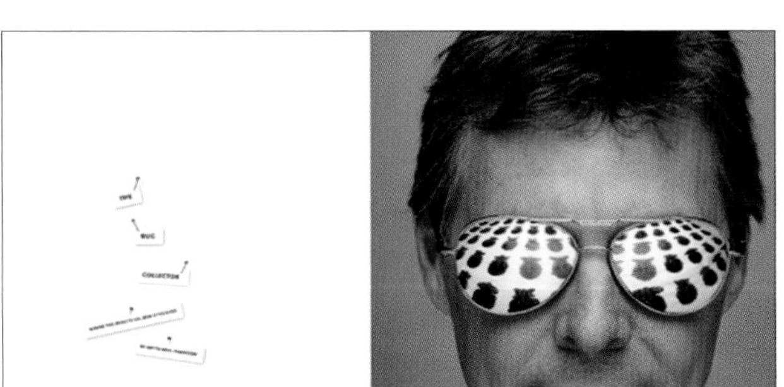

150

153

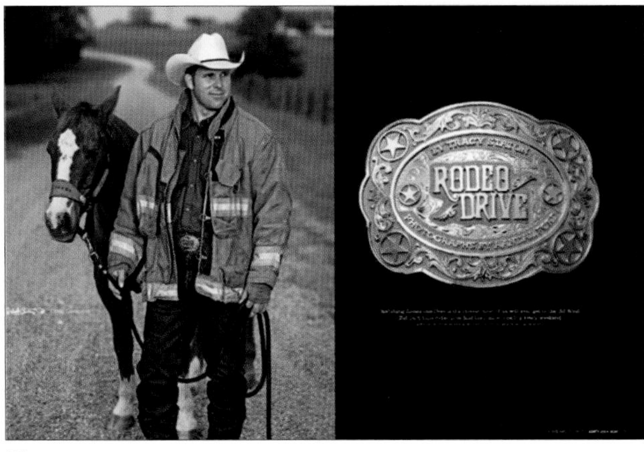

151

154

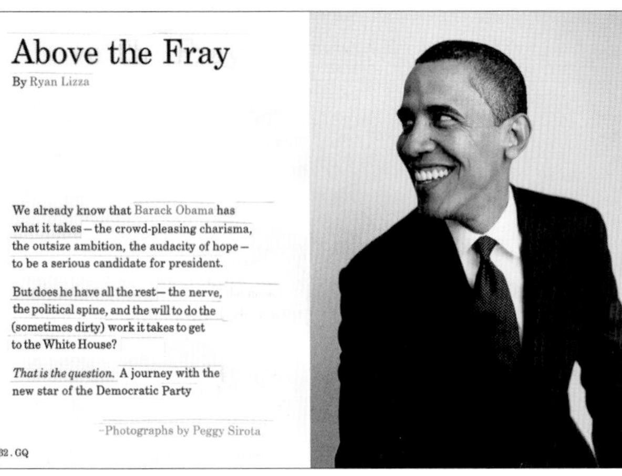

Above the Fray

By Ryan Lizza

We already know that Barack Obama has what it takes—the crowd-pleasing charisma, the outsize ambition, the audacity of hope—to be a serious candidate for president.

But does he have all the rest—the nerve, the political spine, and the will to do the (sometimes dirty) work it takes to get to the White House?

That is the question. A journey with the new star of the Democratic Party

—Photographs by Peggy Sirota

332. GQ

152

Gone Flat

When a trio of would-be corporate spies tried to steal secrets from Coca-Cola, their caper fizzled out fast.

BY CAROLINE WILBERT

155

150 ILLUMINATION

Art Director_**Blake Dinsdale**
Designer_**Blake Dinsdale**
Photographer_**Rob Hill**
Editor-In-Chief_**Charles Reineke**
Publisher_**University of Missouri**
Issue_**Fall 2007**
Category_**Design: Feature: Spread/Single Page**

151 AMERICAN WAY

Design Director_**J.R. Arebalo, Jr.**
Designer_**Caleb Bennett**
Photographers_**Randal Ford, Pat Haverfield**
Publisher_**American Airlines Publishing**
Issue_**February 15, 2007**
Category_**Design: Feature: Spread/Single Page**

152 GQ

Design Director_**Fred Woodward**
Designer_**Chelsea Cardinal**
Director of Photography_**Dora Somosi**
Photographer_**Peggy Sirota**
Publisher_**Condé Nast Publications Inc.**
Issue_**September 2007**
Category_**Design: Feature: Spread/Single Page**

153 MARTHA STEWART LIVING

Creative Director_**Eric A. Pike**
Design Director_**James Dunlinson**
Art Director_**Matthew Axe**
Designers_**Matthew Axe, Lillian Hough**
Director of Photography_**Heloise Goodman**
Associate Photo Editor_**Joni Noe**
Photographer_**Pieter Estersohn**
Stylist_**Edward Ross**
Publisher_**Martha Stewart Living Omnimedia**
Issue_**January 2007**
Category_**Design: Feature: Spread/Single Page**

154 W

Creative Director_**Dennis Freedman**
Design Director_**Edward Leida**
Designer_**Edward Leida**
Photographer_**Steven Klein**
Publisher_**Condé Nast Publications Inc.**
Issue_**August 2007**
Category_**Design: Feature: Spread/Single Page**

155 ATLANTA MAGAZINE

Design Director_**Hector Sanchez**
Designer_**Hector Sanchez**
Photographer_**Norman A. Schwartz**
Digital Imaging **Scott Klingsoehr**
Publisher_**Emmis**
Issue_**January 2007**
Category_**Design: Feature: Spread/Single Page**

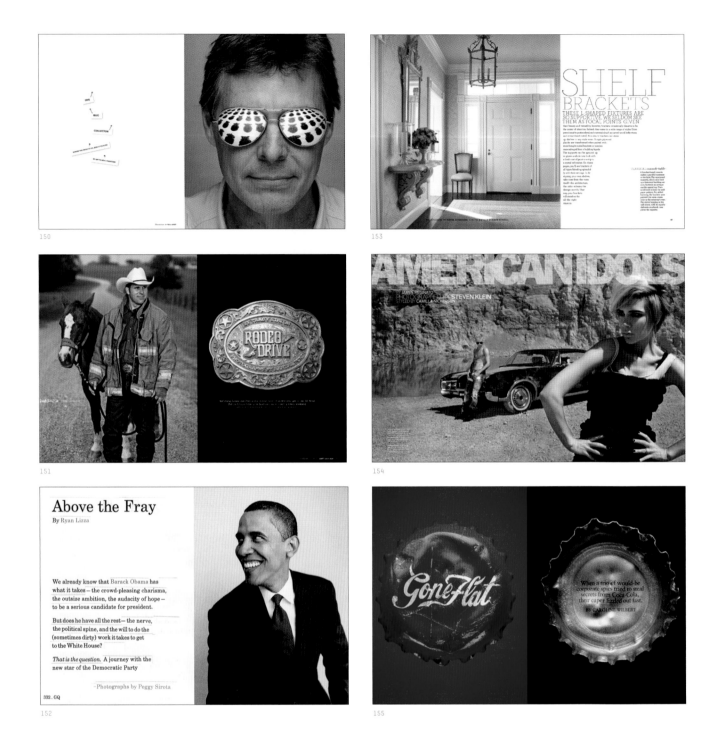

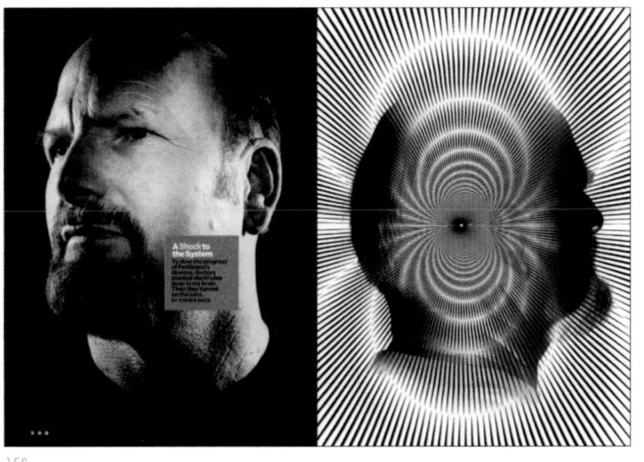

156

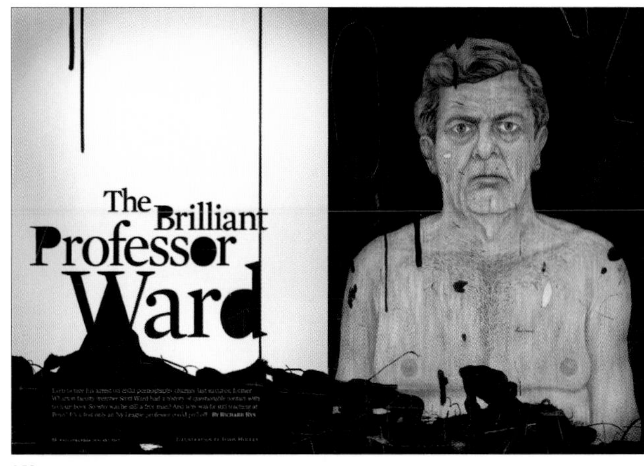

159

157

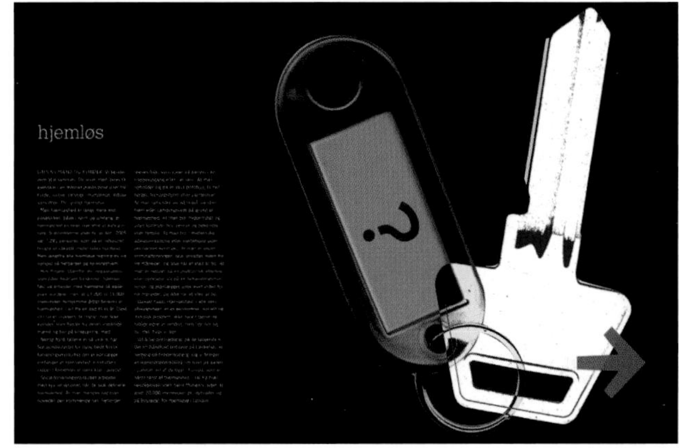

160

158

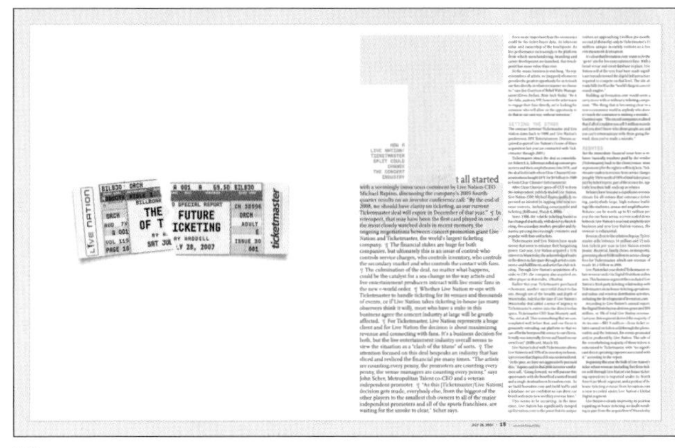

161

156 WIRED

Creative Director_Scott Dadich
Designers_Maili Holiman, Jason Schulte
Photo Editor_Carolyn Rauch
Photographer_Frank W. Ockenfels 3
Publisher_Condé Nast Publications, Inc.
Issue_March 2007
Category_Design: Feature: Spread/Single Page

157 UD&SE

Design Director_Torsten Hogh Rasmussen
Illustrator_Anders Hulgaard
Publisher_DSB Issue_October 2007
Category_Design: Feature: Spread/Single Page

158 CORPORATE LEADER

Creative Director_Florian Bachleda
Photographer_Ian Spanier
Studio_FB Design
Publisher_Doubledown Media
Issue_Premiere
Category_Design: Feature: Spread/Single Page

159 PHILADELPHIA

Design Director_Michael McCormick
Art Director_Andrew Zahn
Designer_Andrew Zahn
Illustrator_Jason Holley
Publisher_Metrocorp Publishing
Issue_January 2007
Category_Design: Feature: Spread/Single Page

160 UD&SE

Design Director_Katinka Bukh
Illustrator_Katinka Bukh
Publisher_DSB Issue_April 2007
Category_Design: Feature: Spread/Single Page

161 BILLBOARD

Creative Director_Josh Klenert
Art Director_Christine Bower
Designer_Greg Grabowy
Photo Editor_Amelia Halverson
Publisher_Nielsen Business Media
Issue_July 28, 2007
Category_Design: Feature: Spread/Single Page

If you don't like the way Dubai looks today, wait a year or two—it's changing fast. Here's a selection of upcoming projects likely to have a big impact on the horizon.

SKYLINE OF TOMORROW

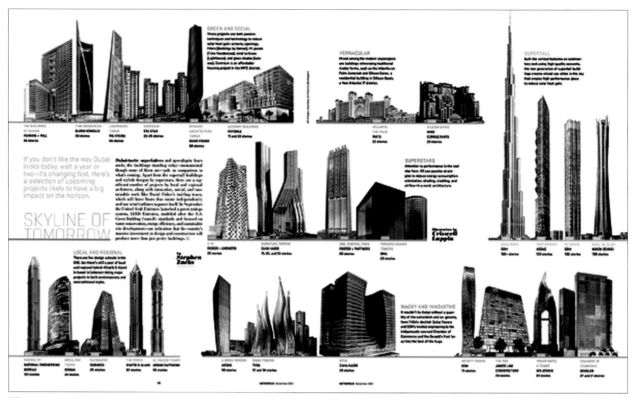

162

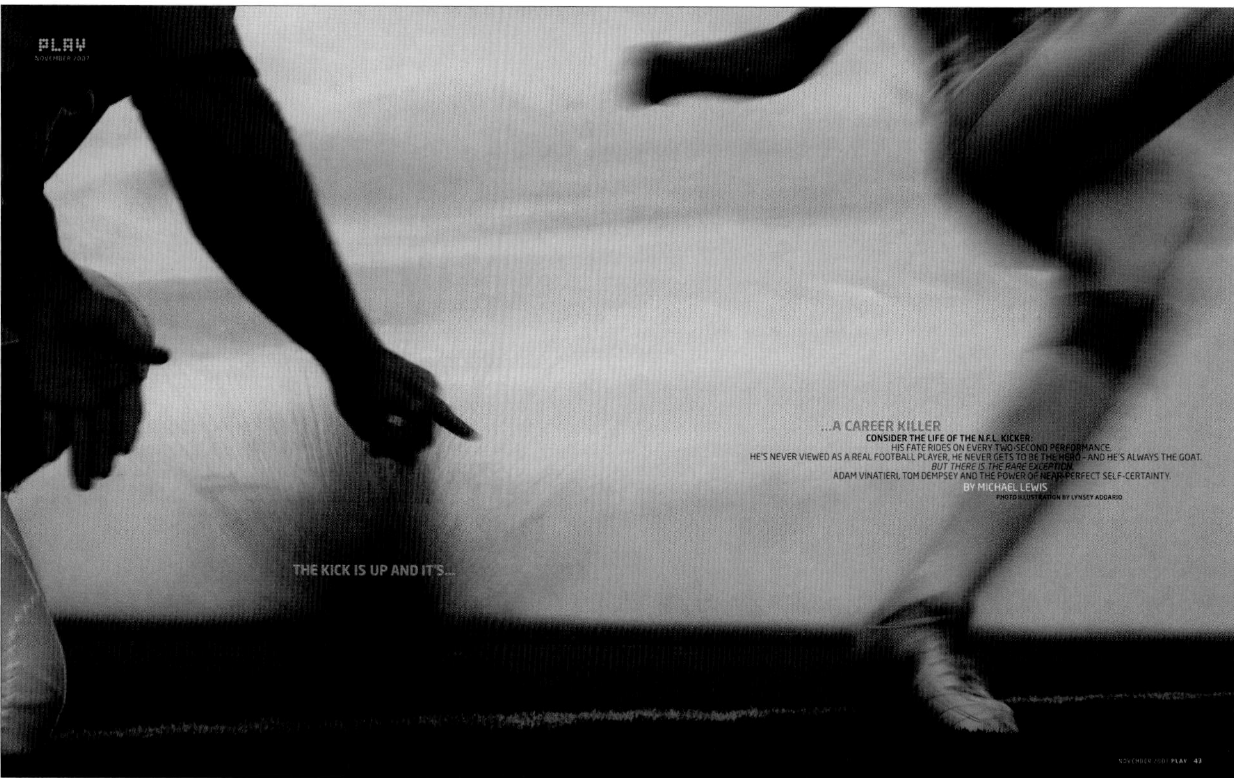

163

162 METROPOLIS

Creative Director_Criswell Lappin
Art Director_Dungjai Pungauthaikan Photo Editor_Bilyana Dimitrova
Publisher_Bellerophon Publications Issue_November 2007
Category_Design: Feature: Spread/Single Page

163 PLAY, THE NEW YORK TIMES SPORTS MAGAZINE

Creative Director_Janet Froelich Art Director_Dirk Barnett
Designer_Dirk Barnett Photo Editor_Kira Pollack
Photographer_Lynsey Addario Publisher_The New York Times
Issue_November 2007 Category_Design: Feature: Spread/Single Page

164

165

164 **GQ**

Design Director_**Fred Woodward** Designer_**Drue Wagner**
Director of Photography_**Dora Somosi** Photographer_**Terry Richardson**
Publisher_**Condé Nast Publications Inc.** Issue_**May 2007**
Category_**Design: Feature: Spread/Single Page**

165 **BLUEPRINT**

Creative Director_**Eric A. Pike** Design Director_**Deb Bishop**
Art Director_**Lisa Thé** Designer_**Lisa Thé**
Director of Photography_**Heloise Goodman**
Assistant Photo Editor_**Darlene Schrack** Photographer_**Johnny Miller**
Editor-In-Chief_**Sarah Humphreys** Publisher_**Martha Stewart Living Omnimedia** Issue_**May/June 2007**
Category_**Design: Feature: Spread/Single Page**

166

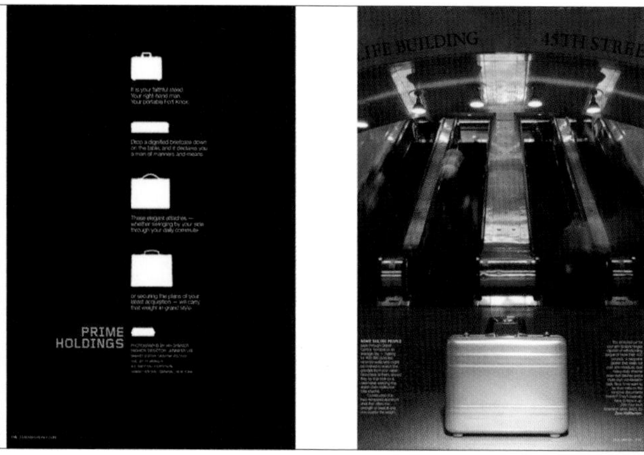

167

169

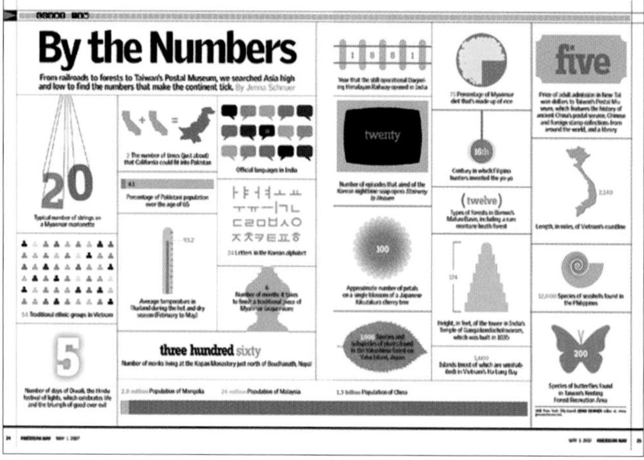

168

170

166 W

Creative Director_Dennis Freedman
Design Director_Edward Leida
Designer_Edward Leida
Photographer_David Sims
Publisher_Condé Nast Publications Inc.
Issue_October 2007
Category_Design: Feature: Spread/Single Page

167 DEALMAKER

Creative Director_Florian Bachleda
Photographer_Ian Spanier
Fashion Director_Jennifer Lee
Studio_FB Design
Publisher_Doubledown Media
Issue_March/April 2007
Category_Design: Feature: Story

168 AMERICAN WAY

Design Director_J.R. Arebalo, Jr.
Art Director_Samuel Solomon
Publisher_American Airlines Publishing
Issue_May 1, 2007
Category_Design: Feature: Spread/Single Page

169 BLUEPRINT

Creative Director_Eric A. Pike
Design Director_Deb Bishop
Designer_Deb Bishop
Director of Photography_Heloise Goodman
Photographer_Johnny Miller
Senior Photo Editor_Mary Cahill
Editor-In-Chief_Sarah Humphreys
Publisher_Martha Stewart Living Omnimedia
Issue_November/December 2007
Category_Design: Feature: Spread/Single Page

170 WIRED

Creative Director_Scott Dadich
Design Director_Wyatt Mitchell
Designer_Scott Dadich
Illustrators_ILM, Ryan Jones, Alex Jaeger, Rick O'Connor, Ron Woodall
Photo Editor_Carolyn Rauch
Photographer_Alessandra Petlin
Publisher_Condé Nast Publications, Inc.
Issue_November 2007
Category_Design: Feature: Spread/Single Page

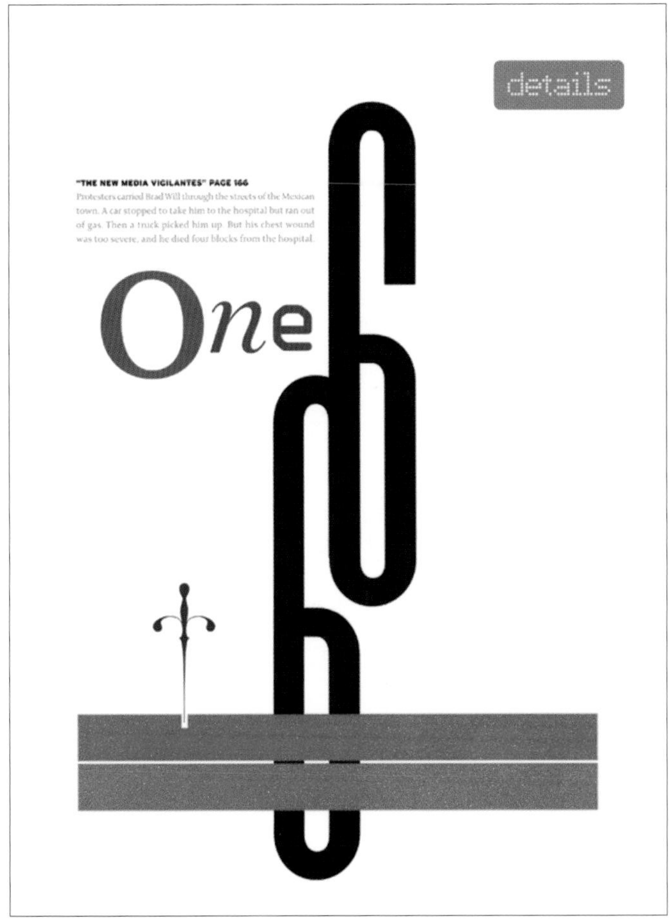

171

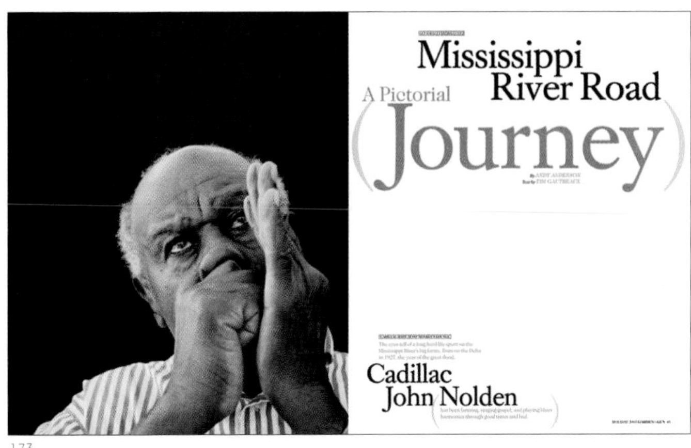

173

174

172

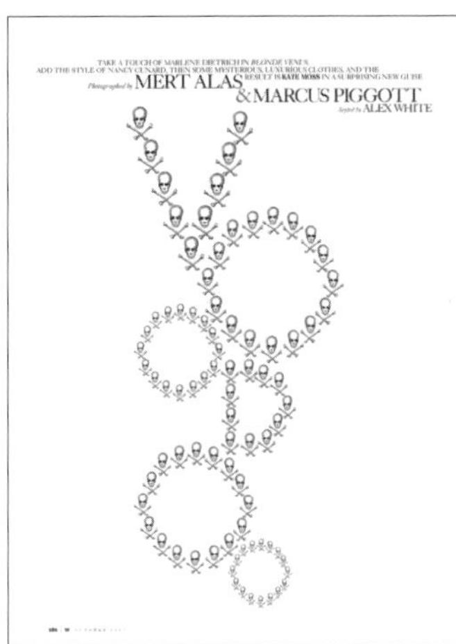

175

171 DETAILS

Creative Director_Rockwell Harwood
Art Director_Andre Jointe
Designer_Rockwell Harwood
Publisher_Condé Nast Publications
Issue_November 2007
Category_Design: Feature: Spread/Single Page

172 GQ

Design Director_Fred Woodward
Designer_Thomas Alberty
Director of Photography_Dora Somosi
Photographer_Nathaniel Goldberg
Publisher_Condé Nast Publications Inc.
Issue_November 2007
Category_Design: Feature: Spread/Single Page

173 GARDEN & GUN

Art Director_Rob Hewitt
Photographer_Andy Anderson
Photography Editor_Maggie Brett Kennedy
Publisher_Event Post Publishing Company
Issue_Holiday 2007
Category_Design: Feature: Spread/Single Page

174 OUTSIDE

Creative Director_Hannah McCaughey
Art Directors_Kate Iltis, John McCauley
Designer_Mace Fleeger
Director of Photography_Lesley Meyer
Photo Editors_Amy Feitelberg, Amber Terranova
Photographer_Philipp Engelhorn
Publisher_Mariah Media, Inc.
Issue_May 2007
Category_Design: Feature: Spread/Single Page

175 W

Creative Director_Dennis Freedman
Design Director_Edward Leida
Art Director_Nathalie Kirsheh
Designer_Edward Leida
Photographers_Mert Alas, Marcus Piggott
Publisher_Condé Nast Publications Inc.
Issue_October 2007
Category_Design: Feature: Spread/Single Page

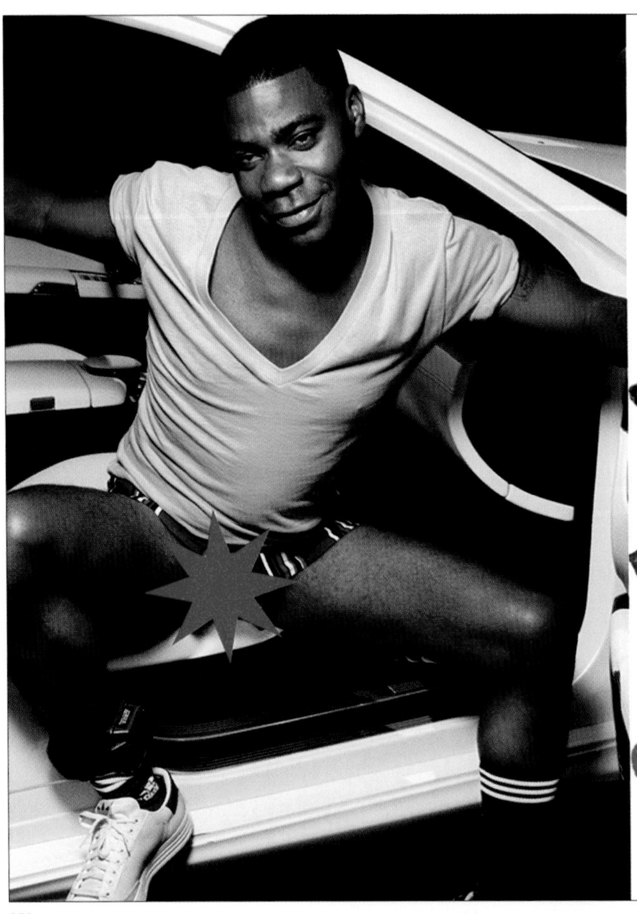

176

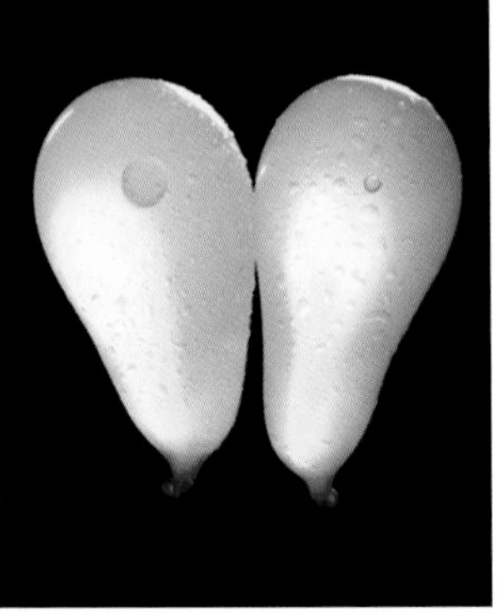

177

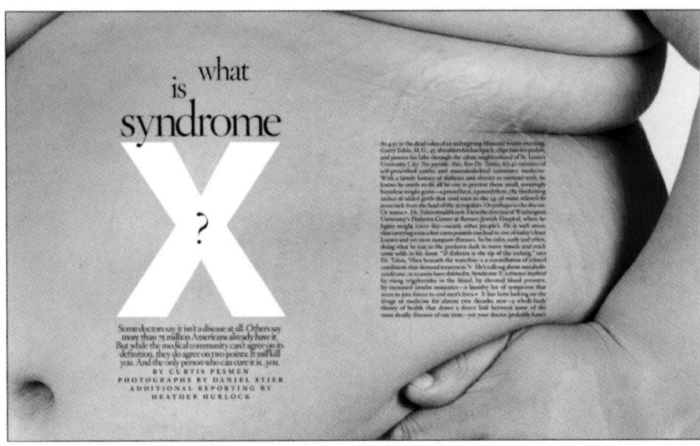

178

176 GQ

Design Director_Fred Woodward Designer_Drue Wagner
Director of Photography_Dora Somosi Photographer_Mark Seliger
Publisher_Condé Nast Publications Inc. Issue_September 2007
Category_Design: Feature: Spread/Single Page

177 COOKIE

Design Director_Kirby Rodriguez Art Director_Alex Grossman
Designers_Shanna Greenberg, Nicolette Berthelot
Photo Editor_Darrick Harris Assistant Photo Editor_Rebecca Ettel
Photographer_Horacio Salinas Editor-In-Chief_Pilar Guzmán
Publisher_Condé Nast Publications Inc. Issue_July/August 2007
Category_Design: Entire Issue

178 BEST LIFE

Art Director_Brandon Kavulla Designer_Heather Jones
Director of Photography_Ryan Cadiz
Photographer_Daniel Srier Publisher_Rodale
Issue_March 2007 Category_Design: Feature: Spread/Single Page

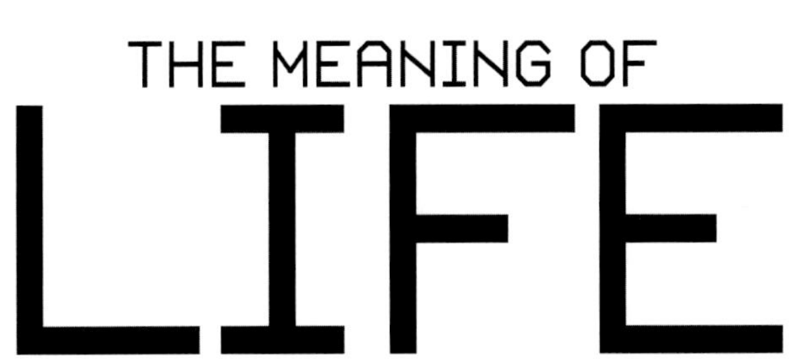

WE CREATE LIFE, WE SEARCH FOR IT, WE MANIPULATE AND REVERE IT.
IS IT POSSIBLE THAT WE HAVEN'T YET DEFINED THE TERM?

Written by Carl Zimmer *Generative Art by Jared Tarbell*

SEED · *July/August 2007* WWW.SEEDMAGAZINE.COM

179

180

181

179 SEED

Art Director_**Adam Billyeald** Designer_**Jared Tarbell**
Editor-In-Chief_**Adam Bly** Publisher Seed_**Media Group**
Issue_**August 2007** Category_**Design: Feature: Story**

180 ATLANTA MAGAZINE

Design Director_**Hector Sanchez** Art Director_**Eric Capossela**
Designer_**Eric Capossela** Publisher_**Emmis**
Issue_**February 2007** Category_**Design: Feature: Spread/Single Page**

181 02138

Creative Director_**Patrick Mitchell** Art Director_**Susannah Haesche**
Director of Photography_**Katharine MacIntyre**
Studio_**PlutoMedia** Publisher_**Atlantic Media** Issue_**Spring 2007**
Category_**Design: Feature: Spread/Single Page**

182

185

183

The New York Times Magazine / DECEMBER 9, 2007

THE 7TH ANNUAL YEAR IN IDEAS

186

184

182 AMERICAN WAY

Design Director_J.R. Arebalo, Jr.
Art Director_Carrie Olivier
Photographer_Justin Stephens
Publisher_American Airlines Publishing
Issue_September 15, 2007
Category_Design: Feature: Spread/Single Page

183 PRIVATE AIR

Creative Director_Florian Bachleda
Art Director_Clare Minges
Photographer_Jimmy Nicol
Studio_FB Design
Publisher_Doubledown Media
Issue_August/September 2007
Category_Design: Feature: Spread/Single Page

184 AMERICAN AIRLINES NEXOS

Design Director_Marco Rosales
Designer_Marco Rosales
Photographer_Kikor
Publisher_American Airlines Publishing
Issue_December 1, 2007
Category_Design: Feature: Spread/Single Page

185 STANFORD MAGAZINE

Art Director_Mairéad Liberace
Designer_Mairéad Liberace
Illustrator_Andy Potts
Publisher_Stanford University
Issue_January/February 2007
Category_Design: Feature: Spread/Single Page

186 THE NEW YORK TIMES MAGAZINE

Creative Director_Janet Froelich
Art Director_Arem Duplessis
Designer_Gail Bichler
Director of Photography_Kathy Ryan
Photo Editor_Joanna Milter
Photographer_Jens Mortensen
Lettering_Carin Goldberg
Editor-In-Chief_Gerry Marzorati
Publisher_The New York Times
Issue_December 9, 2007
Category_Design: Feature: Spread/Single Page

187

189

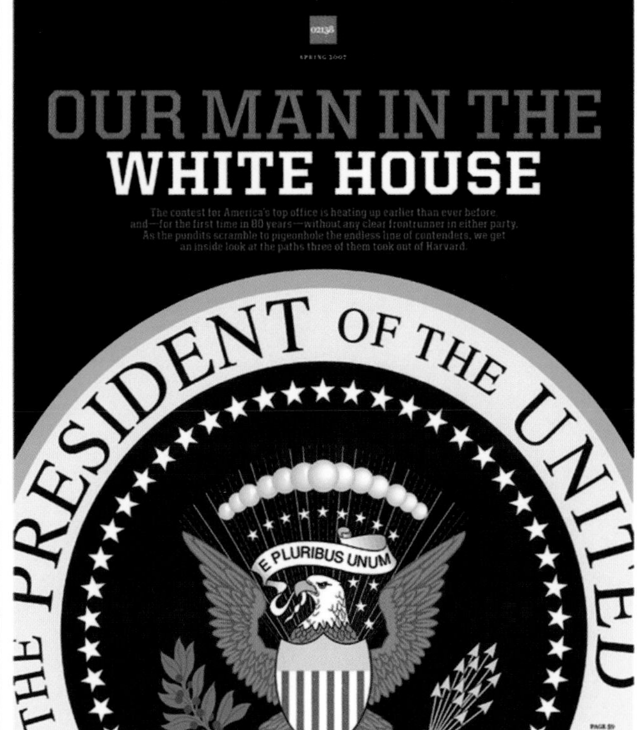

188

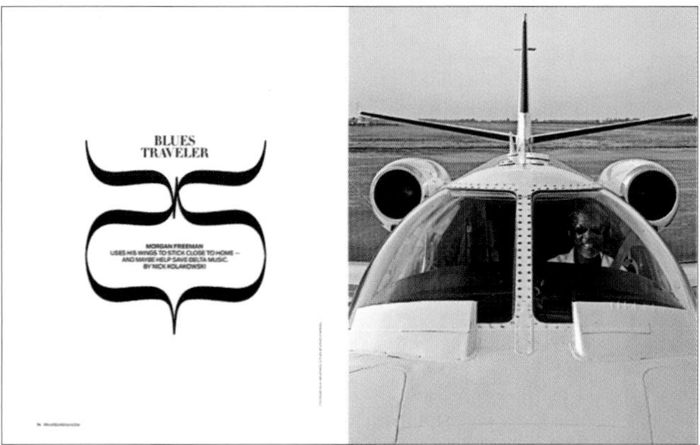

190

191

187 BICYCLING

Design Director_David Speranza
Designer_David Speranza
Director of Photography_Stacey Emenecker
Photographer_Mitch Mandel
Publisher_Rodale, Inc.
Issue_October 2007
Category_Design: Feature: Spread/Single Page

188 02138

Creative Director_Patrick Mitchell
Art Director_Susannah Haesche
Director of Photography_Katharine MacIntyre
Studio_PlutoMedia
Publisher_Atlantic Media
Issue_Spring 2007
Category_Design: Feature: Spread/Single Page

189 HEMISPHERES

Design Director_Jaimey Easler
Art Director_Jennifer Swafford
Designer_Jaimey Easler
Photographer_Adam Voorhes
Senior Art Director_Jody Mustain
Publisher_Pace Communications
Client_United Airlines
Issue_July 2007
Category_Design: Feature: Spread/Single Page

190 PRIVATE AIR

Creative Director_Florian Bachleda
Photographer_Ian Spanier
Studio_FB Design
Publisher_Doubledown Media
Issue_August/September 2007
Category_Design: Feature: Spread/Single Page

191 AMERICAN WAY

Design Director_J.R. Arebalo, Jr.
Art Director_Carrie Olivier
Photographer_Steve Moors
Publisher_American Airlines Publishing
Issue_July 1, 2007
Category_Design: Feature: Spread/Single Page

192

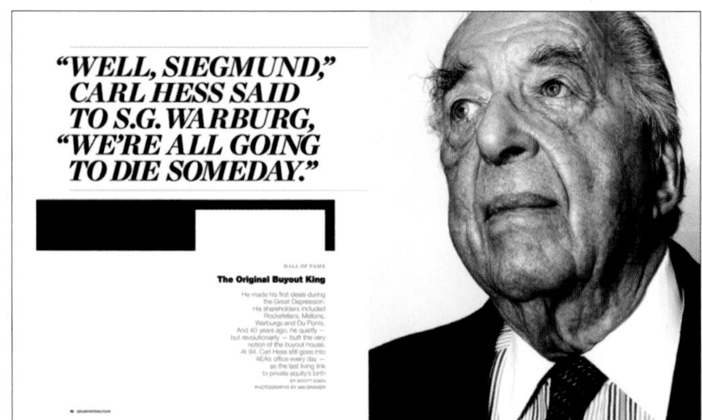

195

193

196

194

197

192 AMERICAN WAY

Design Director_**J.R. Arebalo, Jr.**
Designer_**Caleb Bennett**
Photographer_**Steve Moors**
Publisher_**American Airlines Publishing**
Issue_**December 15, 2007**
Category_**Design: Feature: Spread/Single Page**

193 UD&SE

Design Director_**Torsten Hogh Rasmussen**
Photographer_**Ricky John Molloy**
Publisher_**DSB**
Issue_**October 2007**
Category_**Design: Feature: Spread/Single Page**

194 WIRED

Creative Director_**Scott Dadich**
Art Director_**Carl DeTorres**
Designer_**Carl DeTorres**
Photo Editor_**Carolyn Rauch**
Photographer_**Tony Law**
Publisher_**Condé Nast Publications, Inc.**
Issue_**August 2007**
Category_**Design: Feature: Spread/Single Page**

195 DEALMAKER

Creative Director_**Florian Bachleda**
Photographer_**Ian Spanier**
Studio_**FB Design**
Publisher_**Doubledown Media**
Issue_**March/April 2007**
Category_**Design: Feature: Spread/Single Page**

196 W

Creative Director_**Dennis Freedman**
Design Director_**Edward Leida**
Art Director_**Nathalie Kirsheh**
Designer_**Nathalie Kirsheh**
Photographer_**Juergen Teller**
Publisher_**Condé Nast Publications Inc.**
Issue_**September 2007**
Category_**Design: Feature: Spread/Single Page**

197 SNOWORLD

Creative Director_**Dave Allen**
Designer_**Megan Hixson**
Director of Photography_**Sandra Gnandt**
Photographer_**Will Wissman**
Client_**Warren Miller Films**
Category_**Design: Feature: Spread/Single Page**

198

201

199

202

200

203

198 02138

Creative Director_**Patrick Mitchell**
Art Director_**Susannah Haesche**
Designer_**Ashley Bond** Director of Photography_**Katharine MacIntyre**
Studio_**PlutoMedia**
Publisher_**Atlantic Media**
Issue_**November/December 2007**
Category_**Design: Feature: Spread/Single Page**

199 MINNESOTA MONTHLY

Art Director_**Brian Johnson**
Photographer_**Mike McGregor**
Publisher_**Greenspring Media Group**
Issue_**August 2007**
Category_**Design: Feature: Spread/Single Page**

200 AMERICAN AIRLINES NEXOS

Design Director_**Marco Rosales**
Designer_**Marco Rosales**
Publisher_**American Airlines Publishing**
Issue_**June 1, 2007**
Category **Design: Feature: Spread/Single Page**

201 NYLON GUYS

Design Director_**Michele Outland**
Art Director_**Alexander Chow**
Designer_**Alexander Chow**
Director of Photography_**Stacey Mark**
Photo Editor_**Winona Barton-Ballentine**
Photographer_**Kenneth Cappello**
Publisher_**Nylon LLC**
Issue_**Winter 2007**
Category_**Design: Feature: Spread/Single Page**

202 TEXAS MONTHLY

Art Director_**T.J. Tucker**
Designer_**Andi Beierman**
Illustrators_**Joe Ciardiello, Jonny Hannah**
Publisher_**Emmis Communications Corp.**
Issue_**December 2007**
Category_**Design: Feature: Spread/Single Page**

203 AMERICAN WAY

Design Director_**J.R. Arebalo, Jr.**
Art Director_**Samuel Solomon**
Illustrator_**Darren Booth**
Photographer_**Don Flood**
Publisher_**American Airlines Publishing**
Issue_**February 15, 2007**
Category_**Design: Feature: Spread/Single Page**

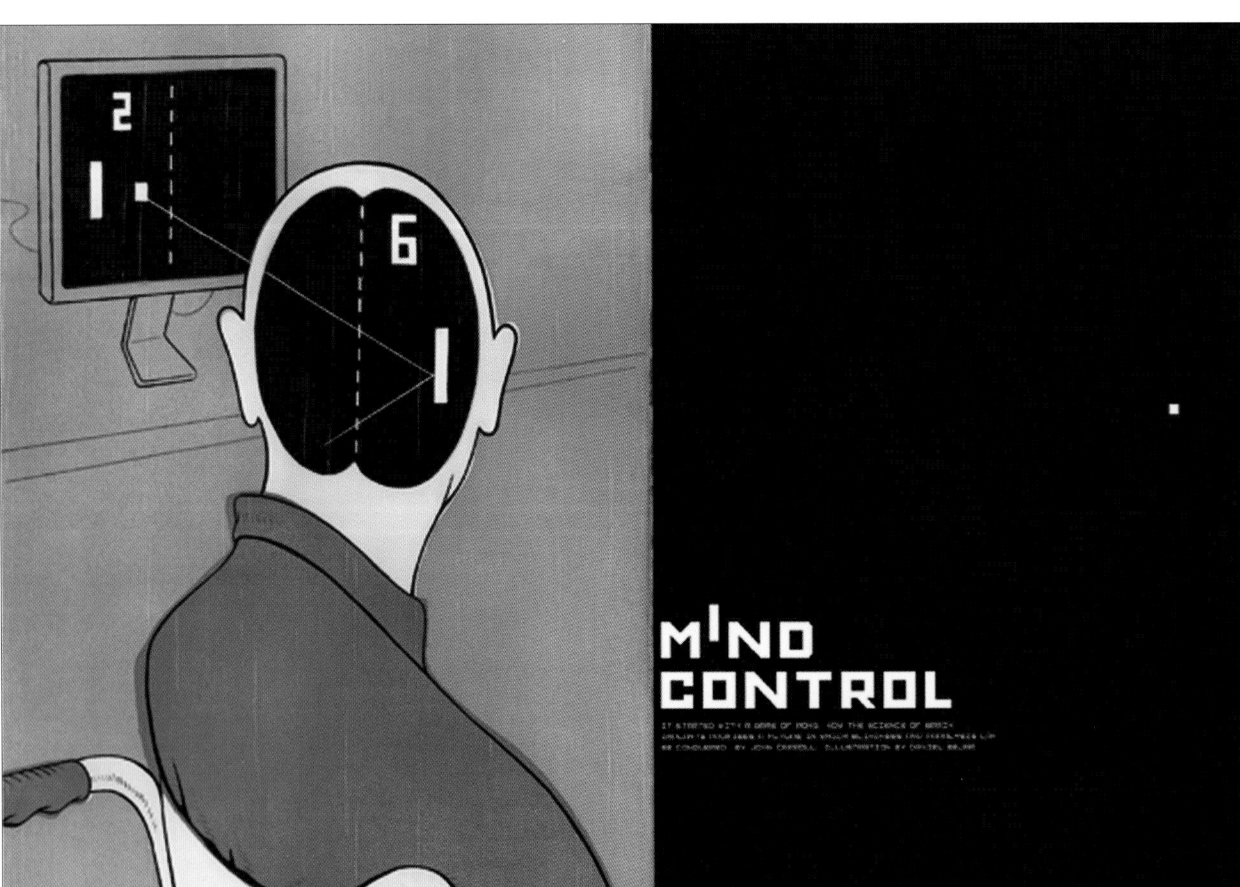

204

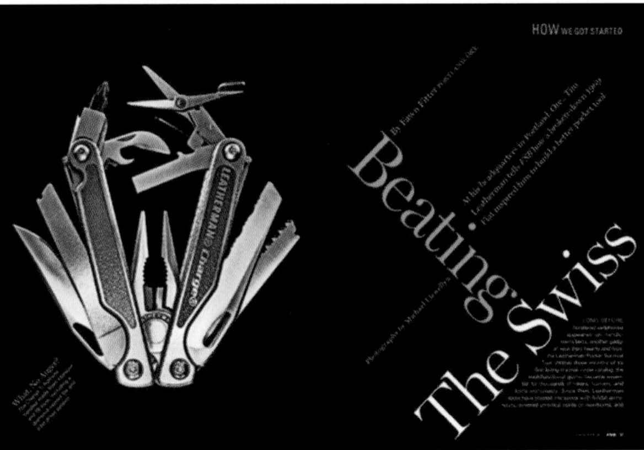

205

206

204 AMERICAN WAY

Design Director_J.R. Arebalo, Jr. Designer_Caleb Bennett
Illustrator_Daniel Bejar Publisher_American Airlines Publishing
Issue_April 15, 2007 Category_Design: Feature: Spread/Single Page

205 FORTUNE SMALL BUSINESS

Art Director_Scott A. Davis Designer_Mike Novak
Director of Photograph_Katy Howe Photographer_Michael Llewellyn
Publisher_Time Inc. Issue_July/August 2007
Category_Design: Feature: Spread/Single Pagel

206 UD&SE

Design Director_Torsten Hogh Rasmussen
Illustrator_Torsten Hogh Rasmussen Publisher_DSB
Issue_June 2007 Category_Design: Feature: Spread/Single Page

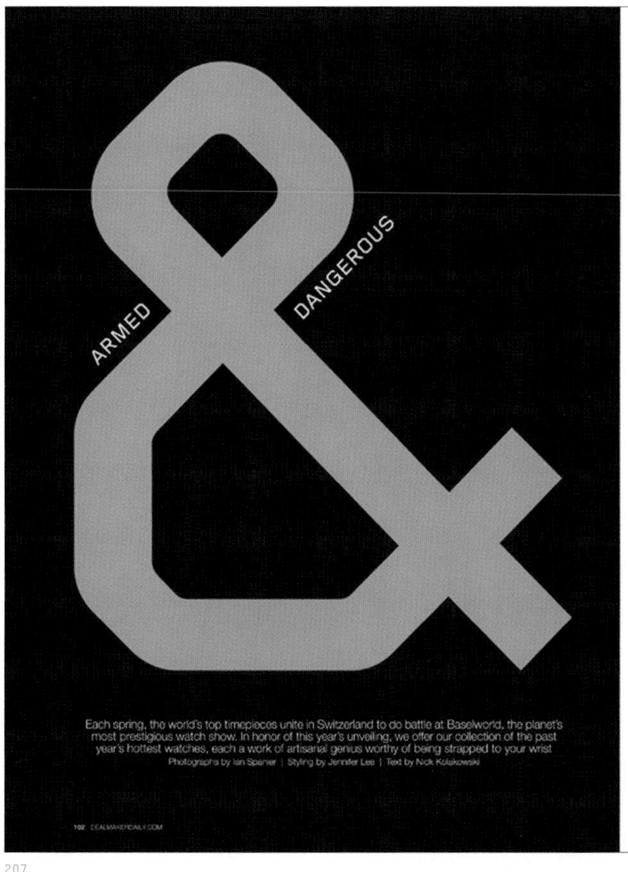

207

208

209

207 DEALMAKER

Creative Director_Florian Bachleda Photographer_Ian Spanier
Fashion Director_Jennifer Lee Studio_FB Design
Publisher_Doubledown Media Issue_May/June 2007
Category_Design: Feature: Spread/Single Page

208 DETAILS

Creative Director_Rockwell Harwood Art Director_Andre Jointe
Designer_Rockwell Harwood Photo Editors_Hali Tara Feldman, Alexandra Ghez, Chandra Glich Photographer_Steven Klein
Publisher_Condé Nast Publications
Issue_November 2007 Category_Design: Feature: Story

209 UD&SE

Design Director_Torsten Hogh Rasmussen
Photographers_Tomas Leth, Anika Lori Publisher_DSB Issue_July 2007
Category_Design: Feature: Spread/Single Page

210

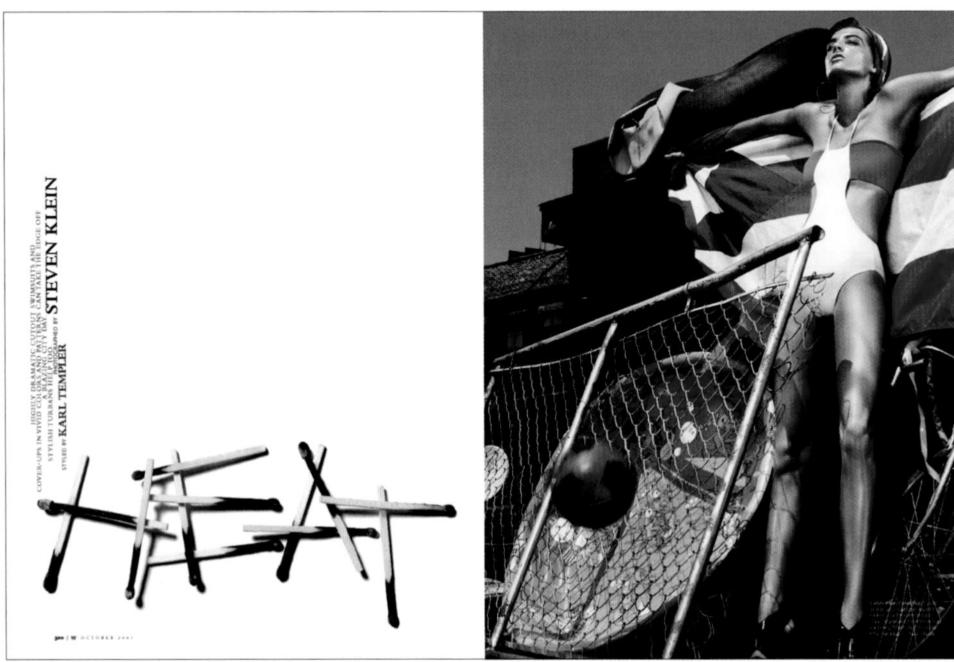

211

210 LIFE & STYLE

Creative Director_Guillermo Caballero
Design Director_Julio Contreras
Designers_Manuela Sanchez, Ixel Osorio, Alfredo Ceballos
Photo Editor_Karen Migoni
Editor-In-Chief_ Carlos Pedroza
Publisher_Grupo Editorial Expansión
Issue_October 2007
Category_Design: Feature: Spread/Single Page

211 W

Creative Director_Dennis Freedman
Design Director_Edward Leida
Designer_Edward Leida
Photographer_Steven Klein
Publisher_Condé Nast Publications Inc.
Issue_October 2007
Category_Design: Feature: Spread/Single Page

212

214

Village Voices LOCAL PROJECTS IS TURNING MUSEUMS INTO PLACES WHERE PEOPLE INTERACT WITH INFORMATION—AND EACH OTHER. ITS LATEST COMMISSION WILL HAVE THE WHOLE COUNTRY JOINING THE CONVERSATION

Photograph by Mark Mahoney

When Jake Barton, the 34-year-old principal of the interactive design firm Local Projects, thinks about what an exhibition can do, he often considers the District Six Museum in Cape Town, South Africa. The museum documents the forced removal of more than 60,000 residents from a mixed-race neighborhood declared a whites-only zone in 1966, and tells the stories of those displaced. In the early '90s, when reclaiming that land was still not an option, the museum kept the issue in the public eye through exhibitions and debate; subsequently, the museum's sister organization helped residents apply to have their land returned. Transforming and healing a community through inclusive storytelling is, in Barton's eyes, the mandate for museums of the 21st century. These days, he has ample reason to meditate on it: In April, he and his seven-person firm received the commission to codesign the permanent exhibition for the World Trade Center Memorial Museum.

By choosing Local Projects, the memorial's directors cast their lot with a new kind of museum that prizes interactivity over top-down presentation. Local Projects insists on a plurality of voices—the exhibitions it creates function as a kind of conversation rather than as repositories of authoritative

215

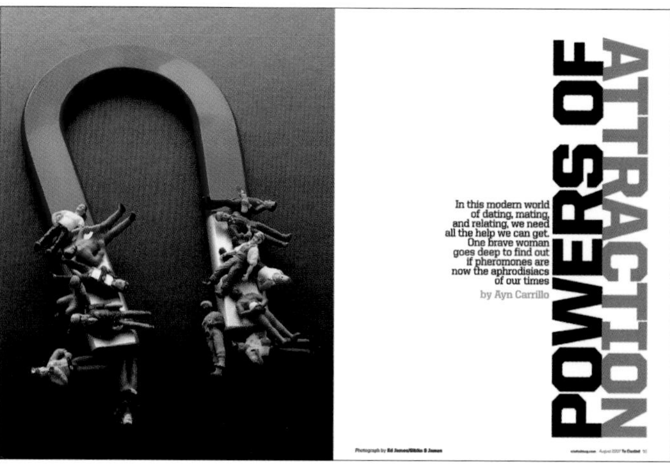

213

216

212 CORPORATE LEADER

Creative Director_**Florian Bachleda**
Design Director_**Ted Keller**
Studio_**FB Design**
Publisher_**Doubledown Media**
Issue_**Premiere Issue**
Category_**Design: Feature: Spread/Single Page**

213 TU CIUDAD

Art Director_**Tom O'Quinn**
Designer_**Tom O'Quinn**
Photo Editor_**Bailey Franklin**
Photographer_**Ed James / Giblin & James**
Publisher_**Emmis**
Issue_**August 2007**
Category_**Design: Feature: Spread/Single Page**

214 ESPN THE MAGAZINE

Creative Director_**Siung Tjia**
Art Director_**Hitomi Sato**
Director of Photography_**Catriona Ni Aolain**
Photo Editor_**Julie Claire**
Photographer_**Morad Bouchakour**
Publisher_**ESPN, Inc.**
Issue_**May 21, 2007**
Category_**Design: Feature: Spread/Single Page**

215 PRINT

Art Director_**Kristina DiMatteo**
Associate Art Director_**Lindsay Ballant**
Designer_**Kristina DiMatteo**
Photographer_**Mark Mahaney**
Editor-In-Chief_**Joyce Rutter Kaye**
Publisher_**F & W Publications**
Issue_**September/October 2007**
Category_**Design: Feature: Spread/Single Page**

216 BICYCLING

Design Director_**David Speranza**
Designer_**David Speranza**
Director of Photography_**Stacey Emenecker**
Photographer_**Jeremy Harris**
Publisher_**Rodale, Inc.**
Issue_**July 2007**
Category_**Design: Feature: Spread/Single Page**

print
Blogging Your Obsessions
Ersatz German Packaging
Overnight Stores Pop Up!
Virtuous Magazines
The Consumption Issue
How Design Drives Spending, Saving, and Desire

217

217

The Obsessives

The four artists whose intent expressions and busy workspaces are pictured at left are, in many ways, quite ordinary. They read, they eat toast, they buy fishing videos. Then they take it a big step further. Kate Bingaman created a dazzling online archive of years' worth of purchases—and bills—all illustrated in minute detail. Designer Nicholas Felton charms the blogosphere yearly with his Feltron Report, an elegant, meticulous annual report of himself. Ellie Harrison, a self-described "recovering data collector," has photographed many dimensions of her life and objects; she also keeps a blog of ideas hatched while drinking tea (she's a Brit). And John D. Freyer made a riveting narrative about selling his possessions on eBay in his book *All My Life for Sale*. We asked all four to document what they consumed for one week. They all produced a vivid record that says volumes about who they are.

217

Shadow Boxer

All James Harvey wanted was to make fine art. Thanks to Andy Warhol, he did—anonymously.

By James Gaddy

ANDY WARHOL

JAMES HARVEY

Photograph by Sasha Nialla

78

217

217 PRINT

Art Director_Kristina DiMatteo Associate Art Director_Lindsay Ballant Designers_Kristina DiMatteo, Lindsay Ballant Illustrators_Happy Pets, Kate Bingaman, Nicholas Felton, Ellie Harrison, John D. Freyer Photographers_Mark Weiss, Erin Gleeson, Brad Dickson, Jason Fulford, Jeon Mee Yoon, Sasha Nialla Editor-In-Chief_Joyce Rutter Kaye Publisher_F & W Publications Issue_July/August 2007 Category_Design: Entire Issue

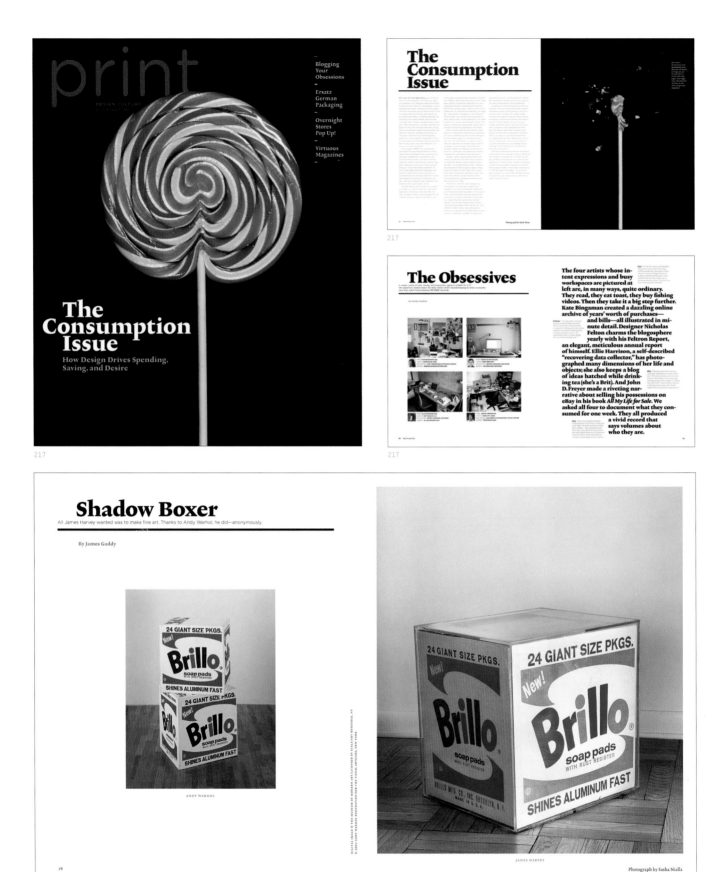

The Architecture Issue

The New York Times Magazine

MAY 20, 2007 · SECTION 6

ECO-TECTURE

Designing and building with the environment in mind.

Why Are the Europeans Greener Than We Are? **By Nicolai Ouroussoff** ... Al Gore's Plans **By James Traub** ... Living in Sustainable Luxury, a proposal **by Diller Scofidio + Renfro** ... The Zero-Energy Home **By Mark Svenvold** ... A Waste-Nothing Builder **By Michael Kimmelman** ... Journey to the World's Greenest City **By Arthur Lubow** ... and more.

218

1

WHY ARE THEY GREENER THAN WE ARE?

218

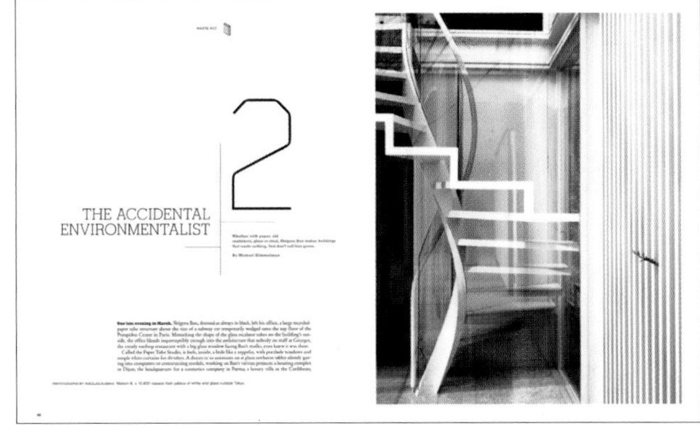
2

THE ACCIDENTAL ENVIRONMENTALIST

218

RECYCLE CITY

For 40 years, a medium-size Brazilian city has set the international standard for environmentally conscious urban planning. But can it grow and remain green?

By Arthur Lubow

3

THE ROAD TO CURITIBA

On Saturday mornings, children gather to paint and draw in the main downtown shopping street of Curitiba, in southern Brazil. More than just a charming tradition, the child's play commemorates a key victory in a hard-fought, ongoing war. Back in 1972, the new mayor of the city, an architect and urban planner named Jaime Lerner, ordered a lightning transformation of six blocks of the street into a pedestrian zone. The change was recommended in a master plan for the city that was approved six years earlier, but fierce objections from the downtown merchants blocked its implementation. Lerner instructed his secretary of public works to institute the change quickly and asked how long it would take. "He said he needed four months," Lerner recalled recently. "I said, 'Forty-eight hours.' He said, 'You're crazy.' I said, 'Yes, I'm crazy, but do it in 48 hours.'" The municipal authorities were able to accomplish it in three days, beginning on a Friday night and

PHOTOGRAPHS BY SIMON NORFOLK A station on Curitiba's rapid-transit-bus system.

218

218 THE NEW YORK TIMES MAGAZINE

Creative Director_**Janet Froelich** Art Director_**Arem Duplessis** Designers_**Gail Bichler, Jeff Docherty**
Director of Photography_**Kathy Ryan** Editor-In-Chief_**Gerry Marzorati** Publisher_**The New York Times**
Issue_**May 20, 2007** Category_**Design: Entire Issue**

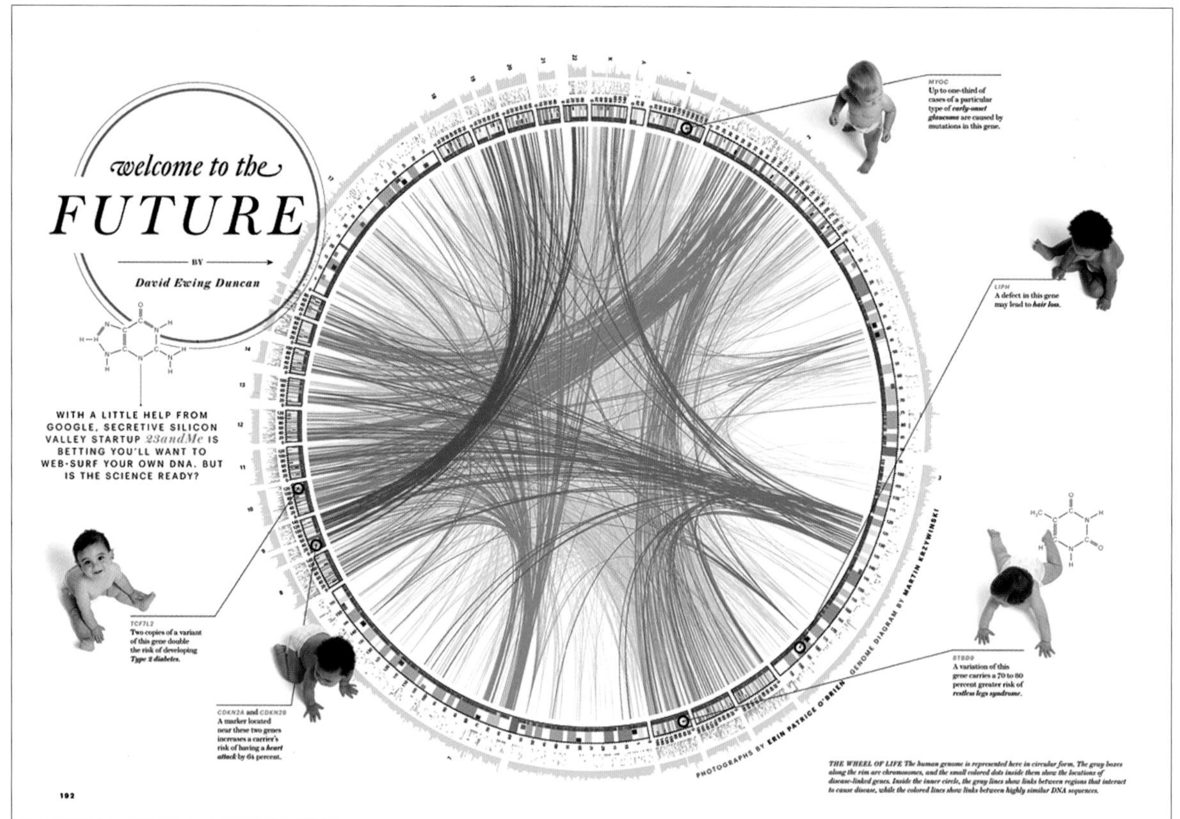

219

219

219 CONDÉ NAST PORTFOLIO

Design Director_Robert Priest Art Director_Grace Lee Deputy Art Director_Sarah Viñas Designers Sarah Viñas, Jana Meier, Rina Kushnir, Grace Martinez Illustrators_Bruce Hutchison, Paul Davis, Kagan McLeod, Jeffrey Decoster, Bryan Christie, Julie Teninbaum, Brian Rea, John Burgoyne, Joel Holland, Roderick Mills, Jonathan Gray, Nick Higgins, Sean McCabe Director of Photography_Lisa Berman Photo Editors Jane Yeomans, Sarah Weissman, Rossana Shokrian, Brian Marcus, Louisa Anderson, John Toolan Deputy Photo Editor_Sarah Czeladnicki Photographers_Rob Howard, Stephen Lewis, Jeff Minton, Dan Winters, Jill Greenberg, Michael Wolf, Misha Gravenor, Ture Lillegraven, Jillian Edelstein, Joe Pugliese, Nikolas Koenig, Brad Bridgers, Levi Brown, Tierney Gearon, Erin Patrice O'Brien, Chris Jordan Information Graphics Director_John Grimwade Editor-In-Chief Joanne Lipman Publisher Condé Nast Publications Inc. Issue November 2007 Category Design: Entire Issue

SKY'S THE LIMIT
Read about Ryan Hall's unprecedented year on page 80.

RUNNING IS A POWERFUL force that offers rewards greater than a trim physique or a finisher's medal. It also has the capacity to transform our minds and spirits, and to improve the lives of others. Take the 34 people we honor here—the RUNNER'S WORLD Heroes of Running 2007. By defying expectations, breaking barriers, and leading future generations, they remind us that the simple act

HEROES

of moving forward can have a profound impact. There's the 88-year-old ultrarunner who's made it his life's work to lead us where no runner had gone before, the cancer survivor who launched a worldwide movement against the disease, and two young superstars who are pumping new life into American distance racing. Through their stories, we hope you'll be inspired to explore the full potential of your running life.

PHOTOGRAPH BY GREGG SEGAL

RUNNER'S WORLD DECEMBER 2007 71

220

Long Time Gone

Quenton Cassidy was once a runner—a great one. Now he was something else. Fortunately, he had always believed in comebacks and second chances

An exclusive excerpt from *Again to Carthage*
By John L. Parker Jr.

THE CABIN SAT BACK OFF THE ROAD IN THE DRIPPING TREES LIKE A PART OF the forest itself, earthy brown, and plain, with a skin of cedar shakes, organic but for its giveaway straight edges. In the gloomy afternoon downpour the familiar shape seemed the essence of refuge. ¶ Could it possibly have been just a year? Yes, and some days. ¶ The screened-in front porch wasn't latched, and he had already retrieved the front door key from his shaving kit, where it had been for more than a year. Cassidy backed in, dragging two big canvas equipment bags, disturbing spiders at work, breathing in the familiar scents of raw lumber, mildew, and the pepper and earthy decay of Spanish

Illustrations by **STERLING HUNDLEY**

RUNNER'S WORLD DECEMBER 2007 99

220

220 RUNNER'S WORLD

Art Director_**Kory Kennedy** Deputy Art Director_**Marc Kauffman** Illustrators_**Andy Martin, Sterling Hundley, Nate Williams** Photo Editor_**Andrea Maurio** Assistant Photo Editor_**Nick Galac** Photographers_**Gregg Segal, Peter Yang, Michael Lavine, Gregg Segal, Amanda Friedman, Michael Lewis** Publisher_**Rodale** Issue_**December 2007** Category_**Design: Entire Issue**

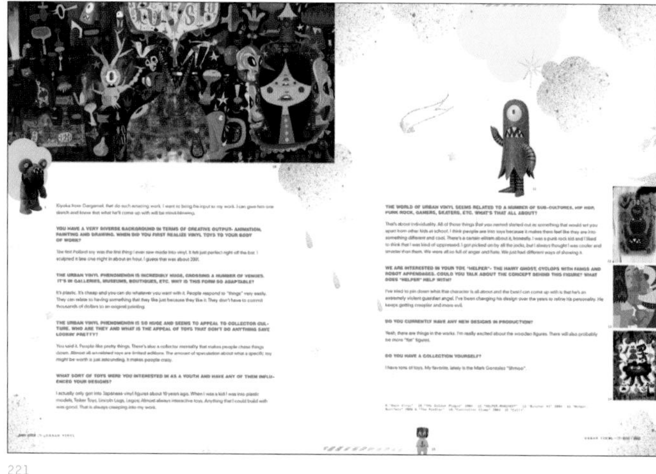

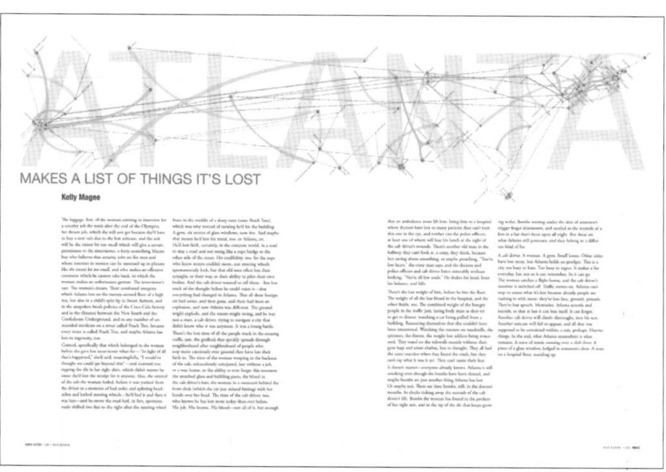

221

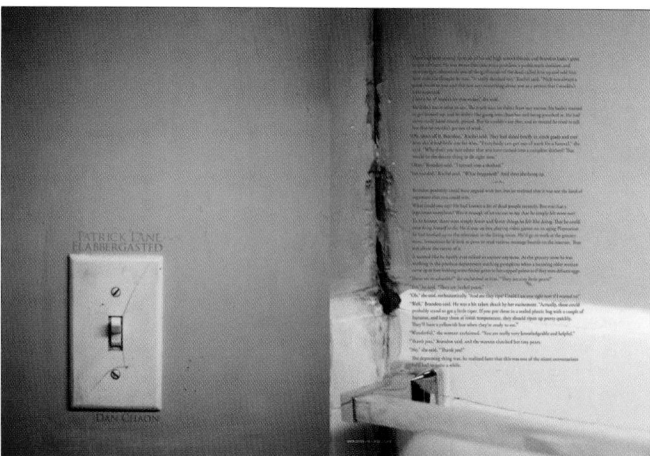

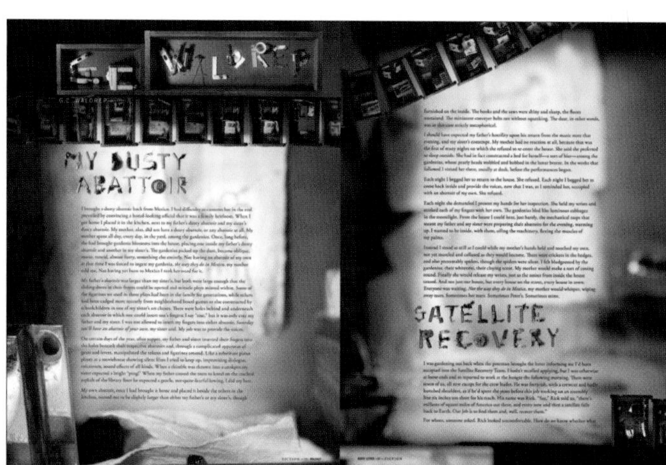

222

223

221 NINTH LETTER LITERARY AND ARTS JOURNAL

Creative Directors_Nan Goggin, Jennifer Gunji, Joseph Squier Design Director_Jennifer Gunji Art Director_Jennifer Gunji Designers_Natalie Berberet, Kyrsten Blinstrup, Laurie Cheng, Sam Copeland, Kelly Cree, Megan Delaney, Fabiola Elias, Diana Jarvis, Jeffrey Jones, Borami Kang, Kristen King, Jonathan Lopez, Clinton Miceli, Hank Patton, Megan Severson, Ashley Skinner, Brett Tabolt, Cathy Wendt, Ho-Mui Wong Editor-In-Chief_Jodee Stanley Publisher_University at Illinois at Urbana Champaign Issue_Spring/Summer 2007, Vol. 4, No. 1 Category_Design: Entire Issue

222 NINTH LETTER LITERARY AND ARTS JOURNAL

Creative Directors_Nan Goggin, Jennifer Gunji, Joseph Squier Design Director_Jennifer Gunji Art Directors_Jennifer Gunji, Daniel Goscha Designers_Travis Austin, Aditya Bhargava, Samuel Copeland, Lauren Emerson, Sarah Esgro, Lauren Ferguson, Adam Fotos, Sarah Kowalis, Jonathan Lopez, Elise McAuley, Archana Shekara, Brett Tabolt, Ho-Mui Wong, Jessica Mullen Publisher_University at Illinois at Urbana Champaign Issue_Fall/Winter 2007, Vol. 4, No. 2 Category_Design: Entire Issue

223 PLAY, THE NEW YORK TIMES SPORTS MAGAZINE

Creative Director_Janet Froelich Art Director_Dirk Barnett Designers_Dirk Barnett, Dragos Lemnei, Julia Moburg Illustrator_+Ism Photo Editor_Kira Pollack Photographers_Finlay MacKay, Larry Sultan Publisher_The New York Times Issue_September 2007 Category_Design: Entire Issue

224

225

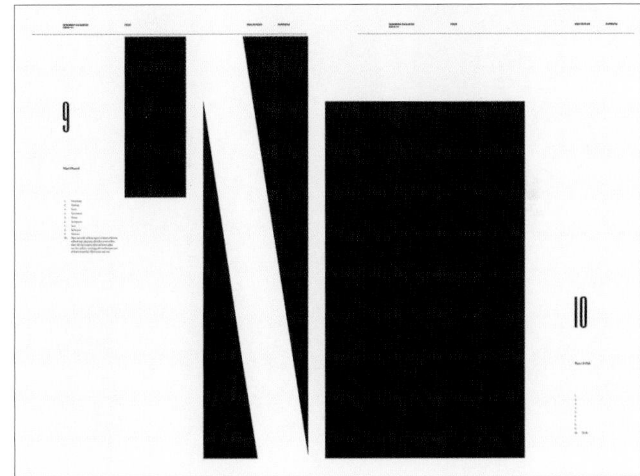

226

224 DEALMAKER

Creative Director_Florian Bachleda Art Director_Clare Minges Director of Photography_Ian Spanier Photographers_Ian Spanier, Jimmy Nicol Fashion Director_Jennifer Lee Studio_FB Design Publisher_Doubledown Media Issue_March/April 2007 Category_Design: Entire Issue

225 GQ

Design Director_Fred Woodward Art Director_Anton Ioukhnovets Deputy Art Director_Thomas Alberty Designers_Drue Wanger, Michael Pangilinan, Rob Hewitt, Chelsea Cardinal, Delgis Canahuate, Eve Binder Illustrators_Christoph Niemann, Jean-Philippe Delhomme, Sean McCabe, Zohar Lazar, John Ueland, John Ritter Director of Photography_Dora Somosi Senior Photo Editor_Krista Prestek Photo Editors_Justin O'Neill, Jesse Lee, Jolanta Bielat, Roberto DeLuna, Halena Green Photographers_Nathaniel Goldberg, Paola Kudacki, Terry Richardson, Matthias Ziegler, Martin Schoeller, Anders Overgaard, Bobby Fisher Creative Director_Jim Moore Editor-In-Chief_Jim Nelson Publisher_Condé Nast Publications Inc. Issue_November 2007 Category_Design: Entire Issue

226 NEWWORK MAGAZINE

Creative Director_Ryotaslu Tanaka Design Director_Ryo Kumazaki Art Director_Hitomi Ishigaki Designer_Aswin Sadha Illustrator_Mario Hugo Director of Photography_Yuji Takenaka Photographer_Tiziano Magni Studio_Studio Newwork Editor-In-Chief_Studio Newwork Issue_December 2007 Category_Design: Entire Issue

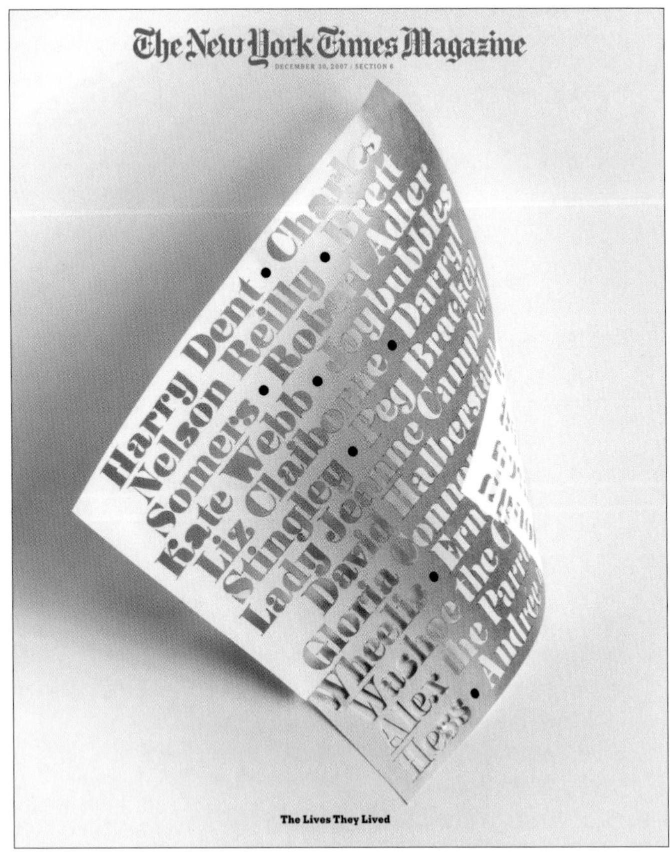

227

The New York Times Magazine

Jack Valenti b.1921
Lady Bird Johnson b.1912
Deborah Kerr b.1921
Molly Ivins b.1944
Norman Mailer b.1923
Tammy Faye Bakker b.1942
Brooke Astor b.1902
Luciano Pavarotti b.1935
Jerry Falwell b.1933
Vincent Sardi Jr. b.1915
Marcel Marceau b.1923
Arthur M. Schlesinger Jr. b.1917
Boris N. Yeltsin b.1931
Ingmar Bergman b.1918
Leona Helmsley b.1920
Michelangelo Antonioni b.1912
Beverly Sills b.1929
Kurt Vonnegut b.1922
Evel Knievel b.1938
Herbert Muschamp b.1947
Ike Turner b.1931

The Lives They Lived

Welcome to the 14th annual Lives They Lived issue. On the last Sunday of each year, we fill these pages with stories of all kinds of people who have died during the last 12 months. It is a daunting task: this newspaper alone published more than 1,000 obituaries, and those only touch on the vast number of notable deaths. In putting together this issue, we shy away from any attempt at being definitive; instead we embrace idiosyncrasy, storytelling and the interests and passions of our editors and writers. This year brought the deaths of many giants of politics and culture, from Arthur M. Schlesinger Jr. to Luciano Pavarotti, from Brooke Astor to Ike Turner, from Lady Bird Johnson to Jack Valenti. But we present some of the lesser-known lives: Harry Dent, who quietly consolidated the South for the Republican Party; Andrée de Jongh, who, at 24, courageously escorted more than 100 soldiers and civilians out of Nazi-occupied Belgium to safety; Gloria Connors, who taught her son Jimmy how to be an unrelenting champion; Ernest Withers, who, as a black photographer, was able to document the civil rights movement from inside. Their stories and those of the two dozen others presented here create a collage of lives well lived.

13

227

LIZ CLAIBORNE | b. 1929

Queen of the Separates

She changed the way working women dressed.

By Rebecca Johnson

Pants, shirt, jacket. No big deal — now. But back in the early 1970s, before Liz Claiborne became a household name, that outfit was not much of an option for women. Out in the world, you wore a dress or a skirt with a matching jacket. At home, you wore slacks or a housedress. You could be dressed up or dressed down, in other words, but "separates," as the fashion industry calls the way women now dress, had yet to become a phenomenon. Until Liz.

As with many figures at the center of a paradigm shift, Claiborne was in the right place at the right time. "I can't tell you we were smart enough back then to say, 'American women are about to join the work force in record numbers, and they're going to need something to wear,'" admits Jerry Chazen, one of Claiborne's original partners. "But there was a busy lady who needed something to wear. We saw a niche."

Claiborne understood that niche because she *was* a busy lady needing something to wear. A Belgian-born high-school dropout who spoke with a kind of accent Americans usually identify as "grand" — "turquoise" was ter-KWAZ — Claiborne began her career as a sketcher and a dress model on Seventh Avenue and worked her way up to designer. Her parents were so opposed to her career choice that her father, a banker, dropped her off on a corner in New York City, handed her $50 and did not speak to her for 20 years. On an interview for a job, Claiborne met the fashion executive Art Ortenberg, and although they were both married to other people at the time, they ended up married to each other shortly thereafter, beginning a lifelong collaboration. Within seven months of starting (along with a handful of investors) Liz Claiborne Inc., they were in the black, an unheard-of feat on Seventh Avenue.

"We started out in the same building," says the designer Stan Herman, who was president of the Council of Fashion Designers of America for 16 years. "I watched her take the fifth floor, then the sixth floor, then the seventh. Finally, they had to move to a new building." The company went public in 1981. Five years later it made the Fortune 500, the first company founded by a woman to do so.

It's not that other companies weren't making clothes for working women. But the clothes they were making looked remarkably similar to the clothes men were wearing — conservative blue or camel's-hair jackets, blouses with bow ties. The message was clear: I may be a woman, but don't worry, I'm not that different from you. Claiborne's clothes were actually quite ordinary — high-waisted pants that flared at the bottom, long-sleeved button-down shirts. The revolution was in the details. A talented seamstress herself, she cared a great deal about fit and comfort.

"She was a pear-shaped woman," says Chazen, "who knew how to design for women, most of whom are also pear-shaped." She was also one of the first to design in color — bright red, yellow and royal blue, the colors female politicians still wear when they want to be taken seriously. Nor did she focus on the East Coast sophisticate. "She also designed for the woman in Dallas, where the light was different," says her design protégée Dana Buchman.

Claiborne also revolutionized the way clothes were sold. Back then, department stores displayed pants with pants, shirts with shirts. She introduced the concept of "outfits." Liz Claiborne pants were sold next to Liz Claiborne shirts with all the dye lots coordinated to match. The innovations made Claiborne a star with a certain generation. "Traveling with her in those days was like traveling with a rock star," Buchman says. "Women were so grateful to her for these clothes."

As it happened, Claiborne did not have the personality of a rock star. Sensing the beginning of what is now the global business of branding, her partners pushed her to become more of a public persona. "We didn't need to spend money on advertising," Chazen says, "because all the magazines wanted to write about Liz or have her clothes in their magazine." But in a business of big egos and flashy personalities, Claiborne was a shy person who preferred staying at home to going out at night. "You never saw Liz at the parties," Stan Herman says. "She was like Garbo."

As the business got bigger and bigger — today Liz Claiborne Inc. is a $5-billion-a-year company and owns the brands Juicy Couture, Lucky Brand Jeans, Dana Buchman, Kate Spade and Ellen Tracy, among others — she grew more and more miserable. "I found myself spending my whole day in elevators," she once lamented in an interview. "Liz was a lovely person," Chazen says. "That was one of the problems with her being a manager. She didn't know how to say something was terrible, because she knew how hard those designers had worked."

In 1989, Claiborne and her husband resigned from the company they started, liquidated their stock and began making grants to wildlife-preservation groups. To date, their foundation has given $40 million away. In this, she was also ahead of her time. "The fashion industry hadn't always been good at giving back," Herman says. "She was among the first." In 2000, the C.F.D.A. recognized that generosity with their Humanitarian Award. Even though the cancer that would eventually kill her was diagnosed three years earlier, Claiborne showed up to accept the award. That night, the woman who built a multibillion-dollar industry on clothes made of bright, happy colors wore black. ■

CLAIBORNE: CHAMPION OF THE BUSY LADY.

22 PHOTOGRAPH FROM LIZ CLAIBORNE INC.

227

227 THE NEW YORK TIMES MAGAZINE

Creative Director_**Janet Froelich** Art Director_**Arem Duplessis** Designer_**Nancy Harris Rouemy** Director of Photography_**Kathy Ryan** Photo Editor_**Clinton Cargill** Editor-In-Chief_**Gerry Marzorati** Publisher_**The New York Times** Issue_**December 30, 2007** Category_**Design: Entire Issue**

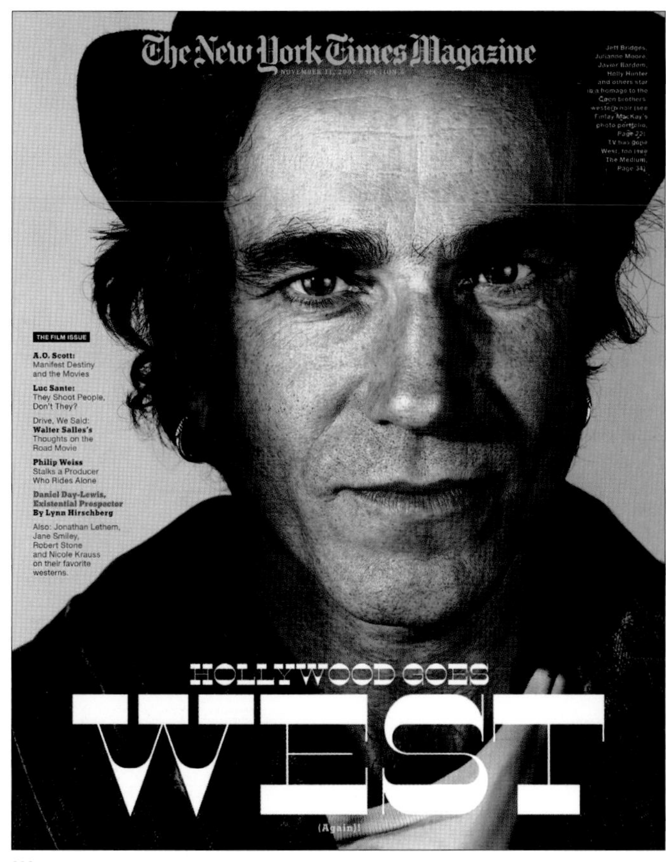

228

The New York Times Magazine / NOVEMBER 11, 2007

HOW THE WESTERN WAS WON

Hollywood's first great genre isn't just about what Americans long for. It's about what the camera longs for.

By A.O. Scott

LIKE A GUNSLINGER standing on a dusty street in a one-horse town, facing down a posse or, if he's wearing a tin star, a gang of outlaws, the western has proved hard to kill. Officially, of course, its death has been documented again and again, with regret and, sometimes, with satisfaction. But as soon as the obsequies have been pronounced and the coffin lowered into the sandy earth, the rumble of hoofbeats sounds on the horizon, and the western rides again. In 1991, for example, the critic J. Hoberman published a thorough and persuasive essay called "How the Western Was Lost," documenting the waning of a once-vigorous form. That same year, however, Kevin Costner's "Dances With Wolves" won the Oscars for Best Picture and Best Director, a feat Clint Eastwood's "Unforgiven" would match two years later. But Hoberman surely had a point. The movie western had retreated from its position as a quintessential and

55

228

Daniel Day-Lewis has always found America — and the American West — a rich vein to mine. In his new movie, he strikes oil. By Lynn Hirschberg

THE NEW FRON-TIER'S MAN

Photograph by Jillian Edelstein Daniel Day-Lewis in the rugged solitude of Luggala, Ireland.

60

228

228 THE NEW YORK TIMES MAGAZINE

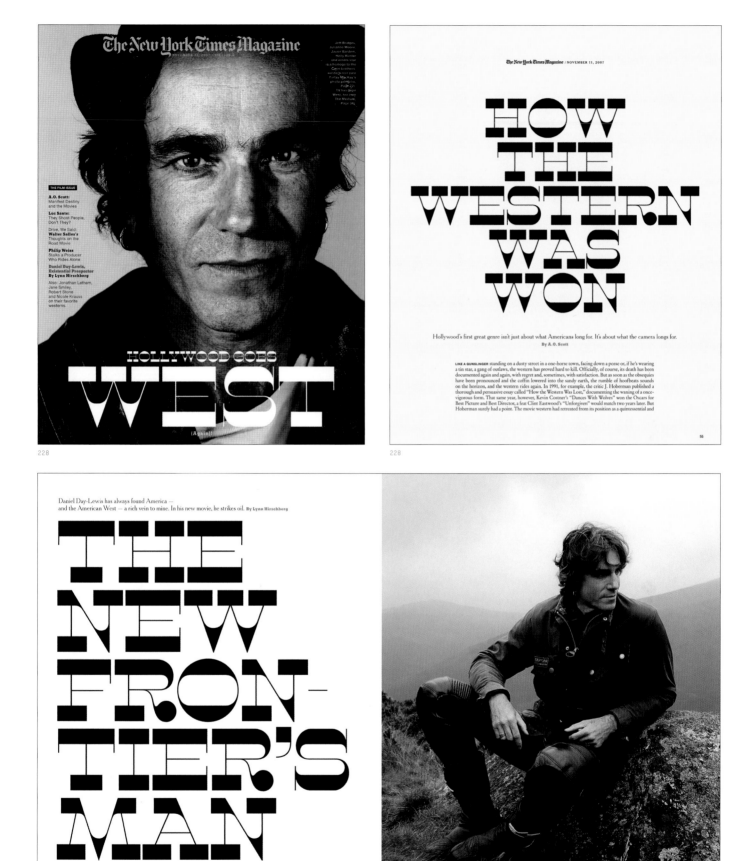

Creative Director_**Janet Froelich** Art Director_**Arem Duplessis** Designer_**Catherine Gilmore-Barnes** Director of Photography_**Kathy Ryan** Photo Editor_**Kira Pollack** Editor-In-Chief_**Gerry Marzorati** Publisher_**The New York Times** Issue_**November 11, 2007** Category_**Design: Entire Issue**

229

229

229

229 GQ

Design Director_Fred Woodward Art Director_Anton Ioukhnovets Deputy Art Director_Thomas Alberty Designers_Drue Wagner, Michael Pangilinan, Chelsea Cardinal, Rob Hewitt, Delgis Cnahuate, Eve Binder Illustrators_Zohar Lazar, Jason Lee, John Ueland, Robert Grossman, Olivier Kugler, Nick Dewar, John Ritter, Jean-Philippe Delhomme, Bryan Christie, Michael Baumgarten, Jill Greenberg, Maciek Kobielski, Matthew Brookes Director of Photography_Dora Somosi Senior Photo Editor_Krista Prestek Photo Editors_Justin O'Neill, Jesse Lee, Jolanta Bielat, Roberto DeLuna, Halena Green Photographers_Brigitte Lacombe, Ellen Von Unwerth, Mark Seliger, Ben Watts, Nathaniel Goldberg, Alexi Lubomirski, Carter Smith, Nadav Kander, Cass Bird, Michael Baumgarten Creative Director_Jim Moore Editor-In-Chief_Jim Nelson Publisher_Condé Nast Publications Inc. Issue_December 2007 Category_Design: Entire Issue

230

230

Added bounce

Bill Gates: "If General Motors [GM] had kept up with technology like the computer industry, we would all be driving $25 cars that go 1,000 miles to the gallon."

John F 'Jack' Smith, former GM chairman: "If GM had developed technology like Microsoft, we would all be driving cars with the following characteristics..."

THE ART of RETORT

"... each time GM introduced a new car, you would have to learn to drive all over again, because none of the controls would operate in the same manner."

"... only one person at a time could use the car, unless you agreed to purchase extra seats."

"... for no apparent reason, your car would sometimes lock you out and refuse to let you in until you simultaneously lifted the door handle, turned the key and grabbed hold of the radio antenna."

"... a routine manoeuvre would often cause your car to shut down and refuse to restart, in which case you would have to reinstall the engine."

"... the air bag system would ask, 'Are you sure?' before deploying."

"... your car would crash twice a day."

NB The cynics on Urban Legends snopes.com maintain this story is just that: it began circulating as a joke some time ago, and quickly mutated into a 'true' story. Whatever the truth, it did no harm to Jack Smith's reputation.

BROUGHT TO YOU BY BDO STOY HAYWARD 16

JOHAN PRAG

The cheque: a brief history

After 2,000 years of evolution, the cheque is headed for the great wallet in the sky. RIP.

AD0001
Romans citizens are converted to the convenience of 'praescriptiones'.

AD250
Persian banks issue letters of credit known as 'sakks'.

1100-1300
The Knights Templar run a primitive cheque system for pilgrims to the Holy Land. Drafts are written in complex codes only Templars can decipher.

1500-1600
More forerunners appear in Britain, issued by 'Money Scriveners' – who are seen as a big improvement on the ranks of 'thievinge broggers' [brokers].

1659
The earliest known handwritten modern cheque is drawn – on Messrs Clayton & Morris of Cornhill, London.

1770
Daily clearings begin. Bank clerks meet at the Five Bells on Lombard St, London.

1800
Spelling standardisation: Britain opts for 'cheque'; the US (re)declares its independence with no-nonsense 'check'.

1860
An enraged taxpayer delivers a 'cheque' written out on 'a large white cow of malevolent aspect' to the Inland Revenue. The story, from *Punch*, was fictitious, but was cited as recently as 2004, during a House of Lords debate.

1914
Growing rates of cheque fraud are accented by Sir Arthur Conan Doyle:
Sherlock Holmes: "I made it my business to hunt down some of Moriarty's cheques. They were drawn on six different banks, does that make any impression on your mind?"
Dr Watson: "Queer, certainly!"
The Valley of Fear

1950s
The advent of mass-banking in spiv Britain leads to a bouncing bonanza. Offending cheques are now posted to their originator for maximum chagrin over the breakfast table.

1970s
Following a banking crisis and recession, the phrase 'the cheque's in the post' takes on new notoriety. Robert Maxwell emerges as 'The Bouncing Czech'. 'Chequebook journalism' takes off proper.

1990
Usage peaks (despite the advent of the ATM) – 11 million are written daily.

2004
After a decade of decline, the arrival of Chip and PIN signals the cheque's death warrant. Chequebook stubs become objects of nostalgia.

2007
Retailers start refusing cheques in droves; BT imposes fees on recusants. APACS reports: "The death of the cheque... is really gathering speed." The Halifax predicts the final cheque will be written in 2020.

JULY
Coutts bucks the trend, reporting a six per cent increase in cheque transactions – its swanky leather chequebooks are a factor?

SEPTEMBER
A grand valedictory gesture! The Government guarantees every UK savings account – the largest blank cheque in history...

BROUGHT TO YOU BY BDO STOY HAYWARD 17

230

230 33 THOUGHTS

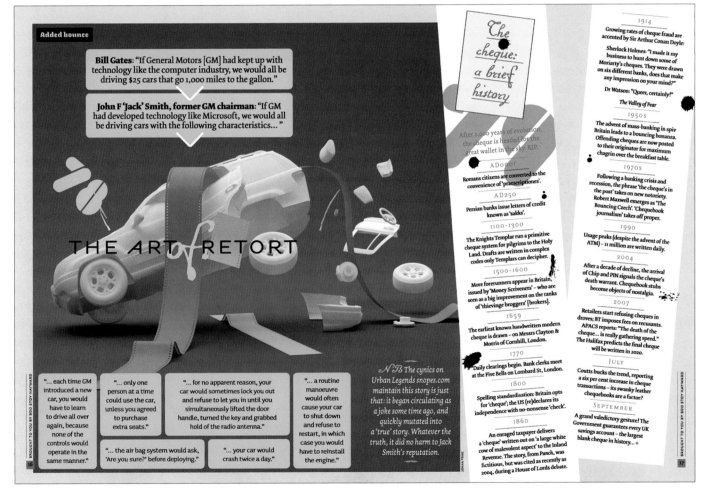

Creative Director_Jeremy Leslie Art Director_James Grubb Designers_Yoko Land, Sandrine Pellettier, McPaul, Johan Prag, Farra Illustrators_Mikko Rantanen, Eskimo Square, Anna Lise Publisher_John Brown Client_BDO Stoy Hayward Issue_Winter 2007 Category_Design: Entire Issue standing natural language, distinguishing a dog from a cat. Despite steady advances in hardware, no machine could think as far as to laugh at a pratfall or make a bad pun.

In pursuing human-style intelligence, the geeks blundered into the deepest, densest, darkest thickets of metaphysics: consciousness, cognition, perception, self-awareness, and how "we" manage to "know" what we know. It turns out that activities like playing chess—things that require sorting and searching—are relatively easy to program, whereas tasks that require some understanding of the world at large, like doing the laundry, are unbearably complex. The metaphysical issues around AI are at a standstill, mainly because metaphysics is old and canny and doesn't move forward in the linear manner of technology. Researchers, their grand illusions and ambitions dashed, fell into a long "AI winter" of shrunken budgets and general indifference.

Nowadays, Google "knows" pretty much anything you ask it. But its insanely fast and powerful work is modestly described as data-mining, not thinking. That vast, globe-spanning, superpowerful, ultrawealthy Web spider has yet to awaken and declare, "I am Google."

But if it starts writing philosophy, all bets are off.

Brain Age »

Geeks have always known that videogames make you smarter, but now the rest of the world is catching on as well, thanks to Nintendo's *Brain Age*. Created in collaboration with neuroscientist Ryuta Kawashima, the DS Lite software has sold millions of copies worldwide. Timed drills—solving math problems, reading aloud, counting stick figures—aim to keep your cerebral muscles toned, and randomized tests assign you a "brain age" that represents your mental fitness. *Brain Age* has pioneered a genre of DS Lite games that appeals to teachers, doctors, businesspeople, and grandmas. Public schools in Japan are even distributing the handhelds to students. Hey, maybe they would release textbooks in game format, too.

Brain implants

Forget about therapy. Never mind pills. Some day soon, a long list of mental ailments may be best solved by sticking a chip in your brain. Neural stimulators—tiny systems that deliver electric current directly to cells—have shown promise in alleviating Parkinson's tremors, short-circuiting epileptic seizures, and stemming the verbal diarrhea of Tourette's. They may even help with depression, obsessive-compulsive disorder, and migraines. Future devices will have bidirectional signals to sense misfiring neurons and selectively zap them into submission. The bad news is, these implants typically cost upwards of $15,000 and come with possible side effects: hallucinations and difficulty finding words. Oh, and don't forget to replace the batteries every five to 10 years.

A B C D E F G H I J K L M N O P Q R S T U V W X Y Z

B

Ballmer, Steve

"Ebullient, focused, funny, passionate, sincere, hard-charging and dynamic." That's how Microsoft describes CEO Steve Ballmer in his official bio, but it hardly does justice to his many layers. There's the Ballmer who, less than a year after taking the reins at Microsoft in January 2000, tried to retool the behemoth and instead presided over its stock's collapse from $57 to $21. There's the Ballmer who, through cunning management, pulled the stock back above $30. There's the chair-tossing Ballmer who screamed that he would "fucking kill Google"; the fist-pumping Ballmer who danced sweatily at a developers conference; and the crow-eating Ballmer who knocked $7 billion off his company's market value by chiding Wall Street for being too bullish on Vista. Today, Ballmer is steering Microsoft away from the desktop and into other areas—enterprise software, health care, robotics. But his true value to his employer may be simpler: The company would be a lot duller without him.

Banksy

This thirtysomething Brit is best known for graffiti, but he can turn anything into art: Paris Hilton CDs, elephants, even the odd canvas. Banksy (real moniker unknown) has made his name by defacing public spaces with arresting images and subversive slogans, like placing a mannequin clad in a Gitmo jumpsuit along Disneyland's Big Thunder Mountain Railroad. Which is not to say he doesn't show in museums. In 2005, Banksy surreptitiously installed a painted rock at the British Museum; it depicts a primitive human pushing a shopping cart. Upon discovering the prank, the museum promptly added the artifact to its permanent collection.

BANKSY

BitTorrent

For years, the movie and music industries have battled peer-to-peer file-sharing systems. In BitTorrent, though, they've found a P2P protocol they can tolerate, if not love. How is it different? It's free, open source, and phenomenally popular, accounting for 35 percent of all Net traffic by some estimates, which makes it an easy and cheap way for content providers to distribute their wares; P2P passes along the bandwidth cost of sending digital media to swarms of peers. And because content providers can run BitTorrent software on their own servers, they can control which users get what data. So even as BitTorrent undergirds scofflaw sites like the aptly named Pirate Bay, it's being used to distribute *World of Warcraft* updates and by Warner Bros. to sell movies and TV online. Seems a little copyright infringement can be forgiven if there's a buck to be made.

Blu-ray

With support from major movie studios, Sony's Blu-ray disc format is poised to defeat its competitor, HD-DVD. But the victory will likely prove Pyrrhic. Already, upstarts like China's Enhanced Versatile Disc are touting equivalent resolution with DRM-free content and cheap players. More important, ultra-advanced disc formats may be moot. Broadband Net access and inexpensive online data storage will soon render plastic discs all but obsolete. What if they launched a format war and nobody came?

Blogosphere

There is unrest in the Galactic Senate. The Blogosphere, under the leadership of rebel commander Nick Denton, has declared its intention to secede from the Mainstream Media. The separatist movement comes at a terrible time for the MSM. Weakened by plagiarists and the dark lords of craigslist, the old guard has been slow to respond to the challenge. Meanwhile, the New Media realms have built a populist regime of citizen journalism and user-generated content. It might even be called a New Hope.

ILLUSTRATION BY **Bryan Christie**

WIRED Geekipedia

231

Facebook

In the beginning, there was Friendster. And Friendster begat MySpace, which drew many disciples and towered over other social networks like tiny Facebook. But Facebook's founder, Mark Zuckerberg, was prideful and refused to sell his company, not even for a reported billion dollars. And, yea, in the spring of 2007, Facebook pulled off a miracle, transubstantiating into a platform for independent developers. And village elder Marc Andreessen declared Facebook "a dramatic leap forward for the Internet industry." And the wise men and women of Silicon Valley began to think that MySpace was not the final word on social networks after all, but merely the first testament.

Faith smackdown

FRANCIS COLLINS VS. RICHARD DAWKINS

Francis Collins, former head of the Human Genome Project (and onetime atheist), rejects the notion that science is sufficient to disprove the existence of God. Biologist Richard Dawkins, a.k.a Darwin's Rottweiler, insists that anyone who believes in an omnipotent creator is suffering a "delusion." Can the gloves of God defeat the punch of proof?

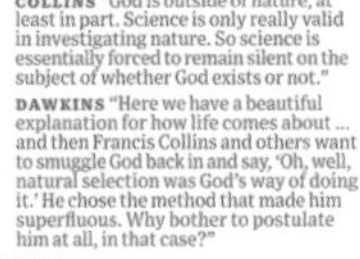

ROUND 1

COLLINS "To say 'There can be no God, and I know that's the case' falls apart on the altar of logical debate—and really, I think, ought to be considered as its own form of blind faith."

DAWKINS "The onus is on somebody who says, 'I want to believe in God,' the Flying Spaghetti Monster, fairies, or whatever it is. It is not up to us to disprove it."

ROUND 2

COLLINS "God is outside of nature, at least in part. Science is only really valid in investigating nature. So science is essentially forced to remain silent on the subject of whether God exists or not."

DAWKINS "Here we have a beautiful explanation for how life comes about ... and then Francis Collins and others want to smuggle God back in and say, 'Oh, well, natural selection was God's way of doing it.' He chose the method that made him superfluous. Why bother to postulate him at all, in that case?"

ROUND 3

COLLINS "God is the answer to all of those 'How must it have come to be?' questions."

DAWKINS "What an incredible evasion of the responsibility to explain. Scientists don't do that. Scientists say, 'We're working on it.'"

DECISION: **GOD ONLY KNOWS**

FRANCIS COLLINS VS RICHARD DAWKINS

Flash

Once, even top Web sites looked like backlit magazine pages. But in 1996, Macromedia acquired a quirky program for drawing animated vector graphics, and the Net has never been the same. Flash gave the medium its own design ethic (and launched a million ill-conceived motion-graphics site intros). The addition of a video codec in 2002 eventually made Flash the standard for streaming clips, thanks to the player's speedy load time and smooth operation. Next up? What else—built-in DRM and forced ad viewing.

« Folksonomy

australia baby china christmas city friends fun germany nature newyork portrait red sanfrancisco water

In the 19th century, scientists hammered out rigid taxonomies to categorize animals, library books, and languages. Today, when anyone on the Web can tag information with words they find descriptive, folksonomies emerge from the collective wisdom of the crowd. The result is an informal, decentralized, evolving classification system. On Flickr, for instance, users adopt one another's tags to create common data sets grouped around even arcane topics like computer recycling. Critics complain of meta-noise, an excess of categories that obscures data instead of revealing it. But for people searching such idiosyncratic topics, the tags are pure signal.

Free

If you build it—and it's cool—they will come. The business model to support it will come later. That's the new economics of the free lunch: Giving away a product or service builds the kind of customer attention and loyalty that rack up earnings. Take a look at Firefox, MySpace, Ubuntu, YouTube, and countless other new-breed products and services that don't cost a penny to use. As scarcity becomes obsolete and bandwidth, storage, and processing grow ever cheaper, old-fashioned vendors will face increasingly skeptical customers asking, what are we paying you for?

Futurism

Futurists enjoy the ultimate job security: The raw material never runs out. The future forever looms ahead, creating a ready market of people who will pay good money for a peek at what's next. The field consists of roughly four schools.

CAPITALISTS US futurists tend to call themselves strategic forecasters, trend spotters, or cool hunters. These market-driven pragmatists write best-selling biz books, moderate scenario-building encounter therapy, and deliver podium-pounding motivational speeches. They consider themselves daring visionaries who tackle unthinkable "wild cards" and "black swans." To the outside world, their prognostications sound like just more America. Major proponent: Global Business Network.

SOCIALISTS Chagrined by the fact that the term *futurism* was invented by Italian proto-fascists, Europeans take an inclusive approach. Their version of futurism has a Teutonically detailed, Brussels-friendly, public policy tinge. At their most daring, they promote notions like "tactical media," "the Multitudes," and a soft-power semiotics designed to turn the whole world European without anybody actually noticing. Major proponent: European Technology Assessment Group.

TOTALITARIANS Futurists of this variety don't merely forecast or speculate. They have a rigid ideological conviction about what the future holds, and they'll happily force it on anyone within reach. Prominent schemes come from situationists, singularity enthusiasts, and transhumanist visionaries who are so desperate to escape the nightmare of history that nobody else can figure out what they're talking about. Major proponent: Project for the New American Century.

APOCALYPTICS Traumatized by breakneck social, political, and technical change, these reactionaries dwell in a faith-based dreamworld where ancient divine revelation is the only source of news. Big-idea apocalyptics promote either the Rapture, where everybody else disappears—thus obviating the need to think about tomorrow—or jihadist martyrdom, where they themselves disappear and take as many unbelievers as possible with them. Major proponents: *Left Behind* fans, al Qaeda.

A B C D E F G H I J K L M N O P Q R S T U V W X Y Z

WIRED Geekipedia

ILLUSTRATION BY **Daniel Adel**

Fake Steve Jobs

It's the rare blogger who knows the power of anonymity. Witness the guessing game over who actually writes the Secret Diary of Steve Jobs. Fake Steve Jobs, or FSJ, uses the Apple CEO as a mask to say what everyone in Silicon Valley would like to, if they weren't too concerned about attracting enemies and bad PR. When the real Jobs released a dry critique of DRM software, Fake Steve Jobs distilled it into its essence: "DRM sucks. You know it. I know it. But the record companies are assholes." The release of FSJ's book this fall could force the parodist into a life less anonymous. Given his skill at speaking truth to power—and making it laugh—that may not matter. Unless, of course, Fake Steve Jobs is none other than Steve Jobs himself.

231

231 WIRED

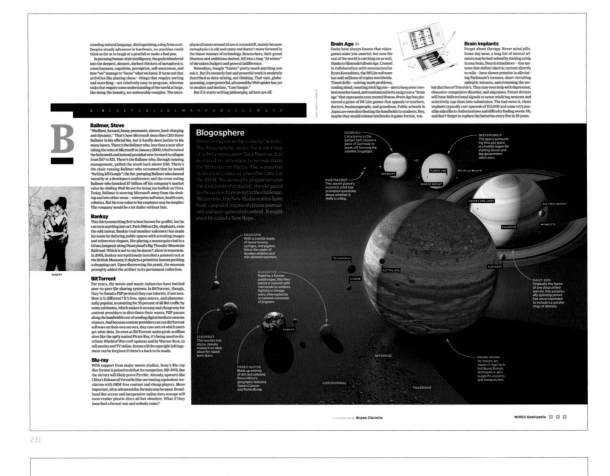

Creative Director_**Scott Dadich** Art Director_**Margaret Swart** Illustrator_**Peter Stemmler** Photo Editor_**Zana Woods** Photographers_**Stephen Lewis, Baerbel Schmidt, R.J. Muna** Publisher_**Condé Nast Publications, Inc.** Issue_**October 2007** Category_**Design: Entire Issue**

Little Ajax photographs by Steve Mundinger

PETER GLUCK'S SOCIAL WORK

by Stephen Zacks

An outspoken architect points the way to socially responsible practice by building his own designs.

Peter Gluck has a problem with the AIA. He has a problem with architectural education too. Really he has a problem with the whole profession of architecture as it is currently practiced. Economic exploitation of youth. Big ideas in service of the highest bidder. Callow young CAD monkeys trained in archispeak. Designers who don't know how to build. Engineers rescuing forms untethered from reality. He doesn't seem like an angry person: he's a sort of laid-back father figure with a gentle demeanor who appears to relish his work. But don't get him started on the irresponsibility of architects and the way the profession is practiced. Or do get him started: you might learn something.

"I don't belong to the AIA," Gluck says during a BMW station-wagon tour of his recent New York projects, among them a campus for Bronx Prep, a charter school for 800 students in the South Bronx, and a center for the Little Sisters of the Assumption Family Health Service, a nonprofit that works with poor families and immigrants in East Harlem. "I think they're the problem, not the solution. It's a group of people who get together to promote themselves; they're not interested in really looking at the profession and trying to see where its problems are."

The Little Ajax Affordable Housing project pivots at the base of a mountain on the edge of downtown Aspen.

138 METROPOLIS September 2007 139

232

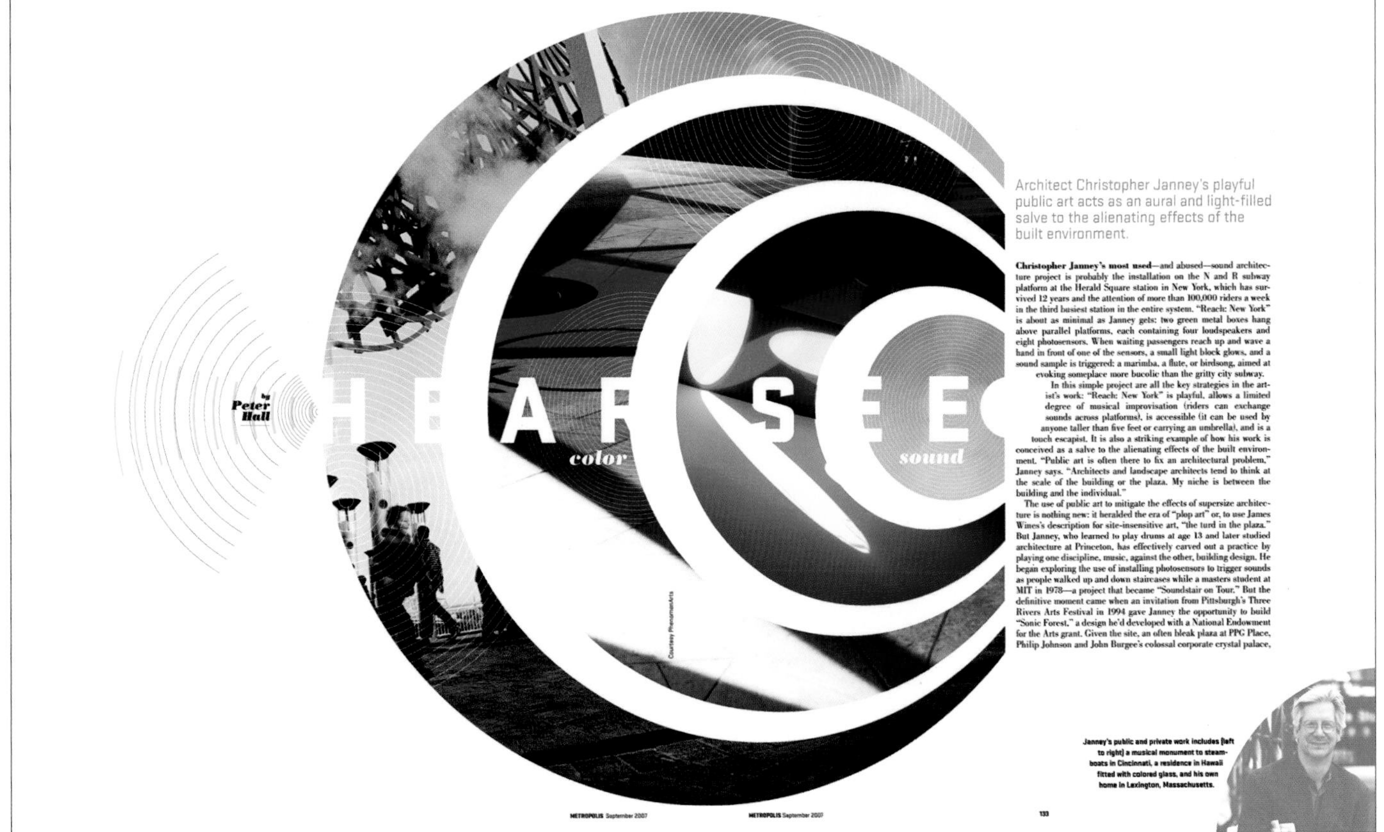

by Peter Hall

HEAR SEE

color *sound*

Architect Christopher Janney's playful public art acts as an aural and light-filled salve to the alienating effects of the built environment.

Christopher Janney's most used—and abused—sound architecture project is probably the installation on the N and R subway platform at the Herald Square station in New York, which has survived 12 years and the attention of more than 100,000 riders a week in the third busiest station in the entire system. "Reach: New York" is about as minimal as Janney gets: two green metal boxes hang above parallel platforms, each containing four loudspeakers and eight photosensors. When waiting passengers reach up and wave a hand in front of one of the sensors, a small light block glows, and a sound sample is triggered: a marimba, a flute, or birdsong, aimed at evoking someplace more bucolic than the gritty city subway.

In this simple project are all the key strategies in the artist's work: "Reach: New York" is playful, allows a limited degree of musical improvisation (riders can exchange sounds across platforms), is accessible (it can be used by anyone taller than five feet or carrying an umbrella), and is a touch escapist. It is also a striking example of how his work is conceived as a salve to the alienating effects of the built environment. "Public art is often there to fix an architectural problem," Janney says. "Architects and landscape architects tend to think at the scale of the building or the plaza. My niche is between the building and the individual."

The use of public art to mitigate the effects of supersize architecture is nothing new: it heralded the era of "plop art" or, to use James Wines's description for site-insensitive art, "the turd in the plaza." But Janney, who learned to play drums at age 13 and later studied architecture at Princeton, has effectively carved out a practice by playing one discipline, music, against the other, building design. He began exploring the use of installing photosensors to trigger sounds as people walked up and down staircases while a masters student at MIT in 1978—a project that became "Soundstair on Tour." But the definitive moment came when an invitation from Pittsburgh's Three Rivers Arts Festival in 1994 gave Janney the opportunity to build "Sonic Forest," a design he'd developed with a National Endowment for the Arts grant. Given the site, an often bleak plaza at PPG Place, Philip Johnson and John Burgee's colossal corporate crystal palace,

Courtesy PhenomenArts

Janney's public and private work includes (left to right) a musical monument to steamboats in Cincinnati, a residence in Hawaii fitted with colored glass, and his own home in Lexington, Massachusetts.

METROPOLIS September 2007 METROPOLIS September 2007 133

232

232 METROPOLIS

Creative Director_Criswell Lappin Art Director_Dungjai Punganthaikan Designer_Erich Nagler Illustrator_Andrew Taray Photo Editor_Bilyana Dimitrova Photographers_Steve Mundinger, Jona Ellis, Julius Sahlman Publisher_Bellerophon Publications Issue_September 2007 Category_Design: Entire Issue

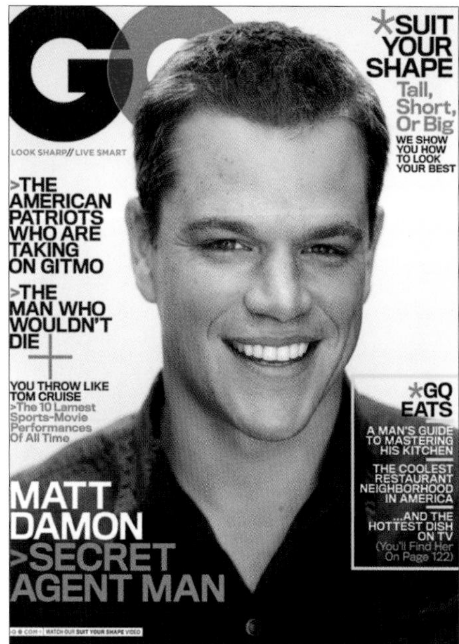

233

233

A MAN'S PLACE IS IN THE

KITCHEN

Guess what, guys. It's no longer enough to just bring home the bacon. It's time you took control of your kitchen. We asked some of the food world's foremost experts to show you how

GQ EATS

It's time to stop thinking of your kitchen as just another room in your house and start thinking of it as a workspace. Like your garage or toolshed, it's about producing and creating. It's about grabbing that dumbbell-heavy meat tenderizer and pounding the crap out of a chicken cutlet; it's about reaching for your ten-inch cook's knife and going to town on a Vidalia onion the size of a grapefruit. It's about taking control. Of course, this does not mean you should make your kitchen *look* like your garage. It should be stylish yet functional. Kind of like your wardrobe. And really, you should be as knowledgeable about the space you cook in as the clothes you wear. You should know which tools to rely on, how to get the most out of the time you spend in your kitchen, and how to make it the most efficient room under your supervision. And why shouldn't it be under your watch? You're the man of the house—why not also be the cook of the house?

PHOTOGRAPHS Sivan Lewin DATE 8/07 PAGE # 109

233

233 GQ

Design Director_**Fred Woodward** Art Director_**Anton Ioukhnovets** Deputy Art Director_**Thomas Alberty** Designers_**Michael Pangilinan, Drue Wagner, Chelsea Cardinal, Rob Hewitt, Eve Binder, Delgis Canahuate** Illustrators_**Jean-Philippe Delhomme, John Ritter, John Ueland, Zohar Lazar** Director of Photography_**Dora Somosi** Senior Photo Editor_**Krista Prestek** Photo Editors_**Justin O'Neill, Jesse Lee, Jolanta Bielat, Halena Green** Photographers_**Alexi Lubomirski, Cass Bird, Nathaniel Goldberg, Ditte Isager, Gillian Laub** Creative Director_**Jim Moore** Editor-In-Chief_**Jim Nelson** Publisher_**Condé Nast Publications Inc.** Issue_**August 2007** Category_**Design: Entire Issue**

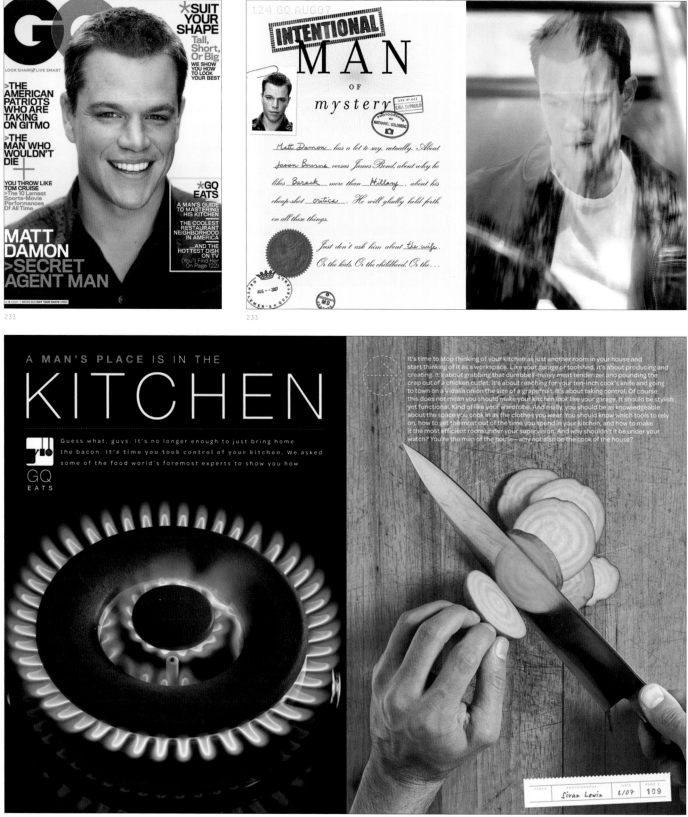

234

234

●●●●●●●

BY DAVID KUSHNER | PHOTOGRAPHS BY BRENT HUMPHREYS

In 2006, a mysterious stalker commandeered the email, cell phone, and PayPal accounts of Talinda and Chester Bennington.

A PASSWORD. 7 SIMPLE LETTERS, A HACKER'S LUCKY GUESS. AND SUDDENLY THE FRONTMAN FOR LINKIN PARK WAS LIVING A NIGHTMARE. FINDING THE STALKER WOULD BECOME A MATTER OF NATIONAL SECURITY.

■■■

234

234 WIRED

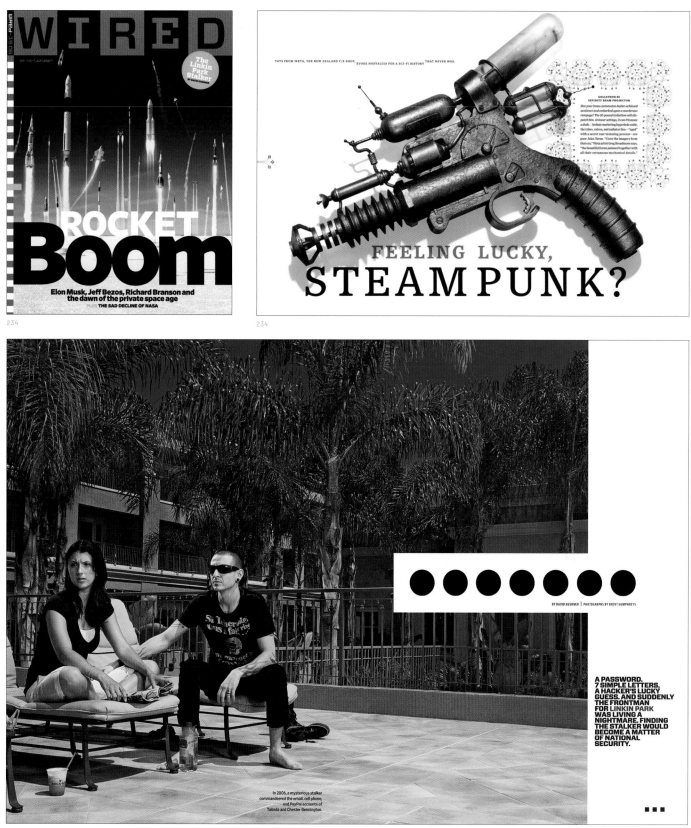

Creative Director_Scott Dadich Art Directors_Maili Holiman, Jeremy LaCroix Designers_Chris Imlay, Carl DeTorres, Victor Krummenacher Illustrators_Bryan Christie, Dan Marsiglio, Saddington & Baynes, Armstrong+White, Riccardo Vecchio Photo Editors_Zana Woods, Carolyn Rauch, Anna Goldwater Alexander Photographers_Brent Humphreys, Bruce Gilden, Ofer Wolberger, Dan Forbes, Brain Finke, Don Foley Publisher_Condé Nast Publications, Inc. Issue_June 2007 Category_Design: Entire Issue

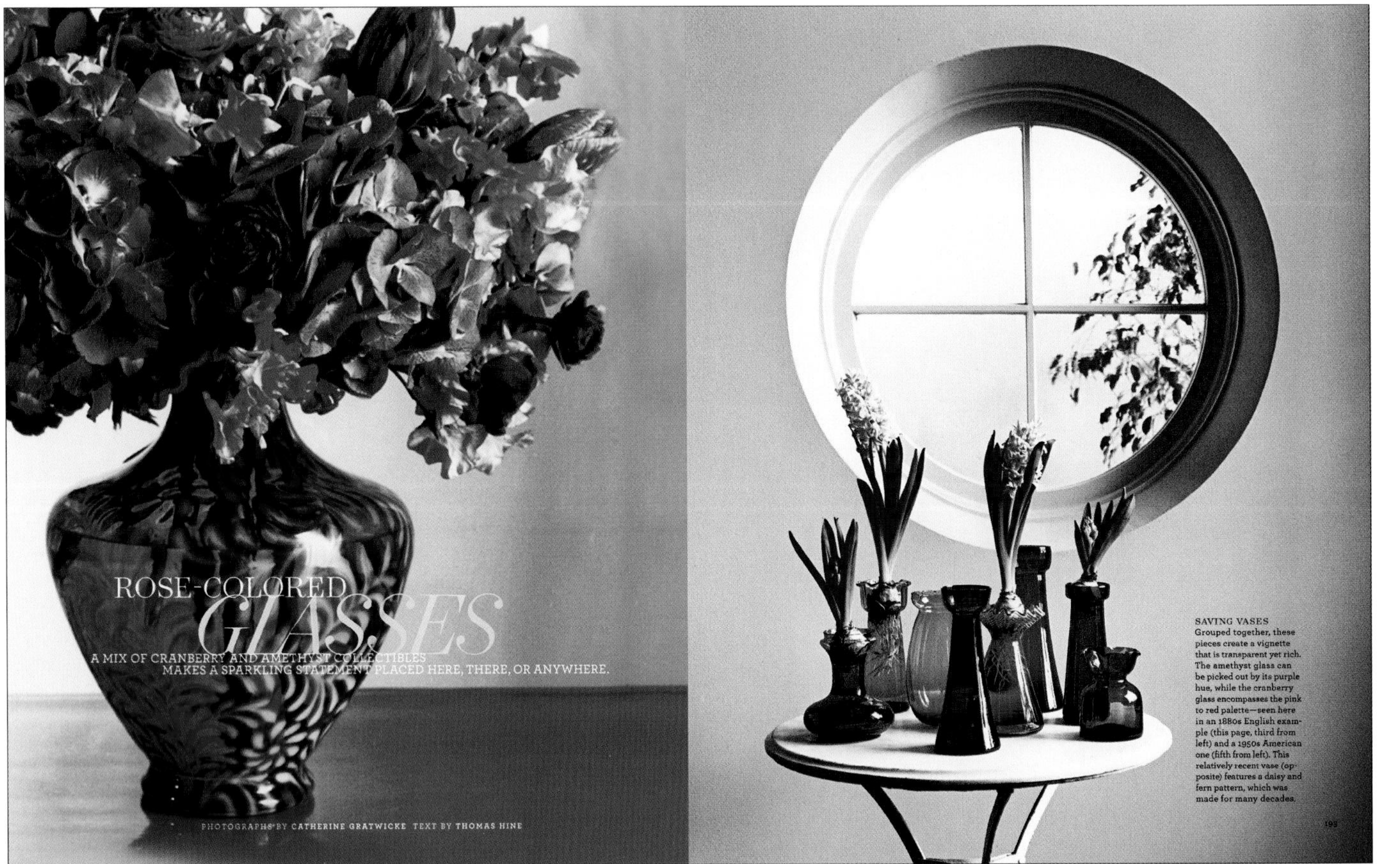

235

235

235 MARTHA STEWART LIVING

Creative Director_**Eric A. Pike** Design Director_**James Dunlinson** Designers_**Matthew Axe, Kevin Brainard, Amber Blakesley, Abbey Kuster-Prokell, Isabel Abdai, Stephen Johnson, Cameron King, Linsey Laidlaw, Mary Jane Callister** Director of Photography_**Heloise Goodman** Senior Photo Editor_**Andrea Bakacs** Associate Photo Editor_**Joni Noe** Photographers_**Pieter Estersohn, Sang An, Dana Gallagher, Hans Gissinger, Catherine Gratwicke** Editor-in-Chief_**Michael Boodro** Editorial Director_**Margaret Roach** Publisher_**Martha Stewart Living Omnimedia** Issue_**May 2007** Category_**Design: Entire Issue**

236

236

236 T, THE NEW YORK TIMES STYLE MAGAZINE

Creative Director_Janet Froelich Senior Art Director_David Sebbah Art Director_Christopher Martinez
Designer_Elizabeth Spiridakis Photo Editors_Judith Puckett-Rinella, Scott Hall Editor-In-Chief_Stefano Tonchi
Publisher_The New York Times Issue_September 16, 2007 Category_Design: Entire Issue

SECTION
DESIGN

AWARD
MERIT

CATEGORY
ENTIRE ISSUE

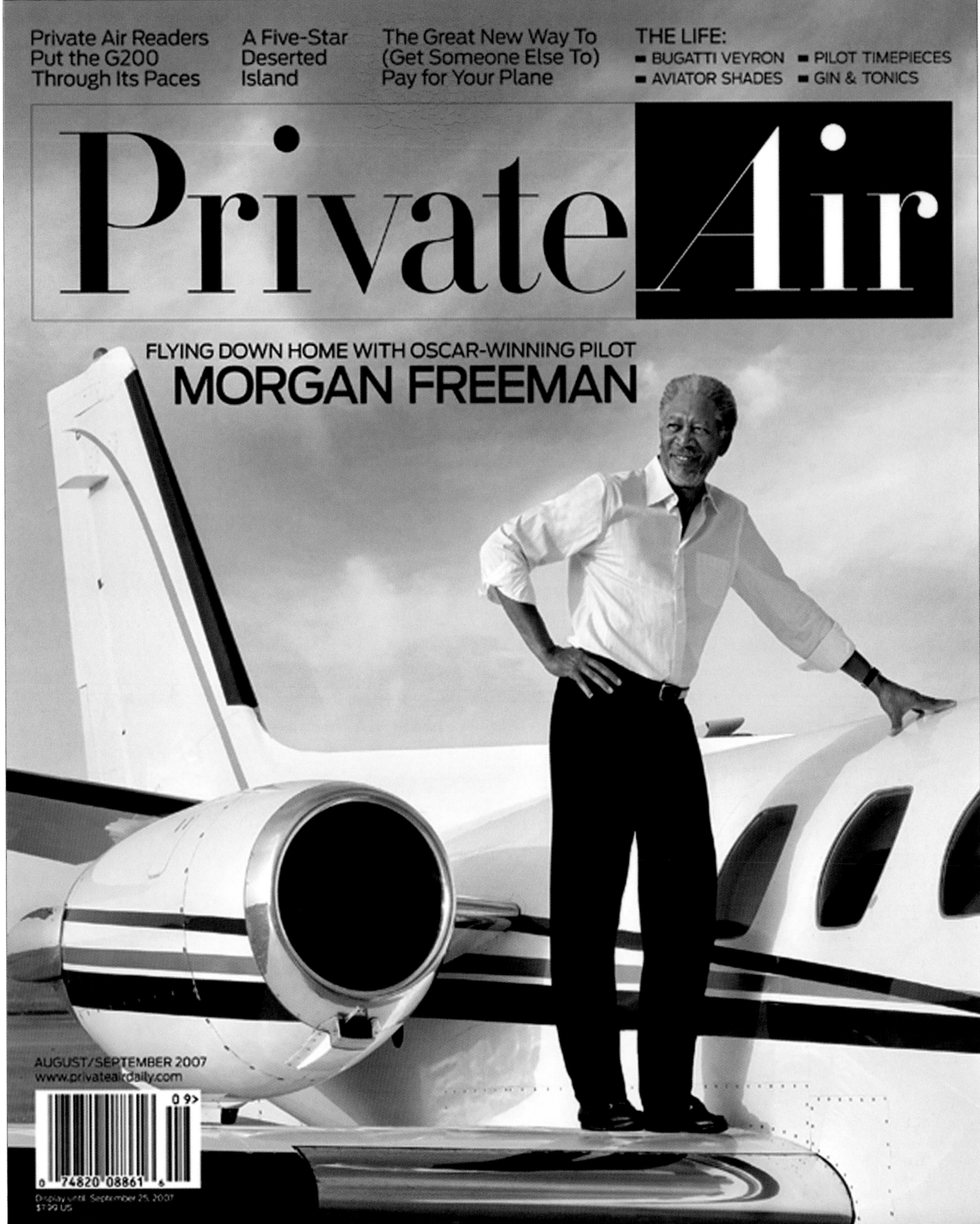

237

237 PRIVATE AIR

Creative Director_Florian Bachleda Art Directors_Clare Minges, Alice Alves Director of Photography_Ian Spanier Photographers_Ian Spanier, Jimmy Nicol, Matt Furman Studio_FB Design Publisher_Doubledown Media Issue_August/September 2007 Category_Design: Entire Issue

238

238

239

239

240

240

238 HALLMARK MAGAZINE

Creative Director_Michelle Egan Design Director_Dan Josephs Art Director_Alden Wallace Illustrators_Maria O'Keefe, Trina Dalziel, Ramone Olivera, Oliver Christianson, Cathy Liesner, Renee Andriani, Ken Sheldon, Amy Kraus Rosenthal Photo Editors_Shelley Knapp, Lisa Vosper Photographers_Scott Gibbons, Jane Kortright, Jake Johnson, Erika McConnell, Ken Sabatini Editor-In-Chief_Lisa Beneson Publisher_Hallmark Publishing Holdings, LLC Issue_July/August 2007 Category_Design: Entire Issue

239 MARTHA STEWART LIVING

Creative Director_Eric A. Pike Design Director_James Dunlinson Designers Matthew Axe, Kevin Brainard, Amber Blakesley, Abbey Kuster-Prokell, Isabel Abdai, Stephen Johnson, Cameron King, Linsey Laidlaw, Mary Jane Callister Director of Photography_Heloise Goodman Senior Photo Editor_Andrea Bakacs Associate Photo Editor_Joni Noe Photographers_Marion Brenner, Maria Robledo, Anna Williams, Anita Calero, Gemma Comas, Lisa Hubbard Editor-In-Chie_Margaret Roach Publisher_Martha Stewart Living Omnimedia Issue_March 2007 Category_Design: Entire Issue

240 EVERYDAY FOOD

Creative Director_Eric A. Pike Art Director_Alberto Capolino Associate Art Director_Maggie Boroujerdi Designer_Alberto Capolino Director of Photography_Heloise Goodman Photo Editor Andrea Bakacs Photographer_Marcus Nilsson Food Editor_Sandra Gluck Food Stylist_CTD Raftus McDowell Editor-In-Chief_Debra Puchalla Publisher_Martha Stewart Omnimedia Issue_July/August 2007 Category_Design: Entire Issue

GET ORGANIZED WITH CHALKBOARD PAINT

If you thought chalkboards were just for schoolrooms, think again. These wipe-off writing surfaces make handy helpers around the home, too. Thanks to paint that dries into a chalkboard finish, your "board" can be whatever size you desire and placed wherever you like. Store-bought formulas come in traditional green and black. But you can also follow our recipe to mix your own batch in any shade. Cleverly applied chalkboard paint means new places to track appointments, keep lists, and leave messages. Or simply use the surface to draw or doodle, which will appeal to kids—and the kid in everyone.

PHOTOGRAPHS BY **ERIC PIASECKI**
TEXT BY **KIMBERLY FUSARO**

WALL CALENDAR

A home office is the ideal spot for a family planner (opposite). Six weeks' worth of squares in a variety of shades can accommodate several schedules. The entire wall is also coated with chalkboard paint for more memos. Start with a base coat of store-bought black chalkboard paint, and then mix in varying amounts of white chalkboard paint for lighter squares. For the how-to, see page 134.

131

241

SUM AND SUBSTANCE
Earthy yellow beets are the primary ingredient of a [illegible] vegetable soup that also features leeks, carrots, and snippings of chives. A bracing squirt of lime—a culinary touch borrowed from Latin American and Southeast Asian soup makers—brightens the whole bowl.

GOLDEN BEET SOUP
with chives and lime wedges

A REFRESHING APPROACH

SPA-INSPIRED RECIPES RESTORE AND RENEW WITH A BOLD PALETTE OF VIBRANT FLAVORS.

Winter's comfort foods—creamy potpies, roasted birds, braised meats—are the culinary equivalents of wrapping ourselves up in a warm, fuzzy blanket for a nap by a crackling fire. But soon enough, we awaken from the slumber, eager for energizing dishes that sparkle with sharp, in-focus flavors and pop with saturated color.

Markets might seem leaner in cold-weather months, but a closer look reveals strong selections. Citrus fruits arrive in a brilliant cascade of colors at just the right moment. And while spices, herbs, and the vast family of onions and garlic are at our fingertips year-round, they're a particular boon now, steering the season's humble root vegetables and leafy greens in exciting directions. Far Eastern and Middle Eastern cooks (and savvy spa chefs) have always known that such emphatic ingredients can stand in for fats and salt, satiating us without weighing us down. Whether it's the tickle of pink peppercorns against bitter endive and sweet-sour grapefruit, the zing of lime and chives in beet soup, or the hum of cumin and coriander in carrot-coconut chicken, these seasonings resonate long after we've cleaned the plate. In the Mediterranean, simple but assured ingredients form whole symphonies of flavor, as in a rousing mix of whole-wheat pasta, Meyer lemon, arugula, and pistachios.

Our seven recipes, then, aren't about deprivation but appreciation. These are foods that make eating right an enticing enterprise. Lusty whole grains, bright-tasting vegetables, and wild fish also are on the menu. Like a brisk walk on a luminous winter morning, each dish will invigorate you.

PHOTOGRAPHS BY **ANNA WILLIAMS** TEXT BY **DANA BOWEN**

105

241

241 MARTHA STEWART LIVING

Creative Director_**Eric A. Pike** Design Director_**James Dunlinson** Designers_**Matthew Axe, Amber Blakesley, Abbey Kuster-Prokell, Isabel Abdai, Stephen Johnson, Cameron King, Linsey Laidlaw, Mary Jane Callister, David Meredith** Director of Photography_**Heloise Goodman** Senior Photo Editor_**Andrea Bakacs** Photographers_**Pieter Estersohn, Anna Williams, William Abranowicz, John Kernick, Eric Piasecki** Editor-In-Chief_**Margaret Roach** Publisher_**Martha Stewart Living Omnimedia** Issue_**January 2007** Category_**Design: Entire Issue**

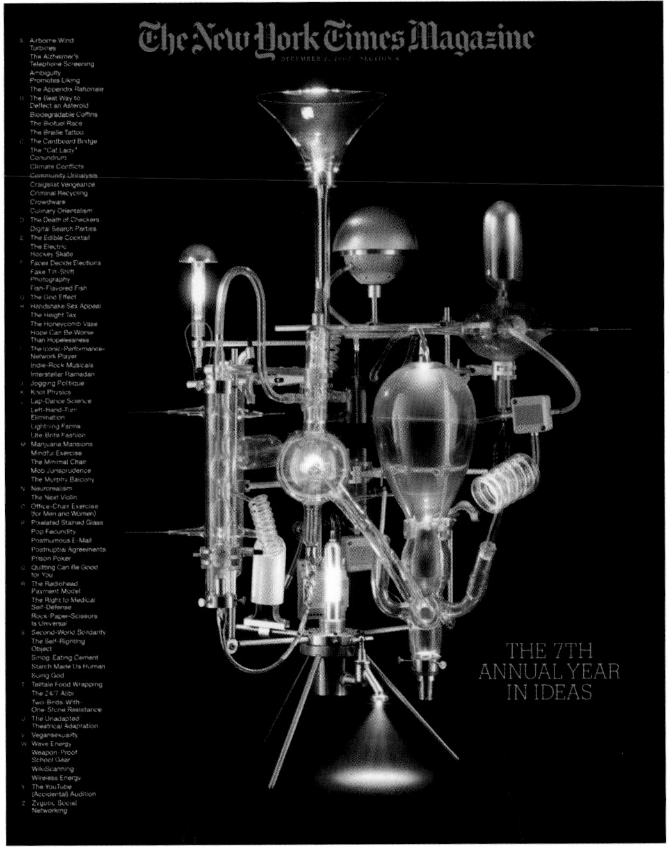

242

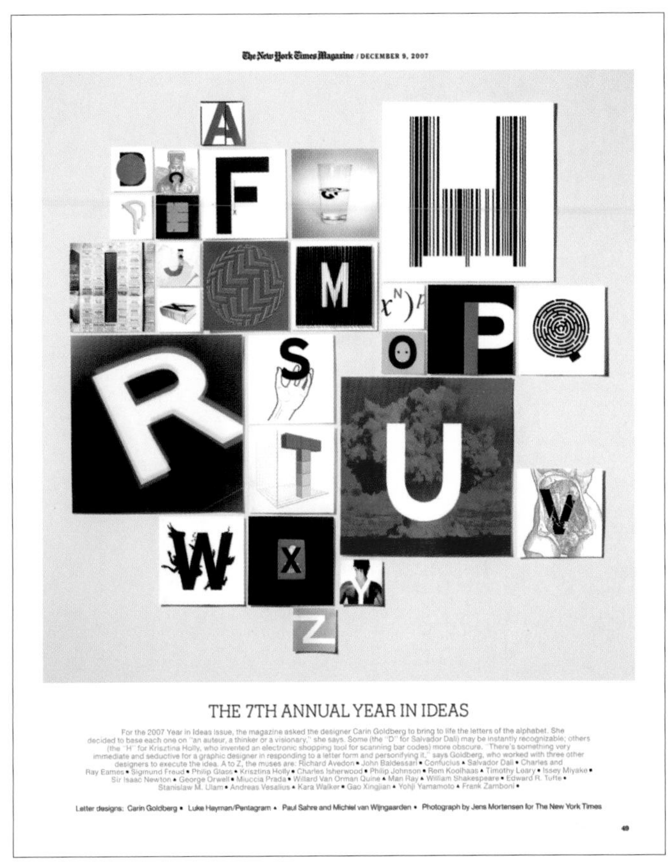
The New York Times Magazine / DECEMBER 9, 2007

THE 7TH ANNUAL YEAR IN IDEAS

For the 2007 Year in Ideas issue, the magazine asked the designer Carin Goldberg to bring to life the letters of the alphabet. She decided to base each one on "an auteur, a thinker or a visionary," she says. Some (the "D" for Salvador Dali) may be instantly recognizable; others (the "H" for Krisztina Holly, who invented an electronic shopping tool for scanning bar codes) more obscure. "There's something very immediate and seductive for a graphic designer in responding to a letter form and personifying it," says Goldberg, who worked with three other designers to execute the idea. A to Z, the muses are: Richard Avedon • John Baldessari • Confucius • Salvador Dali • Charles and Ray Eames • Sigmund Freud • Philip Glass • Krisztina Holly • Charles Isherwood • Philip Johnson • Rem Koolhaas • Timothy Leary • Issey Miyake • Sir Isaac Newton • George Orwell • Miuccia Prada • Willard Van Orman Quine • Man Ray • William Shakespeare • Edward R. Tufte • Stanislaw M. Ulam • Andreas Vesalius • Kara Walker • Gao Xingjian • Yohji Yamamoto • Frank Zamboni •

Letter designs: Carin Goldberg • Luke Hayman/Pentagram • Paul Sahre and Michiel van Wijngaarden • Photograph by Jens Mortensen for The New York Times

49

242

BIODEGRADABLE COFFINS PHOTOGRAPH BY REINHARD HUNGER

PROP STYLIST: FRANZISKA KERN

BIODEGRADABLE COFFINS 6 BIOFUEL RACE, THE 7

BIODEGRADABLE COFFINS [6] This July, when Jorgi Wu was laid to rest in central California, she became the first American to be buried in an Ecopod — a 100 percent biodegradable coffin made of recycled paper. The seed-pod-shaped coffin is designed to be planted in the ground, dissolve and replenish the earth with its nutrient-rich contents. Who needs embalming, cement vaults or herbicide-based lawn care?

Interest in "green" burials has been increasing in recent years, and the Ecopod is one of the first coffins to fit the environmentally conscious consumer niche. Originally developed in England, it is sold in the United States by the Portland-based Natural Burial Company. Visitors to the company's showroom will soon be able to see a variety of other biodegradable coffins made of paper, formaldehyde-free plywood, fair-trade-certified bamboo and hand-woven Somerset willow.

These coffins are the antithesis of the funeral industry's usual rain-forest mahogany and steel caskets, which are held together by formaldehyde-infused glue and hermetically sealed to keep nature *out*. According to Cynthia Beal, the founder of the Natural Burial Company, this preservation process has turned modern cemeteries into "parking lots" for the dead. She says she hopes her products will push the trend toward natural burial parks — currently there are just a handful in the country.

While the Ecopod triumphs in simplicity, it does not skimp on style. It is available in multiple colors — and can be silk-screened with doves, Aztec suns or other designs, and lined with cream or blue feathers, so that customers can choose the Ecopod that best reflects their personalities. Wu chose the forest green model — with a Celtic cross on top. APRIL DEMBOSKY

BIOFUEL RACE, THE [7] For millennia, civilization's main event, the harvest, has focused our attention upon the fruit of our agricultural efforts — the kernel, the grain, busheled and bagged. So it's no surprise that the fledgling biofuel industry has been similarly focused: America's favorite biofuels come mostly from corn and from soy. But when food crops are used as fuel, difficulties may follow. The vogue for corn ethanol has driven up the price of corn around the world, putting the poor in jeopardy. (An expert affiliated with the United Nations went so far as to label the production of biofuels derived from food stock "a crime against humanity.") Corn ethanol is also astonishingly inefficient: because vast amounts of fossil fuels are required for its manufacture, every 1 unit of energy nets a mere 1.3 units of ethanol.

Is there a better way? In 2007, significant steps were taken toward a potentially great second harvest, some of it coming from the byproducts of animals, some of it from municipal waste and garbage but the bulk of it coming from plant biomass, which is really about breaking down cellulose, the key structural component of all plant cell walls and the most abundant of all naturally occurring organic compounds on earth. A recent Department of Energy study found the United States can produce a billion tons of plant biomass annually, yet 400 million years of evolution has made cellulose resistant — the term of art is "recalcitrant" — to manipulation. Unlocking its complex compounds of sugars, whose potential yield is 4 times that of corn on a gallons-per-acre basis, typically requires an aggressive, four-step thermo-chemical process. Taken together, these steps have been too costly or too energy intensive for cellulosic fuel production to become economically viable. Cracking the conundrum of plant cell walls cheaply has become a Brigadoon-like dream that has been "5 years away," as one wry observer put it, "for the last 30 years."

Until now — at least if you believe Vinod Khosla, one of the best-known venture capitalists in America, who was a founder of Sun Microsystems and an early investor in Google, and who has in recent years invested hundreds of millions of dollars into a dozen different biofuel companies using new and potentially revolutionary techniques. In November, a Khosla-backed firm called Range Fuels broke ground on the first cellulosic ethanol plant in the country. The plant, located in Georgia, employs an effi-

THE BIOFUEL RACE ILLUSTRATION BY TAMARA SHOPSIN

PHOTOGRAPH BY JENS MORTENSEN FOR THE NEW YORK TIMES

THE NEW YORK TIMES MAGAZINE / DECEMBER 9, 2007 57

242

242 THE NEW YORK TIMES MAGAZINE

Creative Director_**Janet Froelich** Art Director_**Arem Duplessis** Designer_**Gail Bichler** Director of Photography_**Kathy Ryan** Photo Editors_**Joanna Milter, Kira Pollack** Editor-In-Chief_**Gerry Marzorati** Publisher_**The New York Times** Issue_**December 9, 2007** Category_**Design: Entire Issue**

Arrange Your Action Figures

Careful, those aren't toys! **Tom Root** and **Douglas Goldstein**, the two head writers for the Adult Swim figure-fest *Robot Chicken*, offer advanced tips on curating your cubicle tchotchkes.

1 **MAKE** sure they stay standing. As figures get more and more intricate, they're more and more likely to fall over. Hit the feet with some adhesive pads or sticky tack.

2 **PUT** some thought into the groupings. Nothing says "I don't care" like jumbling together *Star Trek: TOS* with *Star Trek: TNG*. And watch out for bad symbolism: If you work in HR, don't put Darth-anything on your desk.

3 **AVOID** excessively gory figures. Rule of thumb: If you can see brains and/or viscera, don't display it. Also, ixnay on the scantily clad Playmates or porn stars—you'll just look desperate and lonely. Finally, eschew cutesy figures. If the best you can do is Papa Smurf with a fishing pole, just forget it. (Irony is no defense.)

4 **HIDE** the accessories. Most action figures come with tiny accoutrements that are almost certain to get lost. Leave these precious extras at home where they're safe. "Take it from a guy who's still mourning the loss of his Bespin Luke's yellow lightsaber," Root says.

5 **SPREAD** out the toys so that if one does fall, it won't start a domino effect. You don't want to return from lunch to find Robin's face in Batman's crotch.

6 **NEVER** pose figures in compromising positions. Sure, it's funny to make He-Man and She-Ra get all buck wild ... until you're slapped with a harassment lawsuit.

how to...

DRESS LIKE A PROFESSIONAL

"WE HAVE BECOME a nation of slobs," says Tim Gunn, chair of fashion design at the Parsons School and mentor on *Project Runway*. "I regularly see people in sweatpants and flip-flops, even on Seventh Avenue." If this reminds you of some schlump in your office, Gunn has remedial wardrobe tips to pass along. 1. **BUSINESS CASUAL** means a suit and shirt (no tie), not a schwag Dell tee. Minimum specs would be dark dress pants and a long-sleeved shirt with a collar. 2. **KHAKIS** and a white oxford-cloth shirt should be in everyone's inventory. Level it up with a seersucker blazer. 3. **JEANS** are compatible with casual Fridays, but opt for darker washes. Equip a colorful striped shirt for a set bonus.

Choose Gifts for Office Parties Remember, it's *not* the thought that counts. No one wants your papier-mâché bust of Linus Torvalds, even though it took you the whole weekend to make. If you don't know the recipient's tastes, keep it simple. (Maybe you'll regret giving a *Porky's* DVD to a fundamentalist or a bottle of scotch to a 12-stepper.) Still at a loss? Borders or Starbucks gift cards are hard to screw up.

KEEP 'EM *Honest*

ARE YOUR COWORKERS skimping when it comes to the donation jar next to the office coffeemaker? Research shows that a picture of a face—or even just eyes—will inspire people to fork over 30 percent more money. Something about being watched, even though the conscious mind knows it's just a picture, seems to enhance altruism. Test it yourself: Paste this image on your donation or tip jar and watch the dollar bills crowd out the coins.

USE LINKEDIN

Unless you're a tween, social networking sites are kinda lame. Except for LinkedIn, a professional-contact database that rewards users for sharing good advice. **David Nason,** one of the site's top-ranked advice-givers, explains how to leverage it.

1 **EXTEND** invites only to people you know or are fairly confident would like to build a relationship with you. And be selective when accepting a request to link—this isn't a popularity contest.

2 **FILL OUT** your job history. Pay special attention to searchable keywords like "project management" and "Perl." Don't forget to add an elevator statement—a one-sentence pitch for yourself.

3 **SOLICIT** some plaudits. LinkedIn lets users recommend one another. Don't seek raves just from bosses—sometimes peers, clients, and subordinates can offer a better picture of you.

4 **ANSWER** questions posed by other users. Thoughtful responses can earn Best Answer expertise points, which increase your ranking (and status).

AUGUST 2007

243

1

The Gunslinger Born

Graphic virtuoso Jae Lee's latest work is more than an epic homage to Stephen King's original *Dark Tower* opus. It's the origin story of gritty post-apocalyptic protagonist Roland Deschain, chronicling his teenage years just before he embarks on his Tower quest. Adapted by King expert Robin Furth and approved by the macabre maestro himself, the first seven-issue comic series will wrap up in August, with Lee currently inking the second set of installments—news for which King fans say *thankee-sai*.

PLAY

Playlist | WHAT'S WIRED THIS MONTH

AUGUST 2007

243

Mr. Know-It-All | BRENDAN I. KOERNER

Hey, You, Get Off of My Blog

Is it OK to ban someone from posting comments on my blog?

A personal blog is pretty much an autocracy, so you're technically free to ban whoever rubs you the wrong way. But going all Joe Stalin on your commenters—even the ones who annoy you with their nit-picking or wacko views—doesn't jibe with the Internet's spirit of openness. The best blogs are supposed to be a conversation. And anyway, if you're going to publish what you write, accept the fact that the responses are going to be neither 100 percent positive nor 100 percent civil. Journalists have known this since the invention of the letter to the editor. It doesn't mean, however, that you're obliged to let a potty-mouthed commenter ruin your blog. If a recalcitrant troll is scaring off your readers or dragging the discourse into the gutter, a permanent ban may be the only solution. "I view the commenters on my blog like they're guests at a party," says Eugene Volokh, a professor at UCLA School of Law and founder of the Volokh Conspiracy group blog. And if a racist, abusive, or otherwise abhorrent guest is putting a damper on your shindig, you're well within your rights to kick the hooligan to the curb.

As for what constitutes bannable behavior, that's completely your call. Some people prefer running dinner-party-style blogs, where even a little swearing can kill the intellectual vibe. Others aim for the equivalent of a kegger, meaning that only the most egregious speech is barred. Figure out what sort of atmosphere you're gunning for and craft some commenting guidelines accordingly. Repeat violators should get the heave-ho.

The key word here is *repeat*. "From time to time, everyone gets angry and clicks Publish before thinking about it enough," says Dale Carpenter, a University of Minnesota Law School professor and a Volokh Conspiracy contributor. "A person who is uncivil and nonsubstantive one day may have something very important to say the next." Give the commenter a warning before pronouncing him dead to you. If he crosses the line again, you can disappear him with Mr. Know-It-All's blessing.

Every so often I get email asking me to help rescue a Nigerian's long-lost loot. Is it safe to tease these con artists?

The practice you're referring to is known as scam baiting: messing with those email fraudsters

AUGUST 2007

ILLUSTRATIONS BY **Christoph Niemann**

243

243 WIRED

Creative Director_Scott Dadich Art Directors_Maili Holiman, Jeremy LaCroix Designers_Chris Imlay, Carl DeTorres, Margaret Swart, Christy Sheppard Illustrators_Eddie Guy, Bryan Christie, Seth Ferris, Christoph Niemann, Bruce Hutchison, Pietari Posti Photo Editors_Anna Goldwater Alexander, Zana Woods, Carolyn Rauch Photographers_Jill Greenberg, Baerbel Schmidt, John Clard, Darren Braun, Todd Hido Publisher_Condé Nast Publications, Inc. Issue_August 2007 Category_Design: Entire Issue

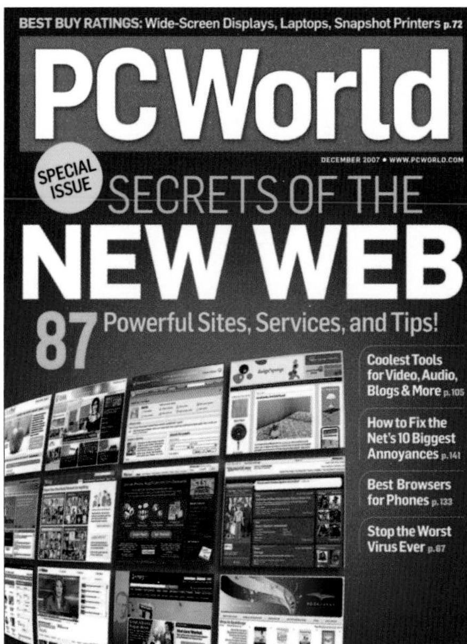

244

Reviews & Rankings

INSIDE

NAVIGON 7100 · APPLE IPOD TOUCH · HTC ADVANTAGE X7501 · MICROSOFT MOBILE MEMORY MOUSE

22-Inch LCDs: More Screen for Less Green

Basic 22-inch wide-screen LCDs are a steal for under $300, and decked-out ones are tempting, too, at less than $400.

HAVE YOU BEEN holding out for the right wide-screen monitor? The big manufacturers are releasing a torrent of new 22-inch wide-screen models, starting at around $270, that may just persuade you to open your wallet. And though any of these models will expand your desktop view, they're far less likely than a 24-inch-plus display to empty your pockets.

The PC World Test Center subjected seven new 22-inch wide-screen monitors to a plethora of viewing tests. Our hawk-eyed jurors scrutinized various text documents and graphics to see which monitors were pleasing and which merely middling. Our Best Buy award went to the good-looking HP w2207 monitor. Priced at $360 (as of October 9), this display combines beauty and substance. Though it trailed others in graphics and text quality, it still performed well enough to earn scores of Very Good and Good, respectively, on those two measures. And its many features, such as a pivoting panel and USB ports, helped it overcome its minor shortcomings in performance. ViewSonic's VG2230wm finished close behind, thanks to good performance and an even better price ($319).

Nipping at the heels of the top two was the Samsung SyncMaster 2232GW. The best graphics and text performer, this monitor will satisfy both casual users and graphics pros. AG Neovo's H-W22, which ranks a respectable fourth, carries a budget price ($269) that belies its impressive showing in our tests. It trumped many of the more expensive displays with accurate and attractive renderings of graphics and text. To boot, its minimalist design will suit users who want to simplify the appearance of their desks. Dell's staid-looking E228WFP rounded out our Top 5 with test scores confirming it as a serious workhorse for users who don't consider design a priority.

We also tested the Envision G218a1 and the Acer P221W, but neither of them captured spots our chart. Though inexpensive ($280) and fairly well designed, the Envision display suffered from so-so graphics performance and a paucity of extra features. Meanwhile, the Acer's performance was okay, but not nearly enough to compensate for its $500 price.

HP SELLS OPTIONAL Easy Clip accessories that attach to the sides of its w2207 display.

The Office Workers' New Desk Friend

For a time, many manufacturers were pushing 19-inch wide screens, already a consumer hit because of their low price and broad spread, to businesses. But that market hasn't taken off as expected. Tom Mainelli, senior research analyst for monitors at IDC (and a *PC World* contributor), sees monitor manufacturers responding by producing a raft of 22-inch wide-screen models that may soon emerge as "blockbuster" performers for office use. "Twenty-two-inch wide monitors have been [in the market] for a while," he observes, but demand for them only recently "started gaining some traction primarily because of the dramatic price difference between 20- and 24-inch wide screens."

Currently you can buy a no-frills 22-incher for as little as $250, while few 24-inch monitors cost less than $500. Mainelli says the price difference reflects the fact that "monitor vendors have kept 24- to 30-inch [displays] as premium monitors, [so] customers are more likely to expect extras" such as high-definition video connectors, pivoting panels, TV tuners, and multiple physical adjustments. If you don't need these frills, however, you can parlay a budget for one 24-inch monitor into an enviable double-22-inch-monitor configuration. Moreover, even though 22-inch models have the »

MORE ONLINE

Visit find.pcworld.com/58685 for a full review of each 22-inch wide-screen model in our Top 5 chart. You'll also find Best Buy charts for flat-panel displays with screen sizes ranging from 17 to 24 inches.

PC WORLD TOP 5 22-INCH WIDE-SCREEN LCD MONITORS

	Model	PCW Rating
1	HP w2207 $360 NEW	79
2	ViewSonic VG2230wm $319 NEW	78
3	Samsung SyncMaster 2232GW $380 NEW	77
4	AG Neovo H-W22 $269 NEW	75
5	Dell E228WFP $300 NEW	74

BOTTOM LINE: This extremely thin-looking monitor is a no-frills performer good for minimalists and budget-conscious offices.

72 | WWW.PCWORLD.COM DECEMBER 2007 — DECEMBER 2007 WWW.PCWORLD.COM | 73

244

GOOD — the High Tech / Low Tech issue

it's all true: THE OLDEST PROFESSION(S) 72 · GET A SECOND LIFE 76 · L.A.'S URBAN CATASTROPHE 102

This man predicts the future (correctly)

How game theory can tell us who the next president will be, if we'll bomb Iran, and the outcome of other world events

245

High Tech / Low Tech

The hollow promise of the internet's Next Big Thing

Get a Life

by MORGAN CLENDANIEL

"Dude, did you lose your dick?"

That is the first thing anyone says to me in Second Life. I am standing naked in a bordello, conspicuously lacking the cartoonish satyr-like genitalia sported by the other male patrons. I have come here with visions of a place where I will no longer be hindered by the chafing constraints of our physical world. Here, I can fly, I can walk through cities wielding a giant sword, I can be the kind of guy who goes to sex clubs. But first, apparently, I have to find a penis. ▸

245

244 PC WORLD

Art Director_Barbara Adamson Designers_Beth Kamoroff, Jeff Berlin, Greg Silva Illustrators_Mick Wiggins, Harry Campbell, Thomas Fuchs, Gordon Studer, John Cuneo Photographers_Robert Cardin, Marc Simon Editor-In-Chief_Hanna McCracken Publisher_International Data Group Issue_December 2007 Category_Design: Entire Issue

245 GOOD

Creative Director_Casey Caplowe Design Director_Scott Stowell Designers_Susan Barber, Rob DiLeso, Gary Fogelson, Carol Hayes, Serifcan Özcan, Nick Rock, Scott Stowell, Ryan Thacker Director of Photography_Joaquin Trujillo Studio_Open Publisher_Good Magazine, LLC Issue_November/December 2007 Category_Design: Entire Issue

WHAT YOU ARE

WHO YOU ARE

246

YOUR DNA DECODED: A $1,000 TEST CAN GIVE YOU A PEEK AT YOUR GENOME—AND AT YOUR RISK OF DEVELOPING CANCER AND OTHER DISEASES. NOW WE JUST HAVE TO FIGURE OUT WHAT TO DO WITH ALL THAT INFORMATION.

BY THOMAS GOETZ | PHOTOGRAPHS BY BRENT HUMPHREYS

A

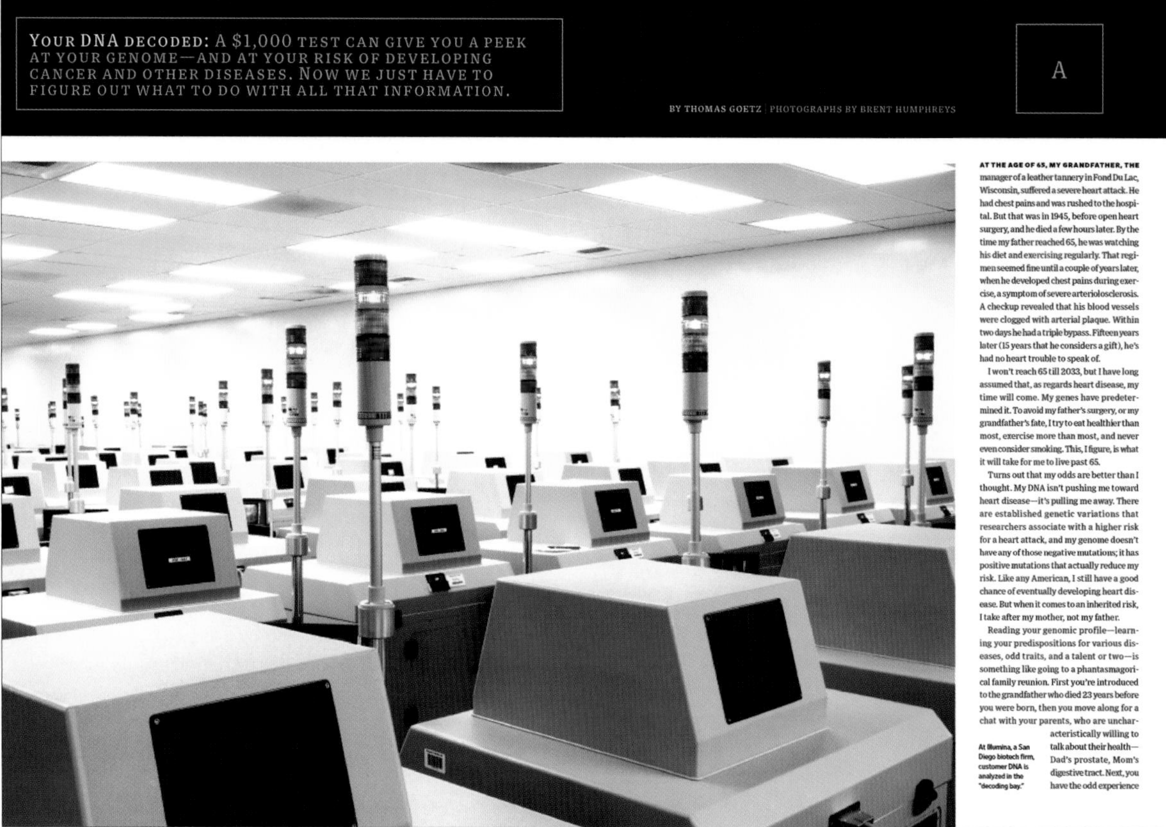

AT THE AGE OF 65, MY GRANDFATHER, THE manager of a leather tannery in Fond Du Lac, Wisconsin, suffered a severe heart attack. He had chest pains and was rushed to the hospital. But that was in 1945, before open heart surgery, and he died a few hours later. By the time my father reached 65, he was watching his diet and exercising regularly. That regimen seemed fine until a couple of years later, when he developed chest pains during exercise, a symptom of severe arteriolosclerosis. A checkup revealed that his blood vessels were clogged with arterial plaque. Within two days he had a triple bypass. Fifteen years later (15 years that he considers a gift), he's had no heart trouble to speak of.

I won't reach 65 till 2033, but I have long assumed that, as regards heart disease, my time will come. My genes have predetermined it. To avoid my father's surgery, or my grandfather's fate, I try to eat healthier than most, exercise more than most, and never even consider smoking. This, I figure, is what it will take for me to live past 65.

Turns out that my odds are better than I thought. My DNA isn't pushing me toward heart disease—it's pulling me away. There are established genetic variations that researchers associate with a higher risk for a heart attack, and my genome doesn't have any of those negative mutations; it has positive mutations that actually reduce my risk. Like any American, I still have a good chance of eventually developing heart disease. But when it comes to an inherited risk, I take after my mother, not my father.

Reading your genomic profile—learning your predispositions for various diseases, odd traits, and a talent or two—is something like going to a phantasmagorical family reunion. First you're introduced to the grandfather who died 23 years before you were born, then you move along for a chat with your parents, who are uncharacteristically willing to talk about their health—Dad's prostate, Mom's digestive tract. Next, you have the odd experience

At Illumina, a San Diego biotech firm, customer DNA is analyzed in the "decoding bay."

246

246 WIRED

Creative Director_Scott Dadich Design Director_Wyatt Mitchell Designer_Wyatt Mitchell
Illustrators_ILM, Ryan Jones, Alex Jaeger, Rick O'Connor, Ron Woodall Photo Editor_Carolyn Rauch Photographers_Frank Schwere, Brent Humphreys
Publisher_Condé Nast Publications, Inc. Issue_December 2007 Category_Design: Feature: Story

162
05-07-GQ

THE GQ PRESIDENTIAL CANDIDATE QUESTIONNAIRE

THE REAL COLBERT REPORT

Let's face it: This country needs a president. And only one man is fit for the job. The guy you're looking at: Comedy Central pundit STEPHEN COLBERT. But to be sure that he possesses the moral authority America so desperately needs, we subjected him to a highly confidential background check. Then, because we are the media and have no morals, we decided to betray his trust and publish his answers

SECTION 1: Candidate Information

1. (a) Last Name
COLBERT

(b) First Name
STEPHEN

2. (a) Office Sought
PRESIDENT OF THE UNITED STATES

(b) Year of Election
2008

3. Photographs by Mark Seliger

247

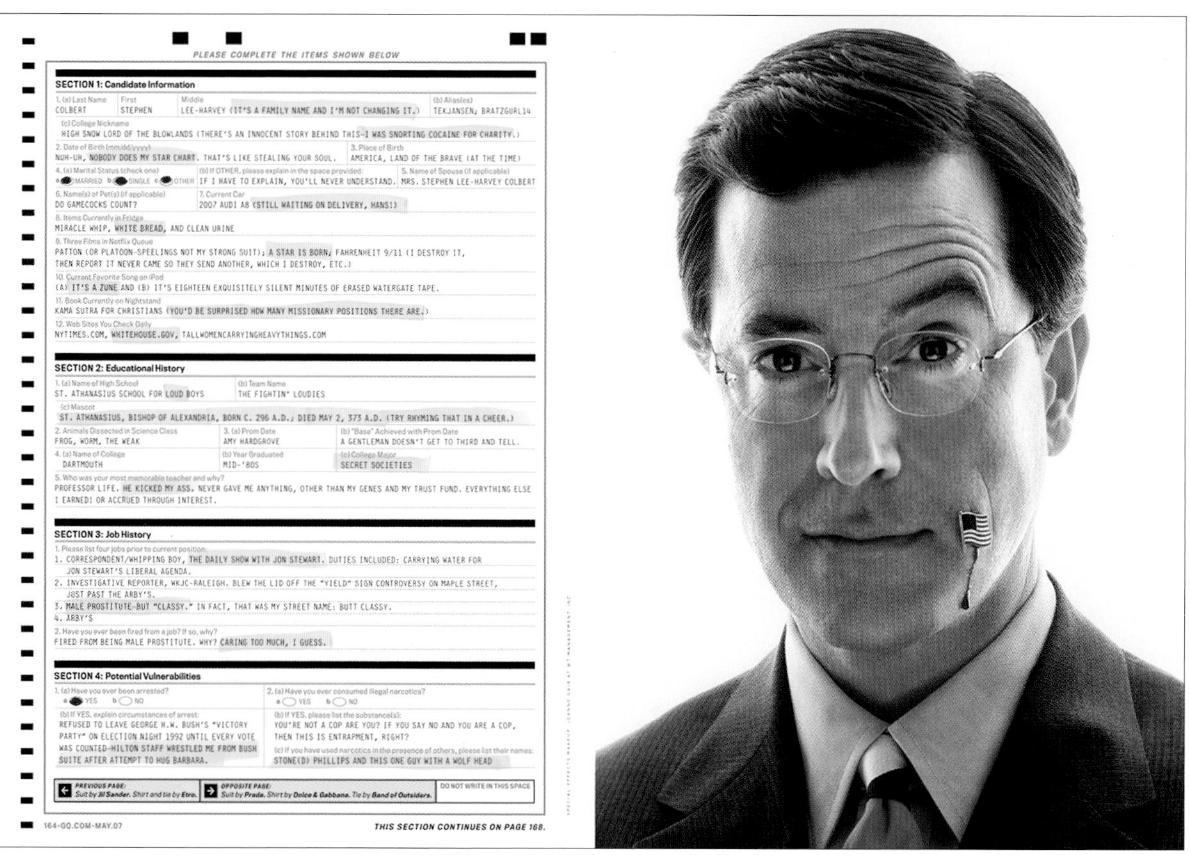

PLEASE COMPLETE THE ITEMS SHOWN BELOW

SECTION 1: Candidate Information

1. (a) Last Name: COLBERT | First: STEPHEN | Middle: LEE-HARVEY (IT'S A FAMILY NAME AND I'M NOT CHANGING IT.) | (b) Alias(es): TEKJANSEN; BRATZGURL14

(c) College Nickname: HIGH SNOW LORD OF THE BLOWLANDS (THERE'S AN INNOCENT STORY BEHIND THIS—I WAS SNORTING COCAINE FOR CHARITY.)

2. Date of Birth (mm/dd/yyyy): NUH-UH, NOBODY DOES MY STAR CHART. THAT'S LIKE STEALING YOUR SOUL.

3. Place of Birth: AMERICA, LAND OF THE BRAVE (AT THE TIME)

4. (a) Marital Status (check one): a MARRIED b SINGLE c OTHER

(b) If OTHER, please explain in the space provided: IF I HAVE TO EXPLAIN, YOU'LL NEVER UNDERSTAND.

5. Name of Spouse (if applicable): MRS. STEPHEN LEE-HARVEY COLBERT

6. Name(s) of Pet(s) (if applicable): DO GAMECOCKS COUNT?

7. Current Car: 2007 AUDI A8 (STILL WAITING ON DELIVERY, HANS!)

8. Items Currently in Fridge: MIRACLE WHIP, WHITE BREAD, AND CLEAN URINE

9. Three Films in Netflix Queue: PATTON (OR PLATOON—SPEELINGS NOT MY STRONG SUIT); A STAR IS BORN; FAHRENHEIT 9/11 (I DESTROY IT, THEN REPORT IT NEVER CAME SO THEY SEND ANOTHER, WHICH I DESTROY, ETC.)

10. Current Favorite Song on iPod: (A) IT'S A ZUNE AND (B) IT'S EIGHTEEN EXQUISITELY SILENT MINUTES OF ERASED WATERGATE TAPE.

11. Book Currently on Nightstand: KAMA SUTRA FOR CHRISTIANS (YOU'D BE SURPRISED HOW MANY MISSIONARY POSITIONS THERE ARE.)

12. Web Sites You Check Daily: NYTIMES.COM, WHITEHOUSE.GOV, TALLWOMENCARRYINGHEAVYTHINGS.COM

SECTION 2: Educational History

1. (a) Name of High School: ST. ATHANASIUS SCHOOL FOR LOUD BOYS | (b) Team Name: THE FIGHTIN' LOUDIES

(c) Mascot: ST. ATHANASIUS, BISHOP OF ALEXANDRIA, BORN C. 296 A.D.; DIED MAY 2, 373 A.D. (TRY RHYMING THAT IN A CHEER.)

2. Animals Dissected in Science Class: FROG, WORM, THE WEAK | 3. (a) Prom Date: AMY HARDGROVE | (b) "Base" Achieved with Prom Date: A GENTLEMAN DOESN'T GET TO THIRD AND TELL.

4. (a) Name of College: DARTMOUTH | (b) Year Graduated: MID-'80S | (c) College Major: SECRET SOCIETIES

5. Who was your most memorable teacher and why? PROFESSOR LIFE. HE KICKED MY ASS. NEVER GAVE ME ANYTHING, OTHER THAN MY GENES AND MY TRUST FUND. EVERYTHING ELSE I EARNED! OR ACCRUED THROUGH INTEREST.

SECTION 3: Job History

1. Please list four jobs prior to current position:
1. CORRESPONDENT/WHIPPING BOY, THE DAILY SHOW WITH JON STEWART. DUTIES INCLUDED: CARRYING WATER FOR JON STEWART'S LIBERAL AGENDA.
2. INVESTIGATIVE REPORTER, WKJC-RALEIGH. BLEW THE LID OFF THE "YIELD" SIGN CONTROVERSY ON MAPLE STREET, JUST PAST THE ARBY'S.
3. MALE PROSTITUTE—BUT "CLASSY." IN FACT, THAT WAS MY STREET NAME: BUTT CLASSY.
4. ARBY'S

2. Have you ever been fired from a job? If so, why? FIRED FROM BEING MALE PROSTITUTE. WHY? CARING TOO MUCH, I GUESS.

SECTION 4: Potential Vulnerabilities

1. (a) Have you ever been arrested? a YES b NO

(b) If YES, explain circumstances of arrest: REFUSED TO LEAVE GEORGE H.W. BUSH'S "VICTORY PARTY" ON ELECTION NIGHT 1992 UNTIL EVERY VOTE WAS COUNTED—HILTON STAFF WRESTLED ME FROM BUSH SUITE AFTER ATTEMPT TO HUG BARBARA.

2. (a) Have you ever consumed illegal narcotics? a YES b NO

(b) If YES, please list the substance(s): YOU'RE NOT A COP ARE YOU? IF YOU SAY NO AND YOU ARE A COP, THEN THIS IS ENTRAPMENT, RIGHT?

(c) If you have used narcotics in the presence of others, please list their names: STONE(D) PHILLIPS AND THIS ONE GUY WITH A WOLF HEAD

PREVIOUS PAGE: Suit by Jil Sander. Shirt and tie by Etro.

OPPOSITE PAGE: Suit by Prada. Shirt by Dolce & Gabbana. Tie by Band of Outsiders.

DO NOT WRITE IN THIS SPACE

164-GQ.COM-MAY.07

THIS SECTION CONTINUES ON PAGE 168.

247

247 GQ

Design Director_Fred Woodward Designer_Thomas Alberty Director of Photography_Dora Somosi
Photographer_Mark Seliger Publisher_Condé Nast Publications Inc.
Issue_May 2007 Category_Design: Feature: Story

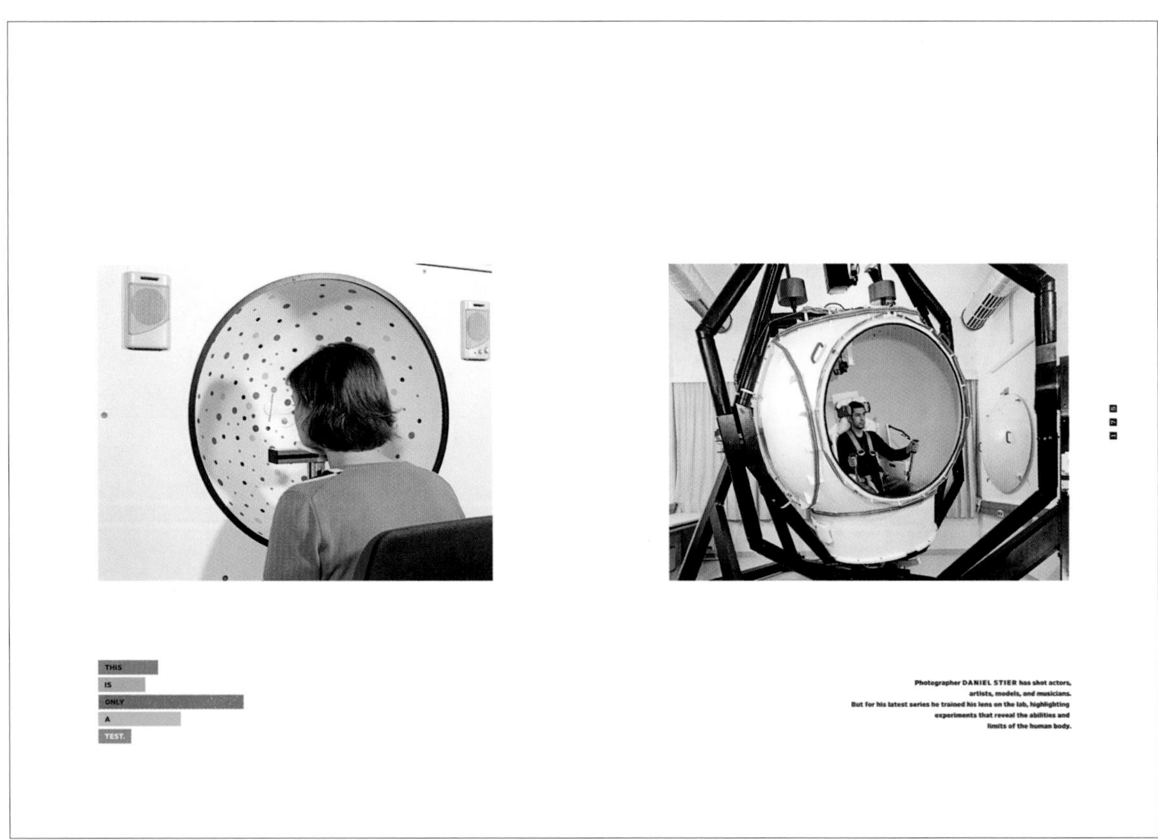

THIS
IS
ONLY
A
TEST.

Photographer DANIEL STIER has shot actors, artists, models, and musicians. But for his latest series he trained his lens on the lab, highlighting experiments that reveal the abilities and limits of the human body.

248

Page 174: In this standard test of the body's balance system, subjects at Ludwig-Maximilians-Universität in Munich sit in front of a field of slowly spinning dots and try to position a needle vertically.

Page 175: At the Universität Tübingen in Germany, researcher Nabil Daddaoua sits in the "turntable," which spins subjects across two axes and measures their eye movements. The goal: to investigate the neural mechanism of balance and space perception.

This page: To study how workers in protective clothing overheat, scientists at the Universität Dortmund in Germany measure heat production and transfer in a variety of simulated climates.

248

248 WIRED

Creative Director_Scott Dadich Designer_Maili Holiman Photo Editor_Carolyn Rauch
Photographer_Daniel Stier Publisher_Condé Nast Publications, Inc.
Issue_September 2007 Category_Design: Feature: Story

GALLERINA
THE DEFINITION OF AVANT-GARDE STYLE, THE GALLERINA INHABITS THE FRONT DESK AS IF SHE WERE A WORK OF ART.
Photographs by PAOLO ROVERSI
DOUBLE EXPOSURE YOHJI YAMAMOTO GRAY FELT HAT, $750, AT YOHJI YAMAMOTO, 103 GRAND STREET. FASHION EDITOR: OLIVIER RIZZO.

249

BLUE PERIOD
JOHN GALLIANO
TAFFETA COAT
GOODMAN.
MULTIMEDIA OSCAR DE LA RENTA SILK FAILLE TOP WITH FEATHERED PEPLUM, $1,190, AT OSCAR DE LA RENTA STORES. MARC JACOBS BLACK RIBBON.

249

249 T, THE NEW YORK TIMES STYLE MAGAZINE

Creative Director_**Janet Froelich** Senior Art Director_**David Sebbah** Art Director_**Christopher Martinez** Designer_**Christopher Martinez** Photo Editor_**Scott Hall** Photographer_**Paolo Roversi** Fashion Editor_**Olivier Rizzo** Editor-In-Chief_**Stefano Tonchi** Publisher_**The New York Times** Issue_**December 2, 2007** Category_**Design: Feature: Story**

250

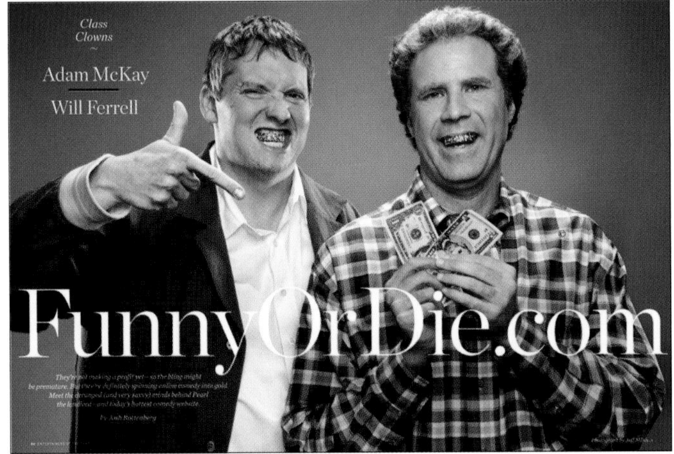

251

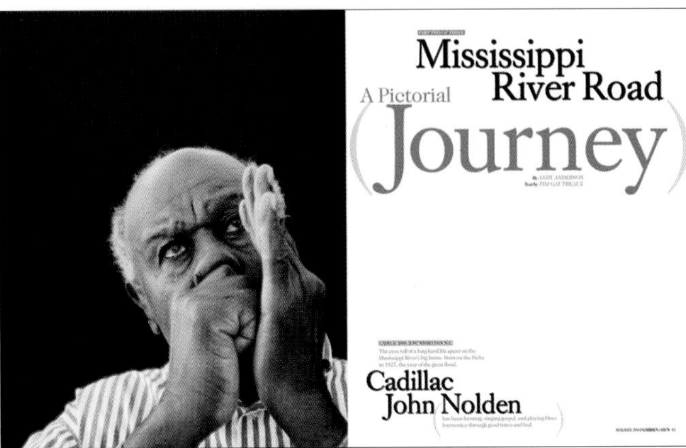

252

250 THE NEW YORK TIMES MAGAZINE

Creative Director_Janet Froelich
Art Director_Arem Duplessis
Designer_Nancy Harris Rouemy
Director of Photography_Kathy Ryan
Photographer_Song Chao
Editor-In-Chief_Gerry Marzorati
Publisher_The New York Times
Issue_February 25, 2007
Category_Design: Feature: Story

251 ENTERTAINMENT WEEKLY

Design Director_Geraldine Hessler
Art Director_Theresa Griggs
Director of Photography_Fiona McDonagh
Managing Editor_Rick Tetzeli
Publisher_Time Inc.
Issue_November 30, 2007
Category_Design: Feature: Story

252 GARDEN & GUN

Art Director_Rob Hewitt
Photographer_Andy Anderson
Photo Editor_Maggie Brett Kennedy
Publisher_Event Post Publishing Company
Issue_Holiday 2007
Category_Design: Feature: Story

how to...

MAKE EVERYTHING BETTER

Don't let the blond 'do and the pressed shirt fool you: Martha Stewart has DIY in her DNA. (When was the last time *you* rewired a lamp or built a lath house?) She's also a gadget freak, buying new digicams and cell phones as fast as manufacturers can spit them out. And when it comes to making things, she's been giving instruction since most of us were messing with Play-Doh. So Stewart seemed perfect to host our 2007 How To issue. To interview her, we called on MARK FRAUENFELDER, a WIRED correspondent and the editor of *Make* magazine. As they sat down in her office, Stewart put her RAZR and BlackBerry on the table in front of her—and then geeked out about home music setups, rude technologies, and Marthapedia.

253

254

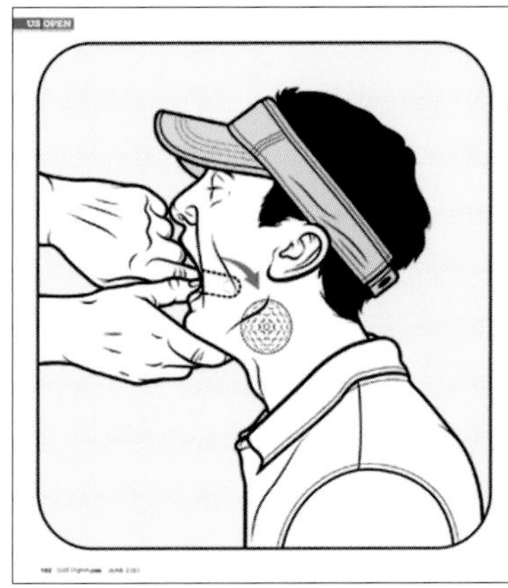
BY JAIME DIAZ

"Put that coffee down! Coffee's for closers only!" So begins Alec Baldwin—as the slickly superior corporate boss Blake—in a brutally calculating humiliation of a group of beaten-down real-estate salesmen in the film of David Mamet's "Glengarry Glen Ross." When two Willy Loman types scoff, Blake explodes with a torrent of abuse that concludes in a course crescendo: "You can't close s—, you *are* s—. Hit the bricks, pal, and beat it, 'cause you are going out!" Ouch. Then again, it was only a slightly dramatized version of professional sports. *Closing, the moment of truth, getting it done, manning up, gut check* and *finishing* are all variations of the blunt and unforgiving jargon athletes in the most demanding arenas use to describe the response that defines the difference between who wins and who loses, who is remembered and who is forgotten, who relishes and who regrets. Being a closer is the intangible quality every aspiring champion most desires; it's the hunger that drove a young Tom Watson, in the midst of his classic duel with Jack Nicklaus at the 1977 British Open at Turnberry, to ask the older champion with Pattonesque wonder, "This is what it's all about, isn't it?" The answer was never more clear than in the endgame of last year's U.S. Open at Winged Foot. Of the five players near the lead at the end—Padraig Harrington, Jim Furyk, Colin Montgomerie, Geoff Ogilvy and Phil Mickelson—only the winner, Ogilvy, was able to par the 72nd

255

253 WIRED

Creative Director_Scott Dadich
Art Director_Maili Holiman
Designers_Carl DeTorres, Maili Holiman
Illustrators_Bruce Hutchinson, Seth Ferris
Photo Editor_Carolyn Rauch
Photographer_Jill Greenberg
Publisher_Condé Nast Publications, Inc.
Issue_August 2007
Category_Design: Feature: Story

254 NATURE CONSERVANCY

Art Director_Weapon of Choice
Designers_Todd Albertson, Tom Brown
Photo Editor_Melissa Ryan
Editor-In-Chief_Teresa Duran
Publisher_The Nature Conservancy
Issue_Winter 2007
Category_Design: Feature: Story

255 GOLF DIGEST

Design Director_Ken DeLago
Designer_Ken DeLago
Illustrator_Jameson Simpson
Publisher_Condé Nast Publications Inc.
Issue_June 2007
Category_Design: Feature: Spread/Single Page

256

256 MARTHA STEWART LIVING

Creative Director_**Eric A. Pike** Design Director_**James Dunlinson** Art Director_**Eric A. Pike** Designers_**Elizabeth Ackerman Valins, Kevin Brainard** Director of Photography_**Heloise Goodman** Senior Photo Editor_**Andrea Bakacs** Photographer_**Charles Masters** Stylists_**Marcie McGoldrick, Blake Ramsey** Editor-In-Chief_**Michael Boodro** Publisher_**Martha Stewart Living Omnimedia** Issue_**December 2007** Category_**Design: Feature: Story**

Far West

by Colin Berry

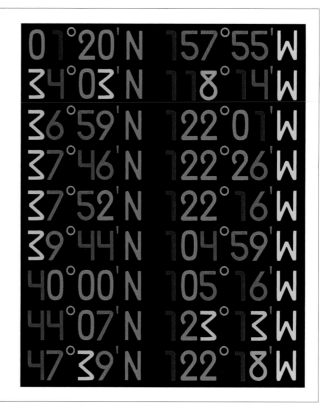

From the Rockies to Diamond Head, designers across the West describe business in one word: thriving. "It's great to be a designer in Denver right now," says Joe Conrad, a partner at Cactus, a 24-person studio in the city's Lower Downtown district. "The country is starting to realize this is a great place to live, and the design community is right in tune."

Independent designer Chirag Ahir agrees. "You see very contemporary, very modern styles here," he says, noting the Denver Art Museum's new building designed by Daniel Libeskind. "Denver is becoming a bridge between east and west." Other parts of Colorado are budding too. TDA Advertising & Design art director Jonathan Schoenberg jokes that Boulder "used to be known as a good place to buy weed. Now it's a much more cultured place."

Development has been key. "Business in Vegas is just like our population—constantly growing," says Glendon Scott, a senior art director at R&R Partners. "New opportunities are popping up all the time." Clean and modern graphics are displacing rustic "Western" motifs, and innovations in digital photography are on the rise. "Digital's functionality gives art directors the chance to play around when we're shooting," Scott says.

In Salt Lake City, Letter 23's creative director, Sage Turk, suggests designers are drawn to smaller cities by the lower cost of living and the intimacy of the profession. "We're like one big dysfunctional family," he says, smiling. "You know all the people in the other houses, and you see their work and say to yourself, 'I'm gonna do it better!'" Jeff Sutherland, a partner at Salty Design Factory in Coeur d'Alene, Idaho, is just as upbeat. "We want to bring national-level design to a small town," he says.

In California, design is similarly humming. "We're definitely at the 'feast' end of the spectrum," reports Kimberly Varella, a partner at Department of Graphic Sciences, a small studio in L.A.'s Chinatown. Sounding like the ultimate Californian, she adds, "Sending out good psychic energy put our business on a total reverse." She's not alone in her experience. Mel Lim, who runs Joy, a three-year-old, three-person studio in San Diego, has expanded her colorful stationery line into baby clothes, pillows, bags, even underwear. Design blogs, she says, have helped build her international fan base: "One mention gets us 5,000 hits a day."

Yet quantity may not be keeping up with quality. "In this industry, with people so used to having something *now*, attention to detail can get lost," argues Erik Miller, design director at TBWA\Chiat\Day in Los Angeles. "My question always is, 'Are we proud of what we've created?' I don't see that at a lot of other agencies. They tend to pump out crap."

Here's one explanation: In Southern California at least, the entertainment industry's reliance on animation and digital graphics adds jobs but dilutes graphic excellence. Dustin Arnold, a consultant in Glendale who has worked for Hermès and H&M, says younger designers like him have forgotten—or may have never known—how to design without technology. "Some people might think I'm neo-Amish, but it's nice to have an experience without being plugged in," he says.

Although clients are trusting designers more to deliver high-level concepts, Eric Heiman, a partner at Volume Inc. in San Francisco, worries about consolidation in the market. "Is a small firm like ours going to be around in 10 years?" he asks. "As design becomes more accessible, and more people think, 'I can do that,' it becomes a double-edged sword."

Still, it's no time for funerals. Illustrator Ward Schumaker, who has ridden his industry's waves for decades, says things are "going crazy" these days, allowing him to expand into calligraphy and fine art. His only gripe is that the new generation of artists seems less interested in craft, relying heavily on what he perceives as *heta-uma*—badly drawn on purpose. "Sometimes I wonder whether or not it's intentional," he says.

In Oregon and Washington, the music industry continues to energize visual culture. Designers raised on anime and Asian-flavored graphic novels, like Junichi Tsuneoka, who runs Studio Stubborn Sideburn in Seattle, are using these influences to inject fresh perspectives. "Art Chantry, [Sub Pop's] Jeff Kleinsmith, and Modern Dog are still the Northwest's biggest influences," says Tsuneoka. "But I'm trying to break the chain."

Lastly, 2,700 miles further west, Honolulu-based Info Grafik reports its best year ever. So are there any Hawaiian visual trends? "Trends are like dandelions, drifting easily across land and ocean," says founder Oren Schlieman via e-mail. Before signing off, he adds: "If you want to talk more, please call my cell phone. I'll be at the beach this afternoon. Aloha."

Art by
Tauba Auerbach
San Francisco, CA

Tauba Auerbach is an artist who lives in San Francisco. Her work is concept-based rather than aesthetic and is shown in galleries internationally. Before moving on to make art full-time, she worked in an old-fashioned sign shop where she hand-painted and gilded signs. She released her first book, *How to Spell the Alphabet* (Deitch Projects) in 2006.

Southwest

by Angela Voulangas

This year's canvassing of designers across the Southwest yielded a rush of enthusiastic reports. Sentiments ranged from formal satisfaction ("Business is outstanding") to harried excitement ("It's been crazy here") to giddy exuberance ("Through the roof!"). So it seems odd that this positive flush didn't translate into a deluge of entries to the Annual. On the contrary, submissions were down for most areas of the Southwest. Few seemed able to offer any real insight into this apparent contradiction. Steve Sturges, partner at Visual Image Advertising in Oklahoma City, suggests, "Big agencies are feeling the pinch. Technology has allowed the best talent to migrate to smaller, more creative shops, but small agencies are less comfortable entering their work in award shows and design annuals." Another explanation comes from Rex Peteet, partner at Sibley/Peteet Design in Austin: "The culprit may be that folks are just really busy." Fair enough.

A population surge, a real estate boom, and a wealth of new businesses are recurring themes for the entire region. In particular, Austin and Albuquerque are experiencing seismic shifts. DJ Stout, a partner at Pentagram Design, explains that Austin's skyline is rapidly changing, with attention turning toward downtown, an area that traditionally emptied out in the evening. With the influx of high-end business and residential construction, says Stout, has come "lots of collateral and identity work"—witness the Spring Condominiums marketing brochure, one of Pentagram's four winning submissions.

Last year, Donna Romano of Ripe Inc. let us know that Albuquerque was a city to watch. How right she was! Stories of expansion came from all sides this time around. Tim McGrath and Sam Maclay of 3, a design studio, say they've tripled their personnel in the space of two years. Bart Cleveland of McKee Wallwork Cleveland was one of several people to point out that the movie industry is putting down more roots in the area: Lions Gate Entertainment reportedly has plans to build a new studio in nearby Rio Rancho, and a large new production facility built in Mesa del Sol earlier this year is already fully booked.

Many designers in the Southwest mentioned signs of digital evolution. Peteet explains that, in his experience, the web has influenced the world of identity design. "Dimension, reflectivity, kinetics, and complexity are now mainstream," he says. Aaron Opsal, owner and creative director of Dallas's The Brand Hatchery, says that almost every new assignment has some digital component. And Brandon Murphy of Squires & Company, which has offices in both Dallas and Albuquerque, posits that annual reports, that oft-maligned corporate staple, will increasingly go digital as well: "Think rich media, streaming video, or sound."

There were fewer significant stylistic trends this year. Bo Bothe, managing partner at Brand Extract in Houston, notes, "The whole flowery-flourishy design trend seems to be coming to an end." It's true that many Southwest winners evince a top note of sleekness. A case in point is the silk-screened aluminum invitation for the Dallas Cowboys by Rovillo + Reitmayer, which is bold and Texas-sized but also spare and sophisticated—it's an elegant statement for an industry that often chooses flash over refinement for its graphics.

Other outstanding entries from the Southwest include a pair of stylistic opposites: "Weeping Mary," Pentagram's emotionally affecting photographic document of a rural Texas town settled by former slaves, and Squires & Company's vibrant and visually complex brochure for a wood products company that records a charity home renovation project. The Richards Group of Dallas created a simple yet sophisticated poster series for immigration lawyer Kam Naidoo that features coloring-book outlines of such American icons as the Statue of Liberty and encourages viewers to "just add color." Sanders/Wingo's invitation for the Austin Ad Federation takes the shape of a diminutive voodoo doll—the perforation is slyly positioned to run across the figure's neck.

This year, as always, we asked designers to give us their thoughts on any issues that stood out. Apparently, green production methods have been on many people's minds. Allyson Lack, of Principle in Houston, notes that designers are "paying more attention to the materials they specify and what happens at the end of the life-cycle of their printed matter." And Brandon Murphy thinks that "the new buzzword of the year is 'sustainability'." But one wonders whether this phenomenon, like blurred type and bird silhouettes, will be one more passing fad.

Art by
Matthew Rodriguez
Austin, TX

Matthew Rodriguez's posters of rainbow monsters and frowning candy corns, and the faces he draws on trees, piles, and poles can be seen on the streets of every city he visits. In February, some of his work will be indoors, at New York's Rare gallery.

257 PRINT

Art Director_**Kristina DiMatteo** Associate Art Director_**Lindsay Ballant** Designers_**Kristina DiMatteo, Lindsay Ballant**
Illustrators_**Tauba Auerbach, Matthew Rodriguez, Rick Valicenti, Friends With You, Adam Larson, Michael Bierut** Editor-In-Chief_**Joyce Rutter Kaye**
Publisher_**F & W Publications** Issue_**November/December 2007** Category_**Design: Feature: Story**

258

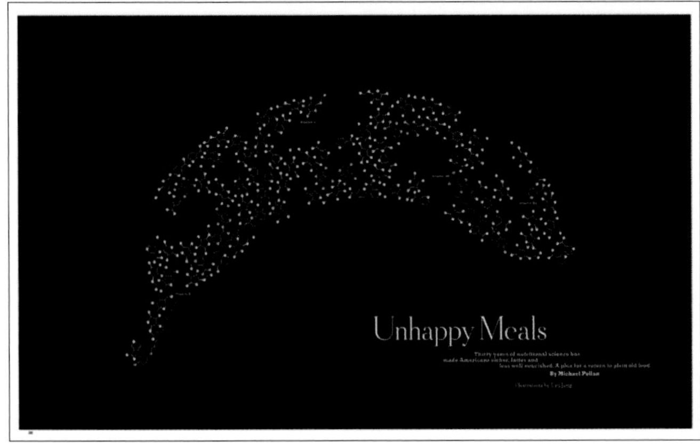

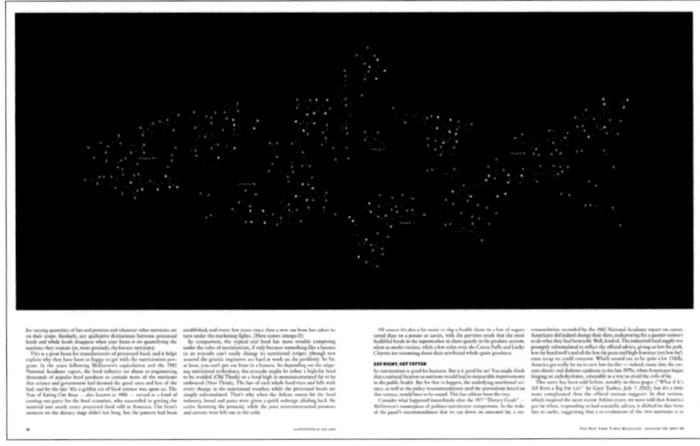

259

260

258 METROPOLIS

Creative Director_**Criswell Lappin**
Designer_**Tom Madriejos**
Photo Editor_**Bilyana Dimitrova**
Publisher_**Bellerophon Publications**
Issue_**July 2007**
Category_**Design: Feature: Story**

259 THE NEW YORK TIMES MAGAZINE

Creative Director_**Janet Froelich** Art Director_**Arem Duplessis**
Designer_**Leo Jung**
Illustrator_**Leo Jung**
Editor-In-Chief_**Gerry Marzorati**
Publisher_**The New York Times**
Issue_**January 28, 2007**
Category_**Design: Feature: Story**

260 LOOP

Creative Director_**Guillermo Caballero**
Design Director_**Roberto Gutierrez**
Designer_**Jose Blenda**
Illustrator_**Ulises Culebro**
Photo Editor_**Ilan Rabchinskey**
Photographer_**Bertha Herrera**
Editor-In-Chief_**Rafael LaFarga**
Issue_**July 2007**
Category_**Design: Feature: Story**

261

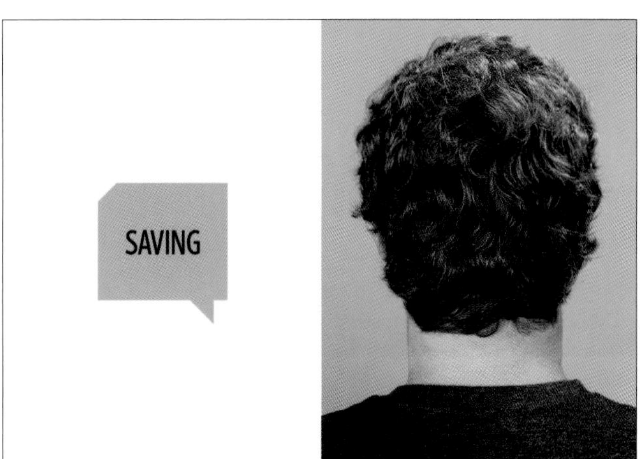

262

263

261 DEPARTURES

Creative Director_Bernard Scharf
Art Director_Adam Bookbinder
Associate Art Director_Lou Corredor
Director of Photography Jennifer Laski
Photo Editors_Jennifer Geaney, Brandon Perlman
Photographer _Frédéric Lagrange
Publisher_American Express Publishing Co.
Issue_January/February 2007
Category Design: Feature: Story

262 WIRED

Creative Director_Scott Dadich
Art Director_Maili Holiman
Designer_Maili Holiman
Photo Editor_Carolyn Rauch
Photographer_Emily Shur
Publisher_Condé Nast Publications, Inc.
Issue_October 2007
Category_Design: Feature: Story

263 ENTERTAINMENT WEEKLY

Design Director_Geraldine Hessler
Art Director_Brian Anstey
Illustrators_Tavis Coburn, Gary Taxali, Eddie Guy, Jonathan Rosen, Josh Cochran, Hanoch Piven, Oksana Badrak Director of Photography_Fiona McDonagh
Managing Editor_Rick Tetzeli
Publisher_Time Inc.
Issue_December 28, 2007 - January 4, 2008
Category_Design: Feature: Story

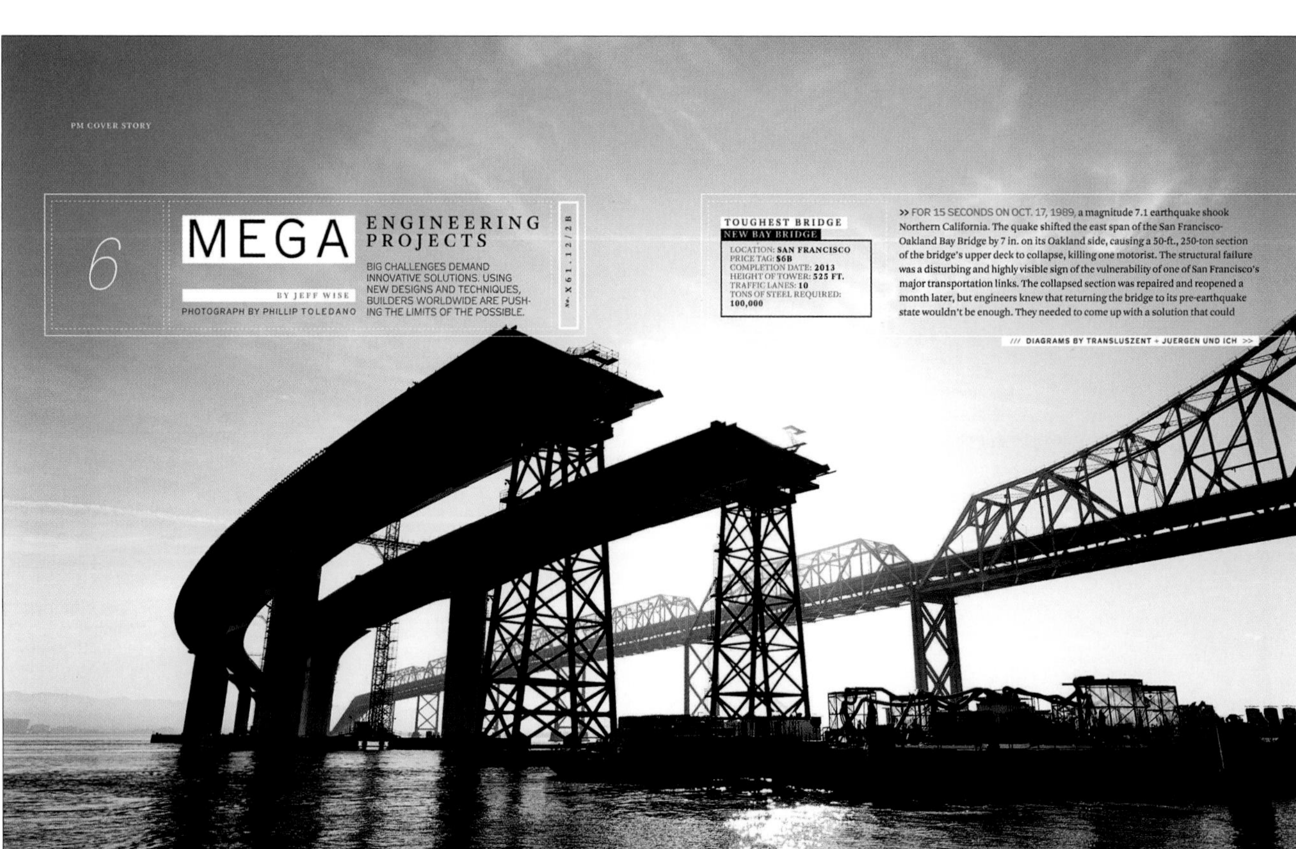

PM COVER STORY

6

MEGA ENGINEERING PROJECTS

BIG CHALLENGES DEMAND INNOVATIVE SOLUTIONS. USING NEW DESIGNS AND TECHNIQUES, BUILDERS WORLDWIDE ARE PUSHING THE LIMITS OF THE POSSIBLE.

BY JEFF WISE

PHOTOGRAPH BY PHILLIP TOLEDANO

TOUGHEST BRIDGE
NEW BAY BRIDGE
LOCATION: **SAN FRANCISCO**
PRICE TAG: **$6B**
COMPLETION DATE: **2013**
HEIGHT OF TOWER: **525 FT.**
TRAFFIC LANES: **10**
TONS OF STEEL REQUIRED: **100,000**

>> FOR 15 SECONDS ON OCT. 17, 1989, a magnitude 7.1 earthquake shook Northern California. The quake shifted the east span of the San Francisco-Oakland Bay Bridge by 7 in. on its Oakland side, causing a 50-ft., 250-ton section of the bridge's upper deck to collapse, killing one motorist. The structural failure was a disturbing and highly visible sign of the vulnerability of one of San Francisco's major transportation links. The collapsed section was repaired and reopened a month later, but engineers knew that returning the bridge to its pre-earthquake state wouldn't be enough. They needed to come up with a solution that could

/// DIAGRAMS BY TRANSLUSZENT + JUERGEN UND ICH >>

THE REPLACEMENT FOR THE ORIGINAL SAN FRANCISCO-OAKLAND BAY BRIDGE, SEEN HERE IN THE BACKGROUND, IS SEISMICALLY REVOLUTIONARY. IT'S DESIGNED TO LAST FOR 150 YEARS.

ON THE WEB /// popularmechanics.com/megaengineering

POPULARMECHANICS.COM | JUNE 2007 87

266

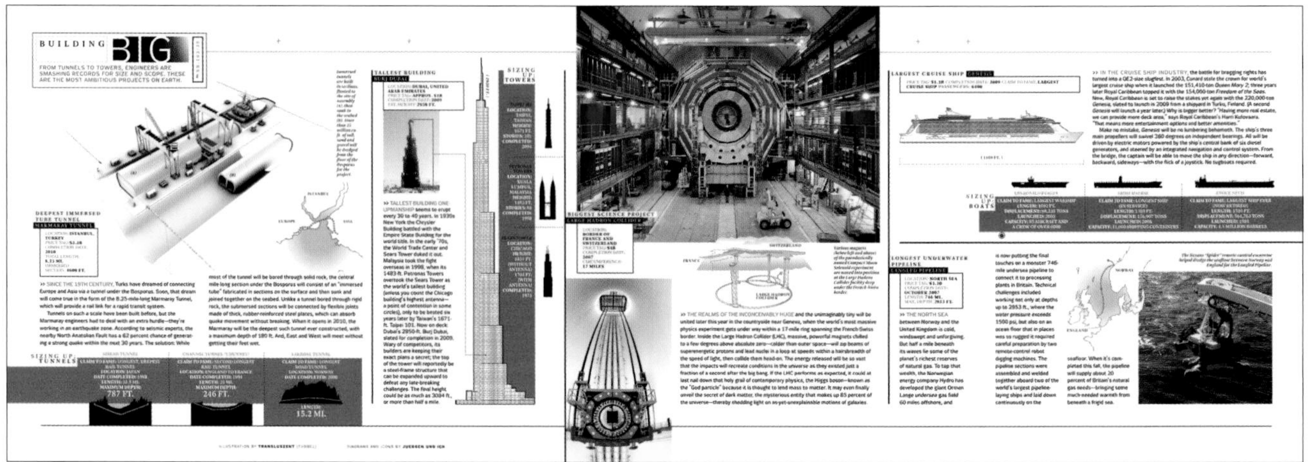

BUILDING BIG

266

266 POPULAR MECHANICS

Design Director_**Michael Lawton**
Art Director_**Peter Herbert**
Assistant Art Director_**Michael Friel**
Illustrators_**Translucent, Juergen Und Ich**
Director of Photography_**Allyson Torrisi**
Associate Photo Editor_**Alison Unterreiner**
Photographer_**Philip Toledano**
Publisher_**The Hearst Corporation-Magazines Division**
Issue_**June 2007**
Category_**Design: Feature: Story**

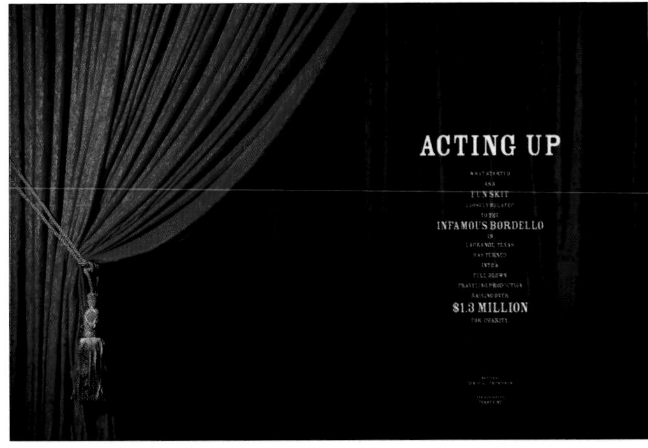

267

267

268

268

269

269

267 RIGAMAROLE

Creative Director_Thomas Hull
Designer_Thomas Hull
Director of Photography_Thomas Hull
Photographer_Terry Vine
Studio_Rigsby Hull
Client_Diamond Offshore Drilling, Inc.
Issue_Spring 2007
Category_Design: Feature: Story

268 WIRED

Creative Director_Scott Dadich
Designer_Scott Dadich
Illustrator_Bryan Christie
Photo Editor_Anna Goldwater Alexander
Photographer_Todd Hido
Publisher_Condé Nast Publications, Inc.
Issue_August 2007
Category_Design: Feature: Story

269 GQ

Design Director_Fred Woodward
Designers_Anton Ioukhnovets, Michael Pangilinan
Director of Photography_Dora Somosi
Photo Editors_Krista Prestek, Justin O'Neill
Photographers_Sivan Lewin, Ditte Isager, Greg Kadel Editor-In-Chief_Jim Nelson
Publisher_Condé Nast Publications Inc.
Issue_August 2007
Category_Design: Feature: Story

270

270

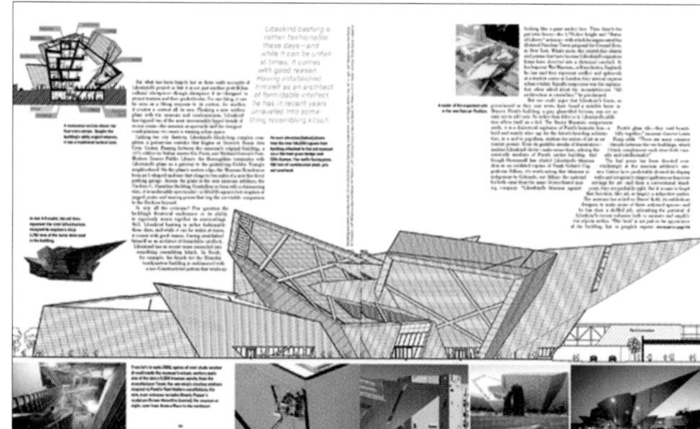

271

271

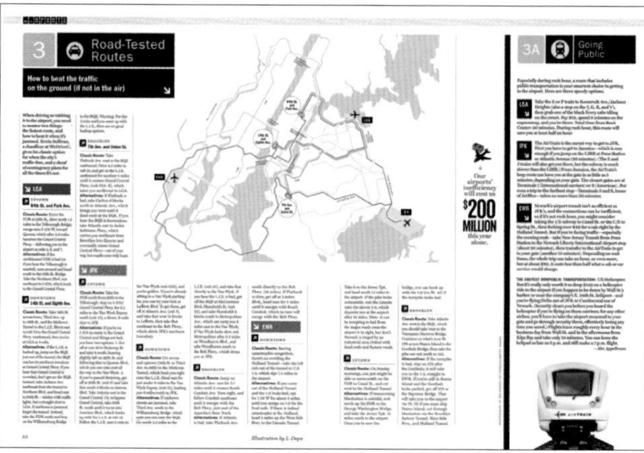

272

272

270 WIRED

Creative Director_Scott Dadich
Art Director_Maili Holiman
Designer_ Maili Holiman
Photo Editor_Carolyn Rauch
Photographer_Brian Finke
Publisher_Condé Nast Publications, Inc.
Issue_June 2007
Category_Design: Feature: Story

271 METROPOLIS

Creative Director_Criswell Lappin
Design Director_Nancy Nowacek
Art Director_Erich Nagler
Photo Editor_Bilyana Dimitrova
Photographer_Jeff Goldberg
Publisher_Bellerophon Publications
Issue_March 2007
Category_Design: Feature: Story

272 NEW YORK

Design Director_Chris Dixon
Art Directors_Randy Minor, Kate Elazegui
Associate Art Director_Robert Vargas
Designers_Robert Vargas, Kate Elazegui
Illustrators_Jason Lee, L-Dopa
Director of Photography_Jody Quon
Photographers_Vincent Laforet, Jeff Mermelstein
Editor-In-Chief_Adam Moss
Publisher_New York Magazine Holdings, LLC
Issue_November 12, 2007
Category_Design: Feature: Story

273

273

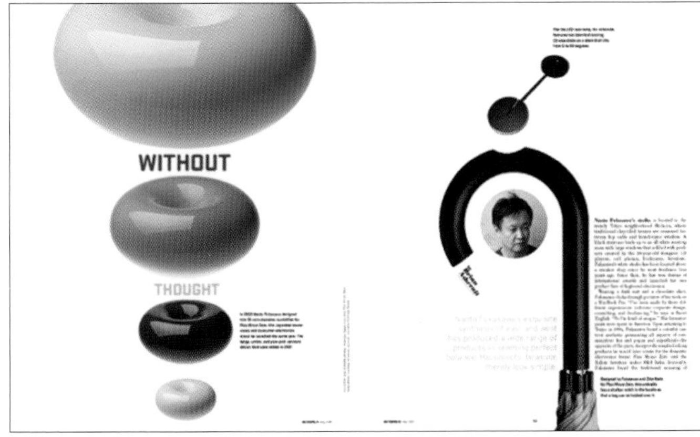

274

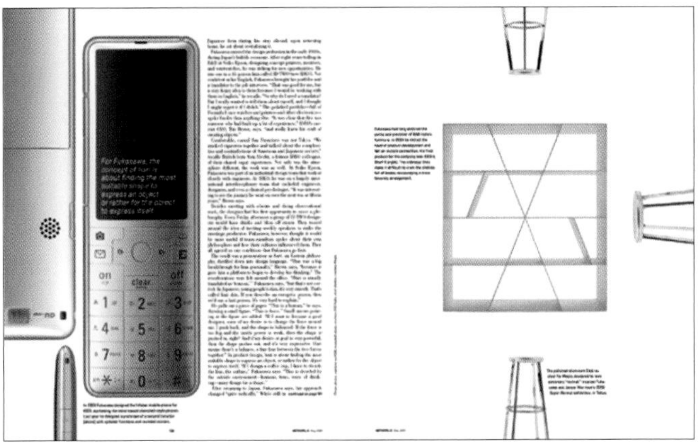

274

275

275

273 METROPOLIS

Creative Director_Criswell Lappin
Design Director_Erich Nagler
Photo Editor_Bilyana Dimitrova
Photographer_John Ellis
Publisher_Bellerophon Publications
Issue_April 2007
Category_Design: Feature: Story

274 METROPOLIS

Creative Director_Criswell Lappin
Art Director_Erich Nagler
Photo Editor_Bilyana Dimitrova
Photographer_Hidetoyo Sasaki
Publisher_Bellerophon Publications
Issue_May 2007
Category_Design: Feature: Story

275 DEPARTURES

Creative Director_Bernard Scharf
Art Director_Adam Bookbinder
Associate Art Director_Lou Corredor
Director of Photography_Jennifer Laski
Photo Editors_Jennifer Geaney, Brandon Perlman
Photographer_Michael Kenna
Publisher_American Express Publishing Co.
Issue_October 2007
Category_Design: Feature: Story

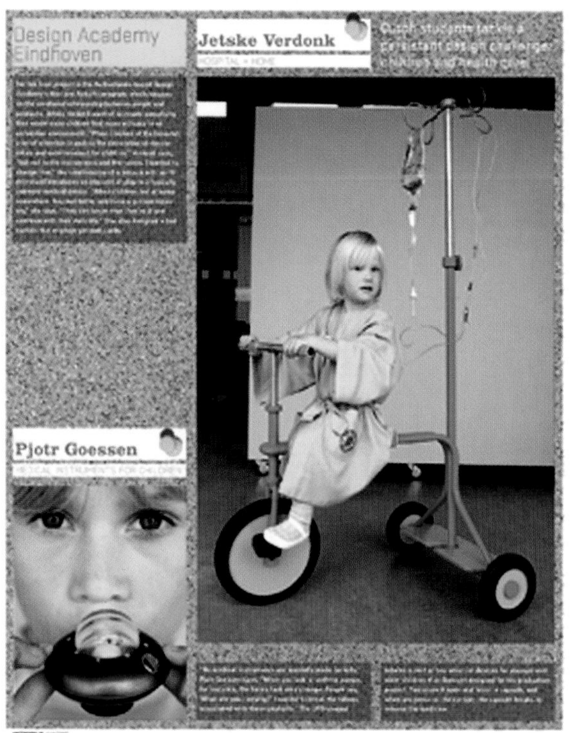

276

276

276 METROPOLIS

Creative Director_Criswell Lappin Art Director_Erich Nagler Photo Editor_Bilyana Dimitrova
Publisher_Bellerophon Publications Issue_April 2007 Category_Design: Feature: Story

277

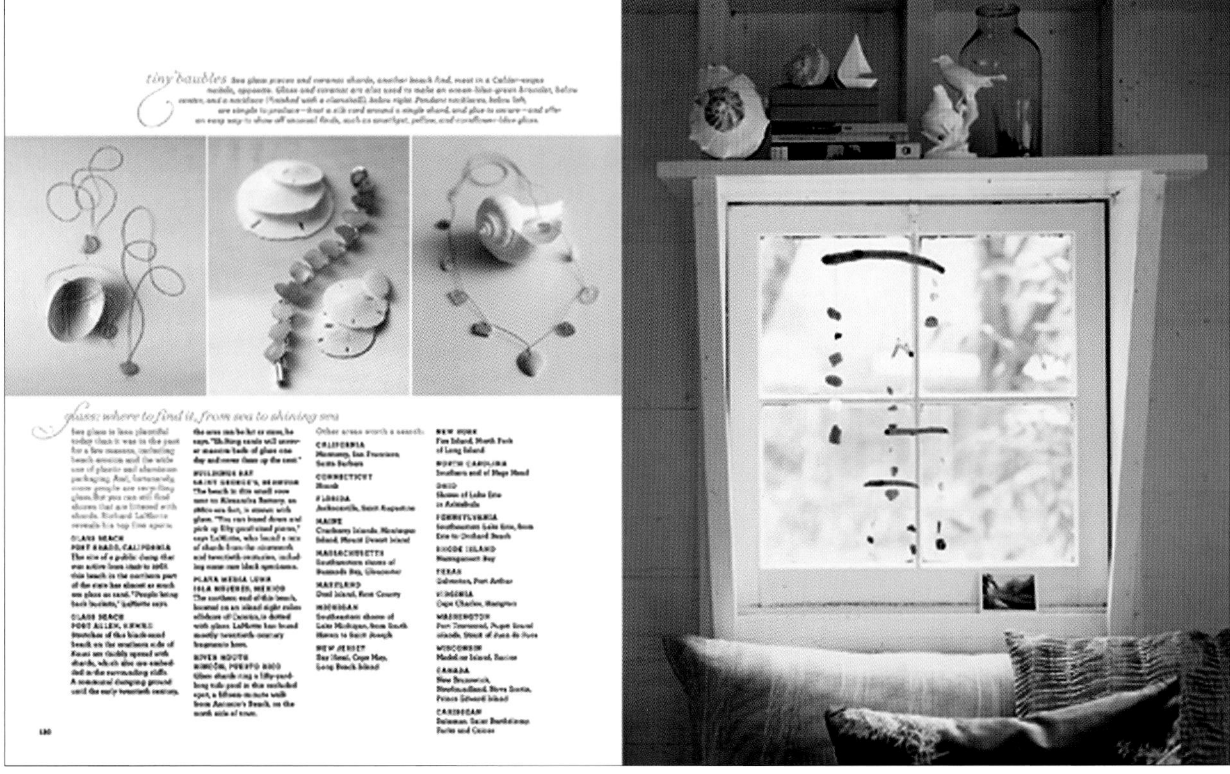

277

277 MARTHA STEWART LIVING

Creative Director_**Eric A. Pike** Design Director_**James Dunlinson** Art Director_**Eric A. Pike** Designer_**Linsey Laidlaw** Director of Photography_**Heloise Goodman** Senior Photo Editor_**Andrea Bakacs** Photographer_**Rick Lew** Stylists_**Hannah Milman, Ayesha Patel, Laura Normandin** Editor-In-Chief_**Michael Boodro** Publisher_**Martha Stewart Living Omnimedia** Issue_**August 2007** Category_**Design: Feature: Story**

LONDON '007 A MAN'S GUIDE TO THE COOLEST CITY ON THE PLANET

NOT SINCE THE SWINGIN' SIXTIES HAS ENGLAND'S CAPITAL BEEN SO VITAL. THE RESTAURANTS NOW RIVAL THE WORLD'S BEST (SERIOUSLY, NO JOKE) YOU WON'T FIND A BETTER ART SCENE AND THE STYLE, AS ALWAYS, IS TOPS. YES, IT'S BLOODY EXPENSIVE- BUT NOW IT'S WORTH IT ••• Photographs by BOBBY FISHER

278

BECAUSE THERE'S ALWAYS A NEW NEIGHBOURHOOD HEATING UP

278

Style

The Strong, Not So Silent Type

279

279

GUCCI UNZIPPED

280

SINCE taking control of PPR in 2005, Pinault has replaced much of the management team his father assembled.

280

278 GQ

Design Director_**Fred Woodward**
Designer_**Michael Pangilinan**
Director of Photography_**Dora Somosi**
Photo Editor_**Krista Prestek**
Photographer_**Bobby Fisher**
Editor-In-Chief_**Jim Nelson**
Publisher_**Condé Nast Publications Inc.**
Issue_**November 2007**
Category_**Design: Feature: Story**

279 THE NEW YORK TIMES MAGAZINE

Creative Director_**Janet Froelich**
Art Director_**Arem Duplessis**
Designer_**Nancy Harris Rouemy**
Director of Photography_**Kathy Ryan**
Photographers_**Inez van Lamsweerde, Vinoodh Matadin**
Editor-In-Chief_**Gerry Marzorati**
Publisher_**The New York Times**
Issue_**June 3, 2007**
Category_**Design: Feature: Story**

280 CONDÉ NAST PORTFOLIO

Design Director_**Robert Priest**
Art Director_**Grace Lee**
Designer_**Grace Lee**
Director of Photography_**Lisa Berman**
Photo Editor_**Jane Yeomans**
Deputy Photo Editor_**Sarah Czeladnicki**
Photographer_**Pascal Chevallier**
Editor-In-Chief_**Joanne Lipman**
Publisher_**Condé Nast Publications Inc.**
Issue_**September 2007**
Category_**Design: Feature: Story**

281

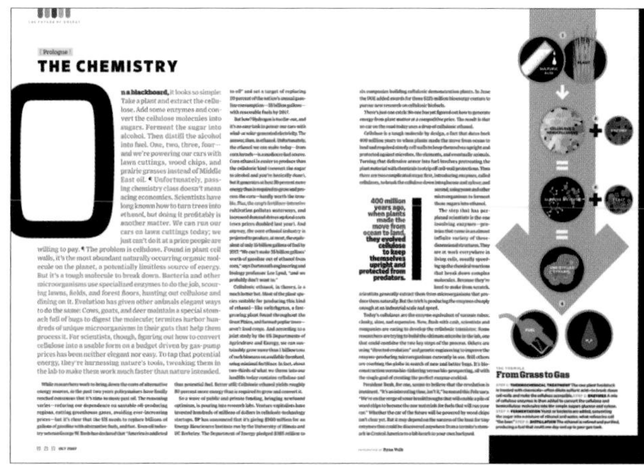

281

282

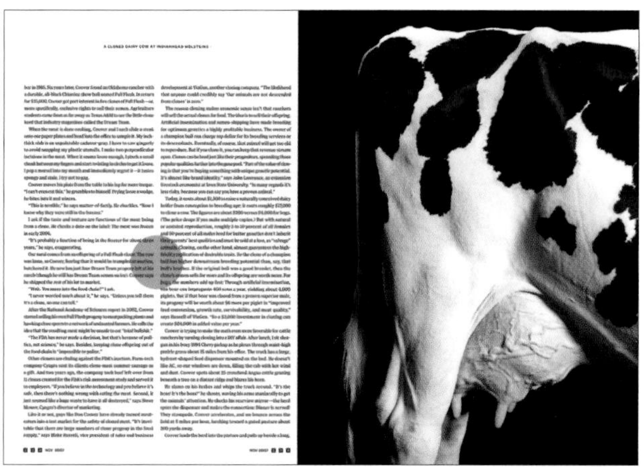

282

THE POWER OF ONE

283

283

281 WIRED

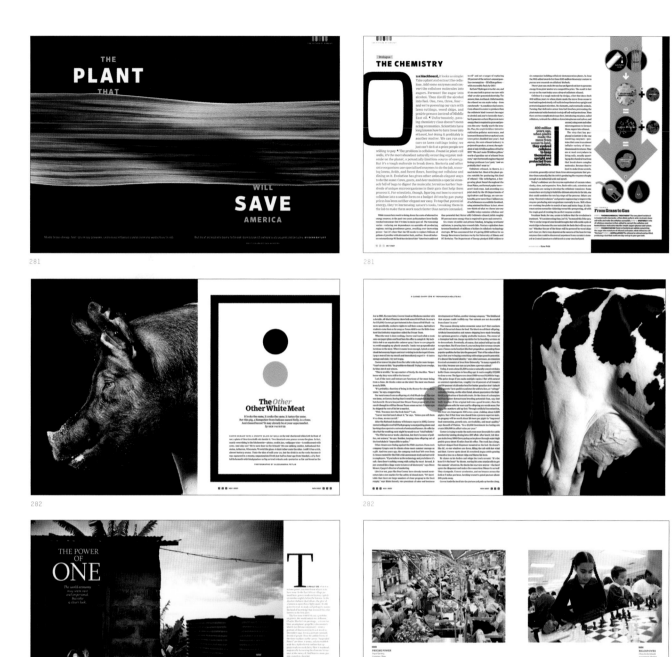

Creative Director_Scott Dadich
Art Director_Maili Holiman
Designers_Maili Holiman, Scott Dadich, Chris Imlay
Illustrator_Ryan Vulk
Photo Editor_Anna Goldwater Alexander
Photographers_Dan Winters, Peter Yang
Publisher_Condé Nast Publications, Inc.
Issue_October 2007
Category_Design: Feature: Story

282 WIRED

Creative Director_Scott Dadich
Design Director_Wyatt Mitchell
Designer_Scott Dadich
Photo Editor_Carolyn Rauch
Photographer_Alessandra Petlin
Publisher_Condé Nast Publications, Inc.
Issue_November 2007
Category_Design: Feature: Story

283 FORTUNE

Design Director_Robert Perino
Art Director_Deanna Lowe
Designer_Alice Alves
Director of Photography_Greg Pond
Photo Editor_Mia Diehl
Photographers_J. Carrier, Kristen Ashburn, Samantha Appleton, Lynsey Addario, Stanley Greene, Lars Tunbjork
Editor-In-Chief_Andy Serwer
Publisher_Time Inc.
Issue_December 10, 2007
Category_Design: Feature: Story

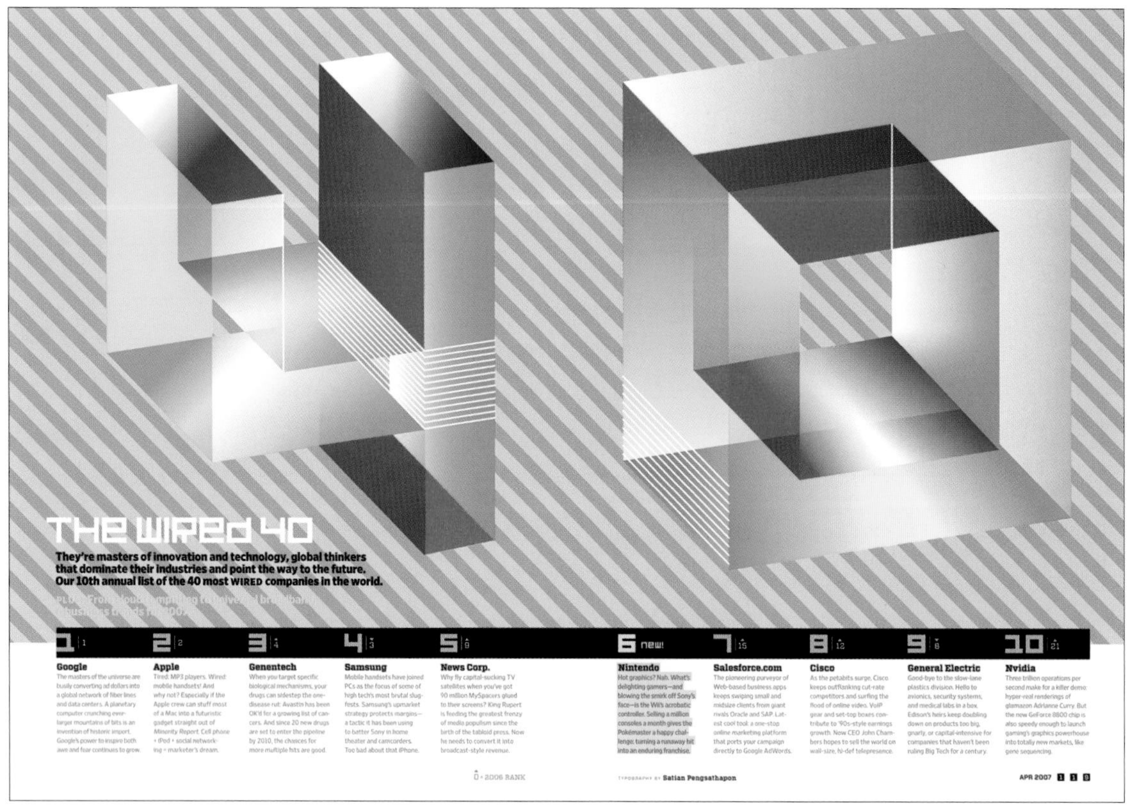

THE WIRED 40

They're masters of innovation and technology, global thinkers that dominate their industries and point the way to the future. Our 10th annual list of the 40 most WIRED companies in the world.

1 | 1 **Google** The masters of the universe are busily converting ad dollars into a global network of fiber lines and data centers. A planetary computer crunching ever-larger mountains of bits is an invention of historic import. Google's power to inspire both awe and fear continues to grow.

2 | 2 **Apple** Tired: MP3 players. Wired: mobile handsets! And why not? Especially if the Apple crew can stuff most of a Mac into a futuristic gadget straight out of *Minority Report*. Cell phone + iPod + social networking = marketer's dream.

3 | 4 **Genentech** When you target specific biological mechanisms, your drugs can sidestep the one-disease rut: Avastin has been OK'd for a growing list of cancers. And since 20 new drugs are set to enter the pipeline by 2010, the chances for more multiple hits are good.

4 | 3 **Samsung** Mobile handsets have joined PCs as the focus of some of high tech's most brutal slugfests. Samsung's upmarket strategy protects margins—a tactic it has been using to batter Sony in home theater and camcorders. Too bad about that iPhone.

5 | 9 **News Corp.** Why fly capital-sucking TV satellites when you've got 90 million MySpacers glued to their screens? King Rupert is feeding the greatest frenzy of media populism since the birth of the tabloid press. Now he needs to convert it into broadcast-style revenue.

6 new! **Nintendo** Hot graphics? Nah. What's delighting gamers—and blowing the smirk off Sony's face—is the Wii's acrobatic controller. Selling a million consoles a month gives the Pokémaster a happy challenge: turning a runaway hit into an enduring franchise.

7 | 15 **Salesforce.com** The pioneering purveyor of Web-based business apps keeps swiping small and midsize clients from giant rivals Oracle and SAP. Latest cool tool: a one-stop online marketing platform that ports your campaign directly to Google AdWords.

8 | 12 **Cisco** As the petabits surge, Cisco keeps outflanking cut-rate competitors and surfing the flood of online video. VoIP gear and set-top boxes contribute to '90s-style earnings growth. Now CEO John Chambers hopes to sell the world on wall-size, hi-def telepresence.

9 | 8 **General Electric** Good-bye to the slow-lane plastics division. Hello to avionics, security systems, and medical labs in a box. Edison's heirs keep doubling down on products too big, gnarly, or capital-intensive for companies that haven't been ruling Big Tech for a century.

10 | 21 **Nvidia** Three trillion operations per second make for a killer demo: hyper-real renderings of glamazon Adrianne Curry. But the new GeForce 8800 chip is also speedy enough to launch gaming's graphics powerhouse into totally new markets, like gene sequencing.

0 = 2006 RANK

TYPOGRAPHY BY **Satian Pengsathapon**

APR 2007 1 1 9

284

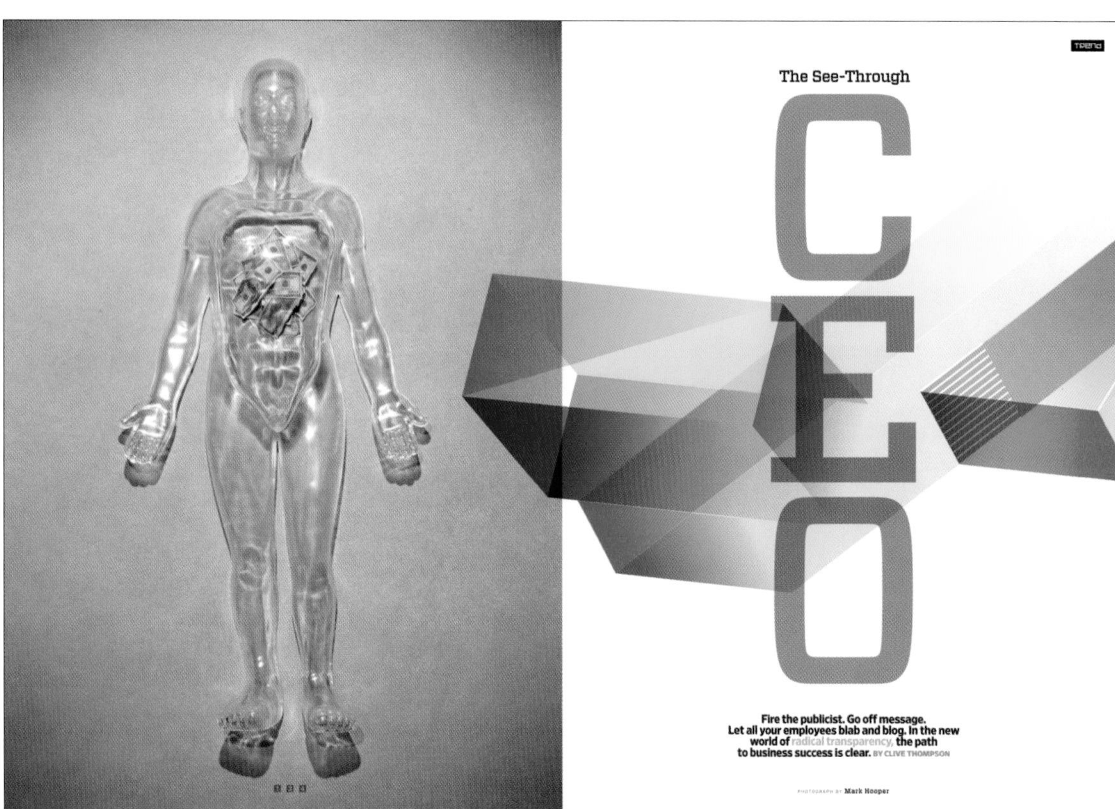

TREND

The See-Through

CEO

Fire the publicist. Go off message. Let all your employees blab and blog. In the new world of radical transparency, **the path to business success is clear.** BY CLIVE THOMPSON

PHOTOGRAPH BY **Mark Hooper**

284

284 WIRED

Creative Director_**Scott Dadich** Art Director_**Maili Holiman** Designer_**Maili Holiman**
Illustrator_**Satian Pengsathapon** Photo Editor_**Anna Goldwater Alexander** Photographers_**Mark Hooper, Michael Elins**
Publisher_**Condé Nast Publications, Inc.** Issue_**April 2007** Category_**Design: Feature: Story**

MONEY, GUNS, GOD

Inside the apocalyptic—and profitable—gun empire of JUSTIN MOON, the C.E.O. who may someday lead the Unification Church

BY *Christopher S. Stewart*

On a blustery night in December 1999, Danny Guzman left his house in Worcester, Massachusetts, and headed downtown to Tropigala, his cousin's nightclub. Tropigala occupied a bunkerlike, one-story brick building on Main South, a street that was home to shuttered storefronts, rooming houses, and a creeping underworld of drug dealing and prostitution, punctuated by the occasional shooting. Despite the upcoming holiday, Tropigala was packed with its usual, mostly Hispanic, crowd, and Guzman, a handsome 26-year-old with a muscular build and

Research BY *Paul Smalera*
PHOTOGRAPH *by* SIVAN LEWIN

201

285

the end-of-time empire

Since founding the Unification Church in the mid-1950s, the Reverend Sun Myung Moon has created a worldwide commercial empire. The idea, according to former members, is to prepare his followers for the end of days. When the global economy fails, Moon will have the resources needed to seize the reins of civilization.

A SAMPLING OF WHAT MOON HAS ASSEMBLED:

(food) Founded in the 1970s, TRUE WORLD FOODS is one of the largest distributors of seafood in the U.S., supplying the bulk of the nation's sushi-grade fish.

(transportation) PYONGHWA MOTORS, Moon's South Korean auto-manufacturing venture, expanded into North Korea in 2000. In addition, Moon companies operate a number of deepwater ports and hold shipbuilding and repair contracts with the Navy and Coast Guard.

(media) Moon owns both the WASHINGTON TIMES and UNITED PRESS INTERNATIONAL, as well as ATLANTIC VIDEO, one of the biggest independent broadcasting facilities in the country.

(sports) The SUN MOON SOCCER FOUNDATION owns two professional soccer teams, one in Brazil and the other in South Korea. Moon's Atlantic Video produces a number of ESPN television programs.

(property) The Moon empire has real estate holdings worth hundreds of millions in the U.S., including the New Yorker hotel in Manhattan, as well as various properties worldwide. Moon also owns an estimated 1.7 million acres of land straddling the border of Brazil and Paraguay.

(banking) In 1982, Moon's Unification Church purchased Uruguay's BANCO DE CREDITO. In 2002, the bank was closed, and its assets were liquidated.

(weapons) KAHR ARMS, a company founded by Moon's son Justin, manufactures the K9 pistol. When it first came out, it was the most easily concealed 9-millimeter handgun on the market.

firing line
Kahr Arms executive Frank Harris, photographed at a shooting range in Pearl River, New York, on May 16.

thousands of followers or tens of thousands; the exact number remains a mystery. Among believers, Justin's mother and father are known as the True Parents, an acknowledgment of the reverend's distinctive relationship with God; he claims to have spoken to Jesus.

Justin and his siblings are considered just as holy. They are called the True Children, and they have lived their lives accordingly. "The Moon kids acted like royalty," Graham Lester, who was a member of the Unification Church from 1979 to 1995, tells me. "From their viewpoint, everyone else was a different species. Other people were not a part of God's realm."

Home for the True Family was a guarded 18-acre mini-castle in Irvington, New York, a tony suburb located along a sweep of the Hudson River. Named East Garden, after Eden, the estate included two smaller houses and a three-story brick mansion with 12 bedrooms, seven baths, a bowling alley, and a dining room equipped with a waterfall and pond. There were other castles and mansions too—in South Korea, Germany, Scotland, England—and few expenses were spared. The children had tutors from Japan, purebred horses, motorbikes, sports cars, and first-class vacations with blank-check spending. "The kids got whatever they wanted," says Donna Collins, who grew up in the church. "At one point, the Moon kids were each getting $40,000 or $50,000 a month for allowance. They had wads of cash. I remember once in London where [one of Justin's sisters] spent like $2,000 a day; I saw a drawer filled with Rolexes and diamonds."

Justin, however, doesn't remember that kind of indulgence. "I got nothing when I was young," he says. "I didn't get one dollar. I drove a beat-up Datsun."

The True Parents were rarely around; they were off building a religion, expanding businesses, and recruiting more followers to work at those businesses. Justin grew up among church members, though the adults around him acted less like elders and more like servants, bowing as he came and went, rarely looking him in the eye.

At times, his parents' absence seemed to take a toll on him. "For me as a child, it was very difficult to understand why our True Parents have always been away," he said in a speech to Unification members in the Philippines. "It is difficult not to be able to have time to share your difficulties with your parents." Only after much "reflection," he explained, did he understand why they "had to live their life."

Justin attended Hackley, an elite prep school in Tarrytown, New York. Girls were verboten for the Moon boys; Reverend Moon had banned premarital sexual relations for all of the church's adherents. The Moon brothers were athletic, good-looking, trained in martial arts, and suspicious of outsiders, according to former church members. Now and then, they got into scuffles on the playground, and on one occasion, Justin's older brother Hyo Jin brought a BB gun to school and shot at students, for which he was expelled.

By the age of 14, Justin had become interested in guns. "My brothers introduced me to shooting," he tells me. "We'd shoot pistols and rifles, go target shooting and hunting." There was a range at the church's seminary in Barrytown, New York, and the family took hunting trips to Alaska. "Hunting was a spiritual event for the Moons," Graham Lester says. "The bigger the beast, the more evil killed."

It was around this time that Tim Porter entered Justin's life. From ages 16 to 20, Porter was considered one of Justin's "expected" friends—local church members summoned to the Moon compound to keep the True Children company. "It was never friendship," Porter recalls one night over drinks in Manhattan. "Think of it as a bunch of people meant to keep the prince happy. We were beneath him and there to serve, to laugh at his jokes, be abused by him, be his yes-men. It was a nightmare."

Porter was born into the Moonie world, the son of high-ranking church members. When he was called to East Garden, he would join the Moon kids in target shooting, tackle football, wrestling. "Sometimes [Justin] would bring in his younger brothers and have them beat us up," Porter says. "His point was that we were wussies and he wanted us to be stronger. It was like military training, getting us ready for the time when we would take on the unbelievers." According to Porter, Justin regularly reminded him and the other members' kids about his father's elevated place in God's drama. "He would always philosophize about the world ending," Porter says, "and how great his father was. That's why he did all this stuff with guns. He believes that they're going to take over the world. He would say this all the time."

Of the 13 children, Justin was considered the most transfixed by his father's messianic claims—a view that would later make Moonie watchers think he could one day become the church's leader.

Later on, there was the fight club. It was Justin's idea, Porter says, and he held sessions at his parents' compound in Seoul. "There were five or six of us, and we'd fight without gloves until we were bloody," Porter says. Justin officiated and fought, but he didn't always play by the rules. As one fight was starting, he unleashed a head kick. "This guy Isaac was just waiting for the fight to begin, and Justin leaped up and did this crazy swinging kick," Porter remembers. "It landed in the guy's face, and it looked like the guy was airborne forever, like he was levitating, until he finally dropped to the floor. It was cool. But it wasn't an emotional thing with [Justin]. He was very calculated about his violence. He had to be the best."

I ask Porter what would have happened had he refused to come one day when the True Family called. "You didn't say no," he says flatly.

Asked about the fight club, Justin acknowledges participating in martial arts training but says he "never officiated." He adds that he isn't sure about his brothers or sisters. "I'm one of 13 siblings. We all had our own lives, and I don't know what they did."

At 18, Justin got a license to carry a handgun, co-signed by one of his *(continued on page 216)*

a death in worcester
BELOW, TOP: The Tropigala nightclub in Worcester, Massachusetts, where patron Danny Guzman was killed in December 1999. BOTTOM: Attorney Hector Piñeiro holds up a photograph of a Kahr handgun similar to the one used to shoot Guzman. In the background are Guzman's daughter and mother.

kahr gun patents

Justin Moon's company, Kahr Arms, has thrived in part because these five patented innovations allow for a smaller weapon

PATENT — **staggered barrel-locking lug:** allows for a much shorter gun.
PATENT — **inertia-fired striker:** streamlines the gun's firing mechanism.
PATENT — **method of retaining a trigger bar onto a trigger:** makes for a thinner gun that keeps its proportions even at a compact size.
PATENT — **striker activation system:** simultaneously activates the firing pin and disarms the safety.
PATENT — **extractor design:** renders the gun practically jam-proof.

204 Condé Nast Portfolio.October.07 — October.07.Condé Nast Portfolio 205

285

285 CONDÉ NAST PORTFOLIO

Design Director_**Robert Priest** Art Director_**Grace Lee** Designer_**Grace Lee** Director of Photography_**Lisa Berman**
Photo Editors_**Jane Yeomans, Sarah Weissman** Deputy Photo Editor_**Sarah Czeladnicki** Photographers_**Sivan Lewin, Henry Leutwyler**
Editor-In-Chief_**Joanne Lipman** Publisher_**Condé Nast Publications Inc.** Issue_**October 2007** Category_**Design: Feature: Story**

286

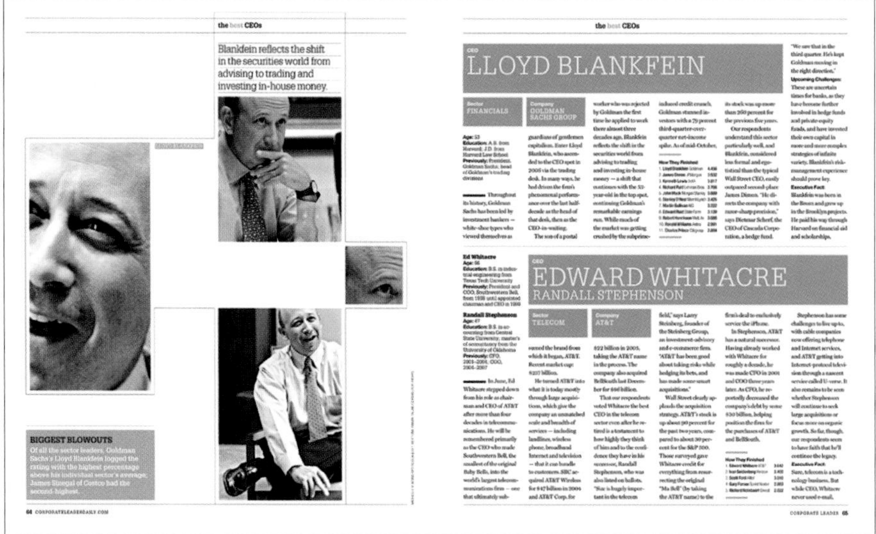

286

287

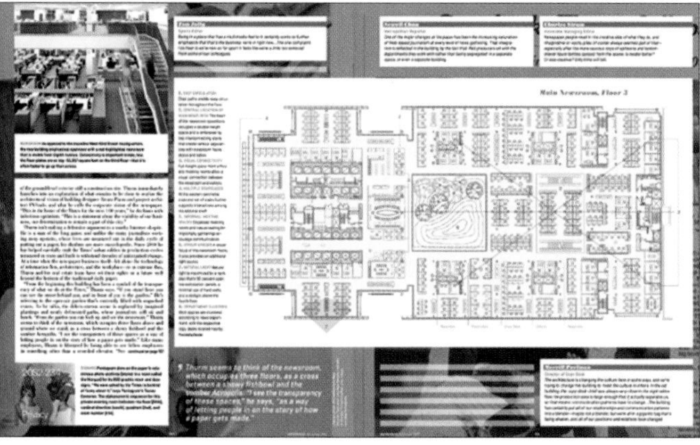

287

FREEZE FRAME

Adult iced desserts well deserving of a close-up

288

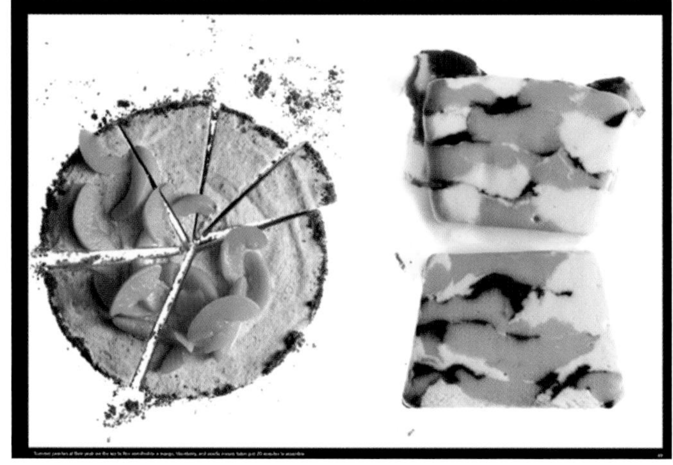

288

286 CORPORATE LEADER

Creative Director_**Florian Bachleda**
Design Director_**Ted Keller**
Studio_**FB Design**
Publisher_**Doubledown Media**
Issue_**Premiere**
Category_**Design: Feature: Story**

287 METROPOLIS

Creative Director_**Criswell Lappin**
Art Director_**Dungjai Pungauthaikan**
Photo Editor_**Bilyana Dimitrova**
Photographers_**Peter Maus, Whitney Cox**
Publisher_**Bellerophon Publications**
Issue_**November 2007**
Category_**Design: Feature: Story**

288 GOURMET

Creative Director_**Richard Ferretti**
Art Director_**Erika Oliveira**
Designer_**Erika Oliveira**
Photo Editors_**Amy Koblenzer, Megan M. Re**
Photographer_**Romulo Yanes**
Editor-In-Chief_**Ruth Reichl**
Publisher_**Condé Nast Publications, Inc.**
Issue_**July 2007**
Category_**Design: Feature: Story**

289

289

290

290

291

291

289 02138

Creative Director Patrick Mitchell
Art Director_Susannah Haesche
Director of Photography_Katharine MacIntyre
Studio_PlutoMedia
Publisher_Atlantic Media
Issue_September/October 2007
Category_Design: Feature: Story

290 SELF

Creative Director_Cynthia Searight
Art Director_Petra Kobayashi
Designer_Duane Thomas
Photo Editor_Kristen Mulvihill
Photographer_Jorg Badura
Editor-In-Chief_Lucy Danziger
Publisher_Condé Nast Publications Inc.
Issue_August 2007
Category_Design: Feature: Story

291 METROPOLIS

Creative Director_Criswell Lappin
Art Director_Dungjai Pungauthaikan
Photo Editor_Bilyana Dimitrova
Photographer_Siobhan Ridgway
Publisher_Bellerophon Publications
Issue_December 2007
Category_Design: Feature: Story

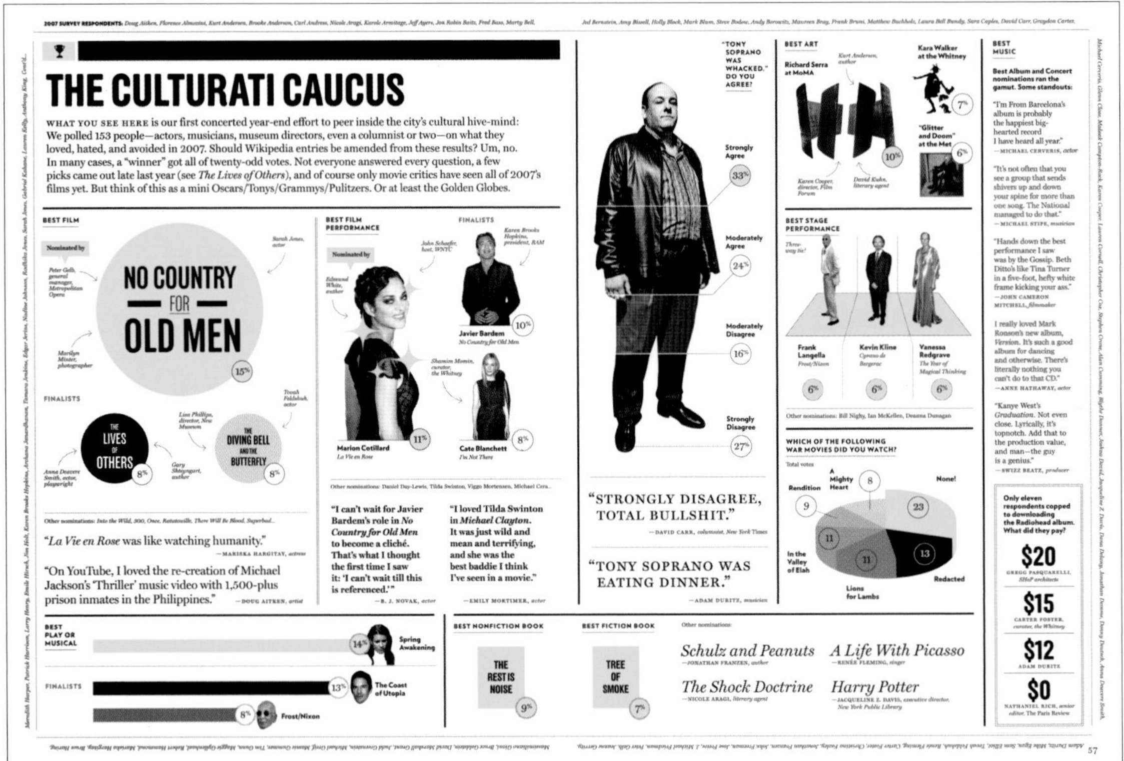

THE CULTURATI CAUCUS

WHAT YOU SEE HERE is our first concerted year-end effort to peer inside the city's cultural hive-mind: We polled 153 people—actors, musicians, museum directors, even a columnist or two—on what they loved, hated, and avoided in 2007. Should Wikipedia entries be amended from these results? Um, no. In many cases, a "winner" got all of twenty-odd votes. Not everyone answered every question, a few picks came out late last year (see *The Lives of Others*), and of course only movie critics have seen all of 2007's films yet. But think of this as a mini Oscars/Tonys/Grammys/Pulitzers. Or at least the Golden Globes.

BEST FILM: NO COUNTRY FOR OLD MEN 15%
FINALISTS: THE LIVES OF OTHERS 8%; THE DIVING BELL AND THE BUTTERFLY 8%

"*La Vie en Rose* was like watching humanity." —MARISKA HARGITAY, actress

"On YouTube, I loved the re-creation of Michael Jackson's 'Thriller' music video with 1,500-plus prison inmates in the Philippines." —DOUG AITKEN, artist

BEST FILM PERFORMANCE: Marion Cotillard, *La Vie en Rose* 11%
FINALISTS: Javier Bardem, *No Country for Old Men* 10%; Cate Blanchett, *I'm Not There* 8%

"I can't wait for Javier Bardem's role in *No Country for Old Men* to become a cliché. That's what I thought the first time I saw it: 'I can't wait till this is referenced.'" —B. J. NOVAK, actor

"I loved Tilda Swinton in *Michael Clayton*. It was just wild and mean and terrifying, and she was the best baddie I think I've seen in a movie." —EMILY MORTIMER, actor

"TONY SOPRANO WAS WHACKED." DO YOU AGREE? Strongly Agree 33%; Moderately Agree 24%; Moderately Disagree 16%; Strongly Disagree 27%

"STRONGLY DISAGREE, TOTAL BULLSHIT." —DAVID CARR, columnist, New York Times

"TONY SOPRANO WAS EATING DINNER." —ADAM DURITZ, musician

BEST ART: Richard Serra at MoMA 10%; Kara Walker at the Whitney 7%; "Glitter and Doom" at the Met 6%

BEST STAGE PERFORMANCE: Frank Langella 6%; Kevin Kline 6%; Vanessa Redgrave 6%

WHICH OF THE FOLLOWING WAR MOVIES DID YOU WATCH? Rendition 9; A Mighty Heart 8; None! 23; In the Valley of Elah 11; Lions for Lambs 11; Redacted 13

BEST MUSIC: Best Album and Concert nominations ran the gamut. Some standouts:

"I'm From Barcelona's album is probably the happiest big-hearted record I have heard all year." —MICHAEL CERVERIS, actor

"It's not often that you see a group that sends shivers up and down your spine for more than one song. The National managed to do that." —MICHAEL STIPE, musician

"Hands down the best performance I saw was by the Gossip. Beth Ditto's like Tina Turner in a five-foot, hefty white frame kicking your ass." —JOHN CAMERON MITCHELL, filmmaker

I really loved Mark Ronson's new album, *Version*. It's such a good album for dancing and otherwise. There's literally nothing you can't do that that CD." —ANNE HATHAWAY, actor

"Kanye West's *Graduation*. Not even close. Lyrically, it's topnotch. Add that to the production value, and man—the guy is a genius." —SWIZZ BEATZ, producer

Only eleven respondents copped to downloading the Radiohead album. What did they pay? $20; $15; $12; $0

BEST PLAY OR MUSICAL: Spring Awakening 14%
FINALISTS: The Coast of Utopia 13%; Frost/Nixon 8%

BEST NONFICTION BOOK: THE REST IS NOISE 9%

BEST FICTION BOOK: TREE OF SMOKE 7%

Other nominations: *Schulz and Peanuts*; *A Life With Picasso*; *The Shock Doctrine*; *Harry Potter*

292

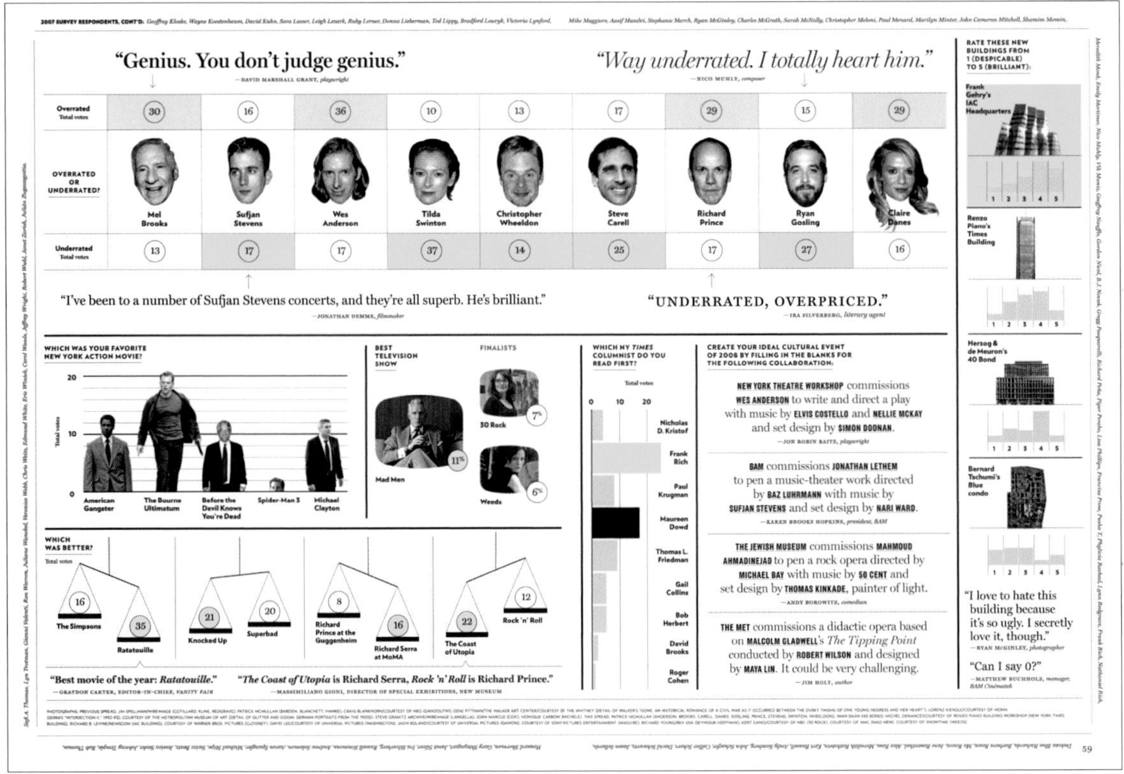

"Genius. You don't judge genius." —DAVID MARSHALL GRANT, playwright

"*Way underrated. I totally heart him.*" —NICO MUHLY, composer

OVERRATED OR UNDERRATED?

	Mel Brooks	Sufjan Stevens	Wes Anderson	Tilda Swinton	Christopher Wheeldon	Steve Carell	Richard Prince	Ryan Gosling	Claire Danes
Overrated (Total votes)	30	16	36	10	13	17	29	15	29
Underrated (Total votes)	13	17	17	37	14	25	17	27	16

"I've been to a number of Sufjan Stevens concerts, and they're all superb. He's brilliant." —JONATHAN DEMME, filmmaker

"UNDERRATED, OVERPRICED." —IRA SILVERBERG, literary agent

WHICH WAS YOUR FAVORITE NEW YORK ACTION MOVIE? American Gangster; The Bourne Ultimatum; Before the Devil Knows You're Dead; Spider-Man 3; Michael Clayton

BEST TELEVISION SHOW: Mad Men 11%
FINALISTS: 30 Rock 7%; Weeds 6%

WHICH NY TIMES COLUMNIST DO YOU READ FIRST? Nicholas D. Kristof; Frank Rich; Paul Krugman; Maureen Dowd; Thomas L. Friedman; Gail Collins; Bob Herbert; David Brooks; Roger Cohen

CREATE YOUR IDEAL CULTURAL EVENT OF 2008 BY FILLING IN THE BLANKS FOR THE FOLLOWING COLLABORATION:

NEW YORK THEATRE WORKSHOP commissions WES ANDERSON to write and direct a play with music by ELVIS COSTELLO and NELLIE MCKAY and set design by SIMON DOONAN.

BAM commissions JONATHAN LETHEM to pen a music-theater work directed by BAZ LUHRMANN with music by SUFJAN STEVENS and set design by NARI WARD. —KAREN BROOKS HOPKINS, president, BAM

THE JEWISH MUSEUM commissions MAHMOUD AHMADINEJAD to pen a rock opera directed by MICHAEL BAY with music by 50 CENT and set design by THOMAS KINKADE, painter of light. —ANDY BOROWITZ, comedian

THE MET commissions a didactic opera based on MALCOLM GLADWELL's *The Tipping Point* conducted by ROBERT WILSON and designed by MAYA LIN. It could be very challenging. —JIM HOLT, author

WHICH WAS BETTER? The Simpsons 16 / Ratatouille 35; Knocked Up 21 / Superbad 20; Richard Prince at the Guggenheim 8 / Richard Serra at MoMA 16; The Coast of Utopia 22 / Rock 'n' Roll 12

"Best movie of the year: *Ratatouille*." —GRAYDON CARTER, EDITOR-IN-CHIEF, VANITY FAIR

"*The Coast of Utopia* is Richard Serra, *Rock 'n' Roll* is Richard Prince." —MASSIMILIANO GIONI, DIRECTOR OF SPECIAL EXHIBITIONS, NEW MUSEUM

RATE THESE NEW BUILDINGS FROM 1 (DESPICABLE) TO 5 (BRILLIANT): Frank Gehry's IAC Headquarters; Renzo Piano's Times Building; Herzog & de Meuron's 40 Bond; Bernard Tschumi's Blue condo

"I love to hate this building because it's so ugly. I secretly love it, though." —RYAN MCGINLEY, photographer

"Can I say 0?" —MATTHEW BUCHHOLZ, manager, BAM Cinématek

292

292 NEW YORK

Design Director_Chris Dixon Art Directors_Randy Minor, Kate Elazegui Designer_Robert Vargas
Director of Photography_Jody Quon Publisher_New York Magazine Holdings, LLC Issue_December 17, 2007
Category_Design: Feature: Story

AMERICAN BRANDSCAPE

FORTUNE 500

IT'S NOT JUST THE SIZE OF THE REVENUE BUT THE BREADTH OF PRODUCTS THAT MAKES A FORTUNE 500 COMPANY IMPRESSIVE. FIRST UP IN THE SHOWCASE:

PEPSICO

NO. 63

Coke may still have the upper hand in the cola wars, but PepsiCo is the master of the snack attack. Today 36% of its revenue comes through Frito-Lay North America and Quaker Foods, which it bought in 2001. And as sales of sodas stall, Pepsi's noncarbonated-beverage portfolio—which includes Aquafina, Gatorade, and recent natural-drinks acquisition Naked Juice—is on the move. It commanded 48.9% market share, vs. Coke's 25.4%, in 2005—proof that it pays to diversify. *—Eugenia Levenson*

1. **Old-School Pop** *Pepsi first hit the market in 1898, 12 years after Coke. Since 1964 it has introduced 26 cola varieties—Crystal Pepsi, anyone?—of which 14 remain in stores today.*
2. **Frito-versary** *The corn chips, now sold in four flavors and three shapes in the U.S., turn 75 this year. Frito-Lay pulled ads featuring the Frito Bandito off the air 37 years ago.*
3. **Serious Jack** *Frito-Lay bought the 111-year-old brand in 1997. Cracker Jack's most valuable prize? A 1914 baseball card set, listed at $45,000 in Beckett price guides.*
4. **Thirst Quencher** *Created in the 1960s by University of Florida scientists, Gatorade is sold in 80 countries and in over 50 flavors, including Red Orange in Italy.*
5. **Bullwinkle's Bro** *Cap'n Crunch cereal's erstwhile mascot, Cap'n Horatio Crunch, was created by Jay Ward, who also drew Rocky and Bullwinkle and Dudley Do-Right.*
6. **Bran Extension** *Quaker Oats became the first breakfast cereal to receive a registered trademark in 1877. After oatmeal, oats are used most often in cookies, then meatloaf.*

94 • FORTUNE April 30, 2007

(continues on page 130)

293

AMERICAN BRANDSCAPE

FORTUNE 500

DEERE

NO. 98

Some 170 years ago, blacksmith John Deere built a steel plow to sell to farmers in Grand Detour, Ill. Since then Deere has grown into a $22 billion company, with 48 factories stretching from Brazil to China. Nearly half the company's sales still come from equipping farmers, but today's customers are as likely to till the soil abroad as on the prairie. Product lines have expanded beyond tractors to the point that Deere's vehicles go everywhere, from construction sites to golf greens. *—Eugenia Levenson*

1. **Lawn Care** *In 1963 a seven-horsepower lawn tractor marked the start of Deere's consumer division, now 18% of revenue. Today Deere sells 32 models, including this X700.*
2. **Logs-R-Us** *Deere's green and yellow color scheme, here seen on a grapple skidder, goes deep into the woods. The forestry and construction unit is second largest by sales.*
3. **Tractor Pull** *In 1918, Deere jumped into the tractor business by acquiring Waterloo Boy Tractor. Back then, Ford Motor sold six times as many machines as Waterloo.*
4. **Big Diggers** *At 4,173 pounds, the 17D is the baby of Deere's excavator family. Big brother 850D LC is the company's heaviest product, tipping the scales at 185,874 pounds.*
5. **Fat Wheels** *The tires on Deere's 400D articulated dump trucks are over six feet high and 30 inches wide, the largest on any Deere machine. Each tire weighs 1,300 pounds.*
6. **Engine-uity** *The company built its first diesel engine in 1949 and has since sold six million units. On its current roster: 25 models, including several marine engines for yachts.*

130 • FORTUNE April 30, 2007

(continues on page 158)

293

293 FORTUNE

Design Director_Robert Perino Art Director_Deanna Lowe Designers_Alice Alves, Tony Mikolajczyk, Linda Rubes, Robert Dominguez, Nai Lee Lum, Vito Zarkovic, John Tomanio, Sarah Slobin, Maria Keehan, Kalyn McCutcheon, Macaulay Campbell Director of Photography_Greg Pond Photo Editors_Scott Thode, Alix Colow, Mia Diehl, Armin Harris, Nancy Jo Johnson, Lauren Winfield, Leslie Dela Vega Editor-In-Chief_Andy Serwer Publisher_Time Inc. Issue_December 10, 2007 Category_Design: Redesign

294

294

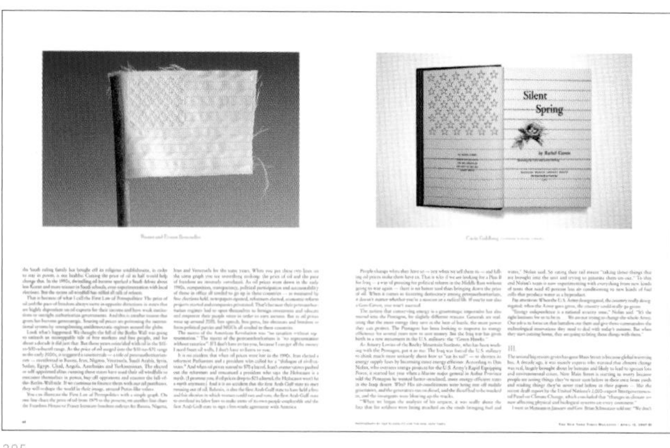

295

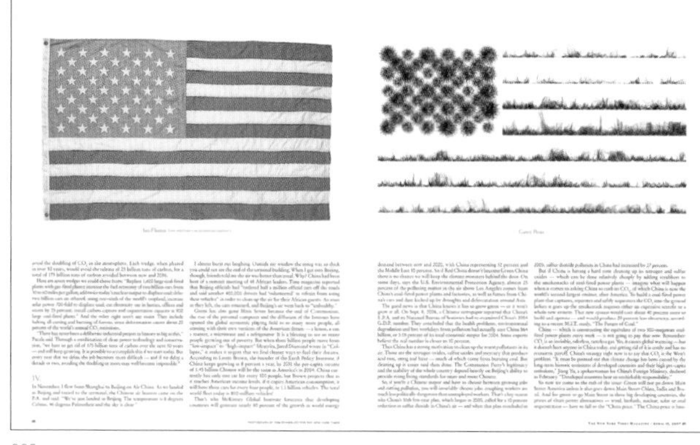

295

296

296

294 GOLF DIGEST

Design Director_Ken DeLago
Designer_Ken DeLago
Publisher_Condé Nast Publications Inc.
Issue_October 2007
Category_Design: Feature: Spread/Single Page

295 THE NEW YORK TIMES MAGAZINE

Creative Director_Janet Froelich
Art Director_Arem Duplessis
Designers_Arem Duplessis, Gail Bichler
Director of Photography_Kathy Ryan
Photo Editor_Kira Pollack
Editor-In-Chief_Gerry Marzorati
Publisher_The New York Times
Issue_April 15, 2007
Category_Design: Feature: Story

296 NEW YORK

Design Director_Chris Dixon
Art Directors_Randy Minor, Kate Elazegui
Designer_Kate Elazegui
Director of Photography_Jody Quon
Photographer_Andrew Eccles
Editor-In-Chief_Adam Moss
Publisher_New York Magazine Holdings, LLC
Issue_July 23, 2007
Category_Design: Feature: Story

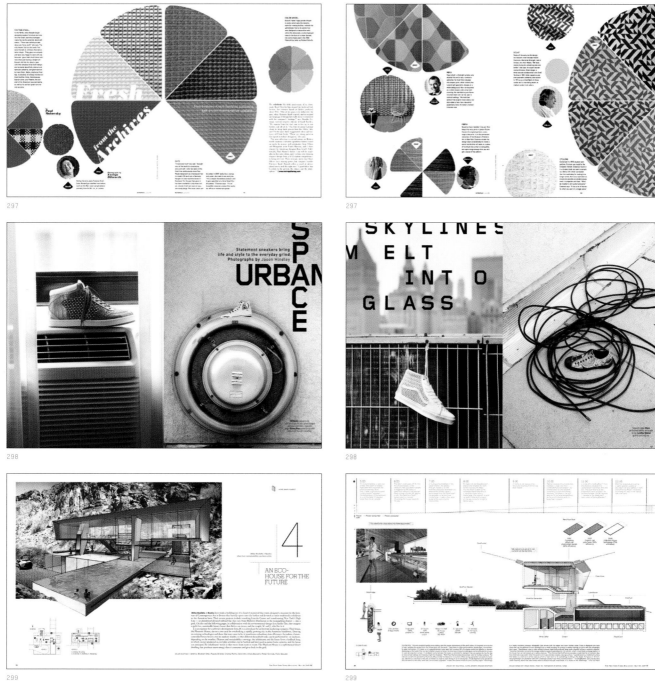

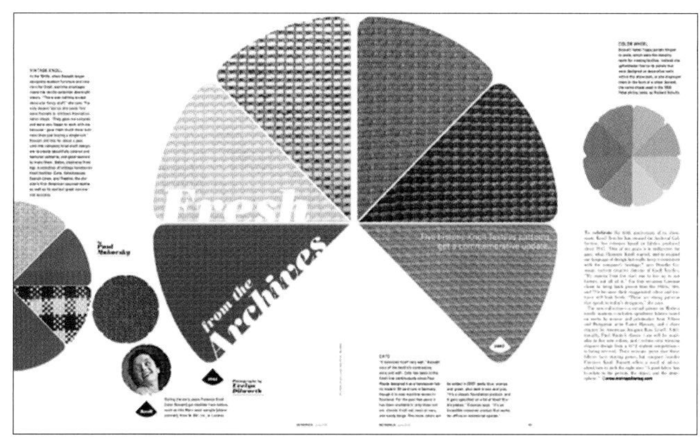

297

297

298

298

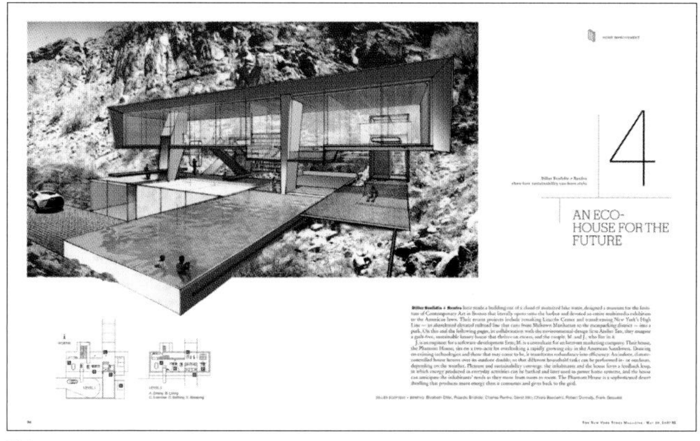

299

299

297 METROPOLIS

Creative Director_Criswell Lappin
Photo Editor_Bilyana Dimitrova
Photographer_Evelyn Dilworth
Publisher_Bellerophon Publications
Issue_June 2007
Category_Design: Feature: Story

298 TREAD

Creative Director_Nancy Campbell
Art Director_Trevett McCandliss
Designer_Trevett McCandliss
Photographer_Jason Hindley
Issue_July 2007
Category_Design: Feature: Story

299 THE NEW YORK TIMES MAGAZINE

Creative Director_Janet Froelich
Art Director_Arem Duplessis
Designers_Gail Bichler, Jeff Docherty
Illustrators_Diller Scofidio + Renfro, Jeff Docherty
Director of Photography_Kathy Ryan
Editor-In-Chief_Gerry Marzorati
Publisher_The New York Times
Issue_May 20, 2007
Category_Design: Feature: Story

300

MARCH 2007 ●● INSTITUTIONAL INVESTOR

CONTENTS

FEATURES

32 CHINA
The New Man in Chinese Banking
BY KEVIN HAMLIN
Frank Newman, the first foreigner to run a Chinese bank, inherited a mess. How goes the clean up?

42 CAPITAL MARKETS
Great Scots
BY BEN MCLANNAHAN
Johnny Cameron builds Royal Bank of Scotland into a debt powerhouse. Just don't call him an investment banker.

48 INVESTING
Ready. Set. Goad!
BY DAVID LANCHNER
First Sweden, then the world. The corporate activists at Cevian Capital plot their moves in the rest of Europe.

64 EXCHANGES
Today Chicago. Tomorrow...
BY LOREN FOX
Chicago's futures exchanges are creating a U.S. Goliath. Can they expand overseas and grab part of the OTC market?

72 TURKEY
Keeping the Faith
BY VITA BEKKER
Why bankers' trust hasn't been shaken even though E.U. membership is not a sure thing.

78 CENTRAL EUROPE
The Contrarians
BY JONATHaN KANDELL
As competitors buy up banks in the old Eastern bloc, KBC keeps its check book closed, focusing instead on expanded services.

"WITH THIS MERGER PENDING, MORE PEOPLE ARE THINKING ABOUT HAVING A PLAN B"

VOLUME XXXI, NO.2 • INTERNATIONAL EDITION

March 2007 RESEARCH and RANKINGS ●●

89 The 2007 Emerging EMEA Research Team
In a volatile year for the region's equity markets, we highlight the analysts who, in the eyes of fund managers, excel at identifying valuable opportunities as well as potential risks.

119 Country Credit
China's new economic power helps global creditworthiness rise to a 26-year high, according to our exclusive survey, and offsets a surprising slump in the U.S.'s rating to an all-time low. By Harvey D. Shapiro

300

300

300 INSTITUTIONAL INVESTOR

Creative Director_Tom Brown Art Director_Nathan Sinclair Designers_Nathan Sinclair, Tom Brown, Diana Panfil Illustrators_Andy Martin, Ulla Puggard, Brian Cairns, Daniel Marsiglio, Andre Metzger, Arthur Mount, Barry Falls Director of Photography_Daniella Nilva Photographers_Fredrik Broden, Martin Adolfsson, Tony Law, Ethan Hill, Tom Tavee, Zachary Zavislak Publisher_Institutional Investor Inc. Issue_March 2007 Category_Design: Redesign

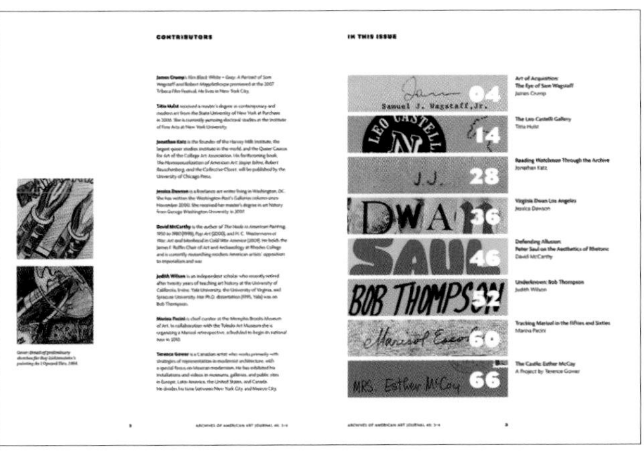
301

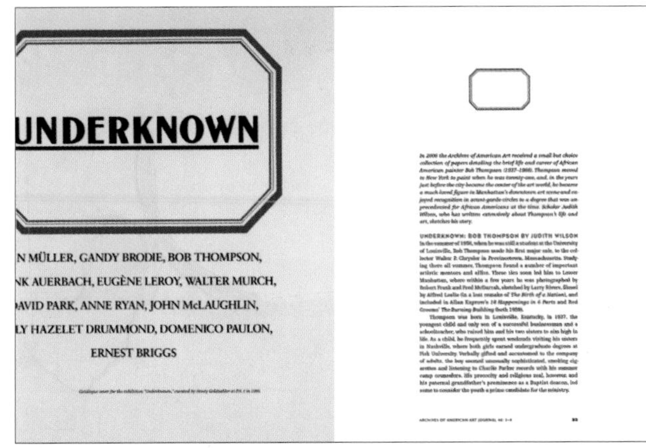

301

302

302

303

303

301 ARCHIVES OF AMERICAN ART JOURNAL

Design Directors_William Drenttel, Jessica Helfand Designers_Teddy Blanks, Jessica Helfand, William Drenttel
Studio_Winterhouse Issue_Fall 2007 Category_Design: Redesign

302 FORTUNE

Design Director_Robert Perino Art Director_Deanna Lowe Designers_Alice Alves, Tony Mikolajczyk, Linda Rubes, Robert Dominguez, Nai Lee Lum, Vito Zarkovic, John Tomanio, Sarah Slobin, Maria Keehan, Kalyn McCutcheon, Macaulay Campbell Director of Photography_Greg Pond Photo Editors_Scott Thode, Alix Colow, Mia Diehl, Armin Harris, Nancy Jo Johnson, Lauren Winfield, Leslie Dela Vega Editor-In-Chief_Andy Serwer Publisher_Time Inc.
Issue_December 10, 2007 Category_Design: Redesign

303 GOLF DIGEST

Design Director_Ken DeLago Designers_Marne Mayer, Tim Oliver, Wendy Reingold, Doug Wheeler Director of Photography_Matthew M. Ginella
Photo Editors_Kerry Brady, Jessica Foster Publisher_Condé Nast Publications Inc. Issue_December 2007 Category_Design: Redesign

FACES

BE SEEN
June 2007

THE PARTIES, THE GOSSIP, THE MOVERS AND SHAKERS

Scene Stealer

21-YEAR OLD JESSICA LEE SHUNNED a career in medicine to follow her passion on the stage and in front of the camera. A graduate of the New York Neighborhood Playhouse Theatre, Lee has made a promising start with several big screen appearances. Her main goal: "To break the Hollywood stereotype of the 'nerdy Asian' or the 'Asian sex kitten.'" Lee cites *Grey's Anatomy*'s Sandra Oh as inspiration: "She plays a character that happens to be Asian rather than an Asian stereotype." When Lee's not treading the boards or on set, she can be found pursuing her other passion: helping the community – she's involved with the International Peer Connection and the Dragon Foundation. Lee divides her time between Vancouver, New York and Hong Kong, where she's fast becoming a hot new face on the scene.

"My goal is to break the stereotype of the 'Asian sex kitten'"

HONG KONG TATLER 49 JUNE 2007

304

STYLE

BEAUTIFUL THINGS TO HAVE AND HOLD

GOTTA HAVE IT
June 2007

BRAVE PERILOUS HEIGHTS THIS SUMMER AS SHOES REACH AN ALL-TIME HIGH. SEE OUR FEATURE ON VERTIGINOUS WEDGES P.264

Jelly platform wedges from Paule Ka

INSIDE
Fine and Dandy P.256
Male Skin P.272
Christoph Wellendorff P.284
Horoscopes P.286
Object of Desire P.288

HONG KONG TATLER 255 JUNE 2007

304

ReDux

Taking their cue from fashion masters like Paul Poiret, Coco Chanel and Gianni Versace, designers this season pay homage to the fabulous fashions of decades past

PHOTOS BY KIM YONG SIK
STYLING BY HAN HYE JIN

1910

Self-proclaimed King of Fashion Paul Poiret liberated women from the corset look and offered dresses that were worked around the body with long, fluid silhouettes

Black strapless dress from Ermano Sevrino; lace shawl from Undercover by Mue; bangles from Chanel; purse from Costume National

304

304 HONG KONG TATLER

Creative Directors_**Maryjane Fahey, Mariana Ochs** Design Directors_**Maryjane Fahey, Mariana Ochs**
Designer_**Ariel Cepeda** Editor-In-Chief_**Sean Fitzpatrick** Publisher_**Edipresse Group** Category_**Design: Redesign**

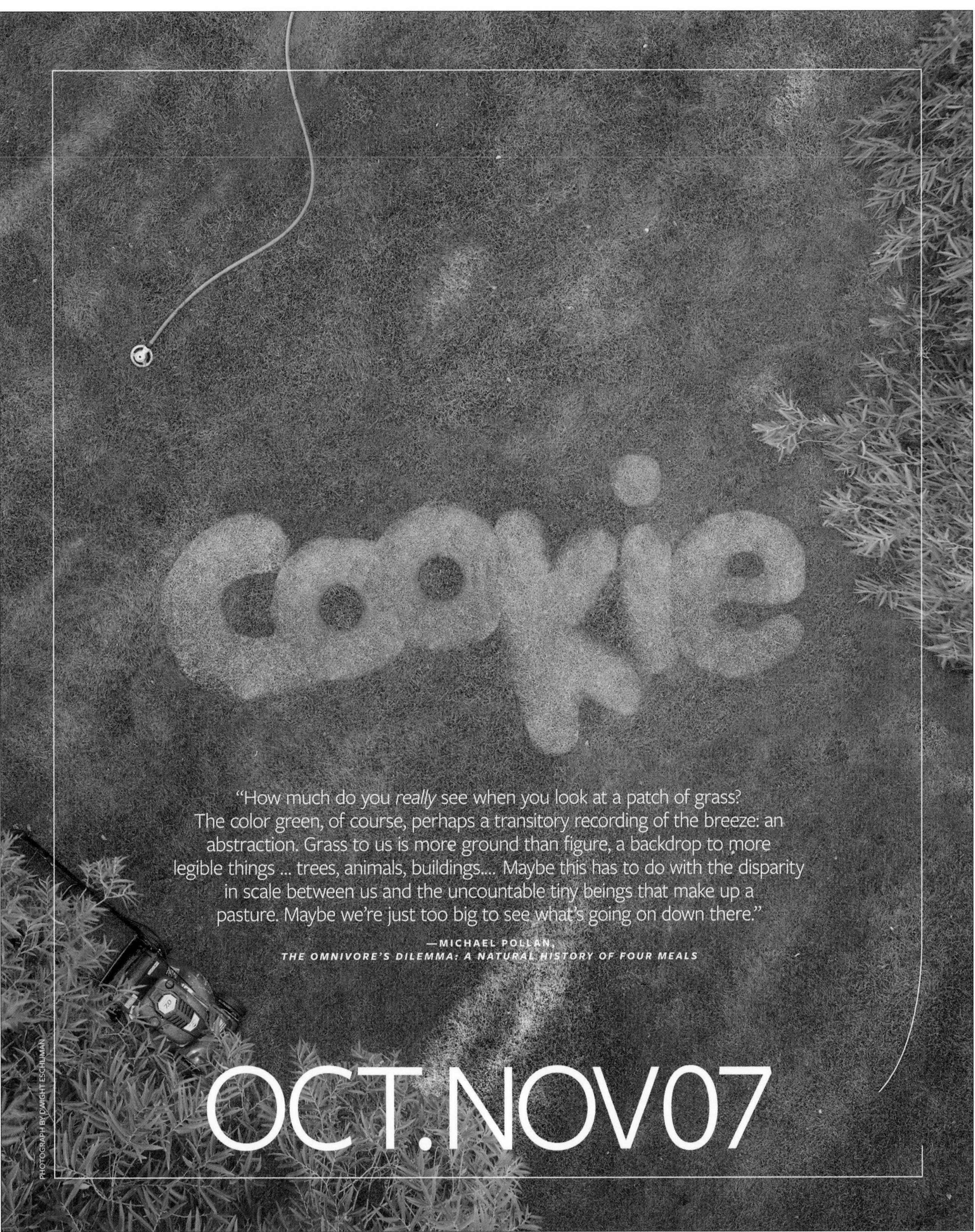

cookie
"How much do you *really* see when you look at a patch of grass? The color green, of course, perhaps a transitory recording of the breeze: an abstraction. Grass to us is more ground than figure, a backdrop to more legible things ... trees, animals, buildings.... Maybe this has to do with the disparity in scale between us and the uncountable tiny beings that make up a pasture. Maybe we're just too big to see what's going on down there."
—MICHAEL POLLAN, *THE OMNIVORE'S DILEMMA: A NATURAL HISTORY OF FOUR MEALS*
OCT.NOV07
PHOTOGRAPH BY DWIGHT ESCHLIMAN

305

305 COOKIE

Design Director Kirby Rodriguez Art Director_Alex Grossman Designers_ Shanna Greenberg, Nicolette Berthelot
Photo Editor_Darrick Harris Assistant Photo Editor_Rebecca Etter Photographers_Horacio Salinas, Dwight Eschliman, Nate Grubbs
Editor-In-Chief_Pilar Guzmán Publisher_Condé Nast Publications Inc. Category_Front of Book/Back of Book

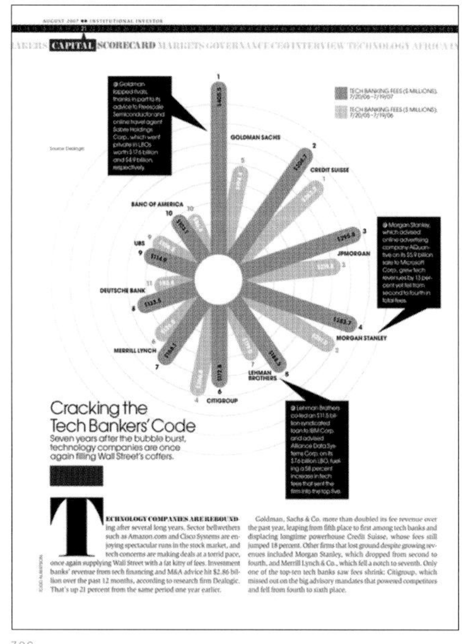

306

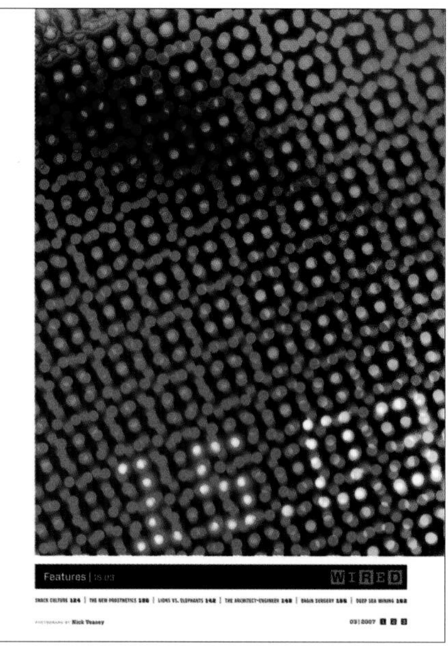

307

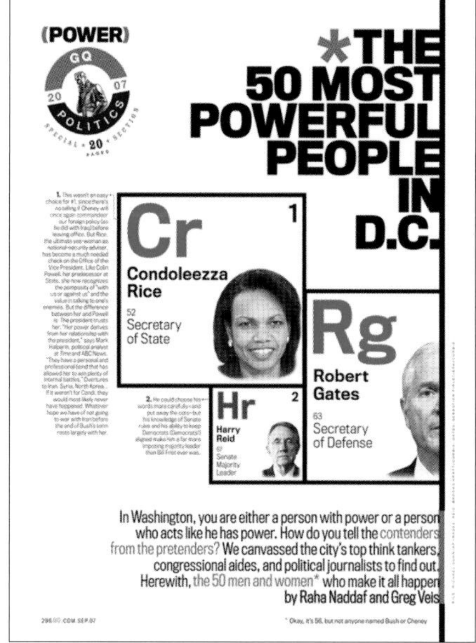

308

306

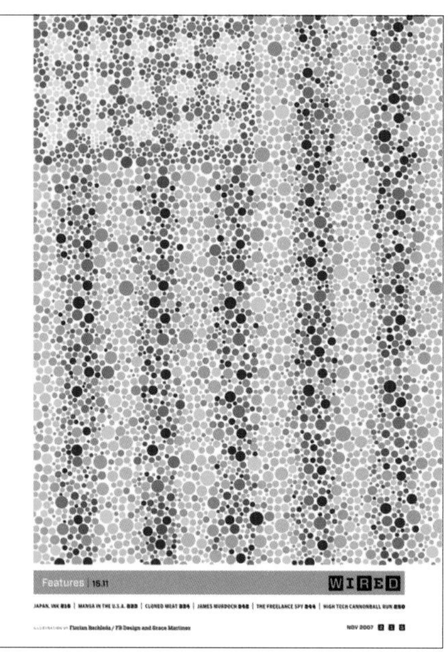

307

(POWER)

THE KEY

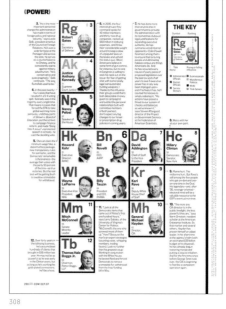

308

306 INSTITUTIONAL INVESTOR

Creative Director_Tom Brown
Art Director_Nathan Sinclair
Designer_Diana Panfil
Illustrators_Todd Albertson, Brian Cairns
Photo Editor_Daniella Nilva
Photographers_Tom Tavee, Zachary Zavislak
Publisher_Institutional Investor Inc.
Issue_October 2007
Category_Front of Book/Back of Book

307 WIRED

Creative Director_Scott Dadich
Illustrators_Nick Veasey, MK12, Paul Pope, Tomato, Florian Bachleda / FB Design & Grace Martinez
Publisher_Condé Nast Publications, Inc.
Issue_March 2007, June 2007, July 2007, September 2007, November 2007
Category_Front of Book/Back of Book

308 GQ

Design Director_Fred Woodward
Designer_Eve Binder
Director of Photography_Dora Somosi
Photo Editors_Roberto DeLuna, Jolanta Bielat
Publisher_Condé Nast Publications Inc.
Issue_September 2007
Category_Front of Book/Back of Book

The New York Times Style Magazine FALL 2007

DESIGN ON THE DOTTED LINE

309

The New York Times Style Magazine WINTER 2007

Who's Your Dada?

T — YOUR GUIDE TO THE UNEXPECTED.

311

The New York Times Style Magazine WINTER 2007

T COZY PIPING HOT, WITH SUGAR.

313

AROUND MY HOUSE

A Toolish Fella

>> Does it really matter if our man hammers with a wrench?

310

WORKSHOP

TECHNIQUES, TIPS AND YOUR QUESTIONS ANSWERED

Ask This Old House

Skill Building

Norm's Notebook

Resource Directory

312

THE REMIX

THE NEED FOR SPEED

Ladies, start your engines. High fashion goes high-octane

Like the Virgins

NOW SEATING | NOGUCHI AND KENMOCHI

314

309 T, THE NEW YORK TIMES STYLE MAGAZINE

Creative Director_Janet Froelich
Senior Art Director_David Sebbah
Art Director_Christopher Martinez
Designer_David Sebbah
Photo Editor_Judith Puckett-Rinella
Photographer_Robin Broadbent
Artwork_Work in Progress
Editor-In-Chief_Stefano Tonchi
Publisher_The New York Times
Issue_April 1, September 23, October 7, November 4, November 18
Category_Front of Book/Back of Book

310 THIS OLD HOUSE

Design Director_Amy Rosenfeld
Art Director_Hylah Hill
Designer_Amy Rosenfeld
Illustrator_Serge Bloch
Photo Editor_Denise Sfraga
Publisher Time Inc.
Issues_June 2007, July 2007, September 2007, December 2007
Category_Front of Book/Back of Book

311 T, THE NEW YORK TIMES STYLE MAGAZINE

Creative Director_Janet Froelich
Senior Art Director_David Sebbah
Art Director_Christopher Martinez
Designer_Christopher Martinez
Photographer and Artist_Dan Tobin Smith
Editor-In-Chief_Stefano Tonchi
Publisher_The New York Times
Issue_November 18, 2007
Category_Front of Book/Back of Book

312 THIS OLD HOUSE

Design Director_Amy Rosenfeld
Art Director_Hylah Hill
Designer_Amy Rosenfeld
Photo Editor_Denise Sfraga
Photographers_Keate, Nigel Cox, Victor Shrager, Plamen Petkov, Beatriz Da Costa
Publisher_Time Inc.
Issues_May 2007, June 2007, September 2007, October 2007, November 2007
Category_Front of Book/Back of Book

313 T, THE NEW YORK TIMES STYLE MAGAZINE

Creative Director_Janet Froelich
Senior Art Director_David Sebbah
Art Director_Christopher Martinez
Designer_David Sebbah
Photo Editor_Judith Puckett-Rinella
Photographer_Robin Broadbent
Artist_Stephanie DeArmond
Editor-In-Chief_Stefano Tonchi
Publisher_The New York Times
Issue_November 4, 2007
Category_Front of Book/Back of Book

314 T, THE NEW YORK TIMES STYLE MAGAZINE

Creative Director_Janet Froelich
Senior Art Director_David Sebbah
Art Director_Christopher Martinez
Designer_Elizabeth Spiridakis
Photo Editor_Scott Hall
Editor-In-Chief_Stefano Tonchi
Publisher_The New York Times
Issue_August 26, 2007
Category_Front of Book/Back of Book

2.25.07 Eat, Memory By Dan Barber

The Great Carrot Caper

Gentle genetic modification yields a nutty harvest.

Last December, right around Christmas, I received a small package from Jean-Marc Montegottero, an artisanal-nut-oil producer in Burgundy. The package contained a shoebox filled with dust. Flummoxed, I phoned his American distributor and importer and our mutual friend, Olivier Wittmann, to inquire about this strange gift.

The dust was almond residue, Olivier said, and he told me about a visit he made to Jean-Marc's on a cold October afternoon. As he walked up the path to his farmhouse, all he could smell was almonds. Figuring that Jean-Marc was making an almond tart for dessert, he opened the door to the kitchen and saw only a large *sautoir* of potatoes simmering gently in duck fat. Confused, he looked at Jean-Marc, who simply smiled. "Sit," he said. "Eat."

The potatoes smelled, and tasted, as Olivier would attest, like almond potatoes. Jean-Marc, a scrupulous recycler, collected the flourlike dust after pressing almonds for the oil and spread it over his potato field like compost. Through a kind of magical osmosis, the almond potatoes were born.

Jean-Marc's gift to me could not have come at a better time. Fall harvest at Stone Barns was a waning memory. Dark clouds of root vegetables and cabbages were on the horizon. I seized on the nut idea — with carrots instead of potatoes. Almonds and carrots are a better pairing, I thought. (Was this becoming competitive?)

Getting the cooks excited about the connections to the farm

Dan Barber is the executive chef and co-owner of Blue Hill and Blue Hill at Stone Barns.

Photograph by Mitchell Feinberg

83

315

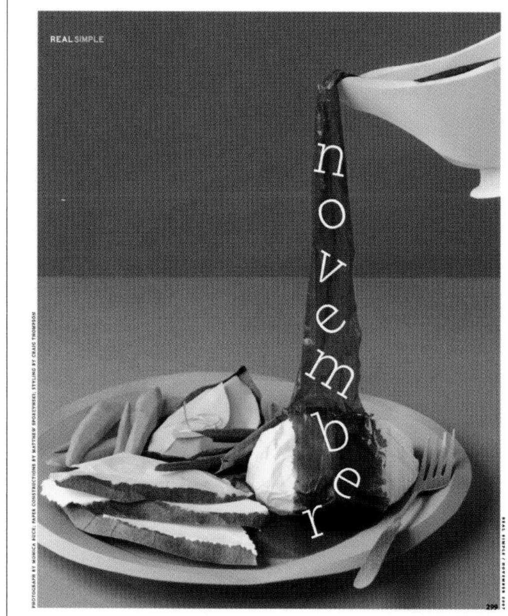

317

316

JOHN CASSIDY

ECONOMICS

His Fault

Blame Greenspan for the credit bubble

ALAN GREENSPAN, April 2005

Alan Greenspan's just-released memoir, *The Age of Turbulence*, is aptly titled. In his two decades as chairman of the Federal Reserve Board, Greenspan presided over Black Monday, the stock market collapse that occurred 20 years ago this month; the Asian financial crisis; the demise of Long-Term Capital Management; and the dotcom bubble.

Greenspan's book will make headlines over the next few weeks, in part because of his surprisingly downbeat assessment of the economy and financial markets. But even though he left the Fed more than a year and a half ago, his recollections aren't of merely historical interest. The current turmoil on Wall Street is largely a result of policy decisions he made during his final years. By keeping interest rates too low for too long, he encouraged a borrowing-fueled speculative binge, which has now given way to a credit squeeze. By failing to crack down on the mortgage industry, he allowed subprime hucksters to peddle dubious loans, which the financial industry's math whizzes packaged for investors. Coming on top of his role in creating

68 Condé Nast Portfolio.October.07

318

315 THE NEW YORK TIMES MAGAZINE

Creative Director_**Janet Froelich** Art Director_**Arem Duplessis** Designer_**Catherine Gilmore-Barnes** Illustrator_**Mitchell Feinberg** Director of Photography_**Kathy Ryan** Photo Editor_**Joanna Milter** Photographer_**Mitchell Feinberg** Editor-In-Chief_**Gerry Marzorati** Publisher_**The New York Times** Issues_**February 25, 2007, May 27, 2007, April 29, 2007** Category_**Front of Book/Back of Book**

316 NEW YORK

Design Director_**Chris Dixon** Art Directors_**Randy Minor, Kate Elazegui** Designer_**John Carbonella** Director of Photography_**Jody Quon** Editor-In-Chief_**Adam Moss** Publisher_**New York Magazine Holdings, LLC** Issue_**May 28, 2007** Category_**Front of Book/Back of Book**

317 REAL SIMPLE

Design Directors **Eva Spring, Ellene Wundrok** Designer_**Eva Spring** Director of Photography_**Casey Tierney** Photo Editor_**Daisy Cajas** Photographer_**Monica Buck** Constructionist_**Matthew Sporzynski** Stylist_**Craig Thompson** Publisher_**Time Inc.** Issue_**November 2007** Category_**Front of Book/Back of Book**

318 CONDÉ NAST PORTFOLIO

Design Director_**Robert Priest** Art Director_**Grace Lee** Deputy Art Director_**Sarah Viñas** Designers_**Grace Lee, Sarah Viñas, Jana Meier, Paloma Shutes, Rina Kushnir** Director of Photography_**Lisa Berman** Photo Editors_**Jane Yeomans, Sarah Weissman, Rossana Shokrian, Brian Marcus, Louisa Anderson** Deputy Photo Editor_**Sarah Czeladnicki** Photographer_**Jill Greenberg** Information Graphics Director _**John Grimwade** Editor-In-Chief_**Joanne Lipman** Publisher_**Condé Nast Publications Inc.** Issue_**October 2007, December 2007** Category_**Front of Book/Back of Book**

1.28.07

ON LANGUAGE BY WILLIAM SAFIRE

The Democrats make their deadline.

319

321

322

ON LANGUAGE BY WILLIAM SAFIRE

The Gotcha! Gang strikes again.

320

321

322

319 THE NEW YORK TIMES MAGAZINE

Creative Director_Janet Froelich Art Director_Arem Duplessis
Designers_Gail Bichler, Leo Jung Director of Photography_Kathy Ryan
Lettering_Hellovan, Tauba Auerbach Editor-In-Chief_Gerry Marzorati
Publisher_The New York Times Issues_January 28, 2007, May 20, 2007, June 17, 2007, August 26, 2007
Category_Front of Book/Back of Book

320 THE NEW YORK TIMES MAGAZINE

Creative Director_Janet Froelich Art Director_Arem Duplessis
Designers_Leo Jung, Gail Bichler Director of Photography_Kathy Ryan
Lettering_Stiletto NYC, Carson Fox Editor-In-Chief_Gerry Marzorati
Publisher_The New York Times Issues February 11, 2007, July 29, 2007, November 4, 2007, November 25, 2007, December 15, 2007
Category_Front of Book/Back of Book

321 REAL SIMPLE FAMILY

Design Director_Eva Spring Art Director_Eva Spring
Designer_Eva Spring Illustrator_Alli Arnold
Photo Editors_Paula Trotto, Shana Sobel Photographer_Monica Buck
Issue_Spring 2007 Category_Front of Book/Back of Book: up to 5 pages

322 REAL SIMPLE

Design Directors_Eva Spring, Ellene Wundrok Art Director_Eva Spring
Designer_Eva Spring Director of Photography_Casey Tierney
Photo Editor_Daisy Cajas Photographer_Monica Buck
Constructionist_Matthew Sporzynski Stylist_Craig Thompson
Publisher_Time Inc. Issue_July 2007
Category_Front of Book/Back of Book: up to 5 pages

eating

photograph by KENJI TOMA

THE IMPROVISER

the accidental dinner

What you'll need: tomatoes, garlic, and a general acceptance of the fact that life is going to intervene

BY FRANCES BOSWELL

I have to admit that halibut was not what I had in mind when I stocked up on heavy, red, ripe tomatoes one early fall day last year. No, what I was envisioning was a big plate of spaghetti with classic tomato sauce and an even bigger glass of red or rosé. My plan was to peel and quarter the tomatoes, add several cloves of garlic and a devil-be-damned ration of olive oil, and let it all simmer until everything sort of fell apart and came together at the same time. Just minutes into my preparations, my 5-year-old daughter, Sophie, started to complain that the smell of garlic was making her sick and couldn't I please turn it off *now?* Nonsense, I thought. It was only when her protests reached that distinct "maybe something really is wrong" tone that I realized that the poor girl had some horrible 24-hour vomit-fever-type thing, and that she really was miserable.

Several hours and changes of bedsheets later, with everyone but me asleep, I had gone off the idea of eating. So I abandoned my now-cold sauce, figuring there was no harm in leaving tomatoes out overnight—preserved, I reasoned, in a puddle of olive oil. The next day, knowing my husband (who had gone to bed the night before with a piece of cheese) would appreciate a real meal, I bought some nice fish. All I had to do was warm up the tomato sauce, lay the fish on top, cover it for 10 minutes until it was steamed through, then toss in some basil at the end. How I love that a 24-hour flu never lasts that long.

Frances Boswell is the coauthor of Food Adventures: Knowing Good Food from the Start (Kyle Books).

COOKIEMAG.COM

To share tips for your best improvised meals, visit cookiemag.com/go/forums.

112

323

OPEN

INSIDE: TRADING-INSPIRED MASTERWORKS, STEREO OF THE GODS, A WALL STREET POTBOILER

"I'M NOT INFLUENCED BY HYPE OR EMOTION; MARKET PRICE MOVEMENTS DETERMINE MY TRADES. I HAVE THE SAME ATTITUDE ON THE ROCKS: I DON'T WANT EMOTION DISTRACTING ME."

325

DIRECTIONS

INSIDE: TRADING'S TOP FEMALE MINDS, THE TURTLES REVISITED, AN ELECTION MONEY MAP

"I'M A HEAVY-DUTY QUANT FAN, BUT I BELIEVE THE BEST TRADING STRATEGIES ARE A MARRIAGE OF HUMANS AND TECHNOLOGY."

324

WIRED

How Yahoo Blew It 126
Selling ads against search seemed like such a simple thing. But while Yahoo CEO Terry Semel fumbled and bumbled, Google pulled ahead.
BY FRED VOGELSTEIN

The Invisible Enemy 132
The Pentagon created the perfect machine for saving the lives of soldiers wounded in Iraq. But then GIs started getting sick. The culprit: a drug-resistant supergerm infecting the military's evacuation chain.
BY STEVE SILBERMAN

A Second Life for MTV 140
It used to be the last word in youth culture. Now MTV is more about reality shows than rock stars. Can a virtual world of 3-D avatars help the network get its groove back?
BY MARK WALLACE

Inherit the Wind 144
The Gulf Coast is littered with the carcasses of spare oil platforms. Now that equipment is being repurposed to build the first offshore wind farm in the United States.
BY JOHN GEOGHEGAN

104

What We Don't Know
What is the universe made of? Why can't humans regenerate lost body parts? How many licks does it take to get to the center of a Tootsie Pop? *The Daily Show*'s John Hodgman and a who's-who of science thinkers explore dozens of life's mysteries, big and small.

Features | 15.02

PHOTOGRAPH BY Tom Schierlitz

02|2007 0 0 7

326

323 COOKIE

Design Director_Kirby Rodriguez Art Director_Alex Grossman
Designers_Shanna Greenberg, Nicolette Berthelot
Photo Editor_Darrick Harris Assistant Photo Editor_Rebecca Etter
Photographer_Kenji Toma Editor-In-Chief_Pilar Guzmán
Publisher_Condé Nast Publications Inc. Issue_September 2007
Category_Front of Book/Back of Book

324 TRADER MONTHLY

Creative Director_Florian Bachleda Art Director_Clare Minges
Director of Photography_Ian Spanier Photographers_Ian Spanier, Matt Furman, Terry Kuzniar Studio_FB Design
Publisher_Doubledown Media Issue_November/December 2007
Category_Front of Book/Back of Book

325 TRADER MONTHLY

Creative Director_Florian Bachleda Art Director_Clare Minges
Photographers_Ian Spanier, Michael Darter Studio_FB Design
Publisher_Doubledown Media Issue_September 2007
Category_Front of Book/Back of Book

326 WIRED

Creative Director_Scott Dadich Design Director_Wyatt Mitchell
Designers_Christy Sheppard, Maili Holiman, Margaret Swart, Chris Imlay Illustrators_ILM, Ryan Jones, Alex Jaeger, Rick O'Connor, Ron Woodall Photographers_Tom Schierlitz, Ofer Wolberger, Olaf Blecker, Rainer Hosch Publisher_Condé Nast Publications, Inc.
Issue_February 2007, June 2007, July 2007, November 2007, December 2007 Category_Front of Book/Back of Book

327

329

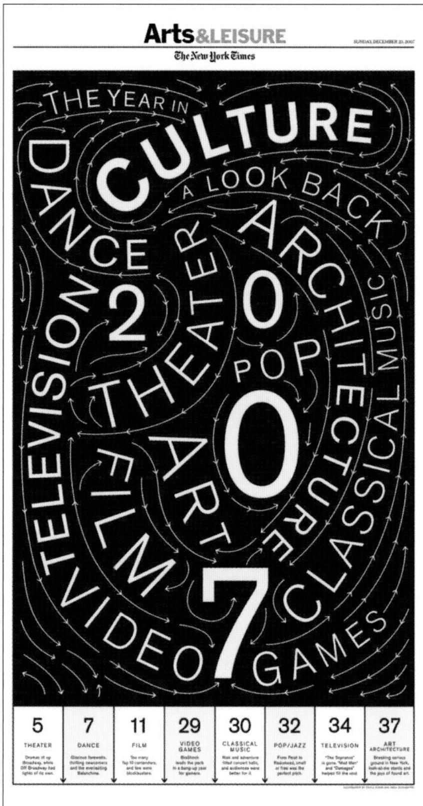

328

Monday 05.03.07 the guardian

A 14-page arts special

The meaning of 'meh' Charlie Brooker Urban cycling: a survival guid

330

327 NEW YORK

Design Director_**Chris Dixon** Director of Photography_**Jody Quon**
Photo Editor_**Leana Alagia** Photographer_**Jake Chessum**
Editor-In-Chief_**Adam Moss** Publisher_**New York Magazine Holdings, LLC**
Issues_**October 22, 2007, December 12, 2007, December 24-31, 2007**
Category_**Front of Book/Back of Book**

328 THE NEW YORK TIMES

Design Director_**Tom Bodkin** Art Director_**Paul Jean**
Designer_**Joon Mo-Kang** Illustrators_**Paula Scher, Drea Zlanabitnig**
Publisher_**The New York Times** Issue_**December 23, 2007**
Category_**Design: Front Page**

329 W

Design Director_**Edward Leida** Art Director_**Nathalie Kirsheh**
Designer_**Nathalie Kirsheh** Photo Editor_**Nadia Vellam**
Photographers_**Thibault Montamat, Monica May, Jen Livingston**
Publisher_**Condé Nast Publications Inc.** Issue_**October 2007**
Category_**Front of Book/Back of Book**

330 THE GUARDIAN

Art Director_**Richard Turley** Illustrator_**Marian Bantjes**
Publisher_**Guardian Newspapers Limited**
Issue_**May 3, 2007** Category **Design: Front Page**

331

331 NEW YORK

Design Director_Chris Dixon Director of Photography_Jody Quon Photo Editors_Caroline Smith, Leana Alagia Photographer_Vincent Laforet
Editor-In-Chief_Adam Moss Publisher_New York Magazine Holdings, LLC Issue_December 24-31, 2007 Category_Photo: Cover

: SECTION
PHOTOGRAPHY

: AWARD
GOLD

: CATEGORY
FEATURE: SPREAD/SINGLE
FEATURE: STORY

332

07 *American Fatherhood*

What Is a Father?

4

The Hero Figure

Aaron Mankin, 25, Marine, Purple Heart recipient, father of one AS TOLD TO JENNIFER WOLFF
PHOTOGRAPH BY MARY ELLEN MARK

Madeline has started to develop this crooked smile that says "I know something you don't." I had that same crooked smile before I was burned.

I was wounded two years ago. We were clearing houses and villages and pinching off the insurgency coming into Iraq from Syria when we rolled over an IED and our vehicle exploded literally 10 feet into the air. More fire came at us, and we thought we were under ambush, but it was our own munitions inside the vehicle cooking off—grenades, bullets, flares. I fell back inside the tank, and the first thing I saw when I opened my eyes was fire. My initial reaction was to gasp, and in doing so, I inhaled flames and smoke and pieces of burned uniform. My goggles and flak jacket protected my eyes and chest, but the rest of my upper body was on fire. I jumped out of the vehicle and tried to put myself out by rolling in the grass, but it was dry grass and it caught fire as I rolled in it. Four Marines died, 11 others were wounded. I was certain I was going to be among the dead. People say your life passes before you. For me, I saw the people who meant the most to me. My mom. My dad. I was only semiconscious. Then, my girlfriend Diana's face popped into my head. I was thinking, *These are my last thoughts. She is my last thought*. And I focused on her face, because if I was going to die in war, I wanted to die with the thought of something worth fighting for, something worth dying for.

Instead, I woke up. The first time I saw Diana three months later, I asked her to marry me. I didn't know what I was capable of as a husband or as a dad. I didn't know what I could bring to the table besides a burned face and scarred arms. My ears, nose, and mouth were gone, as were the thumb and index finger of my right hand. When she said yes, it was a turning point for me. Even though I had a right to be bitter and curse the world, it wasn't what Diana deserved. It wasn't the man she fell in love with.

It was a month and a half before I was ready to look at myself in the mirror. Then one day, I got out of my hospital bed to go to physical therapy and I saw the mirror I'd passed countless times, refusing to see the truth about how hurt I was. I looked over my left shoulder, and there I was—this torn up, frail, thin individual with open wounds on his face that I barely recognized, and my worst imagination became my reality. I cried. Being a Marine, you want to tell yourself you're fine, just walk it off. But I couldn't walk this one off. I covered the bottom half of my face with my elbow, and looking at my eyes and my forehead, I didn't look any different. I knew inside I was still the same man. But not everyone would see that, and I was very concerned when Jake and Maggie, my little brother and sister, then 8 and 7, came to see me in the hospital. I was their big brother. I was in the Marine Corps. I was invincible. That's how they saw me, but I didn't know if they would see me that way anymore. So I asked Jake, "Do you still think Bubba (that's what they call me) is as strong and fast and tough as you used to?" Jake didn't think about it at all. He just said, "Yeah, I think so." And I looked at myself, and I was bandaged up and breathing hard, and I said, "What makes you think that?" And he said back to me, "Well, they tried to blow you up, and they couldn't." I would love it if my daughter would see me that way one day, as "superhuman" in my ability to take care of her, and if she's ever in harm's way, there's a cape to wrap her up and shield her. That cape is me.

My worst fear for her as she grows up is that she will be ridiculed or teased for the way I look. She had nothing to do with this. She can't do anything about my skin. It's not fair for her to carry any kind of burden for me or to feel guilty or bad or "less than" because my face is scarred. On the other hand, I feel lucky that she doesn't know the difference between Daddy now and Daddy then. I see what happens when other officers come home wounded. Their kids are reluctant to hug them because Daddy looks different, and because Daddy has owies and the kids don't want to hurt them. Having a severely wounded father flips a kid's whole world upside down. They don't know what to expect or what's expected of them. In that way, Madeline has been spared.

I never want Madeline to think, *If my daddy weren't hurt, I could....* I want her to see my scars as an advantage. I want her to see that they make me love her more because they make me try harder. And if I can't figure out a way to do something for her, if I can't, say, put together her bike because I'm missing some fingers and I can't manage the little parts, I am not proud, I will ask for help. I will get it done for her somehow. That's on me. That's on my shoulder. She will never go without because I was wounded. I can give you every excuse in my arsenal not to change diapers or do the tough stuff. But the fact that I don't use any of that stuff to my advantage is going to deepen our connection to each other. I can only hope that one day, when she's old enough, she's going to realize that this stuff wasn't easy for her dad, but he did it anyway, because he loved her. ■

122 BEST LIFE JUNE 2007

"If she's ever in harm's way, there's a cape to wrap her up and shield her. That cape is me."

Iraq War veteran Aaron Mankin, with daughter Madeline, 2 months, at their home in Fort Sam Houston, Texas

333

332 GQ

Design Director_**Fred Woodward** Designer_**Anton Ioukhnovets**
Director of Photography_**Dora Somosi** Photo Editor_**Justin O'Neill**
Photographer_**Jill Greenberg** Senior Photo Editor_**Krista Prestek**
Editor-In-Chief_**Jim Nelson** Publisher_**Condé Nast Publications Inc.**
Issue_**June 2007** Category_**Photo: Feature: Spread/Single Page**

333 BEST LIFE

Art Director_**Brandon Kavulla** Designers_**Heather Jones, Dena Verdesca**
Director of Photography_**Ryan Cadiz** Photo Editor_**Jeanne Graves**
Photographer_**Mary Ellen Mark** Publisher_**Rodale**
Issue_**June 2007** Category_**Photo: Feature: Spread/Single Page**

Ved første øjekast ser det frygtindgydende ud. Downtown Tokyo, draperet med lig. Men det er bare sovende mænd. Japanske forretningsfolk fra finansdistriktet **Sjinjuku**, der arbejder så hårdt, at de ikke kan nå hjem til forstæderne, inden de skal til et nyt møde

FOTO CASPER BALSLEV
TEKST KRISTIAN DITLEV JENSEN

*[søvn]

I VESTEN ser de fleste mennesker japanske forretningsfolk som arbejdsnarkomaner. Og selvom loven foreskriver, at man kun behøver at arbejde 40 timer om ugen, er det også rigtigt, at en offentligt ansat funktionær eller en regnskabsmedarbejder i et privat firma i Japan ofte arbejder op imod 50 timer mere om måneden end i vores ende af verden. Det giver ikke sjældent en arbejdsuge på 55 timer. Dertil kommer sociale pligter.

Saito Hironori, der er førstesekretær på den japanske ambassade i København, fortæller, at det i nogle brancher stadig er almindeligt, at man følger med, når chefen inviterer på selskab og sake. Og i fordums tid var det en decideret pligt.

– Det var en del af arbejdet, at man modtog invitationer fra forretningsforbindelser og gik på meget dyre restauranter. Det var også almindeligt, at man drak store mængder alkohol til hverdag. Andre gange var det kollegerne, man gik ud med.

De sovende japanere i habit skyldes i lige så høj grad, at japanerne er rationelle mennesker. Og når man færdes i Sjinjuku Business District, Tokyos larmende, pulserende, neonblinkende, kaotiske finanscentrum, lærer man at optimere døgnets minutter.

– Japan er et meget sikkert samfund, så man kan faktisk →

10 Ud & Se MAJ 2007

334 **UD&SE**

Design Director_**Katinka Bukh**
Photographer_**Casper Balslev**
Publisher_**DSB** Issue_**May 2007**
Category_**Photo: Feature: Story**

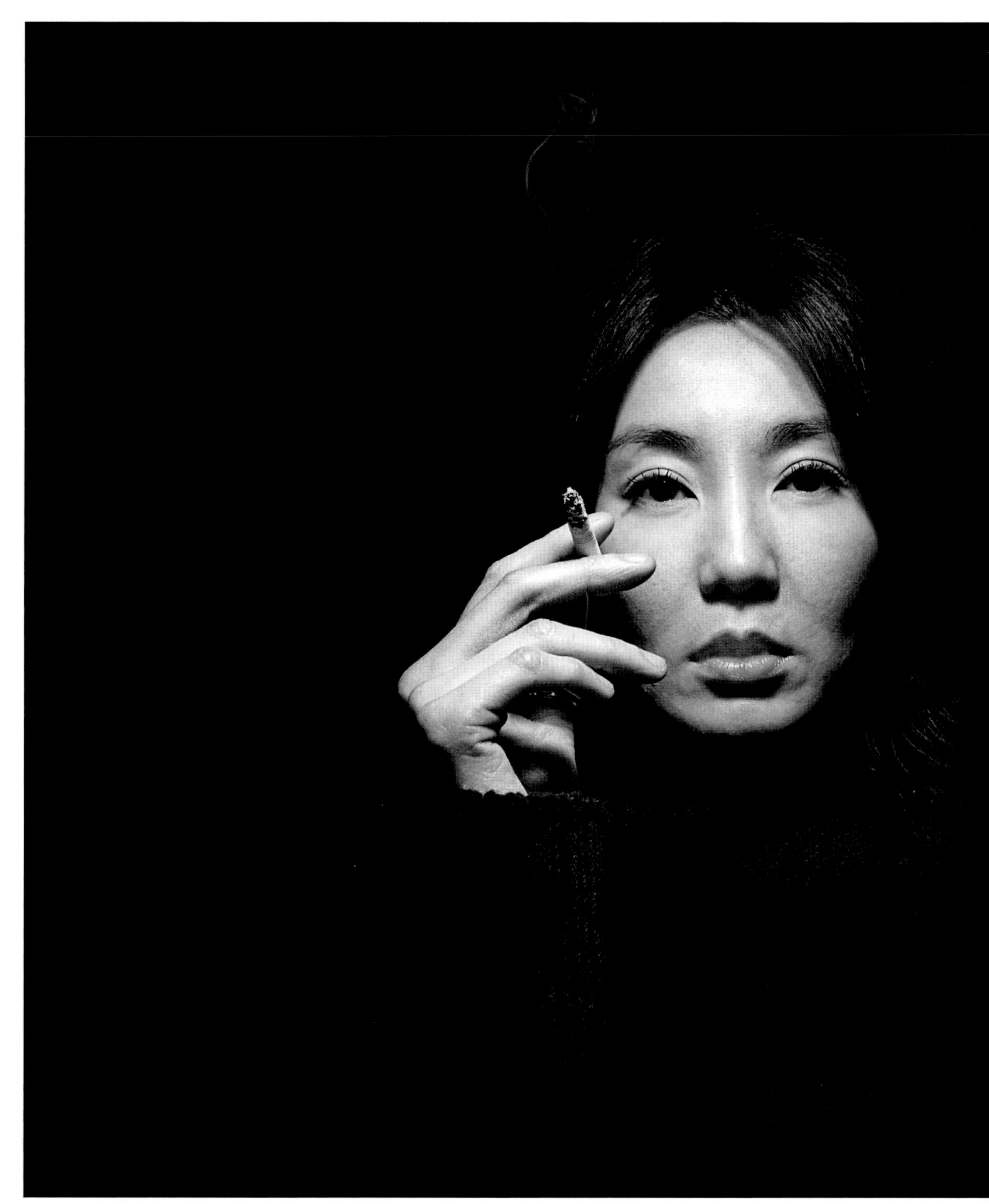

MAGGIE CHEUNG, "CLEAN." PHOTOGRAPH BY PAOLO PELLEGRIN

335 THE NEW YORK TIMES MAGAZINE

Creative Director_**Janet Froelich** Art Director_**Arem Duplessis** Designer_**Catherine Gilmore-Barnes**
Director of Photography_**Kathy Ryan** Photo Editor_**Kira Pollack** Photographers_**Dan Winters, Gareth McConnell, Richard Burbridge, David Sims, Andres Serrano, Paolo Pellegrin, Rineke Dijkstra, Katy Grannan, Gueorgui Pinkhassov, Robert Maxwell**
Editor-In-Chief_**Gerry Marzorati** Publisher_**The New York Times** Issue_**Feburary 11, 2007** Category_**Photo: Entire Issue**

: SECTION
PHOTOGRAPHY

: AWARD
GOLD

: CATEGORY
ENTIRE ISSUE

Crime and Punishment: Jim Dwyer on a Fugitive on the Run for 10 Years; Elizabeth Weil on the Case Against Lethal Injection

The New York Times Magazine

FEBRUARY 11, 2007 / SECTION 6

The 4th Annual Great Performers in Film

A 26-page photographic portfolio of the actors and actresses who defined excellence in the past year.

335

335 THE NEW YORK TIMES MAGAZINE

Creative Director_**Janet Froelich** Art Director_**Arem Duplessis** Designer_**Catherine Gilmore-Barnes**
Director of Photography_**Kathy Ryan** Photo Editor_**Kira Pollack** Photographers_**Dan Winters, Gareth McConnell, Richard Burbridge, David Sims, Andres Serrano, Paolo Pellegrin, Rineke Dijkstra, Katy Grannan, Gueorgui Pinkhassov, Robert Maxwell**
Editor-In-Chief_**Gerry Marzorati** Publisher_**The New York Times** Issue_**Feburary 11, 2007** Category_**Photo: Entire Issue**

RYAN GOSLING, "HALF NELSON." PHOTOGRAPH BY GARETH McCONNELL

60

LEONARDO DiCAPRIO, "THE DEPARTED." PHOTOGRAPH BY RICHARD BURBRIDGE

335

JENNIFER HUDSON, "DREAMGIRLS." PHOTOGRAPH BY KATY GRANNAN

80

SACHA BARON COHEN, "BORAT." PHOTOGRAPH BY RICHARD BURBRIDGE

335

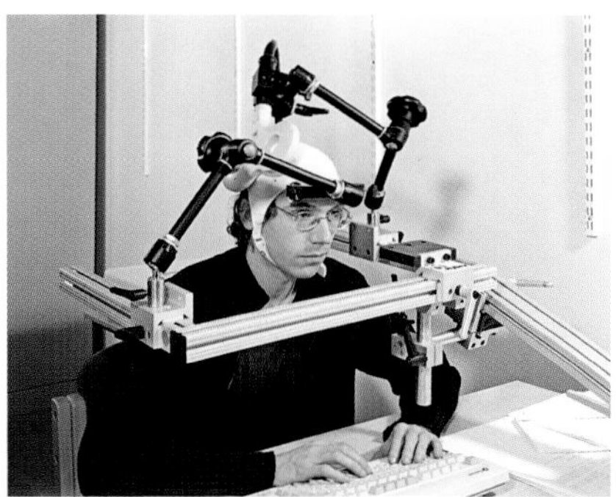

Left: At the University of Birmingham in the UK, Wouter Braet models a brain-stimulating magnet that he uses to identify which regions of the visual cortex are most crucial to word recognition.

Right: Michael Falkenstein at the Universität Dortmund studies how older and younger people process information differently. Here he demonstrates an EEG that records brain activity while subjects interact with a computer.

336

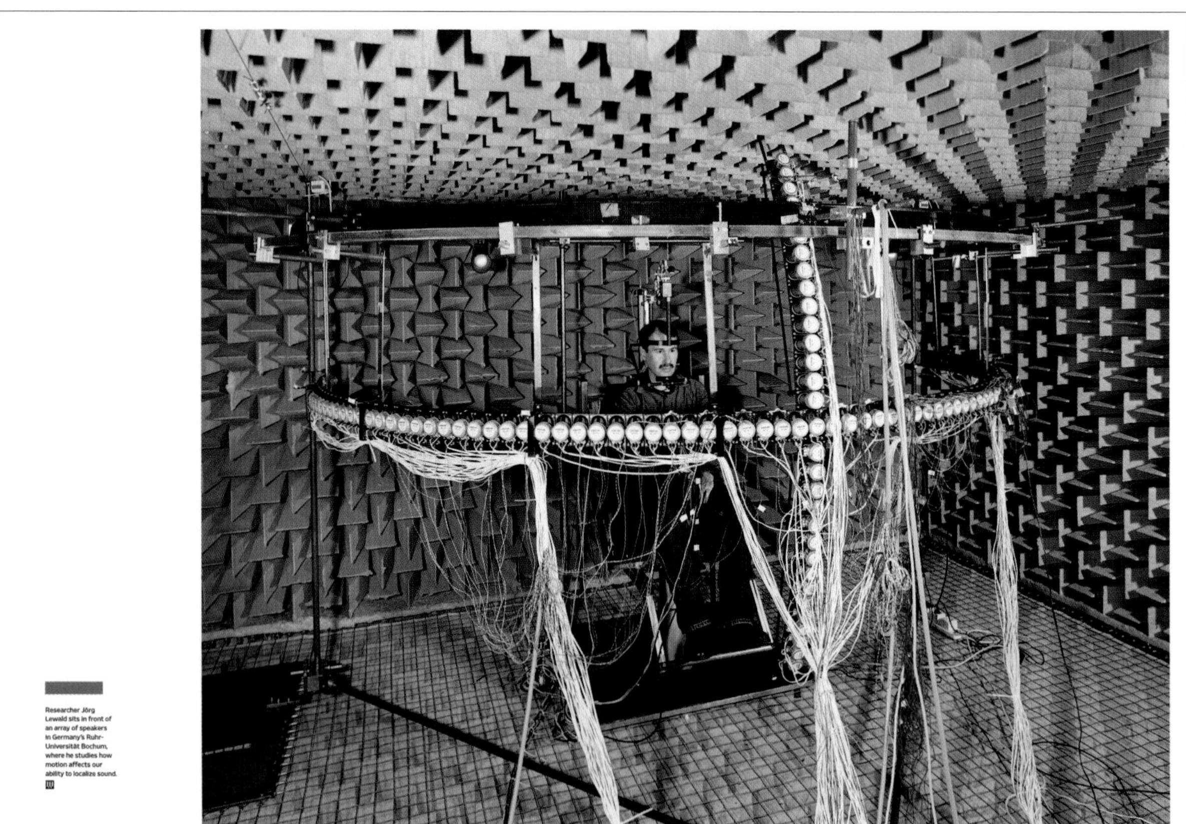

Researcher Jörg Lewald sits in front of an array of speakers in Germany's Ruhr-Universität Bochum, where he studies how motion affects our ability to localize sound.

336

336 WIRED

Creative Director_**Scott Dadich** Designer_**Maili Holiman**
Photo Editor_**Carolyn Rauch** Photographer_**Daniel Stier**
Publisher_**Condé Nast Publications, Inc.**
Issue_**September 2007** Category_**Photo: Feature: Story**

The Yves Saint Laurent show at the Grand Palais, Paris, October 4.

SPRING 2008 | NEW YORK LOOK 95

337

Magdalena Frackowiak is rosy perfection backstage at Viktor & Rolf, Paris, October 2.

SPRING 2008 | NEW YORK LOOK 97

337

337 NEW YORK LOOK

Design Director_**Chris Dixon** Director of Photography_**Jody Quon**
Photo Editors_**Lea Golis, Nadia Lachance** Photographer_**Paolo Pellegrin**
Editor-In-Chief_**Adam Moss** Publisher_**New York Magazine Holdings, LLC**
Issue_**Fall 2007** Category_**Photo: Feature: Story**

338

338 GQ

Design Director_**Fred Woodward** Designer_**Thomas Alberty** Director of Photography_**Dora Somosi** Photographer_**Nathaniel Goldberg**
Editor-In-Chief_**Jim Nelson** Publisher_**Condé Nast Publications Inc.** Issue_**December 2007** Category_**Photo: Cover**

THE INTERROGATION

INT. HOLLYWOOD PRECINCT HOUSE—NIGHT

Detective James Archer (**Alec Baldwin**), of the L.A.P.D. homicide squad, hears out the soliloquy of surprise informant Muriel Slade (**Jennifer Connelly**), twin sister of the murdered man. Her story holds together very well—too well, in fact. Beat cop Mack Shaughnessy (**Aaron Eckhart**) keeps a grip on his stick, just in case her tale starts making even more sense.

Det. Archer: Murder is a savage affair, Miss Slade.

Muriel: And what kind of affairs do you prefer, Detective?

Det. Archer: That's my own business, Miss Slade.

Muriel: Your own business, huh? Any chance I could make partner?

Det. Archer: Lady, your partner is murder. And it's a silent partner.

Shaughnessy (thinking): If it's silent, why don't you two lovebirds shut it? This ain't the El Havana.

Wipe to . . .

www.vanityfair.com | VANITY FAIR | 413

339

THE GETAWAY

INT./EXT. MULHOLLAND DRIVE—NIGHT

Cue swirling, maddening violins. Tilda Lydeker (**Helen Mirren**), aunt to Laura Lydeker, paramour to three-fourths of Beverly Hills circa 1929, and the brains behind the city's third-largest citrus fortune, must drive, and she must drive fast. She knows just how lemonade is made in this town, and she knows Oscar learned the tricks of her trade all too well, and she knows how it all went sour. Oscar may have been just some low-life private dick, and he may have been too free with his fists, but sometimes a woman needs a man who's man enough to remind her that she's a woman—that is, if she's woman enough to take it. And Tilda could take it. Oh, how she could take it. She took it, and she took it, and she took it again. And then once more for laughs.

Along for the ride is Tilda's older half-sister, Alma (**Judi Dench**), issue of their father's youthful dalliance—or was it something more sinister?—with the beautiful daughter of migrant citrus pickers. They say Alma's "slow," but, like her half-sister, when it comes to trouble she's awfully swift on the pickup.

www.vanityfair.com | VANITY FAIR | 423

339

339 VANITY FAIR

Design Director_**David Harris** Designer_**Chris Mueller** Director of Photography_**Susan White** Photo Editor_**Kathryn MacLeod** Photographer_**Annie Leibovitz** Editor-In-Chief_**Graydon Carter** Publisher_**Condé Nast Publications Inc.** Issue_**March 2007** Category_**Photo: Feature: Story**

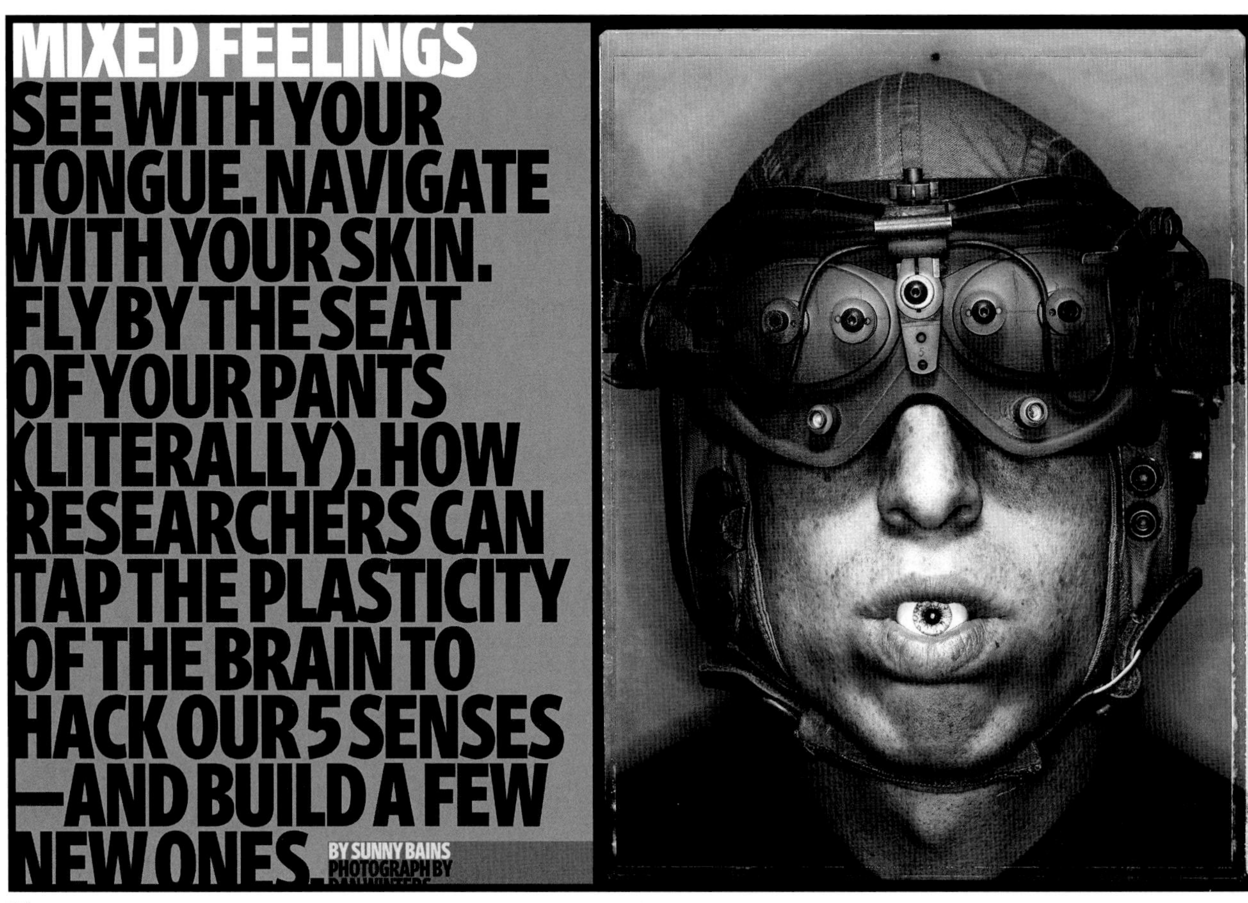

MIXED FEELINGS
SEE WITH YOUR TONGUE. NAVIGATE WITH YOUR SKIN. FLY BY THE SEAT OF YOUR PANTS (LITERALLY). HOW RESEARCHERS CAN TAP THE PLASTICITY OF THE BRAIN TO HACK OUR 5 SENSES —AND BUILD A FEW NEW ONES.
BY SUNNY BAINS
PHOTOGRAPH BY

340

6.3.07 Style
The Strong,
Not So Silent
Type
M/M (Paris) didn't become the fashion world's go-to graphic design duo by being polite. But fonts speak louder than words.
By Alix Browne
Photograph by Inez van Lamsweerde and Vinoodh Matadin
M/M (PARIS): MICHAEL AMZALAG (LEFT) AND MATHIAS AUGUSTYNIAK
52

341

340 WIRED

Creative Director_Scott Dadich Designer_Scott Dadich Photo Editor_Carolyn Rauch Photographer_Dan Winters Publisher_Condé Nast Publications, Inc. Issue_April 2007 Category_Photo-Illustration: Single Page/Spread/Story

341 THE NEW YORK TIMES MAGAZINE

Creative Director_Janet Froelich Art Director_Arem Duplessis Designer_Nancy Harris Rouemy Director of Photography_Kathy Ryan Photographers_Inez van Lamsweerde, Vinoodh Matadin Editor-In-Chief_Gerry Marzorati Publisher_The New York Times Issue_June 3, 2007 Category_Photo: Feature: Spread/Single Page

The New York Times Magazine

AUGUST 26, 2007 / SECTION 6

There will be
another Katrina (or worse).
It will cost insurers
and governments a fortune
(or worse). Some
hedge-fund managers are
betting on it.

The Natural-Catastrophe Casino
By Michael Lewis

Fred Kaplan: Did We Have the Right Kind of Generals in Iraq? Noah Feldman: A Secular Place for Religion in Public Schools

342

342 THE NEW YORK TIMES MAGAZINE

Creative Director_**Janet Froelich** Art Director_**Arem Duplessis** Designer_**Gail Bichler**
Director of Photography_**Kathy Ryan** Photographer_**Sasha Bezzubov** Editor-In-Chief_**Gerry Marzorati** Publisher_**The New York Times**
Issue_**August 26, 2007** Category_**Photo: Cover**

: SECTION
PHOTOGRAPHY

: AWARD
SILVER

: CATEGORY
COVER
FEATURE: SPREAD/SINGLE

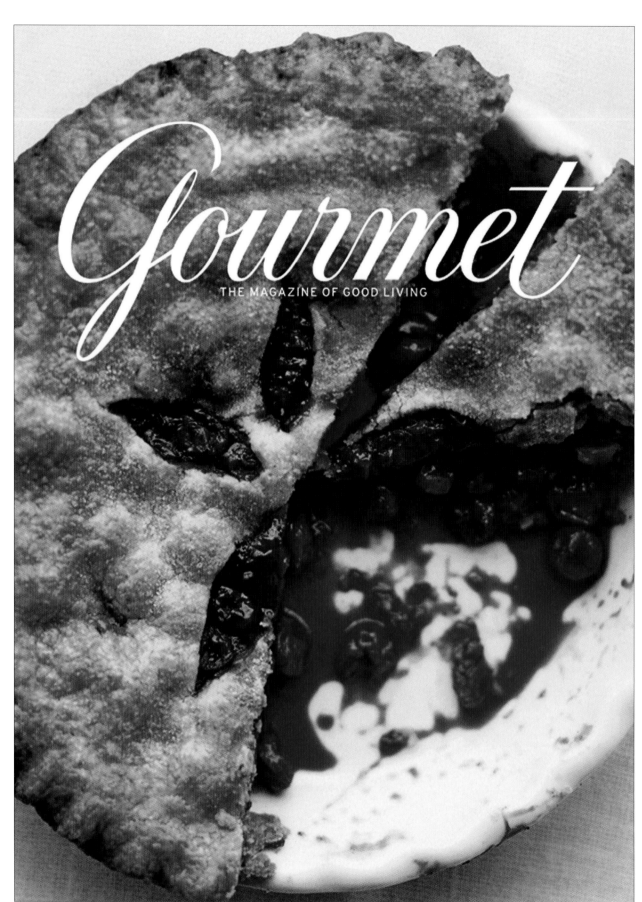

Gourmet
THE MAGAZINE OF GOOD LIVING

343

GOURMET

Creative Director_**Richard Ferretti** Art Director_**Erika Oliveira** Designer_**Richard Ferretti** Director of Photography_**Amy Koblenzer** Photographer_**Mikkel Vang** Editor-In-Chief_**Ruth Reichl** Publisher_**Condé Nast Publications, Inc.** Issue_**July 2007** Category_**Photo: Cover**

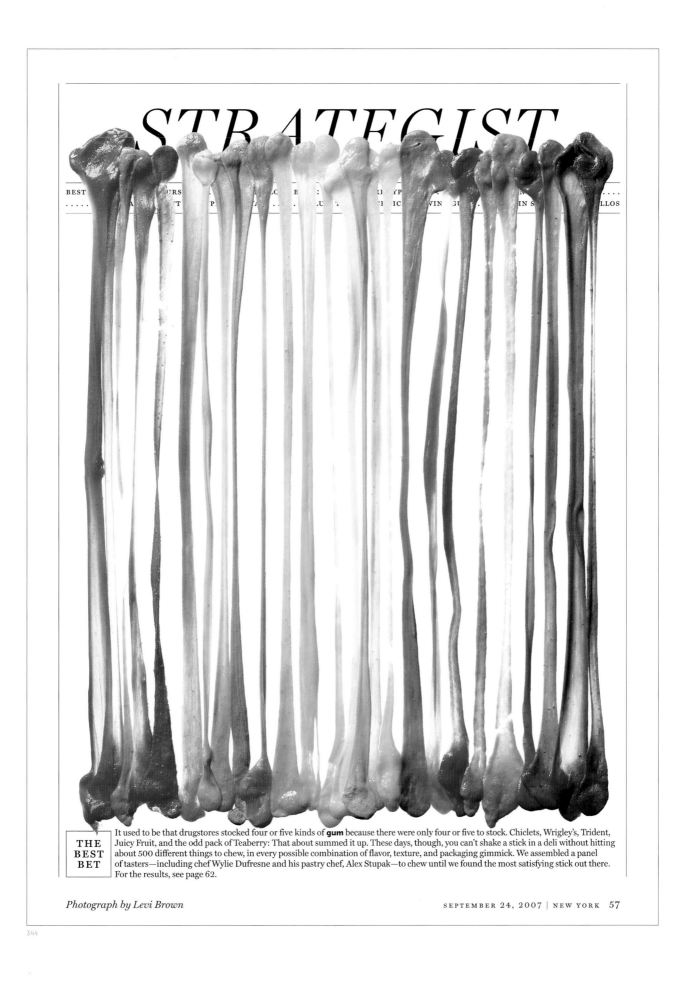

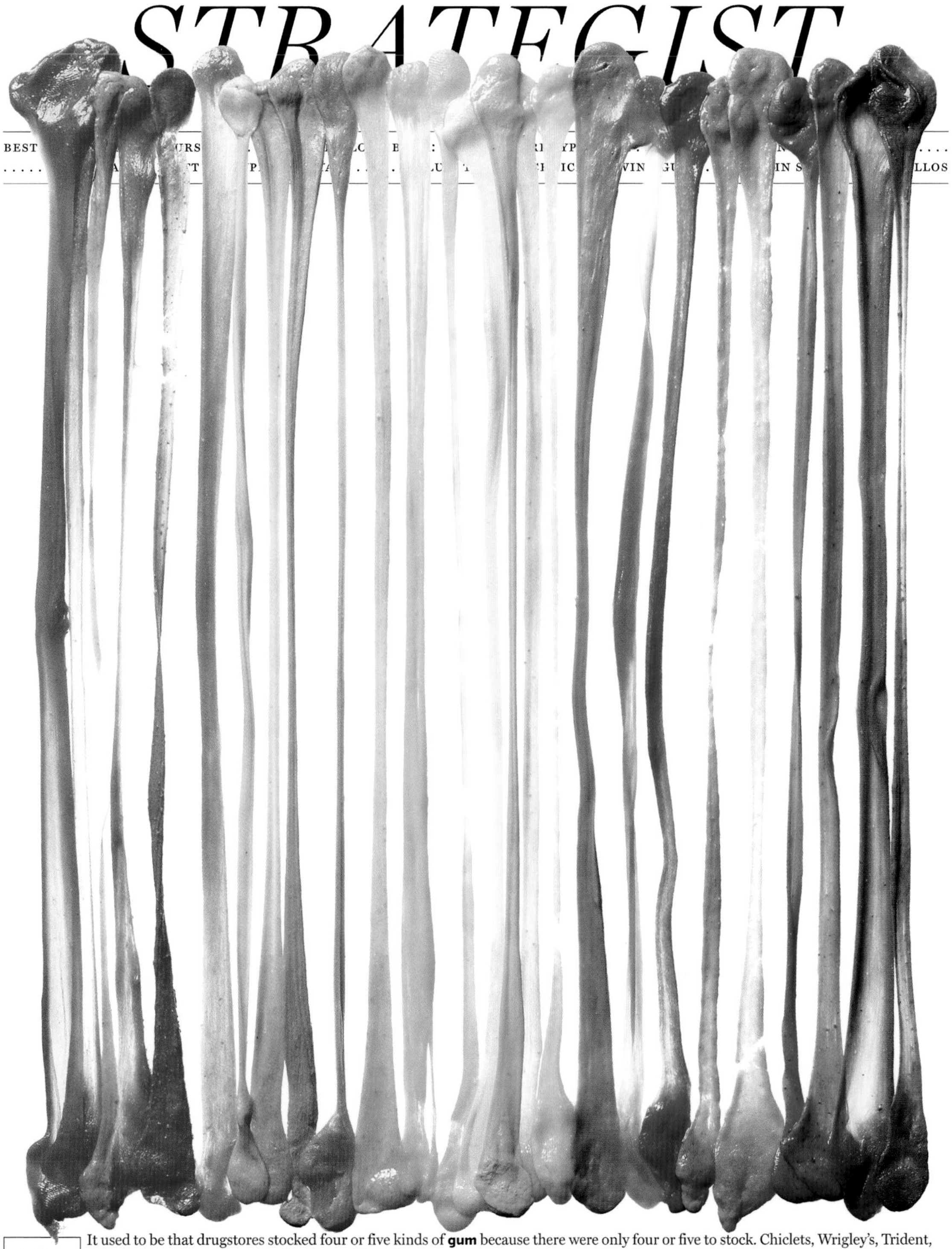

STRATEGIST

THE BEST BET

It used to be that drugstores stocked four or five kinds of **gum** because there were only four or five to stock. Chiclets, Wrigley's, Trident, Juicy Fruit, and the odd pack of Teaberry: That about summed it up. These days, though, you can't shake a stick in a deli without hitting about 500 different things to chew, in every possible combination of flavor, texture, and packaging gimmick. We assembled a panel of tasters—including chef Wylie Dufresne and his pastry chef, Alex Stupak—to chew until we found the most satisfying stick out there. For the results, see page 62.

Photograph by Levi Brown

NEW YORK

Design Director_Chris Dixon Director of Photography_Jody Quon Photo Editor_Leana Alagia Photographer_Levi Brown
Editor-In-Chief_Adam Moss Publisher_New York Magazine Holdings, LLC Issue_September 24, 2007 Category_Photo: Feature: Spread/Single Page

PORTFOLIO

A Really Big Show

THE THRILL OF VICTORY. THE AGONY OF DEFEAT. THE VOYEURISTIC PLEASURE OF HAVING THE BEST EYE IN THE HOUSE AT THE MAJOR EVENTS IN SPORTS.

Photographs by **VINCENT LAFORET**

United States Open Women's Final, Sept. 9, 2006, New York City
Maria Sharapova defeats Justine Henin-Hardenne for her second Grand Slam title.

JUNE 2007 **PLAY** 65

345

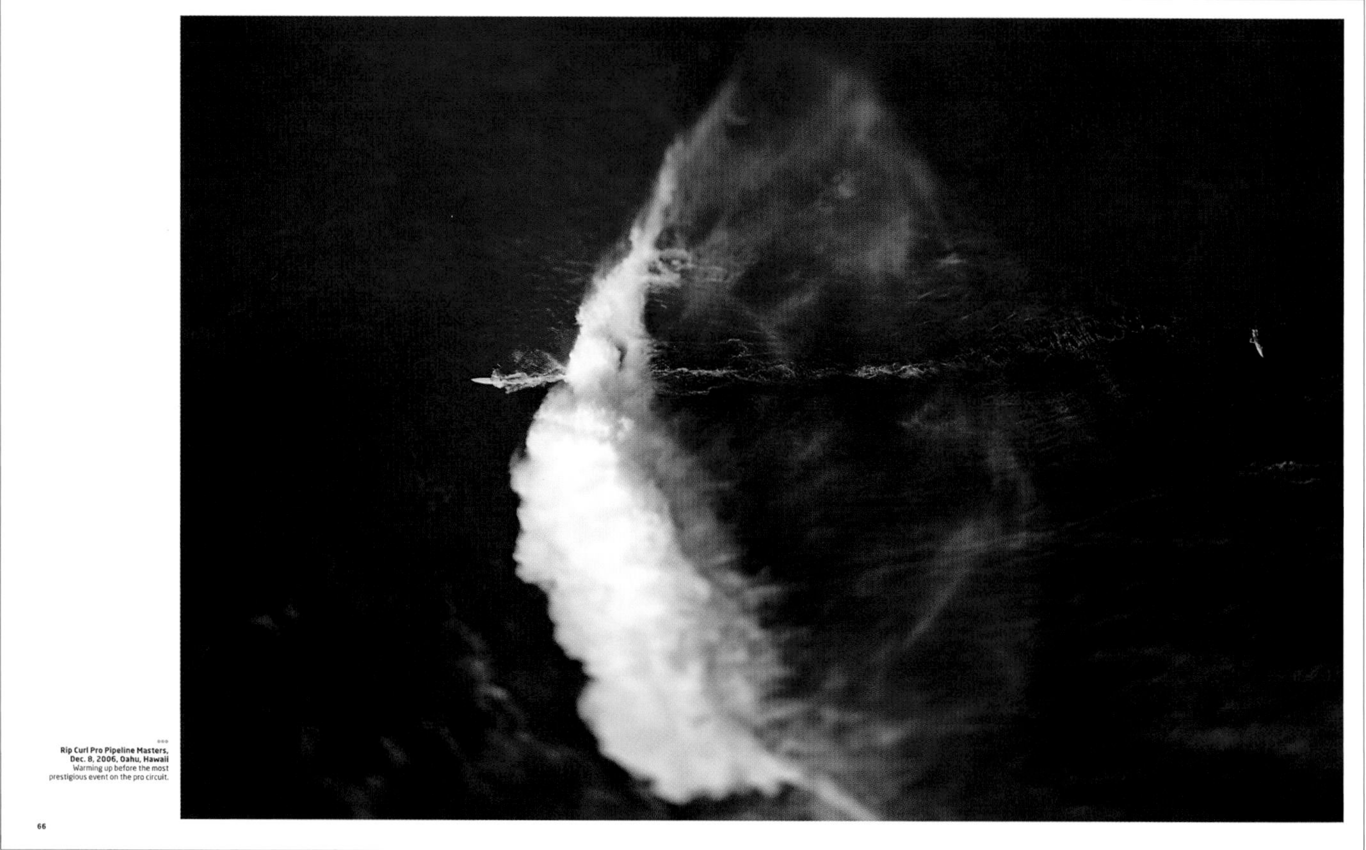

Rip Curl Pro Pipeline Masters, Dec. 8, 2006, Oahu, Hawaii
Warming up before the most prestigious event on the pro circuit.

66

345

345 PLAY, THE NEW YORK TIMES SPORTS MAGAZINE

Creative Director_**Janet Froelich** Art Director_**Christopher Martinez** Designer_**Christopher Martinez** Photo Editor_**Kira Pollack** Photographer_**Vincent Laforet** Publisher_**The New York Times** Issue_**June 2007** Category_**Photo: Feature: Story**

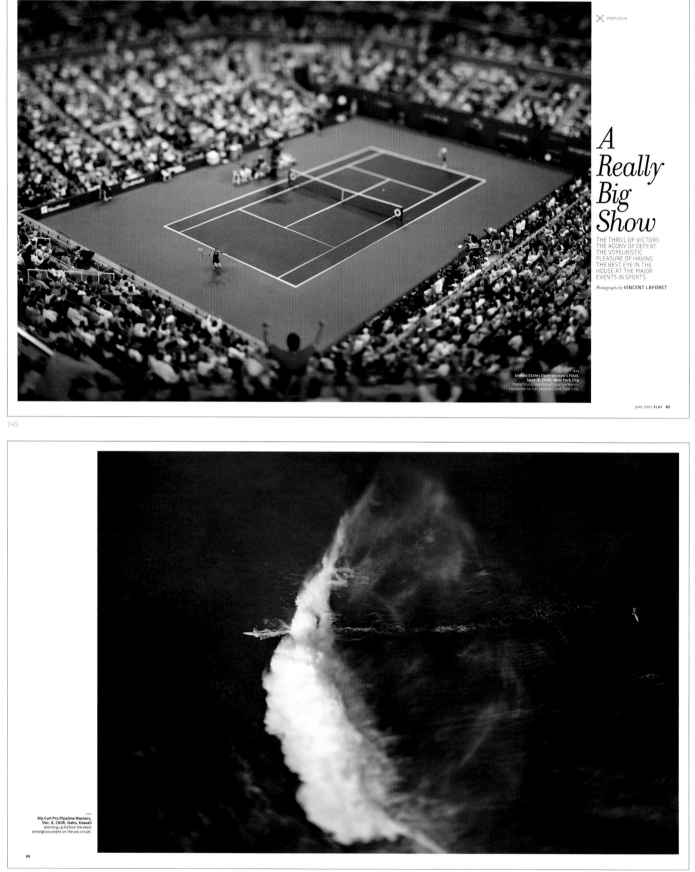

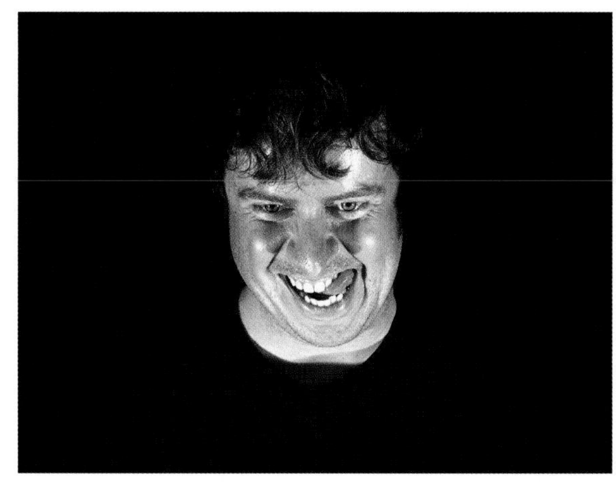

game faces

PHOTOGRAPHS BY PHILLIP TOLEDANO

APR 2007

346

"During a videogame," photographer Phillip Toledano says, "people disappear down a rabbit hole. They drop their public face, and all you see is this really raw emotion." To capture that energy, Toledano set up an Xbox in his girlfriend's apartment and rigged up a strobe light. He asked friends (and friends of friends) to come in and play *Dead or Alive*, a popular fighting game. **Then he started to shoot.**

346

WIRED

Creative Director_Scott Dadich Designer_Scott Dadich Photo Editor_Carolyn Rauch
Photographer_Phillip Toledano Publisher_Condé Nast Publications, Inc. Issue_April 2007 Category_Photo: Feature: Story

: SECTION
PHOTOGRAPHY

: AWARD
SILVER

: CATEGORY
ENTIRE ISSUE
FEATURE: SPREAD/SINGLE

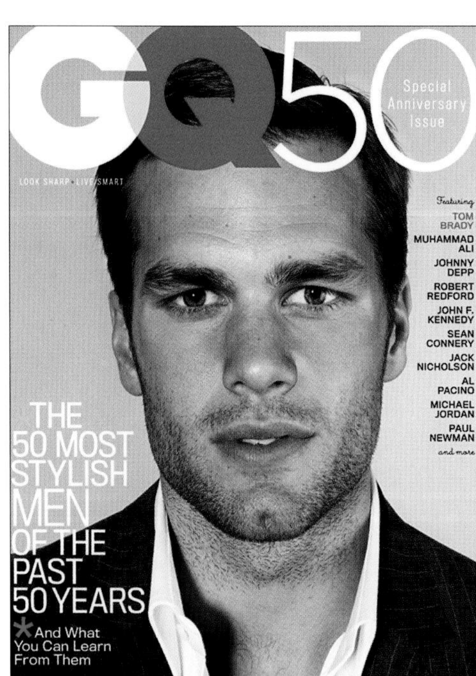

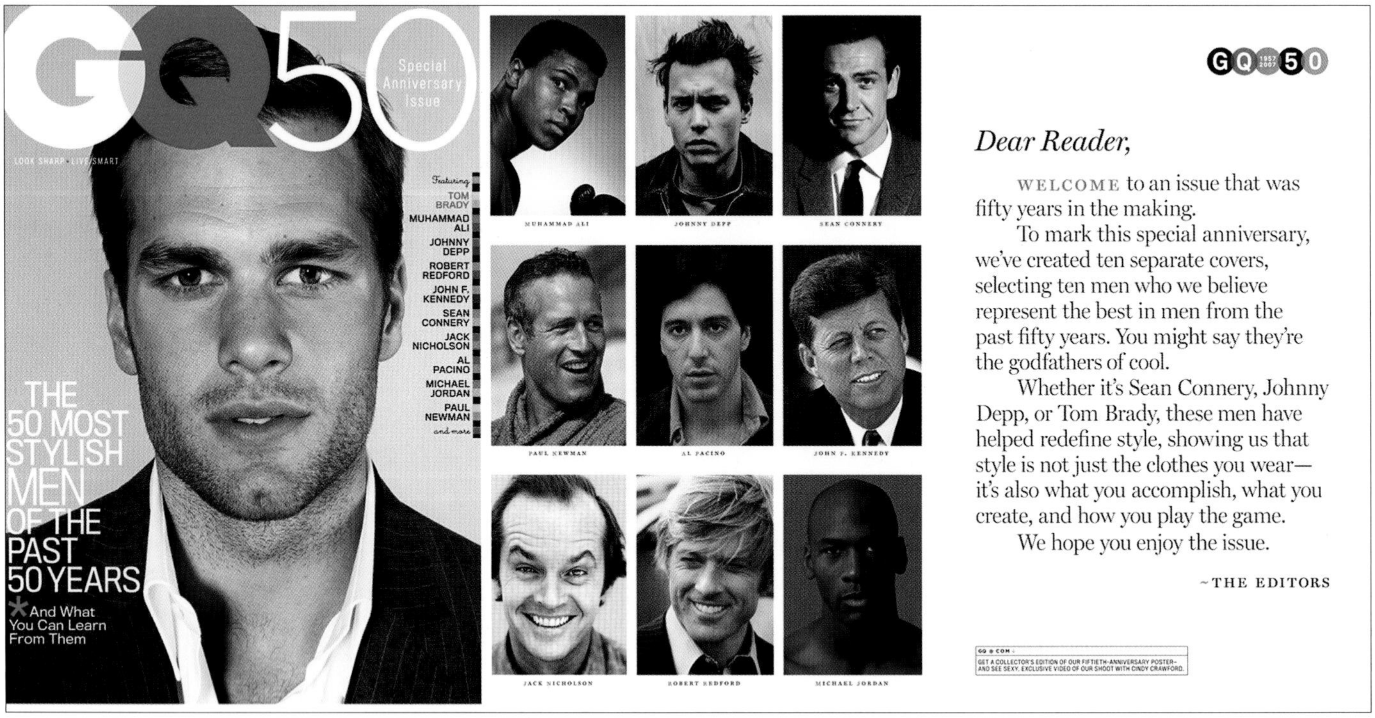

MUHAMMAD ALI · JOHNNY DEPP · SEAN CONNERY · PAUL NEWMAN · AL PACINO · JOHN F. KENNEDY · JACK NICHOLSON · ROBERT REDFORD · MICHAEL JORDAN

GQ 1957 2007 50

Dear Reader,

WELCOME to an issue that was fifty years in the making.

To mark this special anniversary, we've created ten separate covers, selecting ten men who we believe represent the best in men from the past fifty years. You might say they're the godfathers of cool.

Whether it's Sean Connery, Johnny Depp, or Tom Brady, these men have helped redefine style, showing us that style is not just the clothes you wear—it's also what you accomplish, what you create, and how you play the game.

We hope you enjoy the issue.

~THE EDITORS

GQ @ COM: GET A COLLECTOR'S EDITION OF OUR FIFTIETH-ANNIVERSARY POSTER—AND SEE SEXY, EXCLUSIVE VIDEO OF OUR SHOOT WITH CINDY CRAWFORD.

347

LeBRON JAMES

22 | Baller

• For at least eighty-two nights a year, LeBron James walks onto a basketball court and is better at his chosen profession than anyone else on earth. Can you even begin to imagine what that feels like? In his first four seasons, he's racked up 26.7 points per game, a Rookie of the Year award, an All-Star MVP award, and nearly every record that could be preceded by the words *youngest ever*. He's gone through stretches (like the end of Game 5 of this year's conference finals against the Pistons, when he scored the Cavs' final *twenty-five* points) where twenty-footers are automatic. And by some strange blip in the space-time continuum, he's still only 22. Which means we have about fifteen more years to marvel at his dominance while he tries to slay the ghosts of roundball past: Jordan, Magic, Oscar Robertson. Still, LeBron sees a future not just of basketball hegemony but also of world domination. He sees sports' first billionaire. The world's greatest global icon, bigger even than Jordan, because LeBron is coming up in the age of instant, boundary-less media, and unlike other megastars (say, Tiger or Beckham), he shows traces of being a real person. "Growing up," he says, "I didn't understand the business side. All I could understand was how to be able to jump over four or five people and dunk the basketball." Now LeBron talks about "maximizing my opportunities," like his buddy Jay-Z. He agreed to host the ESPYs and *Saturday Night Live* because he's looking "to get my personality out there." And like his pal Warren Buffett (seriously), he's learning to trust his gut when it comes to investments. "In twenty years, I want to do business like Buffett and have swagger like Jay-Z," he says. If King James looks out over the world and says, "Mine," who are we to disagree?

CLOTHES AND SNEAKERS BY **NIKE**

347

GQ

Design Director_**Fred Woodward** Art Director_**Anton Ioukhnovets** Deputy Art Director_**Thomas Alberty** Designers_**Michael Pangilinan, Drue Wagner, Chelsea Cardinal, Rob Hewitt, Eve Binder, Delgis Canahuate, Liana Zamora** Director of Photography_**Dora Somosi** Senior Photo Editor_**Krista Prestek** Photo Editors_**Justin O'Neill, Halena Green, Jess Lee, Roberto De Luna, Jolanta Bielat, Melissa Goldstein** Photographers_**Richard Burbridge, Nathaniel Goldberg, Danielle Levitt, Platon, Terry Richardson, Jeff Riedel, Ilan Rubin, Zachary Scott, Max Vadukul** Creative Director_**Jim Moore** Editor-In-Chief_**Jim Nelson** Publisher_**Condé Nast Publications Inc.** Issue_**October 2007** Category_**Photo: Entire Issue**

347

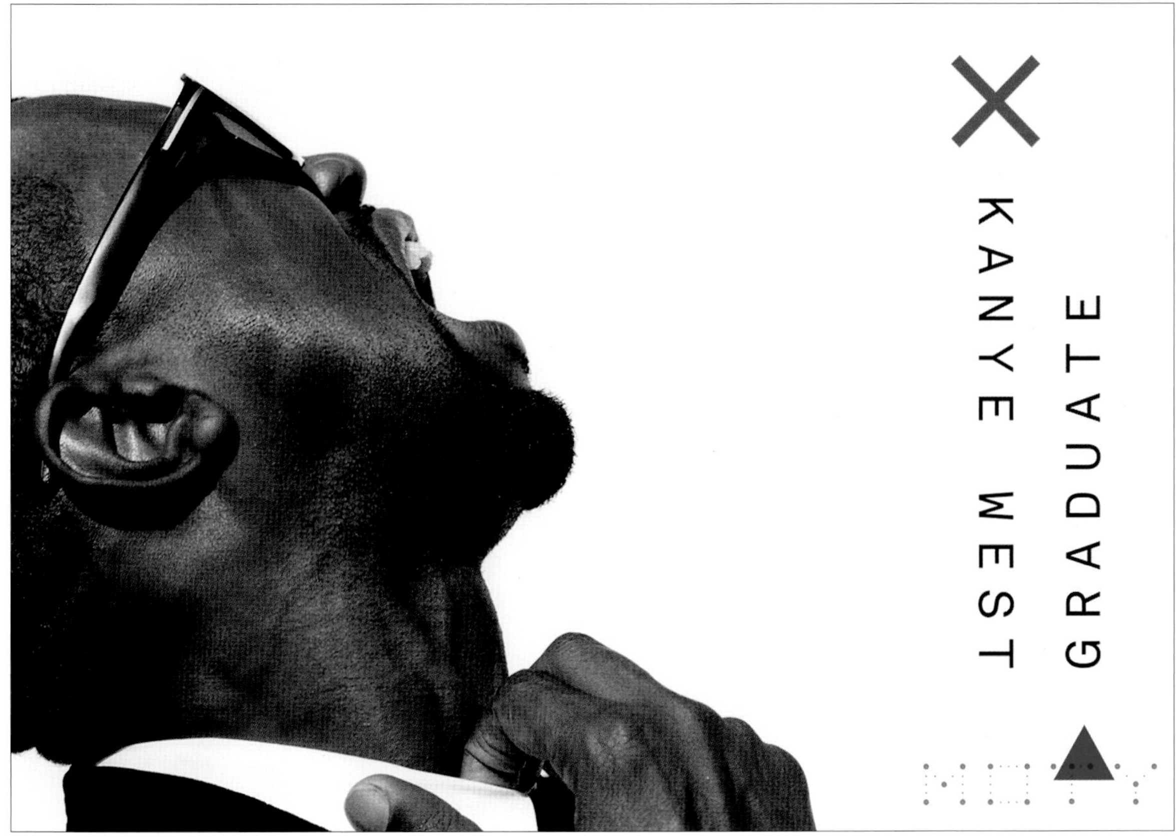

348

348 GQ

Design Director_Fred Woodward Designer_Anton Ioukhnovets
Director of Photography_Dora Somosi Photographer_Nathaniel Goldberg
Editor-In-Chief_Jim Nelson Publisher_Condé Nast Publications Inc.
Issue_December 2007 Category_Photo: Feature: Spread/Single Page

John **Baldessari**

ONE OF THE MOST INFLUENTIAL ARTISTS TO EMERGE SINCE THE MID-SIXTIES, JOHN BALDESSARI HAS PRODUCED WORK RANGING FROM PHOTOTEXT PAINTINGS TO INSTALLATION AND VIDEO. HERE, IN COLLABORATION WITH PHOTOGRAPHER

MARIO **SORRENTI,**

HE TURNS HIS EYE TO FASHION.

ADDITIONAL IMAGES FROM THE ARCHIVES OF *WOMEN'S WEAR DAILY*

CURATED BY **DENNIS FREEDMAN + NEVILLE WAKEFIELD**

YVES SAINT LAURENT'S LIGHT BLUE EMBOSSED LUREX DRESS, AT SELECT YVES SAINT LAURENT STORES, YSL.COM. M&J SAVITT NECKLACE.

286 | **W** NOVEMBER 2007

349

FROM LEFT: **OMO NORMA KAMALI'S** BLACK SILK AND NYLON LACE AND NUDE NYLON AND LYCRA SPANDEX MAILLOT, AT NORMA KAMALI, NEW YORK, 800.8KAMALI, NORMAKAMALI COLLECTION.COM; **CALVIN KLEIN'S** GRAY WOOL TWEED SKIRT, AT CALVIN KLEIN COLLECTION, NEW YORK. **CALVIN KLEIN'S** GRAY SILK JERSEY SHIRT, AT CALVIN KLEIN COLLECTION, NEW YORK; **MOSCHINO'S** BLACK WOOL BOUCLE SKIRT, AT BERGDORF GOODMAN, NEW YORK. YVES SAINT LAURENT SHOES. **ETRO'S** GRAY WOOL PANTS, AT ETRO, NEW YORK AND LOS ANGELES.

349

W

Creative Director_**Dennis Freedman** Design Director_**Edward Leida** Art Director_**Nathalie Kirsheh** Designers_**Edward Leida, Nathalie Kirsheh** Photographer_**Mario Sorrenti** Artist_**John Baldessari** Publisher_**Condé Nast Publications Inc.** Issue_**November 2007** Category_**Photo: Feature: Story**

GARBAGE IN, GARBAGE OUT
Landfills, part I: There is a big difference between landfills in developing countries and those in industrialized nations. In most third world countries, severely poor people live off of the trash in landfills (like this one in Phnom Penh, Cambodia), digging through them and taking items that can be recycled or sold.
AMERICAN WAY

350

E-waste: This trash is one of the negative aspects of the electronic age. The European Union estimates the amount of e-waste is growing at a rate three times faster than that of other types of trash.
Improperly-disposed-of trash: Wastewater treatment plants must spend time and money to remove trash that has washed into drains or been flushed down the toilet.
Glass beach: The "sand" on this beach in Kauai is made almost entirely of pieces of bottles that ended up in the ocean instead of in a trash can.
Landfills, part II: This landfill in Dallas is a far cry from the one in Phnom Penh, but we can do more to reduce the amount of trash that ends up here.
32 AMERICAN WAY OCTOBER 1, 2007
OCTOBER 1, 2007 AMERICAN WAY 33

350

350 AMERICAN WAY

Design Director_J.R. Arebalo, Jr. Art Director_Samuel Solomon Photographer_Beth Callahan
Publisher_American Airlines Publishing Issue_October 1, 2007 Category_Photo: Feature: Story

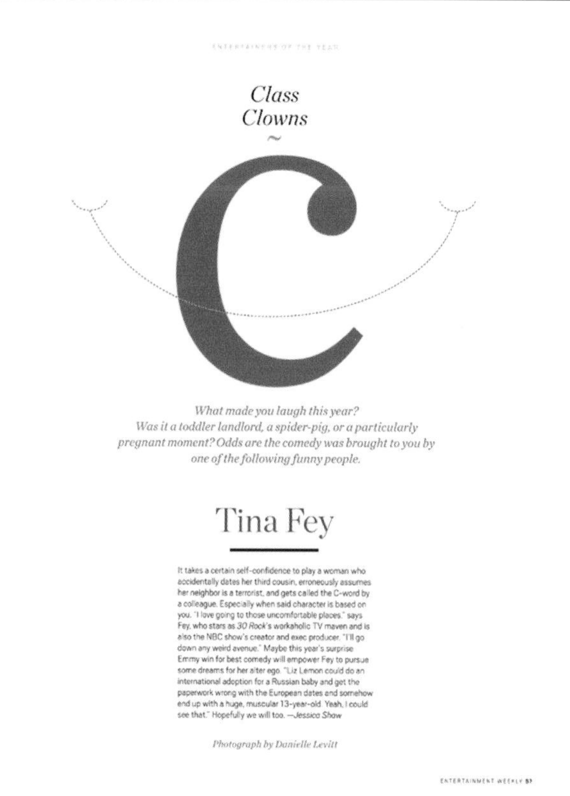

ENTERTAINERS OF THE YEAR

Class Clowns

C

What made you laugh this year? Was it a toddler landlord, a spider-pig, or a particularly pregnant moment? Odds are the comedy was brought to you by one of the following funny people.

Tina Fey

It takes a certain self-confidence to play a woman who accidentally dates her third cousin, erroneously assumes her neighbor is a terrorist, and gets called the C-word by a colleague. Especially when said character is based on you. "I love going to those uncomfortable places," says Fey, who stars as *30 Rock*'s workaholic TV maven and is also the NBC show's creator and exec producer. "I'll go down any weird avenue." Maybe this year's surprise Emmy win for best comedy will empower Fey to pursue some dreams for her alter ego. "Liz Lemon could do an international adoption for a Russian baby and get the paperwork wrong with the European dates and somehow end up with a huge, muscular 13-year-old. Yeah, I could see that." Hopefully we will too. —*Jessica Shaw*

Photograph by Danielle Levitt

ENTERTAINMENT WEEKLY 51

351

352

IF THE ENTERTAINMENT industry implodes in a paroxysm of labor disputes this fall, blame Tyra Banks. Last summer, the 34-year-old supermodel-turned-TV host unwittingly became the eye of a highly publicized storm. The writers of her reality show, *America's Next Top Model*, staged a mini-strike, claiming that, even though contestants are making up their own words, the ideas and the structure of the series belong to the writing room. The *ANTM* staffers wanted to be recognized as television scribes by the Writers Guild of America, with union pay and benefits. At one major rally, nearly a thousand West Coast WGA members turned out in support. But the wordsmiths' rhetoric strayed from the issue at hand into a *Network*-style rant about the real anxiety among all showbiz creatives. "Digital downloads! Internet video-on-demand! This is the future!" shouted Phil Alden Robinson, screenwriter of *Field of Dreams*. "If we're not united, we're not going to get a good deal!" »

Hollywood's Massive Rewrite

Downloads! Video-on-demand! Webisodes! The writers want a cut. by Nancy Miller

WIRED

PHOTOGRAPH BY John Clark

AUGUST 2007

353

ENTERTAINMENT WEEKLY

Design Director_**Geraldine Hessler**
Art Director_**Theresa Griggs**
Director of Photography_**Fiona McDonagh**
Photo Editor_**Suzanne Regan**
Photographer_**Danielle Levitt**
Publisher_**Time Inc.** Issue_**November 30, 2007**
Category_**Photo: Feature: Spread/Single Page**

THE NEW YORK TIMES MAGAZINE

Creative Director_**Janet Froelich**
Art Director_**Arem Duplessis**
Designers_**Leo Jung, Arem Duplessis**
Director of Photography_**Kathy Ryan**
Photo Editor_**Clinton Cargill**
Photographer_**Horacio Salinas**
Editor-In-Chief_**Gerry Marzorati**
Publisher_**The New York Times**
Issue_**May 6, 2007** Category_**Photo: Cover**

WIRED

Creative Director_**Scott Dadich**
Designer_**Chris Imlay**
Photo Editor_**Anna Goldwater Alexander**
Photographer_**John Clark**
Publisher_**Condé Nast Publications, Inc.**
Issue_**August 2007** Category_**Photo-Illustration: Single Page/Spread/Story**

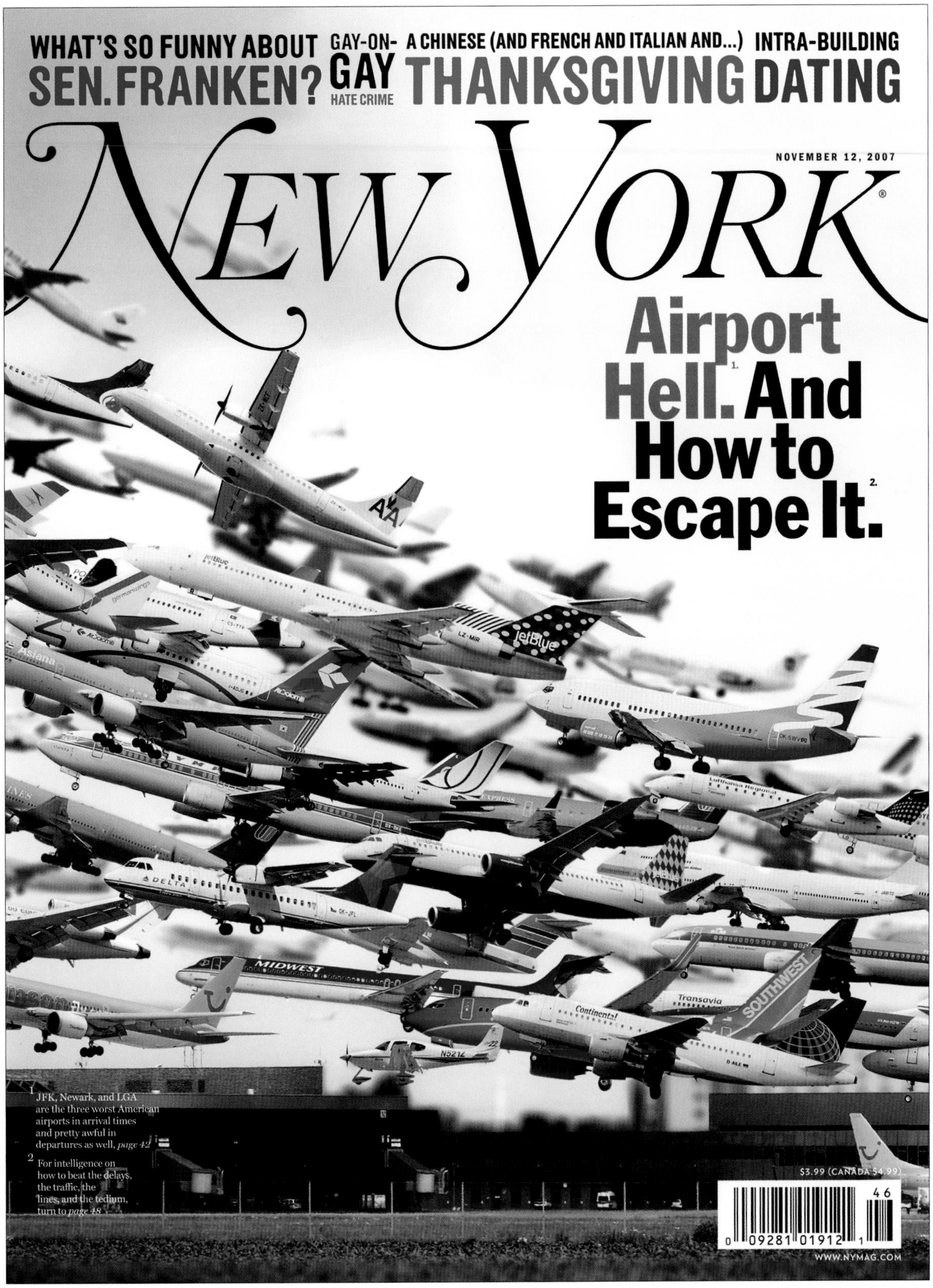

WHAT'S SO FUNNY ABOUT SEN. FRANKEN?
GAY-ON-GAY HATE CRIME
A CHINESE (AND FRENCH AND ITALIAN AND...) THANKSGIVING
INTRA-BUILDING DATING

NEW YORK

NOVEMBER 12, 2007

Airport Hell.[1] And How to Escape It.[2]

1 JFK, Newark, and LGA are the three worst American airports in arrival times and pretty awful in departures as well, page 42

2 For intelligence on how to beat the delays, the traffic, the lines, and the tedium, turn to page 48

$3.99 (CANADA $4.99)

46

0 09281 01912 1

WWW.NYMAG.COM

354

 NEW YORK

Design Director_Chris Dixon
Director of Photography_Jody Quon
Photo Editor_Alexandra Pollack
Photographer_Ho-Yeol Ryu
Editor-In-Chief_Adam Moss
Publisher_New York Magazine Holdings, LLC
Issue_November 12, 2007 Category_Photo: Cover

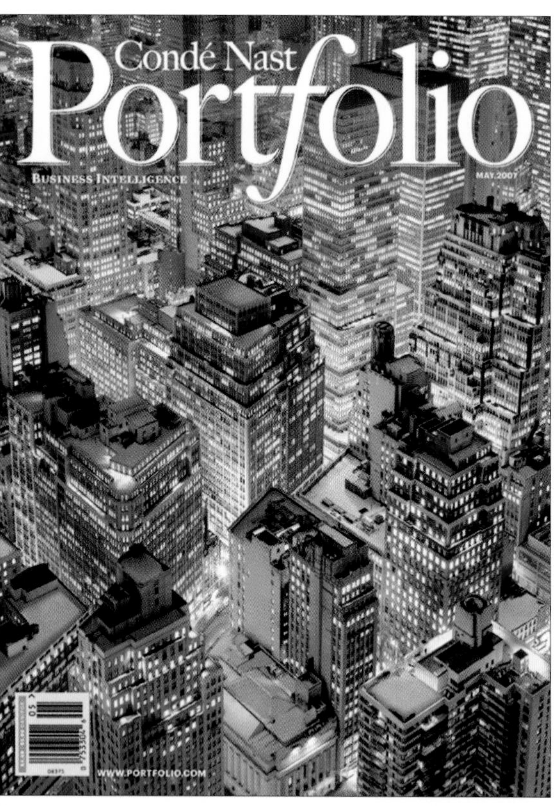

355

357

356

358

355 CONDÉ NAST PORTFOLIO

Design Director_**Robert Priest**
Art Director_**Grace Lee** Designers_**Robert Priest, Grace Lee**
Director of Photography_**Lisa Berman** Photo Editor_**Rossana Shokrian**
Deputy Photo Editor_**Sarah Czeladnicki** Photographer_**Scott Peterman**
Editor-In-Chief_**Joanne Lipman** Publisher_**Condé Nast Publications Inc.**
Issue_**May 2007** Category_**Photo: Cover**

356 FAST COMPANY

Art Director_**Dean Markadakis** Director of Photography_**Meghan Hurley**
Photographer_**Platon** Publisher_**Mansueto Ventures, LLC**
Issue_**February 2007** Category_**Photo: Cover**

357 DETAILS

Creative Director_**Rockwell Harwood** Art Director_**Andre Jointe**
Photographer_**Steven Klein** Senior Photo Editor_**Hali Tara Feldman**
Publisher_**Condé Nast Publications** Issue_**October 2007**
Category **Photo: Cover**

358 T, THE NEW YORK TIMES STYLE MAGAZINE

Creative Director_**Janet Froelich** Senior Art Director_**David Sebbah**
Art Director **Christopher Martinez** Designer_**David Sebbah**
Photo Editor_**Judith Puckett-Rinella** Photographer_**Norbert Schoerner**
Fashion Editor_**Charlotte Stockdale** Editor-In-Chief_**Stefano Tonchi**
Publisher_**The New York Times** Issue_**May 20, 2007**
Category_**Photo: Cover**

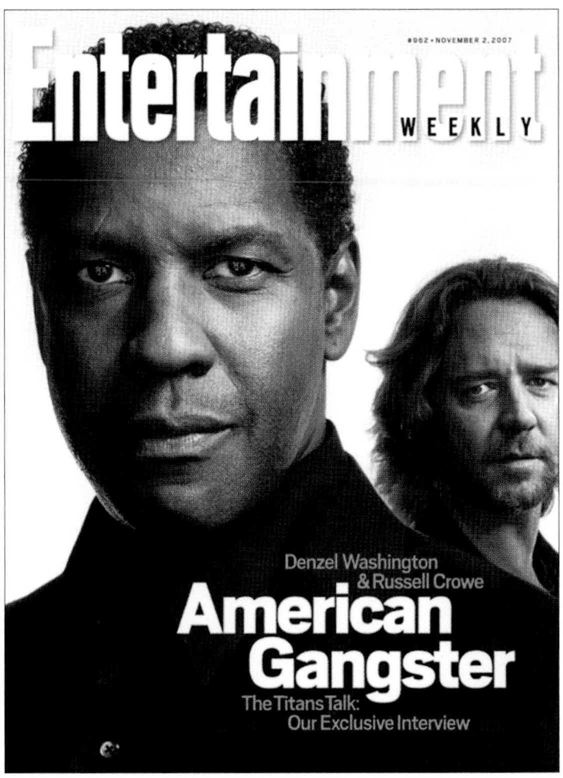

359

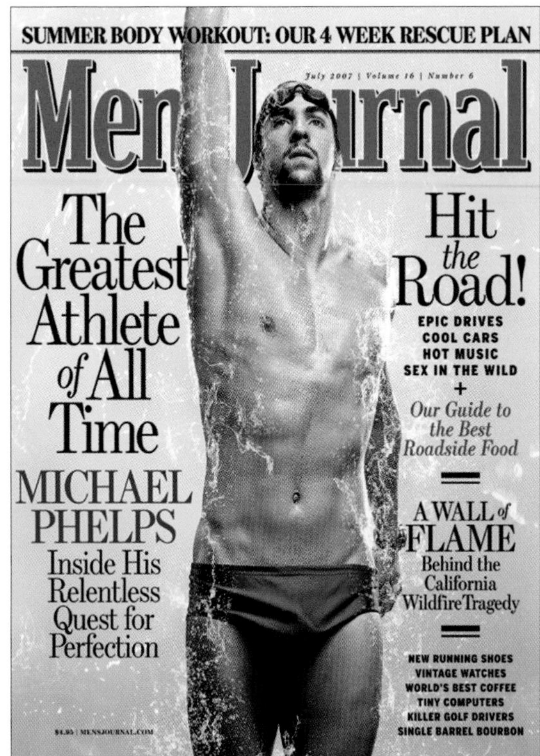

361

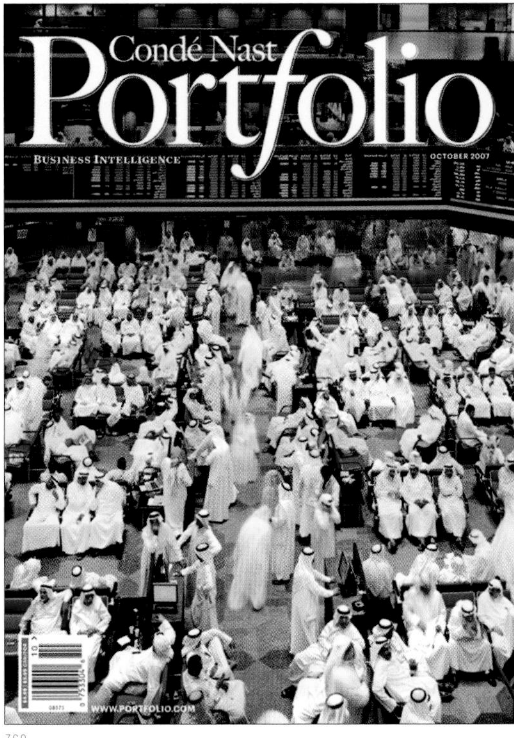

360

362

359 ENTERTAINMENT WEEKLY

Design Director_**Geraldine Hessler** Director of Photography_**Fiona McDonagh** Photographer_**Martin Schoeller** Publisher_**Time Inc.** Issue_**November 2, 2007** Category_**Photo: Cover**

360 CONDÉ NAST PORTFOLIO

Design Director_**Robert Priest** Art Director_**Grace Lee** Designers_**Robert Priest, Grace Lee** Director of Photography_**Lisa Berman** Photo Editor_**Rossana Shokrian** Photographer_**Robert Polidori** Deputy Photo Editor_**Sarah Czeladnicki** Editor-In-Chief_**Joanne Lipman** Publisher_**Condé Nast Publications Inc.** Issue_**October 2007** Category_**Photo: Cover**

361 MEN'S JOURNAL

Creative Director_**Paul Martinez** Director of Photography_**Rob Haggart** Photographer_**Carlos Serrao** Editor-In-Chief_**Jann S. Wenner** Publisher_**Wenner Media LLC** Issue_**July 2007** Category_**Photo: Cover**

362 FORTUNE

Design Director_**Robert Perino** Director of Photography_**Greg Pond** Photo Editor_**Alix Colow** Photographer_**Henry Leutwyler** Publisher_**Time Inc.** Issue_**October 1, 2007** Category_**Photo: Cover**

363

365

364

366

363 MARIE CLAIRE

Creative Director_Michael Picòn Director of Photography_Kristen Schaefer Photo Editors_Andrea Volbrecht, Melanie Chambers Photographer_Mark Abrahams Publisher_The Hearst Corporation-Magazines Div. Issue_October 2007 Category_Photo: Cover

364 NEW YORK

Design Director_Chris Dixon Director of Photography_Jody Quon Photographer_Andrew Eccles Editor-In-Chief_Adam Moss Publisher_New York Magazine Holdings, LLC Issue_July 2-9, 2007 Category_Photo: Cover

365 SKY

Art Director_Ann Harvey Designer_Ann Harvey Photographer_Carl Lessard Editorial Director_Duncan Christy Studio_Pace Communications Publisher_Pace Communications Client_Delta Air Lines Issue_September 2007 Category_Photo: Cover

366 TRAVEL + LEISURE FAMILY

Design Director_Leigh Nelson Director of Photography_Janna Johansson Photo Editor_Catherine Talese Photographer_Richard Fousler Publisher_American Express Publishing Co. Issue_Winter 2007 Category_Photo: Cover

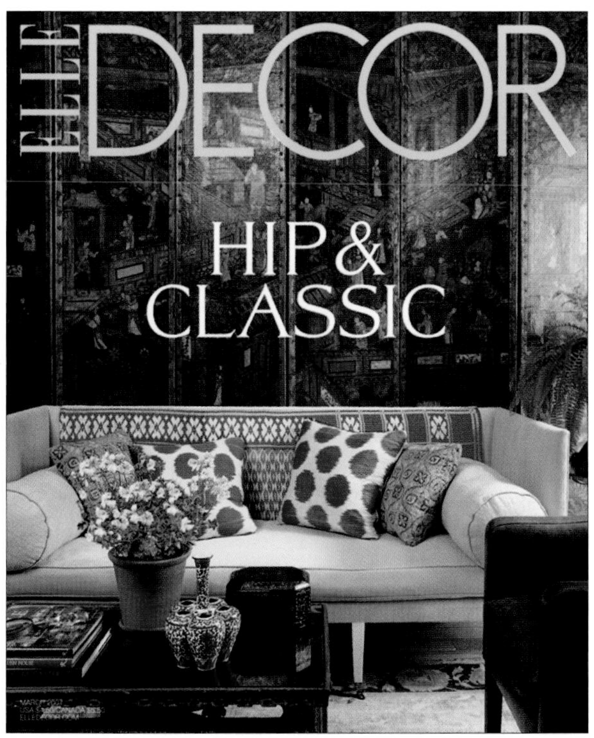

367

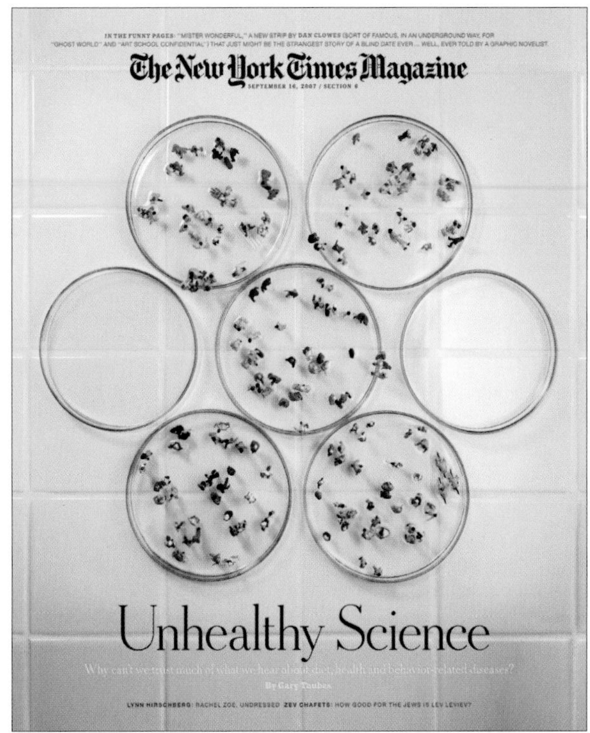

369

368

370

367 ELLE DÉCOR

Art Director_Florentino Pamintuan Photo Editor_Nara Urigoyen
Publisher_Hachette Filipacchi Media U.S. Issue_March 2007
Category_Photo: Cover

368 THE NEW YORK TIMES MAGAZINE

Creative Director_Janet Froelich Art Director_Arem Duplessis
Designer_Catherine Gilmore-Barnes Director of Photography_Kathy Ryan
Photo Editor_Kira Pollack Photographer_Dan Winters
Editor-In-Chief_Gerry Marzorati Publisher_The New York Times
Issue_February 11, 2007 Category_Photo: Cover

369 THE NEW YORK TIMES MAGAZINE

Creative Director_Janet Froelich Art Director_Arem Duplessis
Designer_Gail Bichler Director of Photography_Kathy Ryan
Photo Editor_Joanna Milter Photographer_Reinhard Hunger
Editor-In-Chief_Gerry Marzorati Publisher_The New York Times
Issue_September 16, 2007 Category_Photo: Cover

370 THE NEW YORK TIMES MAGAZINE

Creative Director_Janet Froelich Art Director_Arem Duplessis
Designer_Arem Duplessis Director of Photography_Kathy Ryan
Photo Editor_Kira Pollack Photographer_Dan Winters
Editor-In-Chief_Gerry Marzorati Publisher The_New York Times
Issue_September 2, 2007 Category_Photo: Cover

371

373

375

372

374

376

371 T, THE NEW YORK TIMES STYLE MAGAZINE

Creative Director_**Janet Froelich** Senior Art Director_**David Sebbah** Art Director_**Christopher Martinez** Designer_**David Sebbah** Photo Editor_**Judith Puckett-Rinella** Photographer_**Raymond Meier** Fashion Editor_**Tina Laakkonen** Editor-In-Chief_**Stefano Tonchi** Publisher_**The New York Times** Issue_**November 18, 2007** Category_**Photo: Cover**

372 UCLA MAGAZINE

Design Director_**Charles Hess** Designers_**Alicia Patel, Janet Park** Photo Editor_**Charles Hess** Photographer_**Dave Lauridsen** Studio_**Chess Design** Editor-In-Chief_**Jack Feuer** Publisher_**UCLA** Client_**UCLA** Issue_**October 2007** Category_**Photo: Cover**

373 T, THE NEW YORK TIMES STYLE MAGAZINE

Creative Director_**Janet Froelich** Senior Art Director_**David Sebbah** Art Director_**Christopher Martinez** Designer_**David Sebbah** Photo Editor_**Scott Hall** Photographer_**Raymond Meier** Fashion Editor_**Tina Laakkonen** Editor-In-Chief_**Stefano Tonchi** Publisher_**The New York Times** Issue_**December 2, 2007** Category_**Photo: Cover**

374 TREAD

Creative Director_**Nancy Campbell** Art Director_**Trevett McCandliss** Designer_**Trevett McCandliss** Photographer_**Jason Hindley** Issue_**July 2007** Category_**Photo: Cover**

375 NEW YORK LOOK

Design Director_**Chris Dixon** Art Director_**Randy Minor** Director of Photography_**Jody Quon** Photo Editors_**Lea Golis, Nadia Lachance** Photographer_**Paolo Pellegrin** Editor-In-Chief_**Adam Moss** Publisher_**New York Magazine Holdings, LLC** Issue_**Fall 2007** Category_**Photo: Cover**

376 NEW YORK

Design Directors_**Chris Dixon, Paul Sahre** Director of Photography_**Jody Quon** Photo Editor_**Lisa Corson** Photographer_**Platon** Editor-In-Chief_**Adam Moss** Publisher_**New York Magazine Holdings, LLC** Issue_**April 23, 2007** Category_**Photo: Cover**

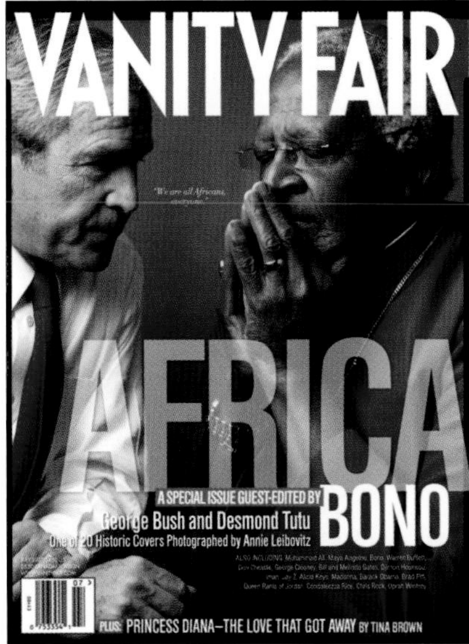

377

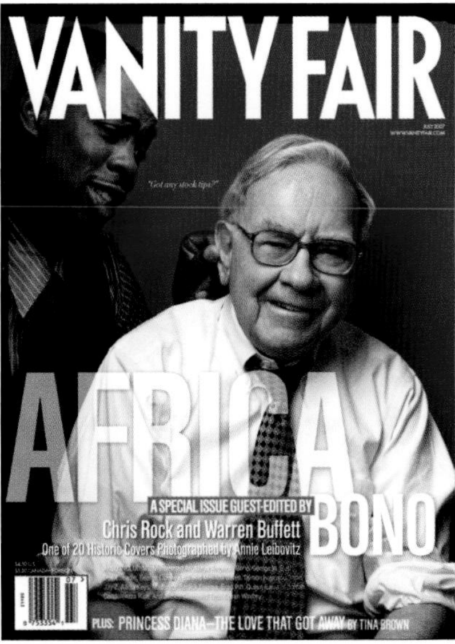

379

381

378

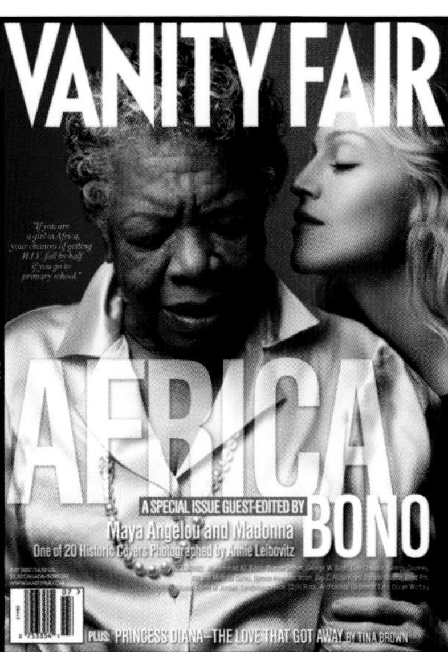

380

382

377 VANITY FAIR

Design Director_**David Harris** Designer_**Chris Mueller**
Director of Photography_**Susan White** Photo Editor_**Kathryn MacLeod**
Photographer_**Annie Leibovitz** Editor-In-Chief_**Graydon Carter**
Publisher_**Condé Nast Publications Inc.** Issue_**July 2007**
Category_**Photo: Cover**

378 VANITY FAIR

Design Director_**David Harris** Designer_**Chris Mueller**
Director of Photography_**Susan White** Photo Editor_**Kathryn MacLeod**
Photographer_**Annie Leibovitz** Editor-In-Chief_**Graydon Carter**
Publisher_**Condé Nast Publications Inc.** Issue_**July 2007**
Category_**Photo: Cover**

379 VANITY FAIR

Design Director_**David Harris** Designer_**Chris Mueller**
Director of Photography_**Susan White** Photo Editor_**Kathryn MacLeod**
Photographer_**Annie Leibovitz** Editor-In-Chief_**Graydon Carter**
Publisher_**Condé Nast Publications Inc.** Issue_**July 2007**
Category_**Photo: Cover**

380 VANITY FAIR

Design Director_**David Harris** Designer_**Chris Mueller**
Director of Photography_**Susan White** Photo Editor_**Kathryn MacLeod**
Photographer_**Annie Leibovitz** Editor-In-Chief_**Graydon Carter**
Publisher_**Condé Nast Publications Inc.** Issue_**July 2007**
Category_**Photo: Cover**

381 GQ

Design Director_**Fred Woodward** Designer_**Thomas Alberty**
Director of Photography_**Dora Somosi** Photographer_**Peggy Sirota**
Editor-In-Chief_**Jim Nelson** Publisher_**Condé Nast Publications Inc.**
Issue_**September 2007** Category_**Photo: Cover**

382 SPIN

Design Director_**Devin Pedzwater** Art Director_**Liz Macfarlane**
Director of Photography_**Michelle Egiziano**
Photo Editors_**Gavin Stevens, Jennifer Edmondson**
Photographer_**Richard Burbridge** Publisher_**Spin Media LLC**
Issue_**June 2007** Category_**Photo: Cover**

Music! Movies! Gift-wrapped manhoods! On the eve of the Grammys, EW gets serious and silly with Justin Timberlake, the boy-band graduate who has turned out to be the real deal.
SEXY BEAST
BY CLARK COLLIS
Photograph by Martin Schoeller

383

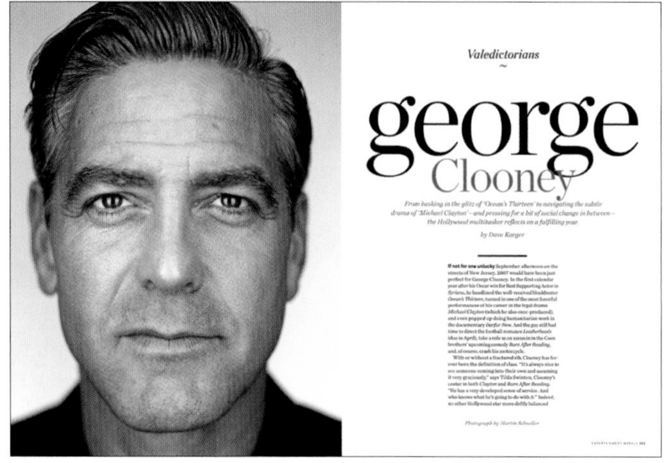

384

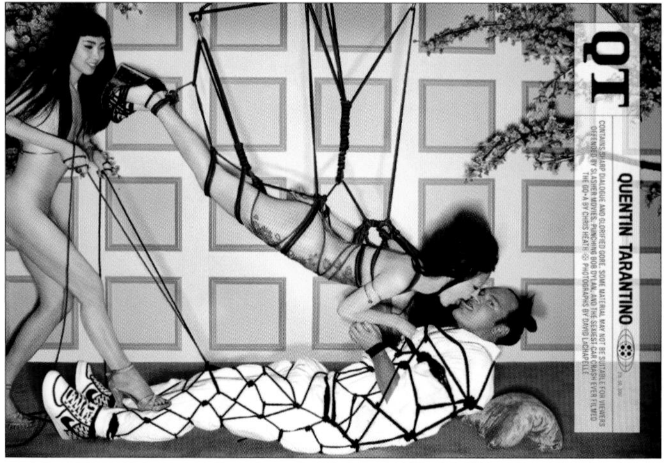

385

383 ENTERTAINMENT WEEKLY

Design Director_Geraldine Hessler
Art Director_Bhairavi Patel
Director of Photography_Fiona McDonagh
Photographer_Martin Schoeller
Publisher_Time Inc.
Issue_February 9, 2007
Category_Photo: Feature: Spread/Single Page

384 ENTERTAINMENT WEEKLY

Design Director_Geraldine Hessler
Art Director_Theresa Griggs
Director of Photography_Fiona McDonagh
Photo Editor_Audrey Landreth
Photographer_Martin Schoeller
Publisher_Time Inc.
Issue_November 30, 2007
Category_Photo: Feature: Spread/Single Page

385 GQ

Design Director_Fred Woodward
Designer_Anton Ioukhnovets
Director of Photography_Dora Somosi
Senior Photo Editor_Krista Prestek
Photographer_David LaChapelle
Editor-In-Chief_Jim Nelson
Publisher_Condé Nast Publications Inc.
Issue_April 2007
Category_Photo: Feature: Spread/Single Page

views of Los Angeles as "really superdorky," and she happily distinguishes it from more fashionable hilltops nearby, "where all the other little star people live."

We sit on the sandy top, and Alba takes advantage of the view to try out some big thoughts. She dismisses her professional restlessness as a thing of the past and pronounces herself happy with who she is right now. "I don't expect other people to do the work for me," she says. "I want variety, and I've done that. And I guess my arms are open to whatever's next." It's just a dog walk on a sunny Friday, a moment to relax at the start of her first week off after months on sets, but here she is, hammering out a personal credo and making a quiet point: What could possibly be wrong with being both hot *and* serious? You get the impression that whatever Alba does—whether it's a superhero franchise or playing along with a photo shoot—she knows exactly what she's doing.

Alba claims to be clumsy, so I lead the way down the mountain. "I fell so many times on *The Eye*, the crew there would get embarrassed for me," she says. "When I first met Alessandro"—Nivola, her costar on the movie—"I fell down the stairs. And then on *Fantastic Four*, I would always twist my ankle and fall down completely. It's just frustrating, always hurting yourself. For *Dark Angel*, Jim Cameron actually made me do gymnastics and dance training so I could be more coordinated."

We reach the parking lot without incident. Back behind the wheel of the Prius, Alba turns onto the empty road, and as she accelerates, she tugs on her sleeves again, revealing her bare shoulders with that same *Flashdance* gesture I'd seen in the morning.

This time, I call her on it.

"Are your hands cold?" I ask.

"It's just a nervous habit," she says. "Thank you for making me aware of it." Her words are kind, but they nevertheless convey a slight edge—something like, "Don't you try that bikini thing on me, too, buddy."

But then she laughs again, and as she slaloms wildly back down Mulholland, she talks about putting a hole in her sleeve for her thumb, so she can just keep it that way.

KEVIN CONLEY *is a GQ correspondent.*

MORE → GQ.COM

JESSICA ALBA IN A SEXY BEHIND-THE-SCENES VIDEO FROM THE SHOOT—AND PHOTOS WE COULDN'T PRINT. PLUS: GO TO GQ.COM/JESSICA TO GET HER GQ POSTER

GQ | 176

386

"I DON'T CONSIDER THE FACT THAT I'VE DATED SEVERAL MEN IN MY LIFE AND NOT MARRIED ONE A FAILURE. I CONSIDER THAT A GOOD TIME!"

387

388

386 GQ

Design Director_Fred Woodward
Designer_Drue Wagner
Director of Photography_Dora Somosi
Photographer_Terry Richardson
Editor-In-Chief_Jim Nelson
Publisher_Condé Nast Publications Inc.
Issue_June 2007
Category_Photo: Feature: Spread/Single Page

387 MORE

Creative Director_Maxine Davidowitz
Art Director_Jose Fernandez
Designer_Maxine Davidowitz
Director of Photography_Karen Frank
Photographer_Fabrizio Ferri
Editor-In-Chief_Peggy Northrop
Publisher_Meredith Corporation
Issue_November 2007
Category_Photo: Feature: Spread/Single Page

388 MORE

Creative Director_Maxine Davidowitz
Art Director_Jose Fernandez
Designer_Jose Fernandez
Director of Photography_Karen Frank
Photo Editor_Jenny Sargent
Photographer_Debra McClinton
Editor-In-Chief_Peggy Northrop
Publisher_Meredith Corporation
Issue_May 2007
Category_Photo: Feature: Spread/Single Page

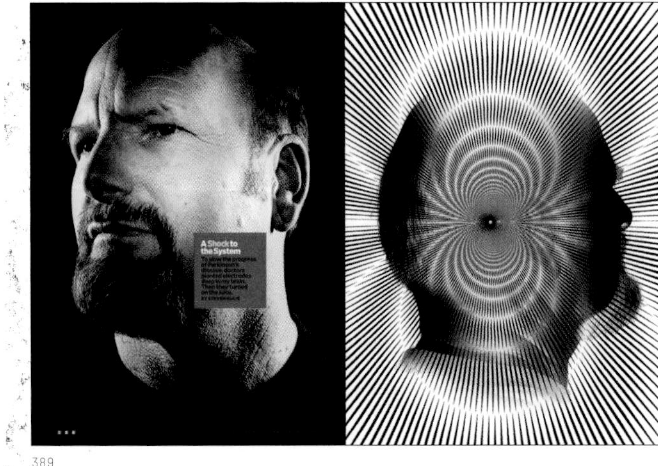

389

392

390

393

391

394

389 WIRED

Creative Director_Scott Dadich
Designers_Maili Holiman, Jason Schulte
Photo Editor_Carolyn Rauch
Photographer_Frank W. Ockenfels 3
Publisher_Condé Nast Publications, Inc.
Issue_March 2007
Category_Photo: Feature: Spread/Single Page

390 ROLLING STONE

Designer_Joe Newton
Director of Photography_Jodi Peckman
Photo Editor_Deborah Dragon
Photographer_Peter Yang
Publisher_Wenner Media
Issue_April 19, 2007
Category_Photo: Feature: Spread/Single Page

391 GLAMOUR

Design Director_Holland Utley
Art Director_Peter Hemmel
Designer_Peter Hemmel
Director of Photography_Suzanne Donaldson
Photo Editor_Stacey Delorenzo
Photographer_Donna Trope
Editor-In-Chief_Cynthia Leive
Publisher_Condé Nast Publications Inc.
Issue_October 2007
Category_Photo: Feature: Spread/Single Page

392 SAMVIRKE

Design Director_Møller Frydkjaer
Photographers_Klavsbo Christensen, Carsten Snejbjerg
Issue_July 2007
Category_Photo: Feature: Spread/Single Page

393 GOLF DIGEST INDEX

Design Director_Ken DeLago
Designer_Ken DeLago
Director of Photography_Matthew M. Ginella
Photo Editor_Kerry Brady
Photographer_Tom Fowlks
Issue_Spring 2007
Category_Photo: Feature: Spread/Single Page

394 TU CIUDAD

Art Director_Tom O'Quinn
Designer_Tom O'Quinn
Photo Editor_Bailey Franklin
Photographer_Robert Trachtenberg
Publisher_Emmis Issue_May 2007
Category Photo: Feature: Spread/Single Page

395

398

Irv Gotti ran one of the world's biggest rap labels, until a high-profile bust nearly cost him everything. With his career in jeopardy and his reputation on the line, can the hip-hop impresario use a VH1 reality show to salvage his empire?
By Margeaux Watson

Frayed Irv

396

Tough Guys Don't Quit

Still sharp and blustery at 83, Norman Mailer weighs in on his provocative new novel, his journalistic legacy, Philip Roth, God, the devil, and his next Big Book.
By Gregory Kirschling

399

397

MAN IN THE MOON

400

395 ENTERTAINMENT WEEKLY

Design Director_Geraldine Hessler
Art Director_Brian Anstey
Director of Photography_Fiona McDonagh
Photo Editors_Freyda Tavin, Audrey Landreth
Photographers_Eric Ogden, Chris Buck
Publisher_Time Inc.
Issue_October 19, 2007
Category_Photo: Feature: Spread/Single Page

396 ENTERTAINMENT WEEKLY

Design Director_Geraldine Hessler
Art Director_Eric Paul
Director of Photography_Fiona McDonagh
Photo Editor_Michele Romero
Photographer_Platon
Publisher_Time Inc.
Issue_December 14, 2007
Category_Photo: Feature: Spread/Single Page

397 GOLF DIGEST

Design Director_Ken DeLago
Designer_Marne Mayer
Director of Photography_Matthew M. Ginella
Photographer_Mark Hooper
Publisher_Condé Nast Publications Inc.
Issue_October 2007
Category_Photo: Feature: Spread/Single Page

398 ENTERTAINMENT WEEKLY

Design Director_Geraldine Hessler
Art Director_Theresa Griggs
Director of Photography_Fiona McDonagh
Photo Editor_Audrey Landreth
Photographer_Ralph Mecke
Publisher_Time Inc.
Issue_February 23, 2007
Category_Photo: Feature: Spread/Single Page

399 ENTERTAINMENT WEEKLY

Design Director_Geraldine Hessler
Art Director_Brian Anstey
Director of Photography_Fiona McDonagh
Photo Editor_Freyda Tavin
Publisher_Time Inc.
Issue_January 19, 2007
Category_Photo: Feature: Spread/Single Page

400 ESPN THE MAGAZINE

Creative Director_Siung Tjia
Designer_Siung Tjia
Director of Photography_Catriona NiAolain
Photo Editors_Amy McNulty, Jim Surber
Photographer_Donald Miralle
Editor-In-Chief_Gary Hoenig
Publisher_ESPN, Inc.
Issue_February 26, 2007
Category_Photo: Feature: Spread/Single Page

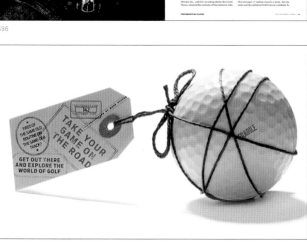

India at Work

From the coal mines of Jharia to the trading floors of Mumbai, *India's 400 million workers are helping build one of the world's fastest-growing economies. That may seem like a paradox in a country where most things, including the traffic, crawl at a snail's pace. But the men and women on these pages—and the stories that follow—paint a portrait of a society on the move.*

Photographs by **BENJAMIN LOWY**

The Taxi Driver
Lala, 17, has been operating an auto rickshaw for two years.
MUMBAI

136 • FORTUNE October 29, 2007

401

GOURMET ENTERTAINS

Caribbean Dreams There are now almost as many people of Puerto Rican descent living in the United States as on the island itself—and our tables are so much the richer for it.

RECIPES AND FOOD STYLING BY MAGGIE RUGGIERO PHOTOGRAPHS BY ROLAND BELLO

The island's sweet scents waft through this menu, from its opening sips of pineapple and mint to desserts lush with tropical fruit.

169

402

401 FORTUNE

Design Director_**Robert Perino** Designer_**Nai Lee Lum**
Director of Photography_**Greg Pond** Photo Editor_**Nancy Jo Johnson**
Photographer_**Benjamin Lowy** Publisher_**Time Inc.**
Issue_**October 29, 2007** Category_**Photo: Feature: Spread/Single Page**

402 GOURMET

Creative Director_**Richard Ferretti** Art Director_**Erika Oliveira**
Designer_**Erika Oliveira** Photo Editor_**Amy Koblenzer**
Photographer_**Roland Bello** Editor-In-Chief_**Ruth Reichl**
Publisher_**Condé Nast Publications, Inc.** Issue_**September 2007**
Category_**Photo: Spread/Single Page**

403

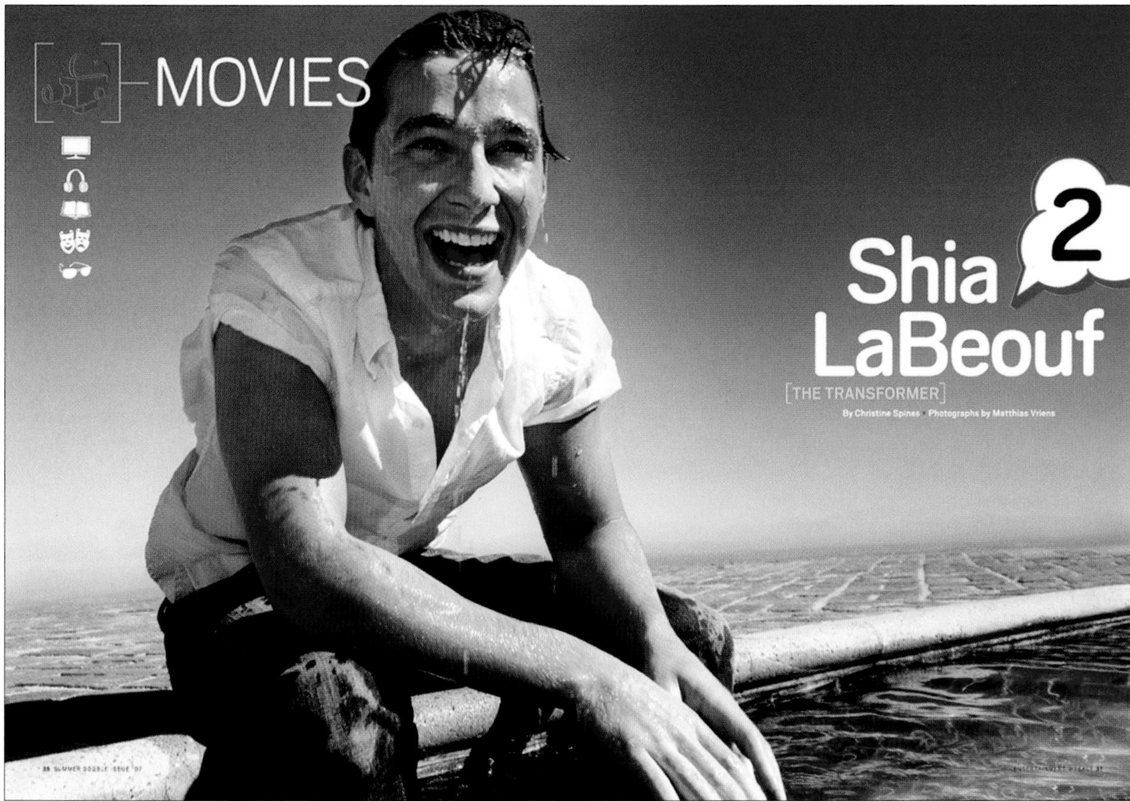

404

403 RUNNER'S WORLD

Art Director_Kory Kennedy Photo Editor_Andrea Maurio
Photographer_J. Carrier Deputy Art Director_Elisa Yoch
Assistant Photo Editor_Nick Galac Publisher_Rodale
Issue_August 2007 Category_Photo: Feature: Spread/Single Page

404 ENTERTAINMENT WEEKLY

Design Director_Geraldine Hessler Art Director_Eric Paul
Director of Photography_Fiona McDonagh
Photo Editor_Michael Kochman Photographer_Matthias Vriens
Publisher_Time Inc. Issue_June 29, 2007
Category_Photo: Feature: Spread/Single Page

405

408

406

409

407

410

405 TIME

Art Director_Arthur Hochstein
Deputy Art Director_Cynthia A. Hoffman
Director of Photography_MaryAnne Golon
Photographer_Nicolas Guerin
Picture Editor_Alice Gabriner
Associate Picture Editor_Jay Colton
Publisher_Time Inc.
Issue_May 14, 2007
Category_Photo: Feature: Spread/Single Page

406 GQ

Design Director_Fred Woodward
Designer_Delgis Canahuate
Director of Photography_Dora Somosi
Photo Editor_Justin O'Neill
Photographer_Tim Richardson
Editor-In-Chief_Jim Nelson
Publisher_Condé Nast Publications Inc.
Issue_June 2007
Category_Photo: Feature: Spread/Single Page

407 GOURMET

Creative Director_Richard Ferretti
Art Director_Erika Oliveira
Designer_Erika Oliveira
Photo Editors_Megan M. Re, Amy Koblenzer
Photographer_Marcus Nilsson
Editor-In-Chief_Ruth Reichl
Publisher_ Condé Nast Publications, Inc.
Issue_December 2007
Category_Photo: Feature: Spread/Single Page

408 POPULAR MECHANICS

Design Director_Michael Lawton
Art Director_Peter Herbert
Assistant Art Director_Michael Friel
Director of Photography_Allyson Torrisi
Associate Photo Editor_Alison Unterreiner
Photographer_Teru Kuwayama
Publisher_The Hearst Corporation-Magazines Div.
Issue_February 2007
Category_Photo: Feature: Spread/Single Page

409 GQ

Design Director_Fred Woodward
Designer_Anton Ioukhnovets
Director of Photography_Dora Somosi
Photo Editor_Justin O'Neill
Photographer_Maciek Kobeilski
Editor-In-Chief_Jim Nelson
Publisher_Condé Nast Publications Inc.
Issue_December 2007
Category_Photo: Feature: Spread/Single Page

410 CORPORATE LEADER

Creative Director_Florian Bachleda
Design Director_Ted Keller
Art Director_Mike Bain
Director of Photography_Ian Spanier
Photographer_Dan Winters
Director of Photography_Leslie DeLa Vega
Studio_FB Design
Publisher_ Doubledown Media
Issue_Premiere
Category_Photo: Feature: Spread/Single Page

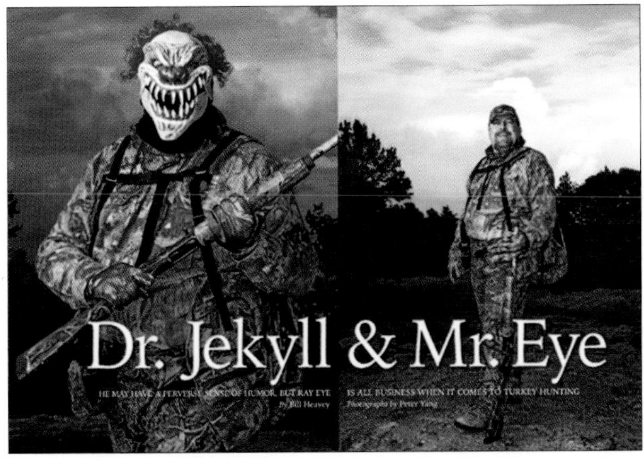

411

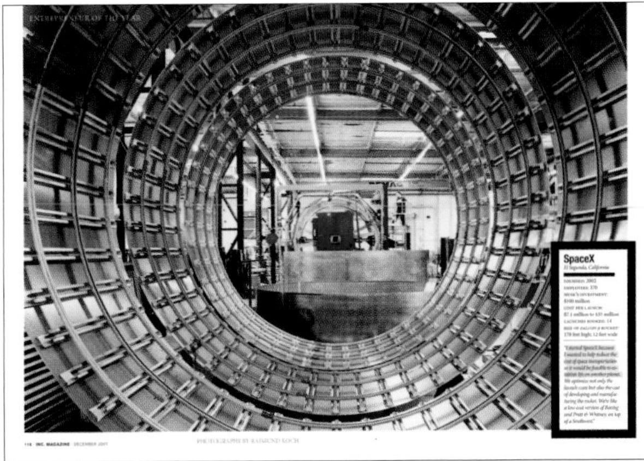

414

412

On the banks of Lake Okeechobee, where the cane grows high and hardship runs deep, the boys of Muck City race through burning fields in pursuit of an elusive prize. Is The Chase why so many of them end up in the NFL? Come see for yourself

415

413

416

411 FIELD & STREAM

Creative Director_Neil Jamieson
Art Director_Ian Brown
Director of Photography_Amy Berkley
Photo Editors_Caitlin Peters, Jaime Santa
Photographer_Peter Yang
Publisher_Time4 Media
Issue_April 2007
Category_Photo: Feature: Spread/Single Page

412 CITY

Creative Director_Fabrice Frere
Design Director_Fabrice Frere
Art Director_Adriana Jacoud
Photo Editor_Anthony Cross
Photographer_Kenji Toma
Publisher_Spark Media
Issue_September 2007
Category_Photo: Feature: Spread/Single Page

413 GARDEN & GUN

Art Director_Tom Brown
Photographer_Michael Eastman
Photography Editor_Maggie Brett Kennedy
Publisher_Event Post Publishing Company
Issue_Summer 2007
Category_Photo: Feature: Spread/Single Page

414 INC.

Creative Director_Blake Taylor
Designer_Blake Taylor
Director of Photography_Travis Ruse
Photographer_Raimund Koch
Editor-In-Chief_Jane Berenstein
Publisher_Mansueto Ventures
Issue December_2007
Category_Photo: Feature: Spread/Single Page

415 ESPN THE MAGAZINE

Creative Director_Siung Tjia
Designer_Siung Tjia
Director of Photography_Catriona NiAolain
Photo Editor_Jim Surber Photographer_Colby Katz
Editor-In-Chief_Gary Hoenig
Publisher_ESPN, Inc.
Issue_April 9, 2007
Category_Photo: Feature: Spread/Single Page

416 CITY

Creative Director_Fabrice Frere
Design Director_Fabrice Frere
Art Director_Adriana Jacoud
Photo Editor_Anthony Cross
Photographer_Phillip Toledano
Publisher_Spark Media
Issue_March 2007
Category_Photo: Feature: Spread/Single Page

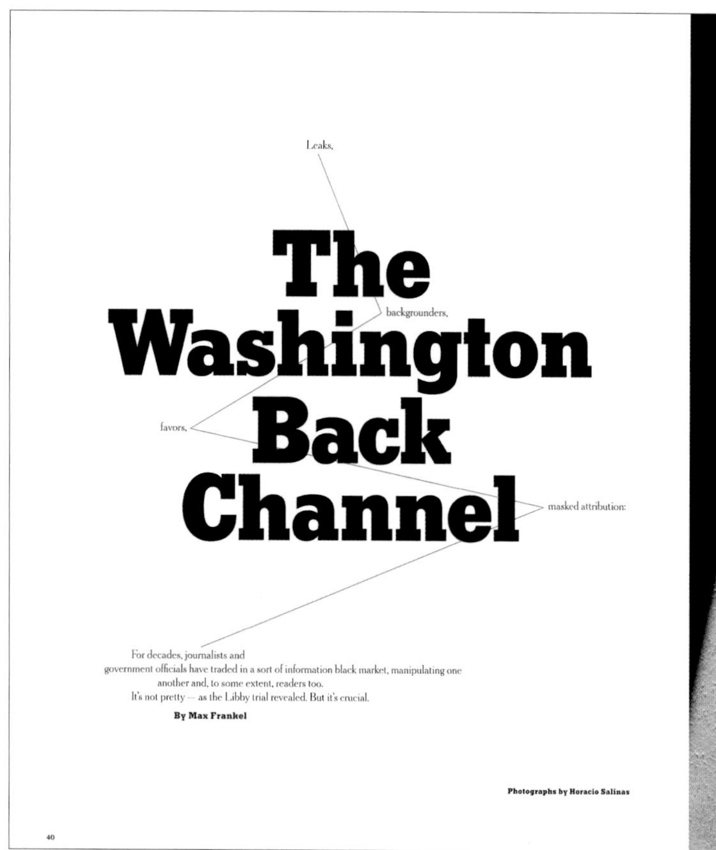

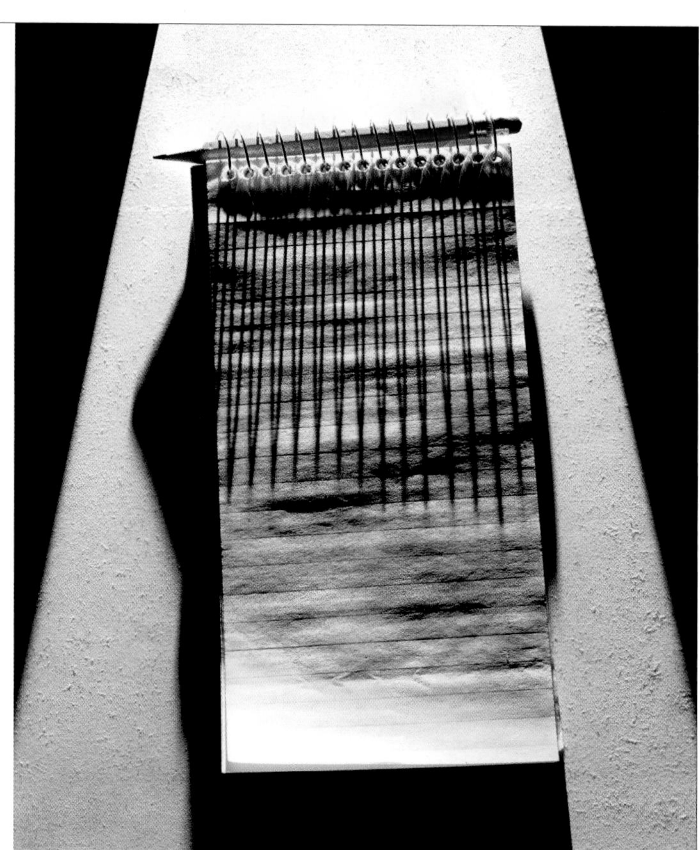

417

418

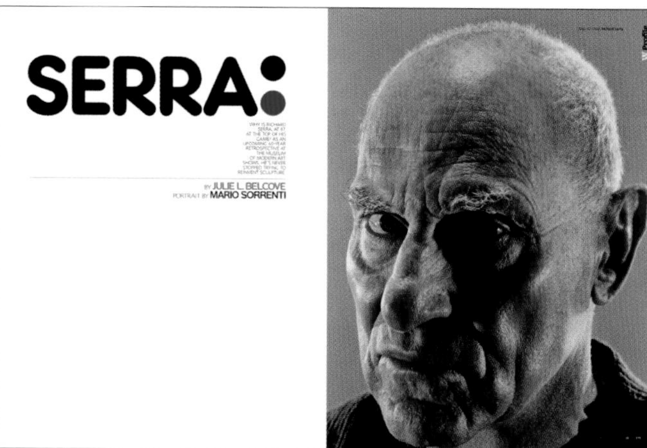

419

417 THE NEW YORK TIMES MAGAZINE

Creative Director_Janet Froelich
Art Director_Arem Duplessis
Designer_Gail Bichler
Director of Photography_Kathy Ryan
Photographer_Horacio Salinas
Editor-In-Chief_Gerry Marzorati
Publisher_The New York Times
Issue_March 25, 2007
Category_Photo: Feature: Spread/Single Page

418 ESPN THE MAGAZINE

Creative Director_Siung Tjia
Designer_Lou Vega
Director of Photography_Catriona NiAolain
Photo Editor_Jim Surber
Photographer_John Loomis
Editor-In-Chief_Gary Hoenig
Publisher_ESPN, Inc.
Issue_May 7, 2007
Category_Photo: Feature: Spread/Single Page

419 W

Creative Director_Dennis Freedman
Design Director_Edward Leida
Art Director_Nathalie Kirsheh
Designer_Nathalie Kirsheh
Photo Editor_Nadia Vellam
Photographer_Mario Sorrenti
Publisher_Condé Nast Publications Inc.
Issue May 2007
Category_Photo: Feature: Spread/Single Page

The Man Who Thinks
He Can Fly

DEAN POTTER'S DAY JOB IS WALKING THE LINE BETWEEN LIFE AND DEATH. SCARILY, THAT'S NOT EVEN CLOSE TO THE CRAZIEST THING ABOUT HIM

BY KATIE ARNOLD
PHOTOGRAPHS BY DAN WINTERS
121

420

2008 INVESTOR'S GUIDE

THE BEST STOCKS FOR 2008

We've found ten stocks that will thrive despite—or even benefit from—the troubles facing the markets next year. BY JON BIRGER

WE'LL SAY THIS FOR the U.S. economy: It can take a punch. ¶ Consider the blows it has absorbed just this year. The worst real estate crash since the Great Depression. *Pow!* Oil prices up from $50 to $90 a barrel since last January. *Bam!* A subprime mortgage mess metastasizing into a full-blown credit crisis, with banks swallowing billions in losses and cutting back on loans. *Baff!* ¶ Yet through all the punishment, the economy has barely flinched. "I'm floored by how resilient it has been," says veteran stock strategist Ed Yardeni of Oak Associates. "Had you told me at the beginning of the year this was going to happen, I doubt I would have been very optimistic."

421

422

420 ESPN THE MAGAZINE

Creative Director_Siung Tjia
Designer_Siung Tjia
Director of Photography_Catriona Ni Aolain
Photo Editor_Maisie Todd
Photographer_Dan Winters
Publisher_ESPN, Inc.
Issue_November 5, 2007
Category_Photo: Feature: Spread/Single Page

421 FORTUNE

Design Director_Robert Perino
Designers_Deanna Lowe, Linda Rubes, Tony Mikolajczyk
Director of Photography_Greg Pond
Photo Editor_Scott Thode
Photographer_Dan Winters
Publisher_Time Inc.
Issue_December 24, 2007
Category_Photo: Feature: Spread/Single Page

422 NATIONAL GEOGRAPHIC

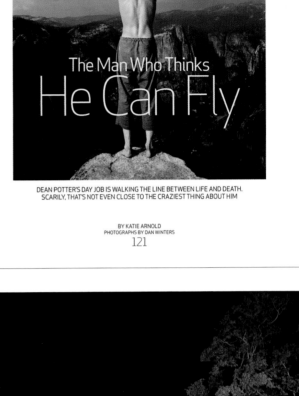

Design Director_David Whitmore
Art Director_Elaine Bradley
Director of Photography_David Griffin
Photo Editor_Kathy Moran
Photographer_Christian Ziegler
Publisher_National Geographic Society
Issue_June 2007
Category_Photo: Feature: Spread/Single Page

THE FAMILY THAT PLAYS TOGETHER
Willis with his "extended family"—ex-wife Demi Moore and her new husband, Ashton Kutcher—off Parrot Cay. "I love Demi," Willis says, "and I know she loves me."

172 | VANITY FAIR | www.vanityfair.com JUNE 2007

JUNE 2007 www.vanityfair.com | VANITY FAIR | 173

423

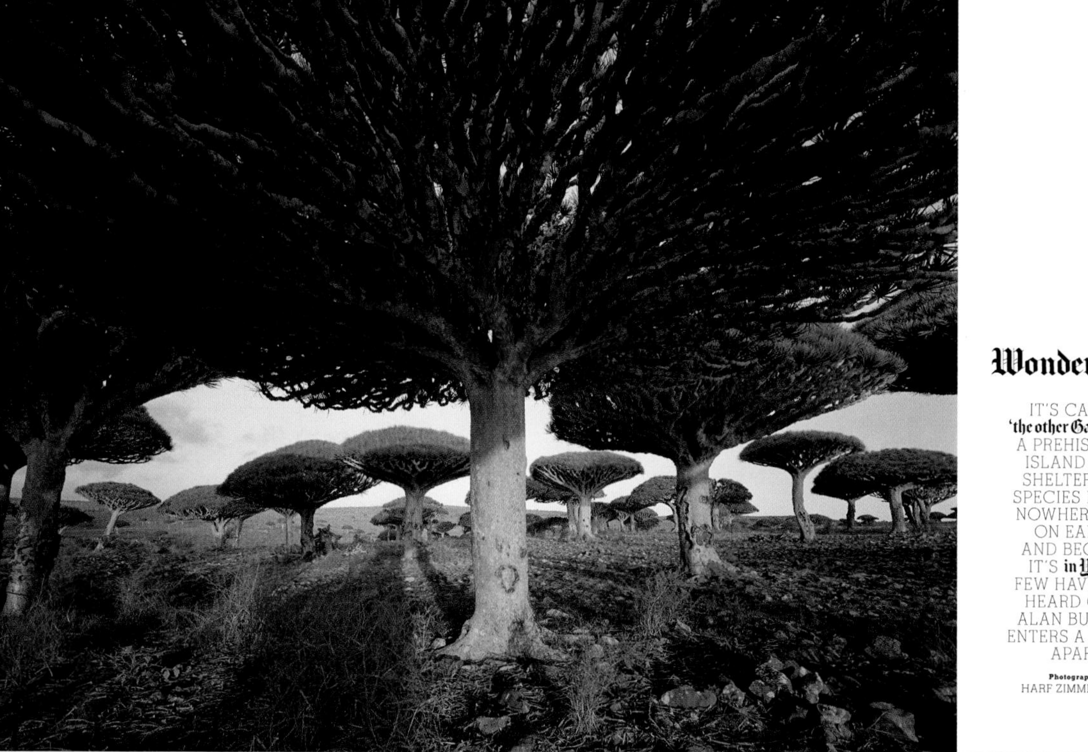

Wonder Land

IT'S CALLED **'the other Galapagos,'** A PREHISTORIC ISLAND THAT SHELTERS 700 SPECIES FOUND NOWHERE ELSE ON EARTH. AND BECAUSE IT'S **in Yemen,** FEW HAVE EVER HEARD OF IT. ALAN BURDICK ENTERS A WORLD APART.

Photographs by HARF ZIMMERMANN

135

424

423 VANITY FAIR

Design Director_David Harris Designer_Chris Mueller
Director of Photography_Susan White Photo Editor_Kathryn MacLeod
Photographer_Annie Leibovitz Editor-In-Chief_Graydon Carter
Publisher_Condé Nast Publications Inc. Issue_June 2007
Category_Photo: Feature: Spread/Single Page

424 T, THE NEW YORK TIMES STYLE MAGAZINE

Creative Director_Janet Froelich Senior Art Director_David Sebbah
Art Director_Christopher Martinez Designer_Christopher Martinez
Photo Editor_Scott Hall Photographer_Harf Zimmerman
Editor-In-Chief_Stefano Tonchi Publisher_The New York Times
Issue_March 25, 2007 Category_Photo: Feature: Spread/Single Page

Certifiable heroes such as GENGHIS KHAN
seem to act as glue for a national identity
that has fragmented since 1990
A cowboy in Kharkorin. Opposite: Wrestlers train at a gym in Ulaanbaatar.

425

Owners Heide Praver Werthamer, Terry Ford, and Lauren Abrams by the pool at Casa Morada.
THUNDERBIRD
The Thunderbird Motel, in Marfa, Texas.
Casa Morada's outdoor front desk.
A guest room at the Thunderbird.
Photographed by BAERBEL SCHMIDT
Photographed by TRUJILLO/PAUMIER 213

024

426

425 TRAVEL + LEISURE

Creative Director_Nora Sheehan Art Director_Katharine van Itallie
Designer_Nora Sheehan Director of Photography_Katie Dunn
Photo Editor_Wendy Ball Photographer Frédéric Lagrange
Publisher_American Express Publishing Co. Issue_February 2007
Category_Photo: Feature: Spread/Single Page

426 TRAVEL + LEISURE

Creative Director_Nora Sheehan Art Director_Katharine Van Itallie
Designer_Howard Greenberg Director of Photography_Katie Dunn
Photo Editor_Malu Alvarez Photographers_Baerbel Schmidt, Tujillo + Paumier Publisher_American Express Publishing Co.
Issue_June 2007 Category_Photo: Feature: Spread/Single Page

427

430

428

431

429

Photo Essay

SCARS OF WAR

432

427 BLENDER

Creative Director_Andy Turnbull
Art Director_Amelia Tubb
Director of Photography_Amy Hoppy
Photographer_Chris Buck
Publisher_Dennis Publishing
Issue_October 2007
Category_Photo: Feature: Spread/Single Page

428 VANITY FAIR

Design Director_David Harris
Director of Photography_Susan White
Photographer_Brigitte Lacombe
Editor-In-Chief_Graydon Carter
Publisher_Condé Nast Publications Inc.
Issue_June 2007
Category_Photo: Feature: Spread/Single Page

429 NEW YORK

Design Director_Chris Dixon
Art Director_Randy Minor
Director of Photography_Jody Quon
Photographer_Katja Rahlwes
Editor-In-Chief_Adam Moss
Publisher_New York Magazine Holdings, LLC
Issue_August 27, 2007
Category_Photo: Feature: Spread/Single Page

430 TOWN & COUNTRY

Creative Director_Mary Shanahan
Art Director_Agnethe Glatved
Director of Photography_Casey Tierney
Photographer_Rob Howard
Publisher_The Hearst Corporation-Magazines Div.
Issue_April 2007
Category_Photo: Feature: Spread/Single Page

431 VANITY FAIR

Design Director_David Harris
Director of Photography_Susan White
Photo Editor_Richard Villani
Photographer_Bruce Weber
Editor-In-Chief_Graydon Carter
Publisher_Condé Nast Publications Inc.
Issue_August 2007
Category_Photo: Feature: Spread/Single Page

432 NEWSWEEK

Creative Director_Amid Capeci
Art Director_Leah Purcell
Director of Photography_Simon Barnett
Photo Editor_Amy Pereira
Photographer_Tim Hetherington – Panos
Publisher_The Washington Post Co.
Issue_March 12, 2007
Category_Photo: Feature: Spread/Single Page

433

436

434

437

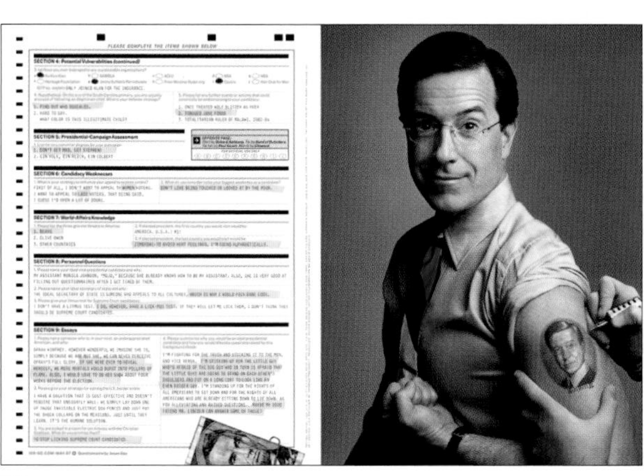

435

438

433 **NEWSWEEK**

Creative Director_Amid Capeci
Art Director_Alex Ho
Director of Photography_Simon Barnett
Photo Editor_James Wellford
Photographer_Gary Knight – VII for Newsweek
Publisher_The Washington Post Co.
Issue_January 29, 2007
Category_Photo: Feature: Spread/Single Page

434 **WIRED**

Creative Director_Scott Dadich
Art Director_ Scott Dadich
Designer_Carl DeTorres
Photo Editor_Carolyn Rauch
Photographer_Brent Humphreys
Publisher_Condé Nast Publications, Inc.
Issue_January 2007
Category_Photo: Feature: Spread/Single Page

435 **GQ**

Design Director_Fred Woodward
Designer_Thomas Alberty
Director of Photography_Dora Somosi
Photographer_Mark Seliger
Editor-In-Chief_Jim Nelson
Publisher_Condé Nast Publications Inc.
Issue_May 2007
Category_Photo: Feature: Spread/Single Page

436 **PRIVATE AIR**

Creative Director_Florian Bachleda
Photographer_Ian Spanier
Studio_FB Design
Publisher_Doubledown Media
Issue_August/September 2007
Category_Photo: Feature: Spread/Single Page

437 **NEWSWEEK**

Creative Director_Amid Capeci
Art Director_Alex Ho
Director of Photography_Simon Barnett
Photo Editors_Beth Ferraro, Michelle Molloy
Photographer_Stephanie Kuykendal for Newsweek
Publisher_The Washington Post Co.
Issue_February 12, 2007
Category_Photo: Feature: Spread/Single Page

438 **STANFORD MAGAZINE**

Art Director_Amy Shroads
Photographer_Glenn Matsumura
Publisher_Stanford University
Issue _January/February 2007
Category_Photo: Feature: Spread/Single Page

The New York Times Magazine / AUGUST 5, 2007

Seeing Iraq as it is (at least through the window of an armored vehicle).

GETTING IRAQ WRONG

WHAT THE WAR HAS TAUGHT ME ABOUT POLITICAL JUDGMENT.

By Michael Ignatieff

The unfolding catastrophe in Iraq has condemned the political judgment of a president. But it has also condemned the judgment of many others, myself included, who as commentators supported the invasion. Many of us believed, as an Iraqi exile friend told me the night the war started, that it was the only chance the members of his generation would have to live in freedom in their own country. How distant a dream that now seems.

Having left an academic post at Harvard in 2005 and returned home to Canada to enter political life, I keep revisiting the Iraq debacle, trying to understand exactly how the judgments I now have to make in the political arena need to improve on the ones I used to offer

Photographs by Benjamin Lowy

26 27

439

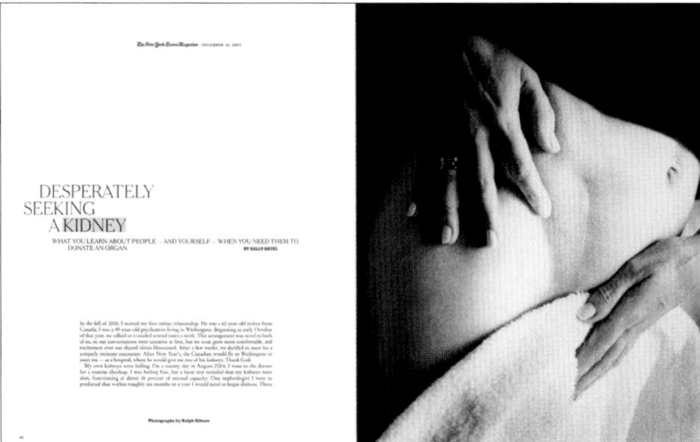

DESPERATELY SEEKING A KIDNEY

440

A Toy Maker's Conscience

441

439 THE NEW YORK TIMES MAGAZINE

Creative Director_Janet Froelich
Art Directors_Arem Duplessis, Gail Bichler
Designer_Jeff Docherty
Director of Photography_Kathy Ryan
Photo Editor_Kira Pollack
Photographer_Benjamin Lowy
Editor-In-Chief_Gerry Marzorati
Publisher_The New York Times
Issue_August 5, 2007
Category_Photo: Feature: Spread/Single Page

440 THE NEW YORK TIMES MAGAZINE

Creative Director_Janet Froelich
Art Director_Arem Duplessis
Designer_Arem Duplessis
Director of Photography_Kathy Ryan
Photo Editor_Clinton Cargill
Photographer_Ralph Gibson
Editor-In-Chief_Gerry Marzorati
Publisher_The New York Times
Issue_December 16, 2007
Category_Photo: Feature: Spread/Single Page

441 THE NEW YORK TIMES MAGAZINE

Creative Director_Janet Froelich
Art Director_Arem Duplessis
Designer_Holly Gressley
Director of Photography_Kathy Ryan
Photo Editor_Leonor Mamanna
Photographer_Horacio Salinas
Editor-In-Chief_Gerry Marzorati
Publisher_The New York Times
Issue_December 23, 2007
Category_Photo: Feature: Spread/Single Page

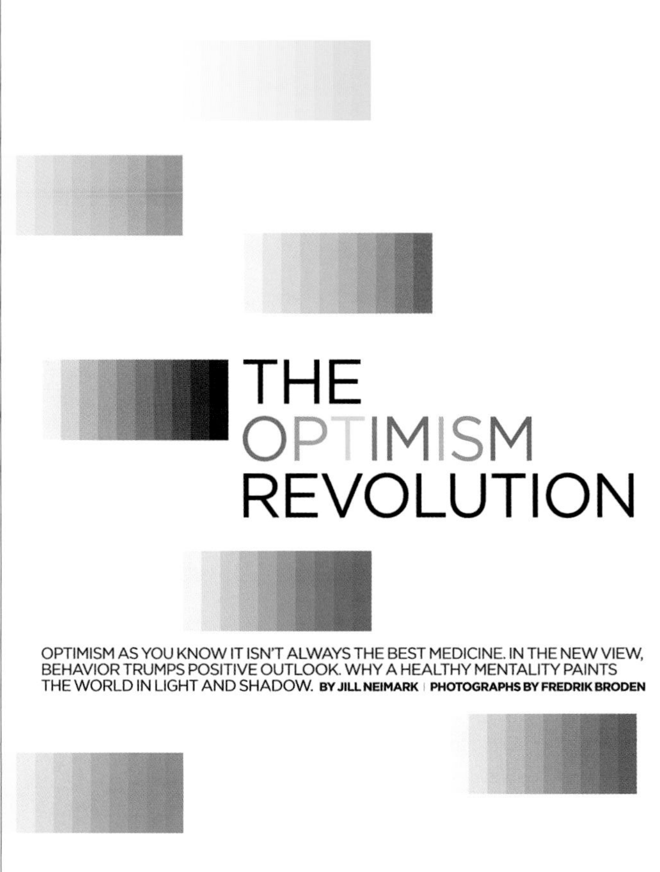

THE
OPTIMISM
REVOLUTION
OPTIMISM AS YOU KNOW IT ISN'T ALWAYS THE BEST MEDICINE. IN THE NEW VIEW, BEHAVIOR TRUMPS POSITIVE OUTLOOK. WHY A HEALTHY MENTALITY PAINTS THE WORLD IN LIGHT AND SHADOW. BY JILL NEIMARK | PHOTOGRAPHS BY FREDRIK BRODEN
88 Psychology Today May/June 2007

442

443

444

442 PSYCHOLOGY TODAY

Creative Director_Edward Levine
Director of Photography_Claudia Stefezius
Photographer_Fredrik Broden
Studio_Levine Design Inc.
Publisher_Sussex Publishers
Client_Psychology Today Issue_May/June 2007
Category_Photo: Feature: Spread/Single Page

443 PSYCHOLOGY TODAY

Creative Director_Edward Levine
Director of Photography_Claudia Stefezius
Photographer_Fredrik Broden
Studio_Levine Design Inc.
Publisher_Sussex Publishers
Client_Psychology Today
Issue_November/December 2007
Category_Photo: Feature: Spread/Single Page

444 O, THE OPRAH MAGAZINE

Design Director_Carla Frank
Designer_Mike Bain
Director of Photography_Jennifer Crandall
Photo Editor_Christina Stephens
Photographer_Alex Beauchesne
Creative Director_Adam Glassman
Editor-In-Chief_Amy Gross
Publisher_The Hearst Corporation-Magazines Div.
Issue_March 2007
Category_Photo: Feature: Spread/Single Page

THE CULTURE PAGES

MOVIES | BOOKS | TV | ART | MATRIX

Is Terence Koh's Sperm Worth $100,000?
Portrait of the artist as a young punk capitalist.
BY MARC SPIEGLER

Terence Koh's artistic coming-out hardly seemed auspicious. It was May 2003. Collector Javier Peres had recently scrapped his international-law career to open Peres Projects gallery. He offered its opening show in Los Angeles to Koh, a young New York artist then known as asianpunkboy, whose track record con-

Photograph by Joseph Maida

JANUARY 15, 2007 | NEW YORK 55

445

447

CHRISTOPHER HITCHENS

On the Limits of Self-Improvement, Part I

There's an entire micro-economy based on the pursuit of betterment. The author—58, full-figured, and ferocious in his consumption of cigarettes and scotch—agreed to test its limits, starting with the Executive De-Stress Treatment at a high-end spa

PHOTOGRAPHS BY ART STREIBER

OCTOBER 2007

449

446

448

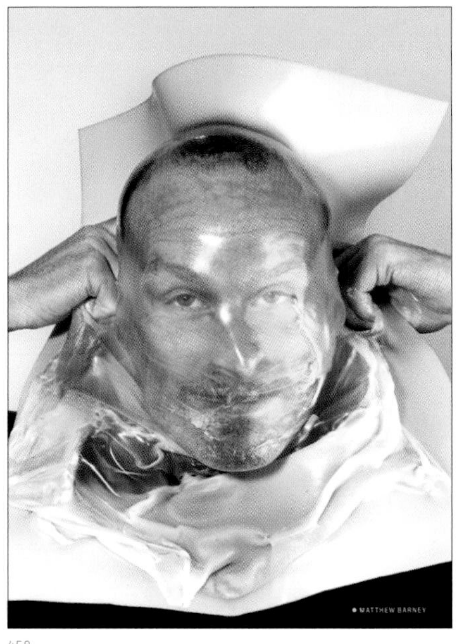

450

445 NEW YORK

Design Director_Chris Dixon
Director of Photography_Jody Quon
Photographer_Joseph Maida
Editor-In-Chief_Adam Moss
Publisher_New York Magazine Holdings, LLC
Issue_January 15, 2007
Category_Photo: Feature: Spread/Single Page

446 GQ

Design Director_Fred Woodward
Designer_Thomas Alberty
Director of Photography_Dora Somosi
Photographer_Richard Burbridge
Editor-In-Chief_Jim Nelson
Publisher_Condé Nast Publications Inc.
Issue_October 2007
Category_Photo: Feature: Spread/Single Page

447 VANITY FAIR

Design Director_David Harris
Director of Photography_Susan White
Photo Editor_SunHee Grinnell
Photographer_Mario Testino
Editor-In-Chief_Graydon Carter
Publisher_Condé Nast Publications Inc.
Issue_February 2007
Category_Photo: Feature: Spread/Single Page

448 GQ

Design Director_Fred Woodward
Designer_Anton Ioukhnovets
Director of Photography_Dora Somosi
Photo Editor_Justin O'Neill
Photographer_Dan Forbes
Editor-In-Chief_Jim Nelson
Publisher_Condé Nast Publications Inc.
Issue_February 2007
Category_Photo: Feature: Spread/Single Page

449 VANITY FAIR

Design Director_David Harris
Director of Photography_Susan White
Photo Editor_Ian Bascetta
Photographer_Art Streiber
Editor-In-Chief_Graydon Carter
Publisher_Condé Nast Publications Inc.
Issue_October 2007
Category_Photo: Feature: Spread/Single Page

450 GQ

Design Director_Fred Woodward
Designer_Thomas Alberty
Director of Photography_Dora Somosi
Photographer_Richard Burbridge
Editor-In-Chief_Jim Nelson
Publisher_Condé Nast Publications Inc.
Issue_October 2007
Category_Photo: Feature: Spread/Single Page

451

453

455

452

454

456

451 TIME

Art Director_Arthur Hochstein
Associate Art Director_Christine Dunleavy
Director of Photography_MaryAnne Golon
Picture Editor_Alice Gabriner
Associate Picture Editor_Marie Tobias
Photographer_Michael Grecco
Publisher_Time Inc. Issue_March 26, 2007
Category_Photo: Feature: Spread/Single Page

452 TIME

Art Director_Arthur Hochstein
Associate Art Director_Christine Dunleavy
Director of Photography_MaryAnne Golon
Picture Editor_Alice Gabriner
Associate Picture Editor_Marie Tobias
Photographer_Michael Grecco
Publisher_Time Inc. Issue_November 26, 2007
Category_Photo: Feature: Spread/Single Page

453 VANITY FAIR

Design Director_David Harris
Director of Photography_Susan White
Photo Editor_Jessica Chatfield
Photographer_Carlyne Cerf de Dudzede
Editor-In-Chief_Graydon Carter
Publisher_Condé Nast Publications Inc.
Issue_September 2007
Category_Photo: Feature: Spread/Single Page

454 GQ

Design Director_Fred Woodward
Designer_Anton Ioukhnovets
Director of Photography_Dora Somosi
Senior Photo Editor_Krista Prestek
Photographer_Jeff Riedel
Editor-In-Chief_Jim Nelson
Publisher_Condé Nast Publications Inc.
Issue_December 2007
Category_Photo: Feature: Spread/Single Page

455 O, THE OPRAH MAGAZINE

Design Director_Carla Frank
Designer_Stravinski Pierre
Director of Photography_Jennifer Crandall
Photo Editor_Christina Stephens
Photographer_Keate
Creative Director_Adam Glassman
Editor-In-Chief_Amy Gross
Publisher_The Hearst Corporation-Magazines Div.
Issue_June 2007
Category_Photo: Feature: Spread/Single Page

456 TOWN & COUNTRY

Art Director_Agnethe Glatved
Designer_Effie Tsu
Photo Editor_Devin Traineau
Photographer_Gabriella Imperatori-Penn
Publisher_The Hearst Corporation-Magazines Div.
Issue_February 2007
Category_Photo: Feature: Spread/Single Page

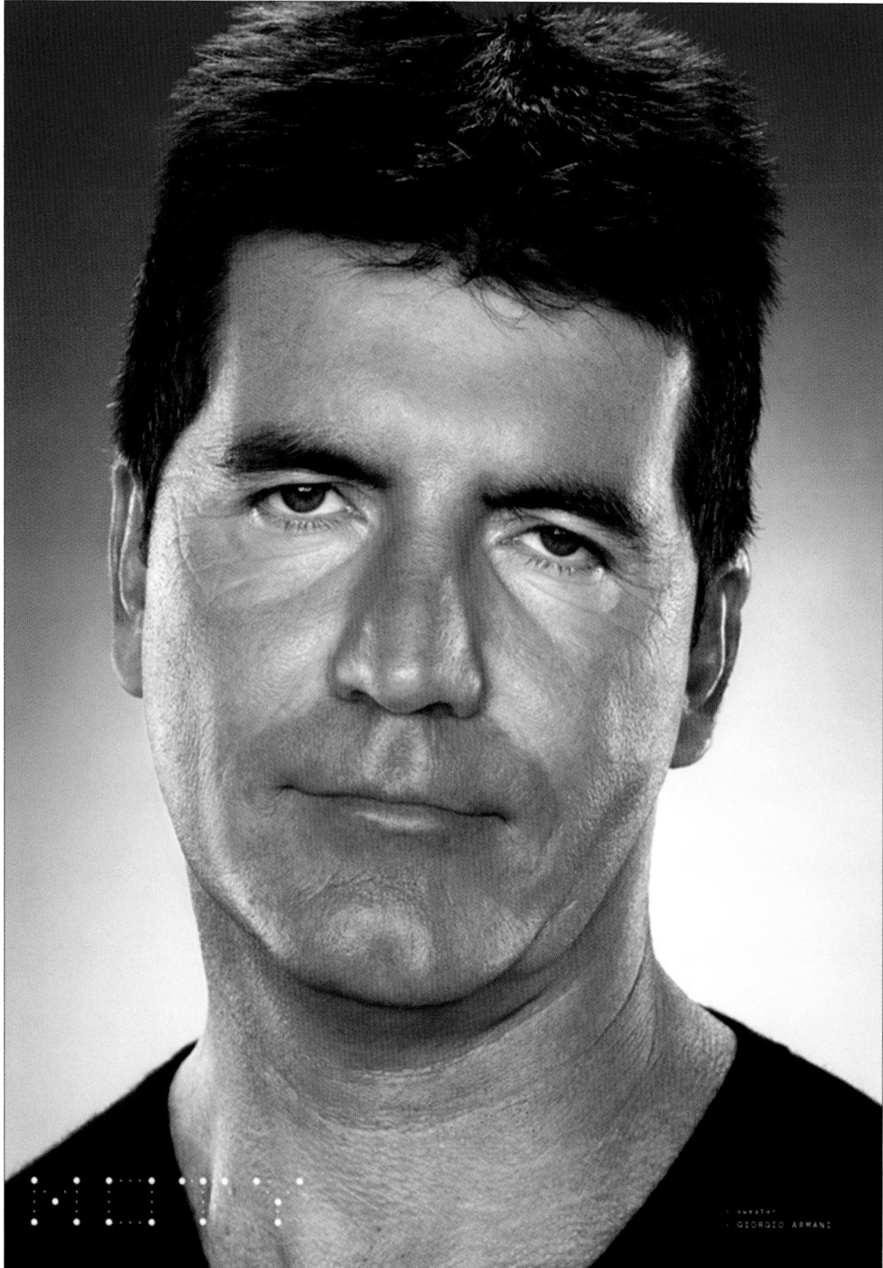

457

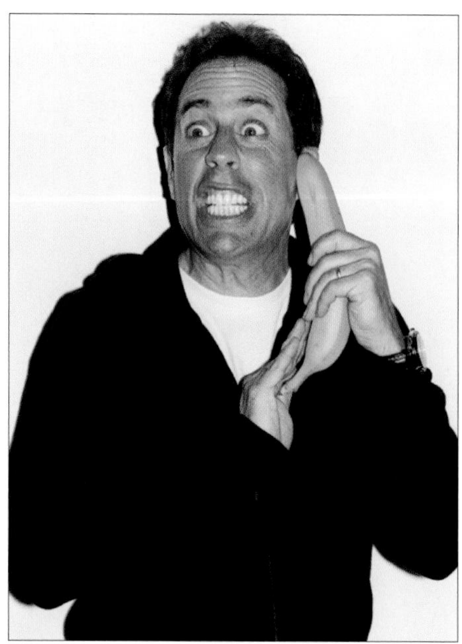

458

459

457 GQ
Design Director_Fred Woodward
Designer_Anton Ioukhnovets
Director of Photography_Dora Somosi
Photo Editor_Justin O'Neill
Photographer_Jill Greenberg
Editor-In-Chief_Jim Nelson
Publisher_Condé Nast Publications Inc.
Issue_December 2007
Category_Photo: Feature: Spread/Single Page

458 GQ
Design Director_Fred Woodward
Designer_Chelsea Cardinal
Director of Photography_Dora Somosi
Photographer_Terry Richardson
Editor-In-Chief_Jim Nelson
Publisher_Condé Nast Publications Inc.
Issue_November 2007
Category_Photo: Feature: Spread/Single Page

459 GQ
Design Director_Fred Woodward
Designer_Chelsea Cardinal
Photographer_Peggy Sirota
Editor-In-Chief_Jim Nelson
Publisher_Condé Nast Publications Inc.
Issue_September 2007
Category_Photo: Feature: Spread/Single Page

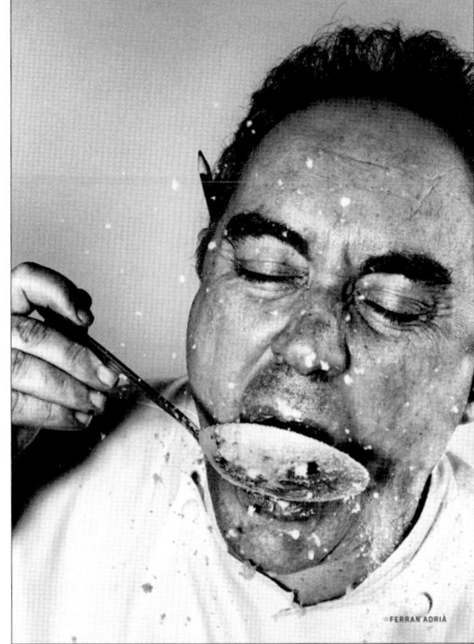

460

461

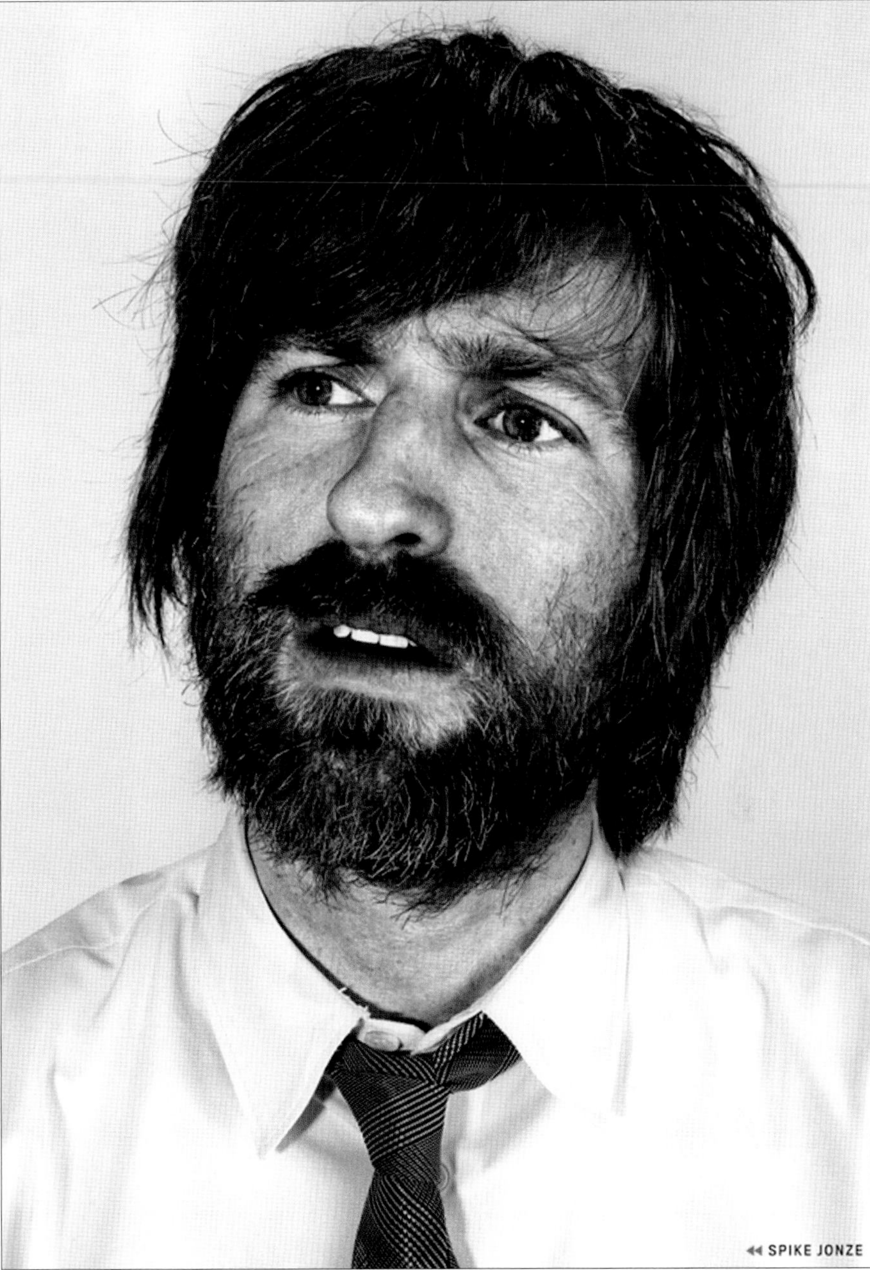

462

460 GQ

Design Director_Fred Woodward
Designer_Thomas Alberty
Director of Photography_Dora Somosi
Photographer_Richard Burbridge
Editor-In-Chief_Jim Nelson
Publisher_Condé Nast Publications Inc.
Issue_October 2007
Category_Photo: Feature: Spread/Single Page

461 GQ

Design Director_Fred Woodward
Designer_Thomas Alberty
Director of Photography_Dora Somosi
Photographer_Richard Burbridge
Editor-In-Chief_Jim Nelson
Publisher_Condé Nast Publications Inc.
Issue_October 2007
Category_Photo: Feature: Spread/Single Page

462 GQ

Design Director_Fred Woodward
Designer_Thomas Alberty
Director of Photography_Dora Somosi
Photographer_Richard Burbridge
Editor-In-Chief_Jim Nelson
Publisher_Condé Nast Publications Inc.
Issue_October 2007
Category_Photo: Feature: Spread/Single Page

463

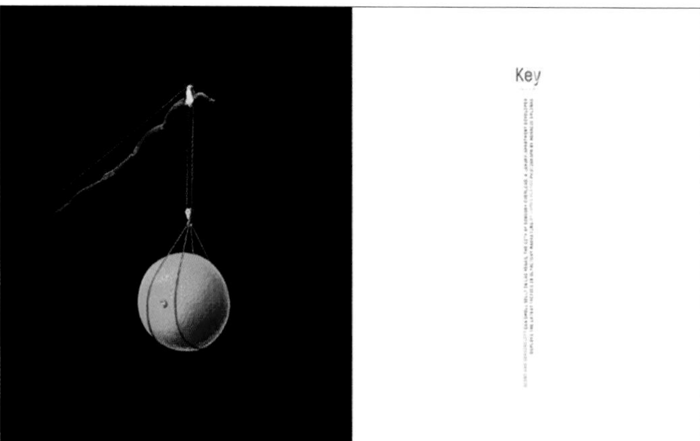

464

465

466

467

463 REAL SIMPLE

Design Director_Ellene Wundrok Designer_ Elsa Mehary
Director of Photography_Casey Tierney Photo Editor_Lauren Epstein
Photographer_Ditte Isager Publisher_Time Inc. Issue_November 2007
Category_Photo: Feature: Spread/Single Page

464 KEY, THE NEW YORK TIMES REAL ESTATE MAGAZINE

Creative Director_Janet Froelich Art Directors_Dirk Barnett, Arem Duplessis Director of Photography_Kathy Ryan
Photo Editor_Joanna Milter Photographer_Horacio Salinas
Editor-In-Chief_Gerry Marzorati Publisher_The New York Times
Issue_Fall 2007 Category_Photo: Feature: Spread/Single Page

465 INC.

Creative Director_Blake Taylor Designer_Jason Miscuka
Director of Photography_Travis Ruse Photo Editor_Kate Spear-Brodsky
Photographer Roark Johnson Editor-In-Chief_Jane Berentson
Publisher_Mansueto Ventures Issue_April 2007
Category_Photo: Feature: Spread/Single Page

466 CONDÉ NAST PORTFOLIO

Design Director_Robert Priest Art Director_Grace Lee
Designer_Jana Meier Director of Photography_Lisa Berman
Photo Editor_Brian Marcus Deputy Photo Editor_Sarah Czeladnicki
Photographer_Kenji Thomas Editor-In-Chief_Joanne Lipman
Publisher_Condé Nast Publications Inc. Issue_December 2007
Category_Photo: Feature: Spread/Single Page

467 NATIONAL GEOGRAPHIC

Design Director_David Whitmore Art Director_Elaine Bradley
Director of Photography_David Griffin Photo Editor_Kathy Moran
Photographer_Paul Nicklen Publisher_National Geographic Society
Issue_June 2007 Category_Photo: Feature: Spread/Single Page

468

469

471

470

472

468 **VANITY FAIR**

Design Director_**David Harris** Director of Photography_**Susan White** Photo Editor_**Kathryn MacLeod** Photographer_**Annie Leibovitz** Editor-In-Chief_**Graydon Carter** Publisher_**Condé Nast Publications Inc.** Issue_**April 2007** Category_**Photo: Feature: Spread/Single Page**

469 **NEW YORK**

Design Director_**Chris Dixon** Director of Photography_**Jody Quon** Photographer_**Hans Gissinger** Editor-In-Chief_**Adam Moss** Publisher_**New York Magazine Holdings, LLC** Issue_**January 22-29, 2007** Category_**Photo: Feature: Spread/Single Page**

470 **ESPN THE MAGAZINE**

Creative Director_**Siung Tjia** Designer_**Robert Festino** Director of Photography_**Catriona Ni Aolain** Photo Editors_**Nancy Weisman, Maisie Todd** Photographer_**Jeff Riedel** Editor-In-Chief_**Gary Hoenig** Publisher_**ESPN, Inc.** Issue_**January 15, 2007** Category_**Photo: Feature: Spread/Single Page**

471 **MEN'S JOURNAL**

Creative Director_**Paul Martinez** Designer_**Paul Martinez** Director of Photography_**Rob Haggart** Photographer_**Carlos Serrao** Editor-In-Chief_**Jann S. Wenner** Publisher_**Wenner Media LLC** Issue_**July 2007** Category_**Photo: Feature: Spread/Single Page**

472 **NATIONAL GEOGRAPHIC**

Design Director_**David Whitmore** Designer_**David Whitmore** Director of Photography _**David Griffin** Photo Editor_**Bill Douthitt** Photographer_**Frans Lanting** Publisher_**National Geographic Society** Issue_**May 2007** Category_**Photo: Feature: Spread/Single Page**

The New York Times Sports Magazine JUNE 2007

PLAY

THE UNENDING HEARTBREAK OF PITCHER KERRY WOOD BY BUZZ BISSINGER

EXCLUSIVE A NEW LEAGUE TARGETS THE N.F.L. BY JOE NOCERA

FAT CATS, AHOY! AMONG THE SWELLS AT THE AMERICA'S CUP BY JOHN TAYMAN

SWIM THE AMAZON, SAVE THE WORLD ONE MAN'S HUMBLE QUEST BY ED ZUCKERMAN

DOPED-UP DNA THE NEXT FRONTIER IN CHEATING

SNEAK PREVIEW TOUR DE FRANCE HOW WE LEARNED TO STOP WORRYING AND LOVE THE RACE

MR. UNPREDICTABLE

CHEER, THEN COVER YOUR EYES. PHIL MICKELSON, GOLF'S NO. 1 WILD CARD, EXPLAINED. BY CHARLES McGRATH

PLUS NEAL POLLACK: SIMULATED BASEBALL: MY SECRET SHAME. GRETCHEN REYNOLDS: WHY YOUNG ATHLETES' HEARTS GIVE OUT. VINCENT LAFORET: THE BIG EVENTS, IN PICTURES. DAVID CARR: THE HBO DRAMA THAT KILLS GIDGET FOR GOOD

473

PLAY

The New York Times Sports Magazine JUNE 2007

52 MY RIGHT ARM
What pitcher Kerry Wood wouldn't give to have the last decade back — to not be the guy about whom teams with a can't-miss prospect wonder, "What went wrong?"
BY BUZZ BISSINGER

58 CAST OFF, CHARACTERS!
It's a four-year, billion-dollar competition that can restore or ruin reputations and turn deep eccentricity into high entertainment. Batten down the hatches for the America's Cup.
BY JOHN TAYMAN

64 A REALLY BIG SHOW
The defining events in sports: Ah, the voyeuristic pleasure of having the best eye in the house.
PHOTOGRAPHS BY VINCENT LAFORET

72 JUST LIKE US – ONLY BETTER
Phil Mickelson may be doomed to play golf's second banana, but that's what makes things so interesting.
BY CHARLES McGRATH

78 OVERCOMING THE U.S. OPEN
Jim Furyk, the 2003 champion, dissects the nerve-fraying course at Oakmont Country Club.
BY DAMON HACK

80 SWIMMING FOR PEACE, THE DALAI LAMA, THE RAIN FOREST. ... WE'LL DRINK TO THAT
It doesn't take much for world-record breaker Martin Strel to get the most out of life.
BY ED ZUCKERMAN

On the cover: Phil Mickelson, photographed by Dan Winters for The New York Times. This page: photograph by Vincent Laforet for The New York Times.

Continued on Page 8

The long view A quiet moment before the Pipeline Masters in Hawaii (Page 64).

6

473

474

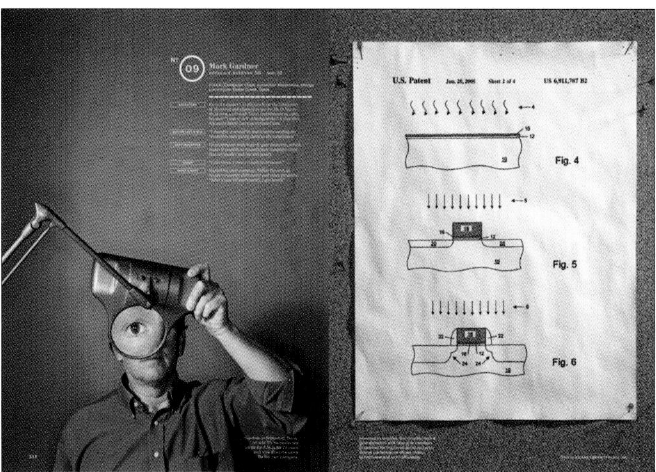

474

473 PLAY, THE NEW YORK TIMES SPORTS MAGAZINE

Creative Director_Janet Froelich Art Director_Christopher Martinez Designers_Christopher Martinez, Dragos Lemnei Photo Editor_Kira Pollack Photographers_Dan Winters, Vincent Laforet Publisher_The New York Times Issue_June 2007 Category_Photo: Entire Issue

474 CONDÉ NAST PORTFOLIO

Design Director_Robert Priest Art Director_Grace Lee Deputy Art Director_Sarah Viñas Designers_ Sarah Viñas, Jana Meier, Rina Kushnir, Grace Martinez Illustrators_Bruce Hutchison, Paul Davis, Kagan Mcleod, Jeffrey Decoster, Bryan Christie, Julie Teninbaum, Brian Rea, John Burgoyne, Joel Holland, Roderick Mills, Jonathan Gray, Nick Higgins, Sean McCabe Director of Photography_Lisa Berman Photo Editors_Jane Yeomans, Sarah Weissman, Rossana Shokrian, Brian Marcus, Louisa Anderson, John Toolan Deputy Photo Editor_Sarah Czeladnicki Photographers_Ron Howard, Stephen Lewis, Jeff Minton, Dan Winters, Jill Greenberg, Michael Wolf, Misha Gravenor, Ture Lillegraven, Jillian Edelstein, Joe Pugliese, Nikolas Koenig, Brad Bridgers, Levi Brown, Tierney Gearon, Chris Jordan, Erin Patrice O'Brien Information Graphics Director_John Grimwade Editor-In-Chief_Joanne Lipman Publisher_Condé Nast Publications Inc. Issue_November 2007 Category_Photo: Entire Issue

475

475

476

476

477

477

475 **PLAY, THE NEW YORK TIMES SPORTS MAGAZINE**

Creative Director_**Janet Froelich** Art Director_**Jeff Glendenning** Designers_**Jeff Glendenning, Jared Ford, Dragos Lemnei** Photo Editor_**Kira Pollack** Photographers_**Arno Rafael Minkkinen, Massimo Vitale, Olaf Blecker, Platon** Publisher_**The New York Times** Issue_**March 2007** Category_**Photo: Entire Issue**

476 **PLAY, THE NEW YORK TIMES SPORTS MAGAZINE**

Creative Director_**Janet Froelich** Art Director_**Dirk Barnett** Designers_**Dirk Barnett, Dragos Lemnei, Julia Moburg** Photo Editor_**Kira Pollack** Photographer_**Simon Norfolk** Publisher_**The New York Times** Issue_**November 2007** Category_**Photo: Entire Issue**

477 **GOURMET**

Creative Director_**Richard Ferretti** Art Director_**Erika Oliveira** Designers_**Flavia Schepmans, Kevin DeMaria** Photo Editors_**Amy Koblenzer, Megan M. Re** Editor-In-Chief_**Ruth Reichl** Publisher_**Condé Nast Publications, Inc.** Issue_**October 2007** Category_**Photo: Entire Issue**

478

478

479

479

480

480

478 NEW YORK LOOK

Design Director_Chris Dixon Art Director_Randy Minor Director of Photography_Jody Quon Photo Editors_Lea Golis, Nadia Lachance Photographer_Paolo Pellegrin Editor-In-Chief_Adam Moss Publisher_New York Magazine Holdings, LLC Issue_Fall 2007 Category_Photo: Entire Issue

479 NEW YORK

Design Director_Chris Dixon Director of Photography_Jody Quon Photo Editors_Alexandra Pollack, Leana Alagia, Caroline Smith, Lea Golis, Lisa Corson Photographers_Andrew Eccles, Katja Rahlwes, Jenny Von Sommers, Rodney Smith, Tierney Gearon, Alex Majoli, Jake Chessum, Jason Kibbler, Christopher Griffith, Andres Sjödin, Graëtan Bernard Editor-In-Chief_Adam Moss Publisher_New York Magazine Holdings, LLC Issue_August 27, 2007 Category Photo: Entire Issue

480 GQ

Design Director_Fred Woodward Art Director_Anton Ioukhnovets Deputy Art Director_Thomas Alberty Designers_Drue Wagner, Michael Pangilinan, Chelsea Cardinal, Rob Hewitt, Delgis Canahuate, Eve Binder Director of Photography_Dora Somosi Senior Photo Editor_Krista Prestek Photo Editors Justin O'Neill, Jesse Lee, Jolanta Bielat, Roberto DeLuna, Halena Green Photographers_Michael Baumgarten, Cass Bird, Matthew Brookes, Jill Greenberg, Nathaniel Goldberg, Nadav Kander, Maciek Kobieleski, Brigitte Lacombe, Alexi Lubomirski, Mark Seliger, Ellen Von Unwerth, Ben Watts Creative Director_Jim Moore Editor-In-Chief_Jim Nelson Publisher Condé Nast Publications Inc. Issue December 2007 Category_Photo: Entire Issue

481

481

482

THE SETTLERS

482

483

483

481 GQ

Design Director_Fred Woodward Art Director_Anton Ioukhnovets Deputy Art Director_Thomas Alberty Designers_Michael Pangilinan, Drue Wagner, Rob Hewitt, Delgis Canahuate, Eve Binder, Chelsea Cardinal Director of Photography_Dora Somosi Senior Photo Editor_Krista Prestek Photo Editors_Justin O'Neill, Halena Green, Jesse Lee, Roberto DeLuna, Jolanta Bielat Photographers_Dan Forbes, David LaChapelle, Terry Richardson, Martin Schoeller, Mark Seliger, Peggy Sirota, Carter Smith Creative Director_Jim Moore Editor-In-Chief_Jim Nelson Publisher_Condé Nast Publications Inc. Issue_April 2007 Category_Photo: Entire Issue

482 THE FADER

Creative Director_Phil Bicker Designers_Si Scott, Marian Bantjes Photographers_Aaron Huey, Jim Marshall, Anna Bauer, Jeremy Sutton-Hibbert, Andrew Dosunmu Issue_May/June 2007 Category_Photo: Entire Issue

483 TIME

Art Director_Arthur Hochstein Deputy Art Directors_D.W. Pine, Cynthia A. Hoffman Director of Photography_MaryAnne Golon Picture Editor_Alice Gabriner Photographers_Platon, Christopher Morris – VII, Yuri Kozyrev – NOOR, Dan Winters, Thomas Dworzak – Magnum, Callie Shell – Aurora, Brooks Kraft – Corbis, Diana Walker – Getty, Anthony Suau, Hector Emanuel Publisher_Time Inc. Issue_December 31, 2007 Category_Photo: Entire Issue

THE OTHER SIDE OF CARBON TRADING

PLANTING TREES IN UGANDA TO OFFSET GREENHOUSE-GAS EMISSIONS IN EUROPE SEEMED LIKE A GOOD IDEA—UNTIL FARMERS WERE EVICTED FROM THEIR LAND TO MAKE ROOM FOR A FOREST.

✲ BY STEPHAN FARIS ✲ PHOTOGRAPHS BY FRANCESCO ZIZOLA

FACE-OFF Farmers stand in a cornfield on contested land in Uganda's Mount Elgon National Park.

FORTUNE • 67

484

UGANDA ✲ CARBON TRADING

INTO THE WOODS A stand of trees near Mount Elgon. Inset: Park warden Masereka with seized lumber.

has since invested $4 million in the project, enough to pay for 3.4 million trees, about a third of what was initially planned. In 2002 the foundation turned to selling carbon credits as a way to fund its projects.

But resentment over the evictions festered. "They were respecting animals rather than human beings," says Yutuko Kimareni, who chairs the Namisindwa Landowners Association, a group of 433 families seeking recognition of their claims. It wasn't until national elections last year resulted in political promises to redraw the park borders that things heated up. That's when Wandeka and his former neighbors got their injunction. And that's when the machetes started flying.

More than half-a-million trees that the Face Foundation had planted were chopped down, and the conflict between the evicted farmers and the paramilitary Ugandan Wildlife Authority got ugly. Wandeka and other farmers allege beatings and torture. In March a ranger was arrested after shooting a man who had chopped at his gun and his forearm with a machete. Johnson Masereka, the park's chief warden, keeps a photograph of another ranger with hack marks on the back of his head. "That's what we face as conservationists," he says. In addition to angry farmers, his rangers fend off timber poachers inside the park, most of them locals trying to earn enough to survive. "The fact is, the population is growing, but the land we have is not elastic."

Masereka maintains that his predecessors acted properly in evicting the farmers, but he acknowledges that more could

72 • FORTUNE September 3, 2007

September 3, 2007 FORTUNE • 73

484

484 FORTUNE

Art Director_Robert Perino Designer_Maria Keehan Director of Photography_Greg Pond Photo Editor_Lauren Winfield Photographer_Francesco Zizola Publisher_Time Inc. Issue_September 3, 2007 Category_Photo: Feature: Story

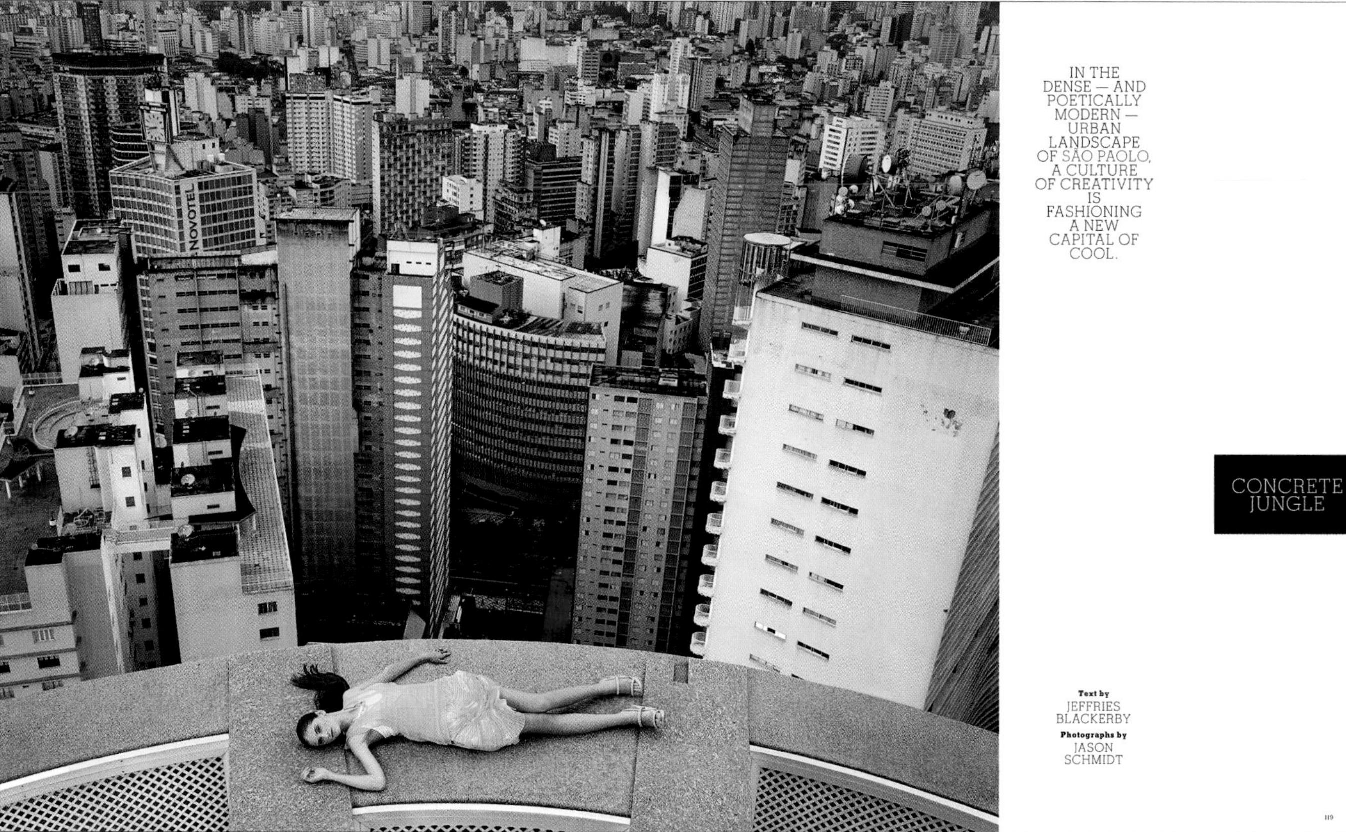
IN THE DENSE — AND POETICALLY MODERN — URBAN LANDSCAPE OF SÃO PAOLO, A CULTURE OF CREATIVITY IS FASHIONING A NEW CAPITAL OF COOL.
CONCRETE JUNGLE
Text by JEFFRIES BLACKERBY
Photographs by JASON SCHMIDT
119

485

of Havaianas flip-flops. Now 11 years old, São Paulo Fashion Week has gone from a novelty to a viable showcase of talent and trends. "The city is really just discovering fashion. It's becoming mainstream," says Cacá Ribeiro, who co-owns the high-end swimwear label Neon and runs a production company that stages fashion shows. (He also recently opened the nightclub Royal downtown. Many Paulistanos seem to have multi-hyphenate careers.) Still, some of Brazilian fashion's most important names — Glória Coelho and Reinaldo Lourenço, both current darlings of Vogue Brasil — are largely unfamiliar outside their country. But international success isn't necessarily the goal for emerging talent; there are plenty of stylish folks right at home. Ribeiro, for his part, says that the success of Neon, now sold in about 60 stores around Brazil, is due solely to the Brazilian market: "Everyone's talking about fashion. You can feel the vibrations of new stuff happening."

The cosmos of style has many orbits, and few are as interconnected as those in São Paulo. In a country where 2.4 percent of the population is wealthy, according to a study from the State University of Campinas, it's no surprise the people with money all seem to know each other. (Paulistanos keep their circles tight for security reasons too; kidnappings and carjackings are a fact of life.) Yet there is a collaborative spirit here that transcends the ordinary social whirl. For example, at a new cultural center called Escola São Paulo, the director Isabella Prata hosts lectures and offers courses to the public ranging from toy design to film directing. In the lounge and garden, students loll about in low-slung chairs; at Escola events, São Paulo's most influential tastemakers — such as the designer Cris Barros, the photographer Bob Wolfenson and the architect Isay Weinfeld — mingle as if they were at a cookout on someone's roof.

Eduardo Brandão, the co-director of Galeria Vermelho, which serves as a similar kind of idea lab for artists of every stripe, suggests that such a collegiate environment might disintegrate in a city with more resources, like New York. Not that São Paulo isn't a place of accomplishment — Vermelho sold almost everything it brought this year to Art Basel Miami, mostly to American collectors. All this bonhomie among the creative class is simply a product of its freshness and enthusiasm.

"In New York," says Jatobá, who lived in Manhattan from 1996 to 2000, "people sniff each other first. Here, we don't sniff. We just circulate. Maybe it's our tropical nature." Or it might be that the circle of tastemakers is small enough that everyone is a friend. (When you spot a Campana brothers' chair in someone's apartment, chances are the owner will tell you the designers are "supernice guys.") In any case, that circle seems to be ever-expanding. "This city demands people to be cultural," Jatobá says, "to be interested in design, film, art, architecture." And in São Paulo, it's not all been done before. ■

Modern romance On the Santa Ifigênia bridge. Marc Jacobs dress, $2,800, and shoes. At Marc Jacobs, Boston.

122

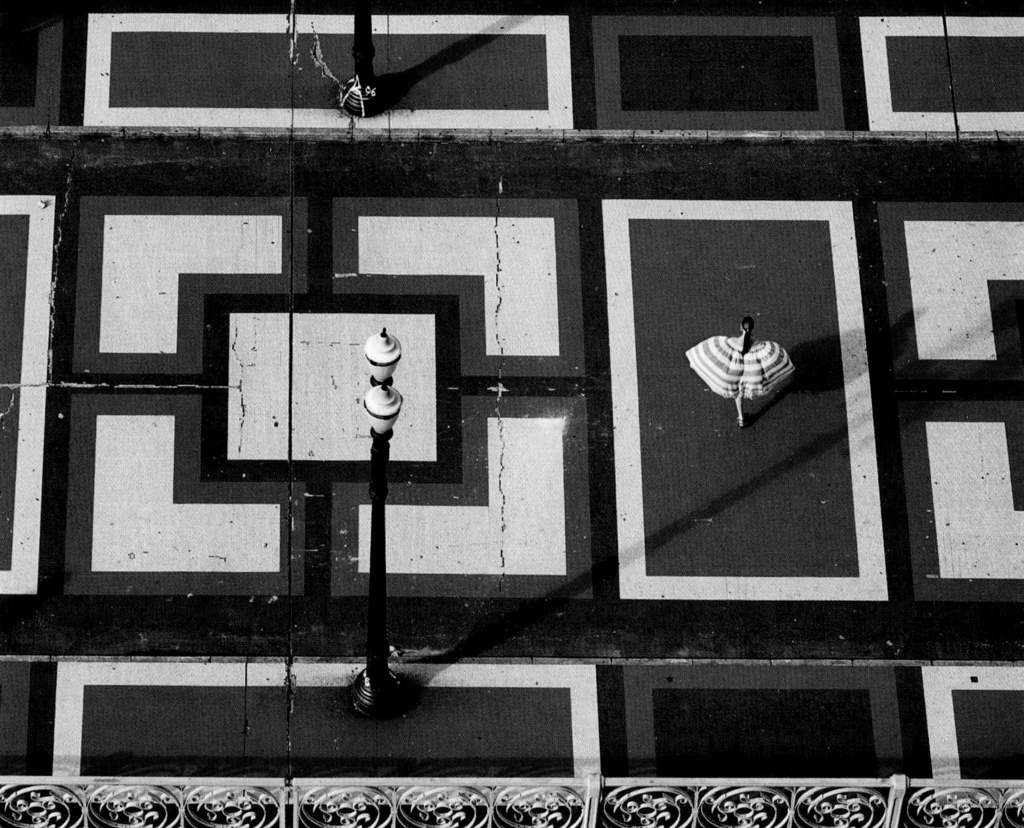

485

485 T, THE NEW YORK TIMES STYLE MAGAZINE

Creative Director_Janet Froelich Senior Art Director_David Sebbah Art Director_Christopher Martinez Designer_Janet Froelich
Photo Editor_Judith Puckett-Rinella Photographer_Jason Schmidt Fashion Editor_Anne Christensen Editor-In-Chief_Stefano Tonchi
Publisher_The New York Times Issue_March 25, 2007 Category Photo: Feature: Story

486

486

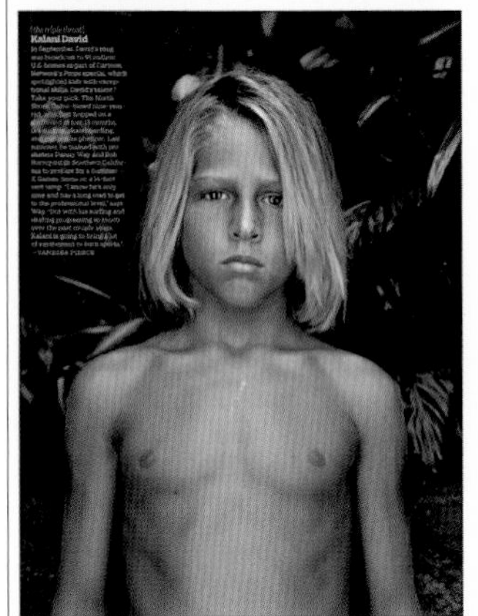

487

487

488

488

486 NEW YORK

Design Director_Chris Dixon Designer_Randy Minor
Director of Photography_Jody Quon Photographer_Tierney Gearon
Editor-In-Chief_Adam Moss Publisher_New York Magazine Holdings, LLC Issue_February 26, 2007 Category_Photo: Feature: Story

487 OUTSIDE

Creative Director_Hannah McCaughey
Art Directors_Kate Iltis, John McCauley Designer_Mace Fleeger
Director of Photography_Lesley Meyer Photo Editors_Amy Feitelberg, Amber Terranova Photographer_Robert Maxwell Publisher_Mariah Media, Inc. Issue_October 2007 Category_Photo: Feature: Story

488 NEWSWEEK

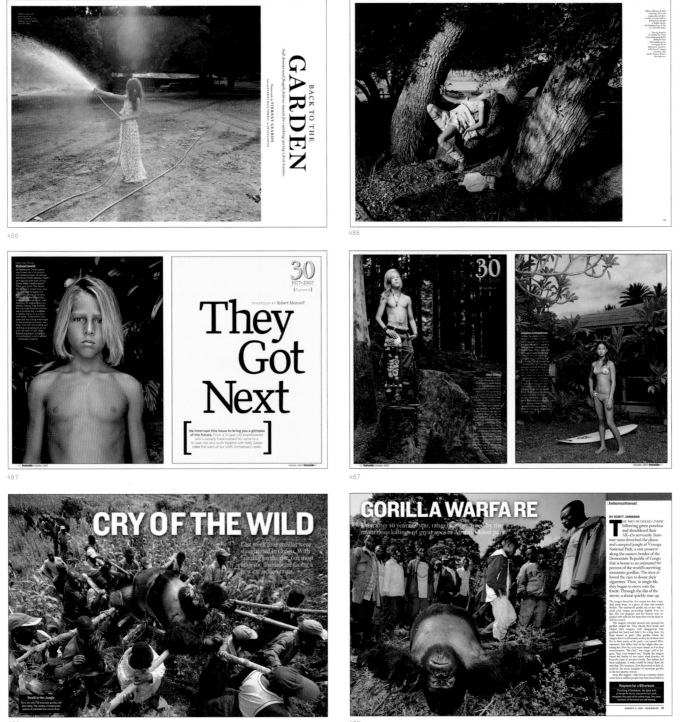

Creative Director_Amid Capeci Art Director_Dan Revitte
Director of Photography_Simon Barnett
Photo Editors_Simon Barnett, James Wellford
Photographer_Brent Stirton – Reportage by Getty Images for Newsweek
Publisher_The Washington Post Co. Issue_August 6, 2007
Category_Photo: Feature: Story

CHILL SEEKERS

Here's to some global cooling so we get a chance to wear winter's hot new coats

PRESERVE the WORLD NOW

489

489

490

490

491

491

489 MARIE CLAIRE

Creative Director_Micael Picón Designer_Shannon Casey
Director of Photography_Kristen Schaefer
Photographer_Mel Karch Fashion Editor_Tracy Taylor
Publisher_The Hearst Corporation-Magazines Div.
Issue_October 2007 Category_Photo: Feature: Story

490 GQ

Design Director_Fred Woodward Designer_Thomas Alberty
Director of Photography_Dora Somosi Photographer_Richard Burbridge
Editor-In-Chief_Jim Nelson Publisher_Condé Nast Publications Inc.
Issue_October 2007 Category_Photo: Feature: Story

491 KEY, THE NEW YORK TIMES REAL ESTATE MAGAZINE

Creative Director_Janet Froelich Art Directors_Dirk Barnett, Arem Duplessis Director of Photography_Kathy Ryan
Photo Editor_Joanna Milter Photographer_Alejandra Laviada
Editor-In-Chief_Gerry Marzorati Publisher_The New York Times
Issue_Fall 2007 Category_Photo: Feature: Story

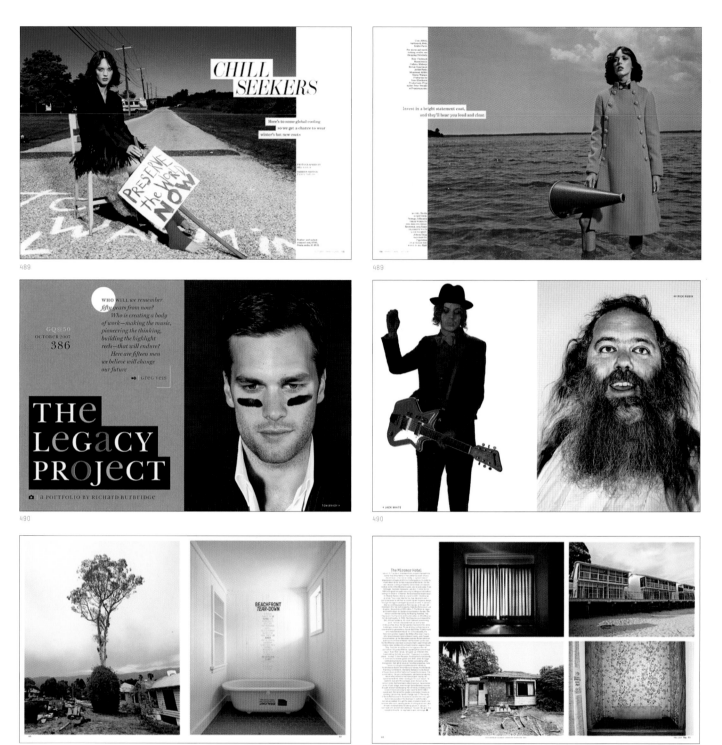

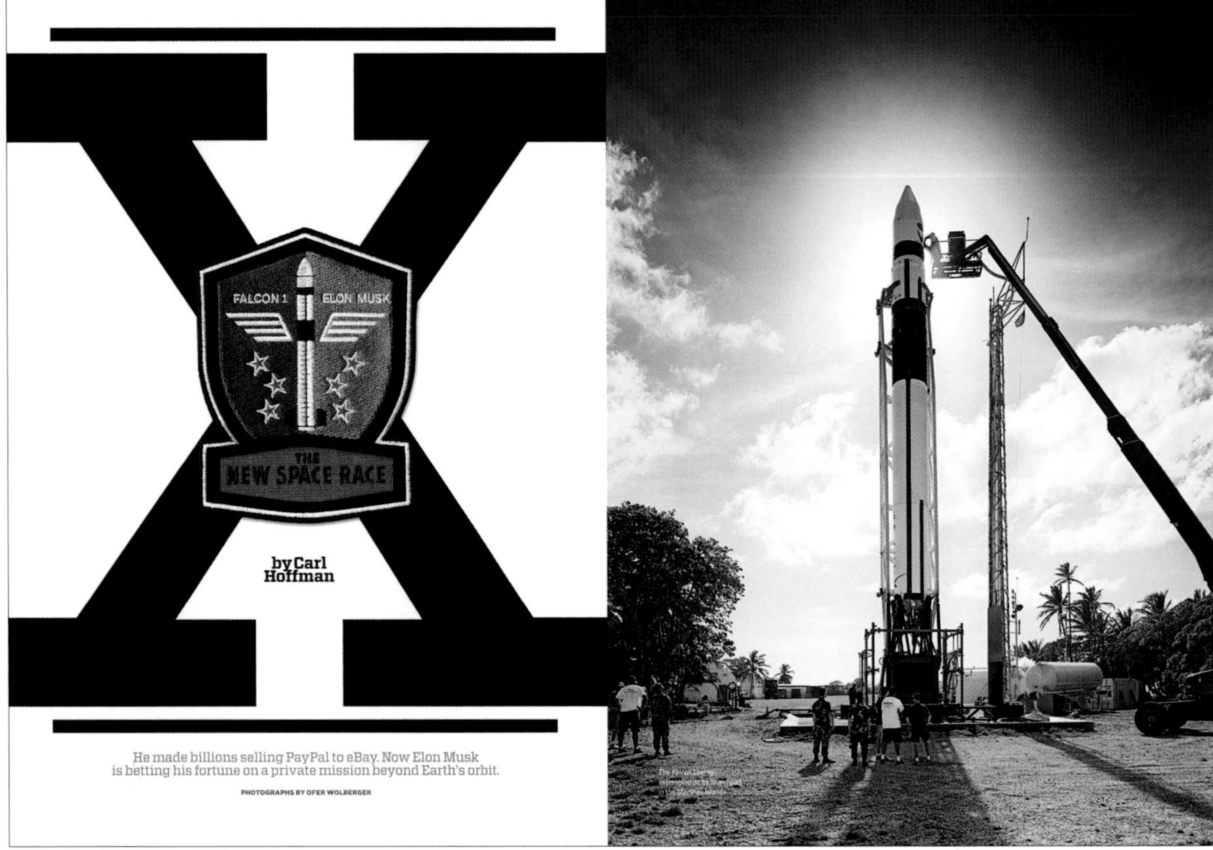

X

by Carl Hoffman

He made billions selling PayPal to eBay. Now Elon Musk is betting his fortune on a private mission beyond Earth's orbit.

PHOTOGRAPHS BY OFER WOLBERGER

492

Figuring

out what went wrong turned out to be easy. SpaceX's computers had gathered a vast amount of data, and multiple video cameras had recorded the launch from every angle. Buzza and Mueller ran the video during the flight back to California and saw the problem right away. Immediately after liftoff, a small fire had broken out on the first-stage engine—they could see it clearly on the video—and it had grown until the engine simply shut down.

They spread printouts of *Falcon*'s telemetry out on the floor of the plane and pored over them on their hands and knees. For good measure, they also combed data from the rocket's static fire, a test during which the countdown proceeds to engine firing for a brief moment, without launch. "Out of 800 data points, there was one blip," Buzza says. "One line went up in the static fire, and that same line on the launch was flat. And we knew exactly what it was. Exactly."

It was a fuel leak. The night before launch, technicians had unscrewed an aluminum nut from the fuel pump to check how secure it was and then torqued it back down. About seven minutes before liftoff, that nut cracked, having corroded in the salty, humid air.

To be sure—and to placate critics—Musk convened his own accident investigation board, headed by Simon Pete Worden, director of the NASA Ames Research Center. The investigation lasted seven months, time spent in meetings and in the lab, endlessly testing various components. In the end, Worden confirmed what Buzza and Mueller had already supposed. The board said that "plumbing lower B-nut failing by corrosion cracking is the single most plausible leak scenario."

The destruction of *Falcon 1*, Musk admitted later, was "a huge blow." But he'd known it was a possibility all along, a potential outcome of the approach he takes to rockets. The space industry was built by huge aerospace companies on government contracts—thousands of people working with hundreds of millions of dollars. Market forces didn't apply. Rockets were launched once and thrown away, high-performance miracles of engineering—race cars. Musk's basic idea was to use his own prodigious fortune to build not touchy Formula One cars

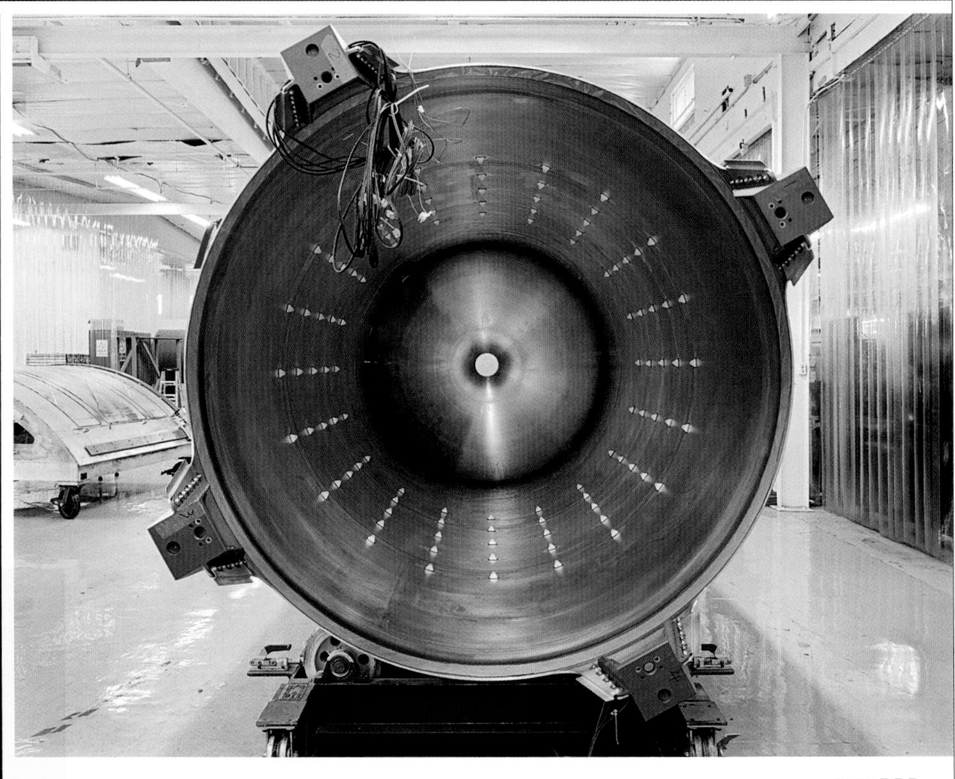

A first-stage *Falcon 1* fuel tank awaits assembly.

JUNE 2007

492

492 WIRED
Creative Director_Scott Dadich Art Director_Maili Holiman Photo Editor_Zana Woods Photographer_Olef Wolberger
Publisher_Condé Nast Publications, Inc. Issue_June 2007 Category_Photo: Feature: Story

'It's a mystical magical animal,' says Chang of the pig. 'It just tastes good.'

493

Chang's soulful cooking challenges the notion that bold flavors and innovation can only come with a hefty price tag.
APPLE SOJU COCKTAILS
PICKLED VEGETABLES
PORK-BELLY BUNS
KING OYSTER MUSHROOMS WITH PISTACHIO PURÉE
ROASTED BRUSSELS SPROUTS
APPLE AND SMOKED-BACON SALAD WITH LYCHEES AND CHILI NUTS
CLAY-POT MISO CHICKEN
STEAMED ASIAN WHITE RICE
SLICED FUYU PERSIMMONS

493

493 GOURMET

Creative Director_**Richard Ferretti** Art Director_**Erika Oliveira** Designer_**Erika Oliveira** Photo Editor_**Amy Koblenzer** Photographer_**Marcus Nilsson** Editor-In-Chief_**Ruth Reichl** Publisher_**Condé Nast Publications, Inc.** Issue_**October 2007** Category_**Photo: Feature: Story**

494 494

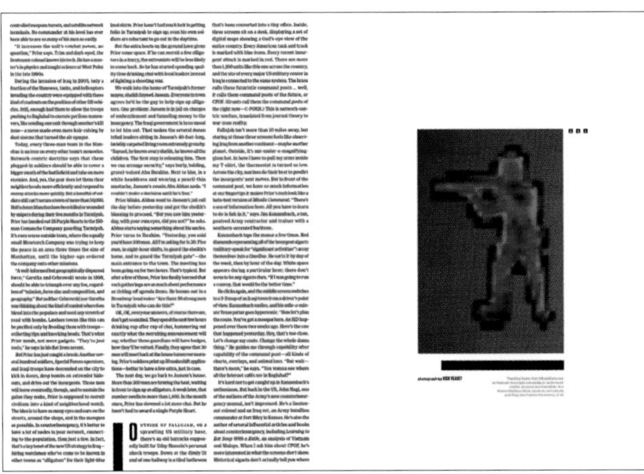

495 495

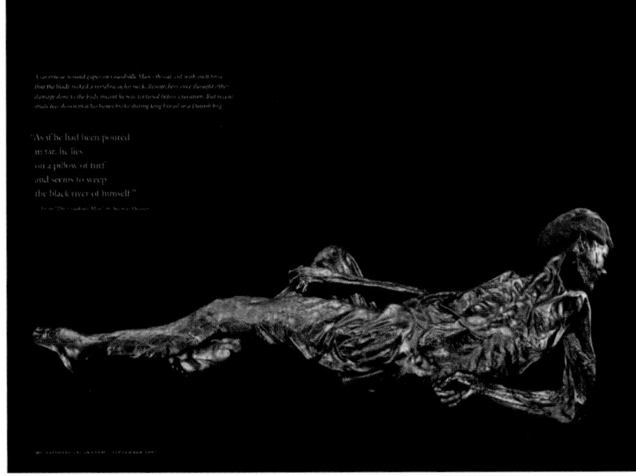

496 496

494 BUST MAGAZINE

Creative Director_Laurie Henzel Designer_Tara Marks
Photographer_Danielle St. Laurent Publisher_Bust Inc.
Issue_October/November 2007 Category_Photo: Feature: Story

495 WIRED

Creative Director_Scott Dadich Design Director_Wyatt Mitchell
Designers_Scott Dadich, Carl DeTorres Photo Editor_Zana Woods
Photographers_Todd Hido, Tom Schierlitz, Nick Veasey, Johan Spanner
Publisher_Condé Nast Publications, Inc. Issue_December 2007
Category_Photo: Feature: Story

496 NATIONAL GEOGRAPHIC

Design Director_David Whitmore Designer_David Whitmore
Director of Photography_David Griffin Photo Editor_Susan Welchman
Photographer_Robert Clark Publisher_National Geographic Society
Issue_September 2007 Category_Photo: Feature: Story

497

497

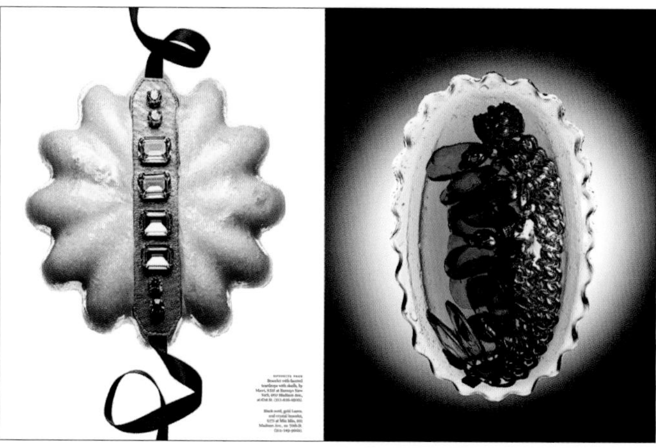

498

498

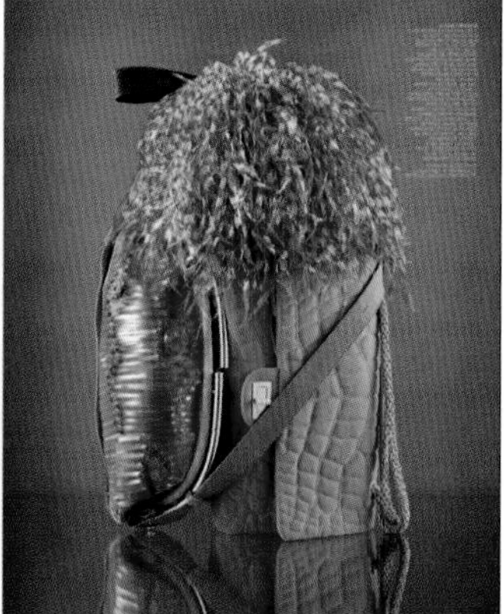

499

499

497 **MEN'S HEALTH**

Design Director_George Karabotsos Art Director_John Dixon Designer_John Dixon Director of Photography_Laurie Kratochvil Photographer_Art Streiber Publisher_Rodale Inc. Issue_March 2007 Category_Photo: Feature: Story

498 **NEW YORK**

Design Director_Chris Dixon Designer_Randy Minor Director of Photography_Jody Quon Photographer_Mitchell Feinberg Editor-In-Chief_Adam Moss Publisher_New York Magazine Holdings, LLC Issue_February 26, 2007 Category_Photo: Feature: Story

499 **T, THE NEW YORK TIMES STYLE MAGAZINE**

Creative Director_Janet Froelich Senior Art Director_David Sebbah Art Director_Christopher Martinez Designer_Christopher Martinez Photo Editor_Scott Hall Photographer_Coppi Barbieri Fashion Editor_Karla M. Martinez Editor-In-Chief_Stefano Tonchi Publisher_The New York Times Issue_August 26, 2007 Category_Photo: Feature: Story

: SECTION
PHOTOGRAPHY

: AWARD
MERIT

: CATEGORY
FEATURE: STORY

500

500

501

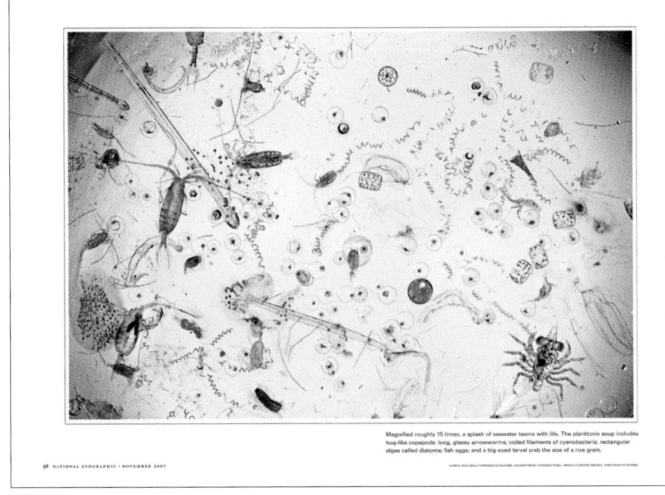

501

502

502

500 DWELL

Design Director_**Kyle Blue** Designers_**Brendan Callahan, Suzanne Lagasa, Emily CM Anderson** Director of Photography_**Kate Stone Foss** Photo Editors_**Andrea Lawson, Alexis Tjian** Photographer_**Sze Tsung Leong** Production_**Kathryn Hansen** Publisher_**Dwell LLC** Issue_**April 2007** Category_**Photo: Feature: Story**

501 NATIONAL GEOGRAPHIC

Design Director_**David Whitmore** Designer_**David Whitmore** Director of Photography_**David Griffin** Photo Editor_**Kathy Moran** Photographer_**David Liitschwager** Publisher_**National Geographic Society** Issue_**November 2007** Category_**Photo: Feature: Story**

502 NEW YORK

Design Director_**Chris Dixon** Art Director_**Randy Minor** Director of Photography_**Jody Quon** Photo Editor_**Leana Alagia** Photographer_**James Welling** Editor-In-Chief_**Adam Moss** Publisher_**New York Magazine Holdings, LLC** Issue_**May 21, 2007** Category_**Photo: Feature: Story**

503 THE NEW YORK TIMES MAGAZINE

Creative Director_**Janet Froelich** Art Director_**Arem Duplessis** Designer_**Nancy Harris Rouemy** Photographer_**Sebastian Kim** Fashion Editors_**Andreas Kokkino, Bifen Xu** Editor-In-Chief_**Gerry Marzorati** Publisher_**The New York Times** Issue_**August 26, 2007** Category_**Photo: Feature: Story**

8.26.07 Style

come as you are

We interrupt our regular coverage of the fall collections with this man- (and woman-) on-the-street report. Coming to you live from the Siren Music Festival at Coney Island, the TV on the Radio concert at the McCarren Park Pool in Williamsburg and P.S.1's annual summer Warm Up in Long Island City, where the personal style quotient was so off the charts that it practically raises the question: Who needs fashion?

Photographs by Sebastian Kim

FASHION EDITORS: ANDREAS KOKKINO AND BIFEN XU

40

503

summer in the city: 2007

43

503

504

504

505

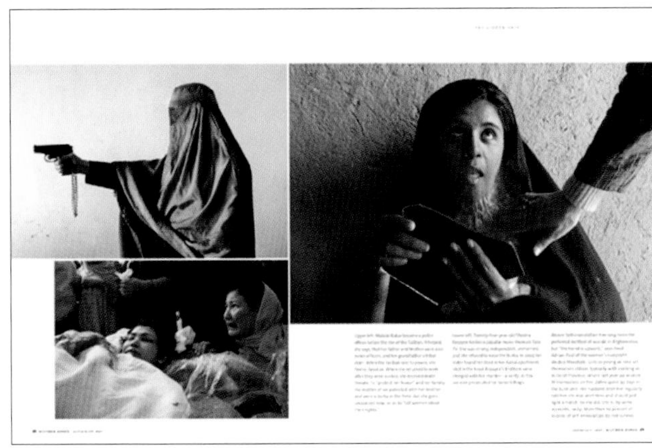

505

506

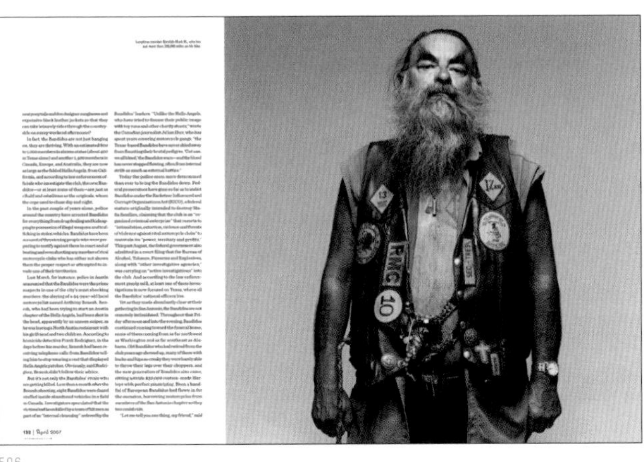

506

504 TREAD

Creative Director_Nancy Campbell
Art Director_Trevett McCandliss
Designer_Trevett McCandliss
Photographer_Jason Hindley
Issue_July 2007
Category_Photo: Feature: Story

505 MOTHER JONES

Creative Director_Susan Scandrett
Art Director_Tim J. Luddy
Designer_Susan Scandrett
Director of Photography_Sarah Kehoe
Photo Editor_Sarah Cross
Photographer_Lana Slezic
Publisher_Foundation for National Progress
Issue_July/August 2007
Category_Photo: Feature: Story

506 TEXAS MONTHLY

Art Director_T.J. Tucker
Designers_Andi Beierman, Rachel Wyatt
Photo Editor_Leslie Baldwin
Photographer_Wyatt McSpadden
Publisher_Emmis Communications Corp.
Issue_April 2007
Category_Photo: Feature: Story

A Complicated Affair

7:38PM Flame of Desire

8:42PM At First Bite

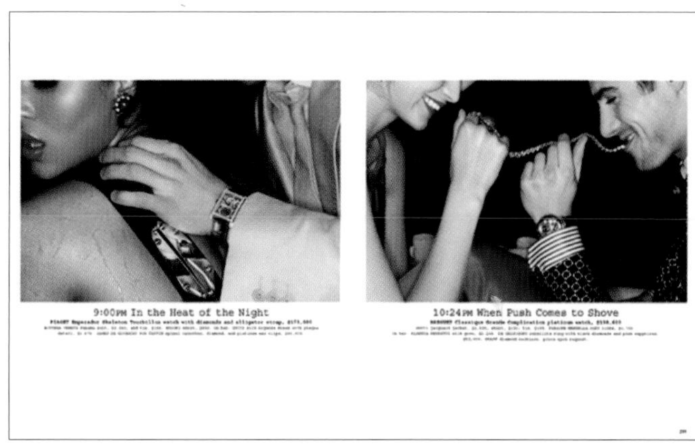
9:00PM In the Heat of the Night

10:24PM When Push Comes to Shove

507

507

Prime Time

Sure, enlightenment comes with age...but so do lines and wrinkles. Six experts offer their strategies and advice on what to ingest, inject, slather on, and work off so you remain forever young.

YOUNG LOVE

PHOTOGRAPHED BY MICHAEL THOMPSON

508

508

JUST BENEATH THE SURFACE

509

509

507 DEPARTURES

Creative Director_Bernard Scharf
Art Director_Adam Bookbinder
Associate Art Director_Lou Corredor
Director of Photography_Jennifer Laski
Photo Editors_Jennifer Geaney, Brandon Perlman
Photographer_Jessica Craig-Martin
Publisher_American Express Publishing Co.
Issue_March/April 2007
Category_Photo: Feature: Story

508 ALLURE

Creative Director_Paul Cavaco
Design Director_Deanna Filippo
Photographer_Michael Thompson
Photo Director_Nadine McCarthy
Editor-In-Chief_Linda Wells
Publisher_Condé Nast Publications Inc.
Issue_April 2007
Category_Photo: Feature: Story

509 THE NEW YORK TIMES MAGAZINE

Creative Director_Janet Froelich
Art Director_Arem Duplessis
Designer_Arem Duplessis
Director of Photography_Kathy Ryan
Photo Editor_Kira Pollack
Photographer_Harf Zimmerman
Editor-In-Chief_Gerry Marzorati
Publisher_The New York Times
Issue_July 8, 2007
Category_Photo: Feature: Story

PHOTOGRAPHS BY Seamus Murphy
A not-always-mythic journey to Shambhala, over sky-high mountains and across vicious deserts, requiring boldness of heart, purity of vision, the recitation of 99 million mantras, and $45 worth of Snickers bars, party balloons, Diamox, and dehydrated soup. By Patrick Symmes
30
1977-2007
[Myths]
The Kingdom of the Lotus
Praying before the Potala, the Dalai Lama's former palace, in Lhasa, Tibet
148 Outside October 2007
October 2007 Outside 149

510

510

510 OUTSIDE

Creative Director_**Hannah McCaughey** Art Directors_**Kate Iltis, John McCauley** Designer_**Mace Fleeger** Director of Photography_**Lesley Meyer** Photo Editors_**Amy Feitelberg, Amber Terranova** Photographer_**Seamus Murphy** Publisher_**Mariah Media, Inc.** Issue_**October 2007** Category_**Photo: Feature: Story**

DANGEROUS WHEN INTERESTED SERENA WILLIAMS IS THE MOST EXCITING PLAYER IN WOMEN'S TENNIS. FOR SOME, THAT'S STILL NOT ENOUGH.

BY SUSAN DOMINUS

PHOTOGRAPHS BY FINLAY MacKAY

PLAY SEPTEMBER 2007

48

511

my life." She no longer sounded like the hard-driving champion convinced she could have taken Wimbledon; she sounded like any other woman struggling with the tedium of trying to stay fit. She watched, perhaps stricken by a small bout of guilt, as a small blond woman with a ponytail jogged down Bedford Avenue. "I need to do what this girl is doing," Williams said without any enthusiasm.

If Serena Williams has had phases of her life when she couldn't face another wind sprint, that would be understandable. When she started playing tennis, at 3 or 4 years old, she probably didn't realize she was signing on for a life of service to the game, as if agreeing at that tender age to a contract with a community that would expect her to play her best for as long as she was physically able.

The Williams family's tennis history, which started in the 1980s, already has the feel of hoary lore: how Richard Williams decided, after watching one woman professional earn more than $40,000 for four days of work, that he and his wife would have two daughters they would train to be tennis stars; how he taught Serena and Venus himself, using videos and books to help guide him. Richard, the son of a sharecropper in Shreveport, La., says he raised his kids as if they were living in the '50s, a bastion of old-fashioned values in the middle of gang-infested Compton, a city south of Los Angeles. After school, Isha, Yetunde and Lyndrea would follow their mother, Oracene, their stepfather and their two younger half-sisters to the court, where they all fed and picked up balls for the girls until it was time to go home. "It wasn't until I got to college that I realized that our lives" — the 10 p.m. mandatory bedtime till age 18, the absence of friends, the family-wide devotion to the two young girls' tennis game — "weren't what other people considered normal," says Isha Price, the oldest surviving sister and an attorney who helps handle some of Venus's and Serena's business affairs. As they got older, their father's tough love materialized on signs he posted around the practice courts. "Venus, when *you* fail, you fail alone," one read.

Discouraged from playing with the other kids in the neighborhood, the five sisters were inseparable. They shared a single room with four beds, meaning Serena bunked with a different sister every night. Serena always particularly admired Venus, only 15 months her senior. She "looked up to Venus so much she *was* Venus," Price says. The family would make Serena order first at restaurants so she wouldn't simply default to her sister's choice; no matter what color she claimed as her favorite, she often chose to wear green, Venus's favorite. Her desire to catch up to Venus in tennis, Serena said at the Australian Open, shaped an ongoing desire to upend expectations — to surprise those who doubted her talents. "I love doubters," she said. "Ever since I was young, even when I came on tour, it was Venus, Venus, Venus, Venus. Oh, and the little sister. My whole goal in life was just to prove people wrong."

Eventually, the little sister prevailed. Today she is considered the stronger player; she heads into the month of the Open ranked No. 8, compared with Venus's rank of 16, despite the victory at Wimbledon.

Richard Williams, now divorced *Continued on page 80*

COURT GESTURE
Serena Williams photographed by Finlay MacKay at the Beverly Hills Country Club on July 12, 2007.

52

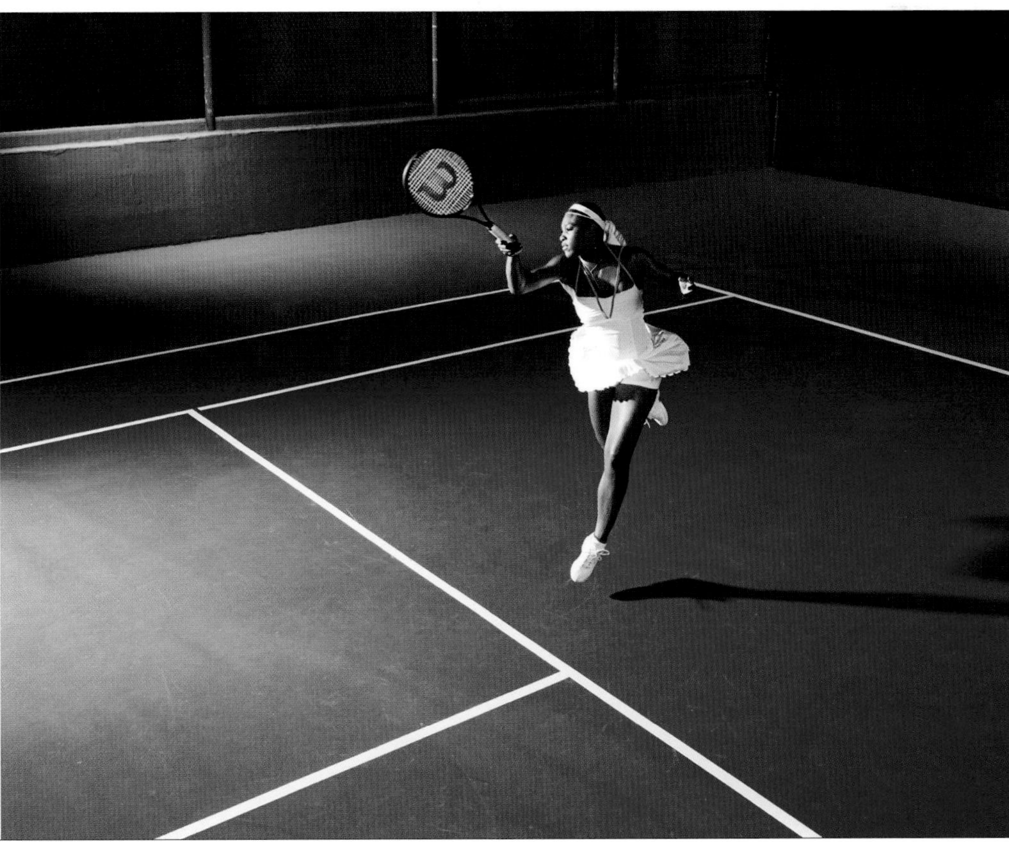

511

511 PLAY, THE NEW YORK TIMES SPORTS MAGAZINE

Creative Director_ Janet Froelich Art Director_ Dirk Barnett Designer_ Dirk Barnett Photo Editor_ Kira Pollack Photographer_ Finlay MacKay Publisher_ The New York Times Issue_ September 2007 Category_ Photo: Feature: Story

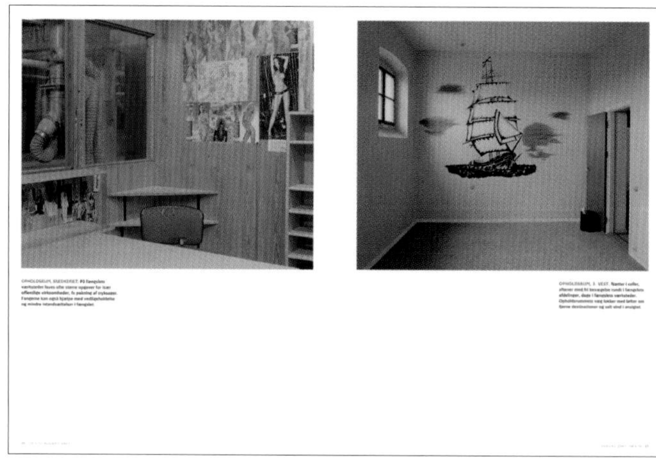

512

512

513

513

514

514

514

SHAWN JOHNSON

512 UD&SE

Design Director_Torsten Hogh Rasmussen
Photographer_Kristian Saderup
Publisher_DSB
Issue_August 2007
Category_Photo: Feature: Story

513 THE NEW YORK TIMES MAGAZINE

Creative Director_Janet Froelich
Art Director_Arem Duplessis
Designer _Gail Bichler
Director of Photography_Kathy Ryan
Photo Editor_Joanna Milter
Photographer_Sasha Bezzubov
Editor-In-Chief_Gerry Marzorati
Publisher_The New York Times
Issue_August 26, 2007
Category_Photo: Feature: Story

514 ESPN THE MAGAZINE

Creative Director_Siung Tjia
Designer_Lou Vega
Director of Photography_Catriona NiAolain
Photo Editor_Julie Claire
Editor-In-Chief_Gary Belsky
Publisher ESPN, Inc.
Issue_December 12, 2007
Category_Photo: Feature: Story

515

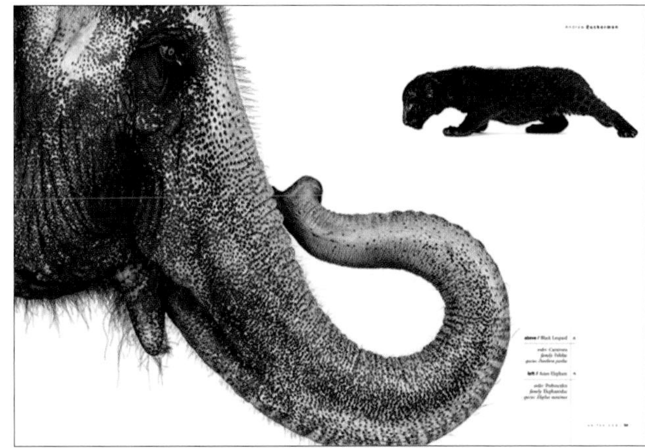

515

516

516

~INLAND~
EMPIRE
Emerging from the long shadow of Soviet Communism, MONGOLIA—with its stark, ravishing landscapes and resurgent Buddhist traditions—is looking west for its future, By PANKAJ MISHRA
Photographed by FRÉDÉRIC LAGRANGE

517

517

515 HEMISPHERES

Design Director_Jaimey Easler
Art Director_Jennifer Swafford
Designer_Jody Mustain
Photographer_Andrew Zuckerman
Senior Art Director_Jody Mustain
Publisher_Pace Communications
Client_United Airlines
Issue_September 2007
Category_Photo: Feature: Story

516 TIME

Art Director_Arthur Hochstein
Associate Art Director_Janet Michaud
Director of Photography_MaryAnne Golon
Picture Editor_Alice Gabriner
Deputy Picture Editor_Dietmar Liz-Lepiorz
Photographers_Yuri Kozyrev – NOOR, Callie Shell – Aurora, Christopher Morris – VII, Brooks Kraft – Corbis, Diana Walker – Getty, Anthony Suau, Hector Emanuel
Publisher_Time Inc. Issue_December 31, 2007
Category_Photo: Feature: Story

517 TRAVEL + LEISURE

Creative Director_Nora Sheehan
Design Director_Katharine Van Itallie
Director of Photography_Katie Dunn
Photo Editor_Wendy Ball
Photographer_Frédéric Lagrange
Publisher_American Express Publishing Co.
Issue_February 2007
Category_Photo: Feature: Story

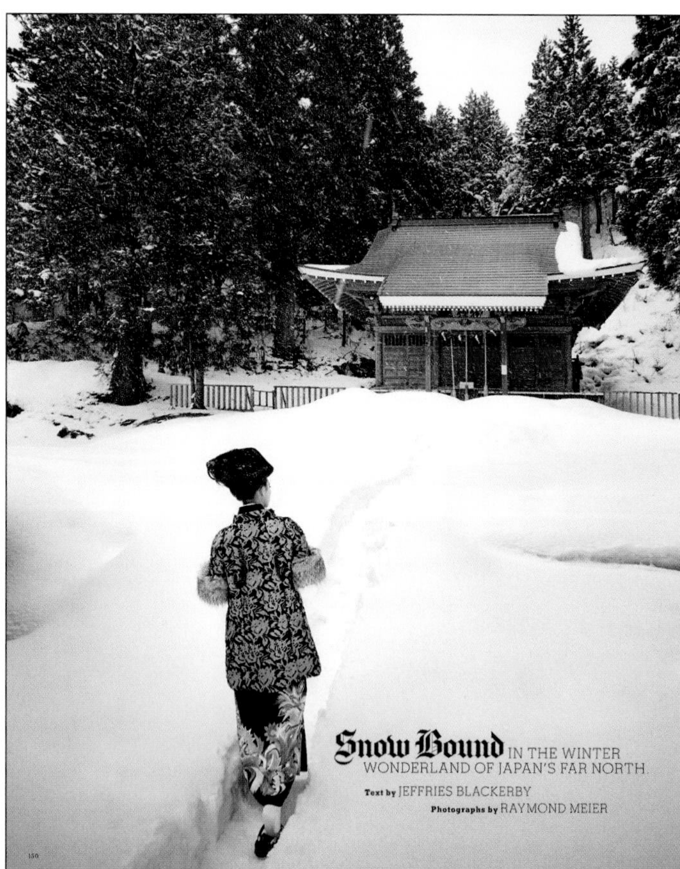
Snow Bound IN THE WINTER WONDERLAND OF JAPAN'S FAR NORTH
Text by JEFFRIES BLACKERBY
Photographs by RAYMOND MEIER
158

ICE QUEEN THE MODEL ANNE WATANABE AT TSURUNOYU ONSEN, ONE OF JAPAN'S MOST HISTORIC HOT-SPRING INNS, IN AKITA PREFECTURE. PROENZA SCHOULER COAT WITH FUR TRIM, $3,425, AT BERGDORF GOODMAN. GIANFRANCO FERRE BELT. WOLFORD HOSIERY. GIAMBATTISTA VALLI SHOES. TRADITIONAL PAPER UMBRELLA FROM THE ONSEN. OPPOSITE: AT GOZANOISHI SHRINE, ON THE NORTH SHORE OF LAKE TAZAWA, JAPAN'S DEEPEST. CHRISTIAN LACROIX WOOL COAT WITH GOLD LAMÉ SCROLLS AND FUR MUFFS, $8,087, AT CHRISTIAN LACROIX, 36 EAST 57TH STREET. ALL VINTAGE CLOTHING THROUGHOUT THESE PAGES FROM TANSU-YA IN TOKYO.
FASHION EDITOR: TIINA LAAKKONEN.

518

BODY BEAUTIFUL IN TSURUNOYU
ONSEN'S MAIN BATHING POOL
GUESTS SOAK FOR HOURS
THE HOT (AND SUPPOSEDLY
BENEFICIAL) WATERS.
IN A ROOM AT THE ONSEN.
JOHN GALLIANO SILK-AND-FOX
COAT, MADE TO ORDER. GO
TO WWW.JOHNGALLIANO.COM.

518

519 519

520 520

521 521

518 T, THE NEW YORK TIMES STYLE MAGAZINE

Creative Director_**Janet Froelich** Senior Art Director_**David Sebbah**
Art Director_**Christopher Martinez** Designer_**Christopher Martinez**
Photo Editor_**Judith Puckett-Rinella** Photographer_**Raymond Meier**
Fashion Editor_**Tina Laakkonen** Editor-In-Chief_**Stefano Tonchi**
Publisher_**The New York Times** Issue_**November 18, 2007**
Category_**Photo: Feature: Story**

519 THE NEW YORK TIMES MAGAZINE

Creative Director_**Janet Froelich** Art Director_**Arem Duplessis**
Designer_**Leo Jung** Director of Photography_**Kathy Ryan**
Photo Editor_**Luise Stauss** Photographer_**Katy Grannan**
Editor-In-Chief_**Gerry Marzorati** Publisher_**The New York Times**
Issue_**March 18, 2007** Category_**Photo: Feature: Story**

520 O, THE OPRAH MAGAZINE

Design Director_**Carla Frank** Designer_**Burgan Shealy**
Director of Photography_**Jennifer Crandall**
Photographer_**Geof Kern** Editor-In-Chief_**Amy Gross**
Publisher_**The Hearst Corporation- Magazines Div.**
Issue_**August 2007** Category_**Photo: Feature: Story**

521 T, THE NEW YORK TIMES STYLE MAGAZINE

Creative Director_**Janet Froelich** Senior Art Director_**David Sebbah**
Art Director_**Christopher Martinez** Designer_**Christopher Martinez**
Photo Editor_**Judith Puckett-Rinella** Photographer_**Raymond Meier**
Fashion Editor_**Tina Laakkonen** Editor-In-Chief_**Stefano Tonchi**
Publisher_**The New York Times** Issue_**October 21, 2007**
Category_**Photo: Feature: Story**

BY CHARLES BOWDEN
PHOTOGRAPHS BY
DIANE COOK AND LEN JENSHEL
A WALL ALONG THE U.S.-MEXICO
BORDER PROMPTS DIVIDED FEELINGS:
IT OFFENDS PEOPLE. IT COMFORTS
PEOPLE. AND IT KEEPS EXPANDING.
Our
Wall

522

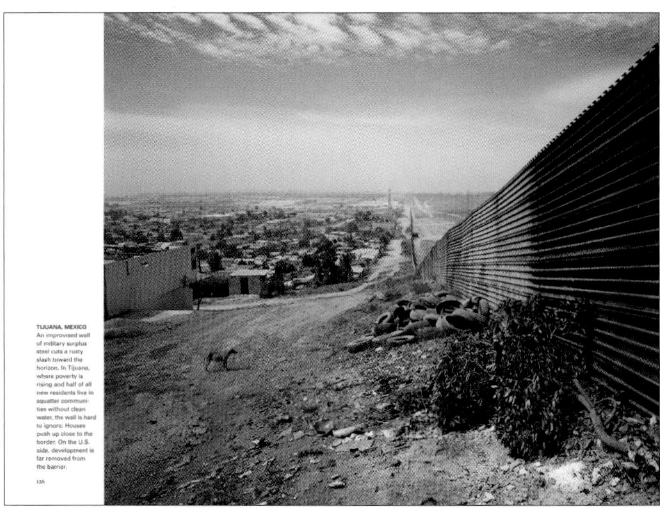

TIJUANA, MEXICO
An improvised wall of military surplus steel cuts a rusty slash toward the horizon. In Tijuana, where poverty is rising and half of all new residents live in squatter communities without clean water, the wall is hard to ignore. Houses push up close to the border. On the U.S. side, development is far removed from the barrier.
126

522

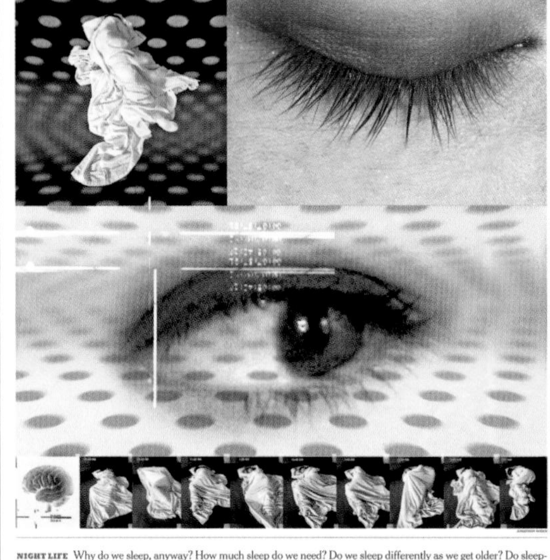

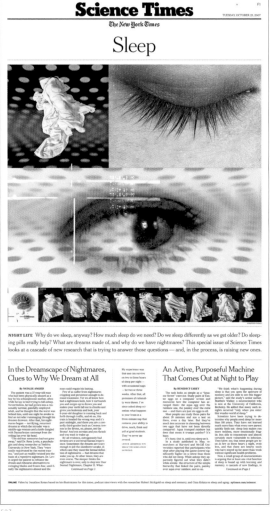

Science Times F1

TUESDAY, OCTOBER 23, 2007

The New York Times

Sleep

NIGHT LIFE Why do we sleep, anyway? How much sleep do we need? Do we sleep differently as we get older? Do sleeping pills really help? What are dreams made of, and why do we have nightmares? This special issue of Science Times looks at a cascade of new research that is trying to answer those questions — and, in the process, is raising new ones.

In the Dreamscape of Nightmares, Clues to Why We Dream at All

By NATALIE ANGIER

The patient was a 37-year-old man who had been physically abused as a boy by his schizophrenic mother, often while he lay in bed trying to fall asleep. Nevertheless, he had grown into a reasonably normal, gainfully employed adult, and he thought that the worst was behind him, until one night he awoke to find an intruder rummaging through his dresser drawers. After that, his nightmares began — terrifying, recurrent dreams in which the intruder was a middle-age woman and a knife dangled with Damoclesian contempt from the ceiling fan over his head.

"The old fear memories had not gone away," said Dr. Ross Levin, a psychologist and sleep researcher at Yeshiva University in New York. They "were easily reactivated by the recent trauma," and just as readily twisted into the basis of a repetitive nightmare. Dr. Levin urged the patient to reframe the dream and rehearse alternatives to swinging blades and frozen fear, until finally the nightmares abated and the man could regain his footing.

Few of us suffer from nightmares crippling and persistent enough to demand treatment. Yet we all know how bad a nightmare feels, how it surrounds you and surges up to drown you and makes your teeth fall out in chunks and gives you leukemia and look, your 6-year-old daughter is running back and forth through traffic, and oh no, this train is headed the wrong way and it's past midnight, and there you are a cowardly third-grader back on Creston Avenue in the Bronx, no, please, not the Bronx! And you scream and you thrash and you want to wake up.

By all evidence, outrageously bad dreams are a universal human experience. Sometimes the dreams are scary enough to jolt the slumberer awake, in which case they meet the formal definition of nightmares — bad dreams that wake you up. At other times, they are even worse. The sleeper thinks the nightmare is over, only to step into Your Nested Nightmare, Chapter II. What-

Continued on Page 3

My experience was that one can survive on two to three hours of sleep per night — with occasional naps — for two or three weeks. After that, all pretenses of rationality were blown. I've since asked sleep scientists what happens to your brain in a three-minute nap that restores your ability to drive, teach, think and yell at grad students. They've never answered.

LEON M. LEDERMAN, WINNER OF THE NOBEL PRIZE IN PHYSICS

An Active, Purposeful Machine That Comes Out at Night to Play

By BENEDICT CAREY

The task looks as simple as a "Sesame Street" exercise. Study pairs of Easter eggs on a computer screen and memorize how the computer has arranged them: the aqua egg over the rainbow one, the paisley over the coral one — and there are just six eggs in all.

Most people can study these pairs for about 20 minutes and ace a test on them, even a day later. But they're much less accurate in choosing between two eggs that have not been directly compared: Aqua trumped rainbow but does that mean it trumps paisley? It's hazy.

It's hazy, that is, until you sleep on it.

In a study published in May, researchers at Harvard and McGill Universities reported that participants who slept after playing this game scored significantly higher on a retest than those who did not sleep. While asleep they apparently figured out what they didn't while awake: the structure of the simple hierarchy that linked the pairs, paisley over aqua over rainbow, and so on.

"We think what's happening during sleep is that you open the aperture of memory and are able to see this bigger picture," said the study's senior author, Matthew Walker, a neuroscientist who is now at the University of California, Berkeley. He added that many such insights occurred "only when you enter this wonder-world of sleep."

Scientists have been trying to determine why people need sleep for more than 100 years. They have not learned much more than what every new parent quickly finds out: sleep loss makes you more reckless, more emotionally fragile, less able to concentrate and almost certainly more vulnerable to infection. They know, too, that some people get by on as few as three hours a night, even less, and that there are hearty souls who have stayed up for more than week without significant health problems.

Now, a small group of neuroscientists is arguing that at least one vital function of sleep is bound up with learning and memory. A cascade of new findings, in

Continued on Page 2

ONLINE Video by Jonathon Rosen based on his illustrations for this issue; podcast interviews with the researcher Robert Stickgold on sleep and memory, and Gina Kolata on sleep and aging: **nytimes.com/science**.

523

524

524

522 NATIONAL GEOGRAPHIC

Design Director_**David Whitmore**
Art Director_**Elaine Bradley**
Director of Photography_**David Griffin**
Photo Editor_**Sarah Leen**
Photographers_**Diane Cook, Len Jenshel**
Publisher_**National Geographic Society**
Issue_**May 2007**
Category_**Photo: Feature: Story**

523 THE NEW YORK TIMES

Design Director_**Tom Bodkin**
Art Director_**Kelly Doe**
Designer_**Kelly Doe**
Illustrator_**Jonathon Rosen**
Director of Photography_**Soo-Jeong Kang**
Publisher_**The New York Times**
Issue_**October 23, 2007**
Category_**Photo: Feature: Story**

524 WOMEN'S HEALTH

Creative Director_**Andrea Dunham**
Designer_**Andrea Dunham**
Director of Photography_**Sarah Rozen**
Photographer_**Jill Greenberg**
Publisher_**Rodale**
Issue_**January/February 2007**
Category_**Photo: Feature: Story**

525

525

526

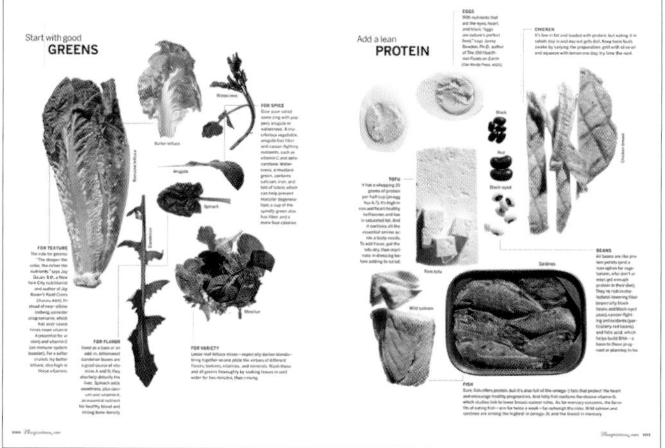

526

527

527

525 CITY

Creative Director_Fabrice Frere
Design Director_Fabrice Frere
Art Director_Adriana Jacoud
Photo Editor_Anthony Cross
Photographer_Kenny Thomas
Publisher_Spark Media
Issue_March 2007
Category_Photo: Feature: Story

526 BLUEPRINT

Creative Director_Eric A. Pike
Design Director_Deb Bishop
Art Director_Cybele Grandjean
Designer_Cybele Grandjean
Director of Photography_Heloise Goodman
Senior Photo Editor_Mary Cahill
Photographer_Charles Masters
Editor-In-Chief_Sarah Humphreys
Publisher_Martha Stewart Living Omnimedia
Issue_May/June 2007
Category_Photo: Feature: Story

527 WIRED

Creative Director_Scott Dadich
Design Director_Wyatt Mitchell
Designer_Scott Dadich
Photo Editor_Carolyn Rauch
Photographer_Alessandra Petlin
Publisher_Condé Nast Publications, Inc.
Issue_November 2007
Category_Photo: Feature: Story

GOURMET ENTERTAINS

CHILD'S PLAY

Costumes! Cake! Action! When food is this good, the guests get to feel like it's their birthday too—even the adults. Recipes by Gina Marie Miraglia Eriquez Photographs by Roland Bello

MENU SERVES 20
(10 CHILDREN, 10 ADULTS)
GINGER CARROT DIP WITH CRUDITÉS
CHERRY LIME VIRGIN RICKEYS
MEATBALL SLIDERS
MACARONI AND CHEESE
BREADED ONION RINGS
FRUIT CUP WITH LIME SYRUP
ICE-CREAM-CONE CAKE

80

Do you dream in chocolate or vanilla? Kids can take their pick with a Mad Hatter sweet that brings new imagination to the idea of ice cream cake.

528

84

You can spot the queen because she's the one with the golden rings—even if, in this case, they're of the onion variety and fit more like bracelets.

528

528 GOURMET

Creative Director_**Richard Ferretti** Art Director_**Erika Oliveira** Designer_**Erika Oliveira** Photo Editor_**Amy Koblenzer** Photographer_**Roland Bello** Editor-In-Chief_**Ruth Reichl** Publisher_**Condé Nast Publications, Inc.** Issue_**August 2007** Category_**Photo: Feature: Story**

SUIT BY VALENTINO
RYAN GOSLING WANTS TO HIDE FROM US.
HE PLAYS WEIRDOS AND SOCIOPATHS IN SMALL-BUDGET FILMS.
HE GUARDS HIS PERSONAL LIFE FIERCELY. HE'S NEVER IN THE GOSSIP RAGS.
SO HOW DID HE GET THIS FAMOUS?
BY BEING ONE OF THE FINEST ACTORS OF OUR TIME, FOR STARTERS
BY ALEX PAPPADEMAS
PHOTOGRAPHS BY NATHANIEL GOLDBERG
the LONER
NOV.07 GQ 217

529

SUIT BY TOM FORD

thing was performing an air-band version of Billy Joel's deathless class-struggle anthem "Uptown Girl." Hoping to get next to her, Gosling volunteered his services as a backup dancer. There was no choreography, so Gosling just did what he felt:

"I go up onstage and start, like, dry-humping the stage. I'm grabbing my stuff, I'm licking my fingers, I'm going up to grown women and trying to grind their faces. Meanwhile, I'm like, *7*, y'know?"

You were 7—were you emulating behavior you'd seen somewhere else? On TV, maybe?

"No. I was just inherently filthy," Gosling says. "I was born inherently filthy. And then we *won*. And we got on the front page of the newspaper. And because I was so young, and what I was doing was so sexual, people really liked it. They really *supported* it. And then because I won that, I got on a TV show that was like *Star Search*. My parents were like, 'You have to come up with a real routine.' And—honestly—I said, 'That's what I do, it's my thing.' And they were like, 'But it's *disgusting*. You can't do that.' "

Were you aware that it was disgusting? Or did you think that if you were being rewarded for it, it was okay?

"Yeah," Gosling says. "In my little mind, I was giving the people what they wanted. *Who are you, as my parents, to keep the people from getting their medicine, my filthy 7-year-old Move?* I made up a routine that didn't have the Move in it. They locked me in the basement until I figured it out, and then they made me do it twice to make sure it was an actual routine. Then I went on the show—and I did the Move. And I won!"

So you were getting the wrong message.

"I was fighting The Man," Gosling says. "So then—are you interested in this?"

Totally.

"Okay," Gosling says, throwing one arm over the back of the booth. "Because it's the *truth*. I'm gonna tell you the truth."

He kept winning. People would see him on the streets of his little town, ask him to do the Move. With time the Move evolved: "It was very emotional," Gosling says. "The main thing was I would pick a girl, or a grown woman, from the audience, and I would just attack her sexually. I would make filthy love to her. I'd mock-take-off her clothes. I would show her what I, as a 7-year-old, would do to her if I could get her alone. The whole thing.

"I got kinda famous for it," he says. "I got beat up a lot for it, too. But it was worth it, because I knew it was my ticket outta there."

In his final appearance on the TV show, Gosling says, "I was facing these twin sisters. They were 8 years old. And they do 'Two Hearts,' the Phil Collins song. They're wearing heart outfits. Big pink heart-shaped bows

220 GQ NOV.07

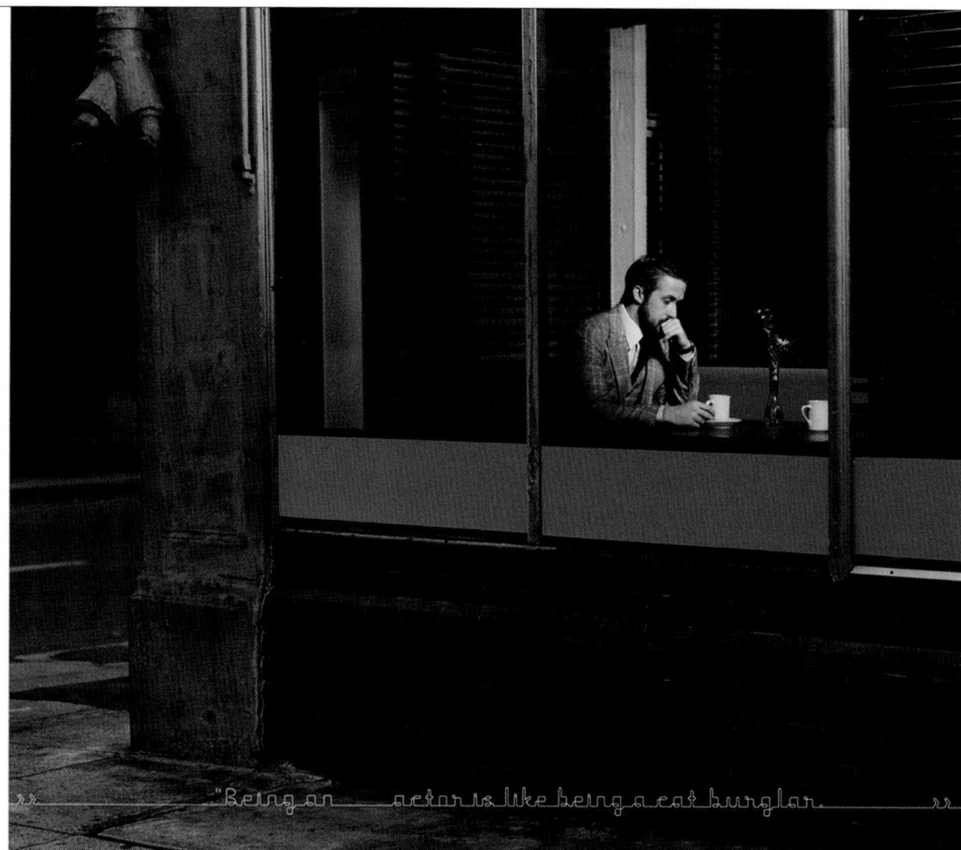

"Being an actor is like being a cat burglar.

529

Design Director_Fred Woodward Designer_Thomas Alberty Director of Photography_Dora Somosi Photographer_Nathaniel Goldberg
Editor-In-Chief_Jim Nelson Publisher_Condé Nast Publications Inc. Issue_November 2007 Category_Photo: Feature: Story

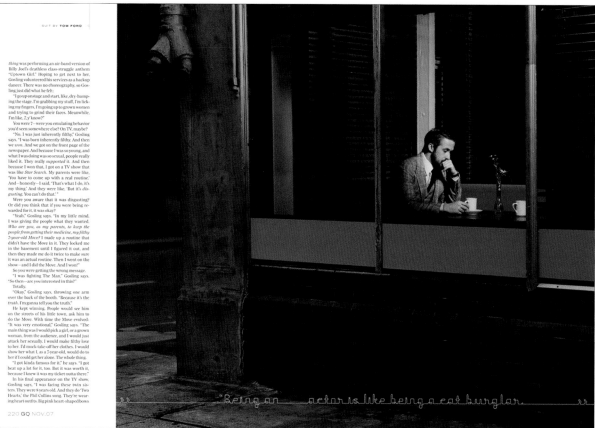

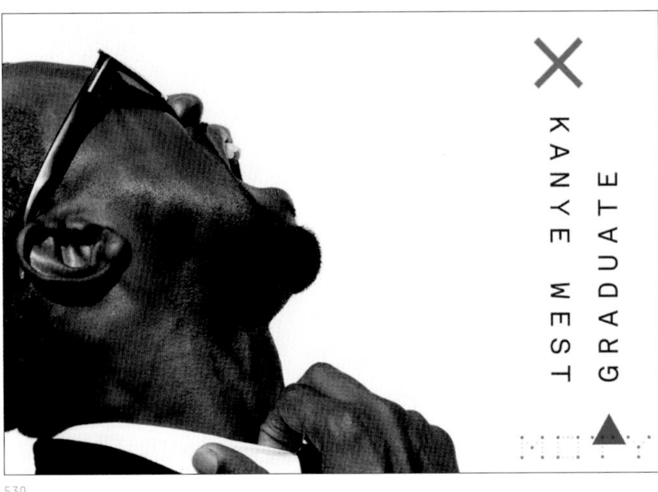

530

530

531

531

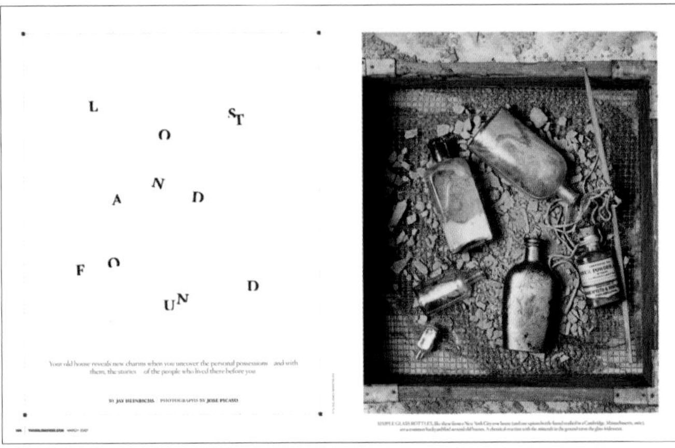

532

532

530 GQ

Design Director_Fred Woodward
Designer_Anton Ioukhnovets
Director of Photography_Dora Somosi
Editor-In-Chief_Jim Nelson
Publisher_Condé Nast Publications Inc.
Issue_December 2007
Category_Photo: Feature: Story

531 MARIE CLAIRE

Creative Director_Paul Martinez
Design Director_Jenny Leigh Thompson
Director of Photography_Alix Campbell
Photo Editors_Andrea Volbrecht, Melanie Chambers
Photographer_Ruven Afanador
Publisher_The Hearst Corporation-Magazines Div. Issue_January 2007
Category_Photo: Feature: Story

532 THIS OLD HOUSE

Design Director_Amy Rosenfeld
Art Director_Hylah Hill
Designer_Hylah Hill
Photo Editor_Denise Sfraga
Photographer_Jose Picayo
Publisher_Time Inc.
Issue_March 2007
Category_Photo: Feature: Story

533

533

534

534

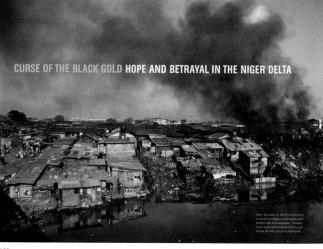

CURSE OF THE BLACK GOLD HOPE AND BETRAYAL IN THE NIGER DELTA

535

535

533 DEPARTURES

Creative Director_Bernard Scharf
Art Director_Adam Bookbinder
Associate Art Director_Lou Corredor
Director of Photography_Jennifer Laski
Photo Editors_Jennifer Geaney, Brandon Perlman
Photographer_ Bill Phelps
Publisher_American Express Publishing Co.
Issue_September 2007
Category_ Photo: Feature: Story

534 GQ

Design Director_Fred Woodward
Designer_Drue Wagner
Director of Photography_Dora Somosi
Senior Photo Editor_Krista Prestek
Photographer_Zachary Scott
Editor-In-Chief_Jim Nelson
Publisher_Condé Nast Publications Inc.
Issue_October 2007
Category_Photo: Feature: Story

535 NATIONAL GEOGRAPHIC

Design Director_David Whitmore
Art Director_Elaine Bradley
Director of Photography_David Griffin
Photo Editor_Kurt Mutcher
Photographer_Ed Kashi
Publisher_National Geographic Society
Issue_February 2007
Category_Photo: Feature: Story

536

536

537

537

538

538

536 NATIONAL GEOGRAPHIC

Design Director_**David Whitmore** Designer_**David Whitmore**
Director of Photography_**David Griffin** Photo Editor_**Sarah Leen**
Photographer_**Jonas Bendiksen** Publisher_**National Geographic Society**
Issue_**May 2007** Category_**Photo: Feature: Story**

537 SOUTHWEST AIRLINES SPIRIT MAGAZINE

Design Director_**Kevin de Miranda**
Designers_**Brody Price, Emily Buxkemper** Photo Editor_**Lauren Chesnutt**
Photographer_**Thomas Allen** Studio_**Pace Communications**
Publisher_**Pace Communications** Client_**Southwest Airlines**
Issue_**December 2007** Category_**Photo: Feature: Story**

538 COOKIE

Design Director_**Kirby Rodriguez** Art Director_**Alex Grossman**
Designers_**Shanna Greenberg, Nicolette Berthelot**
Photo Editor _**Darrick Harris** Assistant Photo Editor_**Rebecca Etter**
Photographer_**Benoit Paverelli** Editor-In-Chief_**Pilar Guzmán**
Publisher_**Condé Nast Publications Inc.** Issue **September 2007**
Category_**Photo: Feature: Story**

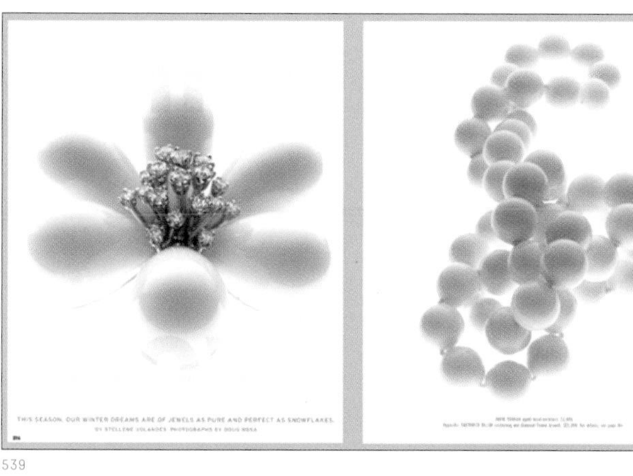

539

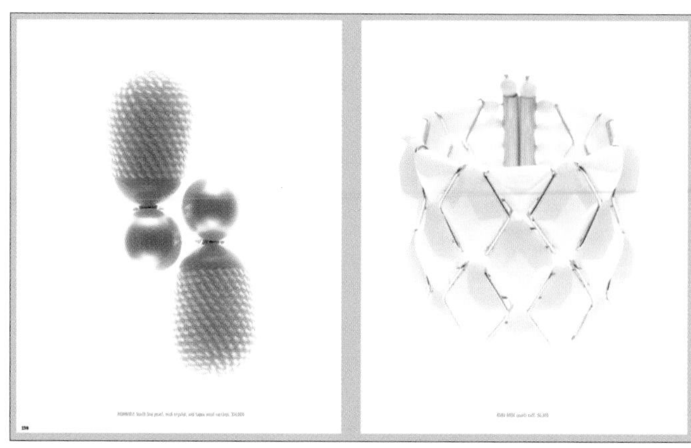

539

540

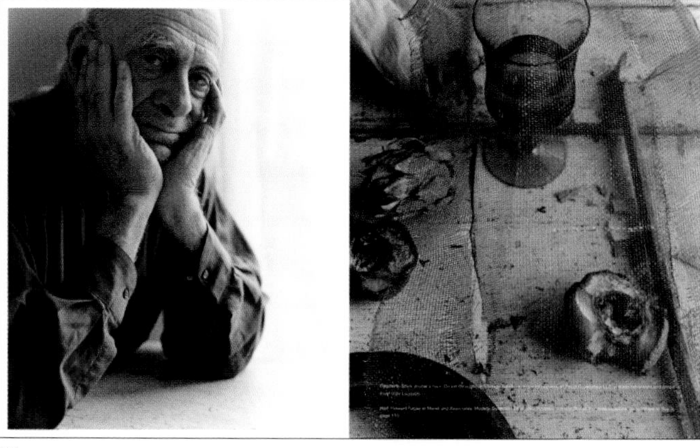

540

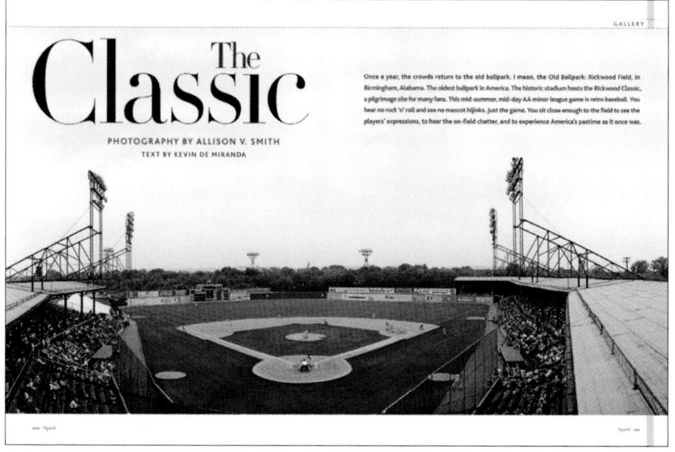

541

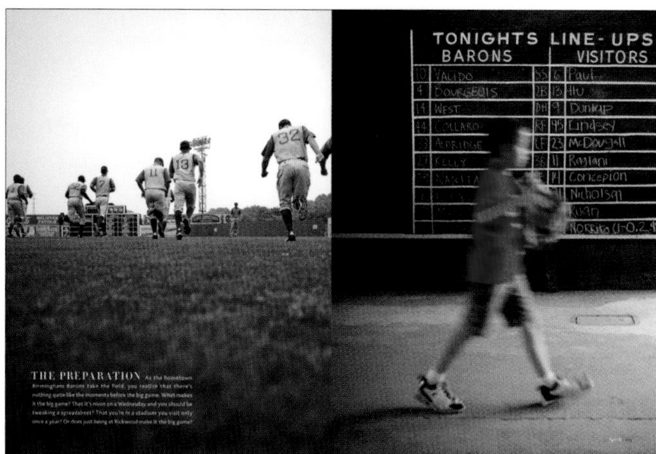

541

539 DEPARTURES

Creative Director_**Bernard Scharf**
Art Director_**Adam Bookbinder** Associate Art Director_**Lou Corredor**
Director of Photography_**Jennifer Laski**
Photo Editors_**Jennifer Geaney, Brandon Perlman**
Photographer_**Doug Rosa** Publisher_**American Express Publishing Co.**
Issue_**January/February 2007** Category_**Photo: Feature: Story**

540 CITY

Creative Director_**Fabrice Frere** Design Director_**Fabrice Frere**
Art Director_**Adriana Jacoud** Photo Editor_**Anthony Cross**
Photographer_**Martyn Thompson** Publisher_**Spark Media**
Issue_**July/August 2007** Category_**Photo: Feature: Story**

541 SOUTHWEST AIRLINES SPIRIT MAGAZINE

Design Director_**Kevin de Miranda**
Designers_**Brody Price, Emily Buxkemper** Photo Editor_**Lauren Chesnutt**
Photographer_**Allison V. Smith** Studio_**Pace Communications**
Publisher_**Pace Communications** Client_**Southwest Airlines**
Issue_**September 2007** Category_**Photo: Feature: Story**

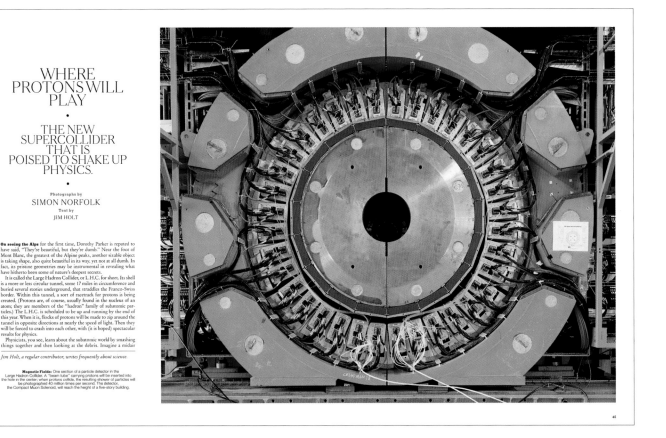

WHERE PROTONS WILL PLAY

•

THE NEW SUPERCOLLIDER THAT IS POISED TO SHAKE UP PHYSICS.

•

Photographs by
SIMON NORFOLK
Text by
JIM HOLT

On seeing the Alps for the first time, Dorothy Parker is reputed to have said, "They're beautiful, but they're dumb." Near the foot of Mont Blanc, the greatest of the Alpine peaks, another sizable object is taking shape, also quite beautiful in its way, yet not at all dumb. In fact, its pristine geometries may be instrumental in revealing what have hitherto been some of nature's deepest secrets.

It is called the Large Hadron Collider, or L.H.C. for short. Its shell is a more or less circular tunnel, some 17 miles in circumference and buried several stories underground, that straddles the Franco-Swiss border. Within this tunnel, a sort of racetrack for protons is being created. (Protons are, of course, usually found in the nucleus of an atom; they are members of the "hadron" family of subatomic particles.) The L.H.C. is scheduled to be up and running by the end of this year. When it is, flocks of protons will be made to zip around the tunnel in opposite directions at nearly the speed of light. Then they will be forced to crash into each other, with (it is hoped) spectacular results for physics.

Physicists, you see, learn about the subatomic world by smashing things together and then looking at the debris. Imagine a midair

Jim Holt, a regular contributor, writes frequently about science.

Magnetic Fields: One section of a particle detector in the Large Hadron Collider. A "beam tube" carrying protons will be inserted into the hole in the center; when protons collide, the resulting shower of particles will be photographed 40 million times per second. The detector, the Compact Muon Solenoid, will reach the height of a five-story building.

44 45

542

Discography: Views of the collider's particle detectors. Each section will be lowered 100 meters beneath the ground into a cavern. The photograph at the bottom left is taken from the floor of the cavern looking up. The red objects are fire extinguishers — in an emergency, they will emit enough breathable foam to fill the cathedral-size cavern within seven minutes. The foam allows workers to breathe freely even as it puts out fires.

46 PHOTOGRAPHS BY SIMON NORFOLK FOR THE NEW YORK TIMES

THE NEW YORK TIMES MAGAZINE / JANUARY 14, 2007 47

542

542 THE NEW YORK TIMES MAGAZINE

Creative Director_Janet Froelich Art Director_Arem Duplessis Designer_Catherine Gilmore-Barnes
Director of Photography_Kathy Ryan Photo Editor_Joanna Milter Photographer_Simon Norfolk Editor-In-Chief_Gerry Marzorati
Publisher_The New York Times Issue_January 14, 2007 Category_Photo: Feature: Story

BUSINESS

On The Job in China

A wave of more than 100 million rural workers has flocked to cities for factory work, fed by Western demand for cheap goods. If conditions aren't ideal, they are often better than farm life

PHOTOGRAPHS BY EDWARD BURTYNSKY

Handsets, handmade *At Bird Mobile's factory near Shanghai, workers assemble phones headed for the domestic market*

543

Roll call *A pep talk starts the day at the Cankun factory in Zhangzhou, opposite Taiwan. It's the No. 1 producer of irons and coffeemakers in the world*

Pierce work *Making shish kebab at the Deda plant north of Beijing, near the North Korean border. Employees process 330,000 chickens a day*

Fast food *The 10-hr. workdays at Youngor Textiles in the seaport city of Ningbo, near Shanghai, are punctuated by 20-min. meal breaks*

Close quarters *Most factory workers live in dorms—like this one in the southeast, near Hong Kong—that house up to 1,000 employees*

IMAGES COURTESY OF THE ARTIST AND CHARLES COWLES GALLERY, NEW YORK/ROBERT KOCH GALLERY, SAN FRANCISCO/NICHOLAS METIVIER GALLERY, TORONTO

543

543 TIME

Art Director_Arthur Hochstein Deputy Art Director_D.W. Pine Director of Photography_MaryAnne Golon Picture Editor_Alice Gabriner Deputy Picture Editor_Dietmar Liz-Lepiorz Photographer_Edward Burtynsky Publisher_Time Inc. Issue_July 9, 2007 Category_Photo: Feature: Story

549

549

550

A Budding Pedophile

A Kid With Real Boundary Problems?

550

551

PINNED

Underwater in a Kayak

STRANDED

In the Snow for 8 Days

HELD CAPTIVE

In a Serbian Jail

551

549 THE NEW YORK TIMES MAGAZINE

Creative Director_Janet Froelich
Art Director_Arem Duplessis
Designer_Arem Duplessis
Director of Photography_Kathy Ryan
Photo Editor_Kira Pollack
Photographer_Dan Winters
Editor-In-Chief_Gerry Marzorati
Publisher_The New York Times
Issue_September 2, 2007
Category_Photo: Feature: Story

550 THE NEW YORK TIMES MAGAZINE

Creative Director_Janet Froelich
Art Directors_Arem Duplessis, Gail Bichler
Designer Leo Jung
Director of Photography_Kathy Ryan
Photo Editor_Clinton Cargill
Photographer_Eric Tucker
Editor-In-Chief_Gerry Marzorati
Publisher_The New York Times
Issue_July 22, 2007
Category_Photo: Feature: Story

551 OUTSIDE

Creative Director_Hannah McCaughey
Art Directors_Kate Iltis, John McCauley
Designer_Mace Fleeger
Director of Photography_Lesley Meyer
Photo Editors_Amy Feitelberg, Amber Terranova
Photographer_Joe Baran
Publisher_Mariah Media, Inc.
Issue_November 2007
Category_Photo: Feature: Story

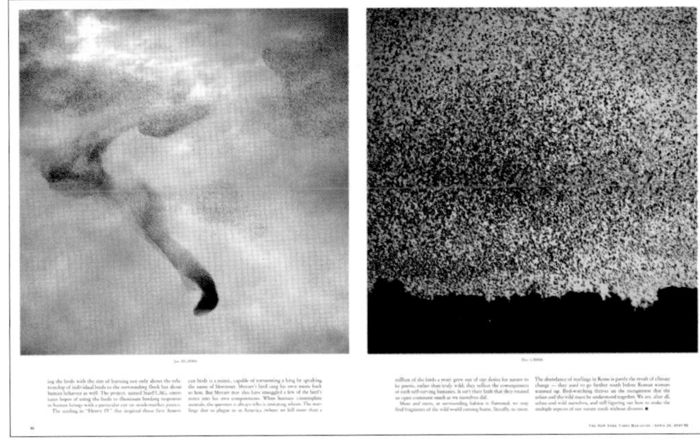

552 552

553 553

554 554

552 THE NEW YORK TIMES MAGAZINE

Creative Director_Janet Froelich
Art Director_Arem Duplessis
Designer_Nancy Harris Rouemy
Director of Photography_Kathy Ryan
Photo Editor_Kira Pollack
Photographer_Richard Barnes
Editor-In-Chief_Gerry Marzorati
Publisher_The New York Times
Issue_April 22, 2007
Category_Photo: Feature: Story

553 MARTHA STEWART LIVING

Creative Director_Eric A. Pike
Design Director_James Dunlinson
Art Director_Matthew Axe
Designer_Matthew Axe
Director of Photography_Heloise Goodman
Senior Photo Editor_Andrea Bakacs
Photographer_Hans Gissinger
Stylists_Lucinda Scala Quinn, Tanya Graff
Editor-In-Chief Margaret Roach
Publisher_Martha Stewart Living Omnimedia
Issue_May 2007 Category_Photo: Feature: Story

554 NEW YORK

Design Director_Chris Dixon
Director of Photography_Jody Quon
Photographers_Richard Avedon, Valérie Belin, Vanessa Beecroft, Marilyn Minter, John Baldessari, Vik Muniz
Editor-In-Chief_Adam Moss
Publisher_New York Magazine Holdings, LLC
Issue_May 14, 2007
Category_Photo: Feature: Story

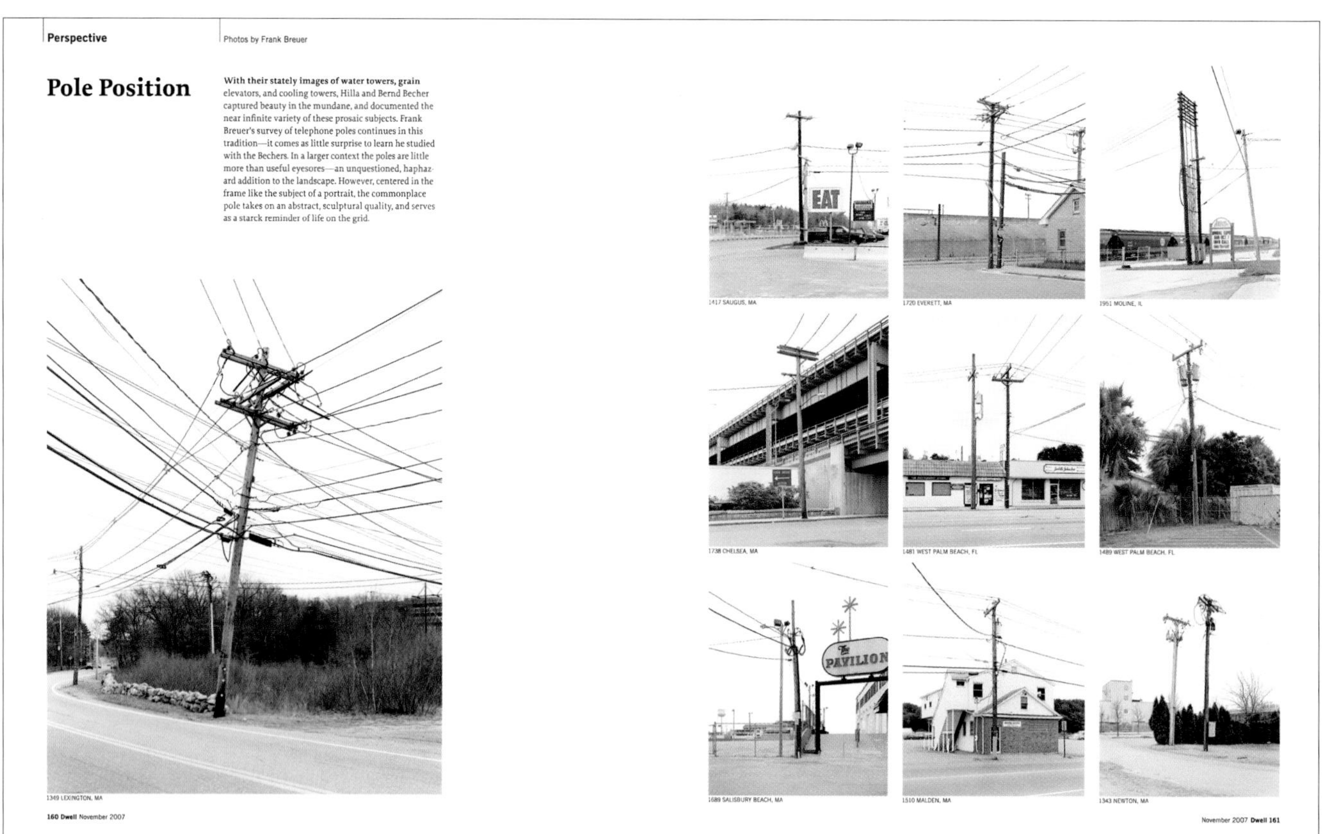

Perspective

Photos by Frank Breuer

Pole Position

With their stately images of water towers, grain elevators, and cooling towers, Hilla and Bernd Becher captured beauty in the mundane, and documented the near infinite variety of these prosaic subjects. Frank Breuer's survey of telephone poles continues in this tradition—it comes as little surprise to learn he studied with the Bechers. In a larger context the poles are little more than useful eyesores—an unquestioned, haphazard addition to the landscape. However, centered in the frame like the subject of a portrait, the commonplace pole takes on an abstract, sculptural quality, and serves as a starck reminder of life on the grid.

1349 LEXINGTON, MA

1417 SAUGUS, MA

1720 EVERETT, MA

1951 MOLINE, IL

1738 CHELSEA, MA

1481 WEST PALM BEACH, FL

1489 WEST PALM BEACH, FL

1689 SALISBURY BEACH, MA

1510 MALDEN, MA

1343 NEWTON, MA

160 Dwell November 2007

November 2007 **Dwell 161**

555

Perspective

1475 SOMERVILLE, MA

1652 GRINNELL, IA

1550 SAUGUS, MA

1405 SAUGUS, MA

1523 PLUM ISLAND, MA

1611 GRINNELL, IA

1537 MALDEN, MA

1332 ARLINGTON, MA

1492 SOUTH OF THE BORDER, SC

1459 WATERTOWN, MA

164 Dwell November 2007

November 2007 **Dwell 165**

555

555 DWELL

Design Director_Kyle Blue Designers_Brendan Callahan, Geoff Halber, Suzanne Lagasa Director of Photography_Kate Stone Foss Photo Editors_Andrea Lawson, Amy Silberman, Alexis Tjian Photographer_Frank Breuer Production_Kathryn Hansen Publisher_Dwell LLC Issue_November 2007 Category_Photo: Feature: Story

556

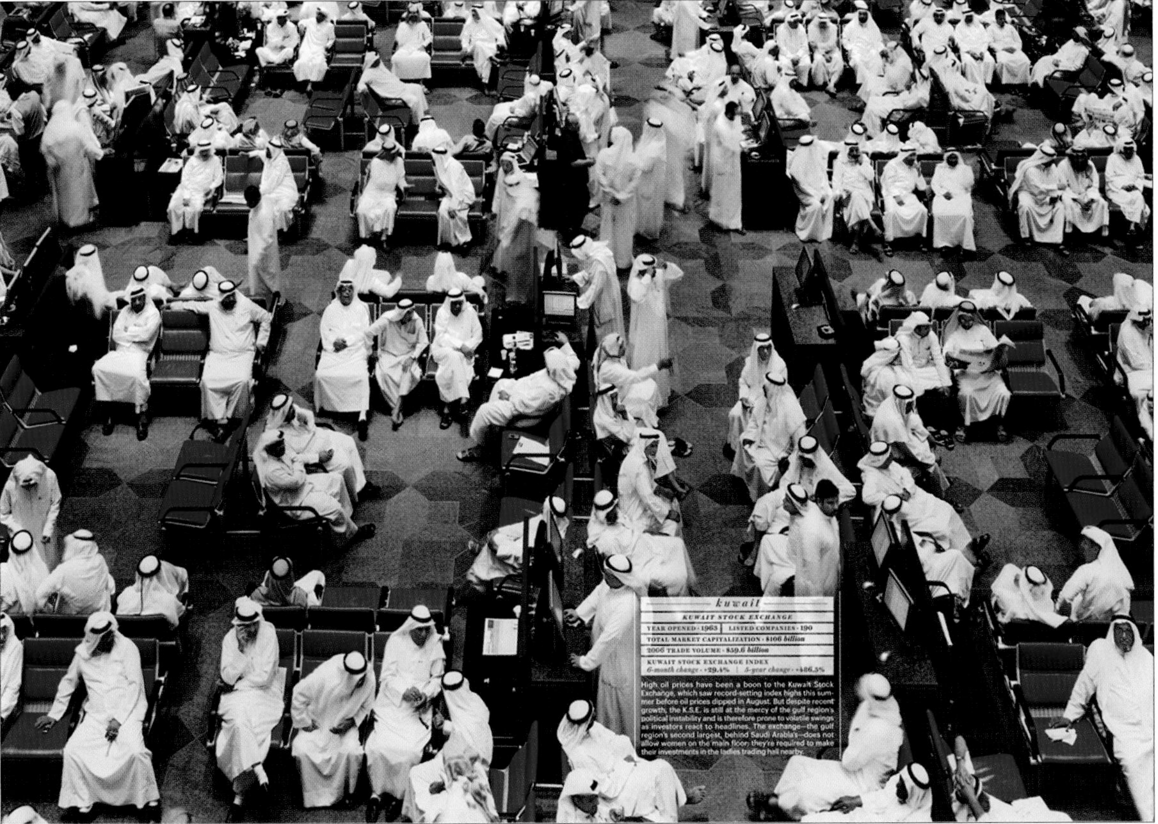

556

556 CONDÉ NAST PORTFOLIO

Design Director_**Robert Priest** Art Director_**Grace Lee** Designer_**Grace Lee** Director of Photography_**Lisa Berman** Photo Editor_**Rossana Shokrian** Deputy Photo Editor_**Sarah Czeladnicki** Photographer_**Robert Polidori** Editor-In-Chief_**Joanne Lipman** Publisher_**Condé Nast Publications Inc.** Issue_**October 2007** Category_**Photo: Feature: Story**

COVER STORY

the coolest girl in the world

557

COVER STORY

557

Cover Story: Pakistan

Islamic militants have spread beyond their tribal bases, and have the run of an unstable, nuclear-armed nation.

Where the Jihad Lives Now

558

PAKISTAN

Visiting Taliban chiefs in Peshawar call reporters to find a cheap hotel, a good restaurant or a new cell phone.

558

Style

SUGAR SHOCK

BY MARTIN PARR

559

559

557 MARIE CLAIRE

Design Director_**Jenny Leigh Thompson**
Director of Photography_**Kristen Schaefer**
Photo Editors_**Andrea Volbrecht, Melanie Chambers**
Photographer_**Ruven Afanador** Fashion Editor_**Tracy Taylor**
Publisher_**The Hearst Corporation-Magazines Div.**
Issue_**September 2007** Category_**Photo: Feature: Story**

558 NEWSWEEK

Creative Director_**Amid Capeci** Art Director_**Alex Ha**
Director of Photography_**Simon Barnett** Photo Editor_**James Wellford**
Photographers_**Bertrand Meunier - Tendance Floue for Newsweek, Aamir Qureshi-AFP-Getty Images** Publisher_**The Washington Post Co.**
Issue_**October 29, 2007** Category_**Photo: Feature: Story**

559 THE NEW YORK TIMES MAGAZINE

Creative Director_**Janet Froelich** Art Director_**Arem Duplessis**
Designer_**Nancy Harris Rouemy** Photographer_**Martin Parr**
Fashion Editor_**Karla M. Martinez** Editor-In-Chief_**Gerry Marzorati**
Publisher_**The New York Times** Issue_**April 8, 2007**
Category_**Photo: Feature: Story**

560

560

561

561

562

562

560 T, THE NEW YORK TIMES STYLE MAGAZINE

Creative Director_**Janet Froelich** Senior Art Director_**David Sebbah**
Art Director_**Christopher Martinez** Designer_**Christopher Martinez**
Photo Editor_**Judith Puckett-Rinella** Photographer_**Coppi Barbieri**
Editor-In-Chief_**Stefano Tonchi** Publisher_**The New York Times**
Issue_**April 15, 2007** Category_**Photo: Feature: Story**

561 GOLF DIGEST INDEX

Design Director_**Ken DeLago** Designer_**Marne Mayer**
Director of Photography_**Ryan Cline** Photographer_**Roxanne Lowit**
Issue_**Fall 2007** Category_**Photo: Feature: Story**

562 THE NEW YORK TIMES MAGAZINE

Creative Director_**Janet Froelich** Art Director_**Arem Duplessis**
Designers_**Leo Jung, Hilary Greenbaum**
Director of Photography_**Kathy Ryan** Photo Editor_**Luise Stauss**
Photographer_**Nadav Kander** Editor-In-Chief_**Gerry Marzorati**
Publisher_**The New York Times** Issue_**October 14, 2007**
Category_**Photo: Feature: Story**

CHIVE BLINI *with crème fraîche, quail eggs, and tarragon*

showstoppers

WHEN YOU ADD ANY OF THESE ELEGANT SEASONAL DISHES TO YOUR HOLIDAY MENU, YOU'RE SURE TO GARNER RAVE REVIEWS.

PHOTOGRAPHS BY JONATHAN LOVEKIN
TEXT BY MEG PETERSON

This spring, embrace the impulse for renewal by debuting some fresh flavors at your holiday table. The many elevated dishes on these pages can help you rethink your routine menu, whether you seek a subtle twist on a classic (an Easter lamb, Passover macaroons) or something a little less expected (individual carrot soufflés, a rustic leek tart). In a nod to the season, every one of these appetizers, entrées, and desserts emphasizes fresh ingredients and includes at least a glimpse of green. Each recipe is practical as well as alluring, containing components that can be made in advance and finished later, in the hours leading up to the meal. Perhaps most enticing, however, is the knowledge that you can add just one new element to your traditional menu and feel as though you've started anew.

CARROT PUDDING SOUFFLÉS *with buttered spring vegetables*

563

LEEK & OLIVE TART *with two cheeses*

POACHED SALMON *with cucumber, cress, and caper sauce*

563

564

564

565

565

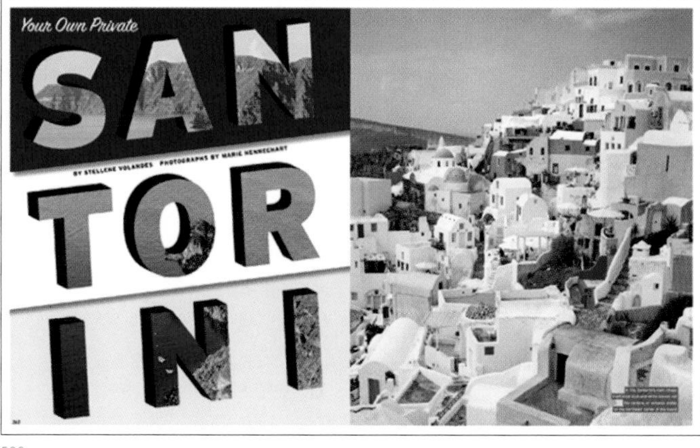

566

566

<u>563</u> MARTHA STEWART LIVING

Creative Director_**Eric A. Pike** Design Director_ **James Dunlinson**
Art Director_**Matthew Axe** Designer_**Matthew Axe**
Director of Photography_**Heloise Goodman**
Senior Photo Editor_**Andrea Bakacs** Photographer_**Jonathan Lovekin**
Stylists_**Pam Morris, Anna Kovel** Editor-In-Chief_**Michael Boodro**
Publisher_**Martha Stewart Living Omnimedia** Issue_**April 2007**
Category_**Photo: Feature: Story**

<u>564</u> NATIONAL GEOGRAPHIC

Design Director_**David Whitmore** Designer_**David Whitmore**
Director of Photography_**David Griffin** Photo Editor_**Kathy Moran**
Photographer_**Michael Nichols** Publisher_**National Geographic Society**
Issue_**March 2007** Category_**Photo: Feature: Story**

<u>565</u> SPIN

Design Director_**Devin Pedzwater** Art Director_**Liz Macfarlane**
Director of Photography_**Michelle Egiziano**
Photo Editors_**Gavin Stevens, Jennifer Edmondson**
Photographer_**Terry Richardson** Publisher_**Spin Media LLC**
Issue_**July 2007** Category_**Photo: Feature: Story**

<u>566</u> DEPARTURES

Creative Director_**Bernard Scharf**
Art Director_**Adam Bookbinder** Associate Art Director_**Lou Corredor**
Director of Photography_**Jennifer Laski**
Photo Editors_**Jennifer Geaney, Brandon Perlman**
Photographer_**Marie Hennechart** Publisher_**American Express Publishing Co.** Issue_**March/April 2007**
Category_**Photo: Feature: Story**

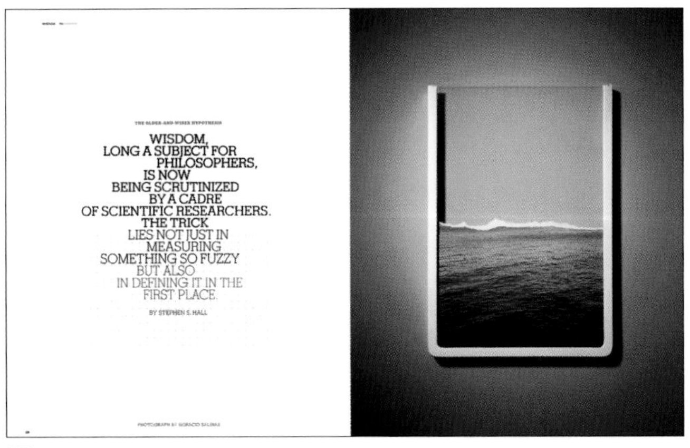

567

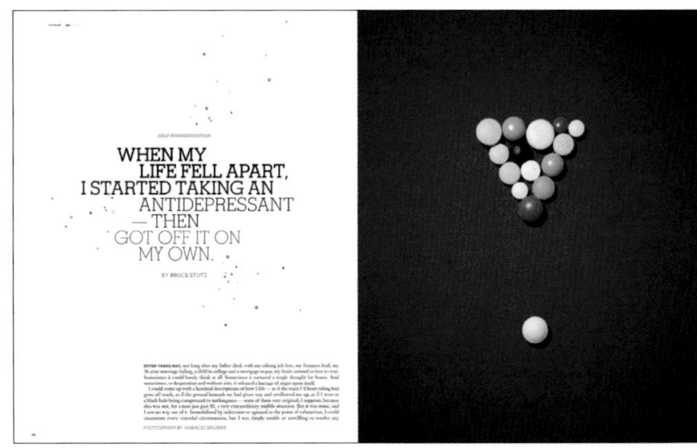

567

568

568

569

569

567 THE NEW YORK TIMES MAGAZINE

Creative Director_**Janet Froelich**
Art Director_**Arem Duplessis**
Designer_**Leo Jung**
Director of Photography_**Kathy Ryan**
Photo Editor_**Clinton Cargill**
Photographer_**Horacio Salinas**
Editor-In-Chief_**Gerry Marzorati**
Publisher_**The New York Times**
Issue_**May 6, 2007**
Category_**Photo: Feature: Story**

568 MEN'S HEALTH

Design Director_**George Karabotsos**
Designer_**Willie Gutierrez**
Director of Photography_**Laurie Kratochvil**
Photo Editor_**Brenda Milis**
Photographer_**Craig Cutler**
Publisher_**Rodale Inc.**
Issue_**December 2007**
Category_**Photo: Feature: Story**

569 MARIE CLAIRE

Creative Director_**Paul Martinez**
Design Director_**Jenny Leigh Thompson**
Director of Photography_**Kristen Schaefer**
Photographer_**Raphael Mazzucco**
Fashion Editor_**Tracy Taylor**
Publisher_**The Hearst Corporation-Magazines Div.**
Issue_**April 2007**
Category_**Photo: Feature: Story**

570

570

571

571

572

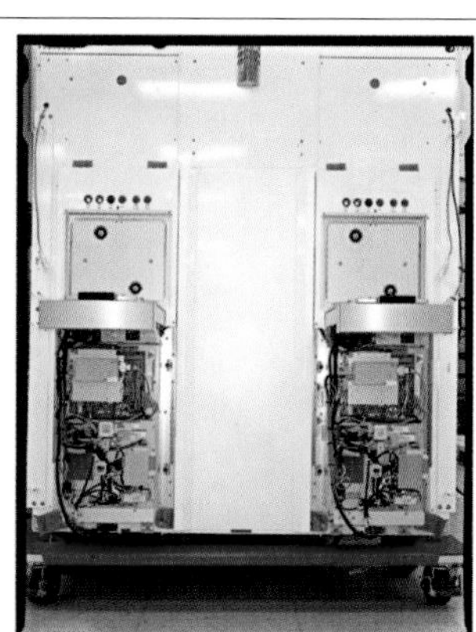

572

570 GQ

Design Director_Fred Woodward
Designer_Rob Hewitt
Director of Photography_Dora Somosi
Senior Photo Editor_Krista Prestek
Photographer_Matthias Ziegler
Editor-In-Chief_Jim Nelson
Publisher_Condé Nast Publications Inc.
Issue_November 2007
Category_Photo: Feature: Story

571 LING

Creative Director_Ricardo Feriche
Art Director_Joel Dalman
Illustrators_Óscar Aragón, Celine Robert, Vincens Castelltorr, Jari Mas
Issue_June 2007
Category_Photo: Feature: Story

572 CORPORATE LEADER

Creative Director_Florian Bachleda
Design Director_Ted Keller
Art Director_Mike Bain
Photo Editors_Ian Spanier, Leslie DeLa Vega
Photographer_Dan Winters
Studio_FB Design
Editor-In-Chief_Randall Lane
Publisher_Doubledown Media
Issue_Premiere Issue
Category_Photo: Feature: Story

573

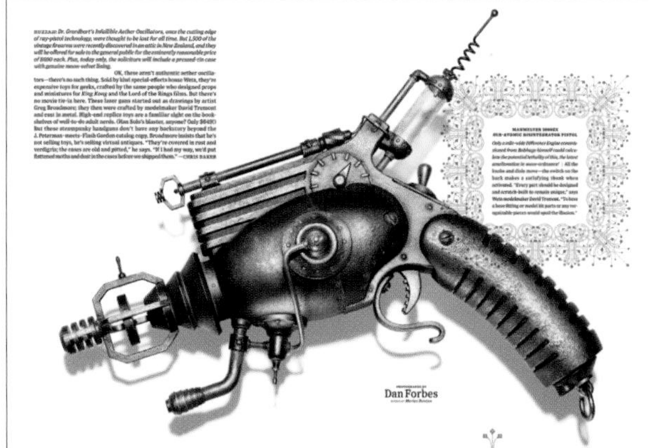

573

574

574

575

575

573 WIRED

Creative Director_Scott Dadich Designers_Chris Imlay, Scott Dadich Illustrator_Marian Bantjes Photo Editor_Carolyn Rauch Photographer_Dan Forbes Publisher_ Condé Nast Publications, Inc. Issue_June 2007 Category_Photo: Feature: Story

574 POPULAR MECHANICS

Design Director_Michael Lawton Art Director_Peter Herbert Assistant Art Director_Michael Friel Director of Photography_Allyson Torrisi Associate Photo Editor_Alison Unterreiner Photographer_Nathaniel Welch Publisher_The Hearst Corporation-Magazines Div. Issue_April 2007 Category_Photo: Feature: Story

575 DWELL

Design Director_Kyle Blue Designers_Brendan Callahan, Geoff Halber, Suzanne Lagasa Director of Photography_Kate Stone Foss Photo Editors_Andrea Lawson, Alexis Tjian Photographers_Catherine Ledner, Julius Shulman Production_Kathryn Hansen Publisher_Dwell LLC Issue_October 2007 Category_Photo: Feature: Story

576

576

577

577

578

578

576 DEPARTURES

Creative Director_Bernard Scharf
Art Director_Adam Bookbinder Associate Art Director _Lou Corredor
Director of Photography_Jennifer Laski Photo Editors_Jennifer Geaney, Brandon Perlman Photographer_Frédéric Lagrange Publisher_American Express Publishing Co. Issue_January/February 2007
Category_Photo: Feature: Story

577 MEN'S HEALTH

Design Director_George Karabotsos Art Director_John Dixon
Designer_John Dixon Illustrator_Jameson Simpson
Director of Photography_Laurie Kratochvil Photo Editor_Brenda Milis
Photographer_Patrik Giardino Publisher_Rodale Inc.
Issue_April 2007 Category_Photo: Feature: Story

578 T, THE NEW YORK TIMES STYLE MAGAZINE

Creative Director_Janet Froelich Senior Art Director_David Sebbah
Art Director_Christopher Martinez Designer_Christopher Martinez
Director of Photography_Kathy Ryan Photographer_Nan Goldin
Fashion Editor_Bruce Pask Editor-In-Chief_Stefano Tonchi
Publisher_The New York Times Issue_September 16, 2007
Category_Photo: Feature: Story

: SECTION **PHOTOGRAPHY** : AWARD **MERIT** : CATEGORY **FEATURE: STORY**

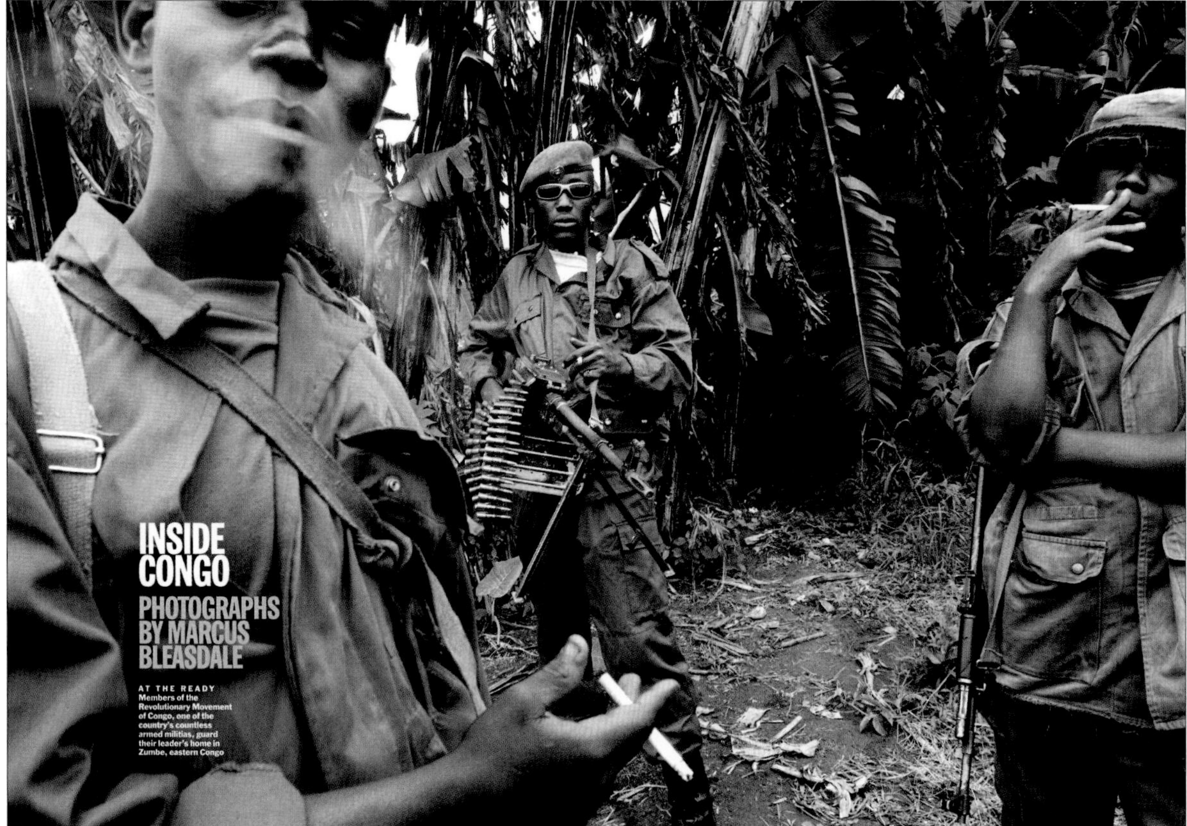

INSIDE
CONGO
PHOTOGRAPHS
BY MARCUS
BLEASDALE
AT THE READY
Members of the
Revolutionary Movement
of Congo, one of the
country's countless
armed militias, guard
their leader's home in
Zumbe, eastern Congo

579

LAST LOOK A woman grieves near the grave of her daughter, 47, one of the millions whose lives have been cut short by war and disease

579

579 TIME

Art Director_**Arthur Hochstein** Deputy Art Director_**D.W. Pine** Director of Photography_**MaryAnne Golon** Picture Editor_**Alice Gabriner** Photographer_**Marcus Bleasdale – VII** Publisher_**Time Inc.** Issue_**January 29, 2007** Category_**Photo: Feature: Story**

580

III.

Waiting for a sign, HOLLY HUNTER studies the landscape as she did in "Raising Arizona." The police might be on their way, or it might be her husband with their stolen baby. Either way, she's ready.

IV.

There's always a heavy, and JON POLITO, who plays some version of a tough guy in many Coen brothers films, is puzzled by the terrorizing nihilism of AIMEE MANN and DAVID THEWLIS in "The Big Lebowski." Like many of California's cultists, their philosophy has gone from dogma to vengeance.

THE NEW YORK TIMES MAGAZINE / NOVEMBER 11, 2007 77

580

580 THE NEW YORK TIMES MAGAZINE

Creative Director_Janet Froelich Art Director_Arem Duplessis Designers_Catherine Gilmore-Barnes, Nancy Harris Rouemy
Director of Photography_Kathy Ryan Photo Editor_Kira Pollack Photographer_Finlay MacKay Fashion Editor_Wendy Schecter
Editor-In-Chief_Gerry Marzorati Publisher_The New York Times Issue_November 11, 2007 Category_Photo: Feature: Story

Octopus
ARMED AND DELICIOUS
By Richard Schweid Photographs by Tom Schierlitz

581

581

582

1948
slow dancing

582

the hills are alive

583

583

581 DEPARTURES

Creative Director_ **Bernard Scharf** Art Director_**Adam Bookbinder** Associate Art Director_**Lou Corredor** Director of Photography_ **Jennifer Laski** Photo Editors_**Jennifer Geaney, Brandon Perlman** Photographer_**Tom Schierlitz** Publisher_**American Express Publishing Co.** Issue_**July/August 2007** Category_**Photo: Feature: Story**

582 CONDÉ NAST PORTFOLIO

Design Director_**Robert Priest** Art Director_**Grace Lee** Deputy Art Director_**Sarah Viñas** Designer_**Sarah Viñas** Director of Photography_ **Lisa Berman** Deputy Photo Editor_**Sarah Czeladnicki** Photo Editor_**Jane Yeomans** Photographers **Leonard Freed, Cornell Capa** Editor-In-Chief_**Joanne Lipman** Publisher **Condé Nast Publications Inc.** Issue_**December 2007** Category_**Photo: Feature: Story**

583 COOKIE

Design Director_**Kirby Rodriguez** Art Director_**Alex Grossman** Designers_**Shanna Greenberg, Nicolette Berthelot** Photo Editor_**Darrick Harris** Assistant Photo Editor_**Rebecca Etter** Photographer_**Thriza Schaap** Editor-In-Chief_**Pilar Guzmán** Publisher_**Condé Nast Publications Inc.** Issue **October/November 2007** Category_**Photo: Feature: Story**

584 MEN'S HEALTH

Design Director_**George Karabotsos** Art Director_**John Dixon** Designer_**John Dixon** Director of Photography_**Laurie Kratochvil** Photo Editor_**Brenda Milis** Publisher_**Rodale Inc.** Issue_**October 2007** Category_**Photo: Feature: Story**

MH SPECIAL SECTION
WOMEN, MONEY, AND FRIENDS COME AND GO, BUT DOGS ARE FOREVER
By Jim Thornton
Photographs by Jill Greenberg
OCTOBER 2007 185

584

"Remember these rules," said my new housemate Adam about my other new housemate, Diablo, a wolf-German shepherd mix who looked as though he had eaten more jugular veins than Snausages. "Don't make quick moves, don't try to touch him, don't look him in the eye, and you'll probably be fine."

I was 6 months out of college and hauling my cheap belongings into a cheaper Salt Lake City bungalow. Adam, an Apache construction worker, explained that he'd rescued his dog from a sadistic drunkard who had beaten the animal half to death with a golf iron. Then Diablo growled as if I were the guy's caddy.

"Quiet," Adam told the beast, not unkindly. Diablo's growling ratcheted down, but only a notch. No wonder the rent was so cheap.

For the next 3 weeks, the growl never stopped. I almost got used to it, the way I almost got used to navigating the bungalow with my eyes trained on the ceiling. Every once in a while, Diablo sniffed my groin with his elongated snout, which could snap moose femurs like pretzel sticks. It was all I could do to keep from fainting.

Our relationship changed one searing afternoon in August. Having come home early for lunch, I heard Diablo snarling at me from his fenced lair in the backyard. His growling carried its usual tone of hatred, but I sensed an additional chord, the barest tone of vulnerability in the heart of the largest carnivore I'd ever lived with.

As slowly and reassuringly as I could, I approached the fence. "It's okay, buddy," I said, trying to channel Saint Francis. "Easy, boy."

Diablo's problem was soon apparent: He'd upended his water dish in the 101° heat. What I decided to do next terrified me, but the alternative—doing nothing—seemed as cruel as beating the brute with a sand wedge. I unlocked the gate and slowly, slowly moved inside his territory. I could feel Diablo's breath on my leg, the guttural vibrations of his growl. Smoothly, slowly, I reached for the water dish, righted it, filled it from the wall spigot, and retreated. The growl was silenced by desperate, maybe even grateful, lapping from the dish.

When I returned home at 6:30 that night, Adam was cooking his dinner, and Diablo was in his usual evening spot beside his master's La-Z-Boy. He was sitting on his haunches, watching me silently. The growl had stopped.

From that point on, our bond deepened.

If you've ever become best friends with a former bully, you know how gratifying it can be. With Diablo beside me, I felt invulnerable—it was as if I'd developed a superpower. In the eons before modern weaponry, dogs like Diablo must have bestowed a sense of invincibility upon those fortunate human beings they trusted.

I got a delicious taste of this a month later, when I was jolted from a deep sleep by the sounds of Diablo in a rage. A couple of my ne'er-do-well friends had broken in at 3 a.m. to invite me out for drinks, which they had hoped I'd pay for. Diablo backed the slackers against a wall.

I gave him an affectionate scratch behind his ears, which, of course, did nothing to calm him. "You know what they say about sleeping dogs, eh, fellas?"

After a quick recitation of Adam's list of "don'ts," I hugged Diablo around his neck and watched my friends slink off into the night. The last thing they heard in retreat was my voice switching to pupspeak.

"Who's a good boy, Diablo? Who's a good boy? You are! Oh, yes you are!"

MY TRANSITION FROM PREY to pal with Diablo mimics the flow of dog-human evolution. Like all good Hollywood buddy films, the relationship between our species opened in deep enmity, slouched toward begrudging tolerance, and only in the final act blossomed into the stuff of—let's admit it—love. Men and dogs now enhance each other's lives in so many ways, from the purely pragmatic to the deeply emotional, that it's hard to imagine any other type of relationship.

In exchange for daily kibble, a place to sleep, and a pat on the head, contemporary canines will do almost anything for us—guide us when we're blind, pull our sleds across the snow-swept tundra, retrieve dead ducks from a lake, even sniff through toxic rubble in search of buried cadavers. As any cop will tell you, the dullest of tail waggers still exceeds by good measure the best burglar alarm ever invented.

Odd to think, then, that *Homo sapiens* and *Canis lupus* first saw each other as enemies: If we could kill and eat a wolf, or vice versa, there was one less meal to find and one

186 OCTOBER 2007

Illustrations by WARD SCHUMAKER

THE MANY FACES OF FIDO

Match the opening mug shot to the mutt

A	B	C
D	E	F

A BOXER
B BLOODHOUND
C ENGLISH BULLDOG
D GREAT DANE
E LABRADOR RETRIEVER
F BEAGLE

JILL GREENBERG
Dog portraits, 1993
"You need a lot of patience to capture the personality of a dog. If you can make a dog sit, you can get a good photograph. They like to be obedient. They like to do what they're trained to do and get praised for it. And dogs are much more focused when you're feeding them."

BRUCE WEBER
Untitled, 1985
Weber photographed Patrick Swayze with the actor's two dogs: a standard poodle and a Rhodesian ridgeback. The ridgeback earned its name from the strip of fur growing in the opposite direction along its spine. As for the standard poodle, the sheared coat was originally intended to help the dogs swim faster to retrieve downed waterfowl.

584

: SECTION
PHOTOGRAPHY

: AWARD
MERIT

: CATEGORY
FEATURE: STORY PHOTO-ILLUSTRATION

585

"DISTURBED" AND "UNDISTURBED" ARE WORDS THAT LANDSCAPE DESIGNER LINDA IVERSON USES FREQUENTLY. "I ALWAYS TRY TO USE WHAT'S INDIGENOUS TO THE SITE, WHETHER IT'S SHRUBS OR TREES OR THE TERRAIN ITSELF," SHE SAYS.

585

In the remote region of the Caucasus Mountains, once part of the Russian empire, lies a centuries-old village still inhabited almost entirely by Jews.
Photography by **Jason Eskenazi**

Jewish HIGH SOCIETY

586

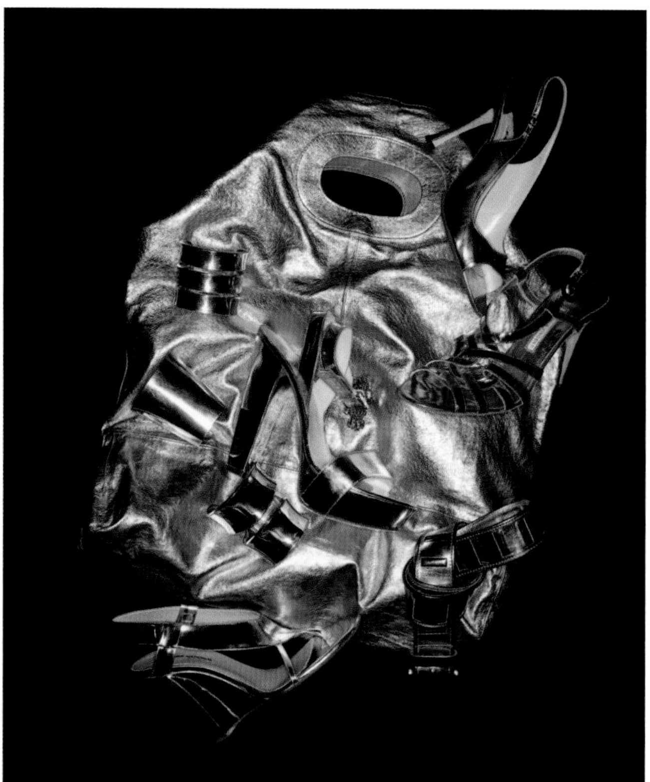

587

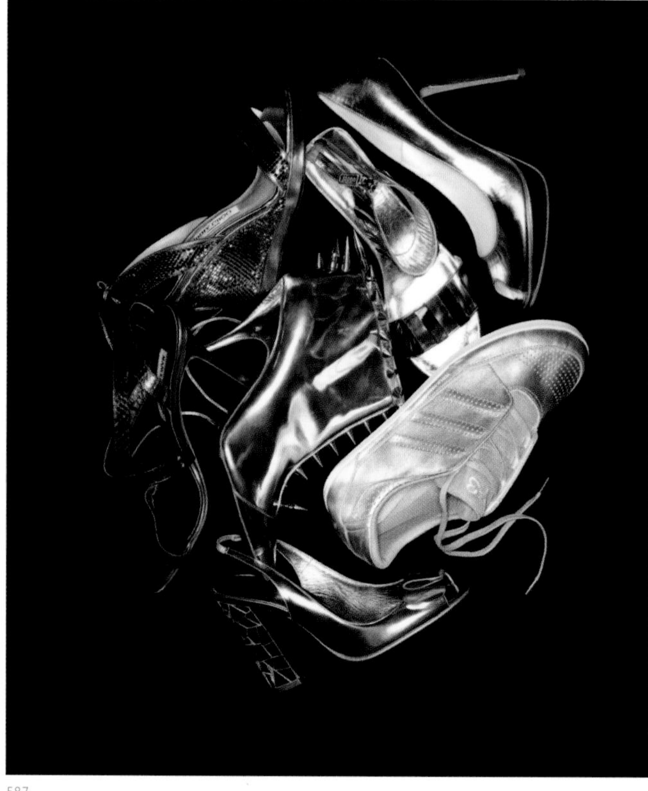

587

585 METROPOLITAN HOME

Art Director_**Keith D'Mello** Designer_**Keith D'Mello**
Photo Editor_**Alexandra Brodsky** Photographer_**Tom Ferris**
Publisher_**Hachette Filipacchi Media U.S.** Issue_**May 2007**
Category_**Photo: Feature: Spread/Single Page**

586 HADASSAH MAGAZINE

Creative Director_**Jodi Rossi** Art Director_**Jodi Rossi**
Photographer_**Jason Eskenazi** Issue_**January 2007**
Category_**Photo: Feature: Story**

587 WEST, THE LOS ANGELES TIMES MAGAZINE

Art Director_**Heidi Volpe** Designers_**Heidi Volpe, Carol Wakano**
Photo Editor_**Heidi Volpe** Photographer_**Charles Masters**
Issue_**March 4, 2007** Category_**Photo: Feature: Story**

588

589

590

591

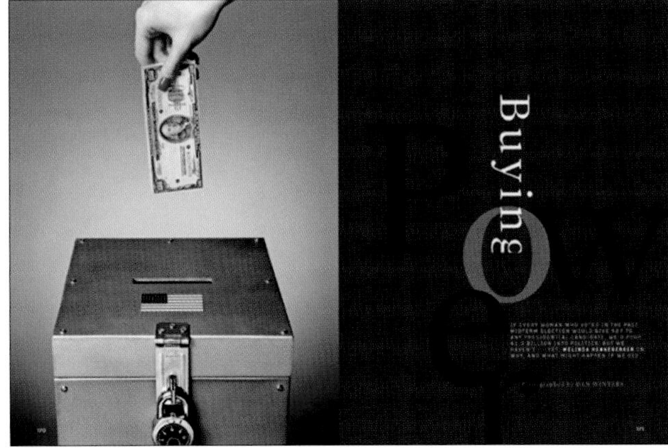

592

588 AARP THE MAGAZINE

Design Director_Andrzej Janerka Art Director_Todd Albertson Designer_Andrzej Janerka Photographer_Jana Leon Editor-In-Chief_Steve Slon Publisher_AARP Publications Issue_July/August 2007 Category_Photo-Illustration: Single Page/Spread/Story

589 INSTITUTIONAL INVESTOR

Creative Director_Tom Brown Art Director_Nathan Sinclair Designer_Stephanie Lora Photo Editor_Daniella Nilva Photographer_Fredrik Broden Publisher_Institutional Investor Inc. Issue_April 2007 Category_Photo-Illustration: Single Page/Spread/Story

590 ROLLING STONE

Designer_Joe Newton Illustrator_Matt Mahurin Director of Photography_Jodi Peckman Publisher_Wenner Media Issue_April 5, 2007 Category_Photo-Illustration: Single Page/Spread/Story

591 GLAMOUR

Design Director_Holland Utley Art Director_Peter Hemmel Designer_Neal Phiefer Illustrator_Laurie Rosenwald Director of Photography_Suzanne Donaldson Photo Editor_Stacey Delorenzo Photographer _Jill Greenberg Editor-In-Chief_Cynthia Leive Publisher_Condé Nast Publications Inc. Issue_March 2007 Category_Photo-Illustration: Single Page/Spread/Story

592 MORE

Creative Director_Maxine Davidowitz Art Director_Jose Fernandez Designer_Jose Fernandez Director of Photography_Karen Frank Photographer_Dan Winters Editor-In-Chief_Peggy Northrop Publisher_Meredith Corporation Issue_September 2007 Category_Photo-Illustration: Single Page/Spread/Story

Billions ov er Baghdad

Between April 2003 and June 2004, $12 billion in U.S. currency—much of it belonging to the Iraqi people—was shipped from the Federal Reserve to Baghdad, where it was dispensed by the Coalition Provisional Authority. Some of the cash went to pay for projects and keep ministries afloat, but, incredibly, at least $9 billion has gone missing, unaccounted for, in a frenzy of mismanagement and greed. Following a trail that leads from a safe in one of Saddam's palaces to a house near San Diego, to a P.O. box in the Bahamas, DONALD L. BARLETT and JAMES B. STEELE discover just how little anyone cared about how the money was handled

BAGHDAD AIRLIFT
In the occupation's first 14 months, C-130 cargo planes flew 363 tons of U.S. currency to Iraq.

336 | VANITY FAIR | www.vanityfair.com OCTOBER 2007 OCTOBER 2007 PHOTO ILLUSTRATION BY JOHN BLACKFORD VANITY FAIR | 337

593

Healthy Living
Doctor/Patient

Living to 100

594

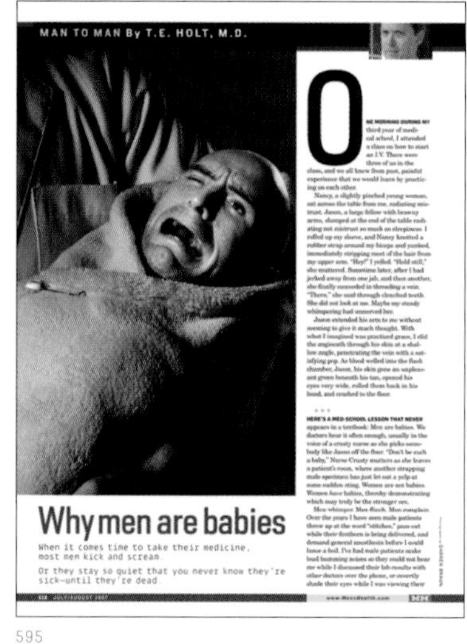

MAN TO MAN By T.E. HOLT, M.D.

Why men are babies

When it comes time to take their medicine, most men kick and scream.
Or they stay so quiet that you never know they're sick—until they're dead

595

THE TALK

Parlor Tricks
AFTER-DINNER GAMES ARE FAR FROM POLITE.
HEIDI JULAVITS PLAYS TO WIN

596

593 VANITY FAIR

Design Director_David Harris Art Director_Julie Weiss
Designer_Julie Weiss Illustrator_John Blackford
Editor-In-Chief_Graydon Carter
Publisher_Condé Nast Publications Inc. Issue_October 2007
Category_Photo-Illustration: Single Page/Spread/Story

594 MARTHA STEWART LIVING

Creative Director_Eric A. Pike Design Director_James Dunlinson
Art Director_Cameron King Designer_Kevin Brainard
Director of Photography_Heloise Goodman
Senior Photo Editor_Andrea Bakacs Photographer_Johnny Miller
Editor-In-Chief_Michael Boodro
Publisher_Martha Stewart Living Omnimedia Issue_September 2007
Category_Photo-Illustration: Single Page/Spread/Story

595 MEN'S HEALTH

Design Director_George Karabotsos Art Director_Vikki Nestico
Designer_Elizabeth Neal Director of Photography_Laurie Kratochvil
Photo Editor_Brenda Milis Photographer_Darren Braun
Publisher_Rodale Inc. Issue_July/August 2007
Category_Photo-Illustration: Single Page/Spread/Story

596 T, THE NEW YORK TIMES STYLE MAGAZINE

Creative Director_Janet Froelich Senior Art Director_David Sebbah
Art Director_Christopher Martinez Designer_Jamie Bartolacci
Illustrator_Joseph Heidecker Editor-In-Chief_Stefano Tonchi
Publisher_The New York Times Issue_November 4, 2007
Category_Photo-Illustration: Single Page/Spread/Story

597

600

598

599

601

597 MEN'S HEALTH

Design Director_**George Karabotsos** Art Director_**John Dixon** Director of Photography_**Laurie Kratochvil** Photo Editor_**Brenda Milis** Photographer_**Geof Kern** Publisher_**Rodale Inc.** Issue_**June 2007** Category_**Photo-Illustration: Single Page/Spread/Story**

598 MEN'S HEALTH

Design Director_**George Karabotsos** Art Director_**Vikki Nestico** Designers_**Vikki Nestico, Elizabeth Neal** Illustrator_**Eddie Guy** Director of Photography_**Laurie Kratochvil** Publisher_**Rodale Inc.** Issue_**July/August 2007** Category_**Photo-Illustration: Single Page/Spread/Story**

599 REAL SIMPLE

Design Director_**Ellene Wundrok** Designer_**Grace Kim** Director of Photography_**Casey Tierney** Photographer_**Marcus Nilsson** Publisher_ **Time Inc.** Issue_**May 2007** Category_**Photo-Illustration: Single Page/Spread/Story**

600 DETAILS

Creative Director_**Rockwell Harwood** Art Director_**Andre Jointe** Designer_**Rockwell Harwood** Illustrator_**Roberto Parada** Photo Editors_**Hali Tara Feldman, Alexandra Ghez** Publisher_**Condé Nast Publications** Issue_**April 2007** Category_**Photo-Illustration: Single Page/Spread/Story**

601 MORE

Creative Director_**Maxine Davidowitz** Art Director_**Jose Fernandez** Designer_**Jenn McManus** Director of Photography_**Karen Frank** Photo Editor_**Jenny Sargent** Photographer_**Plamen Petkov** Editor-In-Chief_**Peggy Northrop** Publisher_**Meredith Corporation** Issue_**September 2007** Category_**Photo-Illustration: Single Page/Spread/Story**

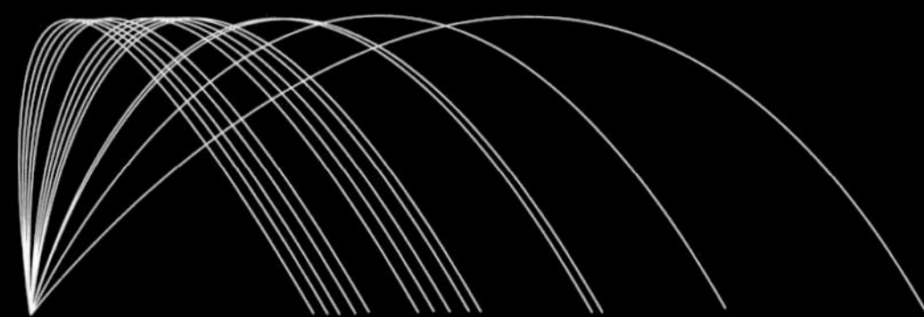

illustration

ENTRIES: 676
CATEGORIES: 3

GOLD: 4
SILVER: 4
MERIT: 37

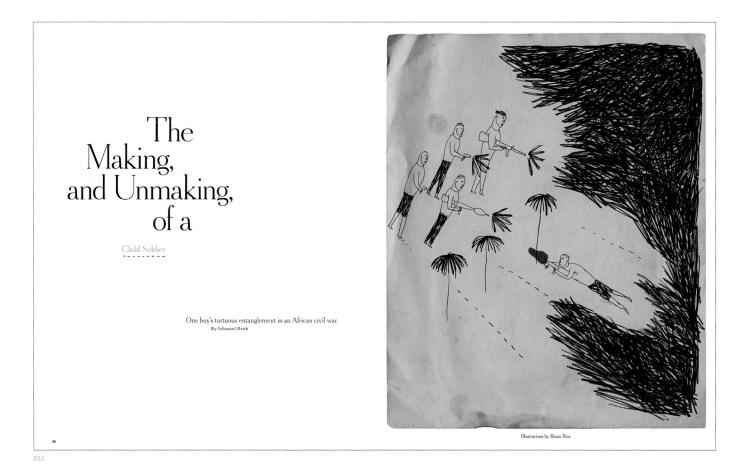

The Making, and Unmaking, of a

Child Soldier

One boy's tortuous entanglement in an African civil war.

By Ishmael Beah

36

Illustrations by Brian Rea

602

to follow the path until we received instructions on what to do next. We walked for long hours and stopped only to eat sardines and corned beef with gari, sniff brown brown and take more white capsules. The combination of these drugs made us fierce. The idea of death didn't cross my mind, and killing had become as easy as drinking water. After that first killing, my mind had stopped making remorseful records, or so it seemed.

Before we got to a rebel camp, we would deviate from the path and walk in the forest. Once the camp was in sight, we would surround it and wait for the lieutenant's command. The rebels roamed about; some sat against walls, dozing off, and others, boys as young as we, stood at guard posts passing around marijuana. Whenever I looked at rebels during raids, my entire body shook with fury; they were the people who had shot my friends and family. So when the lieutenant gave orders, I shot as many as I could, but I didn't feel better. After every gunfight, we would enter the rebel camp, killing those we had wounded. We would then search the houses and gather gallons of gasoline, enormous amounts of marijuana and cocaine, bales of clothes, watches, rice, salt, gari and many other things. We rounded up any civilians — men, women, boys and young girls — hiding in the huts and houses and made them carry our loot back to the base. We shot them if they tried to run away.

On one of these raids, we captured a few rebels after a long gunfight and a lot of civilian casualties. We undressed the prisoners and tied their arms behind their backs until their chests were tight as drums. "Where did you get all this ammunition from?" the corporal asked one of the prisoners, a man with an almost dreadlocked beard. He spat in the corporal's face, and the corporal immediately shot him in the head at close range. He fell to the ground, and blood slowly leaked out of his head. We cheered in admiration of the corporal's action and saluted him as he walked by. Suddenly, a rebel hiding in the bushes shot one of our boys. We dispersed around the village in search of the shooter. When the young muscular rebel was captured, the lieutenant slit his neck with his bayonet. The rebel ran before he fell to the ground and stopped moving. We cheered again, raising our guns in the air, shouting and whistling.

During that time, a lot of things were done with no reason or explanation. Sometimes we were asked to leave for war in the middle of a movie. We would come back hours later after killing many people and continue the movie as if we had just returned from intermission. We were always either on the front lines, watching a war movie or doing drugs. There was no time to be alone or to think. When we conversed with one another, we talked only about the movies and how impressed we were with the way either the lieutenant, the corporal or one of us had killed someone. It was as if nothing else existed.

The villages that we captured and turned into our bases as we went along and the forests that we slept in became my home. My squad was my family, my gun was my provider and protector and my rule was to kill or be killed. The extent of my thoughts didn't go much beyond that. We had been fighting for more than two years, and killing had become a daily activity. I felt no pity for anyone. My childhood had gone by without my knowing, and it seemed as if my heart had frozen. I knew that day and night came and went because of the presence of the moon and the sun, but I had no idea whether it was a Sunday or a Friday.

Taken From the Front

In my head my life was normal. But everything began to change in January 1996. I was 15.

One morning that month, a truck came to the village where we were based. Four men dressed in clean blue jeans and white T-shirts that said "Unicef" in big blue letters jumped out. They were shown to the lieutenant's house. It seemed as if he had been expecting them. As they sat talking on the veranda, we watched them from under the mango tree, where we sat cleaning our guns. Soon all the boys were told to line up for the lieutenant who selected a few of us and asked the adult soldiers to take away our guns and ammunition. A bunch of boys, including my friend Alhaji and me, were ushered to the truck. I stared back at the veranda where the lieutenant now stood, looking in the other direction, toward the forest, his hands crossed behind his back. I still didn't know exactly what was going on, but I was beginning to get angry and anxious. Why had the lieutenant decided to give us up to these civilians? We thought that we were part of the war until the end.

We were on the road for hours. I had gotten used to always moving and hadn't sat in one place idly for a long time. It was night when the truck stopped at a center, where there were other boys whose appearances, red eyes and somber faces resembled ours. Alhaji and I looked at this group, and he asked the boys who they were. A boy who was sitting on the stoop angrily said: "We fought for the R.U.F.; the army is the enemy. We fought for freedom, and the army killed my family and destroyed my village. I will kill any of those army bastards every time I get a chance to do so." The boy took off his shirt to fight, and on his arm was the R.U.F. brand. Mambu, one of the boys on our side, shouted, "They are rebels," and reached for his bayonet, which he had hidden in his army shorts; most of us had hidden either a knife or a grenade before our guns were taken from us. Before Mambu could grab his weapon, the R.U.F. boy punched him in the face. He fell, and when he got up, his nose was bleeding. The rebel boys drew out the few bayonets they had in their shorts and rushed toward us. It was war all over again. Perhaps the naïve men who had taken us to the center thought that removing us from the war would lessen our hatred for the R.U.F. It hadn't crossed their minds that a change of environment wouldn't immediately make us normal boys; we were dangerous, brainwashed to kill.

One boy grabbed my neck from behind. He was squeezing for the kill, and I couldn't use my bayonet effectively, so I elbowed him with all my

40 ILLUSTRATION BY BRIAN REA THE NEW YORK TIMES MAGAZINE / JANUARY 14, 2007 41

602

602 THE NEW YORK TIMES MAGAZINE

Creative Director_Janet Froelich Art Director_Arem Duplessis Designer_Gail Bichler
Illustrator_Brian Rea Editor-In-Chief_Gerry Marzorati Publisher_The New York Times
Issue_January 14, 2007 Category_Illo: Story

: SECTION
ILLUSTRATION

: AWARD
GOLD

: CATEGORY
SPREAD/SINGLE COVER

When a leading bird-watcher in Texas shot one of the feral cats that had been stalking piping plovers, he started the kind of war that only really concerned humans can wage.

By Bruce Barcott

That Kills the Bird?

Illustrations by Jillian Tamaki

46

603

604

THE NEW YORK TIMES MAGAZINE

Creative Director_Janet Froelich Art Director_Arem Duplessis
Designer_Leo Jung Illustrator_Jillian Tamaki
Editor-In-Chief_Gerry Marzorati Publisher_The New York Times
Issue_December 2, 2007 Category_Illo: Spread/Single Page

LING

Creative Director_Ricardo Feriche
Art Director_Joel Dalman Illustrator_HeadsonBoards.com
Issue_November 2007 Category_Illo: Spread/Single Page

A 10TH-CENTURY ROAD TALE! A SWASHBUCKLING, EMPIRE-CHANGING ADVENTURE SET BETWEEN THE BLACK AND CASPIAN SEAS! SILK-ROAD SWORD FIGHTS! KIDNAPPING AND INTRIGUE! AN ABYSSINIAN GIANT! AND MORE!!! THE NEW SUNDAY SERIAL, BY MICHAEL CHABON

The New York Times Magazine

JANUARY 28, 2007 / SECTION 6

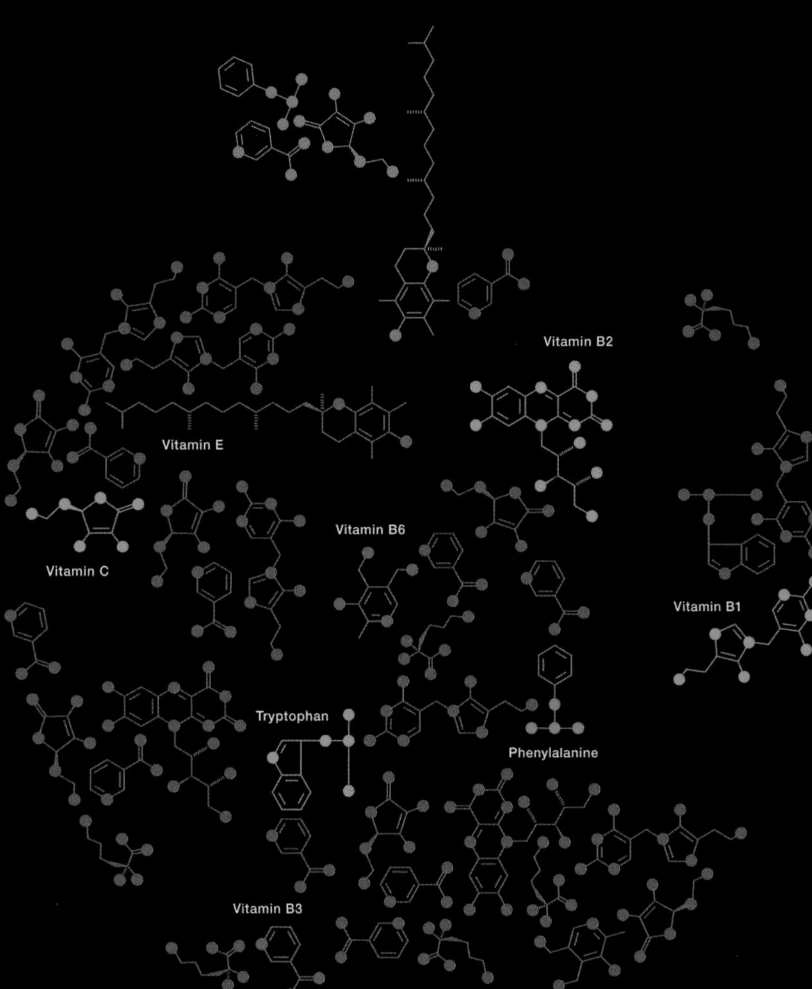

The Age of Nutritionism

How scientists have ruined the way we eat. By Michael Pollan

LAURA SECOR: WHO'S IN CHARGE IN IRAN? **MARK OPPENHEIMER:** HOW WOULD JESUS DANCE?

605

605 THE NEW YORK TIMES MAGAZINE

Creative Director_Janet Froelich Art Director_Arem Duplessis
Designer_Arem Duplessis Illustrator_Leo Jung
Editor-In-Chief_Gerry Marzorati Publisher_The New York Times
Issue_January 28, 2007 Category_Illo: Cover

606

606 WIRED

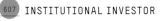

Creative Director_Scott Dadich Design Director_Wyatt Mitchell
Art Director_Carl DeTorres Designers_Scott Dadich, Wyatt Mitchell, Carl DeTorres Illustrator_Yoichiro Ono
Photo Editor_Zana Woods Publisher_Condé Nast Publications, Inc.
Issue_November 2007 Category_Illo: Cover

607 INSTITUTIONAL INVESTOR

Creative Director_Tom Brown Art Director_Nathan Sinclair
Designer_Nathan Sinclair Illustrator_Barry Falls
Publisher_Institutional Investor Inc. Issue_May 2007
Category_Illo: Story

MAY 2007 •• INSTITUTIONAL INVESTOR 180

MONEY MANAGEMENT

Dead Plan Walking

As more companies look to freeze or even terminate their defined benefit pension plans, many are rethinking risk and revolutionizing the way they invest the assets. Money managers must adapt or suffer.

By Virginia Munger Kahn & Michael Shari
ILLUSTRATIONS BY BARRY FALLS

FIRST GENERAL MOTORS CORP. DECIDED TO make life a little tougher for its future retirees. Now it's about to do the same for its money managers.

On January 1, the Detroit automaker froze its defined benefit pension plan for 33,000 salaried workers, cutting benefits for some employees and shifting others into a less costly 401(k) plan. Then in March, GM disclosed that it would dramatically slash the amount of stocks it owns, cutting its equity allocation by 20 percentage points and increasing its fixed-income allocation by the same amount. By the end of the year, GM plans to shift some $21 billion into bonds, costing its investment managers millions of dollars in fees.

There is good reason for the carmaker's suddenly conservative investment posture. After three years of falling stock prices and declining interest rates, the company had to borrow about $13.5 billion in a landmark 2003 bond offering to prop

607

MAY 2007 •• INSTITUTIONAL INVESTOR 182

MONEY MANAGEMENT

up its badly underfunded pension plan. It poured money into stocks and alternative investments, such as hedge funds and private equity, seeking — and getting — strong performance that gave the $101.4 billion plan a $16 billion surplus at the end of last year. Now GM aims to avoid such unpredictable swings in funding.

"The corporation is trying to lower the volatility of that surplus over time," says Nancy Everett, president and CEO of General Motors Asset Management Corp., the GM subsidiary that looks after the pension fund and invests most of its assets with external money managers.

More companies could soon follow GM's lead. Even as surging stock markets and favorable interest rates have restored the health of many plans, defusing fears of an imminent nationwide pension crisis, companies are looking to batten their hatches by freezing or even terminating plans. Roughly 20 to 25 percent of the nation's $2.3 trillion in corporate defined-benefit-plan assets had

measure a plan's funded status and run it through the balance sheet, potentially reducing the company's net worth. In the next three to four years, FASB is widely expected to extend mark-to-market pension accounting to the income statement, a move that could make corporate earnings more volatile.

Whether companies with frozen pension plans will follow GM's lead and dump equities isn't clear yet, but few doubt that the trend will usher in sweeping changes in the way that they manage their assets. "The ground is shifting," says Alec Stais, chief investment officer of the multiproduct investment group at Goldman Sachs Asset Management. "This is a fundamental shift in pension investing."

The implications are profound for the U.S. money management industry, which grew up side by side with defined benefit plans. The number of corporate plans has dropped precipitously, and defined benefit asset growth has slowed dramatically in recent years as

Freezes and terminations were once the hallmark of troubled businesses. Today they come mostly from stable companies.

been frozen by year-end 2006 — meaning some or all employees had stopped accruing benefits — enabling companies to rein in their pension costs. In the next five years, that figure could rise to 40 to 60 percent of defined-benefit-plan assets, McKinsey & Co. estimates. The consulting firm also expects the percentage of assets from terminated pension plans that are managed by insurance companies, which typically pay them out to beneficiaries in the form of annuities, to rise from less than 5 percent of total pension assets to as much as 20 percent. By McKinsey's estimate, then, only 20 to 40 percent of pension assets would remain in active plans.

Once such freezes and terminations were the hallmark of troubled businesses. But today they come mostly from financially stable companies, including Verizon, Citigroup, Hewlett-Packard Co., IBM Corp. and Goodyear Tire and Rubber Co. Typically, such companies switch their workers into defined contribution 401(k) plans, which are less costly.

Ironically, the pension freezes are being driven in part by reform that was originally intended to strengthen defined benefit plans. Last August, President George W. Bush signed into law the Pension Protection Act of 2006, which phases in tighter pension funding rules and will require plan sponsors to value their pension assets and liabilities more frequently, beginning in 2008. The legislation will bring more transparency to pension finances, but it will also make funding requirements more costly and unpredictable.

"The Pension Protection Act effectively sounds the death knell for defined benefit plans," says Robert Pozen, chairman of Boston-based MFS Investment Management.

New rules handed down by the Financial Accounting Standards Board are only adding to the pressure on companies. Until last year plan sponsors could report the net funded status of their pension plans in balance-sheet footnotes and temper, or "smooth," swings in the value of their pension assets and liabilities by amortizing gains and losses over a variable period, typically ten to 15 years. Now they must use the current market value of assets and liabilities to

defined contribution plans and the mutual fund business have notched explosive increases. Nonetheless, the nation's corporate defined benefit plans had some $2.3 trillion in total assets at the end of last year and accounted for about 44 percent of the private sector retirement landscape, according to Cerulli Associates, a Boston-based consulting firm.

"Even though the defined benefit business is in a long, slow decline, it's important to recognize the assets will hang around for many years to come," says Cerulli analyst Daniel Lucey, who covers the retirement and insurance industries.

For decades the most profitable part of the business belonged to traditional, long-only equity managers. No longer. Industry experts predict that these managers will have to adapt or suffer as pension funds reduce purchases of stocks and shift into fixed income, lifting profits for bond houses. At the same time, hedge funds, private equity shops and other alternative managers stand to gain handsomely as pension funds chase alpha.

This is already happening, but the pace is expected to quicken. McKinsey estimates that long-only equity managers will see their fees drop from $2.6 billion in 2006 to $2 billion or less in 2012. Driven by asset growth and increased flows to investment strategies with higher fees, overall money management fees from defined benefit assets will climb from $9.4 billion to $11.8 billion, McKinsey estimates. Meanwhile, fixed-income fees will rise from $1.3 billion to $1.8 billion. Managers of hedge funds, private equity and other alternative products will see spoils grow the most dramatically, with management fees rising from $3.8 billion to $6.5 billion. (The remaining share of fee revenue will flow to passive and quantitative managers.)

Farsighted money managers are not sitting pat. Many have sprung into action in anticipation of new demands from corporate defined benefit clients — and new challenges from competitors. Firms like State Street Global Advisors and Eaton Vance Corp., both based in Boston, and San Francisco-based Barclays Global Investors are introducing new fixed-income products that help pension funds reduce

607

How to Take Care of Your Beautiful Mind

Do you ever have those moments when you feel you're losing it? You're totally overwhelmed, or you're soaking in sadness, or everyone's driving you nuts. You're having a really bad day...
or month...or life. Well, hold on! We've got some important answers for you, starting with a mental health kit of proven techniques to bring you back from the edge, center you, help
you breathe again.... If you think psychotherapy is only for the seriously batty, a psychiatrist in training takes you behind closed doors to hear how three women learned to untangle
the past and live their best lives now. And even for those who have to deal with severe emotional chaos, therapy combined with advances in medication is creating a way out and a way forward—
as a highly successful artist who has bipolar disorder tells us with remarkable candor. Here's to clarity, calm, and the joy and power of knowing yourself. ▸ ILLUSTRATIONS BY BALINT ZSAKO

312 OCTOBER 2007

608

 O, THE OPRAH MAGAZINE

Design Director_**Carla Frank**
Art Director_**Ralph Groom**
Designer_**Ralph Groom**
Illustrator_**Balint Zsako**
Editor-In-Chief_**Amy Gross**
Publisher_**The Hearst Corporation-Magazines Division**
Issue **October_2007**
Category_**Illo: Spread/Single Page**

 THE NEW YORK TIMES MAGAZINE

Creative Director_**Janet Froelich**
Art Director_**Arem Duplessis**
Designers_**Gail Bichler, Arem Duplessis**
Photo Editor_**Kira Pollack**
Photographer_**Vik Muniz**
Artists_**Julian Calderon, Ian Davenport, Robert J. Lang, Ronan and Erwan Bouroullec, Carin Goldberg, Kiki Smith, Ian Flamm, Cuartopiso**
Editor-In-Chief_**Gerry Marzorati**
Publisher_**The New York Times**
Issue_**April 15, 2007**
Category_**Illo: Story**

The Power of Green

What does America need to regain its global stature?

Environmental leadership.

By Thomas L. Friedman

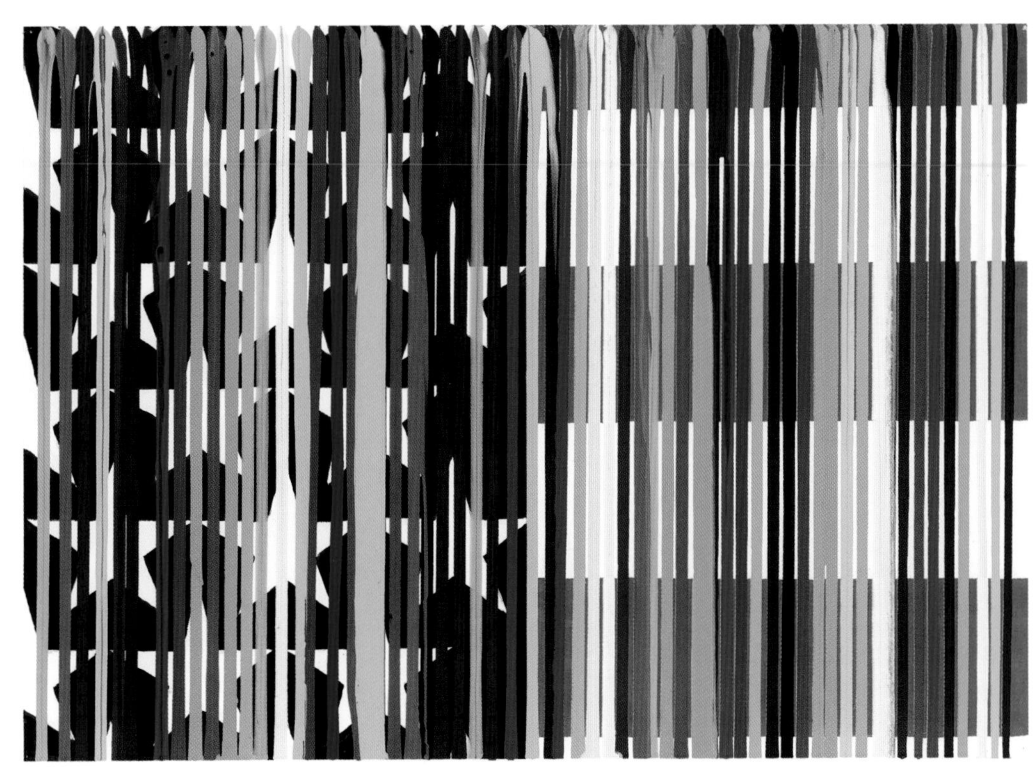

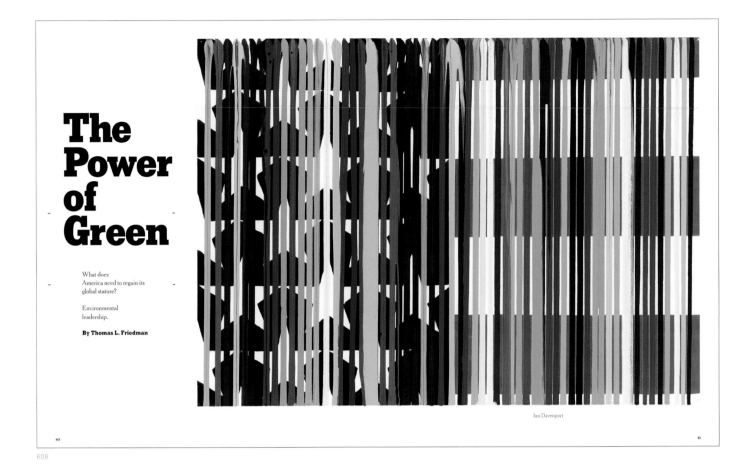

Ian Davenport

I.

One day Iraq, our post-9/11 trauma and the divisiveness of the Bush years

will all be behind us — and America will need, and want, to get its groove back. We will need to find a way to reknit America at home, reconnect America abroad and restore America to its natural place in the global order — as the beacon of progress, hope and inspiration. I have an idea how. It's called "green."

In the world of ideas, to name something is to own it. If you can name an issue, you can own the issue. One thing that always struck me about the term "green" was the degree to which, for so many years, it was defined by its opponents — by the people who wanted to disparage it. And they defined it as "liberal," "tree-hugging," "sissy," "girlie-man," "unpatriotic," "vaguely French."

Well, I want to rename "green." I want to rename it geostrategic, geoeconomic, capitalistic and patriotic. I want to do that because I think that living, working, designing, manufacturing and projecting America in a green way can be the basis of a new unifying political movement for the 21st century. A redefined, broader and more muscular green ideology is not meant to trump the traditional Republican and Democratic agendas but rather to bridge them when it comes to addressing the three major issues facing every American today: jobs, temperature and terrorism.

How do our kids compete in a flatter world? How do they thrive in a warmer world? How do they survive in a more dangerous world? Those are, in a nutshell, the big questions facing America at the dawn of the 21st century. But these problems are so large in scale that they can only be effectively addressed by an America with 50 green states — not an America divided between red and blue states.

Because a new green ideology, properly defined, has the power to mobilize liberals and conservatives, evangelicals and atheists, big business and environmentalists around an agenda that can both pull us together and propel us forward. That's why I say: We don't just need the first black president. We need the first green president. We don't just need the first woman president. We need the first environmental president. We don't just need a president who has been toughened by years as a prisoner of war but a president who is tough enough to level with the American people about the profound economic, geopolitical and climate threats posed by our addiction to oil — and to offer a real plan to reduce our dependence on fossil fuels.

After World War II, President Eisenhower responded to the threat of Communism and the "red menace" with massive spending on an interstate highway system to tie America together, in large part so that we could better move weapons in the event of a war with the Soviets. That highway system, though, helped to enshrine America's car culture (atrophying our railroads) and to lock in suburban sprawl and low-density housing, which all combined to get America addicted to cheap fossil fuels, particularly oil. Many in the world followed our model.

Today, we are paying the accumulated economic, geopolitical and climate prices for that kind of America. I am not proposing that we radically alter our lifestyles. We are who we are — including a car culture. But if we want to continue to be who we are, enjoy the benefits and be able to pass them on to our children, we do need to fuel our future in a cleaner, greener way. Eisenhower rallied us with the red menace. The next president will have to rally us with a green patriotism. Hence my motto: "Green is the new red, white and blue."

The good news is that after traveling around America this past year, looking at how we use energy and the emerging alternatives, I can report that green really has gone Main Street — thanks to the perfect storm created by 9/11, Hurricane Katrina and the Internet revolution. The first flattened the twin towers, the second flattened New Orleans and the third flattened the global economic playing field. The convergence of all three has turned many of our previous assumptions about "green" upside down in a very short period of time, making it much more compelling to many more Americans.

But here's the bad news: While green has hit Main Street — more Americans than ever now identify themselves as greens, or what I call "Geo-Greens" to differentiate their more muscular and strategic green ideology — green has not gone very far down Main Street. It certainly has not gone anywhere near the distance required to preserve our lifestyle. The dirty little secret is that we're fooling ourselves. We in America talk like we're already "the greenest generation," as the business writer Dan Pink once called it. But here's the really inconvenient truth: We have not even begun to be serious about the costs, the effort and the scale of change that will be required to shift our country, and eventually the world, to a largely emissions-free energy infrastructure over the next 50 years.

II.

A few weeks after American forces invaded Afghanistan, I visited the Pakistani frontier town of Peshawar, a hotbed of Islamic radicalism. On the way, I stopped at the famous Darul Uloom Haqqania, the biggest madrasa, or Islamic school, in Pakistan, with 2,800 live-in students. The Taliban leader Mullah Muhammad Omar attended this madrasa as a younger man. My Pakistani friend and I were allowed to observe a class of young boys who sat on the floor, practicing their rote learning of the Koran from texts perched on wooden holders. The air in the Koran class was so thick and stale it felt as if you could have cut it into blocks. The teacher asked an 8-year-old boy to chant a Koranic verse for us, which he did with the elegance of an experienced muezzin. I asked another student, an Afghan refugee, Rahim Kunduz, age 12, what his reaction was to the Sept. 11 attacks, and he said: "Most likely the attack came from Americans inside America. I am pleased that America has had to face pain, because the rest of the world has tasted its pain." A framed sign on the wall said this room was "A gift of the Kingdom of Saudi Arabia."

Sometime after 9/11 — an unprovoked mass murder perpetrated by 19 men, 15 of whom were Saudis — green went geostrategic, as Americans started to realize we were financing both sides in the war on terrorism. We were financing the U.S. military with our tax dollars; and we were financing a transformation of Islam, in favor of its most intolerant strand, with our gasoline purchases. How stupid is that?

Islam has always been practiced in different forms. Some are more embracing of modernity, reinterpretation of the Koran and tolerance of other faiths, like Sufi Islam or the populist Islam of Egypt, Ottoman Turkey and Indonesia. Some strands, like Salafi Islam — followed by the Wahhabis of Saudi Arabia and by Al Qaeda — believe Islam should be returned to an austere form practiced in the time of the Prophet Muhammad, a form hostile to modernity, science, "infidels" and women's rights. By enriching the Saudi and Iranian treasuries via our gasoline purchases, we are financing the export of the Saudi puritanical brand of Sunni Islam and the Iranian fundamentalist brand of Shiite Islam, tilting the Muslim world in a more intolerant direction. At the Muslim fringe, this creates more recruits for the Taliban, Al Qaeda, Hamas, Hezbollah and the Sunni suicide bomb squads of Iraq; at the Muslim center, it creates a much bigger constituency of people who applaud suicide bombers as martyrs.

The Saudi Islamic export drive first went into high gear after extreme fundamentalists challenged the Muslim credentials of the Saudi ruling family by taking over the Grand Mosque of Mecca in 1979 — a year that coincided with the Iranian revolution and a huge rise in oil prices. The attack on the Grand Mosque by these Koran-and-rifle-wielding Islamic militants shook the Saudi ruling family to its core. The al-Sauds responded to this challenge to their religious bona fides by becoming outwardly more religious. They gave their official Wahhabi religious establishment even more power to impose Islam on public life. Awash in cash thanks to the spike in oil prices, the Saudi government and charities also spent hundreds of millions of dollars endowing mosques, youth clubs and Muslim schools all over the world, ensuring that Wahhabi imams, teachers and textbooks would preach Saudi-style Islam. Eventually, notes Lawrence Wright in "The Looming Tower," his history of Al Qaeda, "Saudi Arabia, which constitutes only 1 percent of the world Muslim population, would support 90 percent of the expenses of the entire faith, overriding other traditions of Islam."

Saudi mosques and wealthy donors have also funneled cash to the Sunni insurgents in Iraq. The Associated Press reported from Cairo in December: "Several drivers interviewed by the A.P. in Middle East capitals said Saudis have been using religious events, like the hajj pilgrimage to Mecca and a smaller pilgrimage, as cover for illicit money transfers. Some money, they said, is carried into Iraq on buses with returning pilgrims. 'They sent boxes full of dollars and asked me to deliver them to certain addresses in Iraq,' said one driver. … 'I know it is being sent to the resistance, and if I don't take it with me, they will kill me.'"

No wonder more Americans have concluded that conserving oil to put less money in the hands of hostile forces is now a geostrategic imperative. President Bush's refusal to do anything meaningful after 9/11 to reduce our gasoline usage really amounts to a policy of "No Mullah Left Behind." James Woolsey, the former C.I.A. director, minces no words: "We are funding the rope for the hanging of ourselves."

No, I don't want to bankrupt Saudi Arabia or trigger an Islamist revolt there. Its leadership is more moderate and pro-Western than its people. But the way

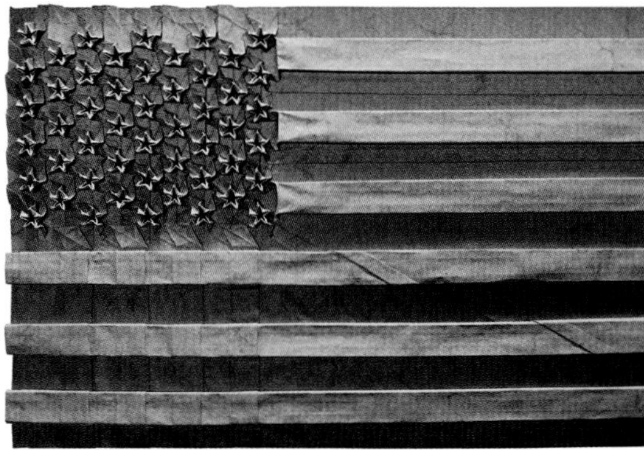

Robert J. Lang

Thomas L. Friedman is a columnist for The New York Times specializing in foreign affairs.

PHOTOGRAPH BY DWIGHT ESCHLIMAN FOR THE NEW YORK TIMES

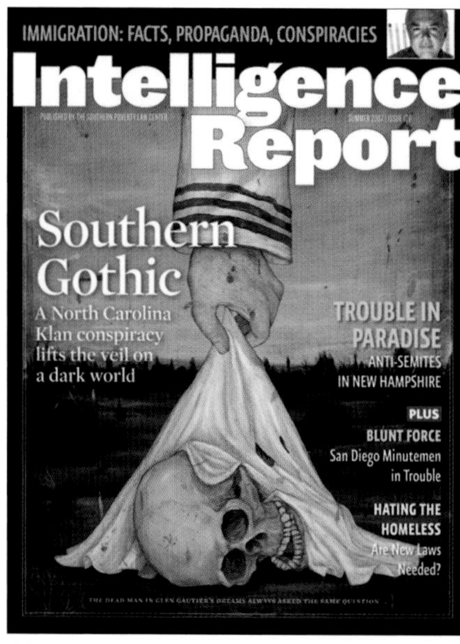

610

612

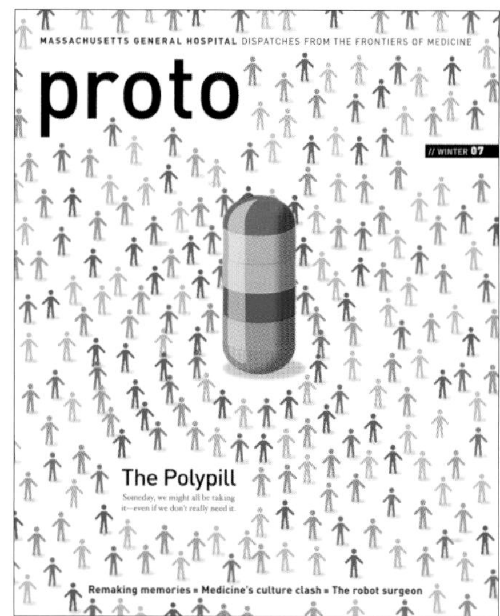

614

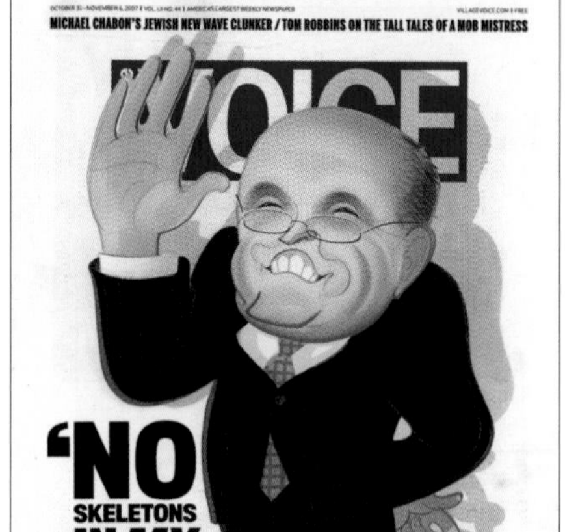

611

613

615

610 INTELLIGENCE REPORT

Creative Director_Russell Estes
Art Director_Valerie Downes
Designer Valerie Downes
Illustrator_Jason Holley
Studio_SPLC Team
Publisher_Southern Poverty Law Center
Client_Intelligence Project
Issue_Summer 2007
Category_Illo: Cover

611 THE VILLAGE VOICE

Creative Director_Ted Keller
Illustrator_Eric Palma
Publisher_Village Voice Media
Issue_November 6, 2007
Category_Illo: Cover

612 TIME OUT NEW YORK

Design Director_Adam Logan Fulrath
Illustrator_Matt Mahurin
Publisher_Time Out New York Partners, L.P.
Issue_June 20, 2007
Category_Illo: Cover

613 METROPOLIS

Creative Director_Criswell Lappin
Art Director_Erich Nagler
Photo Editor_Bilyana Dimitrova
Photographer_Marc Alary
Publisher_Bellerophon Publications
Issue_April 2007
Category_Illo: Cover

614 PROTO

Creative Director_Charlene Benson
Design Director_Alex Knowlton
Designer_Lee Williams
Illustrator_Christoph Niemann
Studio_Time Inc. Content Solutions
Publisher_Time Inc. Strategic Communications
Client_Massachusets General Hospital
Issue_Winter 2007
Category_Illo: Cover

615 METROPOLIS

Creative Director_Criswell Lappin
Art Director_Dungjai Pungauthaikan
Illustrator_Andrew Taray
Photo Editor_Bilyana Dimitrova
Publisher_Bellerophon Publications
Issue_September 2007
Category_Illo: Cover

616

619

617

618

620

616 THE FADER

Creative Director_Phil Bicker
Illustrator_Steven Wilson
Issue_December 2007
Category_Illo: Cover

617 THE NEW YORK TIMES BOOK REVIEW

Design Director_Tom Bodkin
Art Director_Nicholas Blechman
Illustrator_Noma Bar
Publisher_The New York Times
Issue_June 10, 2007
Category_Illo: Cover

618 THE NEW YORK TIMES BOOK REVIEW

Design Director_Tom Bodkin
Art Director_Nicholas Blechman
Illustrator_Christoph Niemann
Publisher_The New York Times
Issue_May 13, 2007 Category_Illo: Cover

619 THE NEW YORK TIMES MAGAZINE

Creative Director_Janet Froelich
Art Director_Arem Duplessis
Designer_Gail Bichler
Illustrator_Balint Zsako
Editor-In-Chief_Gerry Marzorati
Publisher_The New York Times
Issue_July 15, 2007
Category_Illo: Cover

620 WIRED

Creative Director_Scott Dadich
Art Director_Maili Holiman
Illustrators_Armstrong & White, Saddington & Baynes
Photo Editor_Zana Woods
Publisher_Condé Nast Publications, Inc.
Issue_June 2007
Category_Illo: Cover

"THIS ISN'T HELL, YOU BLOODY YOBS. THIS IS ONLY TEXAS."

illustrations by Kako

IN THIS EXCLUSIVE EXCERPT FROM *CUSTER'S BROTHER'S HORSE*, THE NEW NOVEL BY **EDWIN "BUD" SHRAKE**, HONEST MEN ARE MARCHED TO THE GALLOWS BY RED-THROATED UNIONISTS HUNGRY FOR REVENGE.

626

Copyright © 2007 by Edwin Shrake. Used by permission of John M. Hardy Publishing Co.

177

626

625

ILLUSTRATIONS MIXED WITH TEXT HAVE A RICH HISTORY IN JAPAN. TV WAS SLOW TO ARRIVE IN THE COUNTRY AFTER WWII, AND MANGA SOON BECAME THE MOST POPULAR FORM OF ENTERTAINMENT. OSAMU TEZUKA, THE CREATOR OF *TETSUWAN ATOM* WHO IS OFTEN CALLED "THE GOD OF MANGA," HELPED POPULARIZE THE MEDIUM IN THE LATE '40S WITH DYNAMIC STORIES AND AN ART STYLE INFLUENCED BY WALT DISNEY CHARACTERS.

OSAMU TEZUKA

FOREIGNERS IN JAPAN ARE OFTEN AMAZED BY THE VITALITY OF COMICS CULTURE: A JAPANESE BUSINESSMAN SITS ON A TRAIN WITH HIS NOSE BURIED IN A CHILDREN'S COMIC BOOK. THAT SAME COMIC MIGHT SELL 2.5 MILLION COPIES A WEEK.

232

MANGA STORIES ARE USUALLY SERIALIZED IN MAGAZINES, WHICH ARE PRINTED IN BLACK AND WHITE TO KEEP COSTS DOWN. JAPAN'S SMALL SIZE AND DENSE POPULATION MAKES DISTRIBUTING THESE PHONEBOOK-SIZED PERIODICALS EASY.

AFTER APPEARING IN MAGAZINES, MOST POPULAR MANGA TITLES ARE REPRINTED IN PAPERBACKS CALLED TANKOBON. SOME STORIES RUN FOR DECADES—TOTALING THOUSANDS OF PAGES.

EPIC STORY LINES, REVERSED PAGES, BLACK-AND-WHITE ART ... THESE WERE NOT THE SORT OF COMICS THAT AMERICANS WERE USED TO! IN ADDITION, MANGA HAD DEVELOPED ITS OWN DISTINCT SYSTEM OF ICONS AND VISUAL SHORTHAND THAT WAS GUARANTEED TO FLUMMOX FOREIGNERS.

BIG EYES

NOSE BLEED

SPEED LINES

BIG SWEAT DROP

SNOT BUBBLE

ELLIPSES

FOR MANY AMERICANS, FREDERIK SCHODT'S 1983 BOOK *MANGA! MANGA!* PROVIDED AN INTRODUCTION TO THE MEDIUM, OUTLINING A ROBUST ART FORM THAT RANGED FROM SOAP OPERAS TO SPORTS STORIES, FROM HIGH ART TO PORNOGRAPHY.

Manga! Manga! The World of Japanese Comics by frederik l. schodt

IN THE LATE '80S, TRANSLATED MANGA SERIES BEGAN SHOWING UP IN THE U.S. THEY WERE STILL VIRTUALLY INVISIBLE TO THE MAINSTREAM, APPEARING ONLY IN COMICS SHOPS.

MANGA

625

LOCAL HEROES FOOD 2007

Fruits & Vegetables

Beans

Molly Gean's father, Harry Iwamoto, may have been the most famous farmer our markets have seen. Harry's Berries strawberries—Seascape and Gaviota—are the perfectly textured, remarkably sweet, crimson specimens against which all others are measured. Since Harry's death in 1993, Molly and her husband, Rick Gean, along with her brother, Kaz Iwamoto, and his wife, Yoshiko, have been running the family's 30-acre farm in Oxnard. Strawberries are their signature crop, but their Blue Lake beans ("Sweet, juicy, and the best ones to eat raw," says Molly), *haricots verts*, and flat yellow wax Romanos keep chefs like Tom Colicchio and Suzanne Goin coming through the winter. "Everyone else gets happy when they see the movie stars," says Molly. "I get excited when I see the chefs." The farming technique at Harry's Berries is so intensive that despite the relatively small size of the land, it supplies up to 21 farmers' markets each week and often has tomatoes through Thanksgiving. "We try to grow ordinary food with extraordinary flavor," Molly says. "Everyone eats strawberries, everyone eats beans." » At Beverly Hills, Hollywood, Santa Monica (Wed.; Sat., Arizona), and West Hollywood farmers' markets.

Beets

Twenty years ago Jose and Edgar Jaime emigrated with their father from Mexico to start a vegetable farm. Last year Jaime Farms pulled the first crop of beets from its newest growing location, ten acres in Santa Maria. "Our golden beets are the sweetest," says Jose. "They are almost like sweet potatoes—you can put one in the microwave for a minute and eat it right then with a fork." Jaime's beets range from the bloodred Forono to the purple-and-white-striped *chioggia*, with several varieties in between. All four of its fields—in Santa Maria, Lucerne Valley, Yucca Valley, and the City of Industry—operate sustainably, without the use of pesticides. "When there is a pest or disease, it will take the beet when it's big," says Jose. "We pick them early when they're still small and already very sweet." » At Hollywood, Pasadena, and Santa Monica (Wed.) farmers' markets.

Broccoli

It's been 18 months since 350 families were forced to give up a 14-acre urban garden at 41st and Alameda streets in South Los Angeles, where they'd grown food for the community since 1992. But thanks to ten acres leased outside Bakersfield, the South Central Farmers Cooperative is still in business. "We bring in close to a ton of food each week," says SCFC president Tezozomoc, who goes by one name only. Among the most popular fall crops is broccoli, which occupies ten rows of farmland. "When you grow organically, the broccoli heads don't get quite as large as the ones in the grocery stores," says Tezozomoc. "But the customers who buy ours love the taste and texture." Proceeds go to various community outreach programs throughout South Los Angeles, including nutrition education and healthy-cooking demonstrations. » At Atwater Village, Hollywood, Leimert Park, and Watts farmers' markets.

STOCK OPTION

WHEN YOU SUSPECT that pricey imported E.V.O.O. may be hazelnut oil from parts unknown, it's time to look closer to home. Century-old manzanilla, mission, and sivilano trees grow on eight and a half acres of Adams' Olive Ranch in Strathmore, and the morning-picked olives are pressed down the road. The oil rests for 90 days to mellow into flavors ranging from a buttery chardonnay to gin and tonic, and the freshness is apparent in every bottle. In March a 100 percent manzanilla reserve called Ava's Acre makes its debut. » At Santa Monica farmers' markets or adamsoliveranch.com.

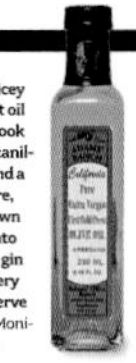

NOVEMBER 2007 | LOS ANGELES | 141

627

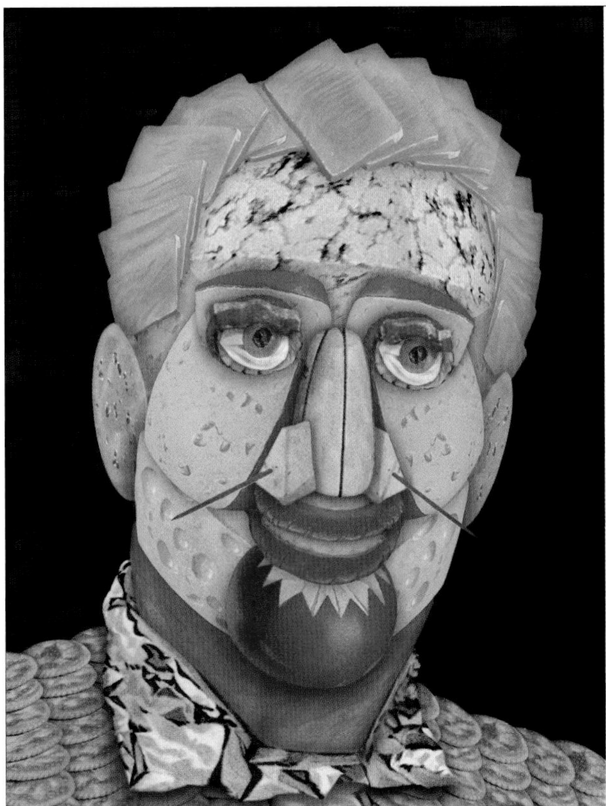

LOCAL HEROES FOOD 2007

Milk, Cheese & Yogurt

Burrata

When Vito Girardi came to the United States from Puglia 15 years ago, he brought with him three generations of cheese-making tradition—and more important, *burrata*. His luscious balloons of cream and curd can be found slumped over dishes at Campanile, Valentino, and Mozza. Inside the Gioia Cheese Company in South El Monte, Girardi forms each piece by hand using cow's milk from a Chino Valley dairy. "It's always been Vito's dream to open in California," says his wife, Monica. "And we were the first to bring burrata here." Gioia also makes mascarpone, ricotta, and smoked mozzarella. » At Bay Cities Italian Deli & Bakery, the Big Cheese, Bristol Farms, Cheese Store of Beverly Hills, Cheese Store of Silverlake, La Brea Bakery, and Wally's Wine Shop.

Feta

Rostom Baghdassarian's grandfather learned the art of yogurt making from the locals in his village in Lebanon. Today family-run Karoun Dairies in Turlock makes a range of Mediterranean fetas, including a double-cream style, a sharp goat's and cow's milk blend, a basket-shaped goat's milk, and a mild, easily crumbled Helena. Each is made with rBST-free milk from Central Valley dairies and comes packed in a generous pool of its own brine, which, says Baghdassarian, "continues to marinate the cheese and keep it moist." His operation once occupied a tiny L.A. plant at Santa Monica Boulevard and Normandie Avenue and today employs more than 80 people. Everything from kefir cheese to kosher yogurt is made here, much of it by hand, along with a new line of Spanish-style cheeses. » At Bristol Farms, Gelson's, and Whole Foods.

Serena

When Marisa Simoes's dad took a farmstead-cheese-making class in 1999, he thought it would be a good way to include his three daughters in his 8,000-cow dairy farm in Lindsay. At the moment, Simoes is the only sibling involved in Three Sisters Farmstead Cheese. Soon after its debut in 2000, her unique Serena—aged one year and reminiscent of a lighter Parmesan—won gold at the World Cheese Awards. "We knew when we started that we wanted to make original cheeses," says Simoes. "We bought 20 different cheeses, laid them out on a table, and picked out all of the characteristics we liked most." Three Sisters cows feed on local citrus, giving the cheese—handcrafted at every stage—a distinctive, sweet, acid-laced aroma. » At Cheese Store of Silverlake.

Gouda

Dutch immigrant Jules Wesselink has been in the California dairy business for more than 50 years, but it wasn't until 1995 that he began making his artisanal Gouda, widely considered the best outside the Netherlands. Today Wesselink's daughter, Valerie Thomas, and her husband, David, run the Winchester Cheese Company, using raw milk from 500 Holsteins and aging the cheese anywhere from 60 days to five years for a range of award-winning farmstead variet-

STOCK OPTION

WHILE WAITING to open a new restaurant, Ludovic Lefebvre, former chef at L'Orangerie and Bastide, has been helping out at friend Eric Payser's Breadbar. Along with "Ludo Bites," a series of weeknight dinners, he was inspired to make pink grapefruit jam. His version, befitting a chef who's paired popcorn with chicken, defies tradition, falling somewhere between a conserve and a marmalade. The rind and pulp of big chunks of fruit are rendered soft and sweet with boiling and can be spread on toast or eaten straight from the jar. » 8718 W. 3rd St., L.A., 310-205-0124 or breadbar.net.

NOVEMBER 2007 | LOS ANGELES | 149

627

625 WIRED

Creative Director_Scott Dadich
Design Director_Wyatt Mitchell
Art Director_Carl DeTorres
Illustrator_Atsuhisa Okura
Publisher_Condé Nast Publications, Inc.
Issue_November 2007 Category_Illo: Story

626 TEXAS MONTHLY

Art Director_T.J. Tucker
Designer_Andi Beierman
Illustrator_Kako
Publisher_Emmis Communications Corp.
Issue_November 2007 Category_Illo: Story

627 LOS ANGELES

Art Director_Joe Kimberling
Designer_Steven Banks
Illustrator_John Craig
Publisher_Emmis Issue_November 2007
Category_Illo: Story

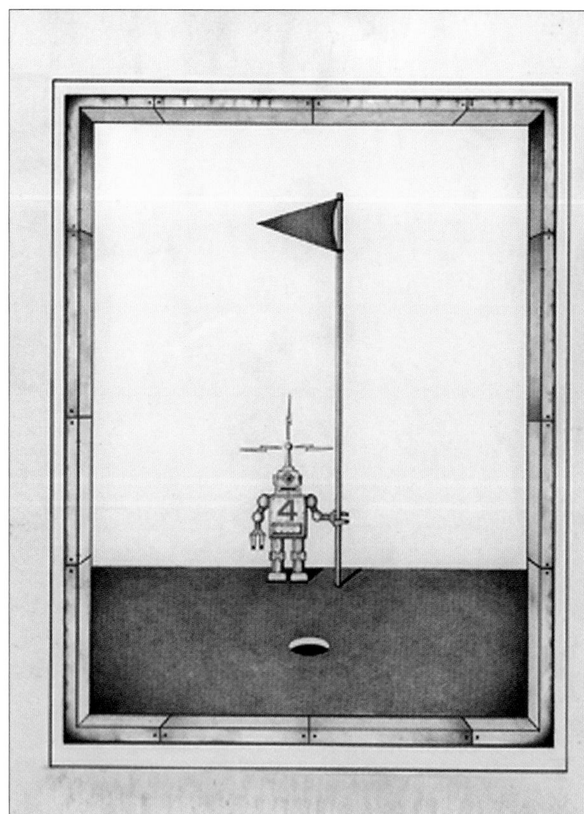

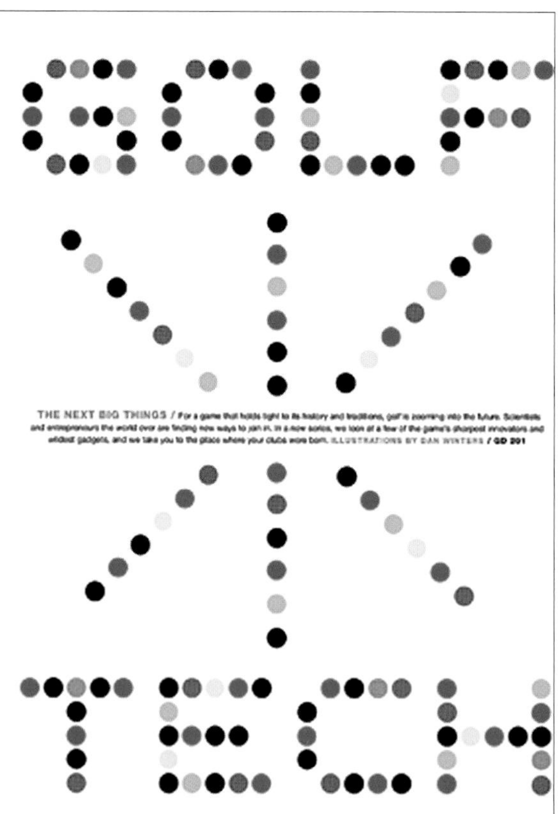

628

THE INNOVATORS

THEY HAVE VASTLY **DIFFERENT BACKGROUNDS**, THEY WORK IN **DIFFERENT FIELDS**, BUT THESE THREE MEN COME TOGETHER AT THE **FOREFRONT OF GOLF TECHNOLOGY**

VISION QUEST

Paul Gagne is brilliant, he speaks with a French-Canadian accent, and he speaks quickly. The layman who asks him for a sampling of his work as a posturologist and exercise kinesiologist with the David Leadbetter Golf Academy is in for a trial. Gagne [GON-ya] begins by describing the misfortune of golfers cursed with "disharmonic feet," and without pausing segues to the nature of parasympathetic brain function and its bearing on cognitive and limbic brain responses. Scarcely taking a breath, he explains why babies who learn to walk before they reach 14 months might develop strong legs but risk having weak spines. You can't get to the subject of his work with 2005 U.S. Open champion Michael Campbell fast enough.

It's worth the wait. Campbell won that Open at Pinehurst with a dazzling back-nine putting display on Sunday. Five times during the final round he dashed into the various portable toilets that dotted the course, in part to use them for their intended purpose but also to perform a peculiar eye exercise prescribed by Gagne that makes the eyes function better together. After emerging from the Port-O-Lets on the 12th and 17th holes, Campbell drained key putts—on No. 17, a 25-footer that clinched the victory. He took only 27 putts that day.

"After doing the exercises, I felt focused and relaxed," says Campbell. "I could really focus on the line of the putts, which was critical on the Pinehurst greens. Doing the exercises took me away from the occasion, the stress, the pressure and put me in the present time."

Campbell's potty breaks are the most curious footnote of the championship, and other Leadbetter students (Michelle Wie among them) have joined him in raving about the effect Gagne's eye exercises have had on their putting. Because the exercises can immediately benefit the everyday golfer, there is hope that Gagne's program could lead to a widespread performance breakthrough in putting.

Gagne, who is based in Montreal, explains the need for the vision exercises with great fervor, as though he discovered them yesterday. In fact, vision has been a component of posturology—Gagne's area of expertise—for several years. He says a posturologist detects and improves abnormalities in posture.

"We've known for a long time that posture is shaped by what we feel through our feet and what we see with our eyes," says Gagne. "With input from optometrists, we're able to discern the nature of the eye problem that leads to poor posture." The first thing Gagne and his associates tested Campbell for was whether his eyes were

292 **PAUL GAGNE** When Gagne's eye exercises helped Michael Campbell win the U.S. Open, the golf world had a new star instructor.

628

628 GOLF DIGEST

Design Director_**Ken DeLago**
Designer_**Tim Oliver**
Illustrator_**Dan Winters**
Publisher_**Condé Nast Publications Inc.**
Issue_**April 2007** Category_**Illo: Story**

SEPTEMBER 2007 •• INSTITUTIONAL INVESTOR

CREDIT MARKETS

SPECIAL REPORT
MARKET TURMOIL

The Ponzi Nation Topples

• This summer's credit crunch was the inevitable result of the reckless buildup of leverage in the global financial system through the use of exotic derivatives and the indulgence of central bankers eager, ironically, to avert a crisis.

By Edward Chancellor
ILLUSTRATIONS BY BARRY FALLS

629

SEPTEMBER 2007 •• INSTITUTIONAL INVESTOR

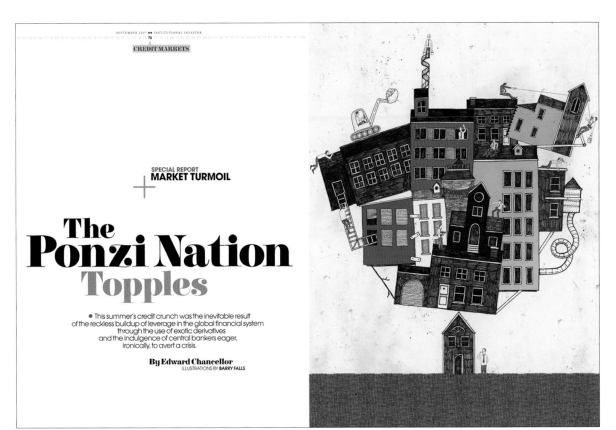

CREDIT MARKETS SPECIAL REPORT MARKET TURMOIL

On August 14, David Viniar, the chief financial officer of Goldman, Sachs & Co., struggled to explain why two hedge funds managed by his firm had suffered severe losses during the first few hectic days of the month. He came up with the rationale that the markets had been hit by a rare "25 standard deviation event." In other words, an occurrence so rare that a person living since the dawn of time would be lucky to have witnessed it. The comment was, of course, far-fetched. History shows that financial crises are as inevitable as death and taxes.

Viniar's comment appears particularly off the mark given the euphoric behavior of the financial markets in the years leading up to this summer's credit crunch. This euphoria was initially induced by a period of low interest rates that followed the collapse of the technology bubble at the turn of the century. That things were carried to an extreme even after the Federal Reserve Board began to raise rates in the summer of 2004 is largely the result of recent changes in the financial system. Credit had became a game of hot potato, with loans passed around and no one taking responsibility for the final outcome. Given this reckless behavior, it was only a matter of time before a crisis appeared.

The credit cycle in history

Recent events in the financial markets have followed a course familiar to students of history. The traditional credit cycle starts with low interest rates. As credit expands, prosperity returns. Over time, lending standards decline. Good bankers have always known that to lend long and borrow short is the fastest way to the bankruptcy court. But when liquidity is abundant, it's easy to roll over short-term loans, and there are fat profits to be made from lending against illiquid collateral. Competition among lenders ensures that those who adhere to conservative practices are pushed aside. Confidence runs high. There is a belief that prosperity will last forever.

But in time prices rise and interest rates follow. It becomes apparent that corners have been cut. "The good times almost always engender much fraud," wrote Walter Bagehot in 1873 in *Lombard Street*. "All people are most credulous when they are most happy; and when money has been made, when some people are really making it, when most people think they are making it, there is a happy opportunity for ingenious mendacity."

A bank, or some other important financial player, suddenly fails. The careless confidence of the boom is replaced by suspicion and fear. No one is sure whom to trust. Everyone seeks the safety of cash. "As credit by growing makes itself grow," wrote the 19th-century economist Alfred Marshall, "so when distrust has taken the place of confidence, failure and panic breed failure and panic." Credit suddenly contracts and liquidity dries up. The central bank is forced to intervene to shore up the financial system.

Historical precedent doesn't help us predict at what exact date a boom will end, which is perhaps why most people on Wall Street don't bother to read up on the past. Still, there are several leading indicators of a crisis. They include the rapid expansion of credit above its long-term trend; financial innovation and deregulation; greater competition among lenders, and the arrival of new entrants; the evolution of fragile debt structures excessively dependent on liquidity; a growing mismatch between assets and liabilities among financial players and a rise in short-term borrowing; falling risk premiums for loans and investments; and, most important of all, the appearance of an asset price boom.

These leading indicators are not precise. Yet when they are present simultaneously, it is pretty likely that a credit crunch will appear at some stage. Given that all these factors were present in the financial markets in the years running up to this summer's events, a crisis was surely inevitable. The only mystery was when it would arrive.

The role of the authorities

In the past it was unusual for one panic to follow hard upon another. Crises tended to appear roughly once a decade — ten years being the amount of time evidently needed for people to forget their previous follies and woes. What's remarkable about this summer's crisis is that it appeared only five years after a the severe credit crunch associated with the collapse of Enron Corp. and WorldCom.

So why did it take a mere five years for the current wave of credit to swell to the breaking point? The shortening of the cycle is largely because of the actions of the Federal Reserve Board, whose monetary policy generated a housing bubble shortly after the end of the dot-com mania. On its own a deflating real estate market would probably have been enough to produce a financial crisis of sorts. But that outcome was assured by the irresponsible behavior of just about every participant in a newly constituted credit system that had been endorsed by the authorities for its superior qualities in managing and distributing risk.

Under then-chairman Alan Greenspan the official policy of the Federal Reserve was that speculative bubbles could not be accurately identified before they popped and, therefore, the authorities should do nothing to hinder their growth. It is enough, the thinking went, for the central bank to deal with the bubble's aftermath. Following this line, the Fed waited for the Internet bubble to burst, which duly happened a few months into the new millennium. Subsequently, interest rates were slashed from 6.5 percent at the end of 2000 to 1 percent in June 2003 and remained at that level for 12 months.

After a brief recession, the U.S. economy recovered. Yet this apparently successful response to a deflating bubble had profound consequences. Low interest rates made it attractive for households to borrow. Cheap mortgages fueled a housing boom and enabled Americans to live above their incomes. "We know," Greenspan declared in February 2004, "that increases in home values and borrowing against home equity likely helped cushion the effects of the declining stock market during 2001 and 2002."

At the time, Greenspan denied that rapidly rising home prices were a cause for concern, claiming, rather implausibly in light of countless past real estate booms and busts, that "houses aren't as prone to bubbles as stocks because high transaction costs and a seller's need of shelter are significant impediments to speculative trading." The housing bulls pointed out that the average price of a U.S. home had never declined and never would (this claim wasn't strictly true, but it served its purpose). Besides, they reasoned, if there were ever any trouble in the housing market, the Federal Reserve would surely lower rates.

The debacle in the subprime mortgage market, which sparked the crisis on Wall Street, has brought a widespread change of opinion. Median U.S. home prices are set to decline this year, according to the National Association of Realtors. The Fed's easy money policy in the wake of the dot-com collapse is now widely held responsible for the housing bubble. Edward Gramlich, a Fed governor from 1997 to 2005, recently told the *Wall Street Journal* that he failed to realize at the time that low rates were making it so easy to issue subprime loans. The *Journal*'s editorial board, formerly a staunch supporter, admits that "the Greenspan Fed is one reason for the current mortgage mess."

Greenspan's policy also fostered an appetite for risk-taking in the financial markets. In the fall of 1998, the prospective collapse of the overleveraged hedge fund Long-Term Capital Management put Wall Street in a deep funk. But the Fed came to the rescue, arranging a bailout for LTCM and twice cutting interest rates. The stock market soon rebounded, and the "Greenspan put" was born. Wall Street learned that panics were likely to be short and relatively painless.

This "put" was exercised again after the failure of Enron. Between 2002 and 2004, short-term interest rates were kept below the rate of inflation. By the summer of 2004, the spread between short- and long-term interest rates was at its highest level in half a century, making it extremely profitable to borrow in the money markets and acquire longer-dated securities. The so-called carry trade became a license for hedge funds, banks and others to print money. Debt leverage, as measured by net borrowing by primary dealers in the repo markets, soared after 2002. The carry trade also provided an incentive for lenders to borrow short and lend long, producing the mismatch of assets and liabilities that generally precedes a financial crisis.

Many expected the carry trade to end after interest rates rose and the yield curve flattened towards the end of 2005. But that didn't happen. It still paid to borrow and acquire riskier debt securities, such as junk bonds and leverage loans, despite the fact their premiums were near record lows. As the "dash to trash" continued, bond market leverage crept upwards.

The Federal Reserve doesn't just set monetary policy. It is also the nation's top bank regulator. In recent years the credit system has changed profoundly. Once, banks played the key role in the credit system, lending and keeping loans on their balance sheets until they were repaid. Now most loans are bundled together, turned into securities and sold in the secondary markets to be bought by hedge funds and others.

Despite the LTCM panic in 1998, Greenspan used his influence to fend off regulation of this new securitized credit system. Hedge funds, he argued, helped to improve the distribution and pricing of risk, producing a more efficient allocation of capital and making the financial system more stable. His views were reiterated by Timothy Geithner, president of the Federal Reserve Bank of New York in May 2005. "By spreading risk more broadly, providing opportunities to manage and hedge risk and making it possible to trade and price credit risk, credit market innovation should help make markets both more efficient and more resilient," he said.

Yet is credit really better priced and distributed than ever before? The activities of lenders and borrowers in the years leading up to this summer's crisis suggest otherwise.

The modern credit system and its flaws

The history of banking has not been without blemish, hence the continual cycle of crises over hundreds of years. Bankers have always moved in shoals, favoring supposedly safe borrowers — whether third-world countries in the 1970s or owners of Japanese real estate in the following decade — only to discover their errors later. As John Maynard Keynes wrote in the 1930s, "A sound banker, alas, is not one who foresees danger and avoids it, but one who, when he is ruined, is ruined in a conventional and orthodox way along with his fellows, so that no one can really blame him."

Despite its flaws, there were certain advantages to traditional banking. Bankers knew their borrowers. They had long-standing relationships that, in theory at least, were based on trust between both parties. Because his employer retained loans until they were repaid, the banker had a career interest in seeing that loans were prudently made. Today participants focus on the fees that they will immediately earn. Incentives have encouraged myopic behavior.

Consider how this works in the mortgage market. A borrower gets an appraisal on a property. In this competitive market, the appraiser with the most generous valuation is likely to land the job. The loan applicant then goes to a mortgage broker, who is paid according to how many loans he or she originates. This creates an incentive to cut corners, possibly exaggerating the borrower's income. The loan application is handed to a bank, which earns a fee from packaging the mortgages together and a profit from selling them to Wall Street. The bonds are sent to the credit agencies, which stamp them with an investment-grade rating in exchange for another fee. Wall Street firms get their revenue from distributing mortgage loans to their clients.

629

629_ INSTITUTIONAL INVESTOR

Creative Director_Tom Brown
Art Director_Nathan Sinclair
Designer_Nathan Sinclair
Illustrator_Barry Falls
Publisher_Institutional Investor Inc.
Issue_September 2007 Category_Illo: Story

: SECTION
ILLUSTRATION

: AWARD
MERIT

: CATEGORY
STORY

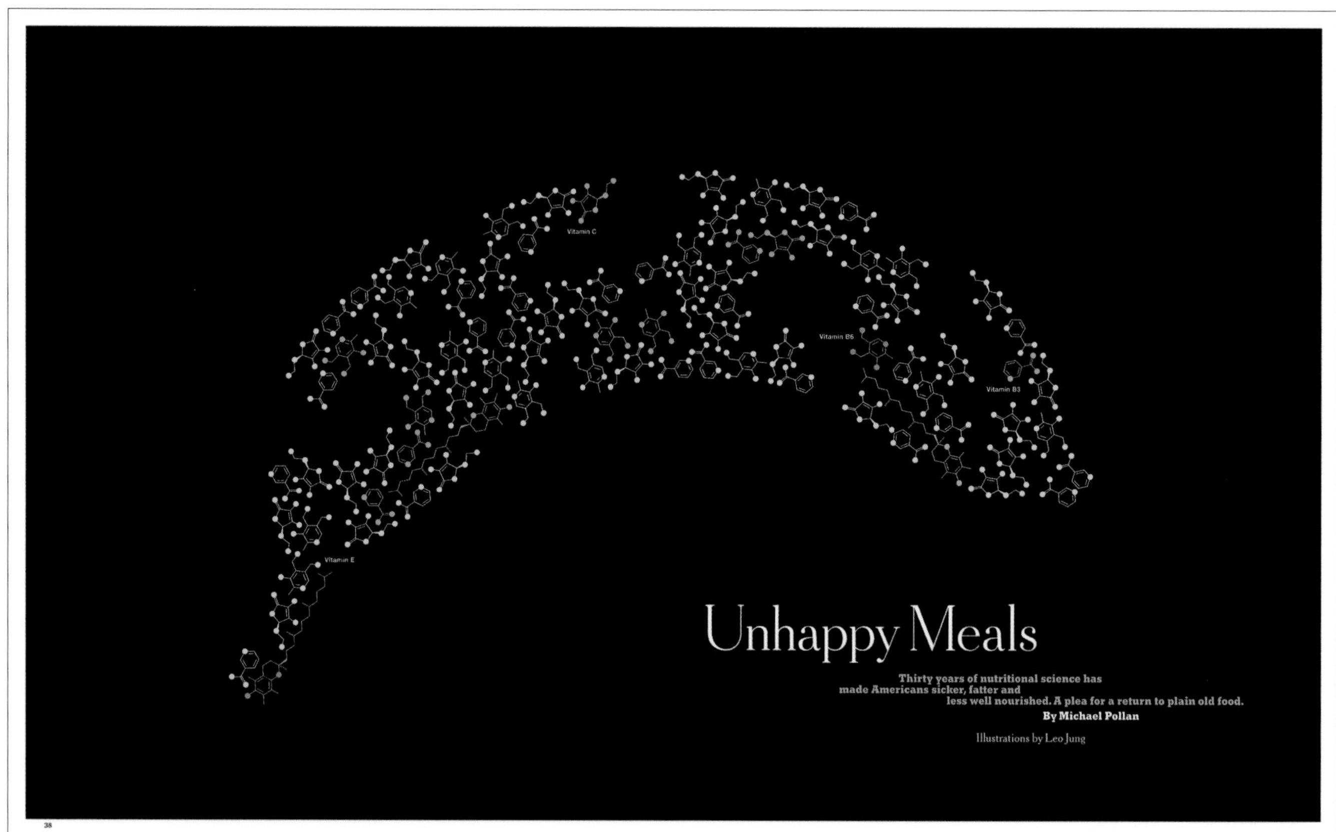

Unhappy Meals

Thirty years of nutritional science has made Americans sicker, fatter and less well nourished. A plea for a return to plain old food.

By Michael Pollan

Illustrations by Leo Jung

38

630

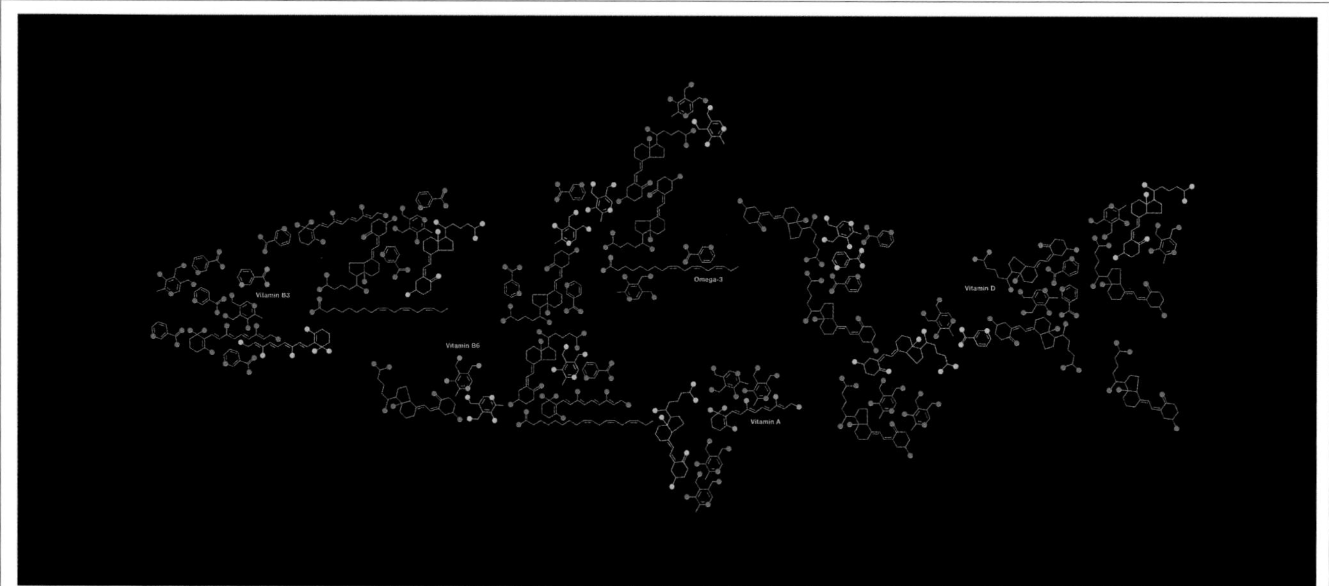

for varying quantities of fats and proteins and whatever other nutrients are on their scope. Similarly, any qualitative distinctions between processed foods and whole foods disappear when your focus is on quantifying the nutrients they contain (or, more precisely, the *known* nutrients).

This is a great boon for manufacturers of processed food, and it helps explain why they have been so happy to get with the nutritionism program. In the years following McGovern's capitulation and the 1982 National Academy report, the food industry set about re-engineering thousands of popular food products to contain more of the nutrients that science and government had deemed the good ones and less of the bad, and by the late '80s a golden era of food science was upon us. The Year of Eating Oat Bran — also known as 1988 — served as a kind of coming-out party for the food scientists, who succeeded in getting the material into nearly every processed food sold in America. Oat bran's moment on the dietary stage didn't last long, but the pattern had been established, and every few years since then a new oat bran has taken its turn under the marketing lights. (Here comes omega-3!)

By comparison, the typical real food has more trouble competing under the rules of nutritionism, if only because something like a banana or an avocado can't easily change its nutritional stripes (though rest assured the genetic engineers are hard at work on the problem). So far, at least, you can't put oat bran in a banana. So depending on the reigning nutritional orthodoxy, the avocado might be either a high-fat food to be avoided (Old Think) or a food high in monounsaturated fat to be embraced (New Think). The fate of each whole food rises and falls with every change in the nutritional weather, while the processed foods are simply reformulated. That's why when the Atkins mania hit the food industry, bread and pasta were given a quick redesign (dialing back the carbs; boosting the protein), while the poor unreconstructed potatoes and carrots were left out in the cold.

Of course it's also a lot easier to slap a health claim on a box of sugary cereal than on a potato or carrot, with the perverse result that the most healthful foods in the supermarket sit there quietly in the produce section, silent as stroke victims, while a few aisles over, the Cocoa Puffs and Lucky Charms are screaming about their newfound whole-grain goodness.

EAT RIGHT, GET FATTER

So nutritionism is good for business. But is it good for us? You might think that a national fixation on nutrients would lead to measurable improvements in the public health. But for that to happen, the underlying nutritional science, as well as the policy recommendations (and the journalism) based on that science, would have to be sound. This has seldom been the case.

Consider what happened immediately after the 1977 "Dietary Goals" — McGovern's masterpiece of politico-nutritionist compromise. In the wake of the panel's recommendation that we cut down on saturated fat, a recommendation seconded by the 1982 National Academy report on cancer, Americans did indeed change their diets, endeavoring for a quarter-century to do what they had been told. Well, kind of. The industrial food supply was promptly reformulated to reflect the official advice, giving us low-fat pork, low-fat Snackwell's and all the low-fat pasta and high-fructose (yet low-fat!) corn syrup we could consume. Which turned out to be quite a lot. Oddly, America got really fat on its new low-fat diet — indeed, many date the current obesity and diabetes epidemic to the late 1970s, when Americans began binging on carbohydrates, ostensibly as a way to avoid the evils of fat.

This story has been told before, notably in these pages ("What if It's All Been a Big Fat Lie?" by Gary Taubes, July 7, 2002), but it's a little more complicated than the official version suggests. In that version, which inspired the most recent Atkins craze, we were told that America got fat when, responding to bad scientific advice, it shifted its diet from fats to carbs, suggesting that a re-evaluation of the two nutrients is in

42 ILLUSTRATION BY LEO JUNG

THE NEW YORK TIMES MAGAZINE / JANUARY 28, 2007 43

630

630 THE NEW YORK TIMES MAGAZINE

Creative Director_**Janet Froelich** Art Director_**Arem Duplessis**
Designer_**Leo Jung** Illustrator_**Leo Jung**
Editor-In-Chief_**Gerry Marzorati** Publisher_**The New York Times**
Issue_**January 28, 2007** Category_**Illo: Story**

MOVIES FOR GROWNUPS™

Attack of the 50-Plus Women!

The sixth annual Movies for Grownups™ Awards

By Bill Newcott

Illustrations by DREW FRIEDMAN

The Last King of Scotland rules as the best movie—but this year it's the women who reign supreme.

Forest Whitaker's ferocious performance as Ugandan despot Idi Amin dominates *Scotland,* winner of our coveted Best Movie for Grownups™ award. But for the first time a quintet of top actresses vied for the Best Actress 50 and Over trophy in five riveting leading roles, a clear sign that Hollywood is softening in its longtime relegation of 50-plus actresses to supporting parts.

It's all part of a steadily evolving attitude shift, one that Hollywood is just beginning to take note of, says Susan Seidelman, writer-director of this year's nominated *The Boynton Beach Club:* "There are a lot of people over 40 or 50 who would go to the movies, but they want to see a movie that reflects their experience as an older person. That's a tough sell for your average Hollywood movie executive, a fetus in a suit."

Best Movie for Grownups

***The Last King of Scotland,* directed by Kevin Macdonald**

As the 1970s Ugandan strongman Idi Amin, Forest Whitaker smiles a thousand-watt grin, reaches out with teddy bear arms—then goes all grizzly on us. Even though we know the

WE'RE BAAAACK! Turning Hollywood precedent upside down, Best Actress Over 50 nominees—*from left,* Helen Mirren, Meryl Streep, Judi Dench, Catherine O'Hara, and Maggie Smith—are redefining the age criteria for leading ladies.

www.aarpmagazine.org **AARP** | 57

631

THE SHOE FITS Actors 50 and over have traditionally had an easier time finding great leading roles. In 2006 Samuel L. Jackson, *left,* and Donald Sutherland made the most of parts that exploited the wisdom of age and experience.

Best Actor 50 and Over

Donald Sutherland, *Aurora Borealis*

Ronald Shorter is trapped. He was once a hard-working hardware salesman, a guy who gave orders and got results. Now he's a prisoner of Parkinson's, a fading shadow shuffling from room to room in his apartment, reporting back to his long-suffering wife about the results of his latest venture into the bathroom. It would be easy to simply pity Ronald, but in the haunting *Aurora Borealis,* Donald Sutherland plays him with such smoldering fire that even as he slowly disappears into himself, Ronald remains defiant, compassionate, and surprisingly triumphant.

Sutherland came very close to passing up the part of Ronald—a man who becomes determined to commit suicide. "I was very, very profoundly depressed for a bunch of reasons," Sutherland says. "Ronald, this character, invaded my person. My father had Parkinson's, my mother died with dementia, and I was pretty familiar with the depression that accompanies people who feel that termination of their life is the most generous thing they can do for the person they love." Yet the film had an unexpected effect. Says Sutherland: "Almost as soon as I started to work on the picture, my depression disappeared, and I haven't been depressed since. So Ronald cured me."

RUNNERS-UP **Gabriel Byrne,** *Wah-Wah:* As a divorced dad living in Africa with a deeply troubled son, Byrne is a man cast adrift at home and in the world...**Samuel L. Jackson,** *Freedomland:* Beneath rumpled clothes and an ill-fitting hat, Jackson brings new life to one of the movies' most durable characters, the world-weary cop...**Peter O'Toole,** *Venus:* The "ick" factor could be high in this tale of an aging thespian smitten with a twentysomething cutie, but O'Toole's charm renders him bulletproof...**Jack Nicholson,** *The Departed:* Few things are scarier than casual brutality. When Nicholson's gangster pulls a ring off a severed hand and gives it to his lackey while saying, "Send it to his wife," we want to run for the exits. *(continued on page 104)*

Visit **www.aarpmagazine.org/movies** *to enter our sweepstakes for a chance to win a 46-inch flat-panel LCD HDTV and movie gift cards. You'll also find Bill Newcott's weekly film reviews and links to his* Movies for Grownups™ *radio program and podcasts.*

No purchase necessary. Purchase will not improve chances of winning. Sweepstakes starts January 25, 2007. All entries must be submitted by no later than 11:59 p.m. EST on March 30, 2007. Estimated odds of winning are 1:20,000. Actual odds of winning depend upon total number of eligible entries received. Sweepstakes is open to legal residents of the United States who are 45 years of age or older and who are not employees or family members of sweepstakes sponsors. Please visit www.aarpmagazine.org/movies to see complete Official Rules. Sweepstakes subject to Official Rules. Void in Puerto Rico and where prohibited.

www.aarpmagazine.org **AARP** | 59

631

AUSTIN POWERS

—images of INFLUENCE and intrigue at the WILD and Woolly eightieth LEGISLATIVE session—

Sketchbook by STEVE BRODNER

Austin has been SAID

632

632

631 AARP THE MAGAZINE

Design Director_Andrzej Janerka Art Director_Todd Albertson
Designer_Todd Albertson Illustrator_Drew Friedman
Editor-In-Chief_Steve Slon Publisher_AARP Publications
Issue_March/April 2007 Category_Illo: Story

632 TEXAS MONTHLY

Art Director_T.J. Tucker Designers_Andi Beierman, Rachel Wyatt
Illustrator_Steve Brodner Photo Editor_Leslie Baldwin
Publisher_Emmis Communications Corp. Issue_July 2007
Category_Illo: Story

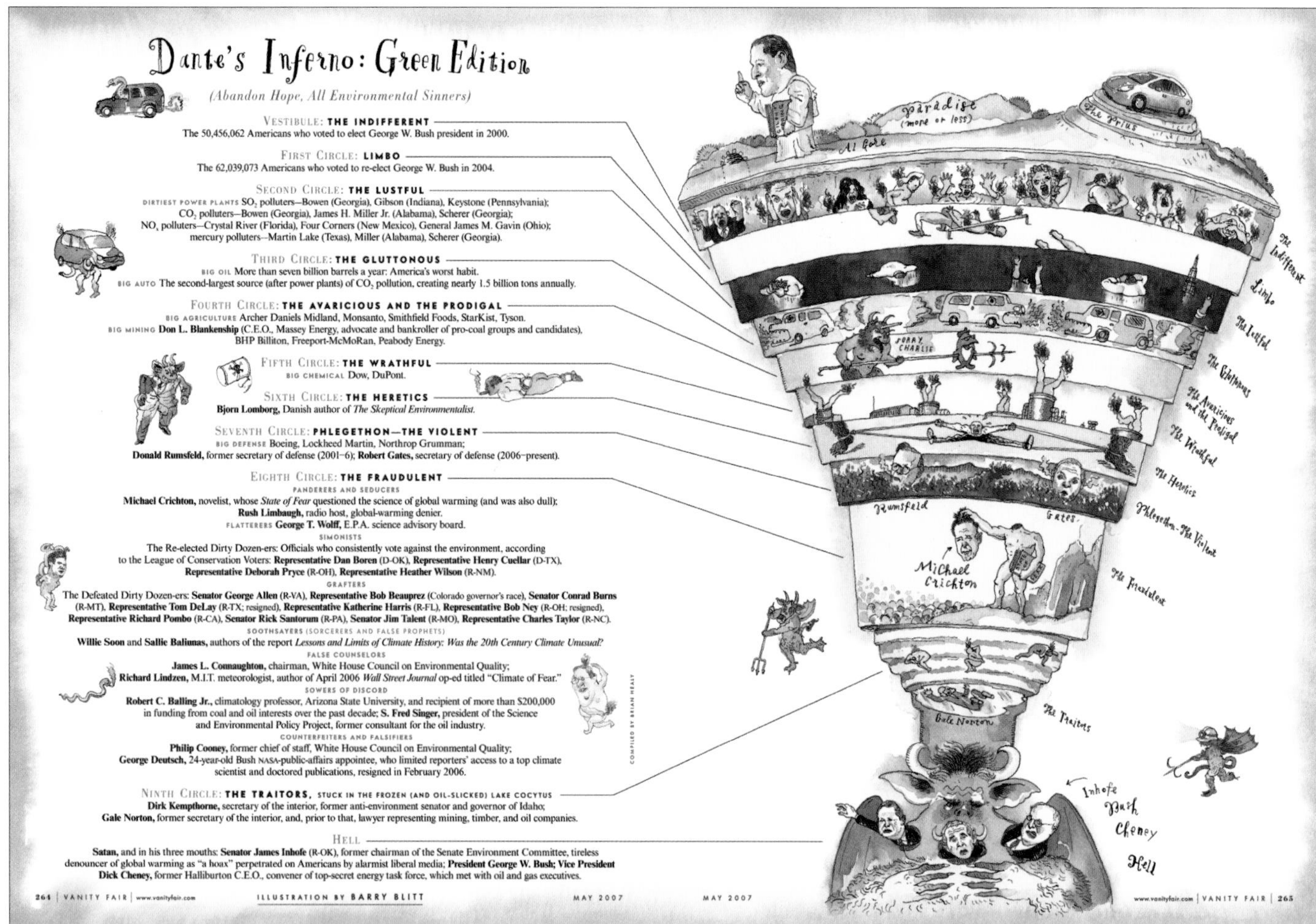

Dante's Inferno: Green Edition

(Abandon Hope, All Environmental Sinners)

VESTIBULE: **THE INDIFFERENT**
The 50,456,062 Americans who voted to elect George W. Bush president in 2000.

FIRST CIRCLE: **LIMBO**
The 62,039,073 Americans who voted to re-elect George W. Bush in 2004.

SECOND CIRCLE: **THE LUSTFUL**
DIRTIEST POWER PLANTS SO_2 polluters—Bowen (Georgia), Gibson (Indiana), Keystone (Pennsylvania); CO_2 polluters—Bowen (Georgia), James H. Miller Jr. (Alabama), Scherer (Georgia); NO_x polluters—Crystal River (Florida), Four Corners (New Mexico), General James M. Gavin (Ohio); mercury polluters—Martin Lake (Texas), Miller (Alabama), Scherer (Georgia).

THIRD CIRCLE: **THE GLUTTONOUS**
BIG OIL More than seven billion barrels a year: America's worst habit.
BIG AUTO The second-largest source (after power plants) of CO_2 pollution, creating nearly 1.5 billion tons annually.

FOURTH CIRCLE: **THE AVARICIOUS AND THE PRODIGAL**
BIG AGRICULTURE Archer Daniels Midland, Monsanto, Smithfield Foods, StarKist, Tyson.
BIG MINING **Don L. Blankenship** (C.E.O., Massey Energy, advocate and bankroller of pro-coal groups and candidates), BHP Billiton, Freeport-McMoRan, Peabody Energy.

FIFTH CIRCLE: **THE WRATHFUL**
BIG CHEMICAL Dow, DuPont.

SIXTH CIRCLE: **THE HERETICS**
Bjorn Lomborg, Danish author of *The Skeptical Environmentalist.*

SEVENTH CIRCLE: **PHLEGETHON—THE VIOLENT**
BIG DEFENSE Boeing, Lockheed Martin, Northrop Grumman;
Donald Rumsfeld, former secretary of defense (2001–6); **Robert Gates,** secretary of defense (2006–present).

EIGHTH CIRCLE: **THE FRAUDULENT**
PANDERERS AND SEDUCERS
Michael Crichton, novelist, whose *State of Fear* questioned the science of global warming (and was also dull);
Rush Limbaugh, radio host, global-warming denier.
FLATTERERS **George T. Wolff,** E.P.A. science advisory board.
SIMONISTS
The Re-elected Dirty Dozen-ers: Officials who consistently vote against the environment, according to the League of Conservation Voters: **Representative Dan Boren** (D-OK), **Representative Henry Cuellar** (D-TX), **Representative Deborah Pryce** (R-OH), **Representative Heather Wilson** (R-NM).
GRAFTERS
The Defeated Dirty Dozen-ers: **Senator George Allen** (R-VA), **Representative Bob Beauprez** (Colorado governor's race), **Senator Conrad Burns** (R-MT), **Representative Tom DeLay** (R-TX; resigned), **Representative Katherine Harris** (R-FL), **Representative Bob Ney** (R-OH; resigned), **Representative Richard Pombo** (R-CA), **Senator Rick Santorum** (R-PA), **Senator Jim Talent** (R-MO), **Representative Charles Taylor** (R-NC).
SOOTHSAYERS (SORCERERS AND FALSE PROPHETS)
Willie Soon and **Sallie Baliunas,** authors of the report *Lessons and Limits of Climate History: Was the 20th Century Climate Unusual?*
FALSE COUNSELORS
James L. Connaughton, chairman, White House Council on Environmental Quality;
Richard Lindzen, M.I.T. meteorologist, author of April 2006 *Wall Street Journal* op-ed titled "Climate of Fear."
SOWERS OF DISCORD
Robert C. Balling Jr., climatology professor, Arizona State University, and recipient of more than $200,000 in funding from coal and oil interests over the past decade; **S. Fred Singer,** president of the Science and Environmental Policy Project, former consultant for the oil industry.
COUNTERFEITERS AND FALSIFIERS
Philip Cooney, former chief of staff, White House Council on Environmental Quality;
George Deutsch, 24-year-old Bush NASA-public-affairs appointee, who limited reporters' access to a top climate scientist and doctored publications, resigned in February 2006.

NINTH CIRCLE: **THE TRAITORS,** STUCK IN THE FROZEN (AND OIL-SLICKED) LAKE COCYTUS
Dirk Kempthorne, secretary of the interior, former anti-environment senator and governor of Idaho;
Gale Norton, former secretary of the interior, and, prior to that, lawyer representing mining, timber, and oil companies.

HELL
Satan, and in his three mouths: **Senator James Inhofe** (R-OK), former chairman of the Senate Environment Committee, tireless denouncer of global warming as "a hoax" perpetrated on Americans by alarmist liberal media; **President George W. Bush; Vice President Dick Cheney,** former Halliburton C.E.O., convener of top-secret energy task force, which met with oil and gas executives.

COMPILED BY BRIAN HEALY

264 | VANITY FAIR | www.vanityfair.com   ILLUSTRATION BY BARRY BLITT   MAY 2007

MAY 2007   www.vanityfair.com | VANITY FAIR | 265

633

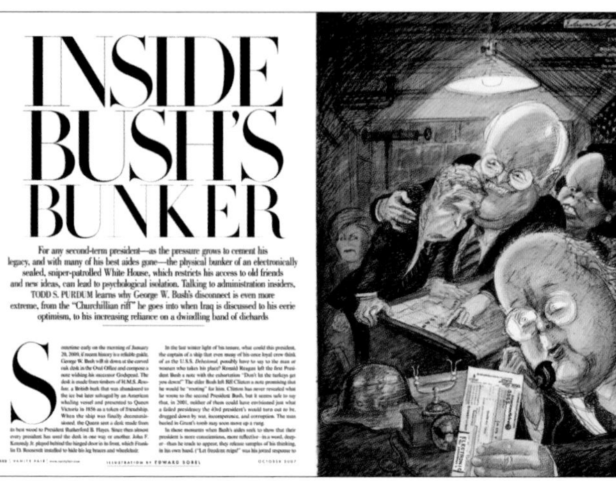

INSIDE BUSH'S BUNKER

For any second-term president—as the pressure grows to cement his legacy, and with many of his best aides gone—the physical bunker of an electronically sealed, sniper-patrolled White House, which restricts his access to old friends and new ideas, can lead to psychological isolation. Talking to administration insiders, TODD S. PURDUM learns why George W. Bush's disconnect is even more extreme, from the "Churchillian riff" he goes into when Iraq is discussed to his eerie optimism, to his increasing reliance on a dwindling band of diehards

634

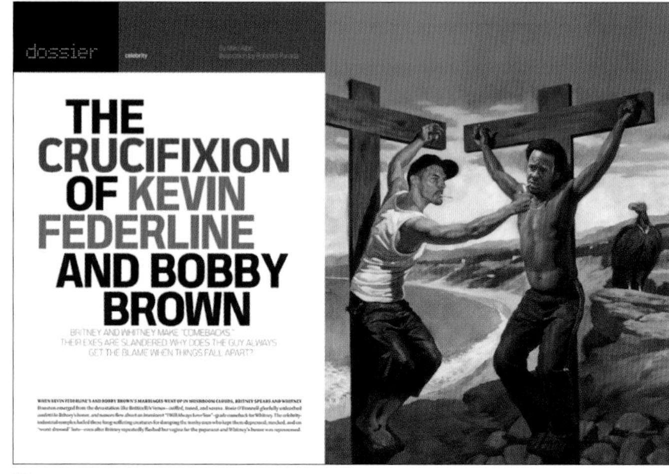

dossier

THE CRUCIFIXION OF KEVIN FEDERLINE AND BOBBY BROWN

BRITNEY AND WHITNEY MAKE "COMEBACKS." THEIR EXES ARE SLANDERED. WHY DOES THE GUY ALWAYS GET THE BLAME WHEN THINGS FALL APART?

635

633 **VANITY FAIR**

Design Director_**David Harris**
Illustrator_**Barry Blitt**
Editor-In-Chief_**Graydon Carter**
Publisher_**Condé Nast Publications Inc.**
Issue_**May 2007**
Category_**Illo: Spread/Single Page**

634 **VANITY FAIR**

Design Director_**David Harris**
Designer_**Lee Ruelle**
Illustrator_**Edward Sorel**
Editor-In-Chief_**Graydon Carter**
Publisher_**Condé Nast Publications Inc.**
Issue_**October 2007**
Category_**Illo: Spread/Single Page**

635 **DETAILS**

Creative Director_**Rockwell Harwood**
Art Director_**Andre Jointe**
Designer_**Rockwell Harwood**
Illustrator_**Roberto Parada**
Photo Editors_**Hali Tara Feldman, Alexandra Ghez**
Publisher_**Condé Nast Publications**
Issue_**January/February 2007**
Category_**Illo: Spread/Single Page**

THE CONVERSATION Donna Brazile and Deborah Tannen discuss

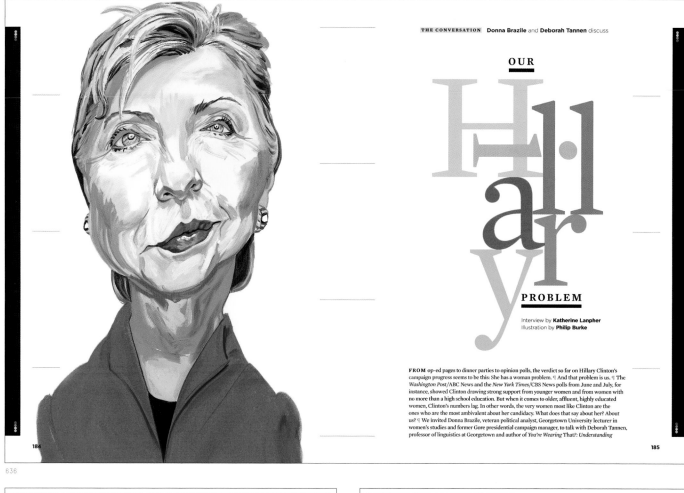

OUR Hillary PROBLEM

Interview by **Katherine Lanpher**
Illustration by **Philip Burke**

FROM op-ed pages to dinner parties to opinion polls, the verdict so far on Hillary Clinton's campaign progress seems to be this: She has a woman problem. ¶ And that problem is us. ¶ The *Washington Post*/ABC News and the *New York Times*/CBS News polls from June and July, for instance, showed Clinton drawing strong support from younger women and from women with no more than a high school education. But when it comes to older, affluent, highly educated women, Clinton's numbers lag. In other words, the very women most like Clinton are the ones who are the most ambivalent about her candidacy. What does that say about her? About us? ¶ We invited Donna Brazile, veteran political analyst, Georgetown University lecturer in women's studies and former Gore presidential campaign manager, to talk with Deborah Tannen, professor of linguistics at Georgetown and author of *You're Wearing That?: Understanding*

184 185

636

NATIONAL AFFAIRS

The GREAT IRAQ SWINDLE

From phony bids to invoicing orgies, how Bush allowed an army of for-profit contractors to invade the U.S. treasury By Matt Taibbi

ILLUSTRATION BY MATT MAHURIN

637

To Catch a Predator claims it is outing dangerous pedophiles. But are the show's faceless vigilantes scarier than their prey? By Vanessa Grigoriadis

The New American Witch Hunt

ILLUSTRATION BY TOMER HANUKA

638

636 MORE

Creative Director_Maxine Davidowitz
Art Director_Jose Fernandez
Designer_Ronald Sequeira
Illustrator_Philip Burke
Director of Photography_Karen Frank
Editor-In-Chief_Peggy Northrop
Publisher_Meredith Corporation
Issue_October 2007
Category_Illo: Spread/Single Page

637 ROLLING STONE

Art Director_Joseph Hutchinson
Designer_Joe Newton
Illustrator_Matt Mahurin
Publisher_Wenner Media
Issue_September 6, 2007
Category_Illo: Spread/Single Page

638 ROLLING STONE

Art Director_Joseph Hutchinson
Designer_Matthew Cooley
Illustrator_Tomer Hanuka
Publisher_Wenner Media
Issue_September 9, 2007
Category_Illo: Spread/Single Page

Dwellings

Illustrations by Leif Parsons

Renovate! Reuse! Recycle!

Recycling soda cans is one thing, but adaptively reusing derelict buildings takes more than just a trip to the curb. Adventurous clients and designers are having a go at architectural dumpster diving, turning sows' ears into silk purses by transforming just about anything into a place called home.

142 Dwell April 2007

April 2007 Dwell 143

639

MONEY MANAGEMENT

The Long & Short of 130/30

Can short-extension funds stay in fashion after this summer's market turmoil?

By Jo Wrighton

640

DON'T Whistle WHILE YOU WORK

641

639 DWELL

Design Director_Kyle Blue Designers_Brendan Callahan, Suzanne Lagasa Illustrator_Leif Parsons Publisher_Dwell LLC Issue_April 2007 Category_Illo: Spread/Single Page

640 INSTITUTIONAL INVESTOR

Creative Director_Tom Brown Art Director_Nathan Sinclair Designer_Lee Wilson Illustrator_Eric Palma Publisher_Institutional Investor Inc. Issue_October 2007 Category_Illo: Spread/Single Page

641 MOTHER JONES

Creative Director_Susan Scandrett Art Director_Tim J Luddy Designer_Tim J Luddy Illustrator_Steve Brodner Director of Photography_Sarah Kehoe Photo Editor_Sarah Cross Publisher_Foundation for National Progress Issue_May/June 2007 Category_Illo: Spread/Single Page

642 NICKELODEON

Design Director_Justine Strasberg Art Director_Chris Duffy Designer_Catherine Tutrone Illustrator_R. Kikuo Johnson Publisher_Nickelodeon, MTV Networks Issue_December 2006/January 2007 Category_Illo: Spread/Single Page

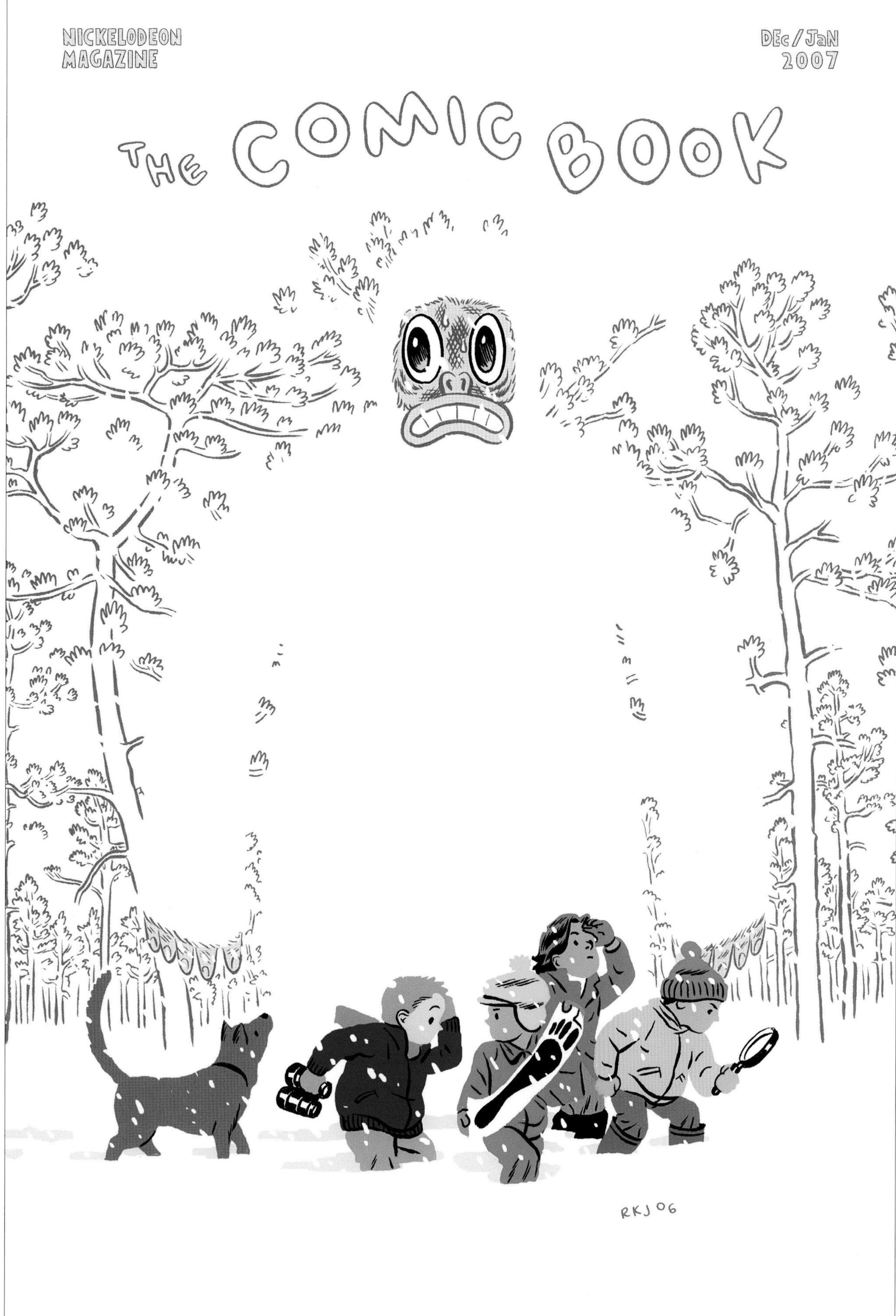
NICKELODEON
MAGAZINE
DEc / JaN
2007
THE COMIC BOOK
RKJ 06

STATE OF PLAY

Governments are giving new funding
and support to European
video games. But what makes a game European?

By Sean Ashcroft

Illustrations by Siggi Eggertsson

77

643

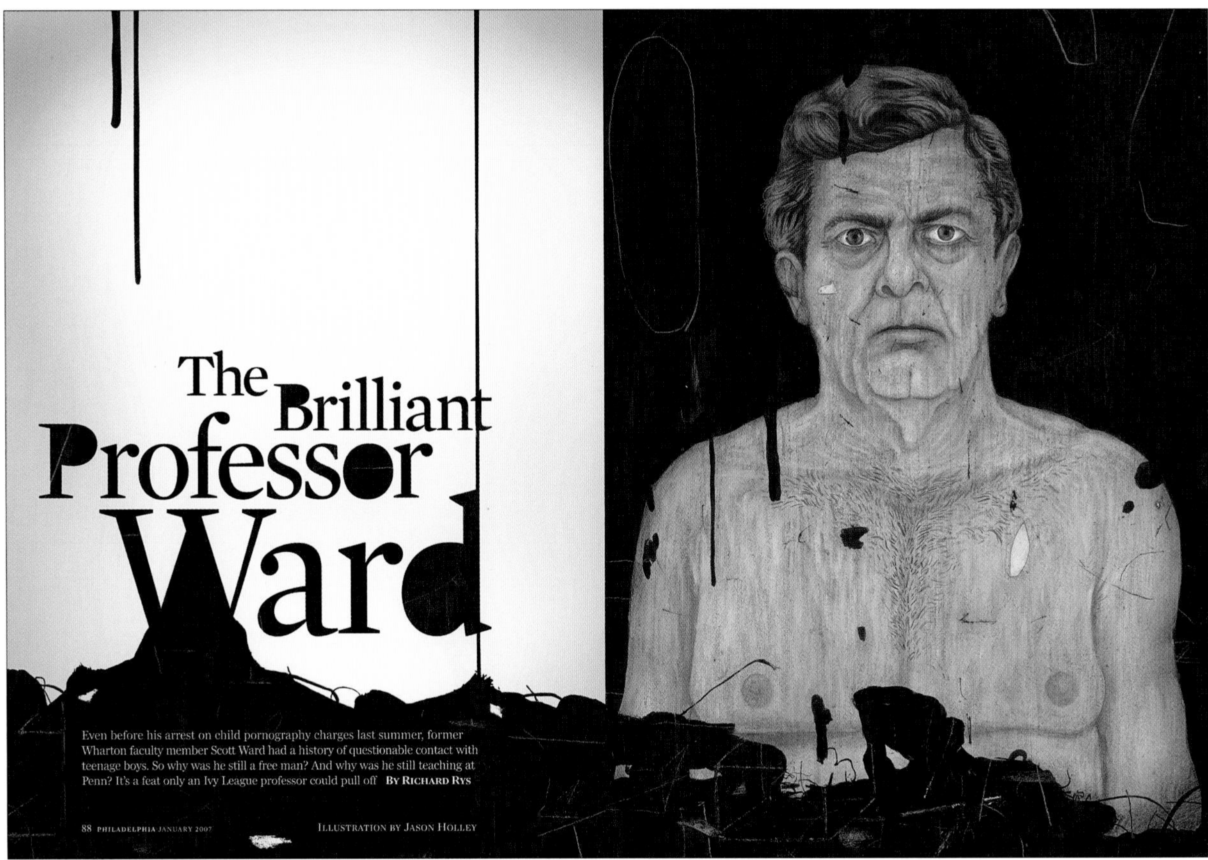

The Brilliant Professor Ward

Even before his arrest on child pornography charges last summer, former Wharton faculty member Scott Ward had a history of questionable contact with teenage boys. So why was he still a free man? And why was he still teaching at Penn? It's a feat only an Ivy League professor could pull off BY RICHARD RYS

88 PHILADELPHIA JANUARY 2007

ILLUSTRATION BY JASON HOLLEY

644

643 PRINT

Art Director_**Kristina DiMatteo**
Associate Art Director_**Lindsay Ballant**
Designer_**Lindsay Ballant** Illustrator_**Siggi Eggertsson**
Editor-In-Chief_**Joyce Rutter Kaye**
Publisher_**F & W Publications** Issue_**June/July 2007**
Category_**Illo: Spread/Single Page**

644 PHILADELPHIA

Design Director_**Michael McCormick**
Art Director_**Andrew Zahn** Designer_**Andrew Zahn**
Illustrator_**Jason Holley** Publisher_**Metrocorp Publishing**
Issue_**January 2007** Category_**Illo: Spread/Single Page**

645

646

645 INTELLIGENCE REPORT

Creative Director_Russell Estes
Designer_Russell Estes Illustrator_Frank Stockton
Studio_SPLC Team Publisher_ Southern Poverty Law Center
Client_Intelligence Project Issue_Winter 2007
Category_Illo: Spread/Single Page

646 LOS ANGELES

Art Director_Joe Kimberling
Designer_Joe Kimberling
Illustrator_Mark Matcho Publisher_Emmis
Issue_January 2007 Category_Illo: Spread/Single Page

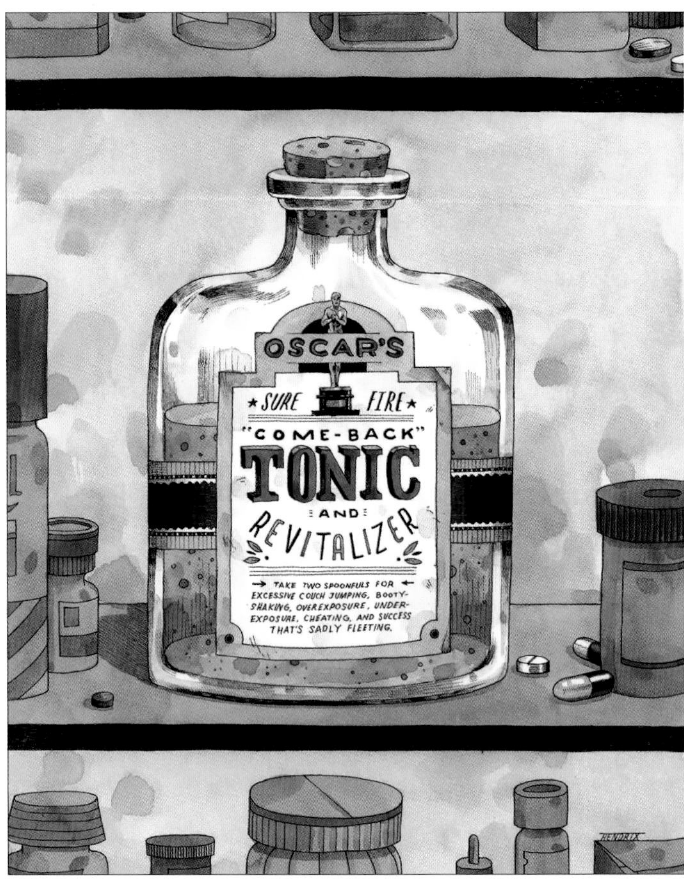

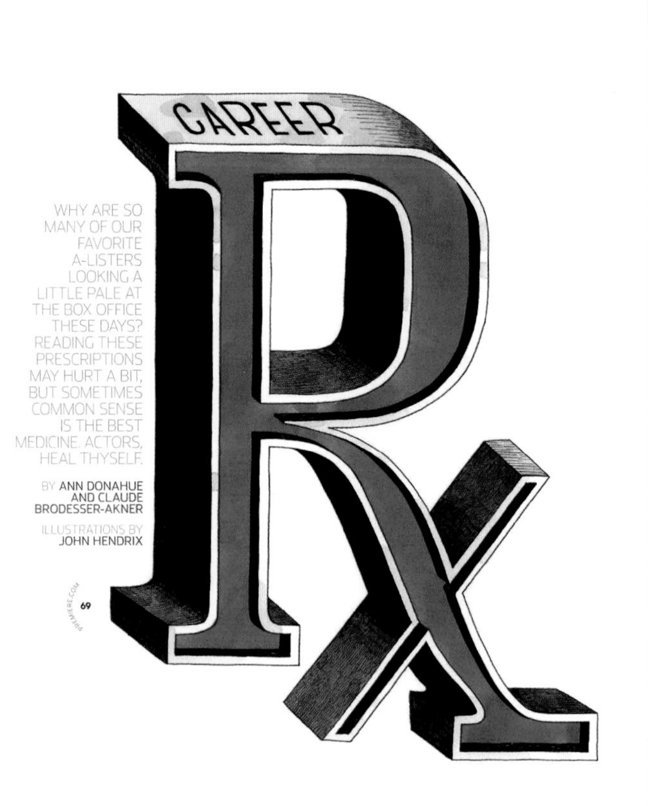
CAREER Rx

WHY ARE SO MANY OF OUR FAVORITE A-LISTERS LOOKING A LITTLE PALE AT THE BOX OFFICE THESE DAYS? READING THESE PRESCRIPTIONS MAY HURT A BIT, BUT SOMETIMES COMMON SENSE IS THE BEST MEDICINE. ACTORS, HEAL THYSELF.

BY ANN DONAHUE AND CLAUDE BRODESSER-AKNER

ILLUSTRATIONS BY JOHN HENDRIX

69

647

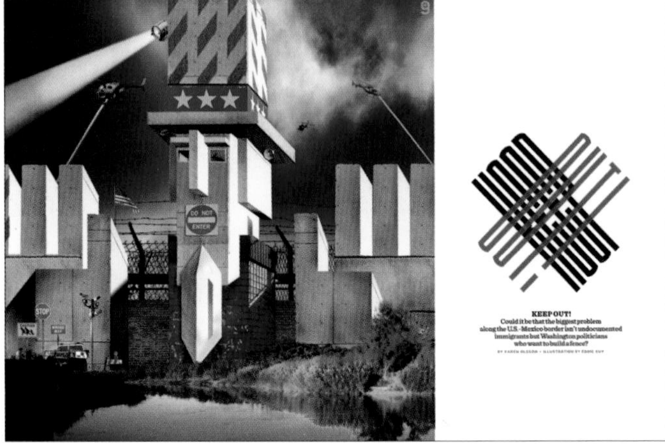
KEEP OUT!

Could it be that the biggest problem along the U.S.-Mexico border isn't undocumented immigrants but Washington politicians who want to build a fence?

648

hillary's prayer

For 15 years, Hillary Clinton has been part of a secretive religious group that seeks to bring Jesus back to Capitol Hill. Is she triangulating—or living her faith?

649

647 PREMIERE

Art Director_Rob Hewitt
Designer_Marina Grinshpun
Illustrator_John Hendrix
Director of Photography_David Carthas
Editor-In-Chief_Peter Herbst
Publisher_Hachette Filipacchi Media U.S.
Issue_April 2007
Category_Illo: Spread/Single Page

648 TEXAS MONTHLY

Art Director_T.J. Tucker
Designer_Andi Beierman
Illustrator_Eddie Guy
Publisher_Emmis Communications Corp.
Issue_November 2007
Category_Illo: Spread/Single Page

649 MOTHER JONES

Creative Director_Susan Scandrett
Art Director_Tim J Luddy
Designer_Tim J Luddy
Illustrator_Andy Friedman
Director of Photography_Sarah Kehoe
Photo Editor_Sarah Cross
Publisher_Foundation for National Progress
Issue_September/October 2007
Category_Illo: Spread/Single Page

by Adam B. Vary *illustration by Brian Cronin*

Out of Sight

Almost two years after 'Brokeback Mountain' raked in $178 million worldwide, no major studio has greenlit a single gay film. What is keeping movies in the closet—and what should Hollywood be learning from TV?

In the weeks before the 78th annual Academy Awards, *Brokeback Mountain* producer Diana Ossana already suspected what few outside Hollywood could imagine: Her film was going to lose the Best Picture race. "Several people told me they knew a lot of Academy voters who just refused to see the film," says Ossana, who also co-wrote the screenplay with Larry McMurtry. This tragic love story between two men had dominated the critics' awards and banked $178 million worldwide. It even captivated sellout crowds in states like Oklahoma and Ohio—just not, apparently, in Academy screening rooms. "What are they afraid of?" McMurtry asked Ossana. "It's just a movie."

But *Brokeback* was more than a movie. It was a phenomenon that commanded the cultural conversation for months, from Jay Leno to YouTube to the cover of *The New Yorker*. More important, it proved that straight audiences would snap up tickets to a same-sex romance. Since then, a few gay-themed films have been released (e.g., *Notes on a Scandal*). But seemingly no studio—nor any studio art-house division—has greenlit a film with a gay lead character. "I don't think any studio responded by saying, 'Quick, dust off whatever gay dramas we have!'" says one former studio head. As surprising as it seemed that *Brokeback* could lose the Oscar to *Crash*, the real shock is just now setting in: *Brokeback* may have changed nothing.

When audiences complain that Hollywood is out of touch with the rest of the country, it's invariably because a movie is deemed too liberal. When it comes

42 NOVEMBER 2, 2007 ENTERTAINMENT WEEKLY 43

650

651

652

650 ENTERTAINMENT WEEKLY

Design Director_Geraldine Hessler
Art Directors_Theresa Griggs, Brian Anstey
Illustrator_Brian Cronin
Director of Photography_Fiona McDonagh
Managing Editor_Rick Tetzeli
Publisher_Time Inc. Issue_November 2, 2007
Category_Illo: Spread/Single Page

651 LOS ANGELES

Art Director_Joe Kimberling
Designer_Joe Kimberling
Illustrator_Dan Adel
Publisher_Emmis Issue_February 2007
Category_Illo: Spread/Single Page

652 MIDDLEBURY MAGAZINE

Art Director_Pamela Fogg
Designer_Pamela Fogg
Illustrator_Chris Buzelli
Editor-In-Chief_Matt Jennings
Publisher_Middlebury College
Issue_Fall 2007
Category_Illo: Spread/Single Page

653

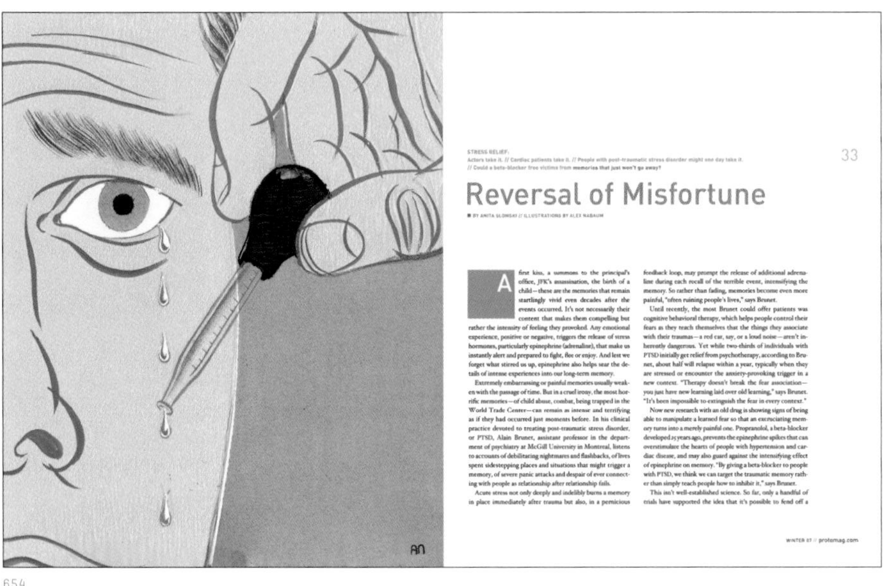

STRESS RELIEF:

33

Reversal of Misfortune

BY AMITA GLOMBAI // ILLUSTRATIONS BY ALEX NABAUM

654

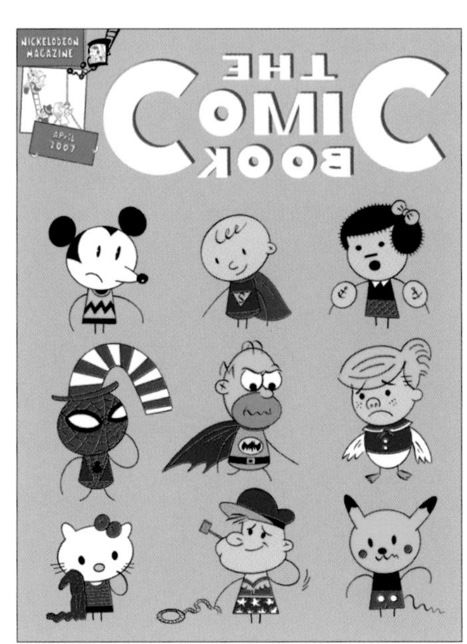

655

653 ROLLING STONE

Art Director_Joseph Hutchinson
Designer_Joe Newton
Illustrator_Benjamin Marra
Publisher_Wenner Media
Issue_November 15, 2007
Category_Illo: Spread/Single Page

654 PROTO

Creative Director_Charlene Benson
Design Director_Alex Knowlton
Designer_Lee Williams
Illustrator_Alex Nabaum
Studio_Time Inc. Content Solutions
Publisher_Time Inc. Strategic Communications
Client_Massachusets General Hospital
Issue_Winter 2007
Category_Illo: Spread/Single Page

655 NICKELODEON

Design Director_Justine Strasberg
Art Director_Chris Duffy
Designer_Catherine Tutrone
Illustrators_Ivan Brunetti, Mark Martin
Publisher_Nickelodeon, MTV Networks
Issue_April 2007
Category_Illo: Spread/Single Page

656

Blogs like Hilton's are increasingly making *fast*, *furious*, and *famous* the marching orders of the mainstream media.

THIS WAS THE YEAR OF...

Perez Hilton

BY TIM STACK

How many times a day do you go online to check it? Once? Twice? Personally, I can't go without visiting PerezHilton.com at least three times daily. But I'm not ashamed. Knowing who Brody Jenner hooked up with at Opera last night or what color baby Uggs Nicole Richie bought yesterday at Kitson is oddly comforting. Useless knowledge, sure, but surprisingly compelling. If Hollywood is high school, like so many celebs claim, then Perez, TMZ.com, and even YouTube are the digital equivalent of the writing on the girls'-bathroom wall, littered with secrets, rumors, and bitchery.

But this year, those scribbles graduated to the front page of the school paper. Yes, these outlets of the tawdry, the titillating, and the tabloid have finally broken through the "legitimate" news-source barrier: In 2007, more than 2,000 news stories were sourced to TMZ. With attention spans dwindling and the appetite for celeb gossip only growing, blogs like Hilton's are increasingly making *fast*, *furious*, and *famous* the marching orders of the mainstream media. Witness the attention placed on – to name just one of 2007's many train wrecks – Paris Hilton's summer jail term. Helicopters. Up-to-the-minute news alerts. Scrums of reporters. Larry King. In their desperate rush to keep up with bloggers like Perez – who, by the way, sat in for a chat with the ladies of *The View* and had his first VH1 special, *What Perez Sez...*, this year – respectable news outlets flushed Ms. Hilton's saga out of the tabloid brush and into the spotlight, where it became a major story.

Gossip is not a new phenomenon, of course. And our burning desire to know whether Britney ran a red light while going chandelier shopping for the third time in one week may eventually flame out. Or not: In July, the month Lindsay Lohan was arrested (again), PerezHilton.com had 60 million page views – a big number for a blog. Perhaps we should appeal to the celebs themselves to change things. Might we suggest that the badly behaved among you clean yourselves up for the sake of the ever-clicking cameras? Or, heaven forbid, stay inside and order delivery instead of driving drunk-enly and sans underwear to Popeyes? Then again, we must admit that a cleaner, gentler Hollywood wouldn't be nearly as much fun. ■

657

656 O, THE OPRAH MAGAZINE

Design Director_Carla Frank
Art Director_Ralph Groom
Designer_Ralph Groom
Illustrator_Serge Bloch
Editor-In-Chief_Amy Gross
Publisher_The Hearst Corporation-Magazines Division Issue_April 2007
Category_Illo: Spread/Single Page

657 ENTERTAINMENT WEEKLY

Design Director_Geraldine Hessler
Art Director_Brian Anstey
Illustrator_Hanoch Piven
Director of Photography_Fiona McDonagh
Managing Editor_Rick Tetzeli
Publisher_Time Inc.
Issue_December 28, 2007
Category_Illo: Spread/Single Page

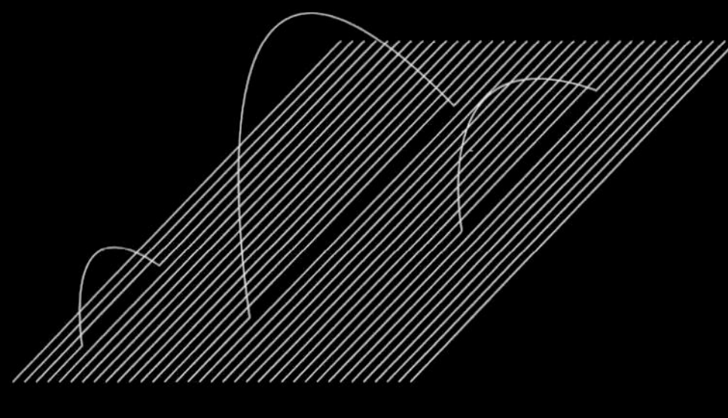

info graphics

ENTRIES: 126
CATEGORIES: 1

GOLD: 1
SILVER: 1
MERIT: 4

online

ENTRIES: 42
CATEGORIES: 4

GOLD: 1
SILVER: 1
MERIT: 4

student

ENTRIES: 239

WINNERS: 6

Op-Chart

ADRIANA LINS de ALBUQUERQUE AND ALICIA CHENG

31 Days in Iraq

In January more than 1,900 people — soldiers, security officers and civilians — were killed in the insurgency in Iraq, up from 800 in January 2006. Many corpses showed signs of torture, meaning the victims were probably killed by religious and tribal death squads.

The map below, based on data from the American, British and Iraqi governments and from news reports, shows the dates, locations and circumstances of deaths for the first month of the year. Given the vast size of Iraq and the communications difficulties inherent in war, the information may be incomplete. Nonetheless, it is our effort to visually depict the continuing human cost of the Iraq war.

AMERICAN FORCES
OTHER COALITION FORCES
IRAQI FORCES
POLICE OFFICER
CIVILIAN

HOSTILE FIRE
CAR BOMB
MORTAR/GRENADE
DECAPITATED/STRANGLED
SUICIDE BOMB
ACCIDENTAL DEATH
IMPROVISED EXPLOSIVE DEVICE

Adriana Lins de Albuquerque is a doctoral student in political science at Columbia. Alicia Cheng is a graphic designer at mgmt. design in Brooklyn.

NICHOLAS D. KRISTOF

Under Bush's Pillow

Dick Cheney as Lord Voldemort?

A reader named Melissa S. e-mailed to say that she explains Iraq policy to her 8-year-old son in terms of Harry Potter characters: "Dick Cheney is Lord Voldemort. George W. Bush is Peter Pettigrew." Don Rumsfeld is Lucius Malfoy, while Cornelius Fudge represents administration supporters who deny that anything is wrong. And, she concludes, "Daily Prophet reporter Rita Skeeter is Fox News."

That was one of the 400 comments from readers offering literary or historical parallels to the Bush administration and Iraq. One of the most commonly cited was Xenophon's ancient warning, in "Anabasis," of how much easier it is to get into a Middle Eastern war than out.

As a reader named John H. summarized "Anabasis": "Ten thousand Greek mercenaries march from Greece to Iran to effect regime change (unseat one emperor and establish his younger brother). They win the first few battles (cakewalk, mission accomplished) but then the younger brother is killed."

So the invaders found themselves without an effective prime minister to hand power to, yet they were stuck deep inside enemy territory. Xenophon's subtext is how the slog of war

From Voldemort to Othello, lessons for the White House.

corrodes soldiers and allows them to do terrible things. Xenophon is particularly pained when recounting a massacre that was the Haditha of its day.

The readers who sent in comments were responding to a column I wrote last month arguing that President Bush is inadvertently a fine education president, because he breathes new life into the classics. Thucydides' account of the failed "surge" in the Sicilian expedition 2,400 years ago is newly relevant, and "Moby Dick" is interesting reading today as a bracing warning of the dangers of an obsessive adventure that casts aside all rules. (You can submit your own favorite literary or historical parallel at nytimes.com/ontheground.)

Perhaps I'm cherry-picking from the classics to support my own opposition to a "surge" in Iraq. In writing this column, I wondered what classics Mr. Bush's supporters would cite to argue for his strategy. Shakespeare's "Henry V"? "Hamlet"?

Yet frankly, it's difficult to find great literature that encourages rulers to invade foreign lands, to escalate when battles go badly, to scorn critics, to be cocksure of themselves in the face of adversity. The themes of the classics tend to be the opposite.

Literature and history invariably counsel doubt and skepticism — even when you think you see Desdemona's infidelity with your own eyes, you don't; even when your advisers are telling you "it's a slam-dunk," it's not. The classics have an overwhelmingly cautionary bias, operating as a check on any impulsive rush to war.

Perhaps that is because, as Foreign Policy argues in its most recent issue, humans have an ingrained psychological tilt to hawkishness. In many ways, the authors note, human decision-making tends to err in ways that magnify conflict and make it difficult to climb down from confrontation.

My hunch is that the classics resonate in part because they are an antidote to that human frailty; literature has generated so many warnings about hubris in part to save us from ourselves.

Eastern classics have that same purpose of trying to tame and restrain us. The central theme of Chinese philosophy is the need for moderation, and Sun Tzu's famous "Art of War" advises generals on how to win without fighting. (Sun Tzu and Julius Caesar alike also appreciated the diplomatic benefits of treating enemy prisoners well; they would be appalled by Abu Ghraib and Guantánamo.)

So Mr. Bush should resolve that for every hour he spends with Mr. Cheney, he will spend another curled up with classical authors like Sophocles. "Antigone," for example, tells of King Creon, a good man who wants the best for his people — and yet ignores public opinion, refuses to admit error, goes double or nothing with his bets, and is slow to adapt to changing circumstance.

Creon's son pleads with his father to be less rigid. The trees that bend survive the seasons, he notes, while those that are inflexible are blown over and destroyed.

Americans today yearn for the same kind of wise leadership that the ancient Greeks did: someone with the wisdom to adjust course, to acknowledge error, to listen to critics, to show compassion as well as strength, to discern moral nuance as well as moral clarity. Alexander the Great used to sleep with the "Iliad" under his pillow; maybe Mr. Bush should try "Antigone."

Oh, and for Mrs. Bush? How about Aristophanes' "Lysistrata"? □

658

658 THE NEW YORK TIMES

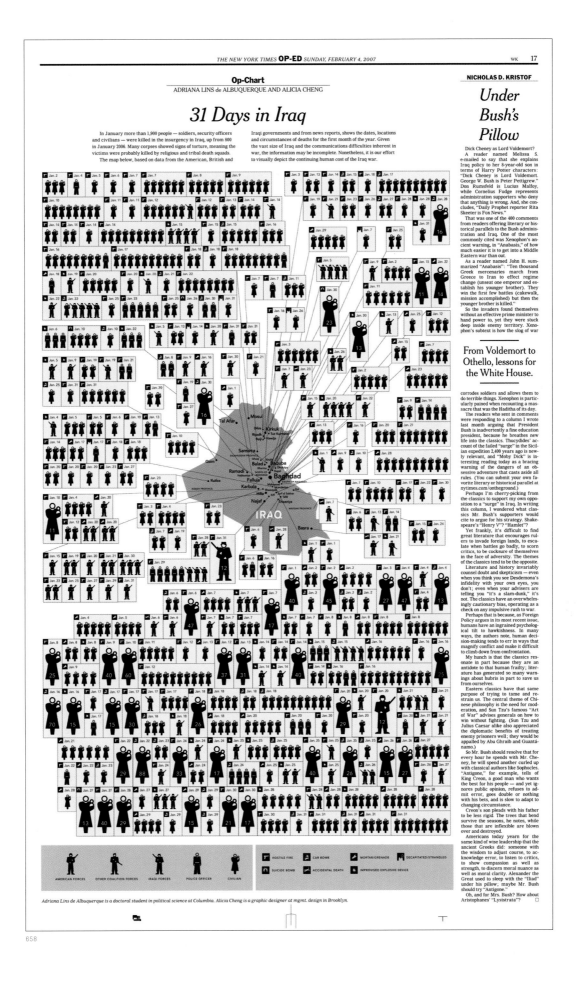

Design Director_Tom Bodkin Art Director_Brian Rea Assistant Art Directors_Sam Weber, Kim Bost Designers_Alicia Cheng, MGMT
Publisher_The New York Times Issue_February 4, 2007 Category_Info Graphics: Single Page/Spread/Story

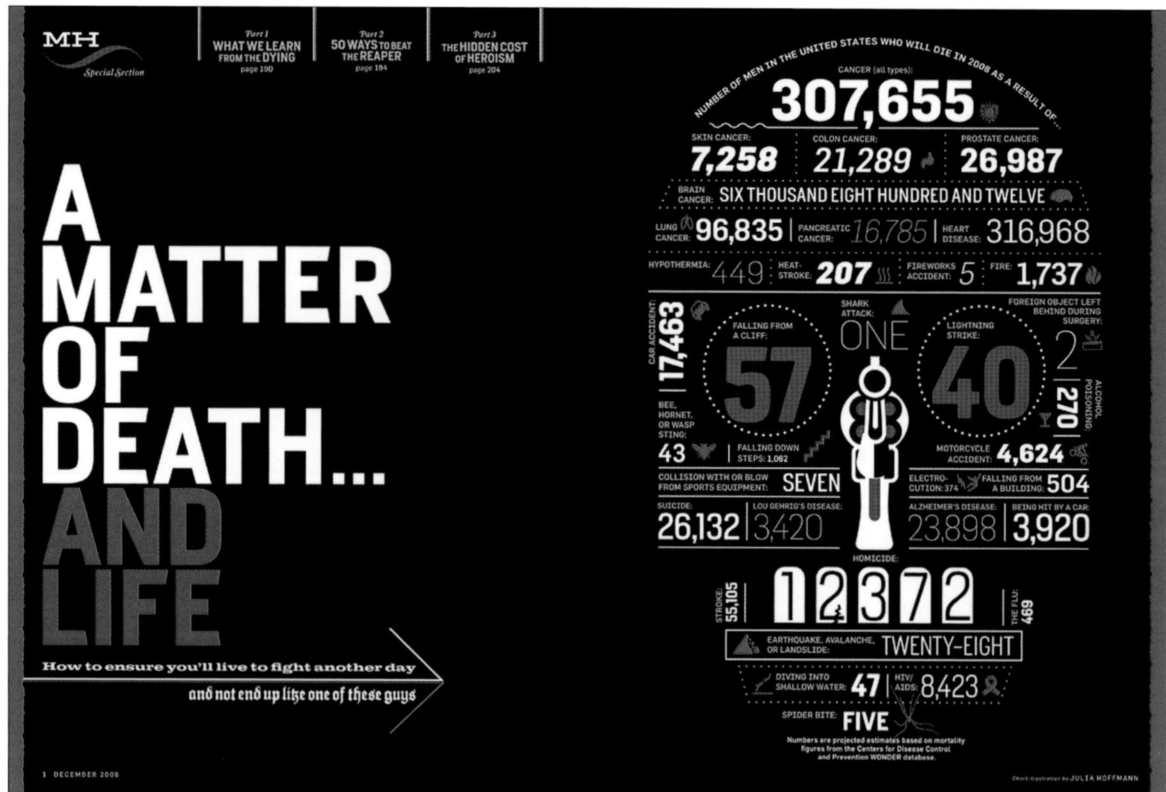

659

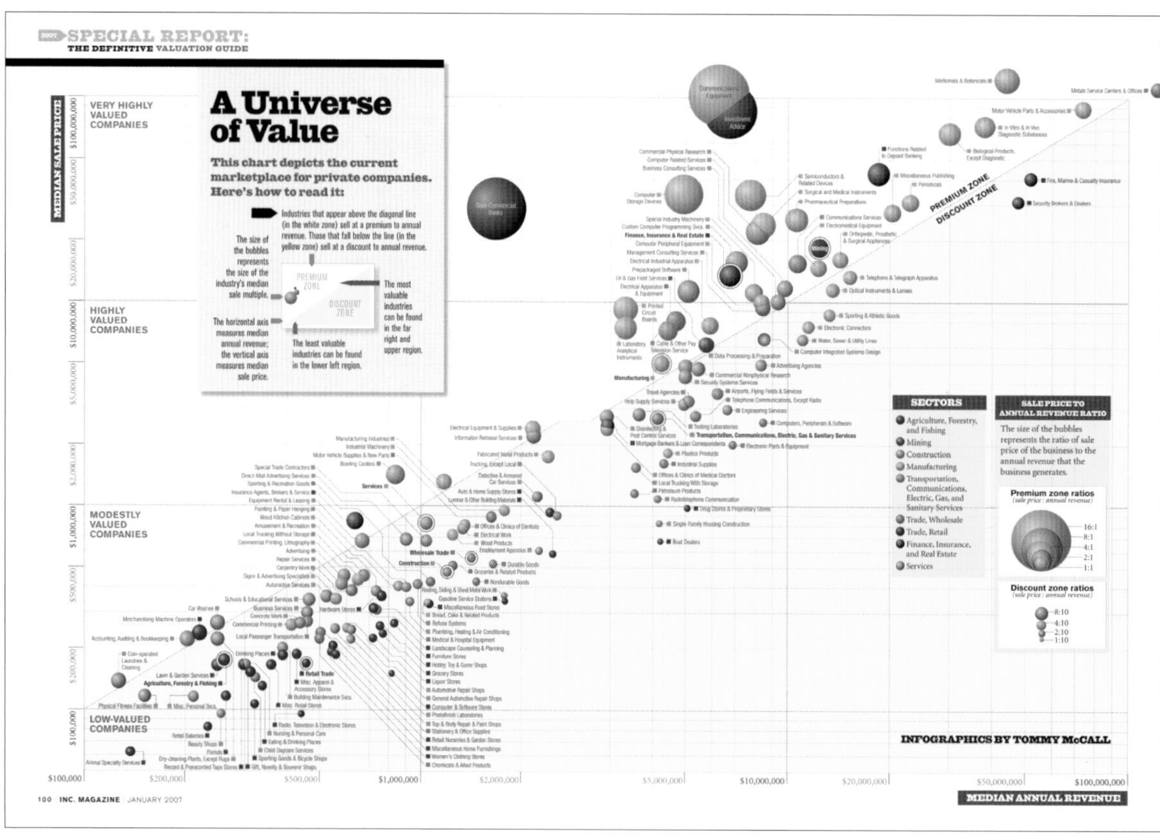

660

659 MEN'S HEALTH

Design Director_George Karabotsos Art Director_John Dixon
Designer_John Dixon Illustrator_Julia Hoffman
Publisher_Rodale Inc. Issue_November 2007
Category_Info Graphics: Single Page/Spread/Story

660 INC.

Creative Director_Blake Taylor
Designer_Lou Vega Illustrator_Tommy McCall
Publisher_Mansueto Ventures Issue_January 2007
Category_Info Graphics: Single Page/Spread/Story

How would you rate your **overall experience** as an undergraduate student?

UNLESS OTHERWISE INDICATED, THESE GRAPHICS REFLECT THE RESULTS OF A NATIONAL POLL OF RECENT COLLEGE GRADUATES BY THE NEW YORK TIMES AND MTVU

Fear and loathing pave the road to college. But ask recent graduates to reflect on their experience, and they advise kids to forget rankings, chill out and get ready to savor the best years of their lives.

By Jacques Steinberg

LAURIE HOACHLANDER'S PARENTS may have spent tens of thousands of dollars on the psychology courses she took as an undergraduate at the University of Pennsylvania, but ask the 27-year-old, a member of the class of 2002, what was most valuable about her college years, and her thoughts drift far beyond the classroom window.

There was her year as a resident adviser to a cluster of freshmen in her dormitory at Penn, an experience colored by the attempted suicide of one of her charges, followed by his recovery and return to the hall. "That taught me a lot about crisis management," she says. Then there was her work as a campus tour guide, which taught her "how to be a better public speaker." That, she says, wound up serving her well in one of her first jobs, as a leader of seminars for real estate brokers: they would interrupt her presentations with offbeat questions,

Infographics by Yokoland

72 LETTERING BY FISHWRAPPERS. PHOTOGRAPHS BY JORGEN GOMNAES.

73

661

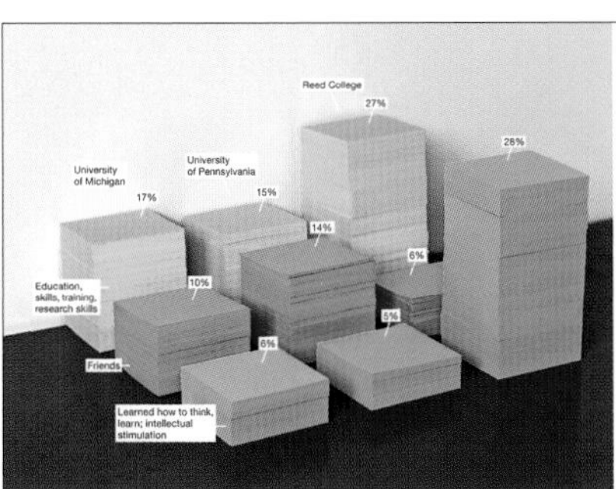

Looking back, what part of your undergraduate college education do you **value most now**?

FROM SURVEYS BY THE TIMES OF RECENT ALUMNI

just like the pesky parents on her tours.

As high-school juniors and seniors descend this fall on fact-finding missions to the nation's colleges and universities — an indispensable part of the uniquely American hazing known as the college-admissions process — a fresh cast of cheerful student tour guides will steer the conversation through familiar scripts. They'll dutifully note the number of volumes in the library and the opportunities for undergraduate research and the ratio of professors to students. Only the most persistent of pesky parents will draw out a story like Hoachlander's of a moment in college life that really made a difference; arguably, it's the rare undergraduate that has the perspective to recognize that moment, let alone go off script to recount it.

But talk to a couple of thousand recent college graduates, as the magazine did this summer — alumni roughly five years out of school, with the perspective that comes from having got a taste of the real world but with memories of freshman and sophomore years still relatively intact — and enough moments spill out to begin to tell a story. Some graduates fondly recall a special professor, others the opportunity to become more self-sufficient. Some say they didn't study hard enough; others, though fewer, regret working themselves too hard and wish they'd taken more time to relax or learn about life from their peers. Yet overall, the story told by these survivors of the admissions process is actually pretty simple: college is great. And their message to those coming up behind them — the classes of 2012 and 2013 and 2014, bigger than any generation of college prospects before them and as anxious as their parents are hovering — is pretty simple, too: chill out.

To an astonishing degree, recent graduates surveyed by The New York Times Poll said that they are satisfied with the choices they made about where to go to college and with the educations they received. That seems to hold true whether they went to big schools or small schools, costly private colleges or somewhat more affordable public universities, their first-choice school or their fourth. Like Laurie Hoachlander, though, the young alums acknowledge, in a variety of their responses, that the qualities they or their parents thought were crucial in choosing a college were not necessarily the things that mattered most once they got there. Magazine rankings and a school's reputation — both extremely important in the minds of many applicants — are often of far less significance to graduates as they reflect on what made their college years worthwhile.

"Now I value the goofy and formative life experiences — driving to Atlantic City on a whim, playing a weekly basketball game with my friends, playing pranks in the dining hall," wrote Dan Diamond, a newsletter editor who was a classmate of Hoachlander's in the class of 2002 at Penn.

Jacques Steinberg is a reporter for The New York Times and the author of "The Gatekeepers: Inside the Admissions Process of a Premier College" (Viking Penguin). Marjorie Connelly of The Times Poll designed the surveys and contributed to this article.

THOUGH A LARGE industry exists to convince teenagers and their parents otherwise, there is not much science in the search for the right college for a particular student. The data that fill many college guidebooks paint a picture of the student body as it passes through the university's front gate, taking the students' measure with SAT scores, class rank and the like. Those lists of "top party schools" or best school for "Birkenstock-wearing, tree-hugging, clove-smoking vegetarians" — an actual category handicapped by The Princeton Review — come from sampling students still in the hazy thick of the college experience. The totemic rankings by U.S. News & World Report add criteria like alumni giving or admissions selectivity to the soup. We thought it might help families making their way through the admissions maze if we could collect the wisdom of students who had made it all the way out into postgraduate life.

So The New York Times conducted a series of surveys over the summer. Telephone polling in conjunction with mtvU, the music channel's on-campus network, produced a sample of 271 college graduates under age 30. (The nationwide poll, conducted June 15 to June 23, has a margin of sampling error of plus or minus six percentage points.) Separately, online surveys by The Times gathered the replies of more than 1,300 graduates, most in the class of 2002, from three institutions generally regarded as among the finest and most selective in the nation: Penn, an Ivy League university in Philadelphia; Reed College, a small liberal arts school in Portland, Ore.; and the University of Michigan in Ann Arbor, a state university. I called a dozen alumni afterward to probe more deeply into their responses to the poll questions.

What qualities were **very or somewhat important** when you were deciding which undergraduate college to attend?

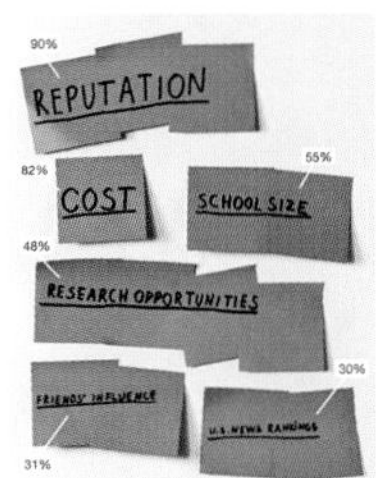

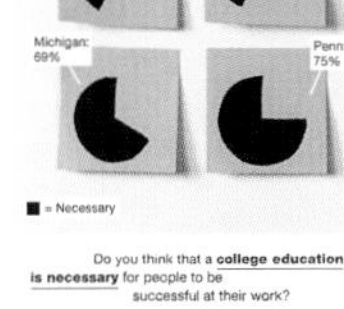

Do you think that a **college education is necessary** for people to be successful at their work?

Much of what the polling found falls safely into the category of "reassuring" — not an adjective that tends to be associated with the college search. Among the group surveyed nationally, 93 percent described their overall undergraduate experience as "excellent" or "good"; the results were comparable for the alumni of Penn (95 percent), Michigan (96 percent) and Reed (98 percent). Likewise, asked if their college education "was worth the money you and your parents paid for it," 89 percent in the national poll said that it was. At Reed and Penn, where tuition bills are among the highest in the nation, 81 percent and 79 percent, respectively, said they got their money's worth. (At Michigan, where tuition is lower for state residents, 84 percent of alumni agreed.) To plumb whether that learning served any practical purpose, those alumni who said they had jobs were asked whether their undergraduate education "prepared you for the work you are currently doing." Seventy-five percent in the national poll said yes — very nearly as positive a response as among the graduates of Penn (82 percent), Michigan (83 percent) and Reed (86 percent.)

(The upbeat responses from alumni of those three colleges come with a caveat: the graduates surveyed chose to be in close-enough touch with their alma mater to at least supply an e-mail address where they could be reached. But their answers were similar enough to those of participants in the national poll — who were part of a random sample — to suggest confidence in the results all around.)

Of course, a high-school student staring at a blank college application may be most interested in the answer to the following question: Why? What made these individuals' college experiences so good? Why was it worth the angst and the hard work and — their parents would probably also want to know — the lingering debts?

For the Penn and Michigan graduates in particular, the answers are not always what they expected back when they were writing essays and filling in SAT bubbles. They recalled being extremely focused on their schools' brand names: 88 percent of the Penn alums said that reputation was "very" important when they were deciding which school to attend, as did 78 percent of the Michigan alums. Similarly, 85 percent of the Penn graduates and 72 percent of the Michigan grads said that their university's ranking by U.S. News & World Report was "somewhat" or "very" important when they were making that decision.

Yet five years after graduating, about one-third at each university said that the rankings seemed "less important" to them now than they did in high school. Asked to volunteer what they valued most about their college experience, 10 percent of the Penn alums — and 5 percent of the Michigan graduates — mentioned their alma mater's reputation. Graduates of both universities were more likely to cite the friendships they made at school. The responses suggest that the critics of college lists are onto something: maybe the devaluing of the rankings can serve as a tonic to the unrelenting obsession they foster among many applicants and their parents.

The Reed alumni teach a different lesson. Reed has long stood opposed to the very idea of college rankings, electing not to provide data to U.S. News, so students in the yearly classes of 300 or so freshman start out picking the school for what it stands for rather than where it stands. And the graduates, looking back, seem to reaffirm the notion that students following their instincts can find their way to the right school. As if parroting the marketing copy in the college's brochure, alums overwhelmingly endorse Reed's "conference" style of learning, in which lessons transmitted in lectures are later reinforced in smaller groups where students engage in spirited debates. Twenty-eight percent of the respondents from Reed said that learning "how to think, to work, to learn" in college was what they valued most now. Another 27 percent cited research skills or other kinds of training.

One was Andrew Schpak, 27, a litigator in Portland who graduated in 2001. He said the school's emphasis on Socratic learning was perhaps as valuable as anything he learned at Cornell law school in preparing him to argue before judges, juries and opposing lawyers. "Reed taught me to think on my feet, to think beyond my gut reaction and to think about what might make me change my mind," he told me in a follow-up interview.

One conclusion to be drawn from Andrew's obvious satisfaction with his education, when laid alongside the responses of so many of his peers, is that the convoluted process of matching students to colleges ultimately does what it is supposed to do. But in the end, I also find myself reflecting on the ongoing regrets expressed by so many of the alumni we contacted — not with their overall college experiences but with the day-to-day choices they made, whether it was the belly-dancing class that one Reed graduate said she missed out on because she was studying too hard or the Greek tragedy that lay untouched on another Reed student's dorm-room bookshelf and now, in all likelihood, will never be opened.

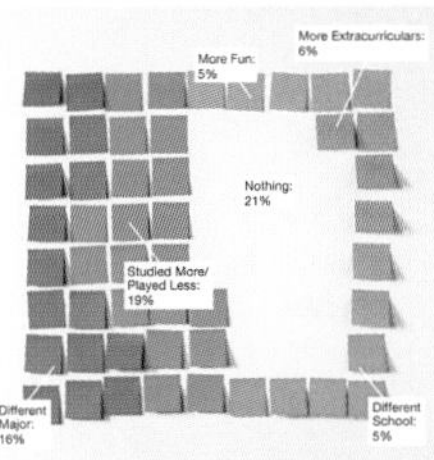

If you could relive your college years, **what would you do differently**?

Perhaps we should be spending a little less time coaching and cajoling high-school students about how to get into college, or even how to identify that mythical "right" college, and instead help them prepare a little better for how to strike a balance, or explore what they hope to accomplish, once they get there. ■

BY THE NUMBERS The complete questionnaire and results of the telephone poll and online surveys, along with an explanation of the methodology by which the polling was conducted: **nytimes.com/magazine**

74 PHOTOGRAPHS BY JORGEN GOMNAES

THE NEW YORK TIMES MAGAZINE / SEPTEMBER 30, 2007 75

661

661 THE NEW YORK TIMES MAGAZINE

Creative Director_Janet Froelich Art Director_Arem Duplessis
Designers_Jeff Glendenning, Arem Duplessis
Infographics_Yokoland Editor-In-Chief_Gerry Marzorati
Publisher_The New York Times Issue_September 30, 2007
Category_Info Graphics: Single Page/Spread/Story

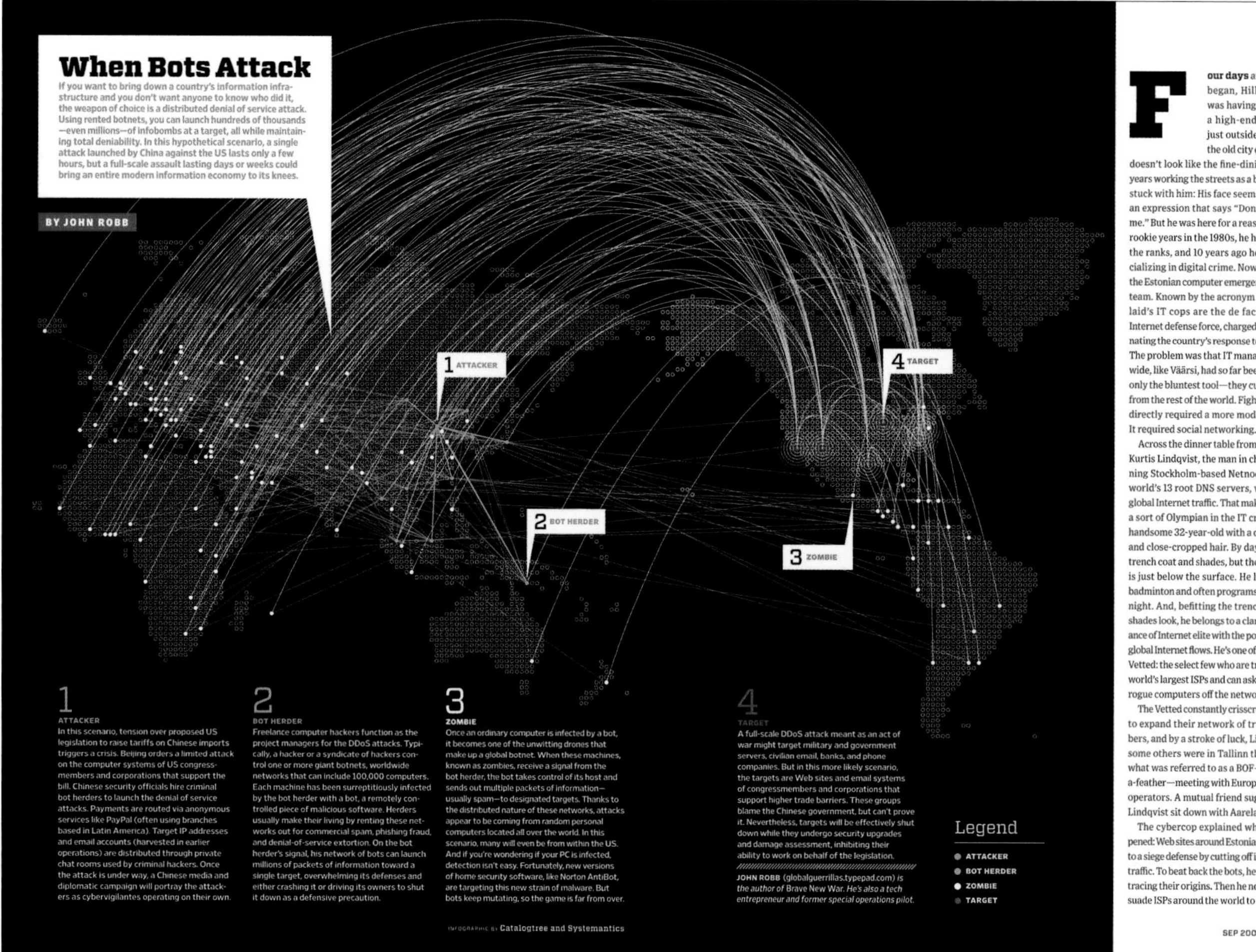

662

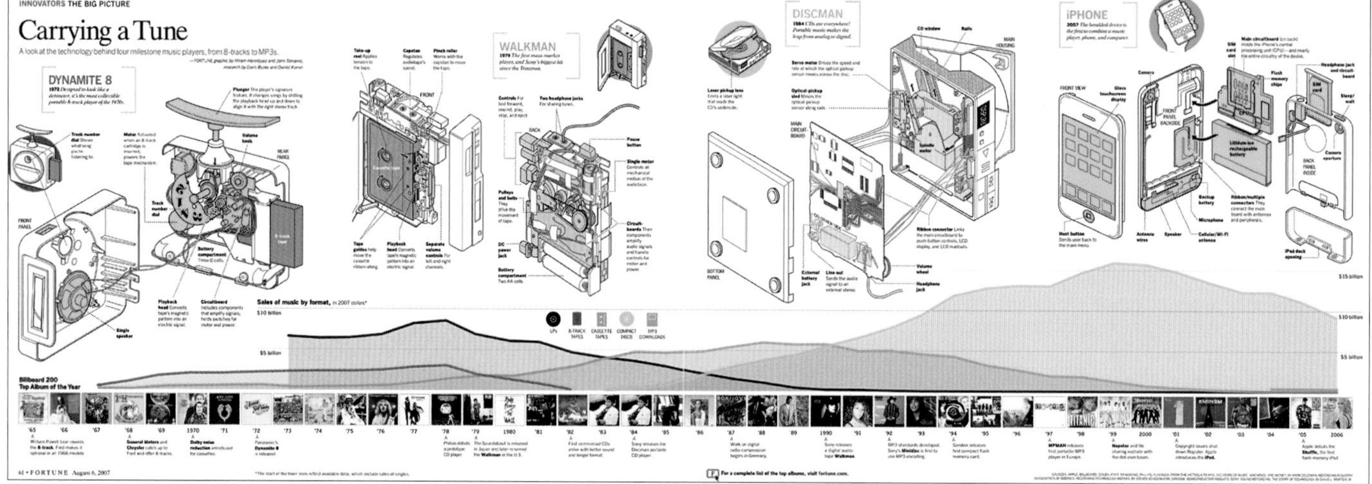

663

662 WIRED

Creative Director_Scott Dadich
Art Director_Maili Holiman Designer_Maili Holiman
Illustrators_Catalogtree, Systemantics
Publisher_Condé Nast Publications, Inc.
Issue_September 2007
Category_Info Graphics: Single Page/Spread/Story

663 FORTUNE

Design Director_Robert Perino
Art Director Deanna Lowe Designers_Sarah Slobin, John Tomanio, Robert Dominguez, Alice Alves
Illustrator_Hiram Henriquez
Director of Photography_Greg Pond
Photo Editor_Armin Harris
Editor-In-Chief_Andy Serwer
Publisher_Time Inc. Issue_August 6, 2007
Category_Info Graphics: Single Page/Spread/Story

COLLEGE HOOPS 2008
YOU CAN GET THERE FROM HERE

BEEN THERE ...

... RECRUITED THAT. NOT ALL COACHES GET THEIR PICK OF THE PREPS EACH YEAR. SOME HAVE TO COUNT ON BEING FIRST TO A NEW HOTBED OR TRUSTING THEIR INSTINCTS ON A SMALL-TOWN UNKNOWN. BY ERIC NEEL | DIAGRAM BY CATALOGTREE

HE'S OUT THERE SOMEWHERE, AND THESE guys know it. Somewhere—maybe a little off the radar or a step out of the spotlight—is the player who will make the difference for their not-quite-top-tier program, the perfect fit for their style and approach. He will be the one who makes it possible to go toe to toe with the biggest of the big names and to dream NCAA Tourney dreams. Their Jimmy Chitwood.

We polled our Bristol experts to identify the most respected recruiters out there, coaches who see prime time where others see pine time. They came back with five: Phil Martelli of St. Joseph's, Boston College's Al Skinner, UNLV's Lon Kruger, Gonzaga's Mark Few and Marquette's Tom Crean. These guys have built what they have from the ground up. In doing so, they've thrown out the traditional map, stretched it beyond recognition and disregarded its borders. Because in the end, their territory is wherever that hidden gem is buried.

PHIL MARTELLI
FIVE-YEAR RECORD: 114–49

When everyone is eyeballing the same players, the question shifts from where you look to what you see. St. Joe's big man, Ahmad Nivins, had a raw offensive game at St. Anthony High in Jersey City, N.J., but what Martelli observed was the kid's work ethic. "It becomes a game of beauty-in-the-eye-of-the-beholder," he says.

Martelli's two most famous finds were, in hindsight, way underrecruited. Delonte West picked Hawk Hill over Manhattan because he wanted the Atlantic 10 TV exposure, and 2003 POY Jameer Nelson picked St. Joe's over Temple (a school used to getting most all the Philly-area kids). Says Martelli, "I see guys like that who just want it more, and I'm smitten."

- **5** N.J. (two from St. Anthony, Jersey City)
- **3** Conn., Pa.
- **1** Del., D.C., Fla., Iowa, Md., W.Va.

AL SKINNER
FIVE-YEAR RECORD: 117–47

If fat-cat programs fill up on top-ranked talent, those looking to take them down have to dig lower down the food chain. Skinner's relentless searching has turned up former Big East POY Troy Bell, current Timberwolves forward Craig Smith and Bobcats first-rounder Jared Dudley. "There are guys out there if you keep working—diamonds in the rough," says Skinner. "Not every kid is well-known and on the circuit." Dudley, who was nabbed the year before our cutoff, was one who hid in plain sight. Because the greatest gifts (court vision, desire to prove himself) the 6'7" tweener from San Diego possesses weren't easy to see, he was recruited only by BC, Creighton and San Diego State. "You don't think about geography," Skinner says. "You're driven by a need to find all the pieces."

- **3** N.J., Texas (two from Dallas Mustangs AAU)
- **2** Colo. (both from Colorado Select AAU)
- **1** Fla., Ill., Mich., N.H., N.Y., R.I., Vt., Va.

LON KRUGER
THREE-YEAR RECORD: 64–34

Fit is the magic word for Kruger, who took over a flagging UNLV program in 2004 with a rep as a top recruiter from his days at Florida and Illinois. In his first seasons in Vegas, he's thought in terms of gathering pieces of the classic hoops puzzle—this year a point guard, next year a big—and about building a certain culture. "We're doing something similar to what you've seen the Spurs do," says Kruger, who has brought in seven juco players (from off-the-map places like Antelope Valley College and Yuba College) since joining the Runnin' Rebs. "We're looking at kids who want to be part of a unit, character guys," he says. "We picture ourselves coming together over time." Last season's 30-7 record was a good one to begin to bond over.

- **6** Calif.
- **4** Texas (three from Houston)
- **3** Utah
- **2** Fla., Kan.
- **1** Ariz., Ill., La., Mich., Nev., N.J., Tenn., Va.

MARK FEW
FIVE-YEAR RECORD: 136–25

When Few began work as a Gonzaga assistant in 1989, the map of Bulldog Country fit in a desktop picture frame. How things have changed. It's no longer easy to hoard Washington's best. So this year's squad features a player from as far away as New Zealand. "We still recruit our backyard," Few says. "We've just moved the fences out a little. We've come to think without boundaries." Assistant Tommy Lloyd, who played professionally in Australia and Germany, is the guy with the international connections (he helped snag foreigners like J.P. Batista and Ronny Turiaf). "You're trying to put together a team full of guys looking to prove the world wrong," says another assistant, Leon Rice. "It's the hungry dogs you're looking for, wherever they are."

- **4** Wash.
- **3** Texas
- **2** Calif., Canada
- **1** Ariz., Col., Fla., Ill., Iowa, Kan., Ore., Pa., Utah, Brazil, New Zealand

TOM CREAN
FIVE-YEAR RECORD: 109–51

Ranking 10-year-old ballers is standard practice these days, but for the coaches who don't make a habit of getting commitments from middle schoolers, feel is a necessary tool. "I go by my gut," Crean says. He calls his recruiting philosophy "inside out." He and his assistants have canvassed Wisconsin and Illinois for talent (Dwyane Wade, Jerel McNeal, Ousmane Barro), but when they exhaust those picked-over avenues, they just extend the search. New Jersey has been a recent hot spot; Crean found two players at St. Benedict's in Newark (David Cubillán, Dwight Burke). "We're not in an area that has huge numbers of major players each year, so we look all over the East Coast, in Texas, overseas," he says. "We'll look anywhere to find the right kid."

- **4** N.J. (two from St. Benedict's, Newark)
- **3** Ill. (two from Chicago)
- **2** Ind., Wis.
- **1** Ala., La., Mass., Minn., Texas

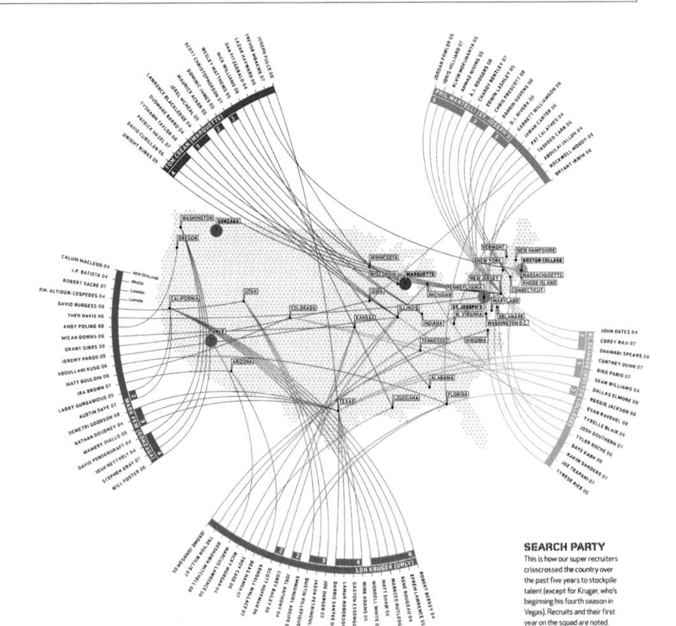

SEARCH PARTY
This is how our super recruiters crisscrossed the country over the past five years to stockpile talent (except for Kruger, who's beginning his fourth season in Vegas). Recruits and their first year on the squad are noted.

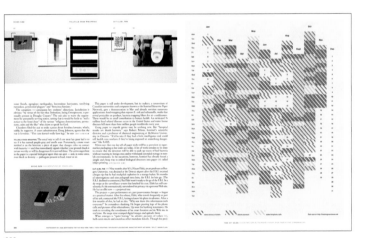

78 | 79

664

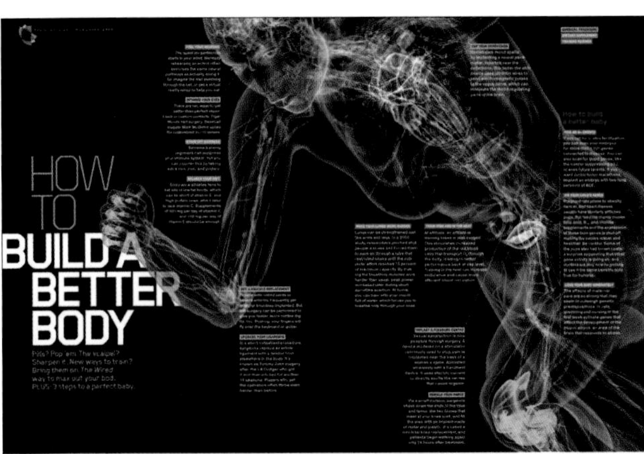

HOW TO
BUILD A BETTER BODY

665

666

664 ESPN THE MAGAZINE

Creative Director_Siung Tjia
Designer_Robert Festino
Illustrator_Catalogtree
Director of Photography_Catriona Ni Aolain
Publisher_ESPN, Inc.
Issue_November 19, 2007
Category_Info Graphics: Single Page/Spread/Story

665 WIRED

Creative Director_Scott Dadich
Art Director_Maili Holiman
Designer_Maili Holiman
Illustrator_Bryan Christie
Publisher_Condé Nast Publications, Inc.
Issue_January 2007
Category_Info Graphics: Single Page/Spread/Story

666 THE NEW YORK TIMES MAGAZINE

Creative Director_Janet Froelich
Art Director_Arem Duplessis
Designer_Gail Bichler
Illustrators_Barbara Hahn, Christine Zimmerman
Editor-In-Chief_Gerry Marzorati
Publisher_The New York Times
Issue_December 9, 2007
Category_Info Graphics: Single Page/Spread/Story

678

678

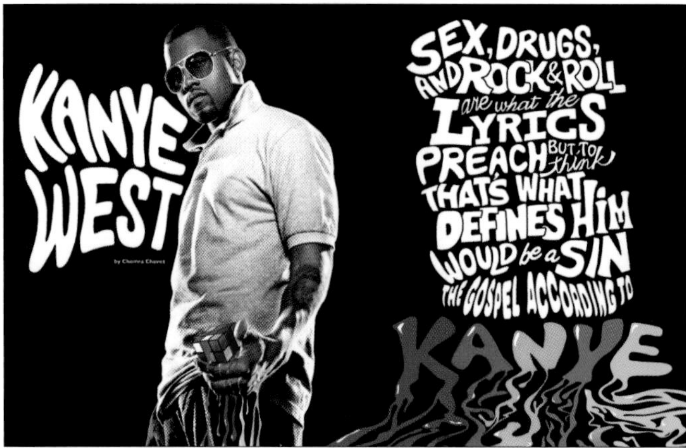

679

679

680

680

678 FIRST PLACE

WINNER OF THE ADOBE SCHOLARSHIP IN HONOR OF B.W. HONEYCUTT

Designer_Paul Johnson
Title_North Dakota
School_Montana State University
Instructor_Jeffrey Conger
Category_Travel

 SECOND PLACE

Designer_Anthony Cruz
Title_Kanye West
School_American Academy of Art
Instructor_Carol Luc
Category_Entertainment / Music

680 THIRD PLACE

Designer_Lauren Turnier
Title_The Gospel According to the Shins
School_Fashion Institute of Technology, New York City
Instructor_Ronald Bacsa
Category_Entertainment / Music

681

681

682

682

683

683

681 1ST HONORABLE MENTION

Designer_Jason Sfetko
Title_Amy Winehouse
School_Rochester Institute of Technology
Instructor_Chris Lyons
Category_Entertainment / Music
IMAGES ID: 904A, 904B

682 2ND HONORABLE MENTION

Designer_Krzysztof Piatkowski
Title_Extreme Rush, Shaun White, Snowboarder
School_School of Visual Arts
Instructor_Mitch Shostak
Category_Sports

683 1ST HONORABLE MENTION

Designer_Yun Soo Yun
Title_Tokyo
School_School of Visual Arts
Instructor_Mitch Shostak
Category_Travel

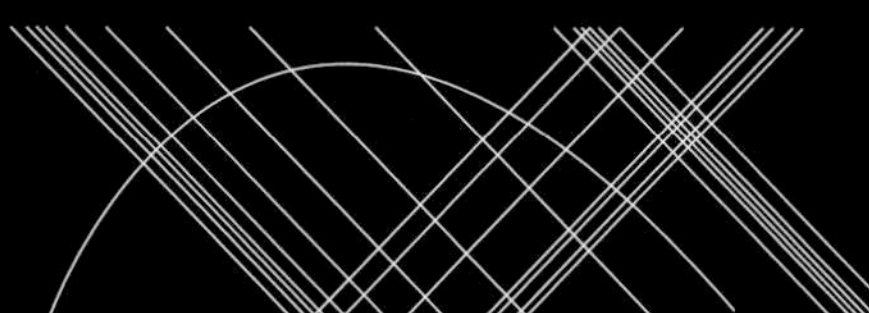

spots

ENTRIES: 627 AWARDS: 100

684

685

687

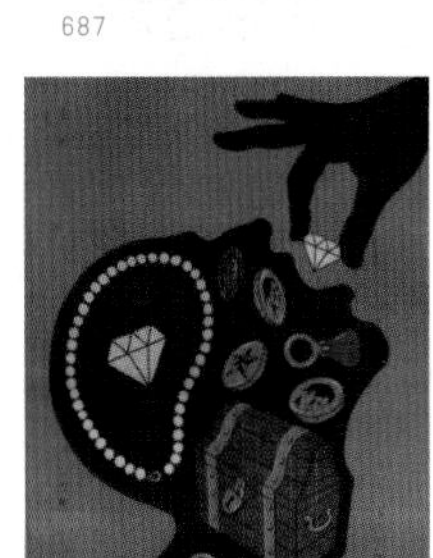
688

686

689

690

691

692

693

694

695

696

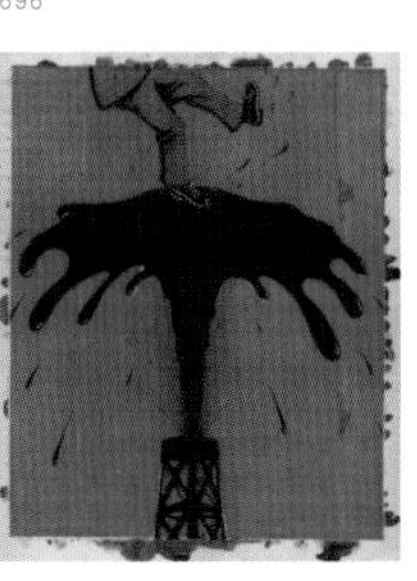
697

684 **PAUL DAVIS**

Title_Bad Vibes Over a Music Deal
Design Director_Robert Priest
Art Director_Grace Lee
Publication_Condé Nast Portfolio
Publisher_Condé Nast Pub. Inc.
Issue_September 2007

685 **DAN ADEL**

Title_Holding Court
Art Director_Dian Holton
Publication_AARP The Magazine
Publisher_AARP Publications
Issue_March/April 2007

686 **CHRIS BUZELLI**

Title_6 Degrees of Irritation
Design Director_Robert Lesser
Art Director_Heather Godin
Publication_CFO
Publisher_CFO Publishing Corp
Issue_March 2007

687 **KAREN CALDICOTT**

Title_Does the Supreme Court Still Matter?
Art Director_D.W. Pine
Publication_TIME Publisher_Time Inc.
Issue_October 22, 2007

688 **MONIKA AICHELE, DANIEL BEJAR, YUKO SHIMIZU, JAMES VICTORE**

Title_Your Money and Your Brain - Fear and Greed Art Director_Davia Smith Publication_Money
Publisher_Time Inc.
Issue_September 2007

689 **MONIKA AICHELE**

Title_Che - Symbol for the Right Wing
Art Directors_Heike Reinsch, Jenny Friedrich-Freska
Publication_Internationaler Kulturaustausch Issue_January 2007

690 **MONIKA AICHELE**

Title_Dead Body in First Class
Art Director_Dieter Roosli
Publication_Annabelle Magazine
Issue_April 2007

691 **BARRY BLITT**

Title_Cruising the Internet at 70 MPH
Art Director_Barbara Adamson
Publication_PC World
Publisher_International Data Group
Issue_May 2007

692 **DAVID M. BRINLEY**

Title_Favorite Card Game
Design Director_Fred Woodward
Publication_GQ
Publisher_Condé Nast Pub. Inc.
Issue_March 2007

693 **JOHN HENDRIX**

Title_Career Rx
Art Director_Marina Grinshpun
Publication_Premiere
Publisher_Hachette Filipacchi Media U.S. Issue_April 2007

694 **GEORGE BATES**

Title_Fidelity's Deafening Silence
Design Director_Robert Perino
Publication_Fortune
Publisher_Time Inc.
Issue_September 17, 2007

695 **JOHN HENDRIX**

Title_Vote for Quirk
Art Director_Melissa Bluey
Publication_The Atlantic
Issue_September 2007

696 **MONIKA AICHELE**

Title_Before I Die
Art Director_Nicholas Blechman
Publication_NYT Book Review
Publisher_The New York Times
Issue_October 14, 2007

697 **DANIEL BEJAR**

Title_Playing the Oil Boom
Art Director_Robert Perino
Publication_Fortune
Publisher_Time Inc.
Issue_November 26, 2007

698

702

699

703

709

710

700

704

706

711

701

705

707

708

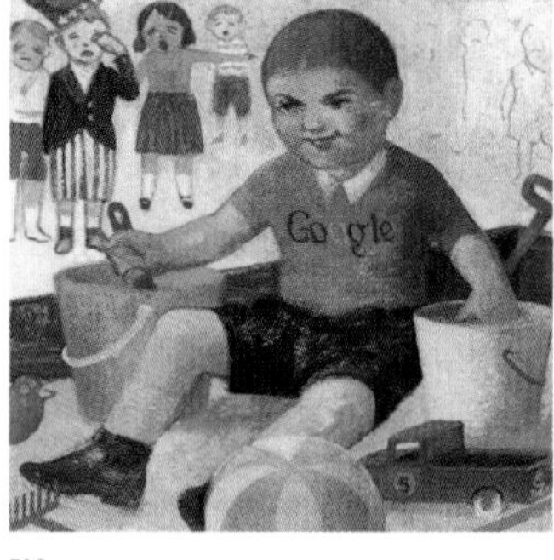

712

698 JOHN CUNEO

Title_Vibrator Withdrawal
Design Director_David Cucurito
Publication_Esquire
Publisher_The Hearst Corporation-Magazines Division Issue_June 2007

699 JOHN CUNEO

Title_Exit Ghost Art Director_Jason Treat Publication_The Atlantic
Issue_October 2007

700 JOHN CUNEO

Title_I'd Rather Eat Chocolate
Design Director_David Cucurito
Publication_Esquire Publisher_The Hearst Corporation-Magazines Division Issue_March 2007

701 JOE MAGEE

Title_Should Prisoners Be Permitted to Participate in Medical Research Trials? Design Director_Alex Knowlton
Publication_PROTO Publisher_Time Inc. Strategic Communications
Issue_Spring 2007

702 JOHN CUNEO

Title_.... A Different Person in Bed
Design Director_David Cucurito
Publication_Esquire
Publisher_The Hearst Corporation-Magazines Division
Issue_January 2007

703 JEAN-PHILIPPE DELHOMME

Title_The Reluctant Hostess
Design Director_Carla Frank
Publication_O, the Oprah Magazine
Publisher_The Hearst Corporation-Magazines Division
Issue_December 2007

704 HARRY CAMPBELL

Title_The Pro Bono Report
Art Director_Joan Ferrell
Publication_The American Lawyer
Publisher_American Lawyer Media
Issue_July 2007

705 JEAN-PHILIPPE DELHOMME

Title_Style Guy: Chillin' in My Bib
Design Director_Fred Woodward
Publication_GQ Publisher_Condé Nast Pub. Inc. Issue_November 2007

706 PAUL BLOW

Title_Help Wanted
Art Director_Jose Fernandez
Publication_More
Publisher_Meredith Corporation
Issue_April 2007

707 TAVIS COBURN

Title_The Coming Robot Army
Art Director_Stacey D. Clarkson
Publication_Harper's Magazine
Issue_February 2007

708 ANDRÉ CARRILHO

Art Director_Stacey D. Clarkson
Publication_Harper's Magazine
Issue_March 2007

709 MARCOS CHIN

Title_Reeling in the Years
Art Director_Jose Fernandez
Publication_More Publisher_Meredith Corporation Issue_October 2007

710 ANDY FRIEDMAN

Title_The Battle for Your Social Circle Design Director_Robert Perino Publication_Fortune
Publisher_Time Inc.

711 ANDY FRIEDMAN

Title_Curators on Commission
Design Director_Robert Priest
Art Director_Grace Lee
Publication_Condé Nast Portfolio
Publisher_Condé Nast Pub. Inc.
Issue_December 2007

712 GERARD DUBOIS

Title_Don't Be Arrogant
Art Director_Robert Perino
Publication_Fortune
Publisher_Time Inc.
Issue_August 20, 2007

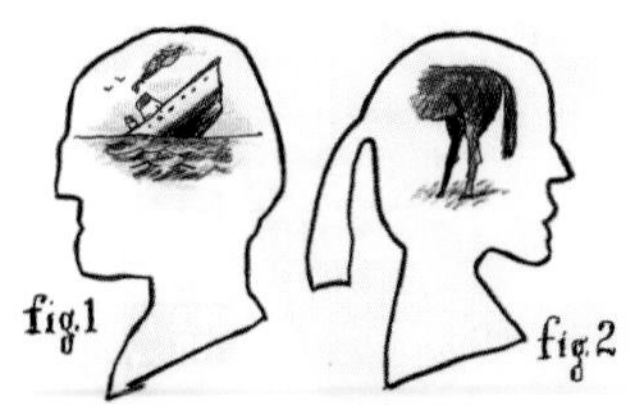

713

714

716

717

719

721

722

723

715

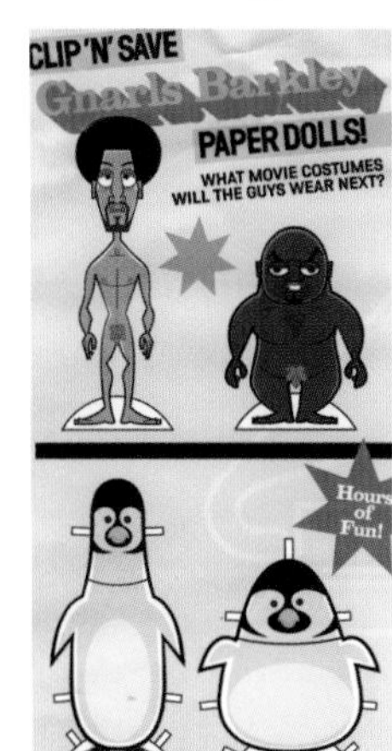

718

720

724

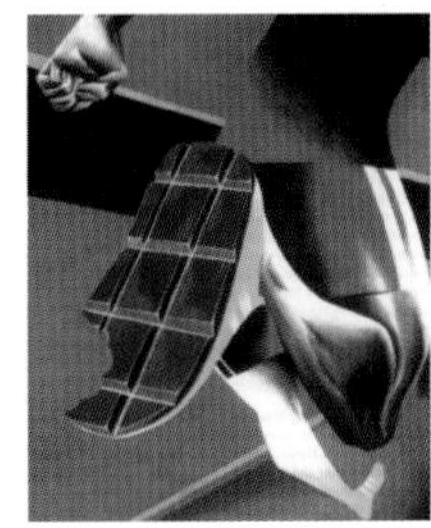
726

725

713 JAMES VICTORE

Title_6 People You Should Never Hire
Art Director_Vikki Nestico
Publication_Men's Health
Publisher_Rodale Inc.
Issue_May 2007

714 ZOHAR LAZAR

Title_Hero
Design Director_Fred Woodward
Publication_GQ
Publisher_Condé Nast Pub. Inc.
Issue_March 2007

715 THOMAS FUCHS

Title_Why the Best Leaders Are Servants Art Director_Sarah Garcea
Publication_Inc. Publisher_Mansueto Ventures Issue_May 2007

716 OLIVIER KUGLER

Title_On My Own
Art Director_Dian Holton
Publication_AARP The Magazine
Publisher_AARP Publications
Issue_September/October 2007

717 PAUL SAHRE

Title_The Black Swan
Design Director_Robert Priest
Art Director_Grace Lee
Publication_Condé Nast Portfolio
Publisher_Condé Nast Pub. Inc.
Issue_May 2007

718 CHIP WASS

Title_Gnarls Barkley Paper Dolls
Art Director_David Schlow
Publication_People Hollywood Daily
Publisher_Time Inc.
Issue_February 2007

719 GARY TAXALI

Title_The Strike Zone
Design Director_Geraldine Hessler
Publication_Entertainment Weekly
Publisher_Time Inc.
Issue_February 23, 2007

720 EMILIANO PONZI

Title_Born on a Blue Day
Art Director_Kelly Kingman
Publication_The Week
Issue_February 16, 2007

721 EDEL RODRIGUEZ

Title_Iraq, Four Years Later
Art Director_Travis Daub
Publication_Foreign Policy
Issue_March 2007

722 TOMER HANUKA

Title_Citigroup
Design Director_Robert Priest
Art Director_Grace Lee
Publication_Condé Nast Portfolio
Publisher_Condé Nast Pub. Inc.
Issue_September 2007

723 JOSH COCHRAN

Title_Cry Wolf
Art Director_Tracy Toscano
Publication_Plenty
Issue_June/July 2007

724 EDEL RODRIGUEZ

Title_Dispatches from the War on Streets
Art Director_Nick Torello
Publication_Business Week
Publisher_McGraw-Hill Companies
Issue_August 6, 2007

725 MARK MATCHO

Title_Break Free!
Art Director_Robert Perino
Publication_Fortune
Publisher_Time Inc.
Issue_October 1, 2007

726 THOMAS FUCHS

Title_Chocolate, Good for You?
Art Director_Kory Kennedy
Publication_Runner's World
Publisher_Rodale
Issue_February 2007

758

755

759

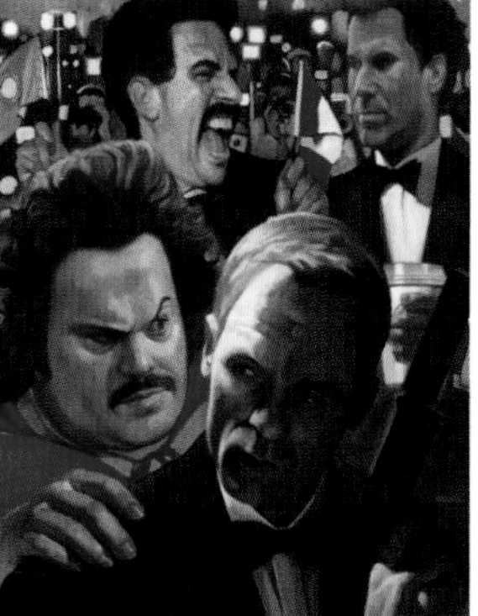

761

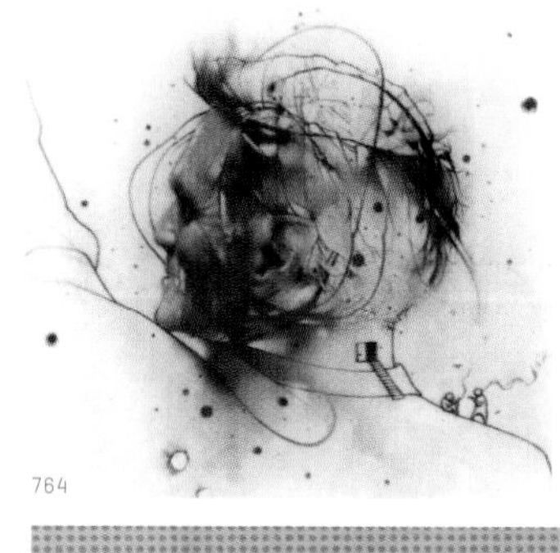

764

765

756

760

762

766

757

763

767

768

755 THILO ROTCHACKER

Title_The Readers Bite Back
Art Director_Michael Schönauer
Publication_Vanity Fair
Publisher_Condé Nast Pub. Inc.
Issue_2007

756 OTTO STEININGER

Title_The Car of the Future
Art Director_Chris Curry
Publication_The New Yorker
Publisher_Condé Nast Pub. Inc.
Issue_November 5, 2007

757 ANDREW ZBIHLYJ

Title_Romney 3000 III
Art Director_Stacey D. Clarkson
Publication_Harper's Magazine
Issue_November 2007

758 MICK WIGGINS

Title_Meeting War Stories
Creative Director_Mitch Shostak
Art Director_Roger J. Greiner
Publication_Convene
Issue_December 2007

759 ISTVAN BANYAI

Title_Enron Suit: A New Tempest for Citi? Art Director_Robert Perino
Publication_Fortune
Publisher_Time Inc.
Issue_December 10, 2007

760 BARRY BLITT

Title_Four Ways to Reclaim Your Digital Rights
Art Director_Barbara Adamson
Publication_PC World
Publisher_International Data Group
Issue_June 2007

761 ROBERTO PARADA

Title_The Men's Health Movie Awards
Art Director_John Dixon
Publication_Men's Health
Publisher_Rodale Inc.
Issue_March 2007

762 JEFFREY DECOSTER

Title_Finding My Stride
Art Director_Kory Kennedy
Publication_Runner's World
Publisher_Rodale
Issue_November 2007

763 ISTVAN BANYAI

Title_Mother's Nature
Art Director_Carla Frank
Publication_O, the Oprah Magazine
Publisher_The Hearst Corporation-Magazines Division
Issue_May 2007

764 ANDREW ZBIHLYJ

Title_Romney 3000 I
Art Director_Stacey D. Clarkson
Publication_Harper's Magazine
Issue_November 2007

765 BRETT RYDER

Title_Lover's Leap
Design Director_Carla Frank
Publication_O, the Oprah Magazine
Publisher_The Hearst Corporation-Magazines Division
Issue_June 2007

766 STEPHEN SAVAGE

Title_Entrepreneurs Inside the Machine
Design Director_Robert Perino
Publication_Fortune
Publisher_Time Inc.
Issue_May 14, 2007

767 ANDREW ZBIHLYJ

Title_Go Forth & Gentrify?
Creative Director_Susan Scandrett
Art Director_Tim J Luddy
Publication_Mother Jones
Publisher_Foundation for National Progress
Issue_July/August 2007

768 ISTVAN BANYAI

Title_And I Have to Spend All Day with These People?
Art Director_Carla Frank
Publication_O, the Oprah Magazine
Publisher_The Hearst Corporation-Magazines Division
Issue_September 2007

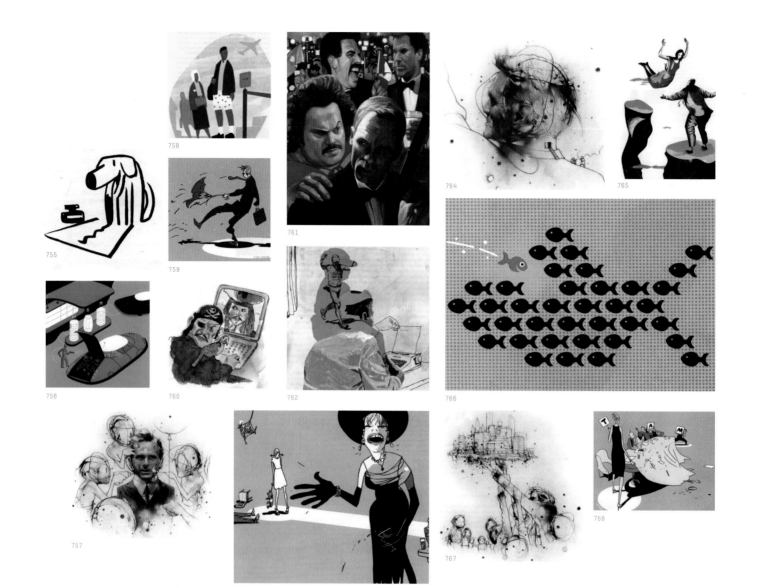

769

772

770

771

773

774

775

776

777

778

779

780

781

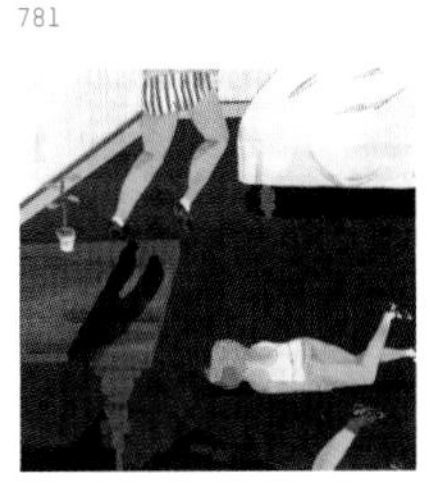

782

769 **SHOUT**
Title_Nice View, Rough Terrain
Art Director_Sarah Garcea
Publication_Inc.
Publisher_Mansueto Ventures
Issue_August 2007

770 **KIRSTEN ULVE**
Title_The Big Night: Oscars 2007
Design Director_Geraldine Hessler
Publication_Entertainment Weekly
Publisher_Time Inc.

771 **SCOTT MENCHIN**
Title_Values Are On the Line
Art Director_Sarah Garcea
Publication_Inc.
Publisher_Mansueto Ventures
Issue_November 2007

772 **MELINDA BECK**
Title_Timing is Everything
Design Director_Soojin Buzelli
Publication_planadviser
Issue_April 17, 2007

773 **JASON HOLLEY**
Title_James Gandolfini
Design Director_Geraldine Hessler
Publication_Entertainment Weekly
Publisher_Time Inc.
Issue_November 23, 2007

774 **SARAH WILKINS**
Title_Free Yourself
Art Director_Ron Escobar
Publication_Yoga Journal
Issue_April 2007

775 **SAM WEBER**
Title_Never Fear
Art Director_Elizabeth Neal
Publication_Men's Health
Publisher_Rodale Inc.
Issue_October 2007

776 **SHOUT**
Title_The Mentor's Manual
Art Director_Jose Fernandez
Publication_More
Publisher_Meredith Corporation
Issue_March 2007

777 **YUKO SHIMIZU**
Title_Cash in the Rebuilding Boom
Design Director_Robert Perino
Publication_Fortune
Publisher_Time Inc.
Issue_October 1, 2007

778 **MARK TODD**
Title_Choice Words
Art Director_Kory Kennedy
Publication_Runner's World
Publisher_Rodale
Issue_May 2007

779 **YUKO SHIMIZU**
Title_Best Jobs in America:
A Parent Going Back to Work
Art Director_Davia Smith
Publication_Money
Publisher Time Inc.
Issue_April 2007

780 **KAGAN MCLEOD**
Title_Bipolar Nation
Design Director_Robert Priest
Art Director_Grace Lee
Publication_Condé Nast Portfolio
Publisher_Condé Nast Pub. Inc.
Issue_September 2007

781 **ANDREA VENTURA**
Title_From the Desk of Daniel Varsky
Art Director_Stacey D. Clarkson
Publication_Harper's Magazine
Issue_June 2007

782 **LUKE BEST**
Title_The Swim Team
Art Director_Stacey D. Clarkson
Publication_Harper's Magazine
Issue_January 2007

index

S

T

U

W

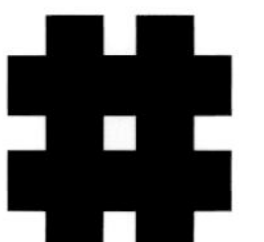

WELCOME DELEGATES! WE HOPE YOU ENJOY THE 43RD PUBLICATION DESIGNERS ANNUAL! YOU HOLD IN YOUR HANDS THE STANDARD-BEARERS OF EDITORIAL DESIGN FROM 2007, CULLED FROM OVER 7,000 ENTRIES. ENJOY!

Dirk Barnett & Scott Dadich
PUB 43 CO-CHAIRS

THE ANNUAL JUDGING would not be possible without the hard work and dedication from so many. Dirk Barnett, Creative Director, Blender, and Scott Dadich, Creative Director, WIRED, (Newsstand Co-Chairs), Francesca Messina, Sr. Art Director, Workman Publishing (Non-Newsstand Chair), Paul Schrynemakers, Creative Director, Rodale Interactive (Online Chair) and Linda Root, Design Director, Studio Incubate (Magazine of the Year Chair) extend an enormous thank-you on behalf of SPD to all the judges and volunteers for an inspiring and rewarding weekend judging almost 7,000 entries at FIT on January 18th, 19th & 20th, 2008.

MANY THANKS ALSO TO:
Mary Oleniczak, Anne Elmer and the staff in the FIT Facilities Office.

Brent Humphreys & Cambria Harkey for the photographs of the judges during the Competition.

Tom Wagner for stage management and production the night of the Gala, and Jon DeLouker for the Gala AV presentation.

Tim Leong and Nancy Stamatopoulos for Captaining the Volunteers the weekend of the judging.

CATALOGTREE for the PUB 43 poster infographics.

Lisa Taner at The New York Times, and Phil Swart from XPEDX for the paper used for the poster and the Gala program.

Andrew Bak of Adamba Imports International for providing cocktails at the Gala.

Tom Brown and Todd Albertson—aka Weapon of Choice—for their consistent dedication and design vigor in producing this beautiful annual for the Society.

Jarik Van Sluijs and Pamela Green of PiC

Gary Van Dis

Claudia de Almeida, Chris Anderson, Gaffney Peglar Barnett, Loan Bedensteiner, Bob Cohn, Alexandra Constantinople, Carl De Torres, Chris Ehrman, Sarah Filippi, Chris Hardwick, Maili Holiman, Victor Krummenacher, Joe Levy, Jeff Lysgaard, Ryan Meith, Wyatt Mitchell, Mike Phirman, Carolyn Rauch, Adam Rogers, Daniel Salo, Shannon Sawtelle, Christy Sheppard, Billy Sorrentino, Margaret Swart, Todd Tankersley, Robert Vargas, Tom Wallace, Rory Walsh, Mike Wodka, Zana Woods, Jacob Young

Amerikom for printing the Call for Entries poster for the Student Competition.

David Rhodes and Richard Wilde of SVA, for providing free summer housing for the winners of the SPD Student Competition.

Linda McNair, Courtney Spain and Joan Bodensteiner of Adobe.

For invaluable help and support in pre-production, Keisha Dean & Mike Ley.

Spots

Chair Jeremy LaCroix led the 21st Annual SPOTS competition this year, championing the little illustrations that say so much. From over 600 entries, the judges selected a class of illustrations that do an excellent job of amplifying the editorial message, from a wide spectrum of publications. Winners are featured in a visual index in this volume, and are celebrated more extensively in a very limited-edition book showcasing both the illustrations and smaller versions of the original editorial pages that featured the work.

SPECIAL THANKS TO THE JUDGES:
Tim Bower
ILLUSTRATOR
Josh Cochran
ILLUSTRATOR
Carl DeTorres
ART DIRECTOR, WIRED
George Lois
Randy Minor
ART DIRECTOR, NEW YORK
Nana Rausch
ILLUSTRATOR

The Student Competition & the Adobe Scholarship in Honor of B.W. Honeycutt

Established in 1995, this competition honors the life and work of B.W. Honeycutt. It recognizes exceptional design by students with awards and three cash prizes: the Adobe Scholarship in Honor of B.W. Honeycutt, the first-place prize of $2500; second-place prize of $1000; and a third-place prize of $500. The top six winners also received summer internships at Martha Stewart Living, New York, Real Simple and W. Chaired by Ian Doherty and Robert Perino, this juried competition acknowledges the student designer and the teachers who develop their unique talents.

In recognizing the promise of each student, Adobe affirms the creative possibilities inherent in the individual. Throughout its partnership with SPD, Adobe is helping shape the next generation of creative professionals. Together we are building the groundwork that will sustain and further artistic accomplishments within the editorial design community.

SPECIAL THANKS TO THE JUDGES:
Florian Bachleda,
CREATIVE DIRECTOR, FB DESIGN
David Curcurito
DESIGN DIRECTOR, ESQUIRE
Luke Hayman,
PARTNER, PENTAGRAM
Nathalie Kirsheh
ART DIRECTOR, W
David McKenna
ART DIRECTOR, NATIONAL GEOGRAPHIC ADVENTURE
Linda Pouder
DESIGN DIRECTOR, STUDIO INCUBATE

The Society thanks our partners for their ongoing support:
Adobe Systems, Inc.
The Heart Agency

The SPD 43rd Publication Design Annual was designed and produced by Tom Brown and Todd Albertson, Weapon of Choice (www.weaponofchoice.ca). With contributing designers Jennifer Roberts & Dian Holton.

Set entirely in T-Star and Colosseum.

First published in the United States of America by:
Rockport Publishers, Inc.
100 Cummings Center, Suite 406-L
Beverly, MA 01915
Tel: 978.282.9590
Fax: 978.283.2742

THE SOCIETY OF PUBLICATION DESIGNERS
27 Union Square West
Suite 207
New York, NY 10003
Tel: 212.223.3332
Fax: 212.223.5880
mail@spd.org
www.spd.org